Lecture Notes in Computer Science   **10343**

Commenced Publication in 1973
Founding and Former Series Editors:
Gerhard Goos, Juris Hartmanis, and Jan van Leeuwen

More information about this series at http://www.springer.com/series/7410

Josef Pieprzyk · Suriadi Suriadi (Eds.)

Information Security and Privacy

22nd Australasian Conference, ACISP 2017
Auckland, New Zealand, July 3–5, 2017
Proceedings, Part II

 Springer

Editors
Josef Pieprzyk 🆔
Queensland University of Technology
Brisbane, QLD
Australia

Suriadi Suriadi 🆔
Queensland University of Technology
Brisbane, QLD
Australia

ISSN 0302-9743　　　　　　ISSN 1611-3349　(electronic)
Lecture Notes in Computer Science
ISBN 978-3-319-59869-7　　ISBN 978-3-319-59870-3　(eBook)
DOI 10.1007/978-3-319-59870-3

Library of Congress Control Number: 2017943039

LNCS Sublibrary: SL4 – Security and Cryptology

Printed on acid-free paper

This Springer imprint is published by Springer Nature
The registered company is Springer International Publishing AG
The registered company address is: Gewerbestrasse 11, 6330 Cham, Switzerland

Preface

The 22nd Australasian Conference on Information Security and Privacy was organized in beautiful New Zealand on the Massey University campus in Auckland, July 3–5, 2017. This was the first time that the conference was organized outside Australia.

This year we received 150 submissions. Each paper got assigned to four referees. In the first stage of the review process, the submitted papers were read and evaluated by the Program Committee members. In the second stage, the papers were scrutinized during an extensive discussion. Finally, the Program Committee chose 45 regular and ten short papers to be included in the conference program. The authors of the accepted papers had ten days for revision and preparation of final versions. The revised papers were not subject to editorial review and the authors bear full responsibility for their contents. The submission and review process was supported by the EasyChair conference submission server. We thank the EasyChair people for letting us use it.

The Program Committee voted for the best paper using the Doodle software. We nominated four papers with best reviews. Out of the four, two papers were the preferred options with no clear winner. We decided to award the ACISP2017 Best Paper Award to the two papers:

- "Dynamic Searchable Symmetric Encryption with Physical Deletion and Small Leakage" by Peng Xu, Shuai Liang, Wei Wang, Willy Susilo, Qianhong Wu and Hai Jin
- "Multi-user Cloud-Based Secure Keyword Search" by Shabnam Kasra Kermanshahi, Joseph K. Liu and Ron Steinfeld

The awards were handed during the conference dinner.

The Jennifer Seberry Lecture this year was delivered by Clark Thomborson from the University of Auckland, New Zealand. The keynote lecture was presented by L. Jean Camp from Indiana University, USA. The program also included invited talks by well-known researchers working in different areas of cybersecurity. They were Dong Seong Kim, University of Canterbury, New Zealand; Dongxi Liu, CSIRO/Data61, Australia; Surya Nepal, CSIRO/Data61, Australia; Paul Pang, Unitec Institute of Technology, New Zealand; Peter Pilley, Department of Internal Affairs, New Zealand; Ian Welch, Victoria University of Wellington, New Zealand and Henry B. Wolfe, University of Otago, New Zealand.

We would like to thank the Program Committee members and the external reviewers for their effort and time to evaluate the submissions. Big thanks go to Julian Jang-Jaccard and Paul Watters for their excellent job in the organization of the conference. We are indebted to the team at Springer for their continuous support of the conference and for their help in the production of the conference proceedings.

July 2017

Josef Pieprzyk
Suriadi Suriadi

ACISP 2017

The 22nd Australasian Conference on Information Security
and Privacy

Massey University, Auckland, New Zealand
July 3–5, 2017

In Co-operation with IACR

Sponsored by Massey University

UNIVERSITY OF NEW ZEALAND

General Co-chairs

Julian Jang-Jaccard   Massey University, New Zealand
Paul Watters   La Trobe University, Australia

Program Co-chairs

Josef Pieprzyk   Queensland University of Technology, Australia
Suriadi Suriadi   Queensland University of Technology, Australia

Program Committee

Cristina Alcaraz   University of Malaga, Spain
Claudio Agostino Ardagna   Università degli Studi di Milano, Italy
Giuseppe Ateniese   Stevens Institute of Technology, USA
Man Ho Au   Hong Kong Polytechnic University, SAR China
Milton Baar   Macquarie University, Australia
Joonsang Baek   Khalifa University of Science, UAE
Lynn Batten   Deakin University, Australia
Colin Boyd   Norwegian University of Science and Technology,
                            Norway
Serdar Boztas   RMIT University, Australia
Alvaro Cardenas   University of Texas at Dallas, USA
Aniello Castiglione   University of Salerno, Italy
Ebrima Ceesay   Leidos and Johns Hopkins University, USA
Jinjun Chen   University Technology Sydney, Australia

Shiping Chen	Data61 - CSIRO, Australia
Xiaofeng Chen	Xidian University, China
Kim-Kwang Raymond Choo	University of Texas at San Antonio, USA
Christophe Doche	Macquarie University, Australia
Ernest Foo	Queensland University of Technology, Australia
David Galindo	University of Birmingham, UK
Colm Gannon	DCET - Internal Affairs, New Zealand
Swee-Huay Heng	Multimedia University, Malaysia
Andreas Holzer	Google Inc., USA
Xinyi Huang	Fujian Normal University, China
Mitsugu Iwamoto	University of Electro-Communications, Japan
Sanjay Jha	University of New South Wales, Australia
Akinori Kawachi	The University of Tokushima, Japan
Peter Kieseberg	SBA Research, Austria
Dong Seong Kim	University of Canterbury, New Zealand
Howon Kim	Pusan National University, South Korea
Jongkil Kim	Data61 - CSIRO, Australia
Ryan Ko	University of Waikato, New Zealand
Marina Krotofil	Hamburg University of Technology, Germany
Noboru Kunihiro	University of Tokyo, Japan
Mirosław Kutyłowski	Wrocław University of Science and Technology, Poland
Junzuo Lai	Singapore Management University, Singapore
Shujun Li	University of Surrey, UK
Kaitai Liang	Aalto University, Finland
Dongxi Liu	Data61 - CSIRO, Australia
Joseph Liu	Monash University, Australia
Shengli Liu	Shanghai Jiao Tong University, China
Javier Lopez	University of Malaga, Spain
Jiqiang Lu	Institute for Infocomm Research, Singapore
Rongxing Lu	University of New Brunswick, Canada
Félix Gómez Mármol	University of Murcia, Spain
Weizhi Meng	Technical University of Denmark, Denmark
Kazuhiko Minematsu	NEC Corporation, Japan
Chris Mitchell	Royal Holloway - University of London, UK
Paweł Morawiecki	Polish Academy of Sciences, Poland
Kirill Morozov	Tokyo Institute of Technology, Japan
Yi Mu	University of Wollongong, Australia
Surya Nepal	Data61 - CSIRO, Australia
Ivica Nikolić	Nanyang Technological University, Singapore
Thomas Peyrin	Nanyang Technological University, Singapore
Man Qi	Canterbury Christ Church University, UK
Kenneth Radke	Queensland University of Technology and CERT Australia, Australia
Reza Reyhanitabar	NEC Laboratories Europe, Germany

Jun Shao	Zhejiang Gongshang University, China
Taeshik Shon	Ajou University, South Korea
Haya Shulman	Fraunhofer SIT, Germany
Tony Skjellum	Auburn University, USA
Ron Steinfeld	Monash University, Australia
Chunhua Su	Japan Advanced Institute of Science and Technology, Japan
Willy Susilo	University of Wollongong, Australia
Shaohua Tang	South China University of Technology, China
Juan Tapiador	Universidad Carlos III de Madrid, Spain
Clark Thomborson	University of Auckland, New Zealand
Fergus Toolan	UCD School of Computer Science, Ireland
Petros Wallden	University of Edinburgh, UK
Cong Wang	City University of Hong Kong, SAR China
Huaxiong Wang	Nanyang Technological University, Singapore
Yu Wang	Deakin University, Australia
George Weir	University of Strathclyde, UK
Sheng Wen	Deakin University, Australia
Henry B. Wolfe	University of Otago, New Zealand
Chi Yang	Unitec Institute of Technology, New Zealand
Guomin Yang	University of Wollongong, Australia
Yanjiang Yang	Huawei Singapore Research Center, Singapore
Wun-She Yap	Universiti Tunku Abdul Rahman, Malaysia
Xun Yi	RMIT University, Australia
Tsz Hon Yuen	Huawei Singapore Research Center, Singapore
Aaram Yun	Ulsan National Institute of Science and Technology, South Korea
Xuyun Zhang	University of Auckland, New Zealand

Additional Reviewers

Fatma Al Maqbali	Ed Dawson	Andrei Kelarev
Janaka Alawatugoda	Nabil El Ioini	Jeongsu Kim
Yoshinori Aono	Gerardo Fernandez	Jianchang Lai
Shahriar Badsha	Filippo Gaudenzi	Anna Lauks-Dutka
Anubhab Baksi	Junqing Gong	Hyung Tae Lee
Arcangelo Castiglione	Zheng Gong	Nan Li
Luigi Catuogno	Fuchun Guo	Xiaoyu Li
Claire Che	Jian Guo	Xingye Lu
Jiahui Chen	Jingjing Guo	Lin Lyu
Jie Chen	Felix Günther	Jinhua Ma
Rongmao Chen	Jinguang Han	Moesfa Soeheila
Ji-Jian Chin	Shuai Han	Mohamad
Craig Costello	Yasufumi Hashimoto	Mihai Moraru
Hui Cui	Shoichi Hirose	Khoa Nguyen

Phuong Ha Nguyen
Tobias Nilges
David Nuñez
Xu Peiming
Jiang Peng
Thye Way Phua
Ananth Raghunathan
Fang-Yu Rao
Juan E. Rubio
Kyoji Shibutani
Siang Meng Sim
Le Su

Bing Sun
Benjamin HongMengTan
Syh-Yuan Tan
Srinivas Vivek
Riad Wahby
Jianfeng Wang
Yunling Wang
Yunhua Wen
Qianhong Wu
Lingling Xu
Rui Xu
Shengmin Xu

Shota Yamada
Xu Yang
Yu Yu
Zuoxia Yu
Shiwei Zhang
Xiao Zhang
Xiaoyu Zhang
Yuexin Zhang
Zongyang Zhang
Peng Zhiniang

Contents – Part II

Privacy

Authentication

Elliptic Curve Cryptography

Short Papers

Contents – Part I

Searchable Encryption

Cryptanalysis

Digital Signatures

Symmetric Cryptography

Analysis of Toeplitz MDS Matrices

Sumanta Sarkar[(✉)] and Habeeb Syed

TCS Innovation Labs, Hyderabad, India
{Sumanta.Sarkar1,Habeeb.Syed}@tcs.com

Abstract. This work considers the problem of constructing efficient MDS matrices over the field $\mathbb{F}_{2^m}$. Efficiency is measured by the metric XOR count which was introduced by Khoo et al. in CHES 2014. Recently Sarkar and Syed (ToSC Vol. 1, 2016) have shown the existence of 4×4 Toeplitz MDS matrices with optimal XOR counts. In this paper, we present some characterizations of Toeplitz matrices in light of MDS property. Our study leads to improving the known bounds of XOR counts of 8×8 MDS matrices by obtaining Toeplitz MDS matrices with lower XOR counts over $\mathbb{F}_{2^4}$ and $\mathbb{F}_{2^8}$.

Keywords: Toeplitz matrix · MDS matrix · XOR count · Lightweight block cipher · Diffusion layer

1 Introduction

Internet of Things (IoT) is a network of interconnected devices that can share data with each other and process when required. IoT applications range from health monitoring and traffic management to several other daily life activities; this is one of the reasons that it also has drawn attention from the industry. The devices used in IoT are mostly RFIDs and sensors, which have very low resources. Thus for ensuring privacy and confidentiality of the data in IoT, classical cryptosystems like AES, RSA are not suitable. To bridge this gap the topic lightweight cryptography has emerged. Lightweight cryptography is mostly based on symmetric key. The eSTREAM finalists `Grain v1` [7], `MICKEY` 2.0 [1], and `Trivium` [18] are examples of lightweight stream ciphers. `CLEFIA` [16], `PRESENT` [5], `PRINCE` [6] are some of the existing lightweight block ciphers.

In this paper we are interested in lightweight block ciphers. Confusion and diffusion layers are the two important building blocks of a block cipher. While confusion layer is responsible for making the relation between key and ciphertext as complex as possible, the diffusion layer spreads the plaintext statistics through the ciphertext. Maximum distance separable (MDS) matrices are a popular choice to build diffusion layer as these matrices achieve the maximum diffusion power. However, constructing an MDS matrix with low implementation cost (as to suit lightweight cryptosystems) is a nontrivial task.

In CHES 2014, [9] introduced the metric XOR count that measures the cost of implementation of a diffusion matrix. A matrix filled with field elements having low Hamming weight may not necessarily result in low hardware cost for the

© Springer International Publishing AG 2017
J. Pieprzyk and S. Suriadi (Eds.): ACISP 2017, Part II, LNCS 10343, pp. 3–18, 2017.
DOI: 10.1007/978-3-319-59870-3_1

implementation of the matrix, which was shown in [9]. This paper measured the number of XORs required to compute the multiplication of a fixed field element and showed that there are MDS diffusion matrices with higher Hamming weight than the AES diffusion matrix, but needed lesser XORs to implement. Then several works [10,11,14,15,17] followed to find MDS matrices with low XOR counts. Search effort for MDS matrices with low XOR count in the previous works have been made in some subclasses of matrices like Hadamard matrices and circulant matrices. Recently [15] settled the question of the minimum XOR counts of 4×4 MDS matrices over $\mathbb{F}_{2^4}$ and $\mathbb{F}_{2^8}$. They showed that matrices achieving the minimum XOR count exist in the class of Toeplitz matrices. This motivates us to study Toeplitz MDS matrices further and analyze several properties of such matrices.

Our Contributions. Since a Toeplitz MDS matrix cannot be involutory [15], there is no scope of getting involutory MDS matrices in the class of Toeplitz matrices. In this work we restrict our study to MDS matrices only. In a Toeplitz matrix, several submatrices repeat. We count the number of distinct $d \times d$, $(1 \leq d \leq n)$ submatrices in Proposition 1; later Theorem 1 shows how many of these distinct submatrices are indeed Toeplitz. One can take the advantage of this redundancy while checking the MDS property of a Toeplitz matrix (see Remark 1). We also study Toeplitz matrices in the class of Cauchy matrices, and prove that a Cauchy-Toeplitz matrix cannot be MDS for dimension greater than 2.

In Sect. 4, we improve the XOR count of 8×8 MDS matrices over $\mathbb{F}_{2^4}$ and $\mathbb{F}_{2^8}$. As the class of all MDS 8×8 matrix is huge, we search in the subclass formed by the Toeplitz matrices. However, it is not easy to exhaust the full class of Toeplitz matrices for these fields. We develop a pruning based search algorithm which enables us to find Toeplitz MDS matrices with lower XOR counts. For $\mathbb{F}_{2^4}$ the lowest XOR count that we obtain is $170 + 8 \cdot 7 \cdot 4$ (earlier known value was $208 + 8 \cdot 7 \cdot 4$), whereas for $\mathbb{F}_{2^8}$ the improved XOR count is $232 + 8 \cdot 7 \cdot 8$ (earlier known value was $240 + 8 \cdot 7 \cdot 8$). Thus we improve the bounds of XOR counts of 8×8 MDS matrices over $\mathbb{F}_{2^4}$ and $\mathbb{F}_{2^8}$.

2   Preliminaries

We denote by $\mathbb{F}_{2^m}$ the finite field with 2^m elements, and by $\mathbb{F}_2^m$ we denote the m-dimensional vector space over $\mathbb{F}_2$. MDS codes are the class of linear codes over the field $\mathbb{F}_{2^m}$ that achieve the Singleton bound, that is for an $[N, K]$ MDS code the minimum distance is $N - K + 1$. An $n \times n$ matrix M over $\mathbb{F}_{2^m}$ is MDS if the $n \times 2n$ matrix $G = [I_n \ M]$ is a generator of a $[2n, n]$ MDS code, where I_n is the $n \times n$ identity matrix. Another characterization of MDS matrices is as follows: M is MDS if and only if every submatrix of M is nonsingular. For details on this one may consult [12]. MDS matrices are popular choice for building diffusion layers of block ciphers, as they attain the maximum diffusion power.

2.1   XOR Counts

The field $\mathbb{F}_{2^m}$ can be identified to the vector space $\mathbb{F}_2^m$, by choosing some basis. There are several kinds of bases for a finite fields, and the mostly used one is the polynomial basis of the form $\{1, \alpha, \ldots, \alpha^{m-1}\}$. To measure the implementation cost of field multiplication [9] proposed the metric XOR count defined as follows.

Definition 1. *Let $P(X)$ be an irreducible polynomial that defines $\mathbb{F}_{2^m}$ and let $\mathcal{B}$ be a basis of $\mathbb{F}_{2^m}$. The XOR count of an element $a \in \mathbb{F}_{2^m}$ with respect to $\mathcal{B}$ is the number of XORs required to implement the multiplication of a with an arbitrary element $b \in \mathbb{F}_{2^m}$. We denote by $XOR(a)$ the XOR count of a.*

Note that $\text{XOR}(0) = 0 = \text{XOR}(1)$. It is mentioned in [9] that low XOR count is strongly correlated to the minimization of hardware area (GE). Thus finding MDS matrices with low XOR count is an active research topic in the context of lightweight cryptography. The set of XOR counts of all the elements of $\mathbb{F}_{2^m}$ is termed as the XOR count distribution which depends on $P(X)$ and $\mathcal{B}$ [14,17]. Note that polynomial basis is a conventional choice for implementation and as noted in [15], we will only be considering polynomial basis. Recently [4] has relooked at XOR count of an element and allowed reuse of repeating terms in the product vector. However, we do not consider such optimization and regard XOR count in its simplified form as given by [9] and many subsequent works [14,15,17].

In [9] the formula for the XOR count of a row of a matrix was derived, later [15] extended it to the full $n \times n$ matrix M defined over $\mathbb{F}_{2^m}$ as

$$\sum_{i=0}^{n-1} \left(\sum_{j=0}^{n-1} \gamma_{ij} + (\ell_i - 1) \cdot m \right) = C(M) + \sum_{i=0}^{n-1} (\ell_i - 1) \cdot m \qquad (1)$$

where γ_{ij} is the XOR count of the j-th entry of the i-th row of the matrix, and ℓ_i is the number of nonzero entries in that row. The term $C(M)$ is the sum of XOR counts of all the entries of M. For an $n \times n$ MDS matrix over $\mathbb{F}_{2^m}$, $\ell_i = n$, so (1) becomes $C(M) + n \cdot (n-1) \cdot m$, and $C(M)$ is the part that varies with the matrices.

3   Toeplitz MDS Matrices

In this section we study Toeplitz MDS matrices in details.

Definition 2. *A matrix is called Toeplitz if every descending diagonal from left to right is constant.*

The following is the general form of an $n \times n$ Toeplitz matrix.

$$T = \begin{bmatrix} a_0 & a_1 & a_2 & \cdots & a_{n-2} & a_{n-1} \\ a_{-1} & a_0 & a_1 & \cdots & a_{n-3} & a_{n-2} \\ \vdots & \vdots & \vdots & \vdots & \vdots & \vdots \\ a_{-(n-1)} & a_{-(n-2)} & a_{-(n-3)} & \cdots & a_{-1} & a_0 \end{bmatrix}. \qquad (2)$$

A Toeplitz matrix is defined by its first row and first column, henceforth we will use

$$\text{Toep}(a_0, a_1, \ldots, a_{n-1}, a_{-1}, a_{-2}, \ldots, a_{-(n-1)}) \tag{3}$$

to describe an $n \times n$ Toeplitz matrix of the form (2). This matrix can also be defined as follows:

$$T = [m_{i,j}], \quad \text{where} \quad m_{i,j} = a_{j-i}. \tag{4}$$

3.1   Properties of a Toeplitz Matrix

To check the MDS property of an $n \times n$ matrix, one has to check if all the submatrices are nonsingular. The total number of such submatrices are $\sum_{i=1}^{n} \binom{n}{i}^2$. However, it is easy to see that in a Toeplitz matrix several sub matrices are duplicates and hence can be ignored while checking MDS property. In this section we compute the number of distinct submatrices of a Toeplitz matrix. Following is a result in this regard proof of which is given in Appendix A.

Lemma 1. *Suppose T is a Toeplitz matrix as given in (2). Every $d \times d$ submatrix of T is equal to a $d \times d$ submatrix T_{sub} such that*

1. *the first row of T_{sub} belongs to the first row of T. Or,*
2. *the first column of T_{sub} belongs to the first column of T.*

Example 1. Consider the following 4×4 Toeplitz matrix T.

$$T = \begin{bmatrix} \boxed{a_0} & a_1 & \boxed{a_2} & a_3 \\ a_{-1} & \textcircled{a_0} & a_1 & \textcircled{a_2} \\ \boxed{a_{-2}} & a_{-1} & \boxed{a_0} & a_1 \\ a_3 & \textcircled{a_{-2}} & a_{-1} & \textcircled{a_0} \end{bmatrix}.$$

The 2×2 submatrix formed by the 2nd and 4th row, and 2nd and 4th column (marked by circles) is equal to the 2×2 submatrix formed by the 1st and 3rd row, and 1st and 3rd column (marked by rectangles).

Let us now count the number of distinct submatrices of a Toeplitz matrices considering that all the a_i's are distinct.

Proposition 1. *Let $T = \text{Toep}(a_0, \ldots, a_{-(n-1)})$ be a Toeplitz matrix in which all a_i's are distinct. Then the number of distinct $d \times d$ submatrices is*

$$\binom{n-1}{d-1}^2 + 2 \binom{n-1}{d-1} \binom{n-1}{d} = \binom{n-1}{d-1}^2 \left(\frac{2n-d}{d} \right). \tag{5}$$

Consequently, the total number of distinct submatrices are

$$\binom{2n-2}{n-1} + 2 \binom{2n-2}{n-2}. \tag{6}$$

Proof. We will count the distinct submatrices as per Lemma 1, i.e., submatrices having elements from the first row or first column. Let $T[0,0]$ be the $(0,0)$-th element of T. We count the number of submatrices with and without $T[0,0]$ separately.

Case 1: When $T[0,0]$ is absent. In this case there are two kinds of submatrices: submatrices that have elements from the first row, but not from the first column, or submatrices that have elements from the first column, but not from the first row. The number of distinct $d \times d$ submatrices that have elements from the first row is $\binom{n-1}{d-1}\binom{n-1}{d}$, and the number of submatrices that have elements from the first column is $\binom{n-1}{d-1}\binom{n-1}{d}$.

Case 2: When $T[0,0]$ is present. In this case the number of distinct $d \times d$ submatrices is $\binom{n-1}{d-1}\binom{n-1}{d-1}$.

Now adding the above two counts we get the number of distinct $d \times d$ submatrices as (5).

Further note that for any positive integer t, $\sum_{i=0}^{t} \binom{t}{i}^2 = \binom{2t}{t}$ and $\sum_{i=0}^{t-1} \binom{t}{i}\binom{t}{i+1} = \binom{2t}{t} + \binom{2t}{t-1}$. Using these, the total number of distinct submatrices is obtained as

$$\sum_{d=1}^{n} \binom{n-1}{d-1}^2 + 2\sum_{d=1}^{n} \binom{n-1}{d-1}\binom{n-1}{d} = \binom{2n-2}{n-1} + 2\binom{2n-2}{n-2}.$$

$\square$

Note that a submatrix of a Toeplitz matrix could also be Toeplitz. Denote by $\text{Row}(S) = (i_0, \ldots, i_{d-1})$, the ordered set of row indices of S and $\text{Col}(S) = (j_0, \ldots, j_{d-1})$ ordered set of column indices of S. We now present a characterization of a submatrix of a Toeplitz matrix to be Toeplitz also.

Proposition 2. *Let $T = Toep(a_0, \ldots, a_{-(n-1)})$ be a Toeplitz matrix in which all a_i's are distinct and S be a $d \times d$ submatrix of T for some $2 \leq d \leq n-1$. Then S is Toeplitz if and only if $\text{Row}(S) = (i_0, \ldots, i_{d-1})$, and $\text{Col}(S) = (j_0, \ldots, j_{d-1})$ satisfy*

$$i_{k+1} - i_k = j_{k+1} - j_k = \rho, \qquad k = 0, \ldots, d-2 \qquad (7)$$

for some integer ρ such that

$$1 \leq \rho \leq \left\lfloor \frac{n-1}{d-1} \right\rfloor. \qquad (8)$$

Proof. Recall that a square matrix $X = [x_{ij}]$ of order n is Toeplitz if and only if for all $0 \leq i, j \leq n-2$

$$x_{i,j} = x_{i+\theta, j+\theta}$$

for every $\theta \geq 1$ is such that $\max\{i+\theta, j+\theta\} \leq n-1$. Now let's prove the lemma. Suppose that S is a $d \times d$ submatrix of T such that $\text{Row}(S)$ and $\text{Col}(S)$ satisfy (7) with ρ as in (8). This implies that for any $i_k \in \text{Row}(S), j_t \in \text{Col}(S), 0 \leq k, t \leq d-2$ we have

$$S_{i_k, j_t} = T_{i_k, j_t} = T_{i_k+\theta, j_t+\theta} = S_{i_k+\theta, j_t+\theta}$$

as S is a submatrix of T which is a Toeplitz matrix. This shows that S is Toeplitz and hence the sufficiency part. Let us prove the necessary part. Suppose S is a $d \times d$ Toeplitz submatrix of T for some $2 \le d \le n - 1$, then we show that $\text{Row}(S), \text{Col}(S)$ satisfy (7) with ρ as in (8). Observe that since (by hypothesis) all the elements of first row and column of T are distinct, it follows from the definition of a Toeplitz matrix that for any $0 \le i, j, i', j' \le n - 1$,

$$T_{i,j} = T_{i',j'} \quad \text{if and only if} \quad j - i = j' - i'. \tag{9}$$

Using this in case of S (which is a Toeplitz submatrix), we have for every element of $\text{Row}(S)$, $\text{Col}(S)$

$$i_k - j_k = i_{k-1} - j_{k-1} \quad \Longrightarrow \quad i_k - i_{k-1} = j_k - j_{k-1},$$

which proves (7). Next suppose $\rho = i_k - i_{k-1}$ then the condition (8) is necessary to make sure that none of the indices of S grows bigger than indices of T. From (7) it follows that

$$i_{d-1} = i_{d-2} + \rho = \ldots = i_0 + \rho(d - 1). \tag{10}$$

Using the facts $2 \le d \le (n - 1)$, $\rho \ge 1$, and $1 \le i_{d-1} \le n - 1$ in (10) we get

$$1 \le 0 + \rho(d - 1) \le (n - 1) \quad \Longrightarrow \quad 1 \le \rho \le \left\lfloor \frac{n-1}{d-1} \right\rfloor.$$

$\square$

In the following we count the number of $d \times d$ Toeplitz submatrices of an $n \times n$ Toeplitz matrix.

Theorem 1. *Let T be an $n \times n$ Toeplitz matrix as given in (2) in which all the elements of first row and first column are distinct. Then the number of distinct $d \times d$ Toeplitz submatrices are*

$$\delta_{d,n} = \begin{cases} 2n - 1 & \text{if } d = 1 \\ (n - d + \tau_{d,n} + 1) \cdot \left\lfloor \frac{n-1}{d-1} \right\rfloor & \text{if } d = 2, \ldots, n \end{cases}, \tag{11}$$

where $\tau_{d,n}$ is given by $n - 1 = \left\lfloor \frac{n-1}{d-1} \right\rfloor (d - 1) + \tau_{d,n}$.

Proof. Suppose S is a $d \times d$ a submatrix of T with $\text{Row}(S) = (i_0, \ldots, i_{d-1})$ and $\text{Col}(S) = (j_0, \ldots, j_{d-1})$. Let

$$\Gamma = \underbrace{\sum_{\theta=1}^{\left\lfloor \frac{n-1}{d-1} \right\rfloor} n - \theta(d - 1)}_{(*)} + \underbrace{\sum_{\theta=1}^{\left\lfloor \frac{n-2}{d-1} \right\rfloor} (n - 1) - \theta(d - 1)}_{(**)}. \tag{12}$$

We will show that the distinct $d \times d$ Toeplitz submatrices of an $n \times n$ Toeplitz matrix T is given by Γ as in (12) and this simplifies to (11). To count distinct submatrices S we use Proposition 1 and consider only those submatrices S for which

$$(i_0 = 0) \text{ or } (i_0 > 0 \text{ and } j_0 = 0),$$

and for each case we count the exact number of Toeplitz submatrices using conditions of Proposition 2 which put together gives (11).

Case 1: When $i_0 = 0$.
This gives the term (*) in (12). In this case for every ρ satisfying (8), the only possibility for $\texttt{Row}(S)$ is $\texttt{Row}(S) = (0, \rho, \ldots, \rho(d-1))$. For every such possible $\texttt{Row}(S)$, the number of possibilities for $\texttt{Col}(S) = (j_0, \ldots, j_{d-1})$ satisfying (7) is $n - \rho(d-1)$. Varying ρ from 1 to $\lfloor \frac{n-1}{d-1} \rfloor$ and summing all the terms we get (*) in (12)

Case 2: When $i_0 > 0$, and $j_0 = 0$.
Let ρ_0 be a value of ρ satisfying (8). One can choose $\texttt{Row}(S) = (i_0, \ldots, i_{d-1})$ satisfying (7) for $\rho = \rho_0$ in exactly $(n-1) - \rho(d-1)$ ways. For every such chosen $\texttt{Row}(S)$ there exits a unique value $\texttt{Col}(S) = (0, j_1, \ldots, j_{d-1})$ (satisfying (7) for $\rho = \rho_0$) which together give a Toeplitz matrix S. Since $i_0 > 0$ total number of available rows is only $n - 1$ and hence the total number of Toeplitz submatrices which do not involve 0 can be obtained by by adding the quantity $[(n-1) - \rho(d-1)]$ for $\rho = 1$ to $\lfloor \frac{n-2}{d-1} \rfloor$ we obtain (**) in (12).

To complete the proof we need to show that Γ in (12) simplifies to (11). This can be easily shown by considering the two cases $\tau_{d,n} > 0$ and $\tau_{d,n} = 0$ separately. $\qquad\square$

Using this result, we compare the number of distinct submatrices of Toeplitz and general matrices in Table 2 in Appendix B.

Remark 1. Given an $n \times n$ matrix, to check the MDS property one needs to verify whether all the $\sum_{i=1}^{n} \binom{n}{i}^2 = \binom{2n}{n} - 1$ square submatrices are nonsingular. However, as we see in Lemma 1 that there are too many redundancies in a Toeplitz matrix, so we need to consider fewer submatrices as opposed to a general matrix. By Proposition 1, we need to consider $\binom{2n-2}{n-1} + 2\binom{2n-2}{n-2}$ submatrices in total for an $n \times n$ Toeplitz matrix.

3.2 Cauchy-Toeplitz Matrices

Cauchy matrices are interesting in the sense that it is easy to construct MDS matrices in this class. A Cauchy matrix over $\mathbb{F}_{2^m}$ is of the form

$$M = [a_{i,j}]_{n \times n}, \text{ where } a_{i,j} = \frac{1}{x_i + y_j}, \quad x_i \neq y_j, \quad 0 \leq i, j \leq n-1. \tag{13}$$

Fact 1. *The Cauchy matrix M is nonsingular if and only if $x_i \neq x_j$ and $y_i \neq y_j$, for all $0 \leq i, j \leq n-1$.*

There have been constructions of MDS matrices which are both Hadamard and Cauchy (see [17] for example). We now analyze the MDS property of matrices which are both Toeplitz and Cauchy. We call matrices which are both Toeplitz and Cauchy as Cauchy-Toeplitz. Example of such a matrix is given in Example 2 in Appendix A.

Theorem 2. *Let T be a $n \times n$ Cauchy-Toeplitz matrix over $\mathbb{F}_{2^m}$. Then the following hold.*

1. *T is symmetric.*
2. *T is singular if $n \geq 3$, and thus T is not MDS if $n \geq 3$.*

Proof. As T is Toeplitz, we must have $T_{i,i} = T_{j,j}$. Then

$$\frac{1}{x_i + y_i} = \frac{1}{x_j + y_j} \implies \frac{1}{x_i + y_j} = \frac{1}{x_j + y_i},$$

that is $T_{i,j} = T_{j,i}$. So T is symmetric.

Next we prove that T is singular whenever $n \geq 3$. Consider a 3×3 Cauchy matrix

$$T_3 = \begin{bmatrix} \frac{1}{x_0+y_0} & \frac{1}{x_0+y_1} & \frac{1}{x_0+y_2} \\ \frac{1}{x_1+y_0} & \frac{1}{x_1+y_1} & \frac{1}{x_1+y_2} \\ \frac{1}{x_2+y_0} & \frac{1}{x_2+y_1} & \frac{1}{x_2+y_2} \end{bmatrix}.$$

By the definition of Cauchy matrix $x_i \neq y_j$ for $i, j = 0, 1, 2$ and from Fact 1 it follows that T_3 is nonsingular if and only if

$$x_i \neq x_j \quad \text{and} \quad y_i \neq y_j \quad \text{for } 0 \leq i < j \leq 2. \tag{14}$$

Suppose that T_3 is Toeplitz, then by Definition 2 we have the following.

$$\begin{aligned} x_0 + y_0 = x_1 + y_1 = x_2 + y_2 &= C_0 \\ x_0 + y_1 = x_1 + y_2 &= C_1 \\ x_1 + y_0 = x_2 + y_1 &= C_2, \end{aligned} \tag{15}$$

for some C_0, C_1 and C_2 in $\mathbb{F}_{2^m}$. As it was proved above that T_3 is symmetric, $C_1 = C_2$ must hold. Using this in (15) we get $x_2 + y_1 = C_1$, and we also have $x_0 + y_1 = C_1$, which together imply $x_0 = x_2$. Then from (14) it follows that T_3 is singular matrix.

Next, for $n > 3$, consider an $n \times n$ Cauchy-Toeplitz matrix T defined by the elements $(x_0, \ldots, x_{n-1})$ and $(y_0, \ldots, y_{n-1})$ of $\mathbb{F}_{2^m}$. Denote by T' the 3×3 submatrix of T consisting of first three rows and columns. Then T' is a Cauchy-Toeplitz matrix defined by the elements (x_0, x_1, x_2) and (y_0, y_1, y_2), and we just proved that $x_0 = x_2$. Consequently using Fact 1 it follows that T is singular. This also shows that T is not MDS.   □

3.3   More Classes of Non-MDS Toeplitz Matrices

We now propose a characterization of Toeplitz matrices that are not MDS. Proofs of these lemmas can be found in Appendix A.

Lemma 2. *The $n \times n$ Toeplitz matrix T as given in (2) is not MDS if for some $i < j$ such that $i + j \leq n - 1$, $a_i = a_j$ and $a_{-i} = a_{-j}$ hold.*

Lemma 3. *The maximum number of occurrences of an element $\beta \in \mathbb{F}_{2^m}$ in a 8×8 MDS matrix is 24.*

4   Searching for MDS Matrices with Low XOR Count

In [15], authors have searched efficiently in the class of 4×4 MDS matrices over $\mathbb{F}_{2^4}$ and $\mathbb{F}_{2^8}$ to obtain the least possible XOR count. However, the space of 8×8 MDS matrices is so vast that it is difficult to exhaust. In this section we search in the class of Toeplitz matrices as 4×4 MDS matrices with the optimal XOR counts in this class [15]. However, the class of 8×8 Toeplitz matrices is also large enough that searching for an improved matrix becomes a challenging task. To tackle this we apply a pruning strategy so that we get search results faster. First we form a search tree as follows.

Forming a Search Tree
A 8×8 Toeplitz matrix T can be defined as $T = \text{Toep}(a_0, \ldots, a_7, a_8, \ldots, a_{14})$. From (1) we have that for any 8×8 matrix M, over $\mathbb{F}_{2^m}$ the sum of XOR counts of all the elements of M is $C(M)$. We define C as the lowest known value of $C(M)$. If we find a Toeplitz MDS matrix T such that

$$C(T) = \sum_{i=0, i \neq 7}^{13} (8 - (i \mod 7))\text{XOR}(a_i) + \text{XOR}(a_7) + \text{XOR}(a_{14}) < \text{C}, \quad (16)$$

we obtain a new MDS matrix with lower XOR count.

Suppose the matrix is defined over the set $U \subseteq \mathbb{F}_{2^m}$. Then every a_i has $|U|$ options to choose from. So the naive search complexity is $|U|^{15}$. Given a_i, for $i = 0, \ldots, 13$, next a_{i+1} will be one of $|U|$ choices, that is, we can view this as a tree where every node has $|U|$ children. As a_0 itself has $|U|$ choices, there will be $|U|$ such trees. Traveling from the root to a leaf will give us one tuple $(a_0, \ldots, a_7, a_8, \ldots, a_{14})$. If $\text{Toep}(a_0, \ldots, a_7, a_8, \ldots, a_{14})$ is MDS, and it also satisfies (16), we get an improved MDS matrix with respect to XOR count. However, if we see that for a choice of a_i, the tuple $(a_0, \ldots, a_i)$ cannot be a part of any $(a_0, \ldots, a_7, a_8, \ldots, a_{14})$ such that $\text{Toep}(a_0, \ldots, a_7, a_8, \ldots, a_{14})$ is not MDS or does not satisfy (16), then we can prune the whole subtree rooted at that a_i, as $\text{Toep}(a_0, \ldots, a_7, a_8, \ldots, a_{14})$ will not improve C for such a choice of a_i. Next we discuss in detail the pruning criteria which we call as E1, E2, E3 and E4.

E1: Occurrence of an element is more than 24 times

Suppose we are at the i-th level, that is with the subtuple $(a_0, \ldots, a_i)$. With this we have a submatrix where each a_r, $0 \le r \le i$ occurs $8 - (r \mod 7)$ times if $r \le 13$ and only once if $r = 14$. We count the number of occurrences of the value of a_i in this submatrix, and if a_i occurs more than 24 times, then by Lemma 3, $(a_0, \ldots, a_i)$ cannot be a part of any Toeplitz MDS matrix $\mathrm{Toep}(a_0, \ldots, a_i, \ldots, a_{14})$. So we prune the subtree rooted at this value of a_i, and switch to the next sibling. Figure 1 in Appendix B describes one such scenario.

E2: XOR count of the submatrix $\ge$ C

First we sort U in ascending order with respect to XOR counts of its elements. Now suppose that we are at the subtuple $(a_0, \ldots, a_i)$ and if

$$\sum_{r=0}^{i}(8 - (r \mod 7))\mathrm{XOR}\,(a_r) \ge \mathtt{C}, \quad \text{for } i < 14, \text{ or}$$

$$\sum_{r=0}^{13}(8 - (r \mod 7))\mathrm{XOR}\,(a_r) + \mathrm{XOR}\,(a_{14}) \ge \mathtt{C}, \quad \text{for } i = 14 \tag{17}$$

holds, then for the current value of a_i, $(a_0, \ldots, a_i)$ cannot be a part of any Toeplitz matrix $\mathrm{Toep}(a_0, \ldots, a_i, \ldots, a_{14}), (a_i \neq 0, \forall i)$ whose XOR count is $<$ C. Since a_i takes values from U which is sorted in increasing order, then all the next siblings will have equal or higher XOR counts, so they will also satisfy (17). Hence we prune the subtree rooted at the current value of a_i and all the other possible subtrees rooted at its next siblings having higher XOR counts. So we move back to a_{i-1} and update it by a new value from U. Figure 2 describes one such scenario.

E3: Submatrices satisfying Lemma 2

Suppose we are with a subtuple $(a_0, \ldots, a_7, \ldots, a_i)$. That is we are now dealing with a $(i-6) \times 8$ Toeplitz submatrix. If $(a_0, \ldots, a_i)$ is such that the condition stated in Lemma 2 is satisfied, then $(a_0, \ldots, a_7, \ldots, a_i)$ cannot be a part of any Toeplitz MDS matrix defined $(a_0, \ldots, a_i, \ldots, a_{14})$. So we prune the subtree rooted at this value of a_i, and switch to the next sibling.

E4: One submatrix is singular

When we are dealing with a $(i-6) \times 8$ Toeplitz submatrix T' formed by $(a_0, \ldots, a_7, \ldots, a_i)$, if one of the submatrices of T' is singular, then we prune the subtree rooted at a_i's current value, and replace it by a new value.

Finally when we land up having a tuple $(a_0, \ldots, a_{14})$ which has survived all the pruning criteria E1, E2, E3, E4 at every level, then we obtain a Toeplitz MDS matrix $T = \mathrm{Toep}(a_0, \ldots, a_{14})$ with lower XOR count than C. Next we replace $\mathtt{C} = C(T)$, and continue the search.

5   MDS Matrices over $\mathbb{F}_{2^4}$ with Improved XOR Count

Using the above mentioned search method we now search for 8×8 Toeplitz MDS matrices over $\mathbb{F}_{2^4}$. The lowest known XOR count of 8×8 MDS matrix is $208 + 7 \cdot 4 \cdot 8$ as reported in [17]. So we set $\mathtt{C} = 208$, and we look for Toeplitz MDS matrices over $\mathbb{F}_{2^4}$ with $C(T) < \mathtt{C}$. We consider $\mathbb{F}_{2^4}$ defined by primitive polynomial $X^4 + X + 1$ whose primitive element is denoted by α. We select $U = \mathbb{F}_{2^4}^*$ that is sorted in ascending order according to the XOR counts of its elements, $U = \{1, \alpha, \alpha^{14}, \alpha^2, \alpha^3, \alpha^{13}, \alpha^4, \alpha^5, \alpha^6, \alpha^7, \alpha^8, \alpha^{12}, \alpha^9, \alpha^{11}, \alpha^{10}\}$. The corresponding XOR counts are $\{0, 1, 1, 2, 3, 3, 5, 5, 5, 6, 6, 6, 8, 8, 9\}$. We apply our search strategy and obtain improved matrices. In fact we obtain several matrices T with $C(T) < 208$, we mention a matrix with least one. The matrix

$$\mathtt{Toep}(\alpha^1, 1, \alpha^4, 1, \alpha^5, \alpha^{14}, \alpha^7, \alpha^8, \alpha^3, \alpha^6, \alpha^{14}, \alpha^{14}, \alpha^8, \alpha^6, \alpha^3) \qquad (18)$$

has XOR count $170 + 7 \cdot 4 \cdot 8$.

The naive search would require to consider $15^{15} = 2^{59}$ elements of $\mathbb{F}_{2^4}$. As our search is applying pruning, thus it ends up considering only

$$22275827417 \approx 2^{35}$$

possible $\mathbb{F}_{2^4}$ elements for the a_i's in total. This explains the effectiveness of our search strategy. As it is observed by [17] that change of irreducible polynomial has effect on the XOR count, so we consider other irreducible polynomials that define $\mathbb{F}_{2^4}$. Note that $X^4 + X^3 + X^2 + X + 1$ is the only such irreducible polynomial apart from $X^4 + X + 1$ up to reciprocal. However, we do not find any better matrix under this irreducible polynomial.

6   MDS Matrices over $\mathbb{F}_{2^8}$ with Lower XOR Count

Next we apply the same search strategy to obtain 8×8 Toeplitz MDS matrices over $\mathbb{F}_{2^8}$. The best known MDS matrix is reported in [11], which is a circulant matrix that has XOR count $240 + 8 \cdot 7 \cdot 8$. We consider $\mathbb{F}_{2^8}$ defined by the primitive polynomial $X^8 + X^7 + X^6 + X + 1$. We take Toeplitz matrices over a subset $U \subset \mathbb{F}_{2^8}$ of 15 elements[1], and sort it according to the XOR counts of the elements in increasing order. Precisely $U = \{x : \mathrm{XOR}\,(x) \leq 10\}$. In this case $|U| = 11$. Our search begins with $\mathtt{C} = 240$. When the search completes the lowest XOR count of Toeplitz MDS matrix that we obtain is $232 + 8 \cdot 7 \cdot 8$, example of such a matrix is

$$\mathtt{Toep}(1, 1, \alpha, \alpha^{253}, 1, \alpha^{253}, \alpha^{252}, \alpha^{157}, \alpha^{158}, \alpha^{253}, \alpha^{254}, \alpha, \alpha^{254}, \alpha^2, \alpha). \qquad (19)$$

As $|U| = 11$, the naive search would require to consider $11^{15} = 2^{43}$ elements from $\mathbb{F}_{2^8}$. Using our pruning strategy, we only need to consider

$$1427292833 \approx 2^{31}$$

---

[1] We do not consider full $\mathbb{F}_{2^8}$ as this leads to a huge search space which will be difficult to complete.

possible $\mathbb{F}_{2^8}$ elements for the a_i's in total. Further with a larger $U = \{x : \text{XOR}\,(x) \leq 12\}$, in which case $|U| = 18$, we do not find any improved matrix. In this case we need to consider approximately 2^{34} elements from $\mathbb{F}_{2^8}$ instead of $15^{18} \approx 2^{71}$ elements. Like $\mathbb{F}_{2^4}$, the search strategy is proving to be effective in case of $\mathbb{F}_{2^8}$ also.

We also consider other primitive polynomials (up to reciprocals) that define $\mathbb{F}_{2^8}$ with small a set U as above. However, we do not obtain any better matrices than the example above.

7   Comparisons

We summarize our findings and compare with the existing results in Table 1.

Table 1. Comparison of XOR count of 8×8 MDS matrices over $\mathbb{F}_{2^8}$ and $\mathbb{F}_{2^4}$ with the previously known values.

Irreducible polynomial	Reference	Matrix type	XOR Counts
$\mathbb{F}_{2^8}$			
$X^8 + X^7 + X^6 + X + 1$	Sect. 6	Toeplitz	$232 + 8 \cdot 7 \cdot 8$
$X^8 + X^7 + X^6 + X + 1$	[11]	Circulant	$240 + 8 \cdot 7 \cdot 8$
$X^8 + X^7 + X^6 + X + 1$	[17]	Hadamard	$320 + 8 \cdot 7 \cdot 8$
$X^8 + X^4 + X^3 + X^2 + 1$	[3]	Circulant	$392 + 8 \cdot 7 \cdot 8$
$\mathbb{F}_{2^4}$			
$X^4 + X + 1$	Sect. 5	Toeplitz	$170 + 8 \cdot 7 \cdot 4$
$X^4 + X + 1$	[17]	Hadamard	$208 + 8 \cdot 7 \cdot 4$
$X^4 + X + 1$	[2]	Hadamard	$264 + 8 \cdot 7 \cdot 4$

8   Conclusions

We have presented an extensive study on Toeplitz MDS matrices theoretically and also in the context of hardware implementation. We have developed an efficient search strategy that has helped find 8×8 Toeplitz MDS matrices with improved XOR count over $\mathbb{F}_{2^4}$ and $\mathbb{F}_{2^8}$. As these matrices are in the Toeplitz class, it restates along with [15] the richness of this class of matrices with respect to containing efficient MDS matrices. On the other hand it will be interesting to have families of efficient (in terms of XOR count) 8×8 MDS matrices. As we have shown that Cauchy-Toeplitz matrices cannot be MDS in general, one has to consider more general matrices for such a construction.

A   Proofs and Example

Proof of Lemma 1

Proof. Consider the following $d \times d$ submatrix A.

$$A = \begin{bmatrix} m_{i_0,j_0} & m_{i_0,j_1} & \cdots & m_{i_0,j_{d-1}} \\ m_{i_1,j_0} & m_{i_1,j_1} & \cdots & m_{i_1,j_{d-1}} \\ \vdots & \vdots & \vdots & \vdots \\ m_{i_{d-1},j_0} & m_{i_{d-1},j_1} & \cdots & m_{i_{d-1},j_{d-1}} \end{bmatrix}.$$

Applying (4), we get the form of this matrix as

$$A = \begin{bmatrix} a_{j_0-i_0} & a_{j_1-i_0} & \cdots & a_{j_{d-1}-i_0} \\ a_{j_0-i_1} & a_{j_1-i_1} & \cdots & a_{j_{d-1}-i_1} \\ \vdots & \vdots & \vdots & \vdots \\ a_{j_0-i_{d-1}} & a_{j_1-i_{d-1}} & \cdots & a_{j_{d-1}-i_{d-1}} \end{bmatrix}. \tag{20}$$

If $j_0 - i_0 \geq 0$, then A is equal to the following submatrix whose first row belongs to the first row of the main matrix T:

$$T_{sub} = \begin{bmatrix} m_{0,j_0-i_0} & m_{0,j_1-i_0} & \cdots & m_{0,j_{d-1}-i_0} \\ m_{i_1-i_0,j_0-i_0} & m_{i_1-i_0,j_1-i_0} & \cdots & m_{i_1-i_0,j_{d-1}-i_0} \\ \vdots & \vdots & \vdots & \vdots \\ m_{i_{d-1}-i_0,j_0-i_0} & m_{i_{d-1}-i_0,j_1-i_0} & \cdots & m_{i_{d-1}-i_0,j_{d-1}-i_0} \end{bmatrix}.$$

On the other hand, if $j_0 - i_0 < 0$, then (20) is equal to the following matrix whose first column belongs to the first column of the main matrix T:

$$T_{sub} = \begin{bmatrix} m_{i_0-j_0,0} & m_{i_0-j_0,j_1-j_0} & \cdots & m_{i_0-j_0,j_{d-1}-j_0} \\ m_{i_1-j_0,0} & m_{i_1-j_0,j_1-j_0} & \cdots & m_{i_1-j_0,j_{d-1}-j_0} \\ \vdots & \vdots & \vdots & \vdots \\ m_{i_{d-1}-j_0,0} & m_{i_{d-1}-j_0,j_1-j_0} & \cdots & m_{i_{d-1}-j_0,j_{d-1}-j_0} \end{bmatrix}.$$

□

Proof of Lemma 2

Proof. As $i + j \leq n - 1$, in the $(i+j)$-th row (row and column number starts from 0), a_{-j} appears in the i-th column, i.e., both a_i and a_{-j} are in the same column. Again in the $(i+j)$-th row, a_{-i} appears in the j-th column, i.e., a_{-i} and a_j are in the same column. Therefore, the 2×2 submatrix of T formed by the $0, (i+j)$-th row and i, j-th column is $\begin{bmatrix} a_i & a_j \\ a_{-j} & a_{-i} \end{bmatrix}$. The determinant of this is $a_i a_{-i} + a_j a_{-j} = 0$ by hypothesis. □

Proof of Lemma 3

Proof. It is easy to check that given an MDS matrix $M = [m_{i,j}]_{n \times n}$ and $\beta \in \mathbb{F}_{2^m}^*$ the matrix $\beta M = [\beta\, m_{i,j}]_{n \times n}$ is also MDS. From [8] it is known that in a 8×8 MDS matrix, 1 can occur at most 24 times. So if there is an element β in an 8×8 MDS matrix V that occurs more than 24 times, then $\beta^{-1}V$ contains 1 more than 24 times, a contradiction.   □

Example 2. Suppose α is a primitive root of $X^4 + X + 1 = 0$ that generates $GF(2^4)$. Consider

$$x_0 = 1, \quad y_0 = \alpha + 1,$$
$$x_1 = \alpha, \quad y_1 = x_0 + y_0 + x_1,$$
$$x_2 = x_0, \quad y_2 = y_0.$$

Then the following is a Cauchy-Toeplitz matrix

$$\begin{bmatrix} a^3 + 1 & 1 & a^3 + 1 \\ 1 & a^3 + 1 & 1 \\ a^3 + 1 & 1 & a^3 + 1 \end{bmatrix}.$$

B   Figures and Tables

Table 2. Number of submatrices of general matrices, and number of general and Toeplitz submatrices of Toeplitz matrices.

Dimension	Submatrices of General matrix	Toeplitz matrix	
		General sub-matrices	Toeplitz submatrices
4×4	69	50	20
5×5	251	182	35
6×6	923	672	55
7×7	3431	2508	81
8×8	12869	9438	113
16×16	601080389	445962870	614

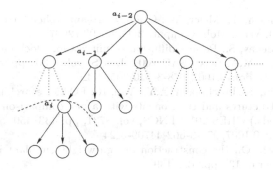

Fig. 1. If the value of a_i occurs more than 24 times then the whole subtree rooted at a_i is pruned.

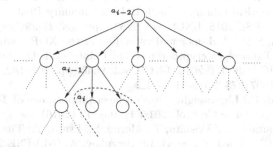

Fig. 2. If the value of a_i satisfies (17), all the subtrees rooted at this a_i and its subsequent siblings are pruned.

References

1. Babbage, S., Dodd, M.: The stream cipher MICKEY 2.0 (2006). http://www.ecrypt.eu.org/stream/mickeypf.html
2. Barreto, P.S.L.M., Nikov, V., Nikova, S., Rijmen, V., Tischhauser, E.: Whirlwind: a new cryptographic hash function. Des. Codes Crypt. **56**(2 3), 141 162 (2010)
3. Barreto, P.S.L.M., Rijmen, V.: Whirlpool. In: van Tilborg, H.C.A., Jajodia, S. (eds.) Encyclopedia of Cryptography and Security, 2nd edn, pp. 1384–1385. Springer, New York (2011)
4. Beierle, C., Kranz, T., Leander, G.: Lightweight multiplication in $GF(2^n)$ with applications to MDS matrices. In: Robshaw, M., Katz, J. (eds.) CRYPTO 2016. LNCS, vol. 9814, pp. 625–653. Springer, Heidelberg (2016). doi:10.1007/978-3-662-53018-4_23
5. Bogdanov, A., Knudsen, L.R., Leander, G., Paar, C., Poschmann, A., Robshaw, M.J.B., Seurin, Y., Vikkelsoe, C.: PRESENT: an ultra-lightweight block cipher. In: Paillier, P., Verbauwhede, I. (eds.) CHES 2007. LNCS, vol. 4727, pp. 450–466. Springer, Heidelberg (2007). doi:10.1007/978-3-540-74735-2_31
6. Borghoff, J., Canteaut, A., Güneysu, T., Kavun, E.B., Knezevic, M., Knudsen, L.R., Leander, G., Nikov, V., Paar, C., Rechberger, C., Rombouts, P., Thomsen, S.S., Yalçın, T.: PRINCE – a low-latency block cipher for pervasive computing applications. In: Wang, X., Sako, K. (eds.) ASIACRYPT 2012. LNCS, vol. 7658, pp. 208–225. Springer, Heidelberg (2012). doi:10.1007/978-3-642-34961-4_14

7. Hell, M., Johansson, T., Meier, W.: Grain: a stream cipher for constrained environments. Int. J. Wire. Mob. Comput. **2**(1), 86–93 (2007)
8. Junod, P., Vaudenay, S.: Perfect diffusion primitives for block ciphers. In: Handschuh, H., Hasan, M.A. (eds.) SAC 2004. LNCS, vol. 3357, pp. 84–99. Springer, Heidelberg (2004). doi:10.1007/978-3-540-30564-4_6
9. Khoo, K., Peyrin, T., Poschmann, A.Y., Yap, H.: FOAM: searching for hardware-optimal SPN structures and components with a fair comparison. In: Batina, L., Robshaw, M. (eds.) CHES 2014. LNCS, vol. 8731, pp. 433–450. Springer, Heidelberg (2014). doi:10.1007/978-3-662-44709-3_24
10. Li, Y., Wang, M.: On the construction of lightweight circulant involutory MDS matrices. In: Peyrin [13], pp. 121–139
11. Liu, M., Sim, S.M.: Lightweight MDS generalized circulant matrices. In: Peyrin [13], pp. 101–120
12. Macwilliams, F.J., Sloane, N.J.A.: The Theory of Error-Correcting Codes (North-Holland Mathematical Library). North Holland, January 1983
13. Peyrin, T. (ed.): FSE 2016. LNCS, vol. 9783. Springer, Heidelberg (2016)
14. Sarkar, S., Sim, S.M.: A deeper understanding of the XOR count distribution in the context of lightweight cryptography. In: Pointcheval, D., Nitaj, A., Rachidi, T. (eds.) AFRICACRYPT 2016. LNCS, vol. 9646, pp. 167–182. Springer, Cham (2016). doi:10.1007/978-3-319-31517-1_9
15. Sarkar, S., Syed, H.: Lightweight diffusion layer: importance of Toeplitz matrices. IACR Trans. Symmetric Cryptol. **2016**(1), 95–113 (2016)
16. Shirai, T., Shibutani, K., Akishita, T., Moriai, S., Iwata, T.: The 128-Bit Blockcipher CLEFIA (Extended Abstract). In: Biryukov, A. (ed.) FSE 2007. LNCS, vol. 4593, pp. 181–195. Springer, Heidelberg (2007). doi:10.1007/978-3-540-74619-5_12
17. Sim, S.M., Khoo, K., Oggier, F., Peyrin, T.: Lightweight MDS involution matrices. In: Leander, G. (ed.) FSE 2015. LNCS, vol. 9054, pp. 471–493. Springer, Heidelberg (2015). doi:10.1007/978-3-662-48116-5_23
18. Tian, Y., Chen, G., Li, J.: On the Design of Trivium. Cryptology ePrint Archive, Report 2009/431 (2009). http://eprint.iacr.org/

Reforgeability of Authenticated Encryption Schemes

Christian Forler[1], Eik List[2], Stefan Lucks[2], and Jakob Wenzel[2([⊠])]

[1] Beuth Hochschule für Technik Berlin, Berlin, Germany
cforler@beuth-hochschule.de
[2] Bauhaus-Universitä Weimar, Weimar, Germany
{eik.list,stefan.lucks,jakob.wenzel}@uni-weimar.de

Abstract. This work pursues the idea of multi-forgery attacks as introduced by Ferguson in 2002. We recoin reforgeability for the complexity of obtaining further forgeries once a first forgery has succeeded. First, we introduce a security notion for the integrity (in terms of reforgeability) of authenticated encryption schemes: j-INT-CTXT, which is derived from the notion INT-CTXT. Second, we define an attack scenario called j-IV-Collision Attack (j-IV-CA), wherein an adversary tries to construct j forgeries provided a first forgery. The term *collision* in the name stems from the fact that we assume the first forgery to be the result from an internal collision within the processing of the associated data and/or the nonce. Next, we analyze the resistance to j-IV-CAs of classical nonce-based AE schemes (CCM, CWC, EAX, GCM) as well as all 3rd-round candidates of the CAESAR competition. The analysis is done in the nonce-respecting and the nonce-ignoring setting. We find that none of the considered AE schemes provides full built-in resistance to j-IV-CAs. Based on this insight, we briefly discuss two alternative design strategies to resist j-IV-CAs.

Keywords: Authenticated encryption · CAESAR · Multi-forgery attack · Reforgeability

1 Introduction

(Nonce-Based) Authenticated Encryption. The goal of authenticated encryption (AE) schemes is to simultaneously protect authenticity and privacy of messages. AE schemes with support for Associated Data (AEAD) provide additional authentication for associated data. The standard security requirement for AE schemes is to prevent leakage of any information about secured messages except for their respective lengths. However, stateless encryption schemes would enable adversaries to detect whether the same associated data and message has been encrypted before under the current key. Thus, Rogaway proposed nonce-based encryption [44], where the user must provide an additional nonce for every message it wants to process – a number used once (nonce). AE schemes that

© Springer International Publishing AG 2017
J. Pieprzyk and S. Suriadi (Eds.): ACISP 2017, Part II, LNCS 10343, pp. 19–37, 2017.
DOI: 10.1007/978-3-319-59870-3_2

require a nonce input are called nonce-based authenticated encryption (nAE) schemes.

Reforgeability. In the cryptographic sense, *reforgeability* refers to the complexity of finding subsequent forgeries once a first forgery has been found. Thus, it defines the hardness of forging a ciphertext after the first forgery succeeded. The first attack known was introduced in 2002 by Ferguson by showing collision attacks on OCB [45] and a Ctr-CBC-like MAC [17]. He showed that finding a collision within the message processing of OCB *"leads to complete loss of an essential function"* (referring to the loss of authenticity/integrity).

Later on, in 2005, the term *multiple forgery attacks* was formed and defined by McGrew and Fluhrer [35]. They introduced the measure of expected number of forgeries and conducted a thorough analysis of GCM [34], HMAC [6], and CBC-MAC [8]. In 2008, Handschuh and Preneel [22] introduced key recovery and universal forgery attacks against several MAC algorithms. The term *Reforgeability* was first formally defined by Black and Cochran in 2009, where they examined common MACs regarding their security to this new measurement [13]. Further, they introduced WMAC, which they argue to be the *"best fit for resource-limited devices"*.

Relevance. For a reforgeability attack to work, an adversary must be provided with a verification oracle in addition to its authentication (and encryption) oracle. In practice, such a setting can, for example, be found when a client tries to authenticate itself to a server and has multiple tries to log in to a system. Thus, the server would be the verification oracle for the client.

Obviously, the same argument holds for the case when the data to be send is of sensitive nature, i.e., the data itself has to be encrypted. Thus, besides the resistance of MACs to reforgeability, also the resistance of AE schemes is of high practical relevance.

Since modern and cryptographically secure AE schemes should provide at least INT-CTXT security in terms of integrity, the first forgery is usually not trivially found and depends on the size of the tag or the internal state. For that reason, reforgeability becomes especially essential when considering resource-constrained devices limited by, e.g., radio power, bandwidth, area, or throughput. This is not uncommon in the area of low-end applications such as sensor networks, VoIP, streaming interfaces, or, for example, devices connected to the Internet of Things (IoT). In these domains, the tag size τ of MACs and AE schemes is usually quite small, e.g., $\tau = 64$ or $\tau = 32$ bits, or even smaller ($\tau = 8$ bits) as mentioned by Ferguson in regard to voice systems [18]. Therefore, even if the AE scheme is secure in the INT-CTXT setting up to τ bits, it is not unreasonable for an adversary to find a forgery for such a scheme in general. Nevertheless, even if finding the first forgery requires a large amount of work, a rising question is, whether it can be exploited to find more forgeries with significantly less than 2^τ queries to an authentication oracle per forgery. For our analysis, we derive a new security notion j-INT-CTXT, which states that an adversary who finds the first forgery using t_1 queries, can generate j

additional forgeries in polynomial time depending on j. In general, the best case would be to find j additional forgeries using $t_1 + j$ queries. Nevertheless, for five schemes (AES-OTR [37], GCM [34], COLM [3], CWC [29], and OCB [30]), there already exist forgery attacks in the literature (see [19] for details) leading to j forgeries using only t_1 queries (thus, the j additional authentication queries are not even required).

Due to the vast number of submissions to the CAESAR competition [10], cryptanalysis proceeds slowly for each individual scheme. For instance, forgery attacks on 3rd-round CAESAR candidates have only been published for AES-COPA [4,32,39], which even might become obsolete since AES-COPA and ELMD [14] have been merged to COLM [3]. Besides looking at 3rd-round CAE-SAR candidates, we also analyze other existing and partially widely-used AE schemes, e.g., GCM, EAX [9], CCM [16], and CWC. Naturally, due to their longer existence, there exist a lot more cryptanalysis on those schemes in comparison to the CAESAR candidates (see [20,27,28,36,42,46] for some examples). The hope is that an INT-CTXT-secure AE scheme does not lose its security when considering reforgeability, i.e., j-INT-CTXT.

We briefly introduce what we mean by *resistant to j-IV-CAs*, whereby we assume the first forgery to be the results from an internal collision of the processing of the associated data and/or the nonce.

- **Nonce-Ignoring:** We call an nAE scheme resistant to j-IV-CAs if the required number of queries of a *nonce-ignoring* j-IV-CA adversary for finding $1 + j$ forgeries (including the first) is greater than $t_1 + j$, where t_1 denotes the number of queries for finding the first forgery.
- **Nonce-Respecting:** We call an nAE scheme resistant to j-IV-CAs if the required number of queries of a *nonce-respecting* j-IV-CA adversary for finding $1 + j$ forgeries (including the first) is greater than $t_1 \cdot j/2$, where t_1 denotes the number of queries for finding the first forgery.

Further, we say that an nAE scheme is *semi-resistant* to j-IV-CAs if the internal state is of wide size and the scheme itself is not trivially insecure in terms of j-IV-CA. Thereby, following a similar approach to the wide-pipe mode introduced for hash functions [33], the internal state of an nAE scheme is at least twice as big as the output, i.e., the tag value. Such a design is, for example, given by the widely used Sponge construction [11]. That would make the search for a generic collision significantly harder than the search for multiple forgeries. We denote the number of queries required for finding a collision within a wide internal state by t_2. Finally, we call an nAE scheme *vulnerable* to j-IV-CAs if it is neither resistant nor semi-resistant to j-IV-CA.

Contribution. This work classifies nonce-based AE schemes depending on the usage of their inputs to the initialization, encryption, and authentication process, and categorize the considered AE schemes regarding to that classification. To allow for a systematic analysis of the reforgeability of AE schemes, we introduce the j-IV-Collision Attack based on the introduced security definition j-INT-CTXT, providing us with expected upper bounds on the hardness of further forgeries (a summary of our results can be found in Table 1). For our attack, we pursue the idea of the message-block-collision attacks presented in [17,45]. However, in contrast, we focus on an internal collision within the processing of the associated data and/or the nonce. In the last section, we provide two approaches to provide resistance in the sense of reforgeability and j-IV-CAs. Moreover, in the full version of this work [19], for AES-OTR, COLM, and OCB, we describe three attacks making multi-forgery attacks more efficient than our generic approach.

Table 1. Expected #oracle queries required for j forgeries for IV/nonce-based classical schemes and 3rd-round CAESAR candidates. By t_1 and t_2, we denote the computational cost for obtaining the first forgery, where t_2 relates to wide-state designs. **NR** = nonce-respecting setting; **NI** = nonce-ignoring setting. Since we obtained the same results for DEOXYS-I and DEOXYS-II, we combine them to DEOXYS in this table. NR-NORX (draft) means the nonce-misuse-resistant version of NORX.

Scheme	NI	NR	Scheme	NI	NR
3rd-round CAESAR candidates					
ACORN [47]	$t_1 + j$	$t_1 \cdot j/2$	KETJE [12]	$t_2 + j$	$t_2 \cdot j/2$
AEGIS [50]	$t_2 + j$	$t_2 \cdot j/2$	KEYAK [21]	$t_2 + j$	$t_2 \cdot j/2$
AES-OTR [37]	t_1	t_1	MORUS [48]	$t_2 + j$	$t_2 \cdot j/2$
AEZv4 [23]	$t_1 + j$	$t_1 \cdot j/2$	NORX [5]	$t_2 + j$	$t_2 \cdot j/2$
ASCON [15]	$t_2 + j$	$t_2 \cdot j/2$	NR-NORX [5]	$t_2 + j$	$t_2 \cdot j$
CLOC [24]	$t_1 + j$	$t_1 \cdot j$	OCB [30]	t_1	t_1
COLM [3]	t_1	$t_1 + j$	SILC [24]	$t_1 + j$	$t_1 \cdot j$
DEOXYS [26]	$t_1 + j$	$t_1 \cdot j$	TIAOXIN [40]	$t_2 + j$	$t_2 \cdot j/2$
JAMBU [49]	$t_1 + j$	$t_1 \cdot j/2$			
Classical schemes					
CWC [29]	t_1	t_1	CCM [16]	$t_1 + j$	$t_1 + j$
EAX [9]	$t_1 + j$	$t_1 \cdot j$	GCM [34]	t_1	t_1

Outline. Section 2 provides necessary preliminaries including our security notions. Section 3 introduces our classification of generic AE schemes. Section 4 presents the j-IV-CA and a generic security analysis. Section 5 contains possible remedies to j-IV-CAs and Sect. 6 concludes our work.

2   Preliminaries

We use lowercase letters x for indices and integers, uppercase letters X, Y for binary strings and functions, and calligraphic uppercase letters $\mathcal{X}, \mathcal{Y}$ for sets and combined functions. We denote the concatenation of binary strings X and Y by

$X \parallel Y$ and the result of their bitwise XOR by $X \oplus Y$. We indicate the length of X in bits by $|X|$, and write X_i for the i-th block (assuming that X can be split into blocks of, e.g., n bits). Furthermore, we denote by $X \leftarrow \mathcal{X}$ that X is chosen uniformly at random from the set $\mathcal{X}$. For an event E, we denote by $\Pr[E]$ the probability of E.

Adversaries and Advantages. An adversary $\mathbf{A}$ is an efficient Turing machine that interacts with a given set of oracles that appear as black boxes to $\mathbf{A}$. We denote by $\mathbf{A}^{\mathcal{O}}$ the output of $\mathbf{A}$ after interacting with some oracle $\mathcal{O}$. We write $\mathbf{Adv}_F^X(\mathbf{A})$ for the advantage $\mathbf{A}$ against a security notion X on a function/scheme F. All probabilities are defined over the random coins of the oracles and those of the adversary, if any. We write $\mathbf{Adv}_F^X(q, \ell, t) = \max_{\mathbf{A}}\{\mathbf{Adv}_F^X(\mathbf{A})\}$ to refer to the maximal advantage over all X-adversaries $\mathbf{A}$ on a given scheme/function F that run in time at most t and pose at most q queries consisting of at most ℓ blocks in total to the available oracles. Wlog., we assume that $\mathbf{A}$ never asks queries to which it already knows the answer, and by $\mathcal{O}_1 \hookrightarrow \mathcal{O}_2$ we denote that $\mathbf{A}$ never queries $\mathcal{O}_2$ with the output of $\mathcal{O}_1$.

We define as (q_E, q_D, ℓ, t)-adversary $\mathbf{A}$ an adversary that asks at most q_E queries to its first oracle, q_D queries to its second oracle, which consist of at most ℓ blocks in sum, where $\mathbf{A}$ runs in time at most t. We define a scheme Π to be $(q_E, q_D, \ell, t, \epsilon)$-X-secure to a notion X if the maximal advantage of all (q_E, q_D, ℓ, t)-X-adversaries on Π is upper bounded by ϵ. During the query phase, we say that an adversary $\mathbf{A}$ maintains a query history $\mathcal{Q}$ collecting all requests together with their corresponding answer. We write $\mathcal{Q}_{|X}$, if we refer only to all entries of type X in the query history. For example, $N_i \notin \mathcal{Q}_{|N}$ denotes that the nonce N_i is not contained in the set of nonces already in the query history.

Nonce-Based AE Schemes. A nonce-based authenticated encryption (nAE) scheme (with associated data) [43] is a tuple $\Pi = (\mathcal{E}, \mathcal{D})$ of a deterministic encryption algorithm $\mathcal{E} : \mathcal{K} \times \mathcal{A} \times \mathcal{N} \times \mathcal{M} \to \mathcal{C} \times \mathcal{T}$, and a deterministic decryption algorithm $\mathcal{D} : \mathcal{K} \times \mathcal{A} \times \mathcal{N} \times \mathcal{C} \times \mathcal{T} \to \mathcal{M} \cup \{\bot\}$, with associated non-empty key space $\mathcal{K}$, associated data space $\mathcal{A} \subseteq \{0,1\}^*$, the non-empty nonce space $\mathcal{N}$, and $\mathcal{M}, \mathcal{C} \subseteq \{0,1\}^*$ denote the message and ciphertext space, respectively. We define a tag space $\mathcal{T} = \{0,1\}^\tau$ for a fixed $\tau \geq 0$. We write $\mathcal{E}_K^{A,N}(M)$ and $\mathcal{D}_K^{A,N}(C,T)$ as short forms of $\mathcal{E}(K, A, N, M)$ and $\mathcal{D}(K, A, N, C, T)$. If a given tuple (A, N, C, T) is valid, $\mathcal{D}_K^{A,N}(C,T)$ returns the corresponding plaintext M, and $\bot$ otherwise. We assume that for all $K \in \mathcal{K}$, $A \in \mathcal{A}$, $N \in \mathcal{N}$, and $M \in \mathcal{M}$ holds *stretch-preservation*: if $\mathcal{E}_K^{A,N}(M) = (C,T)$, then $|C| = |M|$ and $|T| = \tau$, *correctness*: if $\mathcal{E}_K^{A,N}(M) = (C,T)$, then $\mathcal{D}_K^{A,N}(C,T) = M$, and *tidiness*: if $\mathcal{D}_K^{A,N}(C,T) = M \neq \bot$, then $\mathcal{E}_K^{A,N}(M) = (C,T)$, for all $C \in \mathcal{C}$ and $T \in \mathcal{T}$.

Security Notions for Reforgeability. In 2004, Bellare et al. introduced the two security notions INT-PTXT-M and INT-CTXT-M [7]; however, these notions capture the setting that an adversary can pose multiple verification queries for a *single* forgery. In contrast, we are interested in finding *multiple* (in general $j \geq 1$) forgeries based on multiple verification queries. In the scenario of

---

Algorithm 1. The j-INT-CTXT Experiment.

Experiment j-INT-CTXT
1: $K \leftarrow \mathcal{K}$
2: Run $\mathbf{A}^{\mathcal{E}(\cdot),\mathcal{D}(\cdot)}$ such that $\mathbf{A}$ never queries $\mathcal{E} \hookrightarrow \mathcal{D}$
3: **if** $\mathbf{A}$ made j distinct decryption queries (A_i, N_i, C_i, T_i), $1 \leq i \leq j$ such that $\mathcal{D}_K(A_i, N_i, C_i, T_i) \neq \bot$ for all $1 \leq i \leq j$ **then return** 1
4: **return** 0

INT-CTXT, an adversary wins if it can find any valid forgery, that is a tuple (A, N, C, T) for which the decryption returns anything different from the invalid symbol $\bot$ and which has not been previously obtained by $\mathbf{A}$ as response of the encryption oracle. The j-INT-CTXT security notion, as shown in Algorithm 1, is derived from INT-CTXT in the sense that $\mathbf{A}$ now has to provide j distinct valid forgeries that all have not been obtained from the encryption oracle. In the following, we define the j-INT-CTXT Advantage of an adversary.

Definition 1 (j-INT-CTXT Advantage). *Let $\Pi = (\mathcal{E}, \mathcal{D})$ be a nonce-based AE scheme, $K \leftarrow \mathcal{K}$, and $\mathbf{A}$ be a computationally bounded adversary on Π with access to two oracles $\mathcal{E}$ and $\mathcal{D}$ such that $\mathbf{A}$ never queries $\mathcal{E} \hookrightarrow \mathcal{D}$. Then, the j-INT-CTXT advantage of $\mathbf{A}$ on Π defined as*

$$\mathbf{Adv}_{\Pi}^{j\text{-INT-CTXT}}(\mathbf{A}) := \Pr\left[\mathbf{A}^{\mathcal{E},\mathcal{D}} \text{ forges } j \text{ times}\right],$$

where "forges" means that $\mathcal{D}_K$ returns anything other than $\bot$ for a query of $\mathbf{A}$, and "forges j times" means that $\mathbf{A}$ provides j distinct decryption queries (A_i, N_i, C_i, T_i), $1 \leq i \leq j$ such that $\mathcal{D}_K(A_i, N_i, C_i, T_i) \neq \bot$ for all $1 \leq i \leq j$.

We define $\mathbf{Adv}_{\Pi}^{j\text{-INT-CTXT}}(q_E, q_D, \ell, t)$ for the maximal advantage over all adversaries $\mathbf{A}$ on Π that ask at most q_E encryption queries, q_D decryption queries, which sum up to at most ℓ blocks in total, and run in time at most t.

3   Classification of AE Schemes

In our work, we consider AE schemes from a general point of view. Therefore, in comparison to the classification of Namprempre, Rogaway, and Shrimpton [38], we introduce one additional optional input to the tag-generation step (a key-dependent chaining value) and further, we distinguish between the message and the ciphertext being input to the tag generation.

We classify AE schemes according to their inputs to an initialization function F_{IV} and a tag-generation function F_T. Let $\mathcal{K}, \mathcal{A}, \mathcal{N}, \mathcal{IV}, \mathcal{T}, \mathcal{M}, \mathcal{CV}$, and $\mathcal{C}$ define the key, associated data, nonce, IV, tag, message, chaining-value, and ciphertext space, respectively. We define three functions $F_{IV}, \mathcal{E}$, and F_T as follows:

$$F_{IV} : \mathcal{K}[\times\mathcal{A}][\times\mathcal{N}][\times\mathcal{M}] \qquad \rightarrow \mathcal{IV},$$
$$\mathcal{E} : \mathcal{K} \times \mathcal{IV} \times \mathcal{M} \qquad \rightarrow \mathcal{C}[\times\mathcal{CV}],$$
$$F_T : \mathcal{K}[\times\mathcal{CV}][\times\mathcal{M}][\times\mathcal{C}][\times\mathcal{A}][\times\mathcal{N}] \rightarrow \mathcal{T},$$

where $\mathcal{A}, \mathcal{N}, \mathcal{M}, \mathcal{CV}, \mathcal{C} \subseteq \{0,1\}^*$, $\mathcal{T} \subseteq \{0,1\}^\tau$, and $\mathcal{IV} \subseteq \{0,1\}^*$. The expressions (sets) given in brackets are *optional* inputs to the corresponding function, e.g., the function F_{IV} must be provided with at least one input (the key $K \in \mathcal{K}$), but is able to process up to four inputs (including associated data $A \in \mathcal{A}$, nonce $N \in \mathcal{N}$, and message $M \in \mathcal{M}$).

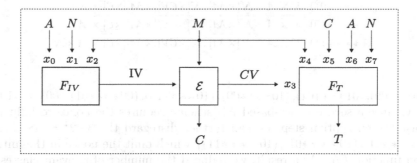

Fig. 1. Generic AE scheme as considered in our analysis.

From this, we introduce a generic classification based on which input is used in F_{IV} and F_T. Note that the encryption algorithm $\mathcal{E}$ is equal for all classes described, i.e., it encrypts a message M under a key K and an $IV \in \mathcal{IV}$, and outputs a ciphertext $C \in \mathcal{C}$. However, the authors of [38] distinguished between IV-based (ivE) and nonce-based (nE) encryption schemes. Such a distinction is covered by our generalized approach since one can simply assume the only input to F_{IV} to be the nonce (and the key) and making F_{IV} itself the identity function, i.e., it forwards the nonce N to the encryption function $\mathcal{E}$. Moreover, AE schemes built from generic composition can be modelled by setting $x_3 = 0$ and assuming F_T to be a PRF-secure MAC (see below for the meaning of x_3).

In the following, we encode the combination of inputs as a sequence of eight bits $x_0, \ldots, x_7$, where each bit denotes whether an input is used (1) or not (0), resulting in a total of $2^8 = 256$ possible classes. More detailed, the first three bits x_0, x_1, x_2 denote whether the associated data A, the nonce N, or the message M is used as input to F_{IV}, respectively. The bits $x_3, \ldots, x_7$ denote whether a key-dependent chaining value CV, M, C, A, or N is used as input to F_T, respectively (see Fig. 1 for a depiction of our generic AE scheme). For example, the string (11010011) represents $F_{IV} : \mathcal{K} \times \mathcal{A} \times \mathcal{N} \to \mathcal{IV}$ and $F_T : \mathcal{K} \times \mathcal{CV} \times \mathcal{A} \times \mathcal{N} \to \mathcal{T}$ as it would be the case for, e.g., POET [2], CLOC, and SILC [24]. Further, we mark a bit position by '∗' if we do not care about whether the specific input is available or not.

Our next step is to significantly reduce the number of possible classes by disregarding those that are trivially insecure. First, we can simply discard $2^4 = 16$ classes of the form $(00 * * * *00)$, where neither the nonce N nor the associated data A is considered as input. Similarly, we can exclude $6 \cdot 2^4 = 96$ classes which lack the use of either the nonce *or* the associated data, i.e.,

Table 2. Overview of accepted classes. All excluded classes are trivially insecure.

Set of classes	Input to F_{IV}	Input to F_T
$(01***10)$	$\mathcal{K} \times \mathcal{N}[\times\mathcal{M}]$	$\mathcal{K}[\times\mathcal{CV}][\times\mathcal{M}][\times\mathcal{C}] \times \mathcal{A}$
$(01***11)$	$\mathcal{K} \times \mathcal{N}[\times\mathcal{M}]$	$\mathcal{K}[\times\mathcal{CV}][\times\mathcal{M}][\times\mathcal{C}] \times \mathcal{A} \times \mathcal{N}$
$(11***00)$	$\mathcal{K} \times \mathcal{A} \times \mathcal{N}[\times\mathcal{M}]$	$\mathcal{K}[\times\mathcal{CV}][\times\mathcal{M}][\times\mathcal{C}]$
$(11***01)$	$\mathcal{K} \times \mathcal{A} \times \mathcal{N}[\times\mathcal{M}]$	$\mathcal{K}[\times\mathcal{CV}][\times\mathcal{M}][\times\mathcal{C}] \times \mathcal{N}$
$(11***10)$	$\mathcal{K} \times \mathcal{A} \times \mathcal{N}[\times\mathcal{M}]$	$\mathcal{K}[\times\mathcal{CV}][\times\mathcal{M}][\times\mathcal{C}] \times \mathcal{A}$
$(11***11)$	$\mathcal{K} \times \mathcal{A} \times \mathcal{N}[\times\mathcal{M}]$	$\mathcal{K}[\times\mathcal{CV}][\times\mathcal{M}][\times\mathcal{C}] \times \mathcal{A} \times \mathcal{N}$

$\{(01***00), (01***01), (10***00), (10***10), (00***01), (00***10)\}$.
Finally, since a secure nonce-based AE scheme requires the nonce to influence at least the encryption step, we can further disregard the $3 \cdot 2^4 = 48$ classes $\{(00***11), (10***01), (10***11)\}$ which omit the nonce in the initialization function F_{IV}. As a result, we reduced the number of relevant classes to 96. An overview can be found in Table 2.

4 j-INT-CTXT-Analysis of nAE Schemes

In this section, we introduce a new attack type called j-IV-Collision Attack (j-IV-CA) as one possible way to analyze the security of a nonce-based AE scheme regarding to reforgeability. We provide two variants (1) for the nonce-ignoring (NI; also known as nonce misuse) and (2) the nonce-respecting (NR) setting.

4.1 j-IV-Collision Attack

The core idea of a j-IV-CA is to (1) assume a first forgery can be found caused by an internal collision within the processing of the associated data A and/or the nonce N and (2) to exploit this collision for efficiently constructing j further forgeries. Depending on the class of an AE scheme, such a collision can occur during the invocation of F_{IV}, F_T, or both.

Due to the character of the attacks presented in this section, we can derive a set of classes $\mathcal{C}_0$ of nAE schemes for which those attacks are trivially applicable. For all schemes belonging to that class, it holds that neither the message M, a message/ciphertext-depending chaining CV, nor the ciphertext C influence the first collision found by our adversary, e.g., if an adversary tries to construct a collision for the outputs of F_{IV}, the only possible inputs to F_{IV} are either the nonce N, the associated data A, or both. Therefore, the set $\mathcal{C}_0$ contains the following 22 classes of AE schemes:

$$\mathcal{C}_0 = \{(110***0*), (01*0001*), (11000011), (11000010)\}.$$

Algorithm 2. j-IV-Collision Attack for nonce-ignoring adversaries.

1: Choose an arbitrary fixed message M
2: $\mathcal{Q} \leftarrow \emptyset$
3: **for** $i \leftarrow 1$ to t_1 **do**
4:     Choose (A_i, N_i) with $(A_i, N_i) \notin \mathcal{Q}_{|A,N}$
5:     Query (A_i, N_i, M) and receive (C_i, T_i).
6:     $\mathcal{Q} \leftarrow \mathcal{Q} \cup \{(A_i, N_i, M, C_i, T_i)\}$
7:     **if** $T_i \in \mathcal{Q}_{|T}$ **then**
8:         Store the tuples (A_i, N_i, M, C_i, T_i) and (A_k, N_k, M, C_k, T_k) for which $T_i = T_k$
9:         **break**
10: **for** $\ell \leftarrow 1$ to j **do**
11:     Choose $M_\ell \notin \mathcal{Q}_{|M}$
12:     Query (A_i, N_i, M_ℓ) and receive (C'_ℓ, T'_ℓ)
13:     $\mathcal{Q} \leftarrow \mathcal{Q} \cup \{(*, *, M_\ell, *, *)\}$
14:     Output the forgery $(A_k, N_k, C'_\ell, T'_\ell)$

Nonce-Ignoring Setting The attack for the nonce-ignoring setting is described in Algorithm 2. An adversary **A** starts by choosing a fixed arbitrary message M and pairs (A_i, N_i) not queried before $((A_i, N_i) \notin \mathcal{Q}_{|A,N}$, see Line 4). That builds up a query (A_i, N_i, M) resulting in an oracle answer (C_i, T_i) which is stored by **A** in the query history $\mathcal{Q}$. Once a collision of two tag values T_i and T_k (implying a collision of two pairs $(A_i, N_i) \neq (A_k, N_k))$[1] was found (Line 7 of Algorithm 2), **A** starts to generate j additionally queries with an effort of $\mathcal{O}(j)$ (Lines 10–14). In Lines 6 and 13, the adversary is collecting all tuples queried so far, where in Line 13 we are only interested in the values of M_ℓ, since these are not allowed to repeat (see Line 11) by the definition of **A**.

It is easy to observe that **A** has to use the same nonce twice, i.e., N_i is chosen in Line 4 and reused in Line 12 of Algorithm 2. Independent from the number of queries of finding the j additional forgeries, **A** always (in the nonce-ignoring as well as in the nonce-respecting setting) has to find a collision for two pairs $(A_i, N_i) \neq (A_k, N_k)$. That number of queries (denoted by t_1 in general, or by t_2 if the scheme employs a wide state of $\geq 2n$ bits (or $\geq 2\tau$ bits, when referring to the size of the tag value), see Table 1) always depends on the concrete instantiation of our generic AE scheme and is usually bounded by at least $\mathcal{O}(q^2/2^n)$ (birthday bound), where q denotes the number of queries and n the state size in bit. In Table 4 of Appendix B, the reader can find the security claims of the considered AE schemes provided by their respective designers.

Nonce-Respecting Setting. The second setting prohibits an adversary from repeating any value N_i during its encryption queries. Therefore, we introduce a

---

[1] Based on our assumption, the case $T_i = T_k$ can be caused by an internal collision of the processing of two pairs $(A_i, N_i) \neq (A_k, N_k)$. Moreover, since we are considering the nonce-ignoring setting allowing an adversary for repeating the values N_i, we can say wlog. That we must have found two associated data values $A_i \neq A_k$ leading to an equal output of the processing of the associated data, e.g., the initialization vector IV (see Fig. 1).

Algorithm 3. j-IV-Collision Attack for nonce-respecting adversaries.

1: Choose an arbitrary fixed message block M
2: $\mathcal{Q} \leftarrow \emptyset$
3: **for** 1 to j **do**
4:    **for** $i \leftarrow 1$ to t_1 **do**
5:       Choose (A_i, N_i) with $(A_i, N_i) \notin \mathcal{Q}_{|A,N}$
6:       Choose P_i with $P_i \notin \mathcal{Q}_{|P}$
7:       Query $(A_i, N_i, M \parallel P_i)$ and receive $(C_i^1 \parallel C_i^{P_i}, T_i)$.
8:       $\mathcal{Q} \leftarrow \mathcal{Q} \cup \{(A_i, N_i, C_i^1 \parallel C_i^{P_i}, T_i)\}$
9:       **if** $C_i^1 \in \mathcal{Q}_{|C^1}$ **then**
10:          **A** outputs the tuples $(A_i, N_i, C_i^1 \parallel C_k^{P_k}, T_k)$ and $(A_k, N_k, C_k^1 \parallel C_i^{P_i}, T_i)$
11:          for which $C_i^1 = C_k^1$ holds
12:          **goto** Step 4

---

modified version of the j-IV-CA as proposed above. Such an attack works for all schemes that allow to observe a collision of the outputs of the IV-generation step by just looking at the ciphertext blocks. Thus, during the first step, we do not care about finding the first forgery but only about the collision during F_{IV} as shown in Algorithm 3. This attacks works also for nAE schemes that consider the associated data A_i only as input to F_T. In such a situation, **A** would leave A_i constant (or empty when considering F_{IV}) and would vary only N_i to find a collision within F_{IV}.

If the number of queries for finding a collision during the processing of the associated data is given by t_1, an adversary requires $j \cdot t_1$ queries in average to obtain $2 \cdot j$ forgeries. Clearly, this attack is weaker than that in the nonce-misuse setting above, but still reduces the number of queries for finding j forgeries from $j \cdot t_1$ to $1/2 \cdot (j \cdot t_1)$.

4.2 Security Analysis

For all nAE schemes which belong to $\mathcal{C}_0$, there exist a straight-forward argument that they are insecure in the nonce-ignoring setting. A j-IV-CA, as defined in Algorithm 2, requires an adversary **A** to choose j pair-wise distinct messages $M_1, \ldots, M_j$. Beforehand, we assume **A** to be successful in finding the first forgery for two distinct pairs (A_i, N_i) and (A_k, N_k) (Lines 3–9 of Algorithm 2) using t_1 queries.

Therefore, the j-IV-CA adversary **A** queries t_1 distinct pairs $(A_i, N_i) \neq (A_k, N_k)$, together with a fixed message M, until an internal collision leads to the case $T_i = T_k$. Since the event of that very first collision does not depend on the message, a chaining value, and/or the ciphertext (requirement for an nAE scheme to be placed in $\mathcal{C}_0$), we can always choose a new message and still can ensure the internal collision for the pairs (A_i, N_i) and (A_k, N_k). Then, **A** only has to query (A_i, N_i, M_ℓ) for a fresh message M_ℓ to the encryption oracle and receives (C'_ℓ, T'_ℓ), where it is trivial to see that the pair (C'_ℓ, T'_ℓ) will also be valid for (A_k, N_k, M_ℓ). **A** then only has to repeat this process for j pairwise distinct messages M_ℓ.

In the case of a nonce-respecting adversary (see Algorithm 3), an internal collision of the processing of $((A_i)$ and) N_i is detected by observing colliding ciphertext blocks (see Line 9). Since the attack requires an internal collision within the IV-generation step and the nonce N_i must not directly influence the tag-generation step F_T, the nonce N_i must be given as input to F_{IV}, but not to F_T. The associated data A_i can be given as input to F_{IV}, F_T, or both. Therefore, the attack described in Algorithm 3 is applicable to all schemes belonging to the subset $\{(11 * * * *00), (11 * * * *00), (01 * * * *10)\}$ of $\mathcal{C}_0$.

All remaining 74 classes in the set $\mathcal{C}_1$ provide resistance to j-IV-CAs from a theoretical point of view, i.e., with regard to our generalized AE scheme as shown in Fig. 1.

$$\mathcal{C}_1 = \{(01 * 0011*), (01 * 0101*), (01 * 0111*), (01 * 1001*), (01 * 1011*),$$
$$(01 * 1101*), (01 * 1111*), (1100011*), (1100101*).(1100111*),$$
$$(1101001*), (1101011*), (1101101*), (1101111*), (111 * * * **)\}$$

However, in practice, their security highly depends on the specific instantiation of F_{IV} and/or F_T. Due to space constraints, the discussion of concrete instantiations from the class $\mathcal{C}_1$ as well as from $\mathcal{C}_0$ when considering classical nAE schemes and 3rd-round CAESAR candidates, is provided in Appendix C.

5   Countermeasures to j-IV-C Attacks

This section describes two possible approaches for providing resistance to j-IV-CAs in the nonce-respecting (NR) as well as in the nonce-ignoring (NI) setting.

Independence of F_{IV} and F_T. For realizing that approach, the pair (A_i, N_i) has to be processed twice. Let $F_{IV}(A_i, N_i, *)$ be the IV-generation step of an nAE scheme processing the tuple $(A_i, N_i, *)$, where '$*$' denotes that F_{IV} can optionally process the message M. Usually, it is proven that F_{IV} behaves like a PRF. Further, let $F_T(*, *, *, A_i, N_i)$ be the tag-generation step of an AE scheme processing the tuple $(*, *, *, A_i, N_i)$, where the first three inputs can be the chaining value CV, the message M, and or the ciphertext C^2, and there exists a proof showing that F_T also behaves like a PRF. Hence, the corresponding scheme would have the class $(11 * * * *11)$ which belongs to $\mathcal{C}_1$. If one can guarantee independence between F_{IV} and F_T, we can say that the outputs of $F_{IV}(A_i, N_i, *)$ and $F_T(*, *, *, A_i, N_i)$ are independent random values. Based on that assumption, a simple collision of the form $F_{IV}(A_i, N_i, *) = F_{IV}(A_k, N_k, *)$ (as required by the j-IV-CA) does not suffice to produce a forgery since it is highly likely that $F_T(A_i, N_i, *) \neq F_T(*, *, *, A_k, N_k)$ and vice versa. Therefore, this *two-pass*

---

[2] Note that at least one of the three inputs must be given since else, the tag would be independent from the message, which would make the scheme trivially insecure.

processing realizes a *domain separation* between the IV-generation and the tag-generation step, providing resistance to j-IV-CAs. One way to achieve that goal can be to invoke the same PRF twice (for F_{IV} and F_T) but always guarantee distinct inputs, e.g., $F_{IV}(A_i, N_i, *, 1)$ and $F_T(*, *, *, A_i, N_i, 2)$. Another approach would be to just use two independent functions.

Wide-State IV. A second approach requires a PRF-processing of the associated data F_{IV} which produces a wide-state output $\tau \leftarrow F_{IV}(A_i, N_i)$ with $|\tau| > n$ bit. For example, for $|\tau| = 2n$, a pair (A_i, N_i) would be processed to two independent n-bit values τ_1 and τ_2. Then, one could use τ_1 as initialization vector to the encryption step and τ_2 as initialization vector to the tag-generation step. Therefore, one can always guarantee domain separation between encryption and tag generation, while remaining a one-pass AE scheme. One possible instantiation for such a MAC (which can be utilized for the processing of the associated data) is PMAC2x [31].

6   Conclusion

In this work, we followed on the idea of multi-forgery attacks first described by Ferguson in 2002 and went on with introducing the j-INT-CTXT notion. Further on, we introduced a classification of nonce-based AE schemes depending of the usage of their inputs to the initialization, encryption, and authentication process, and categorize them regarding to that classification. To allow a systematic analysis of the reforgeability of nonce-based AE schemes, we introduced the j-IV-Collision Attack, providing us with expected upper bounds on the hardness of further forgeries. During our analysis, we found that (1) no considered nAE schemes provides full resistance to j-IV-CA, (2) ACORN, AES-OTR (serial), ASCON, COLM, JAMBU, KETJE, and NORX belong to the class $\mathcal{C}_0$, rendering them implicitly vulnerable to j-IV-CAs, and (3) ASCON, KETJE, KEYAK, MORUS, NORX, NR-NORX, and TIAOXIN are *semi-resistant* to j-IV-CAs since all of them employ a wide state. This has no impact on the applicability of a j-IV-CA itself, but a wide state hardens the computation of the internal collision, e.g., if the internal state is of size $2n$ (wide state) instead of n, a generic collision can be found in 2^n instead of $2^{n/2}$. Finally, we briefly proposed two alternative approaches which would render an nAE scheme resistant to j-IV-CAs in the nonce-respecting as well as the nonce-ignoring setting.

A   Classification of NRS'14 Schemes

This section shows the eleven "favored" nAE schemes considered by [38] and how we map them according to our classification. From Table 3, one can observe that the classes (A1, A7) and (A2, A8) have pairwise the same class according to our generic nAE scheme. That stems from the fact that we do not follow the distinction of nAE schemes from [38] regarding to whether the message/ciphertext can be processed in parallel or if the tag can be truncated. For the scheme N3, it

Table 3. The eleven "favored" nAE schemes considered by the authors of [38] according to our classification.

Name & Class [38]	Class Sect. 3	Name & Class [38]	Class Sect. 3
A1, A1.100111	(01001011)	A7, A3.100111	(01001011)
A2, A1.110111	(11001011)	A8, A3.110111	(11001011)
A3, A1.101111	(01101011)	N1, N1.111	(11100000)
A4, A1.111111	(11101011)	N2, N2.111	(01000111)
A5, A2.100111	(01000111)	N3, N3.111	(01001011)
A6, A2.110111	(11000111)		

holds that $\mathcal{E}$ gets the two separate inputs $F_L(A, N, M)$ and the nonce N. Since there is no segregated tag generation for N3 (the tag is part of the ciphertext), we interpreted F_L as F_{IV} and consider F_{IV} to additionally hand over the nonce N to the encryption $\mathcal{E}$ internally in plain.

B   Security Claims

In Table 4, we state the security as claimed by the authors of the corresponding scheme. We denote by τ, n, c, and r the tag length, block length, capacity, and the rate, respectively.

Table 4. Claimed INT-CTXT bounds. **NR** = nonce-respecting adversary, **NI** = nonce-ignoring adversary, where τ denotes the length of the tag, n the size of the internal state (usually the block size of the internally used block cipher), and c the capacity for sponge-based designs.

Scheme	NI	NR	Scheme	NI	NR
3rd-round CAESAR candidates					
ACORN	–	2^τ	JAMBU	$2^{2n/2}$	$2^{2n/2}$
AEGIS	–	2^τ	KETJE	–	$2^{\min\{\tau, s\}}$
AES-OTR	–	$2^{\tau/2}$	KEYAK	$2^{\min\{c/2, \tau\}}$	$2^{\min\{c/2, \tau\}}$
AEZv4	2^{55}	2^{55}	MORUS	–	2^{128}
ASCON	–	2^τ	OCB	–	2^τ
CLOC	$2^{n/2}$	$2^{n/2}$	SILC	–	$2^{\tau/2}$
COLM	2^{64}	2^{64}	NORX	–	$2^{|\tau|}$
DEOXYS-I	–	2^τ	TIAOXIN	–	2^{128}
DEOXYS-II	$2^{\tau/2}$	$2^{\tau-1}$			
Classical AE schemes					
CCM	–	$2^{n/2}$	CWC	–	$2^{n/2}$
EAX	–	$2^{n/2}$	GCM	–	$2^{n/2}$

C   Concrete Instantiations of $\mathcal{C}_1$ and $\mathcal{C}_0$

The resistance of the classes in $\mathcal{C}_1$ to j-IV-CA regarding to our generalized AE scheme stems from the fact that the message, and/or a chaining value, and/or the ciphertext affect the generation of the IV or the tag, i.e., is input to F_{IV} and/or F_T. However, if we move from our generalized approach to concrete instantiations of these classes, i.e., to existing AE schemes whose structure is defined by a class in $\mathcal{C}_1$, we will see that some of those classes do not provide resistance to j-IV-CAs. However, AE schemes whose classes belong to $\mathcal{C}_0$ are vulnerable to j-IV-CAs in both the NI and the NR setting. In Table 5, we give an overview of the resistance the considered AE schemes to j-IV-CAs and we additionally provide a brief discussion for those cases that are not trivially observable. In addition to the generic j-IV-CAs in this section, we recall stronger multi-forgery attacks on OCB, AES-OTR, and COLM from the literature in the full version of this work [19].

Table 5. j-IV-CA-Resistance of the third-round CAESAR candidates and considered classical AE schemes, in the nonce-ignoring (**NI**) and the nonce-respecting (**NR**) setting. '•' indicates resistance, 'o' vulnerability under certain requirements (e.g., the scheme employs a wide state), and '–' vulnerability. AES-OTR (ser.) means the serial and (par.) the parallel mode.

Scheme	Class	NI	NR	Scheme	Class	NI	NR
3rd-round CAESAR candidates ($\mathcal{C}_0$)				3rd-round CAESAR candidates ($\mathcal{C}_1$)			
ACORN	(11011000)	–	–	AEGIS	(11011010)	o	o
AES-OTR (ser.)	(11001100)	–	–	AES-OTR (par.)	(01001110)	–	–
Ascon	(11010100)	o	o	AEZv4	(11011011)	–	–
COLM	(11011000)	–	–	CLOC	(11010101)	–	•
JAMBU	(11011000)	–	–	Deoxys-I	(01011001)	–	•
Ketje	(11010000)	o	o	Deoxys-II	(01011001)	–	•
NORX	(11010100)	o	o	Keyak	(01011010)	o	o
Classical AE schemes ($\mathcal{C}_1$)				MORUS	(11011010)	o	o
CCM	(01011011)	–	•	NR-NORX	(11110100)	o	•
CWC	(01010110)	–	–	OCB	(01001010)	–	–
EAX	(01000111)	–	•	SILC	(11010101)	–	•
GCM	(01000111)	–	–	Tiaoxin	(11011010)	o	o

AEGIS, MORUS, and TIAOXIN. These schemes provide semi-resistance to j-IV-CAs in the nonce-respecting and the nonce-ignoring setting. This stems from the fact that they employ very wide states, which are initialized by nonce and associated data, and which are more than twice as large as the final ciphertext stretch; therefore, the search for state collisions is at best a task of sophisticated cryptanalysis, and at worst by magnitudes less efficient than the trivial search by querying many forgery attempts. As a side effect, the search for state collisions is restricted to associated data and messages of equal lengths since their lengths are used in F_T (for that reason, we set the bit x_6).

CWC and GCM. In the nonce-ignoring setting, forgeries for CWC and GCM can be obtained with a few queries. The tag-generation procedures of both modes employ a Carter-Wegman MAC consisting of XORing the encrypted nonce with an encrypted hash of associated data and ciphertext. The employed hash are polynomial hashes in both cases, which is well-known to lead to a variety of forgeries after a few queries when nonces are repeated.

In the nonce-respecting setting, both CWC and GCM possess security proofs that show that they provide forgery resistance up to the birthday bound (Iwata et al. [25] invalidated those for GCM and presented revised bounds which still are bound by the birthday paradox). However, a series of works from the past five years [1,41,46] illustrated that the algebraic structure of polynomial hashing may allow to retrieve the hashing key from forgery polynomials with many roots. The most recent work by Abdelraheem et al. [1] proposes universal forgery attacks that work on a weak key set. Thus, a nonce-respecting adversary could find the hash key and possess the power to derive universal forgeries for those schemes, even with significantly less time than our nonce-respecting attack.

AES-OTR and OCB. In the nonce-ignoring setting, these schemes are trivially insecure, as has been clearly stated by their respective authors. We consider OCB as an example, a similar attack can be performed on AES-OTR if nonces are reused. A nonce-ignoring adversary simply performs the following steps:

1. Choose (A, N, M) such that M consists of at least three blocks: $M = (M_1, M_2, \ldots)$, and ask for their authenticated ciphertext $(C_1, C_2, \ldots, T)$.
2. Choose $\Delta \neq 0^n$, and derive $M_1' = M_1 \oplus \Delta$ and $M_2' = M_2 \oplus \Delta$. For $M' = M_1', M_2'$ and $M_i' = M_i$, for $i \geq 3$, ask for the authenticated cipher-text $(C_1', C_2', \ldots, T)$ that corresponds to (A, N, M').
3. Given the authenticated ciphertext (C''', T'') for any further message (A, N, M'') with $M'' = (M_1, M_2, \ldots)$, the adversary can forge the ciphertext by replacing $(C_1'', C_2'') = (C_1, C_2)$ with (C_1', C_2').

Therefore, the complexities for j forgeries under nonce-ignoring adversaries are only t_1 (and not $t_1 + j$, see Table 1). Because of their structure, there exist nonce-respecting forgery attacks on AES-OTR and OCB that are stronger than our generic j-IV-CA. Those can be found in the full version of this work [19].

AEZv4. Since AEZv4 does not separate the domains of (A_i, N_i) for IV and tag generation, our j-IV-CAs work out-of-the box here. More detailed, nonce and associated data are parsed into a string $T_1, \ldots, T_t$ of n-bit strings T_i, and simply hashed in a PHASH-like manner inside AEZ-hash: $\Delta \leftarrow \bigoplus_{i=1}^{t} E_K^{i+2,1}(T_i)$, where E denotes a variant of four-round AES. The adversary can simply ask for the encryption of approximately 2^{64} tuples (A_i, N_i, M) for fixed M. Obtaining a collision for this hash (requiring birthday-bound complexity) can be easily detected when the message is kept constant over all queries. Given such a hash collision for (A_i, N_i) and (A_k, N_k), the adversary can directly construct subsequent forgeries by asking for the encryption of (A_i, N_i, M') and the same ciphertext will be valid for (A_k, N_k, M') for arbitrary M'.

DEOXYS. The nonce-requiring variant of DEOXYS, i.e., DEOXYS-I, possesses a similar structure as OCB. Hence, there are trivial multi-forgery attacks with few queries if nonces repeat:

1. Choose (A, N, M) arbitrarily and ask for (C, T).
2. Choose $A' \neq A$, leave N and M constant and ask for $(C' = C, T')$. Since the tag is computed by the XOR of $\text{Hash}(A)$ with the encrypted checksum under the nonce as tweak, the adversary sees the difference in the hash outputs in the tags: $\text{Hash}(A) \oplus \text{Hash}(A') = T \oplus T'$.
3. Choose (A, N', M') and ask for (C'', T''). It instantly follows that for (A', N', M'), $(C'', T''' = T \oplus T' \oplus T'')$ will be valid.

However, in the nonce-respecting setting, the use of a real tweaked block cipher that employs the nonce in tweak (instead of the XEX construction as in AES-OTR and OCB) prevents the attacks shown in [19]; the tag generation seems surprisingly strong in the sense that an adversary can not detect collisions between two associated data since the hash is XORed with an output of a fresh block cipher (because of the nonce is used as tweak) for every query. Therefore, we indicate that DEOXYS-I provides resistance in the nonce-respecting setting.

DEOXYS-II is a two-pass mode, i.e., the message is processed twice (1) once for the encryption process and (2) for the authentication process. In the nonce-ignoring setting, an adversary can simply fix N_i and vary A_i for finding a collision for Auth, which renders the scheme vulnerable to j-IV-CAs. Therefore, that kind of two-pass scheme (in comparison to SIV, where the message is used as input to F_{IV}), does not implicitly provide resistance to j-IV-CAs.

NORX. The authors of NORX presented a nonce-misuse resistant version of their scheme in Appendix D of [5]. NR-NORX follows the MAC-then-Encrypt paradigm, which yields a two-pass scheme similar to SIV. Therefore, NR-NORX provides at the least resistance to j-IV-CAs in the NR setting, which renders it stronger than NORX. However, this security comes at the cost of being off-line and two-pass.

CCM, EAX, CLOC and SILC. The resistance to j-IV-CAs in the nonce-respecting setting provided by CCM, EAX, CLOC, and SILC stems from similar reasons as for DEOXYS-II; the tag is generated by the XOR of the MAC of the nonce with the MAC of the ciphertext and the MAC of the associated data. Hence, collisions in ciphertext or header can not be easily detected since the MAC of a fresh nonce is XORed to it.

References

1. Abdelraheem, M.A., Beelen, P., Bogdanov, A., Tischhauser, E.: Twisted polynomials and forgery attacks on GCM. In: Oswald, E., Fischlin, M. (eds.) EURO-CRYPT 2015. LNCS, vol. 9056, pp. 762–786. Springer, Heidelberg (2015). doi:10.1007/978-3-662-46800-5_29
2. Abed, F., Fluhrer, S., Foley, J., Forler, C., List, E., Lucks, S., McGrew, D., Wenzel, J.: The POET Family of On-Line Authenticated Encryption Schemes (2014). http://competitions.cr.yp.to/caesar-submissions.html
3. Andreeva, E., Bogdanov, A., Datta, N., Luykx, A., Mennink, B., Nandi, M., Tischhauser, E., Yasuda, K.: COLM v1 (2016). http://competitions.cr.yp.to/caesar-submissions.html
4. Andreeva, E., Bogdanov, A., Luykx, A., Mennink, B., Tischhauser, E., Yasuda, K.: AES-COPA (2014). http://competitions.cr.yp.to/caesar-submissions.html
5. Aumasson, J.-P., Jovanovic, P., Neves, S.: NORX (2016). http://competitions.cr.yp.to/caesar-submissions.html
6. Bellare, M., Canetti, R., Krawczyk, H.: Keying hash functions for message authentication. In: Koblitz, N. (ed.) CRYPTO 1996. LNCS, vol. 1109, pp. 1–15. Springer, Heidelberg (1996). doi:10.1007/3-540-68697-5_1
7. Bellare, M., Goldreich, O., Mityagin, A.: The power of verification queries in message authentication and authenticated encryption. IACR Cryptology ePrint Arch. **2004**, 309 (2004)
8. Bellare, M., Kilian, J., Rogaway, P.: The security of the cipher block chaining message authentication code. J. Comput. Syst. Sci. **61**(3), 362–399 (2000)
9. Bellare, M., Rogaway, P., Wagner, D.: The EAX mode of operation. In: Roy, B., Meier, W. (eds.) FSE 2004. LNCS, vol. 3017, pp. 389–407. Springer, Heidelberg (2004). doi:10.1007/978-3-540-25937-4_25
10. Bernstein, D.J.: CAESAR Call for Submissions, Final, 27 January 2014. http://competitions.cr.yp.to/caesar-call.html
11. Bertoni, G., Daemen, J., Peeters, M., Van Assche, G.: Sponge functions. ECRYPT Hash Function Workshop (2007)
12. Bertoni, G., Daemen, J., Peeters, M., Van Keer, R., Van Assche, G.: CAESAR submission, Ketje v2 (2016). http://competitions.cr.yp.to/caesar-submissions.html
13. Black, J., Cochran, M.: MAC reforgeability. In: Dunkelman, O. (ed.) FSE 2009. LNCS, vol. 5665, pp. 345–362. Springer, Heidelberg (2009). doi:10.1007/978-3-642-03317-9_21
14. Datta, N., Nandi, M.: ELmD (2014). http://competitions.cr.yp.to/caesar-submissions.html
15. Dobraunig, C., Eichlseder, M., Mendel, F., Schläffer, M.: Ascon v1.2 (2016). http://competitions.cr.yp.to/caesar-submissions.html
16. Dworkin, M.J.: SP 800–38C. Recommendation for Block Cipher Modes of Operation: The CCM Mode for Authentication and Confidentiality. Technical report, Gaithersburg, MD, United States (2004)
17. Ferguson, N.: Collision Attacks on OCB. Unpublished manuscript (2002). http://www.cs.ucdavis.edu/rogaway/ocb/links.htm
18. Ferguson, N.: Authentication weaknesses in GCM (2005). http://csrc.nist.gov/groups/ST/toolkit/BCM/documents/comments/CWC-GCM/Ferguson2.pdf
19. Forler, C., List, E., Lucks, S., Wenzel, J.: Reforgeability of Authenticated Encryption Schemes. Cryptology ePrint Archive, Report 2017/332 (2017). http://eprint.iacr.org/2017/332

20. Fouque, P.-A., Martinet, G., Valette, F., Zimmer, S.: On the security of the CCM encryption mode and of a slight variant. In: Bellovin, S.M., Gennaro, R., Keromytis, A., Yung, M. (eds.) ACNS 2008. LNCS, vol. 5037, pp. 411–428. Springer, Heidelberg (2008). doi:10.1007/978-3-540-68914-0_25

21. Peeters, M., Bertoni, G., Daemen, J., Van Assche, G., Van Keer, R.: CAESAR submission, Keyak v2 (2016). http://competitions.cr.yp.to/caesar-submissions.html

22. Handschuh, H., Preneel, B.: Key-recovery attacks on universal hash function based MAC algorithms. In: Wagner, D. (ed.) CRYPTO 2008. LNCS, vol. 5157, pp. 144–161. Springer, Heidelberg (2008). doi:10.1007/978-3-540-85174-5_9

23. Hoang, V.T., Krovetz, T., Rogaway, P.: AEZ v4.2: Authenticated Encryption by Enciphering (2016). http://competitions.cr.yp.to/caesar-submissions.html

24. Iwata, T., Minematsu, K., Guo, J., Morioka, S.: CLOC and SILC v3 (2016). http://competitions.cr.yp.to/caesar-submissions.html

25. Iwata, T., Ohashi, K., Minematsu, K.: Breaking and repairing GCM security proofs. In: Safavi-Naini, R., Canetti, R. (eds.) CRYPTO 2012. LNCS, vol. 7417, pp. 31–49. Springer, Heidelberg (2012). doi:10.1007/978-3-642-32009-5_3

26. Jean, J., Nikolić, I., Peyrin, T., Seurin, Y.: Deoxys v1.41 (2016). http://competitions.cr.yp.to/caesar-submissions.html

27. Westerlund, M., Mattsson, J.: Authentication Key Recovery on Galois Counter Mode (GCM). Cryptology ePrint Archive, Report 2015/477 (2015). http://eprint.iacr.org/2015/477

28. Joux, A.: Authentication Failures in NIST version of GCM. NIST Comment (2006)

29. Kohno, T., Viega, J., Whiting, D.: CWC: a high-performance conventional authenticated encryption mode. In: FSE, pp. 408–426, 2004

30. Krovetz, T., Rogaway, P.: OCB (2016). http://competitions.cr.yp.to/caesar-submissions.html

31. List, E., Nandi, M.: Revisiting full-PRF-secure PMAC and using it for beyond-birthday authenticated encryption. In: Handschuh, H. (ed.) CT-RSA 2017. LNCS, vol. 10159, pp. 258–274. Springer, Cham (2017). doi:10.1007/978-3-319-52153-4_15

32. Jiqiang, L.: On the security of the COPA and marble authenticated encryption algorithms against (almost) universal forgery attack. IACR Cryptology ePrint Arch. 2015, 79 (2015)

33. Lucks, S.: A failure-friendly design principle for hash functions. In: Proceedings of the Advances in Cryptology - ASIACRYPT 2005, 11th International Conference on the Theory and Application of Cryptology and Information Security, Chennai, India, December 4–8, 2005, pp. 474–494 (2005)

34. McGrew, D., Viega, J.: The Galois/Counter Mode of Operation (GCM). Submission to NIST (2004). http://csrc.nist.gov/CryptoToolkit/modes/proposedmodes/gcm/gcm-spec.pdf

35. McGrew, D.A., Fluhrer, S.R.: Multiple forgery attacks against message authentication codes. IACR Cryptology ePrint Arch. 2005, 161 (2005)

36. McGrew, D.A., Viega, J.: The security and performance of the Galois/Counter Mode (GCM) of operation. In: Canteaut, A., Viswanathan, K. (eds.) INDOCRYPT 2004. LNCS, vol. 3348, pp. 343–355. Springer, Heidelberg (2004). doi:10.1007/978-3-540-30556-9_27

37. Minematsu, K.: AES-OTR v3.1 (2016). http://competitions.cr.yp.to/caesar-submissions.html

38. Namprempre, C., Rogaway, P., Shrimpton, T.: Reconsidering generic composition. In: Nguyen, P.Q., Oswald, E. (eds.) EUROCRYPT 2014. LNCS, vol. 8441, pp. 257–274. Springer, Heidelberg (2014). doi:10.1007/978-3-642-55220-5_15

39. Nandi, M.: Revisiting security claims of XLS and COPA. Cryptology ePrint Archive, Report 2015/444 (2015). http://eprint.iacr.org/2015/444
40. Nikolić, I.: Tiaoxin-346 (2016). http://competitions.cr.yp.to/caesar-submissions.html
41. Procter, G., Cid, C.: On weak keys and forgery attacks against polynomial-based MAC schemes. In: Moriai, S. (ed.) FSE 2013. LNCS, vol. 8424, pp. 287–304. Springer, Heidelberg (2014). doi:10.1007/978-3-662-43933-3_15
42. Rogaway, P., Wagner, D.: A Critique of CCM. Cryptology ePrint Archive, Report 2003/070 (2003). http://eprint.iacr.org/2003/070
43. Rogaway, P.: Authenticated-encryption with associated-data. In: ACM Conference on Computer and Communications Security, pp. 98–107 (2002)
44. Rogaway, P.: Nonce-based symmetric encryption. In: Roy, B., Meier, W. (eds.) FSE 2004. LNCS, vol. 3017, pp. 348–358. Springer, Heidelberg (2004). doi:10.1007/978-3-540-25937-4_22
45. Rogaway, P., Bellare, M., Black, J., Krovetz, T.: OCB: a block-cipher mode of operation for efficient authenticated encryption. In: ACM Conference on Computer and Communications Security, pp. 196–205 (2001)
46. Saarinen, M.-J.O.: Cycling attacks on GCM, GHASH and other polynomial MACs and hashes. In: Canteaut, A. (ed.) FSE 2012. LNCS, vol. 7549, pp. 216–225. Springer, Heidelberg (2012). doi:10.1007/978-3-642-34047-5_13
47. Hongjun, W.: A Lightweight Authenticated Cipher (v3) (2016). http://competitions.cr.yp.to/caesar-submissions.html
48. Wu, H., Huang, T.: The Authenticated Cipher MORUS (2016). http://competitions.cr.yp.to/caesar-submissions.html
49. Wu, H., Huang, T.: The JAMBU Lightweight Authentication Encryption Mode (v2.1) (2016). http://competitions.cr.yp.to/caesar-submissions.html
50. Wu, H., Preneel, B.: AEGIS: A Fast Authenticated Encryption Algorithm (v1,1) (2016). http://competitions.cr.yp.to/caesar-submissions.html

Indifferentiability of Double-Block-Length Hash Function Without Feed-Forward Operations

Yusuke Naito[✉]

Mitsubishi Electric Corporation, Kanagawa, Japan
Naito.Yusuke@ce.MitsubishiElectric.co.jp

Abstract. Designing a cryptographic scheme with minimal components is a main theme in cryptographic research. Regarding double-block-length (DBL) hashing, *feed-forward operations* are used to avoid attacks from the blockcipher's decryption function, whereas Özen and Stam showed that by using an iterated structure the feed-forward operations can be eliminated. Precisely, DBL iterated hash functions are collision resistant up to about 2^n query complexity when a blockcipher with n-bit blocks is used.

Regarding the security of hash functions, *pseudorandom-oracle* (PRO) security, which is a stronger security notion than collision resistance, is an important security criterion of hash functions. Though several DBL hash functions with PRO security have been proposed, these use feed-forward operations. Note that Özen-Stam's hash functions are not secure PROs due to the length-extension attack. Hence, it remains an open problem to design a PRO-secure DBL hash function without feed-forward operations.

In this paper, we show that the feed-forward operations in the PRO-secure DBL hash function can be eliminated, that is, the simplified scheme is a secure PRO up to about 2^n query complexity. To our knowledge, this is the first time PRO-secure DBL hash function without feed-forward operations.

Keywords: Double-block-length hash · Blockcipher · Feed-forward operations · Pseudorandom oracle

1 Introduction

Simplification of Cryptographic Scheme. Designing a cryptographic scheme with minimal components is a main theme in cryptographic research, because it offers efficient and/or compact schemes. For example, Even and Mansour [5,6] addressed this problem with respect to blockcipher design in 1991. They were motivated by DESX proposed by Rivest in 1984. DESX was designed to protect DES against exhaustive search attacks by XOR-ing two independent prewhitening and postwhitening keys to the plaintext and ciphertext, respectively. In the Even-Mansour (EM) scheme, the keyed blockcipher is eliminated, where it is replaced with a public random permutation. Another example is

J. Pieprzyk and S. Suriadi (Eds.): ACISP 2017, Part II, LNCS 10343, pp. 38–57, 2017.
DOI: 10.1007/978-3-319-59870-3_3

tweakable blockcipher (TBC) design, e.g., the first TBC called LRW2 [22] has the DESX-style structure, and after that, it has been shown that the blockcipher's key or the output masking can be eliminated [14, 16, 35].

The same research was done in the area of *double-block-length* (DBL) hash design. In this paper, we focus on simplifying DBL-hash constructions.

DBL Hash. DBL hashing is a well-established method for constructing a hash function with $2n$-bit outputs based only on a blockcipher with n-bit blocks. The idea dates back to the designs of MDC-2 and MDC-4 in 1988 by Meyer and Schilling [28]. DBL hash functions have an obvious advantage over classical blockcipher-based functions such as Davies-Meyer and Matyas-Meyer-Oseas, and more generally the PGV class of functions [1, 33, 37]: blockciphers with small blocks can be used such as AES ($n = 128$) [30] and lightweight blockciphers ($n = 64$) e.g., [2, 11, 36, 39], thus implementing both a hash function and an encryption scheme, one can save its memory size by sharing the blockcipher algorithm.

A DBL hash function is mainly designed by the following steps: (1) A collision-resistant DBL compression function (CF) is designed; (2) A DBL hash function is designed by combining the scheme in (1) with a domain extender that preserves the collision security, e.g., the (strengthened) Merkle-Damgård [4, 27]. In the research of DBL hash design, (1) has been mainly studied.

A well-known approach to construct a DBL CF is to use *feed-forward operations* with the aim of avoiding attacks from the blockcipher's decryption function [1, 33, 37]. The following example is Davies-Meyer construction DM : $\{0, 1\}^k \times \{0, 1\}^n \to \{0, 1\}^n$ [33], where a blockcipher $E : \{0, 1\}^k \times \{0, 1\}^n \to \{0, 1\}^n$ with k-bit keys and n-bit blocks is used.

$$\mathsf{DM}(X, Y) = Y \oplus E(X, Y) \text{ where } Y \text{ is feed-forwarded to the output.}$$

Note that the Davies-Meyer construction is a single-block-length scheme, thus the security is ensured up to $2^{n/2}$ query complexity. DBL schemes [7–9, 12, 18–21, 23, 25], in order to avoid the $2^{n/2}$ attack, performs a blockcipher twice to extend its hash size to $2n$ bit. The following construction is Hirose's DBL one [12], where the Davies-Meyer construction is performed twice.

$$\mathsf{Hirose}(X, Y) = \mathsf{DM}(X, Y)\|\mathsf{DM}(X, Y \oplus const)$$

where $k > n$ and *const* is an n-bit non-zero constant value. By the DBL construction, the DBL schemes are collision resistant up to 2^n query complexity.

Simplification of DBL Hash. As mentioned above, in order to avoid attacks from the blockcipher's decryption function, we need to use feed-forward operations. However, Özen and Stam showed that the attacks can be avoided in the iteration even the feed-forward operations are absent [31], which is an extension of Rabin's mode [34] that is a blockcipher-based single-block-length hashing mode (defined as $\mathsf{Rabin}(X, Y) = E(X, Y)$ where X is a message block and Y is a chaining value). Precisely, the DBL iterated hash functions without the feed-forward operations are collision resistant up to about 2^n query complexity. By this simplification, the memory size (or internal state size) and the software/hardware size from the feed-forward operations are reduced.

Open Problem. Since the SHA-3 competition, hash functions have been designed to be a secure pseudorandom oracle (PRO) or indifferentiable from a random oracle [24]. It can be ensured that PRO-secure hash functions have no structural flaw up to the proven bound. Indeed, the SHA-2 hash family includes PRO-secure hash functions, and all hash functions in the SHA-3 family are secure PROs.

Regarding DBL hashing, several schemes that are secure PROs up to 2^n query complexity have been proposed [13, 17, 29]. However, these DBL hash functions use the feed-forward operations. Note that the Özen-Stam's DBL hash function has the iterated structure, thus is not a secure PRO by a so-called length-extension attack [3]. Therefore, the next question naturally arises: *can we securely eliminate feed-forward operations in a PRO-secure DBL hash function?*

Our Contribution. In this paper, we simplify the PRO-secure DBL hash function based on Hirose's CF given in [29], because it is most efficient due to Hirose's construction: in each CF evaluation the same blockcipher's key are inputted to two blockcipher calls, thus the key scheduling of the blockcipher is performed only one time. In the previous scheme, Hirose's CF is iterated, then a finalization function with two blockcipher calls is used in order to avoid the length-extension attack. Note that the finalization function does not use the feed-forward operations. Thus we remove the feed-forward operations in Hirose's CF. We prove that the simplified DBL hash function is a secure PRO up to about 2^n query complexity, thus achieving the same level of PRO security as the previous DBL hash functions.

We next compare our hash function with Özen-Stam's hash function [31] with respect to efficiency. For each message block, both hash functions perform a blockcipher twice. However, after processing message blocks, our hash function requires two blockcipher calls in order to ensure the PRO-security. Hence, our hash function is slightly slower than Özen-Stam's hash function by the finalization procedure. Note that Özen-Stam's hash function is not a secure PRO due to the length extension attack.

Finally, we note that several hashing modes e.g., [3, 15] are secure PROs where the underling CFs are random oracles, and combinations of these and Özen-Stam's hash function, which don't require the finalization procedure, might become secure PROs. In order to prove birthday PRO security, one needs to overcome the PRF/PRP switch regarding the underlying blockcipher. We leave the proof as an open problem from this paper.

Related Works. It was proved that a DBL hash function with the PBGV scheme [32] is a secure PRO up to $2^{n/2}$ query complexity [10]. This scheme uses feed-forward operations and does not achieve 2^n-PRO security. It were proved that MDC4 [28] and Mennink's function [25] are secure PRO up to $2^{n/4}$ and

$2^{n/2}$ query complexities, respectively [26]. These use feed-forward operations and don't achieve 2^n-PRO security.

2   Notation

Let $\{0,1\}^*$ be the set of all bit strings, $\{0,1\}^n$ be the set of all n-bit strings, and $(\{0,1\}^n)^*$ be the set of all strings whose length in bits is a multiple of n, where n is an integer. For a bit string $m \in (\{0,1\}^n)^*$, we write its partition into n-bit strings as $m_1, m_2, \ldots, m_l \xleftarrow{n} m$. For a bit string $x \in \{0,1\}^n$, $x[u,v]$ is a bit string of x from u-th bit to v-th bit, where $1 \leq u \leq v \leq n$. For a bit string y, $x \leftarrow y$ means that y is assigned to x. For a finite set X, $x \xleftarrow{\$} X$ means that an element is sampled uniformly at random from X and is assigned to x. For finite sets $X, Y \leftarrow X$ means that X is assigned to Y, and $Y \xleftarrow{\cup} X$ means that $Y \leftarrow X \cup Y$. For an integer x, $\mathsf{Func}(*, x)$ denotes the set of all functions from $\{0,1\}^*$ to $\{0,1\}^x$, and $\mathsf{Func}(x, y)$ denotes the set of all functions from $\{0,1\}^x$ to $\{0,1\}^y$. For integers k, n, $\mathsf{BC}(k, n)$ denotes the set of all blockciphers with k-bit keys and n-bit blocks.

3   PRO-Secure DBL Hash Function Without Feed-Forward Operations

We define a DBLHF without feed-forward operations. Throughout this paper, a blockcipher with k-bit keys and n-bit blocks is denoted by $E \in \mathsf{BC}(k, n)$, the decryption function is denoted by E^{-1}, and the key length is $k = 2n$.

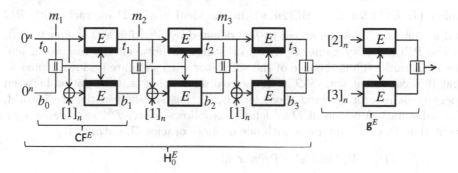

Fig. 1. Hash function F^E with three message blocks $m_1 \| m_2 \| m_3$

3.1   Specification of F

First, a compression function $\mathsf{CF}^E : \{0,1\}^{2n} \times \{0,1\}^n \to \{0,1\}^{2n}$ is defined as

$$\mathsf{CF}^E(t_{i-1} \| b_{i-1}, m_i) = E(m_i \| b_{i-1}, t_{i-1}) \| E(m_i \| b_{i-1}, t_{i-1} \oplus [1]_n)$$

where $[1]_n = 0^{n-1}\|1$. Note that the compression function is Hirose's one [12] without feed-forward operations.

Second, a hash function $H^E : \{0,1\}^* \to \{0,1\}^{2n}$ using CF^E is defined as $H^E(m) = t_l\|b_l$ where $m_1, m_2, \ldots, m_l \overset{n}{\leftarrow} \mathsf{pad}(m)$; $t_0\|b_0 \leftarrow 0^n\|0^n$;

$$t_i\|b_i \leftarrow CF^E(t_{i-1}\|b_{i-1}, m_i) \text{ for } i = 1, \ldots, l.$$

Here, $\mathsf{pad} : \{0,1\}^* \to (\{0,1\}^n)^*$ is an injective padding function. By $H_0^E : (\{0,1\}^n)^* \to \{0,1\}^{2n}$, we denote the function H^E without pad. Hence $H^E(m) = H_0^E(\mathsf{pad}(m))$.

Next, a finalization function $g^E : \{0,1\}^{2n} \to \{0,1\}^{2n}$ is defined as $g^E(x) = E(x, [2]_n)\|E(x, [3]_n)$ where $[2]_n = 0^{n-2}\|10$ and $[3]_n = 0^{n-2}\|11$.

Finally, our hash function $F^E : \{0,1\}^* \to \{0,1\}^{2n}$ is defined as $F^E(m) = g^E(H^E(m))$. By $F^E : (\{0,1\}^n)^* \to \{0,1\}^{2n}$, we denote the function F without pad. Hence $F^E(m) = F^E(\mathsf{pad}(m))$. Figure 1 shows the F^E construction.

3.2   Security of F

We will prove that F^E is a secure pseudo-random oracle (PRO) up to about 2^n query complexity. Before giving the security result, we explain the security notion.

PRO   [24]. In this security, the underlying blockcipher is assumed to be an ideal cipher that is defined as $E \overset{\$}{\leftarrow} BC(2n, n)$. A random oracle $\mathcal{RO}$ is defined as $\mathcal{RO} \overset{\$}{\leftarrow} \mathsf{Func}(*, n)$. The PRO-security game considers the indistinguishability between a real world and an ideal world. Let $\mathcal{D}$ be a distinguisher (algorithm). In the real world, $\mathcal{D}$ interacts with the target hash function F^E and an ideal cipher (E, E^{-1}) for $E \overset{\$}{\leftarrow} BC(2n, n)$. In the ideal world, $\mathcal{D}$ interacts with $\mathcal{RO}$ and a simulator S having access to $\mathcal{RO}$ denoted by $S^{\mathcal{RO}}$ for $\mathcal{RO} \overset{\$}{\leftarrow} \mathsf{Func}(*, 2n)$. In the PRO-security game, $\mathcal{D}$ tries to distinguish between the real world and the ideal world. Thus the role of the simulator is to simulate an ideal cipher so that it is consistent with $\mathcal{RO}$ as in the real world, that is, the relation between query-responses for F^E and those for (E, E^{-1}) is satisfied in the ideal world. The advantage function of $\mathcal{D}$ is defined as follows. Here, $\mathcal{D}^{\mathcal{O}} \Rightarrow 1$ denotes an event that $\mathcal{D}$, which interacts with one or more oracles $\mathcal{O}$, outputs 1.

$$\mathsf{Adv}^{\mathsf{pro}}_{F^E, S}(\mathcal{D}) = \Pr[\mathsf{World_R}] - \Pr[\mathsf{World_I}]$$

$$\text{where } \mathsf{World_R} := \left(E \overset{\$}{\leftarrow} BC(2n, n); \mathcal{D}^{F^E, E, E^{-1}} \Rightarrow 1 \right)$$

$$\mathsf{World_I} := \left(\mathcal{RO} \overset{\$}{\leftarrow} \mathsf{Func}(*, 2n); \mathcal{D}^{\mathcal{RO}, S^{\mathcal{RO}}} \Rightarrow 1 \right)$$

Here, the probabilities are taken over $\mathcal{D}$, E, $\mathcal{RO}$, and S. The security goal is to prove that for any distinguisher $\mathcal{D}$ there exists a simulator S such that the advantage function is upper-bounded by a negligible probability (the birthday bound in this paper).

PRO-Security Bound of F. The upper-bound of the PRO advantage is given in the following.

Theorem 1. *Assume that a distinguisher $\mathcal{D}$ makes q_L queries to F^E of length in blocks at most ℓ (that is, $l \leq \ell$), q_F queries to E, q_I queries to E^{-1}, and runs in time t. Let $\sigma = 2\ell(q_L + 1) + q_F + q_I$ be the maximum number of blockcipher calls by $\mathcal{D}$'s queries. Then for any distinguisher $\mathcal{D}$, there exists a simulator $S = (S_E, S_{E^{-1}})$ such that*

$$\mathsf{Adv}^{\mathsf{pro}}_{F^E,\mathsf{S}}(\mathcal{D}) \leq \frac{48\sigma^2}{(2^n - 4\sigma)^2} + \frac{10\sigma + nq_I}{2^n - 4\sigma} + \left(\frac{16e\sigma}{n(2^n - 4\sigma)}\right)^n.$$

Here, S makes queries to $\mathcal{RO}$ at most $q_F + q_I$ times and runs in time at most $t + \mathcal{O}((q_F + q_I)^2)$.

The above theorem ensures that F^E is a secure PRO as long as (σ, q_I) is less than roughly $(2^n, 2^n/n)$.

Remark 1. The $nq_I/2^n$ term comes from the proof technique where in order to overcome the absence of feed-forward operations, the multi-collision technique given in e.g., [38] is used (See Sect. 4). However, we have not found out the attack matching this term. Hence, this bound might not be tight, and proving the tightness is an open problem from this paper.

4   Proof of Theorem 1

In this proof, we consider the PRO security of F^E instead of F^E, where in the PRO-security game, $\mathcal{D}$ makes a hash query in $(\{0,1\}^n)^*$ to F^E. Since $F^E(m) = F^E(\mathsf{pad}(m))$, $\mathcal{D}$ with access to F^E can obtain outputs of F^E by making queries $\mathsf{pad}(m)$ to F^E. Hence, the PRO-security of F^E implies that of F^E.

First, we introduce a middle world between $\mathsf{World_R}$ and $\mathsf{World_I}$. The middle world uses a hash function $\mathsf{F}_1^{g,E} : (\{0,1\}^n)^* \to \{0,1\}^{2n}$ defined as $\mathsf{F}_1^{g,E}(m) = g(\mathsf{H}_0^E(m))$ for $E \xleftarrow{\$} \mathsf{BC}(2n, n)$ and $g \xleftarrow{\$} \mathsf{Func}(2n, 2n)$.

Then our proof consists of the following three steps.

1. Prove that $\mathsf{F}_1^{g,E}$ is a secure PRO (Lemma 1). Precisely, prove that for any distinguisher $\mathcal{D}$, there exists a simulator S_1 such that the following PRO advantage is upper-bounded by the birthday bound.

   $$\mathsf{Adv}^{\mathsf{pro}}_{\mathsf{F}_1^{g,E},\mathsf{S}_1}(\mathcal{D}) = \Pr[\mathsf{World}^{(1)}_{\mathsf{M}}] - \Pr[\mathsf{World}^{(1)}_{\mathsf{I}}], \text{ where}$$

   $$\mathsf{World}^{(1)}_{\mathsf{M}} := \left(g \xleftarrow{\$} \mathsf{Func}(2n, 2n); E \xleftarrow{\$} \mathsf{BC}(2n, n); \mathcal{D}^{\mathsf{F}_1^{g,E}, g, E, E^{-1}} \Rightarrow 1\right), \text{ and}$$

   $$\mathsf{World}^{(1)}_{\mathsf{I}} := \left(\mathcal{RO} \xleftarrow{\$} \mathsf{Func}(*, 2n); \mathcal{D}^{\mathcal{RO}, \mathsf{S}_1^{\mathcal{RO}}} \Rightarrow 1\right)$$

   Note that the role of the simulator $\mathsf{S}_1 = (\mathsf{S}1_g, \mathsf{S}1_E, \mathsf{S}1_{E^{-1}})$ is to simulate (g, E, E^{-1}) such that it is consistent with $\mathcal{RO}$ as in $\mathsf{World}^{(1)}_{\mathsf{M}}$.

2. Prove that F^E is indifferentiable from $\mathsf{F}_1^{g,E}$ (Lemma 2). Precisely, prove that for any distinguisher $\mathcal{D}$, there exists a simulator S_2 such that the following indifferentiable advantage is upper-bounded by the birthday bound.

$$\mathsf{Adv}_{\mathsf{F}^E,\mathsf{F}_1^{g,E},\mathsf{S}_2}^{\mathsf{indiff}}(\mathcal{D}) = \Pr[\mathsf{World}_\mathsf{R}] - \Pr[\mathsf{World}_\mathsf{M}^{(2)}], \text{ where}$$

$$\mathsf{World}_\mathsf{M}^{(2)} := \left(g \xleftarrow{\$} \mathsf{Func}(2n, 2n); E \xleftarrow{\$} \mathsf{BC}(2n, n); \mathcal{D}^{\mathsf{F}_1^{g,E},\mathsf{S}_2^{g,E,E^{-1}},E,E^{-1}} \Rightarrow 1 \right)$$

Note that the role of the simulator $\mathsf{S}_2 = (\mathsf{S}2_E, \mathsf{S}2_{E^{-1}})$ is to simulate (E, E^{-1}) such that it is consistent with $\mathsf{F}_1^{g,E}$ as in $\mathsf{World}_\mathsf{R}$.

3. Conclude that F^E is a secure PRO from Step 1 and Step 2 via the composition theorem of the indifferentiability [24] up to the proven bounds.

Lemma 1 (Step 1). *Assume that a distinguisher $\mathcal{D}$ runs in time t and makes q_L queries to $\mathsf{F}_1^{g,E}$, q_g queries to g, q_F queries to E, and q_I queries to E^{-1} such that the maximum number of message blocks induced by a query to $\mathsf{F}_1^{g,E}$ is ℓ. Let $\alpha_F = 2(\ell q_L + q_F)$ and $\alpha = 2(\ell q_L + q_F + q_I)$. For any distinguisher $\mathcal{D}$ there exists a simulator S_1 such that*

$$\mathsf{Adv}_{\mathsf{F}_1^{g,E},\mathsf{S}_1}^{\mathsf{pro}}(\mathcal{D}) \leq \frac{\alpha_F(2\alpha_F + 4q_I + q_g - 4)}{(2^n - \alpha)^2} + \frac{\alpha_F + nq_I}{2^n - \alpha} + \left(\frac{2e\alpha_F}{n(2^n - \alpha)} \right)^n.$$

S makes queries to $\mathcal{RO}$ at most q_g times and runs in time at most $t + \mathcal{O}((q_F + q_I)q_g)$.

The proof of Lemma 1 is given in Sect. 4.1.

Lemma 2 (Step 2). *Assume that a distinguisher $\mathcal{D}$ makes q_L queries to F^E, q_F queries to E, and q_I queries to E^{-1} such that the maximum number of message blocks induced by a query to L is ℓ. Let $\beta_F = 2((\ell+1)q_L + q_F)$ and $\beta = 2((\ell+1)q_L + q_F + q_I)$. For any distinguisher $\mathcal{D}$ there exists a simulator S_2 such that*

$$\mathsf{Adv}_{\mathsf{F}^E,\mathsf{F}_1^{g,E},\mathsf{S}_2}^{\mathsf{indiff}}(\mathcal{D}) \leq \frac{6\beta}{2^n - \beta}$$

S makes queries to g at most $q_F + q_I$ times, to E at most $2q_F + q_I$ times and to E^{-1} at most q_I times, and runs in time at most $t + \mathcal{O}(q_F + q_I)$.

The proof of Lemma 1 is given in Subsect. 4.2.

Step 3. By the composition theorem of the indifferentiability [24], for any distinguisher $\mathcal{D}$ there exist distinguishers $\mathcal{D}_1$ and $\mathcal{D}_2$, and a simulator S such that

$$\mathsf{Adv}_{\mathsf{F}^E,\mathsf{S}}^{\mathsf{pro}}(\mathcal{D}) \leq \mathsf{Adv}_{\mathsf{F}_1^{g,E},\mathsf{S}1}^{\mathsf{pro}}(\mathcal{D}_1) + \mathsf{Adv}_{\mathsf{F}^E,\mathsf{F}_1^{g,E},\mathsf{S}2}^{\mathsf{indiff}}(\mathcal{D}_2).$$

Putting the upper-bounds of Lemma 1 and of Lemma 2 into the above gives the upper-bound in Theorem 1. The detail is given in Appendix B.

4.1 Proof of Lemma 1

A simulator S_1 consists of three algorithms $S1_g, S1_E, S1_{E^{-1}}$ that simulate g, E, E^{-1}, respectively. Let $\mathcal{D}$ be a distinguisher which has access to oracles $(L, R_g, R_E, R_{E^{-1}})$, where $(L, R_g, R_E, R_{E^{-1}}) = (\mathsf{F}_1^{g,E}, g, E, E^{-1})$ in $\mathsf{World}_M^{(1)}$, and $(L, R_g, R_E, R_{E^{-1}}) = (\mathcal{RO}, S1_g, S1_E, S1_{E^{-1}})$ in $\mathsf{World}_I^{(1)}$. We denote a query to R_E by (k, x) and the response by y, a query to $R_{E^{-1}}$ by (k, y) and the response by x, and a query to g by w and the response by z. Hence, $y = R_E(k, x)$, $x = R_{E^{-1}}(k, y)$, and $z = g(w)$.

Note that the role of the simulator is to simulate g, E, E^{-1} so that it is consistent with $\mathcal{RO}$ as in $\mathsf{World}_M^{(1)}$. In $\mathsf{World}_M^{(1)}$, there is a relation between queries to L and to $R_g, R_E, R_{E^{-1}}$ with respect to the structure of F_1, thus we need a definition to represent the relation. Let $\mathcal{L}_{qr}$ be a table that keeps query-responses of R_E or of $R_{E^{-1}}$ that have been defined and that is updated by a query to R_E or $R_{E^{-1}}$.

Definition 1 (Block). $w \xrightarrow{m} w'$ *is a block if* $\exists (k, x, y), (k', x', y') \in \mathcal{L}_{qr}$ *s.t.* $w' = \mathsf{CF}^{R_E}(w, m)$, *that is,* $k = k'$, $x = x' \oplus [1]_n$, $w[1, n] = x$, $m = k[1, n]$, $w[n+1, 2n] = k[n+1, 2n]$, *and* $w' = y \| y'$. *w and w' are called "nodes."* $\mathcal{L}_{block}$ *is a table that keeps all blocks.* w *is called the first node and* w' *is called the second node.*

Definition 2 (Path). $0^{2n} \xrightarrow{m_1 \| m_2 \| \cdots \| m_i} w_i$ *is a path if* $\exists 0^{2n} \xrightarrow{m_1} w_1, w_1 \xrightarrow{m_2} w_2, \ldots, w_{i-1} \xrightarrow{m_i} w_i \in \mathcal{L}_{block}$. *$w_i$ is called the "end node."* $\mathcal{L}_{path}$ *is a table that keeps all paths from* $\mathcal{L}_{block}$.

• Simulator

The goal of the simulator is to simulate (g, E, E^{-1}) so that it is consistent with $\mathcal{RO}$ as in $\mathsf{World}_R^{(1)}$, that is, the following relation is satisfied:

$$\forall (0^{2n} \xrightarrow{m} w) \in \mathcal{L}_{path} : L(m) = R_g(w). \tag{1}$$

First $S1_E : \{0,1\}^{2n} \times \{0,1\}^n \to \{0,1\}^n$ and $S1_{E^{-1}} : \{0,1\}^{2n} \times \{0,1\}^n \to \{0,1\}^n$ are defined. They keep query-response triples in $\mathcal{T}_{qr}$ and keep blocks in $\mathcal{T}_{block}$ from $\mathcal{T}_{qr}$. These tables are initialized by empty sets. In these simulators, an ideal cipher $E_S : \{0,1\}^{2n} \times \{0,1\}^n \to \{0,1\}^n$ is implemented by an appropriate way (e.g., lazy sampling), and the simulator responses are defined by using the ideal cipher. When a query-response triple of the simulator is defined, the companion triple is also defined then the corresponding blocks are defined in $\mathcal{T}_{block}$. Note that $\mathcal{T}_{block}$ equals $\mathcal{L}_{block}$, and $\mathcal{T}_{block}$ equals $\mathcal{L}_{path}$.

$S1_E(k, x)$
1. If $\exists (k, x, y) \in \mathcal{T}_{qr}$ then return y
2. $y \leftarrow E_S(k, x);\ x^* \leftarrow x \oplus [1]_n;\ y^* \leftarrow E_S(k, x^*)$
3. $\mathcal{T}_{qr} \xleftarrow{\cup} \{(k, x, y), (k, x^*, y^*)\};$

   $\mathcal{T}_{block} \xleftarrow{\cup} \left\{ x \| k[n+1, 2n] \xrightarrow{k[1,n]} y \| y^*, x^* \| k[n+1, 2n] \xrightarrow{k[1,n]} y^* \| y \right\}$

4. Return y

$-$ $S1_{E^{-1}}(k, y)$

1. If $\exists (k, x, y) \in \mathcal{T}_{qr}$ then return x
2. $x \leftarrow E_S^{-1}(k, y)$; $x^* \leftarrow x \oplus [1]_n$; $y^* \leftarrow E_S(k, x^*)$
3. $\mathcal{T}_{qr} \xleftarrow{\cup} \{(k, x, y), (k, x^*, y^*)\}$;

$$\mathcal{T}_{block} \xleftarrow{\cup} \left\{ x \| k[n+1, 2n] \xrightarrow{k[1,n]} y \| y^*, x^* \| k[n+1, 2n] \xrightarrow{k[1,n]} y^* \| y \right\}$$

4. Return x

Next $S1_g : \{0, 1\}^{2n} \to \{0, 1\}^{2n}$ is defined so that the relation (1) is satisfied, that is,

$$\forall (0^{2n} \xrightarrow{m} w) \in \mathcal{L}_{path} : \mathcal{RO}(m) = S1_g(w).$$

To satisfy the relation, for a query w, $S1_g$ searches a path with the end node w by using $\mathcal{T}_{block}$. If such path, denoted by $0^{2n} \xrightarrow{m} w$, is found, the output is defined by $\mathcal{RO}(m)$. Otherwise, it is randomly drawn from $\{0, 1\}^{2n}$. $S1_g$ keeps query-responses in $\mathcal{T}_g$ which is initialized by an empty set.

$-$ $S1_g(w)$

1. If $(w, z) \in \mathcal{T}_g$ then return z
2. By using $\mathcal{T}_{block}$, search a path with the end node w
3. If such path, denoted by $0^{2n} \xrightarrow{m} w$, is found then $z \leftarrow \mathcal{RO}(m)$; Else
   $z \xleftarrow{\$} \{0, 1\}^{2n}$
4. $\mathcal{T}_g \xleftarrow{\cup} (w, z)$; Return z

In the step 2, a path ending at w can be searched by the following procedure: (1) find a block with the second node w, denoted by $w_1 \xrightarrow{m_1} w$; (2) find a block with the second node w_1, denoted by $w_2 \xrightarrow{m_2} w_1$; (3) repeat this procedure until such block is not found or a block with the first node 0^{2n} is found. Note that if a collision occurs,[1] then $S1_g$ determines that a path is not found.

• **Upper-Bound of** $\mathbf{Adv}_{F_1^{g,E}, S_1}^{pro} (\mathcal{D})$

In order to upper-bound the advantage, the following games are considered, where in Game i, $\mathcal{D}$ has access to oracles $(L, R_g, R_E, R_{E^{-1}})$ that are defined as follows.

$-$ Game 0: $(L, R_g, R_E, R_{E^{-1}}) = (F_1^{g,E}, g, E, E^{-1})$
$-$ Game 1: $(L, R_g, R_E, R_{E^{-1}}) = (F_1^{R_g, R_E}, S1_g, S1_E, S1_{E^{-1}})$
$-$ Game 2: $(L, R_g, R_E, R_{E^{-1}}) = (\mathcal{RO}, S1_g, S1_E, S1_{E^{-1}})$

Note that in Game 1, $F_1^{R_g, R_E}$ is the function F_1 that uses R_g $(= S1_g)$ and R_E $(= S1_E)$ as the underlying primitives, and S_1 has access to $\mathcal{RO}$. Figure 2 shows these games. Let $Gi = (L, R_g, R_E, R_{E^{-1}})$ in Game i. Then we have

---

[1] A collision means that there exist distinct blocks ending at the same node, that is, $u' \xrightarrow{m'} u$ and $u^* \xrightarrow{m^*} u$.

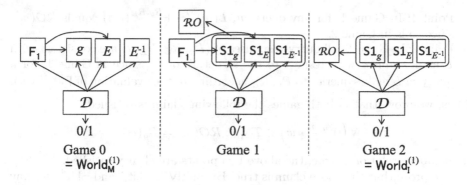

Fig. 2. Games in the proof of step 1

$$\mathsf{Adv}^{\mathsf{pro}}_{\mathsf{F}_1^{g,E},\mathsf{S}_1}(\mathcal{D}) = (\Pr[\mathcal{D}^{G0} \Rightarrow 1] - \Pr[\mathcal{D}^{G1} \Rightarrow 1]) + (\Pr[\mathcal{D}^{G1} \Rightarrow 1] - \Pr[\mathcal{D}^{G2} \Rightarrow 1]).$$

Hereafter, these differences are upper-bounded.

<u>*Upper − Bound of* $\Pr[\mathcal{D}^{G0} \Rightarrow 1] - \Pr[\mathcal{D}^{G1} \Rightarrow 1]$</u>. Since $\mathsf{S1}_E$, $\mathsf{S1}_{E^{-1}}$, and $\mathsf{S1}_g$ behave as E, E^{-1} and g, respectively, we have $\Pr[\mathcal{D}^{G0} \Rightarrow 1] - \Pr[\mathcal{D}^{G1} \Rightarrow 1] = 0$.

<u>*Upper − Bound of* $\Pr[\mathcal{D}^{G1} \Rightarrow 1] - \Pr[\mathcal{D}^{G2} \Rightarrow 1]$</u>. First we prove that Game 1 and Game 2 are indistinguishable unless one of the following events occurs.

- hitIV$^+$ $\Leftrightarrow$ A block $\left(u \xrightarrow{m} v\right)$ is defined by $\mathsf{S1}_E$ such that $v = 0^{2n}$.
- hitIV$^-$ $\Leftrightarrow$ A block $\left(u \xrightarrow{m} v\right)$ is defined by $\mathsf{S1}_{E^{-1}}$ such that $u = 0^{2n}$.
- hit$^+$ $\Leftrightarrow$ When a block $\left(u \xrightarrow{m} v\right)$ is defined by $\mathsf{S1}_E$, there exists a block $\left(u' \xrightarrow{m'} v'\right) \in \mathcal{T}_{block}$ such that $v = u'$ or $v = v'$.
- hit$^-$ $\Leftrightarrow$ When a block $\left(u \xrightarrow{m} v\right)$ is defined by $\mathsf{S1}_{E^{-1}}$, there exists a block $\left(u' \xrightarrow{m'} v'\right) \in \mathcal{T}_{block}$ which was defined by $\mathsf{S1}_E$ such that $u = v'$.
- hitg$^+$ $\Leftrightarrow$ When a block $\left(w' \xrightarrow{m} w\right)$ is defined by $\mathsf{S1}_E$, there exists $(w, z) \in \mathcal{T}_g$.

Let bad = hitIV$^+$ $\vee$ hitIV$^-$ $\vee$ hit$^+$ $\vee$ hit$^-$ $\vee$ hitg$^+$. We assume that bad is a monotone event, that is, firstly bad is false, and if one of the above event occurs, then it becomes true, and after that it will not be changed.

Lemma 3. *Game 1 and Game 2 are indistinguishable as long as* bad = false. ∎

Proof. Assume that bad = false. In Game 1, for a query m, L makes queries to R_E and R_g according to $\mathsf{F}_1^{R_g,R_E}(m)$, whereas in Game 2, L does not make such queries since $L(m) = \mathcal{RO}(m)$. Thus, Game 1 and Game 2 are indistinguishable as long as the structural difference does not affect $\mathcal{D}$'s behavior, that is, the following two points are satisfied.

- Point 1: In Game 1, for any query m, $L(m)$ $(= \mathsf{F}_1^{R_g, R_E}(m))$ equals $\mathcal{RO}(m)$, since so is in Game 2.
- Point 2: In Game 2, all query-responses of $(R_g, R_E, R_{E^{-1}})$ are consistent with L as in Game 1 with respect to the structure of F_1, since in Game 1, for a query m L makes queries to R_g, R_E according to the evaluation of $\mathsf{F}_1^{R_g R_E}(m)$.

Thus, we prove that in both games the following claim is satisfied.

$$\forall \left(0^{2n} \xrightarrow{m} w\right) \in \mathcal{T}_{path} : \mathcal{RO}(m) = R_g(w)$$

If the above relation is true, the above two points are clearly satisfied.

We prove that the above claim is true. By $\neg\mathsf{hitIV}^-$, $\neg\mathsf{hit}^-$ and $\neg\mathsf{hit}^+$, for any path $\left(0^{2n} \xrightarrow{m} w\right) \in \mathcal{T}_{path}$, all blocks in the path are defined by $\mathsf{S1}_E$. By $\neg\mathsf{hitIV}^+$ and $\neg\mathsf{hit}^+$, first the first block (with node 0^{2n}) is defined, second the next block is defined, and the following blocks are defined in sequence. By $\neg\mathsf{hitg}^+$, the path $0^{2n} \xrightarrow{m} w$ was defined before the query w to R_g is made. By $\neg\mathsf{hitIV}^+$ and $\neg\mathsf{hit}^+$, there is no another path with the end node w. Therefore, for the query w to R_g $(= \mathsf{S1}_g)$, $\mathsf{S1}_g$ can find m by the step 2 and defines the output which is equal to $\mathcal{RO}(m)$ by the step 3. Consequently, the above relation is satisfied. □

Let bad_i be an event that $\mathcal{D}$ sets bad in Game i. Analogously, hitIV_i^+, hitIV_i^-, hit_i^+, hit_i^- and hitg_i^+ are defined. The above lemma ensures that $\Pr[\mathcal{D}^{G1} \Rightarrow 1|\mathsf{bad}_1] = \Pr[\mathcal{D}^{G2} \Rightarrow 1|\mathsf{bad}_2]$. Hence we have

$$\Pr[\mathcal{D}^{G1} \Rightarrow 1] - \Pr[\mathcal{D}^{G2} \Rightarrow 1] \leq \max\{\Pr[\mathsf{bad}_1], \Pr[\mathsf{bad}_2]\}.$$

The detail transformation of the inequality is given in Appendix A. Since the numbers of queries to R_E and queries to $R_{E^{-1}}$ in Game 1 are equal to or greater than those in Game 2 due to additional queries by L, we have $\Pr[\mathsf{bad}_2] \leq \Pr[\mathsf{bad}_1]$. Hence $\Pr[\mathsf{bad}_1]$ is upper-bounded.

By $\mathsf{bad}_1 = \mathsf{hitIV}_1^+ \vee \mathsf{hitIV}_1^- \vee \mathsf{hit}_1^+ \vee \mathsf{hit}_1^- \vee \mathsf{hitg}_1^+$, we have

$$\Pr[\mathsf{bad}_1] \leq \Pr[\mathsf{hitIV}_1^+] + \Pr[\mathsf{hitIV}_1^-] + \Pr[\mathsf{hit}_1^+] + \Pr[\mathsf{hit}_1^-] + \Pr[\mathsf{hitg}_1^+].$$

Hereafter, these probabilities are upper-bounded. Recall that $\mathcal{D}$ makes q_L, q_g, q_F, q_I queries to $L, R_g, R_E, R_{E^{-1}}$, respectively, the maximum number of query length in blocks to L is ℓ, $\alpha_F = 2(\ell q_L + q_F)$ (the maximum number of E_S calls in S_E), and $\alpha = 2(\ell q_L + q_F + q_I)$ (the maximum number of E_S calls by all queries).

- $\Pr[\mathsf{hitIV}_1^+]$ is upper-bounded. hitIV_1^+ implies that for some query to R_E $(= \mathsf{S}_E)$, the two outputs of E_S are equal 0^n. Fixing a query, the probability is at most $1/(2^n - \alpha)^2$. We thus have $\Pr[\mathsf{hitIV}_1^+] \leq \alpha_F/(2^n - \alpha)^2$.
- $\Pr[\mathsf{hitIV}_1^-]$ is upper-bounded. hitIV_1^- implies that some response of E_S^{-1} equals 0^n. We thus have $\Pr[\mathsf{hitIV}_1^-] \leq q_I/(2^n - \alpha)$.
- $\Pr[\mathsf{hit}_1^+]$ is upper-bounded. At the i-th query to S_E, at least $2(i - 1 + q_I)$ blocks (with $4(i - 1 + q_I)$ nodes) have been defined, and in S_E two blocks are defined. hit_1^+ implies that for some i-th query to S_E, one of two blocks collide with one of $4(i - 1 + q_I)$ nodes. Since S_E is called $0.5\alpha_F$ times, we have $\Pr[\mathsf{hit}_1^+] \leq \sum_{i=1}^{0.5\alpha_F} 2 \times \frac{4(i-1+q_I)}{(2^n - \alpha)^2} \leq \frac{2\alpha_F^2 + 4\alpha_F(q_I - 1)}{(2^n - \alpha)^2}$.

– $\Pr[\mathsf{hit}_1^-]$ is upper-bounded. First a multi-collision event is defined: $\mathsf{mcoll} \Leftrightarrow \exists (k_1, x_1, y_1), \ldots, (k_n, x_n, y_n) \in \mathcal{T}_{qr}$ such that these triples are defined by E_S and $y_1 = \cdots = y_n$. Then, we have $\Pr[\mathsf{hit}_1^-] \leq \Pr[\mathsf{hit}_1^- | \neg \mathsf{mcoll}] + \Pr[\mathsf{mcoll}]$.

First, $\Pr[\mathsf{hit}_1^- | \neg \mathsf{mcoll}]$ is upper-bounded. Fix $i \in [1, q_I]$. Let $u \xrightarrow{m} v$ be the block defined at the i-th query to $R_{E^{-1}}$. At the i-th query, the number of paths $u' \xrightarrow{m'} v'$ that are defined by S_E and that may satisfy $u = v'$ is at most $n-1$ by $\neg \mathsf{mcoll}$. Hence, we have $\Pr[\mathsf{hit}_1^- | \neg \mathsf{mcoll}] \leq \frac{(n-1)q_I}{2^n - \alpha}$.

Next, $\Pr[\mathsf{mcoll}]$ is upper-bounded. By Stirling's approximation ($x! \geq (x/e)^x$ for any x), we have $\Pr[\mathsf{mcoll}] \leq 2^n \binom{\alpha_F}{n} \left(\frac{1}{2^n - \alpha}\right)^n \leq 2^n \left(\frac{e\alpha_F}{n(2^n - \alpha)}\right)^n$.

Finally we have $\Pr[\mathsf{hit}_1^-] \leq \frac{(n-1)q_I}{2^n - \alpha} + \left(\frac{2e\alpha_F}{n(2^n - \alpha)}\right)^n$.

– $\Pr[\mathsf{hitg}_1^+]$ is upper-bounded. Since there are at most q_g inputs to S_g, we have $\Pr[\mathsf{hitf}_1^+] \leq \sum_{i=1}^{\alpha_F} \frac{q_g}{(2^n - \alpha)^2} = \frac{\alpha_F q_g}{(2^n - \alpha)^2}$.

Summing the above upper-bounds gives

$$\Pr[\mathcal{D}^{G1} \Rightarrow 1] - \Pr[\mathcal{D}^{G2} \Rightarrow 1]$$
$$\leq \frac{\alpha_F(2\alpha_F + 4q_I + q_g - 4)}{(2^n - \alpha)^2} + \frac{\alpha_F + nq_I}{2^n - \alpha} + \left(\frac{2e\alpha_F}{n(2^n - \alpha)}\right)^n.$$

Conclusion of the Proof. Finally, the above upper-bounds give

$$\mathsf{Adv}^{\mathrm{pro}}_{\mathsf{F}_1^{g,E}, S_1}(\mathcal{D}) \leq \frac{\alpha_F(2\alpha_F + 4q_I + q_g - 4)}{(2^n - \alpha)^2} + \frac{\alpha_F + nq_I}{2^n - \alpha} + \left(\frac{2e\alpha_F}{n(2^n - \alpha)}\right)^n.$$

4.2   Proof of Lemma 2

A simulator S_2 consists of two algorithms $S2_E, S2_{E^{-1}}$ that simulate E, E^{-1}, respectively. Let $\mathcal{D}$ be a distinguisher with access to oracles $(L, R_E, R_{E^{-1}})$, where $(L, R_E, R_{E^{-1}}) = (\mathsf{F}^E, E, E^{-1})$ in $\mathsf{World}_\mathsf{R}$, and $(L, R_E, R_{E^{-1}}) = (\mathsf{F}_1^{y,E}, S2_E, S2_{E^{-1}})$ in $\mathsf{World}_\mathsf{M}^{(2)}$. We denote a query to R_E by (k, x) and the response by y, and a query to $R_{E^{-1}}$ by (k, y) and the response by x. Hence, $y = R_E(k, x)$ and $x = R_{E^{-1}}(k, y)$. In this proof, blocks in Definition 1 and paths in Definition 2 are used. Let $\mathcal{L}_{qr}$ be a set of query-responses of R_E and of $R_{E^{-1}}$, $\mathcal{L}_{block}$ be a set of blocks defined by $\mathcal{L}_{qr}$, and $\mathcal{L}_{path}$ be a set of paths defined by $\mathcal{L}_{block}$.

● **Simulator**

The goal of simulator is to simulate (E, E^{-1}) so that the following relation is satisfied (since in $\mathsf{World}_\mathsf{R}$ the relation is satisfied):

$$\forall (0^{2n} \xrightarrow{m} k) \in \mathcal{L}_{path} : L(m) = R_E(k, [2]_n) \| R_E(k, [3]_n).$$

In $\mathsf{World}_\mathsf{M}^{(2)}$, since $L(m) = g(\mathsf{H}_0^E(m))$, in order to satisfy the above relation, we define the simulator so that for a query (k, x) to $S2_E$, if $x = [2]_n$ (resp., $x = [3]_n$), the response is defined so that $S2_E(k, x) = g(k)[1, n]$ (resp., $S2_E(k, x) = g(k)[n+1, 2n]$). Since an output of S_E is defined by g or E, a collision in outputs with the same key of $S2_E$ or of $S2_{E^{-1}}$ might occur, whereas the collision does not occur in $World_R$. We define $S2$ so that if the collision occurs then $S2$ aborts. $S2$ keeps query-responses in $\mathcal{T}_{qr}$ which is initialized by an empty set.

$\underline{S2_E(k, x)}$
1. If $\exists (k, x, y) \in \mathcal{T}_{qr}$ then return y
2. $y_2 \| y_3 \leftarrow g(k)$
3. $\mathcal{T}_{qr} \xleftarrow{\cup} \{(k, [2]_n, y_2), (k, [3]_n, y_3)\}$
4. If $y_2 = y_3$ then abort
5. If $x = [2]_n$ then return y_2
6. If $x = [3]_n$ then return y_3
7. $y \leftarrow E(k, x)$; $y^* \leftarrow E(k, x \oplus [1]_n)$
8. $\mathcal{T}_{qr} \xleftarrow{\cup} \{(k, x, y), (k, x \oplus [1]_n, y^*)\}$
9. If $y = y_2$, $y = y_3$, $y^* = y_2$ or $y^* = y_3$ then abort
10. Return y

$\underline{S2_{E^{-1}}(k, y)}$
1. If $\exists (k, x, y) \in \mathcal{T}_{qr}$ then return x
2. $y_2 \| y_3 \leftarrow g(k)$
3. $\mathcal{T}_{qr} \xleftarrow{\cup} \{(k, [2]_n, y_2), (k, [3]_n, y_3)\}$
4. If $y_2 = y_3$ then abort
5. If $y = y_2$ then return $[2]_n$
6. If $y = y_3$ then return $[3]_n$
7. $x \leftarrow E^{-1}(k, y)$; $y^* \leftarrow E(k, x \oplus [1]_n)$
8. $\mathcal{T}_{qr} \xleftarrow{\cup} \{(k, x, y), (k, x \oplus [1]_n, y^*)\}$
9. If $x = [2]_n$, $x = [3]_n$, $y^* = y_2$ or $y^* = y_3$ then abort
10. Return x

• Upper-Bound of $\mathsf{Adv}^{\mathsf{indiff}}_{\mathsf{F}^E, \mathsf{F}_1^{g, E}, \mathsf{S}_2}(\mathcal{D})$

We consider three games, where in Game i, $\mathcal{D}$ has access to oracle $(L, R_E, R_{E^{-1}})$ defined as follows.

- Game 0: $(L, R_E, R_{E^{-1}}) = (\mathsf{F}^E, E, E^{-1})$
- Game 1: $(L, R_E, R_{E^{-1}}) = (\mathsf{F}^{R_E}, S2_E, S2_{E^{-1}})$
- Game 2: $(L, R_E, R_{E^{-1}}) = (\mathsf{F}_1^{g, E}, S2_E, S2_{E^{-1}})$

Figure 3 shows these games. Note that in Game 1, F^{R_E} is the function F that uses R_E $(= S2_E)$ as the underlying primitives, and $S2_E$ has access to E, E^{-1} and g. Let $Gi = (L, R_E, R_{E^{-1}})$ in Game i. We have

$$\mathsf{Adv}^{\mathsf{indiff}}_{\mathsf{F}^E, \mathsf{F}_1^{g, E}, \mathsf{S}_2}(\mathcal{D})$$
$$= \left(\Pr[\mathcal{D}^{G0} \Rightarrow 1] - \Pr[\mathcal{D}^{G1} \Rightarrow 1]\right) + \left(\Pr[\mathcal{D}^{G1} \Rightarrow 1] - \Pr[\mathcal{D}^{G2} \Rightarrow 1]\right).$$

Hereafter, the two differences are upper-bounded.

Upper − Bound of $\Pr[\mathcal{D}^{G0} \Rightarrow 1] - \Pr[\mathcal{D}^{G1} \Rightarrow 1]$. In this case, Game 0 and Game 1 are indistinguishable as long as S_2 behaves as an ideal cipher. In S_2, outputs are defined by using E, E^{-1} or g, thus outputs with the same key might collide. If the collision occurs, S_2 aborts. Thus S_2 behaves as an ideal cipher as long as it does not abort, that is, $\Pr[\mathcal{D}^{G0} \Rightarrow 1] - \Pr[\mathcal{D}^{G1} \Rightarrow 1]$ is upper-bounded by the probability that S_2 aborts in Game 1.

In the following, the abort probability is evaluated. Note that if one of the following events occurs, then S aborts. Recall that $\mathcal{D}$ makes q_L, q_F and q_I queries to L, R_E and $R_{E^{-1}}$, respectively, the maximum number of blocks of a query to L is ℓ, $\beta_F = 2((\ell + 1)q_L + q_F)$, and $\beta = 2((\ell + 1)q_L + q_F + q_I)$.

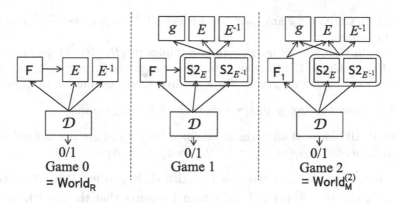

Fig. 3. Games in the proof of step 2

1. In S_E or S_E^{-1}, if $y_2 = y_3$, S_2 aborts. Since the number of queries to g is at most 0.5β, the probability that $y_2 = y_3$ is at most $0.5\beta/2^n$.
2. In S_E, if $y = y_2$, $y = y_3$, $y^* = y_2$ or $y^* = y_3$, S_2 aborts. Since the number of queries to S_E is at most $0.5\beta_F$, the probability that $y = y_2$, $y = y_3$, $y^* = y_2$ or $y^* = y_3$ is at most $2\beta_F/(2^n - \beta)$.
3. In $S_{E^{-1}}$, if $x = [2]_n$, $x = [3]_n$, $y^* = y_2$ or $y^* = y_3$, then S_2 aborts. Since the number of queries to $S_{E^{-1}}$ is at most q_I, the probability that $x = [2]_n$ or $x = [3]_n$ is at most $2q_I/(2^n - \beta)$, and the probability that $y^* = y_2$ or $y^* = y_3$ is at most $2q_I/(2^n - \beta)$.

Hence the probability that S_2 aborts is at most $\frac{0.5\beta+2\beta_F+4q_I}{2^n-\beta}$.

We thus have $\Pr[\mathcal{D}^{G0} \Rightarrow 1] - \Pr[\mathcal{D}^{G1} \Rightarrow 1] \le \frac{0.5\beta+2\beta_F+4q_I}{2^n-\beta}$.

Upper – Bound of $\Pr[\mathcal{D}^{G1} \Rightarrow 1] - \Pr[\mathcal{D}^{G2} \Rightarrow 1]$. First the following events are defined, which ensure that Game 1 and Game 2 are indistinguishable unless one of the events occurs (See Lemma 4).

- abort $\Leftrightarrow$ S_2 aborts.
- hit23$^+$ $\Leftrightarrow$ S_2 makes a query to E such that $[2]_n$ or $[3]_n$ is returned.

Let bad $=$ abort $\vee$ hit23$^+$ be the sum event. We assume that bad is a monotone event, that is, firstly bad is false, and if one of the above event occurs then it becomes true and after that it will not be changed.

Lemma 4. *Game 1 and Game 2 are indistinguishable as long as* bad $=$ false.

Proof. Assume that bad $=$ false. In Game 1, for a query m, L makes queries to R_E according to $\mathsf{F}^{R_E}(m)$, whereas in Game 2, L does not such queries since $L(m) = \mathsf{F}_1^{g,E}(m)$. Thus, Game 1 and Game 2 are indistinguishable as long as the structural difference does not affect $\mathcal{D}$'s behavior, that is, the following two points are satisfied.

- Point 1: In Game 1, for any query m, $L(m)$ $(= \mathsf{F}^{R_E}(m))$ equals $\mathsf{F}_1^{g,E}(m)$, since so is in Game 2.
- Point 2: In Game 2, all query-response triples of $(R_E, R_{E^{-1}})$ are consistent with L as in Game 1 with respect to the structure of F, since in Game 1, for a query m, L makes queries to R_E according to the evaluation of $\mathsf{F}^{R_E}(m)$.

In order to prove the two points, we show the following claims.

- Claim 1: All blocks of all paths are defined by E (and are not defined by g).
- Claim 2: $(w, [2]_n, z_2), (w, [3]_n, z_3) \in \mathcal{T}_{qr} \Rightarrow z_2 \| z_3 = g(w)$.

By the above claims, Point 1 is clearly satisfied. Regarding Point 2, in Game 2, for any path $\left(0^{2n} \xrightarrow{m} w \right) \in \mathcal{T}_{path}$, Claim 1 ensures that the inner blocks are defined by E or E^{-1}, and Claim 2 ensures that for the corresponding pairs $(w, [2]_n, z_2), (w, [3]_n, z_3) \in \mathcal{T}_{qr}$, $z_2 \| z_3 = g(w)$ is satisfied. As a result, $L(m)$ $(= \mathsf{F}_1^{g,E}(m)) = z_2 \| z_3$, that is, all query-response triples of $(R_E, R_{E^{-1}})$ are consistent with L.

Finally, we show that the above claims are valid. Note that the following proofs hold in both Game 1 and Game 2. Consider Claim 1. By $\neg$abort, in S2$_{E^{-1}}$, all outputs of E^{-1} don't equal $[2]_n$ and $[3]_n$. By $\neg$hit23$^+$, in S2$_E$, all outputs of E don't equal $[2]_n$ and $[3]_n$. Thus, for any path $\left(0^{2n} \xrightarrow{m} w \right) \in \mathcal{T}_{path}$, all nodes in the path don't equal $[2]_n$ and $[3]_n$, thus all nodes in the path are defined by E. Hence, Condition 1 is satisfied. Next, consider Claim 2. By $\neg$abort, in S2$_{E^{-1}}$, all outputs of E^{-1} don't equal $[2]_n$ and $[3]_n$, thus any $(w, [2]_n, z_2), (w, [3]_n, z_3) \in \mathcal{T}_{qr}$ are defined by S2$_E$, and by the definition of S2$_E$, $(w, [2]_n, z_2), (w, [3]_n, z_3) \in \mathcal{T}_{qr} \Rightarrow z_2 \| z_3 = g(w)$. $\square$

Let bad_i be an event that $\mathcal{D}$ sets bad in Game i. Similarly, abort_i and $\mathsf{hit23}_i^+$ are defined. By the above lemma, $\Pr[\mathcal{D}^{G1} \Rightarrow 1 | \mathsf{bad}_1] = \Pr[\mathcal{D}^{G2} \Rightarrow 1 | \mathsf{bad}_2]$, thus we have

$$\Pr[\mathcal{D}^{G1} \Rightarrow 1] - \Pr[\mathcal{D}^{G2} \Rightarrow 1] \leq \max\{\Pr[\mathsf{bad}_1], \Pr[\mathsf{bad}_2]\}.$$

The detail of the transformation for the inequality is given in Appendix A. Since the numbers of queries to R_E and to $R_{E^{-1}}$ in Game 1 are equal to or greater than those in Game 2 due to additional queries by L, we have $\Pr[\mathsf{bad}_2] \leq \Pr[\mathsf{bad}_1]$. Note that

$$\Pr[\mathsf{bad}_1] \leq \Pr[\mathsf{abort}_1] + \Pr[\mathsf{hit23}_1^+].$$

The upper-bound of $\Pr[\mathsf{abort}_1]$ is given in the evaluation of $\Pr[\mathcal{D}^{G0} \Rightarrow 1] - \Pr[\mathcal{D}^{G1} \Rightarrow 1]$, where $\Pr[\mathsf{abort}_1] \leq \frac{0.5\beta + 2\beta_F + 4q_I}{2^n - \beta}$. Regarding $\Pr[\mathsf{hit23}^+]$, since an output of E is randomly drawn from at least $2^n - \beta$ values, we have $\Pr[\mathsf{hit23}_1^+] \leq \frac{\beta_F + q_I}{2^n - \beta}$.

Finally, we have

$$\Pr[\mathcal{D}^{G1} \Rightarrow 1] - \Pr[\mathcal{D}^{G2} \Rightarrow 1] \leq \frac{0.5\beta + 2\beta_F + 4q_I}{2^n - \beta} + \frac{\beta_F + q_I}{2^n - \beta}$$

$$= \frac{0.5\beta + 3\beta_F + 5q_I}{2^n - \beta}.$$

Conclusion of the Proof. Finally, the above upper-bounds give

$$\mathsf{Adv}^{\mathsf{indiff}}_{\mathsf{F}^E, \mathsf{F}_1^{g,E}, \mathsf{S}_2}(\mathcal{D}) \leq \frac{0.5\beta + 2\beta_F + 4q_I}{2^n - \beta} + \frac{0.5\beta + 3\beta_F + 5q_I}{2^n - \beta} \leq \frac{6\beta}{2^n - \beta}.$$

A   Upper Bound of $\Pr[\mathcal{D}^{G1} \Rightarrow 1] - \Pr[\mathcal{D}^{G2} \Rightarrow 1]$

Let $\mathsf{G}_i = (\mathcal{D}^{Gi} \Rightarrow 1)$ be an event.

$$\Pr[\mathcal{D}^{G1} \Rightarrow 1] - \Pr[\mathcal{D}^{G2} \Rightarrow 1] = \Pr[\mathsf{G}_1] - \Pr[\mathsf{G}_2]$$

$$= \Pr[\mathsf{G}_1 \wedge \mathsf{bad}_1] + \Pr[\mathsf{G}_1 \wedge \neg\mathsf{bad}_1]$$

$$- (\Pr[\mathsf{G}_2 \wedge \mathsf{bad}_2] + \Pr[\mathsf{G}_2 \wedge \neg\mathsf{bad}_2])$$

$$= \Pr[\mathsf{G}_1|\mathsf{bad}_1]\Pr[\mathsf{bad}_1] + \Pr[\mathsf{G}_1|\neg\mathsf{bad}_1]\Pr[\neg\mathsf{bad}_1]$$

$$- \Pr[\mathsf{G}_2|\mathsf{bad}_2]\Pr[\mathsf{bad}_2] - \Pr[\mathsf{G}_2|\neg\mathsf{bad}_2]\Pr[\neg\mathsf{bad}_2]$$

From $\Pr[\mathsf{G}_1|\neg\mathsf{bad}_1] = \Pr[\mathsf{G}_2|\neg\mathsf{bad}_2]$, we have

$$\Pr[\mathcal{D}^{G1} \Rightarrow 1] - \Pr[\mathcal{D}^{G2} \Rightarrow 1] = \Pr[\mathsf{G}_1|\mathsf{bad}_1]\Pr[\mathsf{bad}_1] - \Pr[\mathsf{G}_2|\mathsf{bad}_2]\Pr[\mathsf{bad}_2]$$

$$+ \Pr[\mathsf{G}_1|\neg\mathsf{bad}_1](\Pr[\neg\mathsf{bad}_1] - \Pr[\neg\mathsf{bad}_2])$$

$$= \Pr[\mathsf{G}_1|\mathsf{bad}_1]\Pr[\mathsf{bad}_1] - \Pr[\mathsf{G}_2|\mathsf{bad}_2]\Pr[\mathsf{bad}_2]$$

$$+ \Pr[\mathsf{G}_1|\neg\mathsf{bad}_1](\Pr[\mathsf{bad}_2] - \Pr[\mathsf{bad}_1])$$

$$\leq \max\{\Pr[\mathsf{bad}_1], \Pr[\mathsf{bad}_2]\}.$$

B   Proof of Theorem 1

We show that for any distinguisher $\mathcal{D}$ there exist distinguishers $\mathcal{D}_1$ and $\mathcal{D}_2$, and a simulator S such that

$$\mathsf{Adv}^{\mathsf{pro}}_{\mathsf{F}^E, \mathsf{S}}(\mathcal{D}) \leq \mathsf{Adv}^{\mathsf{pro}}_{\mathsf{F}^{g,E}, \mathsf{S1}}(\mathcal{D}_1) + \mathsf{Adv}^{\mathsf{indiff}}_{\mathsf{F}^E, \mathsf{F}_1^{g,E}, \mathsf{S2}}(\mathcal{D}_2),$$

where

- $\mathsf{S}^{\mathcal{RO}} = (\mathsf{S}_E^{\mathcal{RO}}, \mathsf{S}_{E-1}^{\mathcal{RO}})$ is a simulator of the PRO security of F^E,
  $\mathsf{S}_1^{\mathcal{RO}} = (\mathsf{S1}_g^{\mathcal{RO}}, \mathsf{S1}_E^{\mathcal{RO}}, \mathsf{S1}_{E-1}^{\mathcal{RO}})$ is a simulator of the PRO security of $\mathsf{F}_1^{g,E}$, and
- $\mathsf{S}_2^{g,E,E^{-1}} = (\mathsf{S2}_E^{g,E,E^{-1}}, \mathsf{S2}_{E-1}^{g,E,E^{-1}})$ is a simulator of the indifferentiability of F^E from $\mathsf{F}_1^{g,E}$.

We first transform the advantage $\mathsf{Adv}^{\mathsf{pro}}_{\mathsf{FE},\mathsf{S}}(\mathcal{D})$ as follows.

$$\mathsf{Adv}^{\mathsf{pro}}_{\mathsf{FE},\mathsf{S}}(\mathcal{D}) = \Pr[\mathcal{D}^{\mathsf{F}^E,E,E^{-1}} \Rightarrow 1] - \Pr[\mathcal{D}^{\mathcal{RO},\mathsf{S}^{\mathcal{RO}}_E,\mathsf{S}^{\mathcal{RO}}_{E^{-1}}} \Rightarrow 1]$$

$$= \left(\Pr[\mathcal{D}^{\mathsf{F}^E,E,E^{-1}} \Rightarrow 1] - \Pr[\mathcal{D}^{\mathsf{F}^{g,E}_1,\mathsf{S2}^{g,E,E^{-1}}_E,\mathsf{S2}^{g,E,E^{-1}}_{E^{-1}}} \Rightarrow 1] \right)$$

$$+ \left(\Pr[\mathcal{D}^{\mathsf{F}^{g,E}_1,\mathsf{S2}^{g,E,E^{-1}}_E,\mathsf{S2}^{g,E,E^{-1}}_{E^{-1}}} \Rightarrow 1] - \Pr[\mathcal{D}^{\mathcal{RO},\mathsf{S}^{\mathcal{RO}}_E,\mathsf{S}^{\mathcal{RO}}_{E^{-1}}} \Rightarrow 1] \right)$$

We then define S and $\mathcal{D}_1$ as

$$\mathsf{S}^{\mathcal{RO}} = (\mathsf{S}^{\mathcal{RO}}_E, \mathsf{S}^{\mathcal{RO}}_{E^{-1}}) = (\mathsf{S2}^{\mathsf{S1}^{\mathcal{RO}}_g,\mathsf{S1}^{\mathcal{RO}}_E,\mathsf{S1}^{\mathcal{RO}}_{E^{-1}}}_E, \mathsf{S2}^{\mathsf{S1}^{\mathcal{RO}}_g,\mathsf{S1}^{\mathcal{RO}}_E,\mathsf{S1}^{\mathcal{RO}}_{E^{-1}}}_{E^{-1}}) \text{ and}$$

$$\mathcal{D}^{L,R_g,R_E,R_{E^{-1}}}_1 = \mathcal{D}^{L,\mathsf{S2}^{R_g,R_E,R_{E^{-1}}}_E,\mathsf{S2}^{R_g,R_E,R_{E^{-1}}}_{E^{-1}}}$$

where $(L, R_g, R_E, R_{E^{-1}})$ is either $(\mathsf{F}^{g,E}_1, g, E, E^{-1})$ or $(\mathcal{RO}, \mathsf{S1}^{\mathcal{RO}}_g, \mathsf{S1}^{\mathcal{RO}}_E, \mathsf{S1}^{\mathcal{RO}}_{E^{-1}})$. Then we have

$$\mathsf{Adv}^{\mathsf{pro}}_{\mathsf{FE},\mathsf{S}}(\mathcal{D}) \leq \left(\Pr[\mathcal{D}^{\mathsf{F}^E,E,E^{-1}} \Rightarrow 1] - \Pr[\mathcal{D}^{\mathsf{F}^{g,E}_1,\mathsf{S2}^{g,E,E^{-1}}_E,\mathsf{S2}^{g,E,E^{-1}}_{E^{-1}}} \Rightarrow 1] \right)$$

$$+ \left(\Pr[\mathcal{D}^{\mathsf{F}^{g,E}_1,g,E,E^{-1}}_1 \Rightarrow 1] - \Pr[\mathcal{D}^{\mathcal{RO},\mathsf{S1}^{\mathcal{RO}}_g,\mathsf{S1}^{\mathcal{RO}}_E,\mathsf{S1}^{\mathcal{RO}}_{E^{-1}}}_1 \Rightarrow 1] \right)$$

We define $\mathcal{D}_2$ as $\mathcal{D}^{L,R_E,R_{E^{-1}}}_2 = \mathcal{D}^{L,R_E,R_{E^{-1}}}$ where $L, R_E, R_{E^{-1}}$ is either $(\mathsf{F}^E, E, E^{-1})$ or $(\mathcal{RO}, \mathsf{S2}^{g,E,E^{-1}}_E, \mathsf{S2}^{g,E,E^{-1}}_{E^{-1}})$. Then we have

$$\mathsf{Adv}^{\mathsf{pro}}_{\mathsf{FE},\mathsf{S}}(\mathcal{D}) \leq \left(\Pr[\mathcal{D}^{\mathsf{F}^E,E,E^{-1}}_2 \Rightarrow 1] - \Pr[\mathcal{D}^{\mathsf{F}^{g,E}_1,\mathsf{S2}^{g,E,E^{-1}}_E,\mathsf{S2}^{g,E,E^{-1}}_{E^{-1}}}_2 \Rightarrow 1] \right)$$

$$+ \left(\Pr[\mathcal{D}^{\mathsf{F}^{g,E}_1,g,E,E^{-1}}_1 \Rightarrow 1] - \Pr[\mathcal{D}^{\mathcal{RO},\mathsf{S1}^{\mathcal{RO}}_g,\mathsf{S1}^{\mathcal{RO}}_E,\mathsf{S1}^{\mathcal{RO}}_{E^{-1}}}_1 \Rightarrow 1] \right)$$

$$= \mathsf{Adv}^{\mathsf{pro}}_{\mathsf{F}^{g,E}_1,\mathsf{S1}_1}(\mathcal{D}_1) + \mathsf{Adv}^{\mathsf{indiff}}_{\mathsf{FE},\mathsf{F}^{g,E}_1,\mathsf{S2}}(\mathcal{D}_2).$$

Next Lemma 1 and Lemma 2 are applied into the above inequation. Assume that $\mathcal{D}$ makes queries to $L, R_E, R_{E^{-1}}$ at most q_L, q_F, q_I, respectively, and the maximum number of message blocks of a query to L is ℓ. In this case,

- $\mathcal{D}_1$ makes queries to $L, R_g, R_E, R_{E^{-1}}$ at most $q_L, q_F + q_I, 2q_F + q_I, q_I$, respectively, and the maximum number of message blocks of a query to L is ℓ, and
- $\mathcal{D}_2$ makes queries to $L, R_E, R_{E^{-1}}$ at most q_L, q_F, q_I, respectively, and the maximum number of message blocks of a query to L is ℓ.

Let $\sigma_F = 2(\ell + 1)q_L + q_F$ be the total number of E calls and $\sigma = \sigma_F + q_I$ the total number of (E, E^{-1}) calls. Then, putting the above parameters into Lemma 1 gives $\alpha_F = 2(\ell q_L + 2q_F + q_I)$, $\alpha = 2(\ell q_L + 2q_F + 2q_I)$, and then

$$\mathsf{Adv}^{\mathrm{pro}}_{\mathsf{F}_1^{g,E},\mathsf{S}_1}(\mathcal{D}_1) \leq \frac{\alpha_F(2\alpha_F + 4q_I + q_g - 4)}{(2^n - \alpha)^2} + \frac{\alpha_F + nq_I}{2^n - \alpha} + \left(\frac{2e\alpha_F}{n(2^n - \alpha)}\right)^n$$

$$= \frac{2(\ell q_L + 2q_F + q_I)(4(\ell q_L + 2q_F + q_I) + 4q_I + (q_F + q_I) - 4)}{(2^n - 2(\ell q_L + 2q_F + 2q_I))^2}$$

$$+ \frac{2(\ell q_L + 2q_F + q_I) + nq_I}{2^n - 2(\ell q_L + 2q_F + 2q_I)} + \left(\frac{2e \cdot 2(\ell q_L + 2q_F + q_I)}{n(2^n - 2(\ell q_L + 2q_F + 2q_I))}\right)^n$$

$$\leq \frac{(\sigma + 3q_F + q_I)(4\sigma + 7q_F + 8q_I)}{(2^n - 4\sigma)^2} + \frac{\sigma + 3q_F + (n + 1)q_I}{2^n - 4\sigma}$$

$$+ \left(\frac{4e(\sigma + 3q_F + q_I)}{n(2^n - 4\sigma)}\right)^n$$

$$\leq \frac{48\sigma^2}{(2^n - 4\sigma)^2} + \frac{4\sigma + nq_I}{2^n - 4\sigma} + \left(\frac{16e\sigma}{n(2^n - 4\sigma)}\right)^n$$

Putting the above parameters into Lemma 2 gives

$$\mathsf{Adv}^{\mathrm{indiff}}_{F^E,\mathsf{F}_1^{g,E},\mathsf{S}_2}(\mathcal{D}_2) \leq \frac{12((\ell + 1)q_L + q_F + q_I)}{2^n - 2((\ell + 1)q_L + q_F + q_I)} \leq \frac{6\sigma}{2^n - \sigma}.$$

Hence we have

$$\mathsf{Adv}^{\mathrm{pro}}_{F^E,\mathsf{S}}(\mathcal{D}) \leq \mathsf{Adv}^{\mathrm{pro}}_{\mathsf{F}_1^{g,E},\mathsf{S}_1}(\mathcal{D}_1) + \mathsf{Adv}^{\mathrm{indiff}}_{F^E,\mathsf{F}_1^{g,E},\mathsf{S}_2}(\mathcal{D}_2)$$

$$\leq \frac{48\sigma^2}{(2^n - 4\sigma)^2} + \frac{10\sigma + nq_I}{2^n - 4\sigma} + \left(\frac{16e\sigma}{n(2^n - 4\sigma)}\right)^n.$$

References

1. Black, J., Rogaway, P., Shrimpton, T.: Black-box analysis of the block-cipher-based hash-function constructions from PGV. In: Yung, M. (ed.) CRYPTO 2002. LNCS, vol. 2442, pp. 320–335. Springer, Heidelberg (2002). doi:10.1007/3-540-45708-9_21
2. Bogdanov, A., Knudsen, L.R., Leander, G., Paar, C., Poschmann, A., Robshaw, M.J.B., Seurin, Y., Vikkelsoe, C.: PRESENT: an ultra-lightweight block cipher. In: Paillier, P., Verbauwhede, I. (eds.) CHES 2007. LNCS, vol. 4727, pp. 450–466. Springer, Heidelberg (2007). doi:10.1007/978-3-540-74735-2_31
3. Coron, J.-S., Dodis, Y., Malinaud, C., Puniya, P.: Merkle-damgård revisited: how to construct a hash function. In: Shoup, V. (ed.) CRYPTO 2005. LNCS, vol. 3621, pp. 430–448. Springer, Heidelberg (2005). doi:10.1007/11535218_26
4. Damgård, I.B.: A design principle for hash functions. In: Brassard, G. (ed.) CRYPTO 1989. LNCS, vol. 435, pp. 416–427. Springer, New York (1990). doi:10.1007/0-387-34805-0_39
5. Even, S., Mansour, Y.: A construction of a cipher from a single pseudorandom permutation. In: Imai, H., Rivest, R.L., Matsumoto, T. (eds.) ASIACRYPT 1991. LNCS, vol. 739, pp. 210–224. Springer, Heidelberg (1993). doi:10.1007/3-540-57332-1_17
6. Even, S., Mansour, Y.: A construction of a cipher from a single pseudorandom permutation. J. Cryptology 10(3), 151–162 (1997)

7. Fleischmann, E., Forler, C., Gorski, M., Lucks, S.: Collision resistant double-length hashing. In: Heng, S.-H., Kurosawa, K. (eds.) ProvSec 2010. LNCS, vol. 6402, pp. 102–118. Springer, Heidelberg (2010). doi:10.1007/978-3-642-16280-0_7

8. Fleischmann, E., Forler, C., Lucks, S., Wenzel, J.: Weimar-DM: a highly secure double-length compression function. In: Susilo, W., Mu, Y., Seberry, J. (eds.) ACISP 2012. LNCS, vol. 7372, pp. 152–165. Springer, Heidelberg (2012). doi:10.1007/978-3-642-31448-3_12

9. Fleischmann, E., Gorski, M., Lucks, S.: Security of cyclic double block length hash functions. In: Parker, M.G. (ed.) IMACC 2009. LNCS, vol. 5921, pp. 153–175. Springer, Heidelberg (2009). doi:10.1007/978-3-642-10868-6_10

10. Gong, Z., Lai, X., Chen, K.: A synthetic indifferentiability analysis of some block-cipher-based hash functions. Des. Codes Crypt. 48(3), 293–305 (2008)

11. Guo, J., Peyrin, T., Poschmann, A., Robshaw, M.: The LED block cipher. In: Preneel, B., Takagi, T. (eds.) CHES 2011. LNCS, vol. 6917, pp. 326–341. Springer, Heidelberg (2011). doi:10.1007/978-3-642-23951-9_22

12. Hirose, S.: Some plausible constructions of double-block-length hash functions. In: Robshaw, M. (ed.) FSE 2006. LNCS, vol. 4047, pp. 210–225. Springer, Heidelberg (2006). doi:10.1007/11799313_14

13. Hirose, S., Kuwakado, H.: A block-cipher-based hash function using an MMO-type double-block compression function. In: Chow, S.S.M., Liu, J.K., Hui, L.C.K., Yiu, S.M. (eds.) ProvSec 2014. LNCS, vol. 8782, pp. 71–86. Springer, Cham (2014). doi:10.1007/978-3-319-12475-9_6

14. Hirose, S., Naito, Y., Sugawara, T.: Output Masking of Tweakable Even-Mansour can be Eliminated for Message Authentication Code. In: SAC 2016. LNCS, Springer (to appear, 2016)

15. Hirose, S., Park, J.H., Yun, A.: A simple variant of the Merkle-Damgård scheme with a permutation. In: Kurosawa, K. (ed.) ASIACRYPT 2007. LNCS, vol. 4833, pp. 113–129. Springer, Heidelberg (2007). doi:10.1007/978-3-540-76900-2_7

16. Kurosawa, K.: Power of a public random permutation and its application to authenticated encryption. IEEE Trans. Inf. Theory 56(10), 5366–5374 (2010)

17. Kuwakado, H., Hirose, S.: Hashing mode using a lightweight blockcipher. In: Stam, M. (ed.) IMACC 2013. LNCS, vol. 8308, pp. 213–231. Springer, Heidelberg (2013). doi:10.1007/978-3-642-45239-0_13

18. Lai, X., Massey, J.L.: Hash functions based on block ciphers. In: Rueppel, R.A. (ed.) EUROCRYPT 1992. LNCS, vol. 658, pp. 55–70. Springer, Heidelberg (1993). doi:10.1007/3-540-47555-9_5

19. Lee, J., Kwon, D.: The security of abreast-DM in the ideal cipher model. IEICE Trans. 94-A(1), 104–109 (2011)

20. Lee, J., Stam, M.: MJH: a faster alternative to MDC-2. Des. Codes Crypt. 76(2), 179–205 (2015)

21. Lee, J., Stam, M., Steinberger, J.: The collision security of tandem-dm in the ideal cipher model. In: Rogaway, P. (ed.) CRYPTO 2011. LNCS, vol. 6841, pp. 561–577. Springer, Heidelberg (2011). doi:10.1007/978-3-642-22792-9_32

22. Liskov, M., Rivest, R.L., Wagner, D.: Tweakable block ciphers. In: Yung, M. (ed.) CRYPTO 2002. LNCS, vol. 2442, pp. 31–46. Springer, Heidelberg (2002). doi:10.1007/3-540-45708-9_3

23. Lucks, S.: A Collision-resistant rate-1 double-block-length hash function. In: Symmetric Cryptography, 07.01. – 12.01.2007. Dagstuhl Seminar Proceedings, vol. 07021. Internationales Begegnungs- und Forschungszentrum fuer Informatik (IBFI), Schloss Dagstuhl, Germany (2007)

24. Maurer, U., Renner, R., Holenstein, C.: Indifferentiability, impossibility results on reductions, and applications to the random oracle methodology. In: Naor, M. (ed.) TCC 2004. LNCS, vol. 2951, pp. 21–39. Springer, Heidelberg (2004). doi:10.1007/978-3-540-24638-1_2
25. Mennink, B.: Optimal collision security in double block length hashing with single length key. In: Wang, X., Sako, K. (eds.) ASIACRYPT 2012. LNCS, vol. 7658, pp. 526–543. Springer, Heidelberg (2012). doi:10.1007/978-3-642-34961-4_32
26. Mennink, B.: Indifferentiability of double length compression functions. In: Stam, M. (ed.) IMACC 2013. LNCS, vol. 8308, pp. 232–251. Springer, Heidelberg (2013). doi:10.1007/978-3-642-45239-0_14
27. Merkle, R.C.: One way hash functions and DES. In: Brassard, G. (ed.) CRYPTO 1989. LNCS, vol. 435, pp. 428–446. Springer, New York (1990). doi:10.1007/0-387-34805-0_40
28. Meyer, C., Matyas, S.: Secure program load with Manipulation Detection Code. In: SECURICOM, pp. 111–130 (1988)
29. Naito, Y.: Blockcipher-based double-length hash functions for pseudorandom oracles. In: Miri, A., Vaudenay, S. (eds.) SAC 2011. LNCS, vol. 7118, pp. 338–355. Springer, Heidelberg (2012). doi:10.1007/978-3-642-28496-0_20
30. NIST: Announcing the Advanced Encryption Standard (AES). In: FIPS 197 (2001)
31. Özen, O., Stam, M.: Another glance at double-length hashing. In: Parker, M.G. (ed.) IMACC 2009. LNCS, vol. 5921, pp. 176–201. Springer, Heidelberg (2009). doi:10.1007/978-3-642-10868-6_11
32. Preneel, B., Bosselaers, A., Govaerts, R., Vandewalle, J.: Collision-free hash functions based on blockcipher algorithms. In: Proceedings of 1989 International Carnahan Conference on Security Technology, pp. 203–210 (1989)
33. Preneel, B., Govaerts, R., Vandewalle, J.: Hash functions based on block ciphers: a synthetic approach. In: Stinson, D.R. (ed.) CRYPTO 1993. LNCS, vol. 773, pp. 368–378. Springer, Heidelberg (1994). doi:10.1007/3-540-48329-2_31
34. Rabin, M.O.: Digitalized signatures. In: Foundations of Secure Computation 1978. pp. 155–166. Academic Press, New York (1978)
35. Rogaway, P.: Efficient instantiations of tweakable blockciphers and refinements to modes OCB and PMAC. In: Lee, P.J. (ed.) ASIACRYPT 2004. LNCS, vol. 3329, pp. 16–31. Springer, Heidelberg (2004). doi:10.1007/978-3-540-30539-2_2
36. Shibutani, K., Isobe, T., Hiwatari, H., Mitsuda, A., Akishita, T., Shirai, T.: *Piccolo*: an ultra-lightweight blockcipher. In: Preneel, B., Takagi, T. (eds.) CHES 2011. LNCS, vol. 6917, pp. 342–357. Springer, Heidelberg (2011). doi:10.1007/978-3-642-23951-9_23
37. Stam, M.: Blockcipher-based hashing revisited. In: Dunkelman, O. (ed.) FSE 2009. LNCS, vol. 5665, pp. 67–83. Springer, Heidelberg (2009). doi:10.1007/978-3-642-03317-9_5
38. Steinberger, J.P.: The collision intractability of MDC-2 in the ideal-cipher model. In: Naor, M. (ed.) EUROCRYPT 2007. LNCS, vol. 4515, pp. 34–51. Springer, Heidelberg (2007). doi:10.1007/978-3-540-72540-4_3
39. Suzaki, T., Minematsu, K., Morioka, S., Kobayashi, E.: TWINE: a lightweight block cipher for multiple platforms. In: Knudsen, L.R., Wu, H. (eds.) SAC 2012. LNCS, vol. 7707, pp. 339–354. Springer, Heidelberg (2013). doi:10.1007/978-3-642-35999-6_22

Software Security

FFFuzzer: Filter Your Fuzz to Get Accuracy, Efficiency and Schedulability

Fan Jiang, Cen Zhang, and Shaoyin Cheng[(✉)]

School of Computer Science and Technology,
University of Science and Technology of China,
Hefei, People's Republic of China
{fjiang,sycheng}@ustc.edu.cn, occia@mail.ustc.edu.cn

Abstract. We present a new black-box mutational fuzzing technology and the corresponding tool which named FFFuzzer to improve the efficiency of fuzzing towards serveral given suspicious vulnerable code blocks.

Our main intuition is by adjusting dynamic taint tracing and doing constraint verification, we can build 2 quite light filters to sieve the mutated input, which is the result of fuzzing's mutation stage, thus FFFuzzer can runs under fuzzing level speed while enjoys better accuracy and schedulability. We collect 14 CVEs that can get enough details to generate a POC from the PDF rendering library *poppler*'s recent 10 years bug list as our benchmark to fully analyzes FFFuzzer's real world challenges. And we build 2 mathematical models to do performance analysis. Analysis and experiments show although FFFuzzer has limitations on fuzzing metadata-related vulnerabilities and its efficiency also depends on seed file like traditional fuzzer, FFFuzzer has much powerful parallellism and it can run an order of magnitude faster than traditional fuzzer.

Keywords: Black-box fuzzing · Dynamic taint analysis · Constraint verification

1 Introduction

1.1 Background

Fuzzing [30] is attractive on its simplicity and effectiveness in bug finding. It is very popular, we can fuzz common software [7,9], network protocol [27], compiler [33] and even operating system [19].

The main course of a single fuzzing run is: given a configuration pair (*program, input*), mutate the input by random and test the program. You can repeat the fuzzing run, deploy fuzzer runs in several machines and once the program under test behaves strangely, e.g. crash, you may find a bug.

Although fuzzing is shiny, plain black-box fuzzing isn't always the best choice for every bug finding scenario. Adjusting fuzzing to improve its efficiency

© Springer International Publishing AG 2017
J. Pieprzyk and S. Suriadi (Eds.): ACISP 2017, Part II, LNCS 10343, pp. 61–79, 2017.
DOI: 10.1007/978-3-319-59870-3_4

under certain application cases is necessary. Considering the following scenario, a binary analyst has targeted some suspicious vulnerable code block using static analysis (maybe just simply target the location where calls an unsafe library function like `strcpy`), and he wants to get the real buggy one, how best can he do? How best can black-box fuzzing do?

To the best of our knowledge, except the scope of scheduling fuzzing, we have 3 solutions and each one has its pros and cons.

– **Dumb fuzzing.** This is the traditional solution but some kind of blindness. Random mutation of the input doesn't target any specific suspicious code block. We have no idea whether suspicious code block is really under testing, and the redundancy between fuzzing machine is exactly a big thing.
– **Taint-based fuzzing.** According to BuzzFuzz [12] and TaintScope [32], we can locate target code block related bytes in seed file using dynamic taint tracing and only fuzz related bytes. This is a brilliant idea but we find that neither the evaluation of its real world limitation nor an analysis of performance in mathematical way has been shown in previous research, especially in black-box scenario. Thus this technology needs more usage instructions.
– **Symbolic execution based fuzzing.** This technology is the most sophisticated one. There are several related research [5,13–15,22]. It has the pontential to traverse every path in the suspicious area. But it is hard to be as popular as fuzzing because of its complexity and performance issue. And to avoid several exponential explosion problem, users have to make much efforts on optimization and use binary analysis to steer the path exploration.

And apparently symbolic execution based fuzzing, which can use path as its basic scheduling unit, has the best schedulability.

So do we have an integrated option that combines fuzzing's speed and modern technology's accuracy and schedulability? If has, how to achieve it by adjusting the existing technology? What challenges are waiting for us in the real world application? And can we quantify the improvement of efficiency comparing with the dumb fuzzing in a mathematical way?

1.2   Our Approach

To answer the above questions, we focus on black-box mutational fuzzing and present the new option – FFFuzzer. The triple F in the name means we add 2 filters to standard fuzzing course. We list the brief introduction of the filters as follows.

– **Taint filter.** We slightly adjust the taint-based fuzzing, collect taint usage in the target code block. The meaning of taint usage is similar as target area related taints in taint-based fuzzing. This filter limits the bytes we can mutate, i.e. we only fuzz the collected taint usage.
– **Constraint filter.** The second filter is inspired by symbolic execution based fuzzing, we set the taint usage as symbolic value and collect their constraints during the symbolic execution, but we leverage the constraints to generate

a constraint verifier instead of calling an SMT solver. This filter sieves the mutated file – we put the mutated input into the verifier, and the real testing comes if verifier returns true, otherwise we regenerate the mutated input.

FFFuzzer's filters are light enough to guarantee the fuzzing speed, this means that the consuming time of a single fuzzing run in FFFuzzer is nearly the same as traditional fuzzing (and even smaller in some cases).

We collect 14 CVEs from *poppler*'s recent 10 years CVE list as our benchmark to analyze the real world challenges of FFFuzzer. From the analysis of the taint filter, we learn that not only FFFuzzer but also all the taint-based fuzzers have problems to handle metadata-related taint propagation. We are the first one use metadata relation to model taint-based fuzzer's common drawback and show why this problem is still hard to handle. And analysis shows the constraint filter can be further optimized when fuzzing at a specific type vulnerability, we present an automatic configuration and optimization method on targeting integer overflow vulnerability.

And we also build 2 mathematical models to analyze the 2 filters' performance respectively. Analysis and experiments prove that FFFuzzer can be at least an order of magnitude faster than dumb fuzzing in finding specific code block's bug.

The rest of the paper is organized as the following. Section 2 discusses related work. Section 3 provides an overview of FFFuzzer with a CVE example. Section 4 discusses FFFuzzer in detail. Section 5 analyzes performance of the filters mathematically. Section 6 shows the experiment. Section 7 concludes and paints the future work.

2   Related Work

As we said before, FFFuzzer is an integrated option of the existing technologies. In this section, we discuss the relations and the differences with the existing researches. We start from the pointer tainting research of Dynamic Taint Analysis (abbreviated as DTA). And then, we review existing works on DTA directed fuzzing. Finally, we discuss researches on symbolic execution based fuzzing.

DTA has some issues which are hard to handle in real world application, roughly speaking, it is the problem of Undertainting and Overtainting [26]. Asia Slowinska et al. [29] defines what is pointer tainting and use a keylogger program to prove that how tough realizing an accurate DTA is. Then Tao Bao et al. [1] and Min Gyung Kang et al. [18] present solutions to the pointer tainting on source code and binary respectively. Our work base on these researches, but the problem we summarized is not limited to the pointer tainting.

BuzzFuzz [12] uses DTA to locate regions of input that influence values used at library calls, which is called taint-based fuzzing which is one of the key component of our FFFuzzer. TaintScope [32] is similar as BuzzFuzz but it operates at binary level and capable of identifying and bypassing checksum checking. But both of them just ignore pointer tainting problem and haven't done a mathematical performance analysis. Part of our work can be seen as a completion to the research of DTA directed fuzzing, let subsequent researchers understand this technology quicker, deeper and more comprehensive.

A lot of researchers are interested in symbolic execution based fuzzing, e.g. SAGE [14], BitScope [2], CUTE [28], DART [13], KLEE [5], EXE [6] and so on. These researches include white-box/black-box fuzzing, symbolic/concolic execution, and offline/online execution. All of the systems are sophisticated and can fuzz at a very accurate way. However, symbolic execution based fuzzing needs much efforts and more computation resources in exchange. And it is difficult to handle a large scale real world program without additional steering work, e.g. SmartFuzz [22] and Dowser [15]. FFFuzzer doesn't like the system mentioned above. We drop the SMT solver, turn the collected constraints into a verifier and let whole system running in fuzzing level speed. Hence the difference between FFFuzzer and the system mentioned above is they are systems in different design philosophy. FFFuzzer is a new option for researchers and bugfinders.

3   FFFuzzer Overview

3.1   Problem Context Declaration

Before fully introducing our approach, we declare the context of our problem in this section.

Black-box mutational fuzzing. To simplify the problem we focus on black-box mutational fuzzing and consider we have a fuzzer like zzuf [20] or BFF [7]. The key difference between mutational fuzzing and generally speaking fuzzing is mutational fuzzing keeps the file length unchanged. Thus mutation can be considered as just reverting some bits in the original input. Generally speaking fuzzing means we can use arbitrary mutation strategy which makes fuzzing hard to model mathematically [8].

This paper assumes the input is in file format, but the analysis and results can be extended to other kinds of input directly.

The fuzzing configuration of black-box mutational fuzzing can be seen as $(\rho, \varsigma, \gamma)$. ρ represents the program under test, ς represents a seed file and γ represents the range of mutation ratio, which is the proportion of the amount of the flipped bits to the input's bit length.

Target area. Note that our background is there is an analyst, he/she locates some suspicious code blocks likely to be vulnerable. Code block can be a set of assembly instructions. Usually, the code blocks you locate for 1 suspicious target are in a single function and let us call it target area. This paper only does analysis on single target area scenario but it is quite straightforward to extend the result in multiple target areas case. And this paper also assumes that we have the seed file that can reach the target area.

Benchmark. *Poppler* is a commonly used PDF rendering library [11], and we collect 14 CVEs of *poppler* as our benchmark. This is not a full list of *poppler*'s recent 10 years' bug, but some of them have too few details to generate a POC. We get details mainly from NVD [24], Mitre [21], Bugzilla [23] and SecurityFocus [31]. We analyze these CVEs, locate their root cause, generate the seedfile and set the target area manually.

```
1  // FoFiType1.cc
2  // parse embeded font file
3  void FoFiType1::parse() {
4     ...
5     // parse encoding array
6     else if (!encoding &&
7     !strncmp(line, "/Encoding 256 array", 19)) {
8        encoding = (char **)gmallocn(256, sizeof(char *));
9        ...
10       for (j = 0, line = getNextLine(line);
11          j < 300 && line && (line1 = getNextLine(line));
12          ++j, line = line1) {
13          ...
14          if (*p2) {
15             ...
16             // vulnerability point, atoi can return negative
17             code = atoi(p);
18             ...
19             if (code < 256) {
20                ...
21                // unsafe addr write that can trigger crash
22                encoding[code] = copyString(p);
23             }
24          ...
25 }
```

Fig. 1. Source code of CVE-2010-3704

3.2 Overview with Example

In this subsection we draw the full picture of our approach and use CVE-2010-3704 [16] as an example to make illustration clearer. Figure 1 shows the source code of the vulnerability.

Example. The root cause of CVE-2010-3704 is the unsafe use of atoi library function. atoi(const char * str) parses C-string str interpreting its content as an integral number, which is returned as a value of type int. This means if atoi function receives a big number (bigger than the macro INT_MAX in limit.h), atoi may return a negative. This leads code < 0 and thus we can write anything in the address smaller than encoding.

To reach line 17's vulnerable code in Fig. 1, the original seed file must have an embedded Type 1 font program including Encoding Array entry in its dictionary [25].

Note that the target area of this example is the entire FoFiType1::parse() function and the parse function only wants to get FontName and Encoding info, it returns immediately when enough info is collected.

Buliding taint filter. First, FFFuzzer treats the whole seed file as initial taints and do dynamic taint tracing in the byte granularity, which means that every

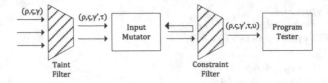

Fig. 2. Work flow of FFFuzzer

byte in the seed file has its own taint color. Taints propagate during the execution and once the program reaches the entry of target area, we start *recording used taints of every executed assembly instruction until the program exits the function.* We say a taint is used if it appears in an instruction's operator except it is going to be cleaned. And taint usage represents all used taints collected in the target area. Note that the taint usage are not only collected from the target area but also collected from the function it calls during its execution. Taint filter sieves input by only mutating the byte which its taint color is collected in the taint usage. As for the example, the original seed file is 13339 bytes. The taint usage we collected covers 1510 bytes, consists of the parsed part of embeded font program and a few metadata field like obj's length, objstm's N.

Remember that the fuzzing configuration is $(\rho, \varsigma, \gamma)$. Now it becomes $(\rho, \varsigma, \gamma, \tau)$ and the new parameter τ represents the taint usage related bytes. And note that the meaning of γ changes. It becomes the range of the proportion of the amount of flipped bits to the bit length of taint usage.

Building constraint filter. Second, FFFuzzer reanalyzes the seed file. And this time it treats the taint usage related bytes as symbolic input, i.e. the 1510 bytes in this example. Like any other symbolic execution system, we deduce new symbol expression according to the instruction's operational semantics along the program's execution and generate a constraint if a conditional branch's choose is influenced by symbol. We stop the execution when it reaches target area and transform the collected constraints into OCaml source code and compile the source code to an executable named constraint verifier. Because the verifier contains all constraints from the program start to the target area, when you input the mutated taint usage value into the verifier it tells you whether the input can let program reaches the target area. And the verification speed is much faster than constraint solving. As for this example, we collect 22679 constraints on the way to `parse`, and we turn it into a verifier that has 60 MB size. It can do 100 times of verification in 4 s. And note that setting all taint usage as symbolic and collect all their constraints is only suitable for a small part of fuzzing target like this example, we show this simply method here just for an illustration. And we discuss a more practical usage in Subsect. 4.2.

Constraint filter uses the verifier to determine whether a mutated file is worth to do real testing. And the fuzzing configuration is changed again – $(\rho, \varsigma, \gamma, \tau, \upsilon)$. The parameter υ represents the verifier.

Table 1. Evaluation of taint filter's capacity

CVE NO.	Vulnerability type	Fully collected	Undertainting type
20082950	Pointer Uninitialization	No	①
20090755	Design Error	No	① ③
20093603	Integer Overflow	Yes	
20093604	Integer Overflow	Yes	
20093606	Integer Overflow	Yes	
20093608	Integer Overflow	Yes	
20093609	Integer Overflow	Yes	
20093938	Buffer Overflow	Yes	
20094035	Buffer Overflow	No	
20103704	Unsafe Use of Library	Yes	
20134472	Race Condition	No	④
20134473	Stack Overflow	Yes	
20134474	Format String	Yes	
20158868	Array Overbound Write	Yes	① ③

Complete course of fuzzing. Figure 2 shows the entire course of FFFuzzer, the shaded trapezoids are the filters we added and the rectangles are the key components in traditional fuzzing. The arrows represent input stream and the fuzzing configuration is commented above the arrows. Filters add new parameters to fuzzing configuration but let mutation be more targeted.

Results. In this example, assuming we have the above fuzzing configuration, and set γ to the range $(0.0165, 0.0331)$. We do a little modification to BFF [7] and let it be our fuzzer, use 1 verification process and 1 fuzzing process. The result shows taint filter let FFFuzzer runs 10 times faster than dumb fuzzing and then constraint filter sieves nearly half of the mutated input.

4 FFFuzzer Details and Discussion

4.1 Taint Filter

Taint filter is mainly based on the well-known technology – dynamic taint analysis, thus we skip the technical details to avoid redundancy with existing researches and only discuss its settings, evaluation and real world challenges.

Settings of taint filter. We see the course of taint filter as 2 parts: taint propagation and taint collection. Hence we discuss their settings separately.

We recommend setting basic tainting [29] as FFFuzzer's default propagation rule. Basic tainting only propagates taints when operation establishes data dependency between source and destination. Apparently this limits the taint filter's capacity, but this is the most suitable choice under existing researches, and we detail the reason later.

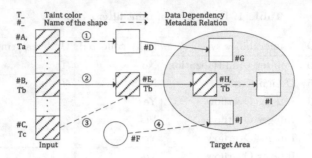

Fig. 3. Taint propagation model in execution

The recommended setting of taint collection has been *emphasized* in Subsect. 3.2.

Evaluation with benchmark. Define the minimum crash bit set [17] as a minimal set of the bits required to be reverted to trigger a bug and let us abbreviate it as MCBS. One bug may has several independent trigger point thus has several MCBSs. We see the evaluation of taint filter's capacity as the evaluation of whether the collected taint usage is a superset of one of the specific bug's MCBS. Table 1 shows the results of testing with our benchmark. The reason also can be divided into 2 parts – problem in taint propagation and problem in taint collection.

Problem in taint propagation. Before we deep into the reason, we detail the conception of advanced tainting first. Advanced tainting is a taint propagation rule concerning tainted addresses and control-flow taint [26]. It is capable of propagating taints when operation establishes some specific metadata relation between operators. Applying advanced tainting accurately is hard because it is difficult to distinguish whether this operation really builds metadata relation in binary level. And simply applying advanced tainting surely leads to taint explosion.

The problem in taint propagation is it is hard to propagate taints accurately concerning metadata relations.

Figure 3 shows the taint propagation model. Square represents a variable in execution, and shaded square means the variable is tainted while empty means it's clean. The ellipse represents the target area and we collect all used taints in the ellipse. The circle represents some data out of the scope of our tainting model. Notice that in the figure we should collect all taints but only catch Tb finally.

Arrow ①, ③, ④ represent 3 types of metadata relation we summarized from analysis. ① represents the case destination is source's metadata, e.g. let #A be an Array, program calculates the length of #A and stores it into #D. ③ represents the case source is destination's metadata, e.g. a string object in PDF file would be (This is a string), and the parentheses surrounding the content is used to indicate its string type. Thus let #B be the content and #C be parentheses,

#C instructs program to parse #B as a String class #E. ④ also represents source is destination's metadata but the source is out of the traditional tainting model hence we can't mark it as a taint, e.g. time, a key metadata for race condition bug. Table 1 also records what kinds of metadata relation the failure CVE should do taint propagation but not.

Theoretically, advanced tainting is capable of fixing the case of ① and ③ if we can distinguish which operation really build a metadata relation. M.G. Kang et al. presents DTA++ [18] that do advanced tainting only in strong condition checked by constraint solving in black-box scenario. It is a fantastic idea but we find it is not very suitable in our scenario because of the performance issue. DTA++ needs us specify a taint and it checks if there exists undertainting in the taint propagation. Look at Fig. 3, we have no idea to recognize which bytes in the input is #A or #C. And it would be very time-consuming if we want to check all taints in the input just assume the length of input file is 2 KB. And we may have dozens of the seed file. Thus this is not a scalable solution.

Problem in taint collection. The intuition of taint collection is function is designed to accomplish some specific task, unlike a piece of suspicious code block, the logic of a function is integrated. Thus the function's entire taint usage is much more likely to be a superset of the bug's MCBS than a code fragment of the function's. This assumption usually works well in our experiment except CVE-2009-4035. The deep reason of the failure is single dynamic trace can't extracts the full information of a function, it needs the help of static binary analysis or many good enough trace or both. Apparently this let FFFuzzer's capability depends on the seed file to some extent if there is no additional auxiliary static analysis.

Note that our collection strategy is not the only choice, you can leverage your own knowledge about the target to customize your strategy.

4.2   Constraint Filter

The main intuition of constraint filter is by turning the constraint solving into constraint verification, we can enjoy more accuracy while keeping the fuzzing level speed. This subsection we first discuss how to use constraint filter better, then give the key points we learned on building constraint filter.

4.2.1   Practical Usage Discussion
False Negative. Verifier may returns false negative results. It means verifier may has unnecessary constraints which may let FFFuzzer misses the mutated input that can expose the vulnerability. Unlike Subsect. 3.2's *dump all constraints in execution* strategy, we maintain a constraint stack along with the program's execution and only collect the constraints from the branches of the path from the program start to the start point of the target area. This strategy reduces a lot of needless constraints but still has two problems.

Firstly, target area is used for specifying the range of taint collection and for preventing the constraints of the path from the start of target area to the real

```
// best border of target
// area: **********

{
  if(x > 0)
  {// **********
  // big x can let buf
  // overbound write
    buf[x] = k;
  }// **********
  ...
}
```

```
{// **********
  if(x == CERTAIN_VALUE)
  {
  // a branch hard to reach,
  // buf is uninitialized
    buf[x] = k;
  }
  else
  {// normal input can reach
    ...
  }
}// **********
```

(a) Buffer Overbound Write   (b) Pointer Uninitialization

Fig. 4. Examples of the best division of target area

trigger point from being collected. But when aiming at different type vulnerability, the best target area division strategy is different. For example, in Fig. 4a, the best division of target area is the trigger point's nearest branch because this can let us get maximum constraints on x. But in Fig. 4b, the best division becomes the function of the trigger point because we need less limitations to let the mutated x has the possibility to reach the trigger point's branch. Thus, we had better choose different division strategy of target area for different fuzzing target to get the best efficiency.

Secondly, there may still exist unnecessary constraints because we only leverage a single execution trace's information, we don't know whether the path forbade by the branches of this path can also reach the target area and trigger the bug. This means a better fuzzing result needs additional static analysis or several valuable seed files.

Filter Ratio. We also need to consider the filter ratio of the verifier – we may not get enough efficiency benefit when the verifier's filter ratio is relatively low. We give an answer about when we can get benefit in Subsect. 5.2 by mathematical analysis.

Optimization on Integer Overflow. We find constraint filter has more advantages in testing suspicious integer overflow. Suspicious integer overflow usually is located by giving some sensitive functions or instructions, and then finding which one can be influenced by user's input, e.g. there may exists integer overflow vulnerability when `malloc`'s size parameter is tainted. Thus the best division way of target area is the sensitive instruction's nearest branch.

The input field related with integer overflow in the seed file (i.e. the taint usage we located) are actually numbers, and the field can be ASCII or binary format in a fixed or variable length. We give its main automatic recognition and optimization method as follows.

First, we recognize whether the field is in ASCII or binary format. We can achieve this easily with the help of protocol reverse technology [4], e.g. if a field's taint is the parameter of `atoi` or all the field's bytes is in the range of 0x30-0x39 and the byte's value is substracted from 0x30 in the execution, we can say this field is in ASCII format. And we can add additional filter rules for the ASCII format field to reject the mutation that contains a byte not in the number range (0x30-0x39).

Second, we recognize whether the field has a fixed or variable length. We insert an extra byte at the beginning of the field and do taint propagation again. The inserted byte is 0x30 or 0x00 according to its format is ASCII or binary. If the taint propagation result shows all bytes (original field bytes and the extra byte) are used in the sensitive instruction, e.g. the `malloc`'s size parameter has all bytes' taint colors, we can say this field has a variable length. The intuition is that a variable length field is distinguished by separators and the inserted byte hasn't broken this field's lexical structure. And even if there is an outside layer's length field and the inserted byte breaks its meaning, the parsing program is still very likely to parse it rightly because the parsing logic for variable length format input usually has a certain degree of fault tolerance.

Finally, if the field has a variable length, we should enlarge its length to let it has enough bytes to express big values, e.g. 0xFFFFFFFF (the border value of 32 bit `int` type) equals 4294967295, it needs 10 bytes in ASCII format. We repeat the insertion operation described in the second step until the field has enough bytes or the inserted byte can't be used together with other bytes of the field in the sensitive instruction.

4.2.2 Verifier Generation

FFFuzzer mainly does 2 kinds of optimization on verifier's generation, one is on constraint generation and the other is on verifier's source code architecture.

Symbolic expression reusing. During the symbolic execution, FFFuzzer deduces new symbolic expression and gives them a unique variable name which called variable definition to prevent the symbolic expression's length grows explosively. We believe not every variable definition is necessary because we are running in binary level and there certainly exists semantic redundancy due to the limitations of assembly language. Thus we create an additional hash table, it records the mapping from symbolic expression to variable name. We check if the symbolic expression has already emerged every time before we want to define a new variable. This technology reduces half of the redundant definition of variable in our statistics.

Constraint folding. This is a technology SAGE [14] first comes up with. FFFuzzer is build on the BAP [3] and runs on BIL[1]. We find that the constraint formulas we generated contain many reducible constant bit extract operations[2]

BAP doesn't do optimization to the BIL lifted from assembly. This is right

---

[1] BAP's intermediate language.
[2] Bap.Std.Bitvector.extract_exn.

as a default behavior but we should work this out. We model the redundancy elimination rules to fold constant operation. As a result, constant folding reduce the whole formulas' length from 14 MB to 8.9 MB in the example of Subsect. 3.2.

Constraint independence. EXE [6] first presents this technology to reduce the pressure of SMT solver, and we find it is also useful in verifier generation. FFFuzzer transforms the constraints to OCaml source codes and compiles them to an executable. Thus spliting the constraints into exclusive subgroups to get more but smaller .ml[3] file is an attractive idea. In the example of Subsect. 3.2, the constraints are divided into more than 100 subgroups.

Source code architecture. FFFuzzer choose OCaml as constraint transformation target language just because we can reuse the library of the core data structure – BAP's *bitvector* instead of finding a similar one in other language. We find that different source code architecture of verifier has very different performance. Ours is just a feasible one and it is not surprising to see you can design a better one than ours, and the speed of yours is surely faster if you choose C++ as transformation's target language.

FFFuzzer keeps the verifier's architecture as simple as possible to make compiler happier. Verifier is designed to do 1 verification per execution. It accepts this-time-value of the symbols as input and loads them to its inner hashtable. Then it begins to repeat the course of calculating the variables used by a constraint and verifying that constraint. Verifier perpares a hashtable for variables too. The constraints are verified linearly and it throws exception immediately once a constraint is unsatisfied, thus returning false is usually faster than returning true because returning true means verifier has finished all constraints' verification.

5   Performance Analysis with Mathematical Model

5.1   Taint Filter

To roughly measure the performance enhancement of taint filter, we do the following assumption and abstraction.

Remember that taint filter's fuzzing configuration is $(\rho, \varsigma, \gamma, \tau)$. We assume the target area really contains a bug and the seed file ς is capable of triggering that bug by flipping bits. We model the fuzzing process as a sequence of Bernoulli trials. The probability of success is p and success result means the input triggers the bug. In our model, trigger a bug means the flipped bits is a superset of one of the bug's trigger point's MCBS. Assume there are totally x_t independent trigger points in the file and the taint filter can catch x_f of them. And we assume the size of every trigger point's MCBS equals h_{min}, this means the hamming distance between the seed file with any minimized crash file is h_{min}. Assume γ is not a range but a small fixed value, i.e. we revert a fixed amount of bits for every

---

[3] OCaml source code filename extension, like .cpp.

mutation, let the amount be $h_{min} + h_a$. Assume l_t represents the seed file's bit length and l_f represents taint usage's.

For traditional fuzzing, p is marked as p_t, for fuzzing with taint filter p is marked as p_f, because γ is small and usually x_t is relatively small to l_t and l_f, thus we ignore the case that mutation covers more than 1 MCBS and calculate their value as:

$$p_t = \frac{x_t \cdot \binom{l_t - h_{min}}{h_a}}{\binom{l_t}{h_{min} + h_a}} , \quad p_f = \frac{x_f \cdot \binom{l_f - h_{min}}{h_a}}{\binom{l_f}{h_{min} + h_a}} \tag{1}$$

Define X as the number of trails we have run to get one success, X obeys the shifted geometric distribution[4]. Let $E[X]$ be the expected value of X, then we get $E[X] = \frac{1}{p}$. Define X_t as X for traditional fuzzing, X_f as X for fuzzing with taint filter, r as the proportion of $E[X_t]$ to $E[X_f]$, we get:

$$E[X_t] = \frac{1}{p_t} , \quad E[X_f] = \frac{1}{p_f} , \quad r = \frac{E[X_t]}{E[X_f]} = \frac{p_f}{p_t}$$

Substitute p_t and p_f, and notice we have the implicit conditions $l_t \geq l_f > 0$ and $h_{min} \geq 1$, r is:

$$r = \frac{x_f \cdot \binom{l_f - h_{min}}{h_a}}{\binom{l_f}{h_{min} + h_a}} \cdot \frac{\binom{l_t}{h_{min} + h_a}}{x_t \cdot \binom{l_t - h_{min}}{h_a}} = \frac{x_f \cdot (l_f - h_{min})! \cdot l_t!}{x_t \cdot l_f! \cdot (l_t - h_{min})!}$$

$$= \frac{x_f}{x_t} \cdot \frac{l_t}{(l_t - h_{min})} \cdot \frac{(l_t - 1)}{(l_t - h_{min} - 1)} \cdots \frac{(l_f + 1)}{(l_f - h_{min} + 1)}$$

r represents the performance enhancement of taint filter fuzzing towards a specific target area. And in real world fuzzing case, the inequation $l_t - l_f \geq h_{min} + 1$ is usually true, thus r can be:

$$r = \frac{x_f}{x_t} \cdot \frac{l_t}{l_f} \cdot \frac{(l_t - 1)}{(l_f - 1)} \cdots \frac{(l_t - h_{min} + 1)}{(l_f - h_{min} + 1)} \geq \frac{x_f}{x_t} \cdot \left(\frac{l_t}{l_f}\right)^{h_{min}} \tag{2}$$

Notice that three of our assumptions are not always true – trigger a bug equals mutation bit set is a superset of MCBS, all MCBS's size equals h_{min} and multiple counting when mutation covers more than 1 MCBS in Eq. 1. Last 2 assumptions perform well when the amount of trigger points is low or just 1. Thus our approximation of r is more accurate when x_t is small.

For example, in CVE-2010-3704, the r_{real} we get from experiments is 9.887, and $\frac{x_f}{x_t} = 1$, $l_t = 13339 \times 8 = 106712$, $l_f = 1510 \times 8 = 12080$, $h_{min} = 1$, thus r_{math} is:

$$r_{math} = \frac{106712}{12080} \approx 8.834$$

What's more, we can analyze the trend of r from Eq. 2. r is an exponential type expression like $k \cdot a^b$. When taint filter catches more trigger point's MCBS,

---

[4] Shifted means X's value starts from 1 not 0, see details in https://en.wikipedia.org/wiki/Geometric_distribution.

k is bigger, and r increases linearly. When the division of the length of seed file to taint usage is bigger, a is bigger, and r increases in power growth speed. When the bug is harder to trigger, b is bigger, and r increases exponentially.

5.2 Constraint Filter

To compare performance about fuzzing with or without a verifier, we do the following abstraction. Consider a single CPU fuzzing machine, it runs every fuzzing iteration independently. Each iteration can return 3 possible results – 2 failure results and 1 success result. Define the possibility of first failure result as p_1, costing time as t_1. And define the second failure result's p_2 and t_2 analogously. Thus the success result's possibility is $(1 - p_1 - p_2)$, and we also define the consuming time as t_3. Let the machine's average running time to get the first success result be T, we get:

$$T = p_1 \cdot (t_1 + T) + p_2 \cdot (t_2 + T) + (1 - p_1 - p_2) \cdot t_3$$
$$= \frac{p_1 \cdot t_1 + p_2 \cdot t_2 + (1 - p_1 - p_2) \cdot t_3}{1 - p_1 - p_2}$$

The first type failure represents the verifier's rejection, and the second type failure represents the situation that mutated input pass the verification but still can't trigger the bug. Let the mean time of a single verification be t_v, the mean time of a single iteration without verification be t_r. Based on the above assumption, when fuzzing with no verifier, we get $t_1 = t_2 = t_3 = t_r$, when fuzzing with a verifier, we get $t_1 = t_v$, $t_2 = t_3 = t_v + t_r$, the machine's average running time under 2 cases are:

$$T_{no\_v} = \frac{t_r}{1 - p_1 - p_2}, \quad T_{one\_v} = \frac{t_v + (1 - p_1) \cdot t_r}{1 - p_1 - p_2}$$

Now the performance analysis question becomes a math inequation, i.e. let T_{one_v} be smaller than T_{no_v}:

$$T_{no\_v} \geq T_{one\_v} \Leftrightarrow \frac{t_r}{1 - p_1 - p_2} \geq \frac{t_v + (1 - p_1) \cdot t_r}{1 - p_1 - p_2} \Leftrightarrow \frac{t_v}{t_r} \leq p_1$$

In this inequation, p_1 is the rejection possibility of verifier, i.e. the filter ratio of constraint filter. It is necessary to mention that p_1 is not a fixed value, there has a positive correlation between p_1 and the mutation ratio range γ – the more bits you flips, the more possible the verification fails.

t_v depends on the amount of constraints and how better the verifier you generated. But remember that our verifier contains more than 20000 constraints only need 0.04 s per run on average.

Different target program has a very different t_r. And t_r also varies when testing different kind vulnerability. For example, the t_r of a command line tool like *pdftotext* is at the same order of magnitudes as t_v, but t_r of a GUI program is usually several seconds, it is dozens times bigger than t_v. And testing bugs related to memory allocation is usually slow and often set a dead time like 3 s.

Thus we should first calculate $\frac{t_v}{t_r}$ and p_1 using a few tests before fuzzing and then determine use a second filter or not.

What we analyzed above is under the single CPU fuzzing machine. But we can leverage constraint filter's concurrency potential under certain scenarios. Some program only can run 1 instance in 1 system simultaneously like most GUI program while we can have several concurrent verification processes. With the help of multiprocessing, at best case we can ignore the consuming time of verification and at most save $\frac{p_1 \cdot t_r}{1 - p_1 - p_2}$ time.

6 Experiment

6.1 Implementation and Experiment Setup

We implement our system on BAP platform in approximately 3000 lines of OCaml. This includes offline taint usage collection module and verifier generation module. We modify the open source pintool [10] to record offline execution trace. And our fuzzer is based on BFF and zzuf but do some modification.

Experiments are prepared to verify 2 things, one is the performance issue we analyzed in Subsect. 5.1, and the other one is the performance enhancement for constraint filter in finding suspicious integer overflow. Each verification has its own experiments.

6.2 Taint Filter

We choose several CVEs from our benchmark to verify the taint filter's performance issue. To verify it more comprehensively, we choose 6 CVEs that each CVE belongs to a different vulnerability type. There are totally 9 types, but some of them are not suited for this experiment – CVE-2013-4472 belongs to race condition which is a vulnerability type out of our fuzzing scope and CVE-2013-4473/4474 are 2 vulnerabilities only triggered by command line input.

For each selected CVE, we manually set its own fuzzing configuration. Because of the randomness of fuzzing, we do 100 fuzzing campaigns for each CVE using taint filter fuzzing and traditional mutational fuzzing and compare the 2 method's performance using the average result. A fuzzing campaign represents the whole course of fuzzing – start and repeat fuzzing iteration, find the specified crash, record crash iteration number and crash time. We write additional scripts to distinguish whether this crash's root cause is actually the target CVE. We adjust the seed file ς and the mutation ratio γ to let fuzzing easier because finish 100 traditional fuzzing campaigns using a hard to crash seed file is too time consuming. In this experiment, every fuzzing machine is set as a single CPU system.

Table 2 shows the related fuzzing parameters and results. Most parameters are the same meaning as Subsect. 5.1, γ means the mutation ratio range, h_{min} means the number of bits needed to be flipped to trigger a crash (it is assumed to be the same value for all trigger points), x means the number of trigger points,

Table 2. Taint filter performance evaluation.

CVE NO.	γ_{trad}	γ_{taint}	h_{min}	x_f/x_t	I_{trad}	I_{taint}	T_{trad}	T_{taint}	r_{math}	r_{real}
20082950	0.00000 0.00017	0.00000 0.00290	1	0.6	11,014	808	928 s	78 s	10.2	13.6
20090755	0.00000 0.00084	0.00000 0.01340	1	a	439	249	68 s	43 s	(16.0 * a)	1.8
20093604	0.00009 0.00151	0.00560 0.09000	1	1	151,310	1,872	62,319 s	982 s	59.3	80.8
20094035	0.00000 0.00073	0.00000 0.00270	1	1	5,684	1,354	684 s	193 s	3.7	4.2
20103704	0.00000 0.00380	0.00000 0.03310	1	1	25,232	2,552	2,354 s	233 s	8.8	9.9
20158868	0.00000 0.00038	0.00000 0.00390	1	a	19,351	6,614	1,602 s	507 s	(10.2 * a)	2.9

I means average triggering iteration number, T means the average triggering time. Some bug's $\frac{x_f}{x_t}$ is too difficult to calculate because there are many ways to trigger it, we mark it as a in the table. Apparently $a < 1$ and we can see their real performance has gotten very limited enhancement. And during the experiment, traditional fuzzing usually has a lot of duplicated crashes which are unrelated with the target bug. That kind of crashes usually are easy to trigger and need additional time do triage thing.

6.3 Constraint Filter

We use all integer overflow vulnerabilities of our benchmark except CVE-2009-3606 to test the constraint filter's performance enhancement. CVE-2009-3606 is excluded because its trigger path is overlapped with CVE-2009-3609 and its constraint set is a subset of CVE-2009-3609's.

This experiment is similar as the taint filter's. We do 100 fuzzing campaigns to get the average result of taint filter only fuzzing and full FFFuzzer's fuzzing. We still set fuzzing machine as a single CPU system but use 1 process do verification and 1 process do the rest of fuzzing. Verification process do the mutation and verification work, it can be seen as a producer and the fuzzing process is the consumer.

Table 3 shows the results. Because we are testing integer overflow and it is related with memory allocation thus the average running time of 1 fuzzing iteration is apparently slower than first experiment's. And due to this, the verification's consuming time can be ignored even we do multiprocessing in a single CPU system. The filter ratio is high even under a low mutation ratio because the inputs are in ASCII format, thus we have the extra rules to reject the mutation

Table 3. Constraint filter performance evaluation

CVE NO.	Mutation ratio	I_{taint}	I_{fffuzz}	T_{taint}	T_{fffuzz}	Filter ratio	Performance enhancement
20093603	(0.00616, 0.09900)	2,351	721	728 s	209 s	0.90	3.26
20093604	(0.00560, 0.09000)	1,872	672	982 s	312 s	0.81	2.79
20093608	(0.01200, 0.13000)	6,554	1,685	4,388 s	1,083 s	0.87	3.89
20093609	(0.01200, 0.13000)	893	390	1,631 s	773 s	0.77	2.29

contains byte that is not in range 0x30-0x39. And the reason that the performance enhancement doesn't equal to $\frac{1}{1-FilterRatio}$ is the extra rules also incur false negative, e.g. 0xb3 represents [3] and it totally equals 0x33, which represents the normal 3, in *poppler*'s parsing logic.

7 Conclusion

This paper presents a new option for fuzzing towards several suspicious code block named FFFuzzer. The key point is by locating taint related bytes and doing constraint verification instead of constraint solving, FFFuzzer can run at fuzzing level speed but more concentrate on the target. Experiments show FFFuzzer can run an order of magnitude faster than traditional fuzzer and it can be further optimized when targeting specific type vulnerability, e.g. the integer overflow. Besides, we use real world CVEs to evaluate FFFuzzer's capability. We are the first one use metadata relation to model the taint-based fuzzer's drawback and point out why it is still hard to be solved efficiently and comprehensively in black-box scenario. And we analyze each filter's performance mathematically.

Our research on constraint verification is ongoing, in future research, we would like to release more potential about constraint filter, e.g. finding more especially suitable vulnerability type or absorbing more assistant technologies to extend its usage. And realizing white-box scenario's FFFuzzer is also promising, we may generate a super lightweight verifier that may only contain thousands of lines of code with the help of compiler.

References

1. Bao, T., Zheng, Y., Lin, Z., Zhang, X., Xu, D.: Strict control dependence and its effect on dynamic information flow analyses. In: Proceedings of the 19th International Symposium on Software Testing and Analysis, ISSTA 2010, pp. 13–24. ACM, New York (2010). http://doi.acm.org/10.1145/1831708.1831711
2. Brumley, D., Hartwig, C., Kang, M.G., Liang, Z., Newsome, J., Poosankam, P., Song, D., Yin, H.: Bitscope: automatically dissecting malicious binaries (2007)
3. Brumley, D., Jager, I., Avgerinos, T., Schwartz, E.J.: BAP: a binary analysis platform. In: Gopalakrishnan, G., Qadeer, S. (eds.) CAV 2011. LNCS, vol. 6806, pp. 463–469. Springer, Heidelberg (2011). doi:10.1007/978-3-642-22110-1_37
4. Caballero, J., Yin, H., Liang, Z., Song, D.: Polyglot: automatic extraction of protocol message format using dynamic binary analysis. In: ACM Conference on Computer and Communications Security, CCS 2007, Alexandria, Virginia, USA, pp. 317–329, October 2007
5. Cadar, C., Dunbar, D., Engler, D.: Klee: unassisted and automatic generation of high-coverage tests for complex systems programs. In: Proceedings of the 8th USENIX Conference on Operating Systems Design and Implementation, OSDI 2008, pp. 209–224. USENIX Association, Berkeley (2008). http://dl.acm.org/citation.cfm?id=1855741.1855756
6. Cadar, C., Ganesh, V., Pawlowski, P.M., Dill, D.L., Engler, D.R.: Exe: automatically generating inputs of death. Acm Trans. Inform. Syst. Secur. 12(2), 1–38 (2008)

7. CERT/CC: Bff. https://www.cert.org/vulnerability-analysis/index.cfm, basic Fuzzing Framework
8. Cha, S.K., Woo, M., Brumley, D.: Program-adaptive mutational fuzzing. In: 2015 IEEE Symposium on Security and Privacy, pp. 725–741, May 2015
9. Eddington, M.: Peach fuzzer. http://www.peachfuzzer.com, grammar based fuzzer
10. feseal: Pin tracer - a tracer based on pin: Intels dynamic binary instrumentation engine (2016). https://github.com/BinaryAnalysisPlatform/bap-pintraces
11. Freedesktop: Pdf rendering library. https://poppler.freedesktop.org/
12. Ganesh, V., Leek, T., Rinard, M.: Taint-based directed whitebox fuzzing. In: Proceedings of the 31st International Conference on Software Engineering, ICSE 2009, pp. 474–484. IEEE Computer Society, Washington, DC (2009). http://dx.doi.org/10.1109/ICSE.2009.5070546
13. Godefroid, P., Klarlund, N., Sen, K.: Dart: directed automated random testing. SIGPLAN Not. **40**(6), 213–223 (2005). http://doi.acm.org/10.1145/1064978.1065036
14. Godefroid, P., Levin, M.Y., Molnar, D.: Sage: whitebox fuzzing for security testing. Commun. ACM **55**(3), 40–44 (2012). http://doi.acm.org/10.1145/2093548.2093564
15. Haller, I., Slowinska, A., Neugschwandtner, M., Bos, H.: Dowsing for overflows: a guided fuzzer to find buffer boundary violations. In: Usenix Conference on Security, pp. 49–64 (2013)
16. Hoger, T.: Array indexing error in xpdf. https://bugzilla.redhat.com/show_bug.cgi?id=638960, bug track in bugzilla
17. Householder, A.: Well theres your problem: Isolating the crash-inducing bits in a fuzzed file. Technical report CMU/SEI-2012-TN-018, Software Engineering Institute, Carnegie Mellon University, Pittsburgh, PA (2012). http://resources.sei.cmu.edu/library/asset-view.cfm?AssetID=28043
18. Kang, M.G., Mccamant, S., Poosankam, P., Song, D.: Dta++: dynamic taint analysis with targeted control-flow propagation. In: Network and Distributed System Security Symposium, NDSS 2011, San Diego, California, USA, February 2011
19. eSage Lab: Ioctl fuzzer. https://github.com/Cr4sh/ioctlfuzzer, windows NT kernel fuzzer
20. Labs, C.: zzuf. http://caca.zoy.org/wiki/zzuf, multi-purpose fuzzer
21. MITRE: Cve: Common vulnerabilities and exposures. https://cve.mitre.org/, the Standard for Information Security Vulnerability Names
22. Molnar, D., Li, X.C., Wagner, D.A.: Dynamic test generation to find integer bugs in x86 binary linux programs. In: Proceedings of the Usenix Security Symposium, Montreal, Canada, 10–14 August 2009, pp. 67–82 (2009)
23. Mozilla: Web-based general-purpose bugtracker and testing tool. https://bugzilla.mozilla.org/
24. NVD: National vulnerability database. https://nvd.nist.gov/home.cfm, automating vulnerability management, security measurement, and compliance checking
25. Press, A.: Adobe Type 1 Font Format, 1st edn. Addison-Wesley Longman Publishing Co. Inc., Boston (1990)
26. Schwartz, E.J., Avgerinos, T., Brumley, D.: All you ever wanted to know about dynamic taint analysis and forward symbolic execution (but might have been afraid to ask). In: 2010 IEEE Symposium on Security and privacy (SP), pp. 317–331. IEEE (2010)
27. Sec, I.: Spike fuzzer. https://www.blackhat.com/presentations/bh-usa-02/bh-us-02-aitel-spike.ppt, network protocol fuzzer

28. Sen, K., Marinov, D., Agha, G.: Cute: a concolic unit testing engine for C. In: Proceedings of the 10th European Software Engineering Conference Held Jointly with 13th ACM SIGSOFT International Symposium on Foundations of Software Engineering, ESEC/FSE-13, pp. 263–272. ACM, New York (2005). http://doi.acm.org/10.1145/1081706.1081750

29. Slowinska, A., Bos, H.: Pointless tainting? evaluating the practicality of pointer tainting. In: Proceedings of the 4th ACM European Conference on Computer Systems, EuroSys 2009, pp. 61–74. ACM, New York (2009). http://doi.acm.org/10.1145/1519065.1519073

30. Sutton, M., Greene, A., Amini, P.: Fuzzing: Brute Force Vulnerability Discovery. Addison-Wesley Professional, Amsterdam (2007)

31. Symantec: Online computer security news portal and purveyor of information security services. http://www.securityfocus.com/

32. Wang, T., Wei, T., Gu, G., Zou, W.: Checksum-aware fuzzing combined with dynamic taint analysis and symbolic execution. ACM Trans. Inf. Syst. Secur. **14**(2), 15:1–15:28 (2011). http://doi.acm.org/10.1145/2019599.2019600

33. Yang, X., Chen, Y., Eide, E., Regehr, J.: Finding and understanding bugs in c compilers. SIGPLAN Not. **46**(6), 283–294 (2011). http://doi.acm.org/10.1145/1993316.1993532

Splitting Third-Party Libraries' Privileges from Android Apps

Jiawei Zhan[1,2,3], Quan Zhou[1,2], Xiaozhuo Gu[1,2], Yuewu Wang[1,2(✉)], and Yingjiao Niu[1,2]

[1] Data Assurance and Communication Security Research Center, CAS, Beijing, China
[2] Institute of Information Engineering, CAS, Beijing, China
wangyuewu@iie.ac.cn
[3] University of Chinese Academy of Sciences, Beijing, China

Abstract. Third-party libraries are very prevalent in the development of Android Apps. However, the wide use of third-party libraries may cause potential violations on user's privacy. In the original Android permission mechanism, host Apps share all permissions with their third-party libraries. Moreover, the details of most third-party libraries are not very clear to developers and malicious code may be contained. With privileges and malicious code, the attack may be conducted. In this paper, we present a novel privilege splitting mechanism for the third-party libraries in Android Apps. Different from other similar approaches, our system makes full use of the original permission mechanism to minimize the attack surface and the impact on Android system. Since the lightweight customization on Android, our system can be easily adapted to both Dalvik and ART (Android Runtime) virtual machines. We deployed a prototype on a real Android device and evaluated it's compatibility, effectiveness and performance. The experiment results show that our system is compatible with existing Apps, splits the third-party libraries' privileges effectively according to the given policies, and works well with negligible performance overhead.

Keywords: Android · Third-party library · Privilege splitting · Fine-grained

1 Introduction

Nowadays, third-party libraries are very widely used by the developers to implement interesting functions in a more cost-efficient way. For example, through including a map library [1], a developer may complete a Location Based Services (LBS) App with only a small amount of code. There are also lots of other prevalent third-party libraries, such as game engine [2], advertisement [3], image processing [4], User Interface (UI) [5], and so on. Unfortunately, third-party libraries may become an appropriate channel for the propagation of mobile malicious code. Generally, the details of third-party libraries are not very clear to

© Springer International Publishing AG 2017
J. Pieprzyk and S. Suriadi (Eds.): ACISP 2017, Part II, LNCS 10343, pp. 80–94, 2017.
DOI: 10.1007/978-3-319-59870-3_5

the App developers, thus various malicious code may be contained and packaged into legitimate Apps unconsciously.

Android provides permission mechanism to restrict the access of system resources and mitigate the attacks. However, permission mechanism only provides access control at App level and cannot enforce special policies on the third-party libraries. The check procedure of Android permission mechanism is based on an App's UID [6]. Every App will be allocated to a unique UID during its installation. As a part of Apps, third-party libraries share the same UID with their host App, and inherit all the permissions. Potential malicious code which hidden in the third-party libraries may use these privileges to access sensitive resources and carry out attacks.

More and more attention has been paid on mitigating the privacy risks posed by the third-party libraries. A great deal of previous works [7,8] load the third-party libraries into a standalone process space, and assign the process with a new UID. Inter-Process Communication (IPC) channel has been introduced between host App and these libraries, therefore host App can work well even divided into different processes. Through these mechanisms, special permission polices can be enforced on the third-party libraries. In those methods, considerable modification on the host App is required. The other methods implement in-App privilege regulation through extending the Android permission mechanism. For example, FLEXDROID [9] introduces a new mechanism (*inter-process stack inspection*) to identify the source of a system resource access, and enforce different access control policies. These approaches are mainly implemented based on the Dalvik VM, and cannot work well on ART. However, Dalvik has been replaced by ART in Android 5.0 or higher version. According to the data provided by Google [10], 64.8% of Android devices run on ART VM by the end of February 2017. Therefore, it is critical that we should take ART into consideration.

In this paper, a fine-grained privilege splitting scheme on third-party libraries is presented. Different from existing solutions, we take full advantages of the permission mechanism to minimize the impact on Android system and adapt our scheme to both Dalvik and ART virtual machines. The key challenge of our scheme is to distinguish the source of a system API call at library level. The library call sequences are stored in the stack of a thread, and can be obtained by the host App process. However, the permission check occurs at an independent *system_server* process. It must be ensured that the stack information of a system call could be transmitted from host App to the permission check point in a trustworthy way. Furthermore, multi-thread and dynamic Java code execution are very popular [9], which may break the permission policy on third-party libraries. It is also important to ensure that our scheme works effectively in such situations.

In our work, we modified the Android system libraries to make sure that the stack information could be fetched by every specific Android API when it is invoked by the host App. Then, we reused the existing service communication channel, so that stack information is packed into a *Parcel* package with the request parameters, and sent to the permission check point to support library-level permission check. We also extended the thread creation and dynamic class loading mechanism to ensure that our library level permission control may not be bypassed through these dynamic features. The *PackageManageService* (PMS) is modified to make sure that the library-level permission check may be performed in a similar way as the App level permission check. Finally, we implement our prototype and evaluate its effectiveness and performance.

In summary, we make the following contributions in this paper.

– Based on the features of Android system, we present a novel privilege splitting mechanism to enforce a fine-grained control on third-party libraries. Most of our extensions are implemented based on the original system modules, and only few mechanisms are newly introduced. Therefore, the potential attack surface of our scheme and its impact on the whole system are minimized.
– Our scheme is well compatible with existing Apps. Since we treated dynamic features carefully, App developers can use multi-thread, dynamic class loading and reflection technologies without any restrictions. In addition, we also extended PMS to make the privileges of third-party libraries can be configured in the same way as the whole App.
– Our system is the first libraries' privilege splitting scheme that can work well on both Dalvik and ART, thus can be deployed on the newer version of Android. We developed a prototype system and evaluated its effectiveness and efficiency. The results show that our scheme can effectively split the third-party libraries from their host App with an ignorable impact on Android system.

The remainder of this paper is organized as follows. Section 2 introduces necessary background knowledge. Section 3 presents the system design. A prototype implementation is detailed in Sect. 4. Section 5 discusses the evaluation of our system. We describe related works in Sect. 6. Finally, we conclude this paper in Sect. 7.

2   Background

2.1   Third-Party Libraries

App development often relies on various libraries. The libraries provided by the Android system are called as system libraries while the libraries developed by other people or organizations are called as third-party libraries. Third-party libraries can be used by Apps in the same way as system libraries. However, contrast to third-party libraries, system libraries are more trustworthy. Moreover, most Android framework APIs are implemented in system libraries.

According to the way of realization, third-party libraries may be classified into two types: Java libraries and native libraries. Java libraries are compiled into bytecode and executed on the virtual machine provided by Android system. Meanwhile, as a Linux-based operating system, Linux dynamic library is well supported in Android. Native libraries are often written in C/C++ and compiled into Linux shared objects (.so). Native libraries are usually called by Java code through Java Native Interface (JNI). With the help of JNI, we can create a specific Java class for a native library, so that host App may access the functions of the native library through this class.

2.2   The Dynamic Features of Third-Party Libraries

In addition to traditional techniques like callback, class inheritance and JNI, there are also many dynamic features in Java programming language including reflection, multi-thread and dynamic code generation.

The wide use of these techniques in current Apps improves the efficiency and flexibility for App development, but also brings new challenges in distinguishing the boundaries between the third-party libraries and their host App. Reflection allows Java code to dynamically modify the access specifiers of member variables and methods at runtime, thus breaks the original encapsulation. Multi-thread allows Apps to execute tasks by creating a lot of new threads. However, the child thread will lose the stack information of its parent thread. Dynamic code generation can dynamically create a new class and load it to VM using class-loader, which compromises the code integrity of the third-party libraries. These dynamic features should be considered when implementing a fine-grained access control on third-party libraries.

2.3   UID Based Access Control in Android

There are many system resources in Android, including location, SMS, contacts, etc. All of these resources are protected by permission mechanism. Developers apply for permissions in a file called *AndroidManifest.xml* which is packed as a part of Android package. When an App is being installed, the requested permissions will be extracted from *AndroidManifest.xml* and displayed to the user. The user can decide to accept all permission requests or reject them (Starting with Android 6.0, permissions are requested and granted to Apps at runtime rather than installation time). If the permission requests are accepted, PMS will store these permission information in a system file named *Package.xml* and index them by App's UID. When Android system is booted, these information will be loaded into the process space of PMS for subsequent permission check.

When an App wants to access protected resources through system APIs, a request will be sent to the corresponding system service provider through binder mechanism. Once receiving the request, the service will communicate with permission checking related service to verify whether corresponding permission is granted to this App according to its UID. Instead of using the system APIs directly, some Apps may access system resources through abnormal ways such as native code, this problem may be solved by [8] and is not considered in this paper.

3   System Design

The system architecture is shown in Fig. 1. The white rectangle is a component that already exists in Android system, the gray part indicates an extended component, the rounded rectangle dedicates an existing component that has been modified. Our system is composed of five components that scatter in different processes and cooperate to enforce fine-grained access control on third-party libraries. The details of each component are described below.

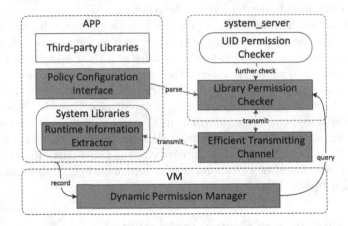

Fig. 1. System architecture

Policy Configuration Interface. App developers are the best candidate for policy configuration on third-party libraries, because they have a clear understanding of what privileges should be granted to a library. In order to be compatible with the existing permission configuration, the interface is also implemented as statements in *AndroidManifest.xml*. The only difference is that the permission statements for libraries are marked with new tags. PMS is extended to be able to parse and extract the libraries' permissions. Since the permissions of the third-party libraries cannot go beyond the scope of their host App, the user's approval on the corresponding statements are no longer required. Thus, our system makes no difference on user's experience.

Runtime Information Extractor. In order to implement a fine-grained permission control, it is necessary to identify the source of a request at library level. The stack information contains the calling sequences of all libraries. Thus, we can get the call traces of an system API clearly through the runtime stack information. As described in Sect. 2, both host App and third-party libraries access system resource via APIs implemented in various system libraries. Therefore, by extending the system libraries, we can extract the stack information when a system API is called.

Efficient Transmitting Channel. Binder is a mechanism for inter-process communication and widely used in the Android system. The communication between system services and Apps is implemented based on binder. Our scheme implements the stack information transmitting based on the extending of service access. In the Java layer, the service request data will be packed in the form of *Parcel* package before being transmitted to service provider. By extending the calling procedure of Android service access communication, we can implement an efficient channel between stack information extractor and permission checker.

Library Permission Checker. This component is introduced in *system_server* process to complete permission check at library level. Library permission checker is serial connected to the original permission checker. After receiving a check request from a system service, the original permission checker will first work based on the App's UID. If passed, library permission checker will be called based on the stack information contained in the request and the related policies configured by developers.

Dynamic Permission Manager. The dynamic features of Java programming language may disturb the library sequences of stack information. The child thread's stack information will be cleared during its creation, this may cause the loss of parent thread's library calling sequences. In addition, libraries can create and use a new class through reflection and dynamic class loading, which breaks the limit of its parent's policy. To solve these problems, we introduce *Dynamic Permission Manager (DPM)* to adjust the permissions of newly-created threads or classes dynamically, ensuring that their privileges cannot be escalated over their parents.

4 Implementation

We have implemented a prototype and the details of critical techniques are given below.

4.1 Library Permission Configuration

We add two tags to announce the application of library permission in *Android-Manifest.xml* file. *lib-permission* tag is used to specify a library, and *allow* sub tag is used to apply for permissions by this library. PMS uses *PackageParser* class to parse the *AndroidManifest.xml* file, and store the data in the form of a *Package* class. *PackageParser* is extended to be able to parse these new tags in *AndroidManifest.xml*. A *HashMap* is introduced into *Package* class as a library permission table. The key of this table is the package name of a third-party library, the value is a set of approved permissions. The data contained in library permission table is also stored in *package.xml* to make library permission configuration is still effective when system is rebooted.

Listing 1.1. Permission Configuration in *AndroidManifest.xml*

```
1 <uses-permission android:name="android.Permission.SEND_SMS" />
2 <uses-permission android:name="android.Permission.READ_SMS" />
3
4 <lib-permission android:name="com.thirdParty.lib">
5     <allow android:permission="android.permission.READ_SMS" />
6 </lib-permission>
```

Listing 1.1 shows an example of configuring permissions for third-party libraries in a *AndroidManifest.xml* file. First two lines are the original permissions application for the whole App. Fourth line indicates that the following permission application is for a library which package name is *"com.thirdParty.lib"*. Subsequent lines are the specific permission applications marked with *allow* sub tag. A third-party library can apply for multiple permissions. According to Listing 1.1, the App needs the permissions to both read and send SMS, but the library which package name is *"com.thirdParty.lib"* only need a permission to read SMS.

4.2   Runtime Stack Information Extracting

The stack of a thread contains the calling sequence of libraries. Each sequence item mainly consists of a package name, a class name and a method name. An example of call stack is shown in Table 1. So, with the stack information, we can identify the call traces of a system API clearly.

Table 1. Call stack information

Description	Call stack
System library	android.telephony.SmsManager.sendTextMessage
Third-party library	com.ThirdPartLib.SmsUtil.senSmsWithDelay
Third-party library	com.ThirdPartLib.MainService.initService
Host code	com.example.hostApp.MainActivity.sendSms
Host code	com.example.hostApp.MainActivity.onCreate

There are two ways to get the stack information of target thread depending on different situations. One is to hook the stack frame pointer of VM by sending a request to target process, but this requires that each App process has the ability to respond such request, and needs the modification to process creation or VM. The other is to use existing system API if the extractor share the same process with target thread, this can be realized utilizing *getStackTrace* method. The former will cause two extra inter-process communications, and need to adapt different VMs. The later has no extra communication, but can only get the stack information of current process.

In our scheme, the second way is adopted. Every App process that created by the zygote process contains an instance of the VM which preloaded a variety of system libraries including Android Framework, runtime libraries, etc. Through the modification to these libraries, we can extract the call stack information when a system API is called.

4.3 Runtime Stack Information Transmitting

We construct the channel between stack information extractor and permission check point based on Android service communication mechanism. Android system services may work in the *system_server* process or other standalone processes, such as Phone and Media. Since the isolation between processes, all these services are accessed by Apps through binder communication.

In the general communication scenarios, system services are responsible to provide access interfaces to protected resources, Apps access these resources by sending request to system services. Figure 2 shows the details of requesting a location resource through binder based Android service communication. *LocationManagerService* is a system service that provides location resource for Apps, it inherits from the *ILocationManager.Stub* class, and acts as a server. *LocationManager* is a system library that provides APIs for apps to request location resource, it contains a *Proxy* class. *Proxy* is an internal class of *ILocationManager.Stub*, and acts as a client. The service request data is packed and sent by *ILocationManager.Stub.Proxy* and the replay data is transmuted with *ILocationManager.Stub*. Through extending these two classes, the stack information can be transmitted along with service parameters.

Similar to most services, *ILocationManager* and all it's inner classes are generated by *ILocationManager.aidl* file. *Android Interface Definition Language (AIDL)* is a Java-based specification Language that supports local and remote procedure calls in Android platform. Some communications of resource access may implement related interface by themselves instead of using AIDL. In this case, the same specification as AIDL must be followed. So, the information transmitting channel of different service accesses may be implemented in a same way.

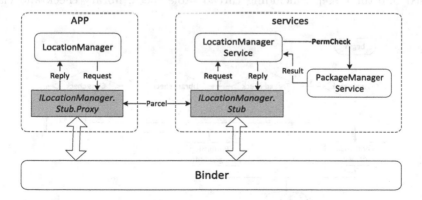

Fig. 2. Location request based on binder

4.4 Dynamic Permission Adjusting

In order to resist the potential collusive attack caused by new thread creation, we record the parent thread information by maintaining a thread table in the global data area of the VM (*DvmGlobals* structure in Dalvik or *runtime* class in ART). The key of thread table is a thread ID, and the value is the call sequence of its parent thread. Thus, when a non-system application (UID greater or equal to 10000) creates a new thread, its current call sequence will be passed to this new thread. There are two kinds of thread in Android. One is the VM thread, this type of thread will automatically be appended to *threadList* (a list to describe the threads in VM) when it is created. The other is native thread which cannot execute Java code unless it has been appended to the *threadlist*. DPM uses the *threadList* as a point to monitor the thread creation, so that every thread creation operation may be recorded in the thread table. With this table, the runtime stack information extractor can work effectively even the multi-thread is adopted in Apps.

For reflection and dynamic class generation, we maintain a class table in the VM. Once a new class is dynamically loaded, the caller's permissions will be passed to the new class based on *Least Privilege Rule*. Dalvik VM uses the *loadClassFromDex* function to load a class, and ART VM uses the other one named *DefineClass*. DPM takes these functions as a monitoring point to ensure that all the dynamic class loading operations can be recorded in class table. With this table, our library-level permission checker can work effectively even in the context of dynamic class generation.

4.5 Library-Level Permission Checking

Library-level permission checker serial connects to the original UID-based permission checker. As showed in Fig. 3, only original permission checking is passed, library-level permission checker begins to work. The whole procedure can be divided into three steps, including thread table check, library check and class

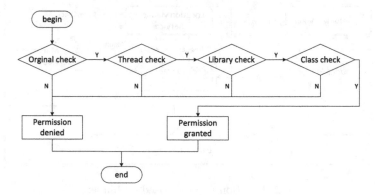

Fig. 3. Procedure of library-level permission checking

table check. The first step aims to identify whether the parent of request thread is granted such permission using the thread table described in Sect. 4.4. The second step is used to judge whether the library calling sequence has the permission violation by utilizing the *HashMap* described in Sect. 4.1. At last, class table described in Sect. 4.4 will be used to check the permission of dynamically loaded class.

5 Evaluation

We evaluate our prototype in four aspects:

(i) demonstrate its compatibility by running existing Apps on our system over Dalvik and ART respectively;
(ii) demonstrate its effectiveness by enforcing fine-grained permission control on the third-party libraries;
(iii) evaluate the performance overhead caused by library permission checker which is the core component of our system;
(iv) evaluate the overall performance of our system.

Our system is mainly deployed on Nexus 6 that has Snapdragon 805 CPU (2.7 GHZ, quad-core) and 3 GB RAM, with Android 5.1.1 (Lollipop) and Linux kernel 3.10.40.

5.1 Compatibility and Effectiveness

To demonstrate the compatibility and effectiveness of our system, we deployed our system on two platforms. The one is the Nexus 6 described above which uses the ART VM. The other is a *qemu* emulator with Android 4.4.4 (KitKat) and Linux kernel 3.4.0, which uses Dalvik VM.

Compatibility with existing Apps. We downloaded 100 popular Apps of various categories from *Google Play* [11] as an experiment sample. We chose *Monkey* [12] as our testing tools which is provided by Google. *Monkey* can send random touch events to Apps automatically, thus help us to find the potential bugs. To improve the validity of the results, we randomly chose 30% of the sample and ran cases manually. Among the sample Apps, no one crashed during the *Monkey* testing on both two platforms. After checking the log and testing them manually, we can conclude that our system is well compatible with existing Apps on both two kinds of Android virtual machines.

Effectiveness on third-party libraries. We chose five third-party libraries to evaluate the effectiveness of our system, the first three libraries are widely used by developers and the others are written by ourselves. As showed in Table 2, every third-party library has the code to access corresponding protected resources, and its host App have all permissions they needed. We blocked the permission of third-party libraries by appending our policy to the *AndroidManifest.xml* using the specific tags described in Sect. 4.1. The result shows that our system can effectively split third-party libraries' permissions from their host App.

Table 2. Effectiveness on third-party libraries

Third-party library	Resource	Blocked permission	Result
com.tencent.mm.sdk.*	Network	ACCESS_NETWORK_STATE	Success
com.amap.api.*	Phone	READ_PHONE_STATE	Success
com.amap.api.location.*	Location	ACCESS_FINE_LOCATION	Success
com.example.readcontacts.*	Contacts	READ_CONTACTS	Success
com.example.sendsms.*	SMS	SEND_SMS	Success

5.2   Permission Check Overhead

Our system aims to provide a fine-grained permission control on third-party libraries, thus the check procedure will be more complicated than the original one. There are three parts may cause extra overhead, one is the stack info extracting, the second is an extra data transmission based on the service access communication, the last but most expensive one is the extra checking operations including library sequence processing and permission matching. We use the pseudo code showed in Listing 1.2 as our experiment procedure.

Listing 1.2. Experiment Procedure

```
startTime = getCurrentTime()
for i = 1 to 10000 do
    check random permission
endTime = getCurrentTime()
runTime = endTime - startTime
averageTime = runTime / 10000
```

In order to ensure the accuracy of result, we conducted this experiment by checking random permissions 10000 times, and compared with the same device which operating system is the original Android 5.1.1 from Android Open Source Project (AOSP). On the original platform without our system, the average time of each permission check is 1234 us. On the platform deployed with our system, it takes 1451 us, which means extra 17.59% overhead. The overhead of permission check in Compac [13] is 22.2%, which is higher than our system. The main reason may be the less Inter-process communication of our system. Although the number seems like a great overhead, but it makes little difference on the whole system. Because the permission check only occurs when accessing system resources, and this would not happen frequently during Apps' runtime.

5.3   Overall Performance

In order to evaluate the overall performance of our system exactly, we chose four benchmarks which are widely used in Android. The experiment result is shown in Table 3, AOSP 5.1.1 means the original Android without our system. Each row of the table represents the result of one benchmark, including the score of each system, the differences and the extra overhead. Antutu produces an holistic score based on various measures, CF Benchmark conducts its evaluation based on Java code and native code, GeekBench and Linpack evaluate the system in single-thread and multi-thread mode separately.

Table 3. Overall performance

Benchmark	AOSP 5.1.1	Our system	Over.	Over.(%)
Antutu 6.1.1	71291	69602	1689	2.37%
CF Benchmark 1.3	36409	36243	166	0.46%
GeekBench 4(GPU)	3537	3457	80	2.26%
GeekBench 4(CPU Single-thread)	1000	986	14	1.40%
GeekBench 4(CPU Multi-thread)	2825	2793	32	1.13%
Linpack 1.4(Single-thread)	5.68	5.67	0.01	0.18%
Linpack 1.4(Multi-thread)	3.24	3.23	0.01	0.31%

From the table, we find that Linkpac produces the overhead less than 0.31% which is negligible to the system. Antutu produces the highest overhead (2.37%), but is also quit close to the original Android. In conclusion, our system produces little impact on the overall performance.

6   Related Work

Inter-process isolation on third-party libraries. This kind of researches split libraries' permissions from their host Apps by moving them to a separate process. AdDroid [14] builds a uniform management platform for advertising functions of Apps by creating a new system service in Android, isolating ad libraries from their original process. AdSplit [7] and AFrame [15] run the ad libraries as a separate application so that developers have no need to apply for any permissions for such libraries, which helps to restrict the malicious behavior of ad libraries effectively. NativeGuard [8] uses a similar approach, but only works on native libraries. LayerCake [16] provides secure third-party libraries that can be embedded in the Apps' user interface by splitting related libraries from their host Apps. However, these approaches require extra IPC when libraries interact with their host Apps. This feature will cause great impact on system performance when using the libraries which interact with Apps frequently.

Inter-component isolation on third-party libraries. Such kind of researches isolate third-party libraries' permissions from their host Apps under the conditions of not migrating libraries to other process. Compac [13] mainly aims at enforcing component level access control in Android, especially for the third-party libraries. FLEXDROID [9] considers the features of JNI and dynamic code execution of Java based on the above approach. However, these approaches

cause extra IPC when check a permission request, and cannot be applied to the
Android 5.0 or higher version (the Dalvik VM has been replaced with ART).

Extra access control in Apps. In order to solve problems caused by the
coarse-grained control of permission mechanism, researchers proposed many
solutions to regulated the behaviors of Apps. Apex [17] and Kirin [18] allow
users to grant part of permissions to Apps, and enforce policies at the installation. Saint [19] provides extra interface to enforce policies at runtime. References [20,21] uses an adaptive approach to dynamically configure App's permissions based on the context. There are also some researches aim to enhance
the system security by introducing mandatory access control (MAC) into the
Android platform. References [22–24] use MAC mechanism to mitigate privilege escalation attacks in Android. SEAndroid [25] extends the SELinux to the
Android system, implementing MAC on both the kernel and framework layer.
FlaskDroid [26,27] and SEDalvik [28] implement MAC for components and virtual machines respectively.

7　Conclusions and Future Work

In this paper, a fine-grained library-level permission control scheme is presented
to resist the potential malicious code contained in third-party libraries. Our
scheme is mainly implemented based on extending the existing modules of current permission mechanism. With the extending of *AndroidManifest.xml* and
PMS, App developers to could configure permission policy at library level. Then,
Android system libraries are extended to make our system has the ability to
extract the runtime libraries sequence information when an system API is called.
Through extending Android service request communication mechanism, a channel between information extracting point and permission checking point is built.
With libraries sequence information, a library-level permission checking is conducted. In addition, dynamic code execution features are considered carefully in
our scheme. We implement a prototype and evaluate it in four aspects, the result
shows that our scheme can work well on Dalvik and ART virtual machines with
reasonable overhead.

　　The code obfuscation technique makes the names of third-party libraries
incomprehensible. Thus, our work may lose effectiveness. Fortunately, the code
obfuscation is usually operated by App developers. They can exclude the suspicious libraries from obfuscation by modifying related configurations. In our
future work, we intend to introduce customized ACL (Access Control List) [29]
to split privileges in native layer without moving libraries to other process.

Acknowledgement. This research was supported by the National Key Research and
Development Program of China (Grant No. 2016YFB0800102), and National Basic
Research Program of China (973 Program No. 2013CB338001)

References

1. android-mapviewballoons. https://github.com/jgilfelt/android-mapviewballoons
2. jmonkeyengine. http://code.google.com/p/jmonkeyengine/
3. Grace, M., Zhou, W., Jiang, X., Sadeghi, A.-R.: Unsafe exposure analysis of mobile in-app. advertisements. In: Proceedings of the Fifth ACM Conference on Security and Privacy in Wireless and Mobile Networks (2012)
4. Opencv for android. http://billmccord.github.com/OpenCV-Android/
5. android-wheel. http://code.google.com/p/android-wheel/
6. Android permissions. https://developer.android.com/guide/topics/security/permissions.html
7. Shekhar, S., Dietz, M., Wallach, D.S.: Adsplit: separating smartphone advertising from applications. In: Presented as part of the 21st USENIX Security Symposium (2012)
8. Sun, M., Tan, G.: Nativeguard: protecting android applications from third-party native libraries. In: Proceedings of the 2014 ACM Conference on Security and Privacy in Wireless & Mobile Networks (2014)
9. Seo, J., Kim, D., Cho, D., Kim, T., Shin, I.: Flexdroid: enforcing in-app. privilege separation in android. In: Proceedings of Annual Network & Distributed System Security Symposium (NDSS) (2016)
10. Android platform versions, February 2017. https://developer.android.com/about/dashboards/index.html
11. Google play. https://play.google.com/store
12. Monkey. https://developer.android.com/studio/test/monkey.html
13. Wang, Y., Hariharan, S., Zhao, C., Liu, J., Du, W.: Compac: enforce component-level access control in android. In: Proceedings of the 4th ACM Conference on Data and Application Security and Privacy (2014)
14. Pearce, P., Felt, A.P., Nunez, G., Wagner, D.: Addroid: privilege separation for applications and advertisers in android. In: Proceedings of the 7th ACM Symposium on Information, Computer and Communications Security (2012)
15. Zhang, X., Ahlawat, A., Du, W.: Aframe: isolating advertisements from mobile applications in android. In: Proceedings of the 29th Annual Computer Security Applications Conference (2013)
16. Roesner, F., Kohno, T.: Securing embedded user interfaces: android and beyond. In: Presented as part of the 22nd USENIX Security Symposium (2013)
17. Nauman, M., Khan, S., Zhang, X.: Apex: extending android permission model and enforcement with user-defined runtime constraints. In: Proceedings of the 5th ACM Symposium on Information, Computer and Communications Security (2010)
18. Enck, W., Ongtang, M., McDaniel, P.: On lightweight mobile phone application certification. In: Proceedings of the 16th ACM Conference on Computer and Communications Security (CCS) (2009)
19. Ongtang, M., McLaughlin, S., Enck, W., McDaniel, P.: Semantically rich application-centric security in android. In: Proceedings of the 2009 Annual Computer Security Applications Conference (ACSA) (2009)
20. Roesner, F., Kohno, T., Moshchuk, A., Parno, B.: User-driven access control: Rethinking permission granting in modern operating systems. In: Proceedings of the 2012 IEEE Symposium on Security and Privacy (2012)
21. Conti, M., Nguyen, V.T.N., Crispo, B.: Crepe: context-related policy enforcement for android. In: Proceedings of the 13th International Conference on Information Security (2010)

22. Bugiel, S., Davi, L., Dmitrienko, A., Fischer, T., Sadeghi, A.R.: Xmandroid: a new android evolution to mitigate privilege escalation attacks (2011)
23. Bugiel, S., Davi, L., Dmitrienko, A., Fischer, T., Sadeghi, A.R., Shastry, B.: Towards taming privilege-escalation attacks on android. In: Proceedings of Annual Network & Distributed System Security Symposium, vol. 130(130), pp. 346–360 (2012)
24. Dietz, M., Shekhar, S., Pisetsky, Y., Shu, A., Wallach, D.S.: Quire: lightweight provenance for smart phone operating systems. Dissertations & Theses - Gradworks, p. 23 (2011)
25. Smalley, S., Craig, R.: Security enhanced (se) android: bringing flexible mac to android. In: Proceedings of 20th Annual Network & Distributed System Security Symposium (NDSS) (2013)
26. Bugiel, S., Heuser, S., Sadeghi, A.R.: Towards a framework for android security modules: Extending se android type enforcement to android middleware. Technical report, Center for Advanced Security Research Darmstadt (2012)
27. Bugiel, S., Heuser, S., Sadeghi, A.R.: Flexible and fine-grained mandatory access control on android for diverse security and privacy policies. In: Usenix Conference on Security, pp. 131–146 (2013)
28. Bousquet, A., Briffaut, J., Clvy, L., Toinard, C., Venelle, B., Bousquet, A., Clvy, L., Venelle, B.: Mandatory access control for the android dalvik virtual machine. In: The Workshop on Usenix Federated Conferences (2013)
29. acl, linux man page. http://linux.die.net/man/5/acl

SafeStack⁺: Enhanced Dual Stack to Combat Data-Flow Hijacking

Yan Lin(✉), Xiaoxiao Tang, and Debin Gao

School of Information Systems, Singapore Management University,
Singapore, Singapore
{yanlin.2016,xxtang.2013,dbgao}@smu.edu.sg

Abstract. SafeStack, initially proposed as a key component of Code Pointer Integrity (CPI), separates the program stack into two distinct regions to provide a safe region for sensitive code pointers. SafeStack can prevent buffer overflow attacks that overwrite sensitive code pointers, e.g., return addresses, to hijack control flow of the program, and has been incorporated into the Clang project of LLVM as a C-based language front-end. In this paper, we propose and implement SafeStack⁺, an enhanced dual stack LLVM plug-in that further protects programs from *data-flow* hijacking. SafeStack⁺ locates data flow sensitive variables on the unsafe stack that could potentially affect evaluation of branching conditions, and adds canaries of random sizes and values to them to detect malicious overwriting. We implement SafeStack⁺ as a plug-in on LLVM 3.8 and perform extensive experiments to justify a lazy checking mechanism that adds on average 3.0% of runtime and 5.3% of memory overhead on top of SafeStack on SPEC CPU2006 benchmark programs. Our security analysis confirms that SafeStack⁺ is effective in detecting *data-flow* hijacking attacks.

Keywords: Buffer overflow · Data flow · Control flow

1 Introduction

Many techniques have been proposed to fight against memory attacks, e.g., Data Execution Prevention (DEP) [8] to prevent code execution in non-executable memory regions, Address Space Layout Randomization (ASLR) [3] to randomize the location where executable is loaded into memory, Control Flow Integrity (CFI) [23,26,31] to prevent redirecting of execution flows. Code Pointer Integrity (CPI) [22] is a recent addition to the family of defenses to provide integrity of code pointers in a program and thereby prevent control-flow hijacking attacks. The core of CPI is a C-based language front-end of LLVM called *SafeStack* that splits the regular stack into two parts: a safe stack and an unsafe stack. All proven-safe objects are placed onto the safe stack while those that cannot be proven safe are placed onto the unsafe stack, such as buffers which may overflow. SafeStack prevents a buffer overflow on the unsafe stack from corrupting

© Springer International Publishing AG 2017
J. Pieprzyk and S. Suriadi (Eds.): ACISP 2017, Part II, LNCS 10343, pp. 95–112, 2017.
DOI: 10.1007/978-3-319-59870-3_6

anything on the safe stack, and thereby prevents control-flow hijacking attacks. It introduces negligible runtime overhead of less than 0.1%, and has been incorporated into the Clang project of LLVM due to its increasing acceptance by developers.

Being proposed as a defense to provide code pointer integrity, SafeStack, however, is susceptible to data-flow hijacking attacks. In particular, objects on the unsafe stack could overwrite each other, and such unsafe objects could potentially be used subsequently in an evaluation of branch conditions, changing which would lead to a successful data-flow hijacking attack. In this paper, we propose SafeStack$^+$, an enhanced dual stack mechanism that works on top of SafeStack to detect data-flow hijacking attacks. The idea of SafeStack$^+$ is to add protections into the unsafe stack rather than leaving it as the attackers' playground. SafeStack$^+$ first locates all variables on the unsafe stack that could potentially affect the execution of conditional branches using a def-use analysis, and then adds canaries of random sizes and values around them. Finally, SafeStack$^+$ adds runtime checks into the program to verify the integrity of the canaries to detect data-flow hijacking attacks.

Although the idea sounds simple, the key to a successful defense of memory attacks that can gain acceptance by developers is a low runtime overhead in the resulting binary executable. To achieve this goal, we implement SafeStack$^+$ on LLVM 3.8 with various canary checking mechanisms to test the corresponding runtime overheads. The extensive experiments show that our *lazy checking* mechanism that verifies the integrity of canaries at the point of branching evaluation results in a small runtime overhead of 3.0% and memory overhead of 5.3% on average on top of SafeStack. We further confirm SafeStack$^+$'s enhanced security with a real-world vulnerability CVE-2013-0230.

In summary, this paper makes the following contributions:

1. We propose SafeStack$^+$, an LLVM plug-in on top of SafeStack that adds canaries around sensitive objects on the unsafe stack to detect data-flow hijacking attacks.
2. We perform extensive testing on various canary checking mechanisms to justify our lazy checking technique, and show that it results in low runtime and memory overhead.
3. We demonstrate that SafeStack$^+$ can be used to effectively defend against data-flow hijacking attacks with a real-world vulnerability.

The remainder of this paper is structured as follows. We first discuss in Sect. 2 the limitation of SafeStack and our motivation. Section 3 introduces the design and implementation of SafeStack$^+$. We demonstrate the efficiency of SafeStack$^+$ with extensive performance evaluations and present the security analysis in Sect. 4. Section 5 briefly introduces the related work on memory corruption countermeasures and points out the limitation of SafeStack$^+$. In the end, we conclude in Sect. 6.

2   SafeStack and Our Motivation

As mentioned in Sect. 1, SafeStack is a core component of Code Pointer Integrity (CPI). In this section, we first briefly discuss how SafeStack works and its limitations. After that, we present our motivation of SafeStack$^+$ in tackling SafeStack's limitations.

2.1   SafeStack

Kuznestsov et al. [22] proposed Code Pointer Integrity (CPI) to guarantee the integrity of all code pointers in a program (e.g., function pointers and saved return addresses) by storing the sensitive pointers and their metadata (which describes the target object on which the sensitive pointer is based) in a safe memory region. Every dereference of a sensitive pointer is instrumented to check at runtime whether it is safe using the metadata associated with the pointer being dereferenced. CPI treats the stack specially, because the safety of most accesses to stack objects requires no runtime checks as they can be checked statically during compilation.

SafeStack is used to protect critical data on the stack by separating the native stack into two areas. There is a safe stack which is used for control flow information and data that is only ever accessed in a safe way (safe in the sense that the pointer dereference is safe – the memory it accessed lies within the target object on which the dereferenced pointer is based). There is an unsafe stack which is used for everything else that is stored on the stack. By arranging information on the two separated stacks, the safe stack can be accessed without any checks. The two stacks are located in different memory regions in the process's address space and thus prevents a buffer overflow on the unsafe stack from corrupting anything on the safe stack.

Listing 1 shows an example where we indicate results of the static analysis in SafeStack as comments below the code lines. We encourage readers to refer to the original paper of CPI [22] and source code of SafeStack [2] for the precise definitions.

SafeStack is implemented as a plug-in of LLVM to statically analyze source code of a program to identify its safe and unsafe objects. After identifying the safe and unsafe objects, SafeStack allocates space for unsafe objects in the unsafe memory region, which is accessible through a dedicated segment register (%gs in x86-32). Unsafe objects are placed onto the unsafe stack next to each other to minimize memory overhead.

Although the design of SafeStack meets the requirement of minimal memory overhead which is likely an important reason why it has been gaining developers' acceptance, it leads to an important limitation – unsafe objects are located at predictable locations on the unsafe stack, and could overwrite one another in a predictable manner.

Figure 1 shows the layout of the safe and unsafe stacks when the code in Listing 1 executes. We notice that all unsafe objects are pushed onto the unsafe stack one next to the other, and other proven-safe objects are stored on the

Listing 1. Example code

```
 1 void determine_privilege_level(int *pl) {
 2     *pl = get_priviliege();
 3 }
 4 int main() {
 5     int i = 0;
 6     int pl;
 7     int *ptr;
 8     char buffer[16];
 9     int p[16];
10     int b = 1;
11     int len;
12
13     ptr = &b;
14     /*b is unsafe -- conservatively assume that storing a pointer is unsafe as
15     there's no way to tell whether it points to a valid object or not.*/
16
17     memset(p,0,20);
18     /*p is unsafe -- the size of memory access region of p is 20, greater than
19     the allocated size of 16.*/
20
21     determine_privilege_level(&pl);
22     /*pl is unsafe -- potential information leak when a pointer to a local
23     variable is passed to another function.*/
24
25     gets(buffer);
26     /*buffer is unsafe -- potential information leak when a pointer to a local
27     variable is passed to another function.*/
28
29     len = pl;
30     if (pl == 0x42)
31         access_file(FILE *f);
32     else
33         printf("Not allowed to access the file");
34
35     return &i;
36     /* i is unsafe -- returning a pointer may cause information leakage.*/
37 }
```

safe stack. This ensures that unsafe objects could not modify objects on the
safe stack; however, e.g., pl can be overwritten by buffer and p in a typical
buffer overflow, and since the offsets between pl and the buffers are fixed and
can be easily learned from the code, the overwriting of pl is easy and its effect
is predictable by an attacker.

To make things worse, pl is a *sensitive* variable in the sense that its value
determines the branching decision at line 30 of Listing 1, which makes the overwriting of pl a successful data-flow hijacking attack.

2.2   Motivation

As shown in Sect. 2.1, SafeStack defeats control-flow hijacking attacks with minimal overhead, but it is vulnerable to data-flow hijacking attacks. This limitation

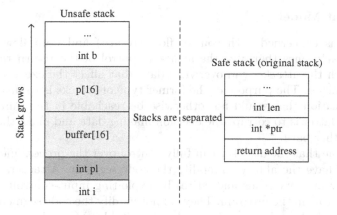

Fig. 1. Layout of the unsafe stack and safe stack

stems from the fact that SafeStack was initially proposed in the project of Code Pointer Integrity (CPI) which concerns only control flow integrity. In this paper, we investigate the possibility of enhancing SafeStack such that it is resistant to data-flow hijacking attacks while retaining the advantages of SafeStack in its negligible runtime overhead.

A simple yet effective way of protecting data-flow sensitive variables is to add canaries around them and to check for integrity of the canaries during program execution. However, in such an approach, it is crucial to precisely identify sensitive data for canary introduction to minimize the potential overheads – runtime overhead for checking their integrity and memory overhead for storing the canaries. Not only that, the runtime checking of the canaries also need to be efficient enough not to cause excessive runtime overheads. In this paper, we focus on protecting data whose values could potentially affect the evaluation of conditional branches (e.g., pl as in Listing 1; referred to as sensitive data in the rest of the paper), since other control-sensitive data (e.g., the return addresses) are already well protected in the safe stack.

3   Design and Implementation of SafeStack+

To show how SafeStack+ achieves its objects in defending against data-flow hijacking attacks, we present our design and implementation of SafeStack+, an enhanced dual stack mechanism built on top of SafeStack. SafeStack+ is an enhancement to SafeStack in the sense that it retains the dual-stack design of SafeStack and its definition of safe and unsafe objects. SafeStack+ achieves its design objective by introducing canaries in the unsafe stack to detect modifications to sensitive data.

In this section, we will begin with the threat model of SafeStack+, and then present its detailed design. We then present some implementation details of SafeStack+ to improve its performance.

3.1 Threat Model

This paper is concerned with control flow (return) and data flow hijacking attacks, namely ones that give the attacker control of the return targets and ones in which the attacker can overwrite data that affect the execution of conditional branches. The purpose of the former type of attacks is to divert control flow to a location that would not otherwise be reachable in the same context, whereas the latter is to corrupt the decision making data and make the program execute another path.

We assume that the attacker can fully control over the process memory, but he does not have the ability to modify the code segment. Attackers can carry out arbitrary memory reads and writes by exploiting input-controlled memory corruption errors in the program. They cannot modify the code segments as code pages are marked read-executable and not writable. Meanwhile, they cannot control the program loading process. These assumptions ensure the integrity of the original program code instrumented at compile time, and enable the program loader to safely configure the dedicated segment register used by the canaries and the unsafe stack.

3.2 Design

The high-level design of SafeStack$^+$ follows that of SafeStack in that both consist of a static analysis pass that identifies important objects in a program P (sensitive unsafe variables in the case of SafeStack$^+$) and an instrumentation pass that rewrites P to protect the important objects. However, SafeStack$^+$ differs from SafeStack in that we introduce canaries to further protect unsafe objects on the unsafe stack. In this section, we present our detailed design of SafeStack$^+$.

Figure 2 shows the workflow of SafeStack$^+$. We run static analysis to find sensitive variables first, and then instrument the code for canary insertion and runtime canary checking.

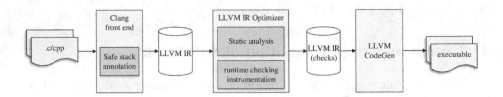

Fig. 2. Illustration of SafeStack$^+$'s workflow

Static Analysis. We determine the set of sensitive variables using def-use analysis in LLVM where a variable is considered sensitive if it affects the execution of conditional branches and it is unsafe. The definition of an unsafe variable follows that in SafeStack that the pointer dereference of it is unsafe – the memory it accessed may not lie within the target object on which the dereferenced pointer is based. We could do this via a forward execution analysis by keeping track of all code locations where an unsafe variable is used (directly and indirectly). If the target location involves a conditional branch, we add the unsafe variable to the sensitive set. Alternatively, we can also perform a backward tracking analysis starting from the sink of conditional branches, and trace back to the unsafe variables as sources. Since we implement SafeStack$^+$ as an LLVM plug-in and perform the static analysis during compilation time, we choose the former method for its simplicity. Note that if an unsafe variable is used as the argument of a call instruction, the analysis needs to jump inside the callee function to check whether the arguments will be used by a conditional branch.

Instrumentation for Runtime Checking. We protect the sensitive unsafe variables by inserting canaries around them and checking the integrity of the canaries at runtime. A canary is a piece of data inserted on the stack to detect memory corruption attacks [13]. For example, if any buffer is overflown in an attack, the canary on the stack is likely overwritten before the sensitive data next to it is modified. Therefore, checking the integrity of the canaries enables detection of memory corruptions. Both inserting and checking the canaries are done via instrumenting the target program during compilation.

As shown in Fig. 3, a canary is added next to the sensitive variable at the lower address (toward the direction of stack growth) to detect overwriting by other unsafe variables from lower addresses. To deal with brute-force attacks, canaries added in SafeStack$^+$ do not have fixed sizes or values. There is a trade-off between security and performance when setting the maximum size of the canaries – bigger size gives better security in that it provides higher entropy to the canary value, but also adds more runtime overhead to checking its integrity and bigger memory usage. SafeStack$^+$ randomly chooses from three different sizes: 4, 8, and 16 bytes (for memory alignment purposes) at compile time. Canaries are accessible through a dedicated segment register (%gs) to prevent attackers from obtaining them easily.

After canaries are inserted next to the sensitive variables, we need to check its integrity at runtime. The time of checking also involves trade-off between security and performance: checking integrity at every access of the sensitive variable (reading from and writing to) gives better security, but the frequent access might introduce prohibitive overhead. We introduce a lazy checking mechanism by delaying the integrity check till the point of conditional branch evaluation. We consider this an acceptable security policy since SafeStack$^+$ is designed to fight against data-flow hijacking attacks, and the lazy checking right before branching satisfies the security requirement. Although it may lead to a delay in detecting the corresponding attack, it could greatly improve performance due to the lower checking frequency.

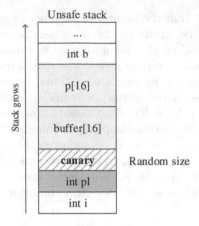

Fig. 3. SafeStack$^+$ approach

Figure 4 shows the different locations to check the integrity of the canary for the sensitive variable pl in the sample code in Listing 1. We can perform checking

– When reading the value of the sensitive variable from memory, see Fig. 4(a);
– When storing the value of the sensitive variable to memory, see Fig. 4(b);
– or, when evaluating the branching condition, see Fig. 4(c).

```
void determine_privilege_level(int *p){
    *pl = get_priviliege();
}
int main(){
    ......
    determine_privilege_level(&pl);
    gets(buffer);
    // canary checking
    len = pl;
    // canary checking
    if ( pl == 0x42 )
        printf("Accessed\n");
    else
        printf("Not allowed to access the file\n");
    return 0;
}
```

```
void determine_privilege_level(int *p){
    *pl = get_priviliege();
    // canary checking
}
int main(){
    ......
    determine_privilege_level(&pl);
    gets(buffer);
    len = pl;
    if ( pl == 0x42 )
        printf("Accessed\n");
    else
        printf("Not allowed to access the file\n");
    return 0;
}
```

```
void determine_privilege_level(int *p){
    *pl = get_priviliege();
}
int main(){
    ......
    determine_privilege_level(&pl);
    gets(buffer);
    len = pl;
    // canary checking
    if ( pl == 0x42 )
        printf("Accessed\n");
    else
        printf("Not allowed to access the file\n");
    return 0;
}
```

(a) When reading from memory,

(b) When storing to memory,

(c) When evaluating branch conditions,

Fig. 4. Lazy checking of integrity of canaries

Intuitively, delaying the checking at branching evaluation might result in the smallest number of checks because each branching evaluation might correspond to multiple reads and writes of the sensitive variable. We delay our further discussion on the design choice to Sect. 4 where we discuss the experiments performed, since we want to measure the amount of saving before making the design decision.

3.3   Implementation

We obtained the source code of SafeStack integrated in LLVM 3.8 compiler infrastructure [5], and added more than 700 lines of code in C++ to implement SafeStack+. Most of the additional code is added to perform static analysis to find instructions that manipulate the sensitive variables and to add instructions to check the value of the canary. Some code is also added to add canaries when allocating space for these sensitive variables. SafeStack+ accepts unmodified C/C++ program source as its input.

Sensitive Variable Analysis. We implement the sensitive data analysis for SafeStack+ as an LLVM pass. The LLVM pass operates on the LLVM Intermediate Representation (IR), which is a low-level strongly-typed language-independent program representation tailored for static analysis and optimization. The LLVM IR is generated from the C/C++ source code by clang [1], which preserves most of the type information that is required by our analysis and the def-use chain can be used easily to get the locations for each variable.

For every unsafe `alloca` instruction that allocates memory on the stack frame, we traverse the list of instructions that make use of it using the def-use chain provided by LLVM. If the corresponding memory is used by a conditional branch, we consider it as sensitive. When checking whether arguments of each function call are involved in the evaluation of a conditional branch, if the caller and callee are located in different modules, it will be difficult to carry out the analysis. We take a simple solution to first compile all source code into one IR file.

Note that the determination of sensitive variables is a conservative process – a sensitive variable may not be overwritten forever as there are no vulnerable buffers being stored beyond it. We leave a more precise static analysis to find sensitive variables our future work.

Canary Insertion and Integrity Check. Canaries on SafeStack+ are stored in the thread control block which can be accessed only directly through one of the segment registers. We implement this by using the `InitialExecTLSModel` flag. To insert a canary to protect a sensitive variable, we modify function `moveStaticAllocasToUnsafeStack()` so that a canary is created right after allocating spaces for unsafe variables on the unsafe stack.

Integrity checking of the canaries at every reading (or writing) of the sensitive variables is implemented by traversing the list of instructions that make use of the corresponding sensitive variable, and inserting a call before (or after) the instruction to check for integrity. Our lazy checking, on the other hand, is implemented by finding conditional branches whose evaluation is affected by sensitive variables and inserting a call before the evaluation to check for integrity of the Canaries. We do not make additional effort to optimize the instrumentation code (e.g., by inlining the code of integrity checking instead of inserting a function call) because the compiler will perform further compilation and optimization after our instrumentation.

4   Evaluation

In this section, we perform a number of experiments to demonstrate the efficiency and effectiveness of SafeStack$^+$. Specifically, we first perform some simple statistical analysis on software programs to find out the number of variables that require protection in order to defend against data-flow hijacking. After that, we empirically test a number of ways of implementing our idea to justify our lazy checking mechanism. Finally, we test SafeStack$^+$'s capability in defending against a suite of security attacks and a real-world data-flow hijacking attack.

All experiments were performed on a desktop computer with an Intel i7 4510u CPU with 8GB of memory running the x86 version of Ubuntu 14.04. All experiments were conducted 10 times, average of which is reported in this paper.

4.1   Variables to be Protected for Data-Flow Hijacking

The first experiment we performed is to find out how many sensitive variables need to be protected to defend against data-flow hijacking. If there are many, then it may make sense to just add canaries for every one and skip the process of locating sensitive ones. Table 1 shows some simple statistics for SPEC CPU2006 programs compiled without optimization. Specifically, we show percentage of unsafe functions (functions with at least one unsafe variable) upon all functions, percentage of unsafe variables upon all variables, and percentage of sensitive variables upon all unsafe variables.

Table 1. Simple statistics of SPEC benchmark programs

Program	Unsafe functions	Unsafe variables	Sensitive variables
bzip2	23.3%	8.3%	44.4%
gcc	13.1%	4.0%	47.0%
mcf	8.3%	4.4%	87.5%
sjeng	27.1%	13.2%	60.4%
libquantum	33.0%	8.6%	14.9%
astar	15.1%	9.7%	21.3%
namd	43.2%	4.6%	78.9%
soplex	11.9%	7.7%	19.5%
lbm	28.5%	8.6%	18.2%
average	22.6%	7.7%	43.6%

The first two columns of results basically show that there are not that many functions requiring an unsafe stack, and there are not that many unsafe variables on the unsafe stack when it is needed. This explains why, in general, SafeStack has small overheads. The last column of results, which are more specifically about SafeStack⁺, show that the percentage of sensitive variables upon all unsafe variables covers a relatively big range from 18% to 87%. That said, the average is still below 50%, which justifies our strategy of locating only sensitive variables for added protection.

Note that the analysis above is purely static, which may not closely correspond to the overhead experienced by end users. We therefore need some dynamic analysis in order to precisely find out the user experience in terms of runtime overhead.

4.2   Dynamic Analysis for Various Strategies of Integrity Check

Having shown that there are fewer than 50% of the unsafe variables requiring protection against data-flow hijacking attacks, we now move on to dynamically analyzing the overhead when the benchmarking programs are running on certain workloads. At the same time, we also want to try out different integrity checking mechanisms to test the extent to which our intuition of lazy checking generating less overhead is correct. Figure 5 shows the results for our three canary integrity checking strategies – before reading sensitive variables from memory, after storing them to memory, and before evaluating branching conditions. Please refer to Sect. 3.2 for more discussions of the three strategies. Note that here we show the additional overhead of dynamically executing the benchmarking programs on SafeStack⁺ over that on SafeStack, when the programs are given the workload of the largest input file under the **ref** folder provided by SPEC CPU2006.

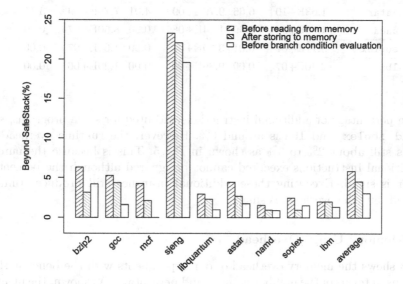

Fig. 5. Additional runtime overhead of SafeStack⁺ over SafeStack

Results show that performing integrity check before branch condition evaluation enjoys a smaller runtime overhead of 3.0% compared to 5.8% and 4.5%, respectively, when checking before reading or after storing the sensitive variables. This confirms our intuition since each branch condition evaluation may correspond to multiple variable reads and writes. We therefore decide that SafeStack$^+$ shall adapt the lazy checking mechanism for improved efficiency. sjeng experiences much higher runtime overhead than other programs. We investigate the detailed execution, and find that this is due to a large number of looping that result in more integrity checking needed. That said, our general finding of lazy checking enjoying better efficiency still holds true for this special case.

Table 2 shows the number of additional instructions executed for integrity checks of the canaries when the benchmarking programs are running the same workload. Results are consistent with those shown in Fig. 5, which, again, confirms our intuition that lazy checking enjoys better efficiency in general.

Table 2. Instructions added for canary integrity check

Program	Reading		Storing		Branch evaluation	
	#	%	#	%	#	%
bzip2	4.56E+09	12.17	1.32E+09	3.53	3.49E+09	9.32
gcc	8.91E+09	3.93	6.22E+09	2.74	5.39E+09	2.38
mcf	1.06E+08	0.28	5.02E+07	0.13	3.57E+07	0.09
sjeng	2.54E+11	38.36	2.39E+11	36.04	2.19E+11	33.01
libquantum	3.29E+11	5.89	3.29E+11	5.90	3.28E+11	5.89
astar	1.63E+10	6.66	9.79E+09	4.01	7.75E+09	3.17
namd	1.60E+08	0.00	1.44E+08	0.00	8.50E+07	0.00
soplex	3.17E+07	0.01	3.59E+06	0.00	1.65E+07	0.00
lbm	2.40E+07	0.00	9.99E+06	0.00	1.29E+06	0.00

The percentage of additional instructions executed for some programs, such as namd, soplex, and lbm is around 0%. However, the runtime overhead for them is still about 2% to 3% as shown in Fig. 5. This is because the number of additional instructions executed cannot be ignored although the percentage number is small. Executing these additional branches still produces runtime overhead, but the overhead is small.

4.3   Memory Usage Overhead

Table 3 shows the memory overhead of our experiments with the benchmarking programs in terms of the number of bytes and percentage. As shown, the memory overhead ranges from 24 bytes to 5,220 bytes with an average of 960 bytes, which is about 5.3%. We find such memory usage overhead acceptable.

Note that the memory usage overhead is proportional to the number of sensitive variables statically found in the program and not dynamically related to the

Table 3. Memory usage overhead

Program	Memory overhead (Bytes)	Percentage (%)
bzip2	224	0.01
gcc	5220	5.76
mcf	52	18.31
sjeng	496	0.18
libquantum	64	6.45
astar	108	1.89
namd	1632	0.13
soplex	820	5.87
lbm	24	9.09
average	960	5.3

specific workload. For example, lbm contains only two sensitive variable, which result in 24 bytes of memory overhead; however, its runtime overhead is still noticeable at 1.3% with some specific workload, as shown in Fig. 5.

Security Evaluation on the RIPE Benchmark. Having shown that SafeStack$^+$ enjoys reasonably small runtime and memory overhead, we now turn to the security evaluation. First, we want to make sure that SafeStack$^+$ is no worse than SafeStack in defending against control-flow hijacking attacks. For this purpose, we use the RIPE [29] benchmark that contains 850 exploits that attempt to perform control-flow hijacking attacks. Table 4 summarizes the evaluation results under three different settings.

Table 4. Statistical results on RIPE Benchmark

System name	# of success	# of failure
RIPE with ASLR	130	720
RIPE with ASLR and compiled with SafeStack	80	770
RIPE with ASLR and compiled with SafeStack$^+$	80	770

Our evaluation shows that SafeStack$^+$ and SafeStack enjoys the same advantages in defending against control-flow hijacking attacks (not only the same number of exploits failed but they are the exact same set). Although this result is as expected, it is interesting to observe the consistency of the behavior of these exploits under SafeStack and SafeStack$^+$, i.e., although the unsafe stack has quite different structure, all the exploits behave in the same way on both SafeStack and SafeStack$^+$.

4.4 Security Evaluation on a Data-Flow Hijacking Attack

In this section, we use a real-world example to show how SafeStack$^+$ defends against a data-flow attack. This experiment was based on CVE-2013-0230 on a memory corruption vulnerability for miniupnpd.

CVE-2013-0230 reports a buffer overflow bug in miniupnpd before version 1.0. The vulnerability can be exploited by overflowing the stack [4] which results in potentially a control-flow hijacking and a data-flow hijacking scenario. We will show how SafeStack$^+$ defends against the data-flow hijacking attack. Listing 2 presents (part of) the source code of miniupnpd 1.0, with line 11 showing a stack-based buffer overflow if methodlen is more than 2048 bytes long.

Listing 2. ExecuteSoapAction

```
1  ExecuteSoapAction(struct upnphttp * h, const char * action, int n)
2  {
3      char * p;
4      char method[2048];
5      int i, len, methodlen;
6      i = 0;
7      p = strchr(action, '#');
8      methodlen = strchr(p, '"') - p - 1;
9      .......
10     memset(method, 0, 2048);
11     memcpy(method, p, methodlen);
12     syslog(LOG_NOTICE,"SoapMethod: Unknown: %s", method);
13
14     SoapError(h, 401,"Invalid Action");
15 }
```

Figure 6 shows the stack layout when function ExecuteSoapAction is called under SafeStack (left) and SafeStack$^+$ (right), respectively. As we can see, HttpCommand[16] and HttpUrl[128] can be overwritten by method[2048] in SafeStack, which may cause a data-flow hijacking since both HttpCommand[16] and HttpUrl[128] are sensitive variables whose values may affect the execution of conditional branches. However, on SafeStack$^+$, we add canaries for these two variables, which can help detecting the overflow of method[2048].

We stress that this is a real-world example of vulnerability and the corresponding data-flow hijacking exploits detected by SafeStack$^+$.

5 Limitations and Related Work

In this section, we briefly discuss limitations of SafeStack$^+$ and some related work.

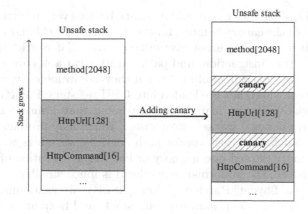

Fig. 6. Layout of unsafe stack

5.1 Limitations

As discussed earlier, the set of sensitive variables we find is an over approximation – a sensitive variable may not be overwritten at all as there are no vulnerable buffers being stored beyond it. We leave it our future work – a more precise static analysis to find the sensitive variables.

A simple idea of attacking SafeStack+ is to brute force the size and value of the canary. With a canary size of 4 bytes, the expected number of tries the attack has to make is 2^{31}. Having a canary of bigger size or multiple canaries (for multiple sensitive variables) makes the attack even more impractical. Memory leakage attacks are possible but very difficult since canaries are only accessible through a dedicated segment register (%gs).

Now we have to find the data-flow vulnerability described in this paper manually, which is time consuming. We leave it our future work – automatically find the data-flow vulnerability that can overwrite the data which could potentially affect evaluation of branching conditions.

5.2 Related Work

Many bounds checking methods are proposed to fight against memory corruptions. Cyclone [21] and CCured [25] fuse pointer values and associated bounds meta information into one unified object. With this, bounds information can be read directly from this object and this information can be used for bounds checking instrumentation. SoftBound [24] and Baggy Bounds Checking [7,15] store the bounds meta information in a shadow space or shadow memory that is separated from the main memory of the program. Shadow memory has better binary compatibility as the layout of objects in main memory is not changed. LowFAT [16] extends the low-fat pointer to stack objects by using pointer mirroring and memory aliasing.

StackGuard [13] patches gcc to add a canary before every return address and checks the value of the canary before a function returns. StackGuard ensures targets of return instructions are not overwritten, while SafeStack$^+$ ensures that both targets of return instructions and path sensitive variables are not overwritten. PointGuard [12] encrypts pointers when they are in memory, and decrypts encrypted pointers when they are loaded into CPU registers. PointGuard is similar to SafeStack$^+$ with the main difference being that PointGuard needs to check when each pointer is loaded into register, which may produce a high runtime overhead. SafeStack$^+$ just checks path sensitive variables when they are loaded from memory (stored into memory or before the execution of conditional branches). Therefore, the performance overhead is much smaller.

Address Space Layout Randomization (ASLR) [3] randomizes the base addresses of the text segment, data segment, stack, and heap at load time. Software diversity [18, 20, 28] implements fine-grained code randomization to mask important details of a program. StackArmor [11] focuses on stack layout randomization. It disrupts the traditional stack organization by making the stack frames and vulnerable buffers neither temporally nor spatially adjacent in memory.

Control Flow Integrity (CFI) [6] ensures that the targets of all indirect branches point to legitimate locations determined statically. However, getting all precise targets for each indirect branch statically is difficult, so many coarse grained CFI methods are proposed [23, 26, 31] to simply include every function in a program in the set of valid targets. CFI could not guarantee protection against all control flow hijacking attacks. Recent results [10, 19, 27] show that many existing CFI solutions can be bypassed in a principled way.

Shadow stack techniques [9, 14, 17, 30] split the stack into two parts: a shadow stack for storing sensitive data such as return addresses and the main stack for storing everything else. SafeStack [22] can be seen as one special case of shadow stack. It stores local variables (called unsafe variables) that may cause memory error onto one unsafe stack (shadow stack), and return addresses and other safe variables are placed onto the main stack. However, this strategy alone does not prevent unsafe variables from attacking each other.

6   Conclusion

This paper presents SafeStack$^+$, which extends SafeStack to make it can defend against both control flow and data flow hijacking attacks. We show that the average runtime and memory overhead of SafeStack$^+$ are 3.0% and 5.3% respectively. In addition, we evaluate how different checking locations would affect the runtime overhead. Results show that, for most programs, checking at memory related operations experiences more runtime overhead and adds more instructions. The security evaluation shows SafeStack$^+$ can effectively counter against both control flow and data flow hijacking attacks.

References

1. Clang: a C language family frontend for LLVM. https://clang.llvm.org/
2. SafeStack.cpp. http://llvm.org/docs/doxygen/html/SafeStack_8cpp_source.html
3. Pax ASLR (Address Space Layout Randomiztion) (2003). https://pax.grsecurity.net/docs/aslr.txt
4. MiniUPnPd 1.0 Stack Buffer Overflow Remote Code Execution (2013). http://www.cvedetails.com/cve/cve-2013-0230
5. The LLVM Compiler Infrastructure (2016). http://llvm.org/
6. Abadi, M., Budiu, M., Erlingsson, U., Ligatti, J.: Control-flow integrity. In: Proceedings of the 12th ACM Conference on Computer and Communications Security, pp. 340–353. ACM (2005)
7. Akritidis, P., Costa, M., Castro, M., Hand, S.: Baggy bounds checking: an efficient and backwards-compatible defense against out-of-bounds errors. In: Proceedings of the 18th USENIX Security Symposium, pp. 51–66 (2009)
8. Andersen, S., Abella, V.: Data execution prevention. Changes to functionality in microsoft windows xp service pack, 2 (2004)
9. Bhatkar, S., DuVarney, D.C., Sekar, R.: Efficient techniques for comprehensive protection from memory error exploits. In: Proceedings of the 14th USENIX Security Symposium (2005)
10. Carlini, N., Wagner, D.: Rop is still dangerous: breaking modern defenses. In: Proceedings of the 23rd USENIX Security Symposium, vol. 14 (2014)
11. Chen, X., Slowinska, A., Andriesse, D., Bos, H., Giuffrida, C.: Stackarmor: comprehensive protection from stack-based memory error vulnerabilities for binaries. In: Symposium on Network and Distributed System Security (2015)
12. Cowan, C., Beattie, S., Johansen, J., Wagle, P.: Pointguard tm: protecting pointers from buffer overflow vulnerabilities. In: Proceedings of the 12th USENIX Security Symposium, vol. 12, pp. 91–104 (2003)
13. Cowan, C., Pu, C., Maier, D., Walpole, J., Bakke, P., Beattie, S., Grier, A., Wagle, P., Zhang, Q., Hinton, H.: Stackguard: automatic adaptive detection and prevention of buffer-overflow attacks. In: Proceedings of the 7th USENIX Security Symposium, vol. 98, pp. 63–78 (1998)
14. Dang, T.H., Maniatis, P., Wagner, D.: The performance cost of shadow stacks and stack canaries. In: Proceedings of the 10th ACM Symposium on Information, Computer and Communications Security, pp. 555–566. ACM (2015)
15. Ding, B., He, Y., Wu, Y., Miller, A., Criswell, J.: Baggy bounds with accurate checking. In: International Symposium on Software Reliability Engineering Workshops, pp. 195–200. IEEE (2012)
16. Duck, G.J., Yap, R.H., Cavallaro, L.: Stack bounds protection with low fat pointers. In: Symposium on Network and Distributed System Security (2017)
17. Erlingsson, Ú., Abadi, M., Vrable, M., Budiu, M., Necula, G.C.: Xfi: software guards for system address spaces. In: Proceedings of the 7th Symposium on Operating Systems Design and Implementation, pp. 75–88. USENIX Association (2006)
18. Fu, J., Lin, Y., Zhang, X.: Code reuse attack mitigation based on function randomization without symbol table. In: Proceeding of the 15th IEEE International Conference on Trust, Security and Privacy in Computing and Communications, pp. 394–401. IEEE (2016)
19. Göktas, E., Athanasopoulos, E., Bos, H., Portokalidis, G.: Out of control: overcoming control-flow integrity. In: Proceedings of the 35th IEEE Symposium on Security and Privacy, pp. 575–589. IEEE (2014)

20. Hiser, J., Nguyen-Tuong, A., Co, M., Hall, M., Davidson, J.W.: Ilr: where'd my gadgets go? In: Proceedings of the 33rd IEEE Symposium on Security and Privacy, pp. 571–585. IEEE (2012)

21. Jim, T., Morrisett, J.G., Grossman, D., Hicks, M.W., Cheney, J., Wang, Y.: Cyclone: a safe dialect of C. In: Proceedings of the USENIX Annual Technical Conference, pp. 275–288 (2002)

22. Kuznetsov, V., Szekeres, L., Payer, M., Candea, G., Sekar, R., Song, D.: Code-pointer integrity. In: Proceedings of the 11th USENIX Symposium on Operating Systems Design and Implementation, vol. 14, pp. 147–163 (2014)

23. Lin, Y., Tang, X., Gao, D., Fu, J.: Control flow integrity enforcement with dynamic code optimization. In: Bishop, M., Nascimento, A.C.A. (eds.) ISC 2016. LNCS, vol. 9866, pp. 366–385. Springer, Cham (2016). doi:10.1007/978-3-319-45871-7_22

24. Nagarakatte, S., Zhao, J., Martin, M.M., Zdancewic, S.: Softbound: highly com-patible and complete spatial memory safety for C. In: ACM Conference on Pro-gramming Language Design and Implementation, vol. 44(6), pp. 245–258 (2009)

25. Necula, G.C., McPeak, S., Weimer, W.: Ccured: type-safe retrofitting of legacy code. In: Proceedings of the 29th ACM Symposium on Principles of Programming Languages, vol. 37, pp. 128–139. ACM (2002)

26. Payer, M., Barresi, A., Gross, T.R.: Fine-grained control-flow integrity through binary hardening. In: Almgren, M., Gulisano, V., Maggi, F. (eds.) DIMVA 2015. LNCS, vol. 9148, pp. 144–164. Springer, Cham (2015). doi:10.1007/978-3-319-20550-2_8

27. Schuster, F., Tendyck, T., Pewny, J., Maaß, A., Steegmanns, M., Contag, M., Holz, T.: Evaluating the effectiveness of current Anti-ROP defenses. In: Stavrou, A., Bos, H., Portokalidis, G. (eds.) RAID 2014. LNCS, vol. 8688, pp. 88–108. Springer, Cham (2014). doi:10.1007/978-3-319-11379-1_5

28. Wartell, R., Mohan, V., Hamlen, K.W., Lin, Z.: Binary stirring: self-randomizing instruction addresses of legacy x86 binary code. In: Proceedings of the 2012 ACM Conference on Computer and Communications Security, pp. 157–168. ACM (2012)

29. Wilander, J., Nikiforakis, N., Younan, Y., Kamkar, M., Joosen, W.: Ripe: run-time intrusion prevention evaluator. In: Proceedings of the 27th Annual Computer Security Applications Conference, pp. 41–50. ACM (2011)

30. Younan, Y., Pozza, D., Piessens, F., Joosen, W.: Extended protection against stack smashing attacks without performance loss. In: Proceedings of the 22nd Annual Computer Security Applications Conference, pp. 429–438. IEEE (2006)

31. Zhang, M., Sekar, R.: Control flow integrity for cots binaries. In: Proceedings of the 22nd USENIX Security Symposium, vol. 13 (2013)

Network Security

Prover Efficient Public Verification of Dense or Sparse/Structured Matrix-Vector Multiplication

Jean-Guillaume Dumas[1($\boxtimes$)] and Vincent Zucca[2]

[1] Université Grenoble Alpes, Laboratoire Jean Kuntzmann,
CNRS, UMR 5224, 700 av. centrale, IMAG - CS 40700, 38058 Grenoble, France
Jean-Guillaume.Dumas@imag.fr
[2] Sorbonne Universités, Univ. Pierre et Marie Curie, Laboratoire LIP6,
CNRS, UMR 7606, 4 place Jussieu, 75252 Paris, France
Vincent.Zucca@lip6.fr

Abstract. With the emergence of cloud computing services, computationally weak devices (Clients) can delegate expensive tasks to more powerful entities (Servers). This raises the question of verifying a result at a lower cost than that of recomputing it. This verification can be private, between the Client and the Server, or public, when the result can be verified by any third party. We here present protocols for the verification of matrix-vector multiplications, that are secure against malicious Servers. The obtained algorithms are essentially optimal in the amortized model: the overhead for the Server is limited to a very small constant factor, even in the sparse or structured matrix case; and the computational time for the public Verifier is linear in the dimension. Our protocols combine probabilistic checks and cryptographic operations, but minimize the latter to preserve practical efficiency. Therefore our protocols are overall more than two orders of magnitude faster than existing ones.

1 Introduction

With the emergence of cloud computing services, computationally weak devices (Clients, such as smart phones or tablets) can delegate expensive tasks to more powerful entities (Servers). Such heavy tasks can, e.g., be cryptographic operations, image manipulation or statistical analysis of large data-sets. This raises the question of verifying a result at a lower cost than that of recomputing it. This verification can be private, between the Client and the Server, or public, when the result can be verified by any third party.

For instance within computer graphics (image compression and geometric transformation), graph theory (studying properties of large networks), big data analysis, one deals with linear transformations of large amount of data, often

This work is partly funded by the OpenDreamKit Horizon 2020 European Research Infrastructures project (#676541).

J. Pieprzyk and S. Suriadi (Eds.): ACISP 2017, Part II, LNCS 10343, pp. 115–134, 2017.
DOI: 10.1007/978-3-319-59870-3_7

arranged in large matrices with large dimensions that are in the order of thousands or millions in some applications. Since a linear transformation on a vector x can be expressed by a matrix-vector multiplication (with a matrix of size $m \times n$), a weak client can use one of the protocols in the literature [4,6,16] to outsource and verify this computation in the optimal time $O(m + n)$, i.e., linear in the input and the output size. However as these protocols use expensive cryptographic operations, such as pairings, the constants hidden in the asymptotic complexity are usually extremely large [15].

In this paper, we propose an alternative protocol, achieving the same optimal behavior, but which is also practical: the overhead for the Prover is now very close to the time required to compute the matrix-vector multiplication, thus gaining two orders of magnitude with respect to the literature. Our protocol not only does this for dense matrices, but is also sensitive to any structure or sparsity of the linear transformation. For this, we first remove any quadratic operation that is not a matrix-vector multiplication (that is we use projections and rank-1 updates) and second we separate operations in the base field from cryptographic operations so as to minimize the latter. More precisely, we first combine rank-one updates of [6] and the projecting idea of [4] with Freivalds' probabilistic check [7]. Second, we use a novel strategy of vectorization. For instance, with a security parameter s (e.g., an $s = 128$-bits equivalent security), exponentiations or pairings operations usually cost about $O(s^3)$ arithmetic operations. To make the whole protocol work practical, we thus reduce its cost from $\mathcal{O}\left(s^3 mn\right)$ to $\mathcal{O}\left(\mu(A) + s^3(m + n^{4/3})\right)$, where $\mu(A) < 2mn$ is the cost of one, potentially structured, matrix-vector multiplication. We also similarly reduce the work of the Verifier. This allows us to gain two orders of magnitude on the Prover's work and therefore on the overall costs of outsourcing, while preserving and sometimes even improving the practical efficiency of the Verifier.

Thus, after some background in Sect. 2, our first improvement is given in a relaxed public verification setting in Sect. 4 via matrix projection and probabilistic checks. Our second improvement is given in Sect. 5 where the verification is bootstrapped efficiently by vectorization. We then show how to combine all improvements in Sect. 6 in order to obtain a complete and provably secure protocol. Finally, we show in Sect. 7 that our novel protocol indeed induces a global overhead factor lower than 3 with respect to non verified computations. This is gaining several orders of magnitude on the Prover side with respect to previously known protocols, while keeping the Verification step an order of magnitude faster.

2   Background and Definitions

In this paper, we want to be able to prove fast that a vector is a solution to a linear system, or equivalently that a vector is the product of another vector by a matrix. This is useful, e.g., to perform some statistical analysis on some medical data. We distinguish the matrix, a static data, from the vectors which are potentially diverse. In the following, $\mathbb{F}_p$ will denote a prime field and we consider:

- Data: matrix $A \in \mathbb{F}_p^{m \times n}$.
- Input: one or several vectors $x_i \in \mathbb{F}_p^n$, for $i = 1..k$.
- Output: one or several vectors $y_i = Ax_i \in \mathbb{F}_p^m$, for $i = 1..k$.

Then, we denote by $\star$ an operation performed in the exponents (for instance, for $u \in \mathbb{G}^n$ and $v \in \mathbb{Z}^n$, the operation $u^T \star v$ actually denotes $\prod_{j=1}^n u[j]^{v[j]}$).

Publicly Verifiable Computation. A publicly verifiable computation scheme, in the formal setting of [13], is in fact four algorithms (*KeyGen, ProbGen, Compute, Verify*), where *KeyGen* is some (amortized) preparation of the data, *ProbGen* is the preparation of the input, *Compute* is the work of the *Prover* and *Verify* is the work of the *Verifier*. Usually the Verifier also executes *KeyGen* and *Prob-Gen* but in a more general setting these can be performed by different entities (respectively called a *Preparator* and a *Trustee*). More formally we define these algorithms as follow:

- *KeyGen*$(1^\lambda, f) \rightarrow (\mathtt{param}, EK_f, VK_f)$: a randomized algorithm run by a *Preparator*, it takes as input a security parameters 1^λ and the function f to be outsourced. It outputs public parameters $\mathtt{param}$ which will be used by the three remaining algorithms, an evaluation key EK_f and a verification key VK_f.
- *ProbGen*$(x) \rightarrow (\sigma_x)$: a randomized algorithm run by a *Trustee* which takes as input an element x in the domain of the outsourced function f. It returns σ_x, an encoded version of the input x.
- *Compute*$(\sigma_x, EK_f) \rightarrow (\sigma_y)$: an algorithm run by the *Prover* to compute an encoded version σ_y of the output $y = f(x)$ given the encoded input σ_x and the evaluation key EK_x.
- *Verify*$(\sigma_y, VK_f) \rightarrow y$ or $\bot$: given the encoded output σ_y and the verification key VK_f, the *Verifier* runs this algorithm to determine whether $y = f(x)$ or not. If the verification passes it returns y otherwise it returns an error $\bot$.

Completeness. A publicly verifiable computation scheme for a family of function $\mathcal{F}$ is considered to be *perfectly complete* (or *correct*) if for every function belonging to $\mathcal{F}$ and for every input in the function domain, an honest *Prover* which runs faithfully the algorithm *Compute* will *always* (with probability 1) output an encoding σ_y which will pass *Verify*.

Soundness. A publicly verifiable computation scheme for a family of function $\mathcal{F}$ is called *sound* when a prover cannot convince a verifier to accept a wrong result $y' \neq y$ except with negligible probability. More formally we evaluate the capability of an adversary $\mathcal{A}$ to deceive the verifier through a *soundness experiment*. In this experiment, we assume that the adversary $\mathcal{A}$ accesses to the output of the algorithm *KeyGen* by calling an oracle $\mathcal{O}_{KeyGen}$ with inputs 1^λ and the function to evaluate f. This oracle $\mathcal{O}_{KeyGen}$ returns public parameters for the protocol $\mathtt{param}$, an evaluation key EK_f and a verification key VK_f. Afterwards the adversary $\mathcal{A}$ sends its challenge input x to an oracle $\mathcal{O}_{ProbGen}$ which returns σ_x. Finally $\mathcal{A}$ outputs an encoding $\sigma_{y^*} \neq \sigma_y$ and runs the *Verify* algorithm on inputs σ_{y^*} and VK_f, whether it outputs y or $\perp$ the experiment has either succeeded or failed.

Definition 1. *A publicly verifiable computation scheme for a family of function $\mathcal{F}$ is sound if and only if for any polynomially bounded adversary $\mathcal{A}$ and for any f in $\mathcal{F}$ the probability that $\mathcal{A}$ succeeds in the soundness experiment is negligible in the security parameter.*

Adversary model. The protocol in [6], see afterwards, is secure against a *malicious Server only*. That is the Client must trust both the Preparator and the Trustee. We will stick to this model of attacker in the remaining of this paper.

Public delegatability. One can also further impose that there is no interaction between the Client and the Trustee after the Client has sent his input to the Server. Publicly verifiable protocols with this property are said to be publicly delegatable [4]. The protocol in [6] does not achieve this property, but some variants in [4,16] already can.

Bilinear Pairings. The protocols we present in this paper use bilinear pairings and their security is based on the co-CDH assumption, for the sake of completeness we recall hereafter these definitions.

Definition 2. (bilinear pairing)
Let $\mathbb{G}_1$, $\mathbb{G}_2$ and $\mathbb{G}_T$ be three groups of prime order p, a bilinear pairing is a map $e : \mathbb{G}_1 \times \mathbb{G}_2 \to \mathbb{G}_T$ with the following properties:

1. *bilinearity: $\forall a, b \in \mathbb{F}_p$, $\forall (g_1, g_2) \in \mathbb{G}_1 \times \mathbb{G}_2$, $e(g_1^a, g_2^b) = e(g_1, g_2)^{ab}$;*
2. *non-degeneracy: if g_1 and g_2 are generators of $\mathbb{G}_1$ and $\mathbb{G}_2$ respectively then $e(g_1, g_2)$ is a generator of $\mathbb{G}_T$;*
3. *computability: $\forall (g_1, g_2) \in \mathbb{G}_1 \times \mathbb{G}_2$, there exist an efficient algorithm to compute $e(g_1, g_2)$.*

Definition 3. (co-CDH assumption)
Let $\mathbb{G}_1$, $\mathbb{G}_2$ and $\mathbb{G}_T$ be three groups of prime order p, such that there exist a bilinear map $e : \mathbb{G}_1 \times \mathbb{G}_2 \to \mathbb{G}_T$. Let $g_1 \in \mathbb{G}_1$, $g_2 \in \mathbb{G}_2$ be generators and $a, b \xleftarrow{\$} \mathbb{F}_p$ be chosen randomly. We say that the co-computational Diffie-Hellman assumption (co-CDH) holds in $\mathbb{G}_1$, if given g_1, g_2, g_1^a, g_2^b the probability to compute g_1^{ab} is negligible.

Fiore and Gennaro's protocol. For the sake of completeness, we briefly remind the original protocol for matrix-vector verification in [6], but with our rank-one update view. It stems from the fact that if s, t, ρ, τ are randomly generated vectors then the function $g^{M[i,j]}$, where $M = s \cdot t^T + \rho \cdot \tau^T$, is a pseudorandom function [6, Theorem 3], provided that the *Decision Linear* assumption [6, Definition 3] (a generalization of the External Diffie-Hellman assumption for pairings), as well as co-CDH, hold.

- *KeyGen*: for $A \in \mathbb{F}_p^{m \times n}$, generate 3 multiplicative groups $(\mathbb{G}_1, \mathbb{G}_2, \mathbb{G}_T)$ of prime order p (g_1, g_2 generating respectively $\mathbb{G}_1$ and $\mathbb{G}_2$) and a bilinear map $e : \mathbb{G}_1 \times \mathbb{G}_2 \to \mathbb{G}_T$. Generate secret random values $s \in \mathbb{F}_p^m, t \in \mathbb{F}_p^n, \rho \in \mathbb{F}_p^m, \tau \in \mathbb{F}_p^n$ and $\alpha \in \mathbb{F}_p$. Compute $W \in \mathbb{G}_1^{m \times n}$ such that $W[i,j] = g_1^{\alpha A[i,j] + s[i]t[j] + \rho[i]\tau[j]}$, give it to the server and publish $a = e(g_1^\alpha; g_2) \in \mathbb{G}_T$.
- *ProbGen*: for $x \in \mathbb{F}_p^n$ a query vector, compute $\mathrm{VK}_x \in \mathbb{G}_T^m$, such that $\mathrm{VK}_x[i] = e(g_1^{(s[i]t^T + \rho[i]\tau^T) \cdot x}; g_2)$. Send x to the server and publish VK_x.
- *Compute*: compute $y = Ax$ and $z = W \star x \in \mathbb{G}_1^m$ (that is $z[i] = \prod_{j=1}^n W[i,j]^{x[j]}$).
- *Verify*: check that $e(z[i]; g_2) = a^{y[i]} \mathrm{VK}_x[i]$, for all $i = 1, \dots, m$.

This protocol is sound, complete and publicly verifiable. It however uses many costly exponentiations and pairings operations that renders it inefficient in practice: even though the Client and Trustee number of operations is linear in the vector size, it takes still way longer time that just computing the matrix-vector product in itself, as shown in the experiment Sect. 7.

Related work. The work of [6] introduced the idea of performing twice the computations, once in the classical setting and once on encrypted values. This enables the Client to only have to check consistency of both results. Then [16] extended the part on matrix-vector multiplication to matrix-matrix while adding public delegatability. Finally, [4] introduced the idea of projecting the random additional matrix and the extra-computations allowing to reduce the cost of the *Verify* algorithm and also to decrease the size of the verification key by a factor m. For an $m \times n$ dense matrix, the protocol in [6] has a constant time overhead for the Prover, but this constant is on the order of cryptographic public-key operations like pairings. Similarly, the Verifier has $\mathcal{O}(mn)$ cryptographic public-key pre-computations and $\mathcal{O}(n)$ of these for the public verification. Unfortunately, these cryptographic operations can then induce some 10^6 slow-down [15] and do no improve even if the initial matrix is sparse or structured (as the rank one updates, $s \cdot t^T$ and $\sigma \cdot \tau^T$, are always dense). Other approaches include follow up of the celebrated PCP theorem [8], with software like Pepper [14], or quadratic arithmetic programs, with software like Pinocchio [12]. These breakthrough suffer however from the same practical slowness [15].

3 Probabilistic Verification and the Random Oracle Model

First we recall that private verification is very fast and does not require any cryptographic routines. Then we show that this allows to obtain a very efficient protocol in the random oracle model, but for a fixed number of inputs.

3.1 Private Verification

Without any recourse to cryptography, it is well known how to privately verify a matrix-vector multiplication. The idea is to use Freivalds test [7], *on the left*, provided that multiplication by the transpose matrix is possible:

> - Verifier to Prover: A, $x_i \in \mathbb{F}_p^n$, for $i = 1, \ldots, k$.
> - Prover to Verifier: $y_i \in \mathbb{F}_p^m$, for $i = 1, \ldots, k$.
> - Verifier verification: random $u \in \mathbb{F}_p^m$, then $w^T = u^T \cdot A$, and finally check, for $i = 1, \ldots, k$, that $w^T \cdot x_i \overset{?}{=\!=} u^T \cdot y_i$ in $\mathbb{F}_p$.

On the one hand, this protocol uses only classical arithmetic and is adaptable to sparse matrices, that is when a matrix vector product costs $\mu(A)$ operations with $\mu(A) < 2mn$ (this is the case for instance if the matrix is not structured but is sparse with $\mu(A)/2 < mn$ non-zero elements). Indeed, in the latter case, the cost for the Prover is $k\mu(A)$, where the cost for the Verifier is $\mu(A) + 4kn$.

On the other hand, the protocol has now Freivalds probability of revealing an error in any of the y_i: $1 - 1/p$, if $\mathbb{F}_p$ is of cardinality p (or $1 - 1/p^\ell$ if u is chosen in an extension of degree ℓ of $\mathbb{F}_p$).

3.2 Public Verification in the Random Oracle Model

Using Fiat-Shamir heuristic [5], the privately verifiable certificate of Sect. 3.1 can be simulated non-interactively: uniformly sampled random values produced by the Verifier are replaced by cryptographic hashes (to prove security in the random oracle model) of the input and of previous messages in the protocol. Complexities are preserved, as producing cryptographically strong pseudo-random bits by a cryptographic hash function (e.g., like the extendable output functions of the SHA-3 family defined in [2,11]), is linear in the size of both its input and output (with atomic operations often even faster than finite field ones):

> - Preparator to Prover: $A \in \mathbb{F}_p^{m \times n}$.
> - Verifier to Prover: $x_i \in \mathbb{F}_p^n$, for $i = 1, \ldots, k$.
> - Prover to Verifier: $y_i \in \mathbb{F}_p^m$, for $i = 1, \ldots, k$.
> - Verifier to Trustee: all the x_i and y_i.
> - Trustee publishes and signs both $u \in \mathbb{F}_p^m$ and $w \in \mathbb{F}_p^n$ such that: $u = Hash(A, x_1, \ldots, x_k, y_1, \ldots, y_k) \in \mathbb{F}_p^m$, then $w^T = u^T \cdot A \in \mathbb{F}_p^n$.
> - Verifier public verification: $w^T \cdot x_i \overset{?}{=\!=} u^T \cdot y_i$ in $\mathbb{F}_p$.

There is no overhead for the Prover; the cost for the Trustee is a single matrix-vector product for any k, plus a linear cost, and the cost for the Verifier is $\mathcal{O}(nk)$. Using Fiat-Shamir heuristic this allows an afterwards public verification but this not possible to test new vectors once u has been revealed.

4 A First Step Towards Public Verifiability

Freivalds' probabilistic verification of matrix multiplications [7] allows for private verifiability of matrix-vector computations. This can be naturally extended in the random oracle model via Fiat-Shamir heuristic [5]. This however forces the vectors to be multiplied to be known in advance, whereas our goal is instead to obtain public verifiability with an *unbounded number of vector inputs*. As an upstart, we thus first present an improvement if the public verification model is slightly relaxed: in this section, we allow the Trustee to perform some operations after the computations of the Server. We will see in next sections how to remove the need for the Trustee's intervention. For this, we combine Freivalds projection (to check that $Ax_i = y_i$, one can first precompute $w^T = u^T A$ and check that $w^T x_i = u^T y_i$) with Fiore & Gennaro's protocol, in order to improve the running time of both the Trustee and the Client: we let the Prover compute its projection in the group. That way most of the pairings computations of the Trustee and Client are transformed to classical operations: the improvement is from $\mathcal{O}(n)$ cryptographic operations to $\mathcal{O}(n)$ classical operations and a single cryptographic one. Further, the projection can be performed beforehand, during the precomputation phase. That way the preparation requires only one matrix-vector for the Freivalds projection and the dense part is reduced to a single vector. The cryptographic operations can still be delayed till the last check on pairings. This is shown in Fig. 1.

- **Preparator:** secret random $u \in \mathbb{F}_p^m$, $t \in \mathbb{F}_p^n$, then $\omega^T = g_1^{u^T A + t^T} \in \mathbb{G}_1^n$.
- **Preparator to Prover:** $A \in \mathbb{F}_p^{m \times n}$, $\omega \in \mathbb{G}_1^n$
- **Preparator to Trustee:** u, t in a secure channel.
- **Verifier to Prover:** $x_i \in \mathbb{F}_p^n$
- **Prover to Verifier:** $y_i \in \mathbb{F}_p^m$, $\zeta_i \in \mathbb{G}_1$ such that $y_i = Ax_i$ and $\zeta_i = \omega^T \star x_i$.
- **Verifier to Trustee:** x_i, y_i
- **Trustee to Verifier:** $h_i = (u^T \cdot y_i) \in \mathbb{F}_p$ and $d_i = (t^T \cdot x_i) \in \mathbb{F}_p$, then send $\eta_i = e(g_1; g_2)^{h_i + d_i} \in \mathbb{G}_T$.
- **Verifier public verification:** $e(\zeta_i; g_2) \overset{?}{=\!=} \eta_i$ in $\mathbb{G}_T$.

Fig. 1. Interactive protocol for Sparse-matrix vector multiplication verification under the co-CDH.

Theorem 1. *The protocol of Fig. 1 is perfectly complete and sound under the co-Computational Diffie-Hellman assumption.*

Proof. For the correctness, we have that: $\zeta_i = g_1^{(u^T A + t^T) \cdot x_i} = g_1^{u^T \cdot y_i + t^T \cdot x_i} = g_1^{h_i} g_1^{d_i} = g_1^{h_i + d_i}$. Then, by bilinearity, $e(\zeta_i; g_2) = e(g_1; g_2)^{h_i + d_i} = \eta_i$.

For the soundness, a malicious Prover can guess the correct output values, but this happens once in the number of elements of $\mathbb{G}_T$. Otherwise he could try to guess some matching h_i and d_i, but that happens less than one in the number of elements of $\mathbb{F}_p$. Finally, the Prover could produce directly ζ_i. Suppose then it is possible to pass our verification scheme for some A, x and $y' \neq y = Ax$. Then without loss of generality, we can suppose that the first coefficients of both vectors are different, $y'[1] \neq y[1]$ (via row permutations) and that $y'[1] - y[1] = 1$ (via a scaling).

Take a co-computational Diffie-Hellman problem (g_1^c, g_2^d), where g_1^{cd} is unknown. Then denote by $a = e(g_1^c; g_2^d) = e(g_1^{cd}; g_2)$ and consider the vector $z^T = [a, e(1; 1), \ldots, e(1; 1)]$. Compute $\chi^T = z^T \star A$. The latter correspond to $\chi^T = e(g_1^{u^T A}; g_2)$ for (a not computed) $u^T = [cd, 0, \ldots, 0]$. Now randomly choose $\psi^T = [\psi_1, \ldots, \psi_n]$ and compute $\omega^T = g_1^{\psi^T}$. Compute also the vector $\phi^T = e(\omega^T; g_2)/\chi^T$ coefficient-wise. The latter correspond to $\phi^T = e(g_1^{t^T}; g_2)$ for $t^T = \psi^T - u^T A$. Finally, compute $\zeta = g_1^{\psi^T \cdot x}$ (indeed, then $\mu = e(\zeta; g_2) = e(g_1^{\psi^T \cdot x}; g_2) = \eta = e(g_1^{u^T \cdot y}; g_2)e(g_1^{t^T \cdot x}; g_2)$, that is $\eta = (\chi^T \star x)(\phi^T \star x)$ is actually $\eta = (z^T \star y)(\phi^T \star x))$. Now, if it is possible to break the scheme, then it is possible to compute ζ' that will pass the verification for y' as Ax, that is $e(\zeta'; g_2) = (z^T \star y')(\phi^T \star x)$. Let $h = u^T y$, $d = t^T x$ and $h' = u^T y'$. Then $e(\zeta; g_2) = e(g_1^h; g_2)e(g_1^d; g_2)$ and $e(\zeta'; g_2) = e(g_1^{h'}; g_2)e(g_1^d; g_2)$. But $h' - h = u^T(y' - y) = cd(y'[1] - y[1]) = cd$ by construction. Therefore $\zeta'/\zeta = g_1^{cd}$, as e is non-degenerate, and the co-CDH is solved.

5   Verifying the Dot-Products by Bootstrapping and Vectorization

To obtain public verifiability and public delegatability, the Client should perform both dot-products, $u^T \cdot y$ and $t^T \cdot x$ (from now on, for the sake of simplicity, we drop the indices on x and y). But as u and t must remain secret, they will be encrypted beforehand. To speed-up the Client computation, the idea is then to let the Server perform the encrypted dot-products and to allow the Client to verify them, mostly with classical operations.

For this trade-off, we use vectorization. That is, for the vectors u and y, we form another representation as $\sqrt{m} \times \sqrt{m}$ matrices:

$$U = \begin{bmatrix} u_1 & \cdots & u_{\sqrt{m}} \\ u_{1+\sqrt{m}} & \cdots & u_{2\sqrt{m}} \\ \cdots & \cdots & \cdots \\ u_{1+m-\sqrt{m}} & \cdots & u_m \end{bmatrix} \text{ and } Y = \begin{bmatrix} y_1 & \cdots & y_{1+m-\sqrt{m}} \\ y_2 & \cdots & y_{2+m-\sqrt{m}} \\ \cdots & \cdots & \cdots \\ y_{\sqrt{m}} & \cdots & y_m \end{bmatrix}.$$

Then $u^T \cdot y = Trace(UY)$. Computing with this representation is in general slower than with the direct dot-product, $\mathcal{O}\left(\sqrt{m}^3\right)$ instead of $\mathcal{O}(m)$. As shown next, this can be circumvented with well-chosen left-hand sides and at least mitigated, with unbalanced dimensions.

5.1   Dot-Product with Rank 1 Left-Hand Side

The first case is if u is of rank 1, that is if in matrix form, u can be represented by a rank one update, $U = \mu \cdot \eta^T$ for $\mu, \eta \in \mathbb{F}_p^{\sqrt{m}}$. Then both representations require roughly the same number of operations to perform a dot-product since then:

$$Trace(\mu \cdot \eta^T \cdot Y) = \eta^T \cdot Y \cdot \mu \tag{1}$$

Therefore, we let the Prover compute $z^T = g_1^{\eta^T} \star Y$, where $z[i] = g_1^{\sum \eta[j]Y[j,i]}$, and then the Verifier can check this value via Freivalds with a random vector v:

$g_1^{\eta^T} \star (Y \cdot v) \overset{?}{=} z^T \star v$. The point is that the Verifier needs now $\mathcal{O}(m)$ operations to compute $(Y \cdot v)$, but these are just classical operations over the field. Then its remaining operations are cryptographic but there is only $\mathcal{O}(\sqrt{m})$ of these. Finally, the Verifier concludes the computation of the dotproduct, still with cryptographic operations, but once again with only $\mathcal{O}(\sqrt{m})$ of them. Indeed, the dot product $d = u^T y = Trace(UY) = Trace(\mu \cdot \eta^T \cdot Y) = \eta^T \cdot Y \cdot \mu$ is checked by $e(g_1^d; g_2) = e(g_1; g_2)^d = \prod_{i=1}^{\sqrt{m}} e(z[i]; g_2^{\mu[i]})$ and the latter is $e(g_1; g_2)^{\sum \sum \mu[i]\eta[j]Y[j,i]} = e(g_1; g_2)^{\eta^T \cdot Y \cdot \mu}$.

- *KeyGen*$(1^\lambda, \mu, \eta)$: given the security parameter 1^λ and vectors $\mu \in \mathbb{F}_p^{b_2}$ and $\eta \in \mathbb{F}_p^{b_1}$ (here $u = \mu \cdot \eta^t$), it selects two cyclic groups $\mathbb{G}_1$ and $\mathbb{G}_2$ of prime order p that admit a bilinear pairing $e : \mathbb{G}_1 \times \mathbb{G}_2 \to \mathbb{G}_T$ and generators g_1, g_2 and g_T of the three groups. Finally it outputs params $= \{b_1, b_2, p, \mathbb{G}_1, \mathbb{G}_2, \mathbb{G}_T, e, g_1, g_2, g_T\}$ and $EK_f = (g_1^{\eta^T})$ and $VK_f = (g_2^\mu)$.
- *ProbGen*(y): from $y \in \mathbb{F}_p^m$ it builds $Y \in \mathbb{F}_p^{b_1 \times b_2}$ and outputs $\sigma_x = Y$.
- *Compute*(σ_x, EK_f): compute $z^T = g_1^{\eta^T} \star Y$ and outputs $\sigma_y = (z^T)$.
- *Verify*(σ_y, VK_f): it starts by sampling randomly a vector $v \in \mathbb{F}_p^{b_2}$ then it checks whether $z^T \star v$ is equal to $g_1^{\eta^T} \star (Yv)$ or not. If the test passes it returns $\prod e(z[i]; g_2^{\mu[i]})$ and if it fails it returns $\perp$.

Fig. 2. Publicly delegatable protocol for the dot-product with a rank-1 left hand side.

In practice, operations in a group can be slightly faster than pairings. Moreover $\lceil \sqrt{m} \rceil^2$ can be quite far off m. Therefore it might be interesting to use a non square vectorization $b_1 \times b_2$, as long as $b_1 b_2 \geq m$ and $b_1 + b_2 = \Theta(\sqrt{m})$ (and 0 padding if needed). Then we have $U \in \mathbb{F}_p^{b_1 \times b_2}$, $\mu \in \mathbb{F}_p^{b_1}$, $\eta \in \mathbb{F}_p^{b_2}$, $Y \in \mathbb{F}_p^{b_2 \times b_1}$ and $z \in \mathbb{G}_2^{b_1}$. The obtained protocol can compute $e(g_1; g_2)^{u^T \cdot y}$ with $\mathcal{O}(\sqrt{m})$ cryptographic operations on the Verifier side and is given in Fig. 2.

Lemma 1. *The protocol of Fig. 2 for publicly delegation of a size m external group dot-product verification with rank-1 left hand side is sound, perfectly complete and requires the following number of operations where $b_1 b_2 \geq m$ and $b_1 + b_2 = \Theta(\sqrt{m})$:*

- *Preparation: $\mathcal{O}(b_1 + b_2)$ in $\mathbb{G}_i$;*
- *Prover: $\mathcal{O}(m)$ in $\mathbb{G}_i$;*
- *Verifier: $\mathcal{O}(m)$ in $\mathbb{F}_p$, $\mathcal{O}(b_1 + b_2)$ in $\mathbb{G}_i$ and $\mathcal{O}(b_1)$ pairings.*

Proof. Correctness is ensured by Eq. (1). Soundness is given by Freivalds check. Complexity is as given in the Lemma: indeed, for the Verifier, we have: for $Y \cdot v$: $\mathcal{O}(b_2 b_1) = \mathcal{O}(m)$ classic operations; for $g_1^{\eta^T} \star (Yv)$: $\mathcal{O}(b_2)$ cryptographic (group) operations; for $z^T \star v$: $\mathcal{O}(b_1)$ cryptographic (group) operations; and for $\prod_{i=1}^{b_1} e(z[i]; g_2^{\mu[i]})$: $\mathcal{O}(b_1)$ cryptographic (pairings) operations. Then the preparation requires to compute $g_1^\eta \in \mathbb{G}_1^{b_2}$ and $g_2^\mu \in \mathbb{G}_1^{b_1}$, while the Prover needs to compute $g_1^{\eta^T} \star Y$ for $Y \in \mathbb{F}_p^{b_2 \times b_1}$ and $b_1 b_2 = \mathcal{O}(m)$.

5.2   Rectangular General Dot-Product

Now if u is not given by a rank 1 update, one can still verify a dot-product with only $\mathcal{O}\left(\sqrt{m}\right)$ pairings operations but as the price of slightly more group operations as given in Fig. 3.

- **KeyGen**($1^\lambda, u$): given the security parameter 1^λ and vector $u \in \mathbb{F}_p^m$, it selects two cyclic groups $\mathbb{G}_1$ and $\mathbb{G}_2$ of prime order p that admit a bilinear pairing $e : \mathbb{G}_1 \times \mathbb{G}_2 \to \mathbb{G}_T$ and generators g_1, g_2 and g_T of the three groups and also integers b_1, b_2 such that $m = b_1 b_2$ and it outputs $\texttt{params} = \{b_1, b_2, p, \mathbb{G}_1, \mathbb{G}_2, \mathbb{G}_T, e, g_1, g_2, g_T\}$. Then it samples a random $w \in \mathbb{F}_p^{b_1}$, creates $U \in \mathbb{F}_p^{b_1 \times b_2}$ from u and finally it outputs and $EK_f = (g_1^U)$ and $VK_f = (g_1^{w^T \cdot U}, g_2^{\omega^T})$.
- **ProbGen**(y): from $y \in \mathbb{F}_p^m$ it builds $Y \in \mathbb{F}_p^{b_2 \times b_1}$ and outputs $\sigma_x = Y$.
- **Compute**(σ_x, EK_f): compute $C = g_1^U \star Y$ and outputs $\sigma_y = (C)$.
- **Verify**(σ_y, VK_f): it starts by sampling randomly a vector $v \in \mathbb{F}_p^{b_1}$ then it computes $z = C \star v$ and checks whether $\prod e(z[i]; g_2^{\omega[i]})$ is equal to $e(g_1^{w^T \cdot U} \star (Yv); g_2)$ or not. If the test passes it returns $Trace(C)$ and if it fails it returns $\perp$.

Fig. 3. Publicly delegatable protocol for the external dot-product.

Lemma 2. *The protocol of Fig. 3 is sound, perfectly complete and requires the following number of operations with $b_1 b_2 \geq m$:*

- *Preparation: $\mathcal{O}(m)$ in $\mathbb{F}_p$ and $\mathcal{O}(m)$ in $\mathbb{G}_i$;*
- *Prover: $\mathcal{O}(mb_1)$ in $\mathbb{G}_1$;*
- *Verifier: $\mathcal{O}(m)$ in $\mathbb{F}_p$, $\mathcal{O}\left(b_1^2 + b_2\right)$ in $\mathbb{G}_i$ and $\mathcal{O}(b_1)$ pairings.*

Proof. Correctness is ensured by the vectorization in Eq. (1). Soundness is given by the Freivalds check. Complexity is as given in the Lemma: indeed, for the Verifier, we have:

1. $Y \cdot v$: $\mathcal{O}(b_2 b_1) = \mathcal{O}(m)$ classic operations;
2. $g_1^{w^T U} \star (Yv)$: $\mathcal{O}(b_2)$ cryptographic (group) operations;
3. $z = C \star v$: $\mathcal{O}(b_1^2)$ cryptographic (group) operations;
4. $\prod_{i=1}^{b_1} e(z[i]; g_2^{w[i]})$: $\mathcal{O}(b_1)$ cryptographic (pairings) operations;

Then the preparation requires to compute $w^T \times U$. This is $\mathcal{O}(b_1 b_2 = m)$ operations. Finally, the Prover needs to compute the matrix multiplication $g_1^U \star Y$ for $U \in \mathbb{F}_p^{b_1 \times b_2}$ and $Y \in \mathbb{F}_p^{b_2 \times b_1}$, in $\mathcal{O}(b_1^2 b_2) = \mathcal{O}(mb_1)$.

Therefore, one can take $b_1 = \mathcal{O}\left(\sqrt[3]{m}\right)$ and $b_2 = \mathcal{O}\left(m^{2/3}\right)$ which gives only $\mathcal{O}\left(m^{2/3}\right)$ cryptographic operations for the Verifier, and $\mathcal{O}\left(m^{4/3}\right)$ cryptographic operations for the Prover.

6   Public Delegatability via Bootstrapping

To recover the public delegatability model, we use the protocol of Fig. 1 but we trade back some cryptographic operations using the protocols of Figs. 2 and 3 to the Verifier. With an initial matrix $A \in \mathbb{F}_p^{m \times n}$ we however trade back only on the order of $\mathcal{O}\left(\sqrt{m} + \sqrt{n}\right)$ cryptographic operations. This gives a slower verification in practice but interaction is not needed anymore. We present our full novel protocol for matrix vector product in Fig. 4 (with the flow of exchanges shown in Fig. 5, next).

- *Keygen*(1^λ, A): given a security parameter 1^λ and a matrix $A \in \mathbb{F}_p^{m \times n}$, it selects two cyclic groups $\mathbb{G}_1$ and $\mathbb{G}_2$ of prime order p that admit a bilinear pairing $e : \mathbb{G}_1 \times \mathbb{G}_2 \to \mathbb{G}_T$. Then it selects generators g_1, g_2 and g_T of the three groups, and integers b_1, b_2, c_1, c_2, d_1, d_2 such that $b_1 b_2 = m$ and $c_1 c_2 = d_1 d_2 = n$ with $b_1 + b_2 \in \mathcal{O}\left(m^{1/2}\right)$, $c_1 + c_2 \in \mathcal{O}\left(n^{1/2}\right)$, $d_1 \in \mathcal{O}\left(n^{1/3}\right)$, $d_2 \in \mathcal{O}\left(n^{2/3}\right)$ and it outputs parameters: $\mathrm{param} = (m, n, b_1, b_2, c_1, c_2, d_1, d_2, p, e, \mathbb{G}_1, \mathbb{G}_2, \mathbb{G}_T, g_1, g_2, g_T)$.
  Then it samples randomly $\mu \in \mathbb{F}_p^{b_1}$, $\eta \in \mathbb{F}_p^{b_2}$, $\rho_1 \in \mathbb{F}_p^{c_1}$, $\rho_2 \in \mathbb{F}_p^{c_1}$, $\tau_1 \in \mathbb{F}_p^{c_2}$, $\tau_2 \in \mathbb{F}_p^{c_2}$, $\varpi \in \mathbb{F}_p^{d_1}$, $(\gamma, \delta) \in \mathbb{F}_p^2$ and $v \in \mathbb{F}_p^n$ with $v \simeq V \in \mathbb{F}_p^{d_1 \times d_2}$.
  Finally it computes $U = \mu \cdot \eta^T \simeq u \in \mathbb{F}_p^n$, $T = \rho_1 \cdot \tau_1^T + \rho_2 \cdot \tau_2^T \simeq t^T \in \mathbb{F}_p^n$, $\omega^T = g_1^{u^T \cdot A + t^T + \gamma \delta v^T} \in \mathbb{F}_p^n$ and publishes:
  $$EK_f = \{A, \omega^T, (g_1^{\tau_1^T}), (g_1^{\tau_2^T}), (g_1^{\eta^T}), (g_1^{\delta \cdot V})\}$$
  $$VK_f = \{(g_1^{\tau_1^T}), (g_1^{\tau_2^T}), (g_2^{\rho_1}), (g_2^{\rho_2}), (g_1^{\eta^T}), (g_2^\mu), (g_1^{\delta \varpi^T \cdot V}), (g_2^{\gamma \varpi}), g_2^\gamma\}.$$
- *ProbGen*(x): given a vector $x \in \mathbb{F}_p^n$, output $\sigma_x = x$.
- *Compute*(σ_x, EK_f): given the encoded input σ_x and the evaluation key EK_f, it computes $y = Ax$, $\zeta = \omega^T \star x$, $s_i^T = g_1^{\tau_i^T} \star X$ for $i \in \{1,2\}$ with $x \simeq X \in \mathbb{F}_p^{c_2 \times c_1}$, $z^T = g_1^{\eta^T} \star Y$ with $y \simeq Y \in \mathbb{F}_p^{b_2 \times b_1}$ and $C = g_1^{\delta \cdot V} \star X$ with $x \simeq X \in \mathbb{F}_p^{d_2 \times d_1}$. Finally it outputs $\sigma_y = \{y, \zeta, s_1^T, s_2^T, z^T, C\}$.
- *Verify*(σ_y, VK_f): it starts by sampling randomly four vectors $(v_1, v_2) \in \mathbb{F}_p^{c_1}$, $v_3 \in \mathbb{F}_p^{b_1}$ and $v_4 \in \mathbb{F}_p^{d_1}$. Then it checks whether $s_1^T \star v_1$ is equal to $g_1^{\tau_1^T} \star (X \cdot v_1)$ or not (and similarly for s_2, v_2, τ_2), then it computes $D_1 = \prod e(s_1[j]; g_2^{\rho_1[j]})$, as well as $D_2 = \prod e(s_2[j]; g_2^{\rho_2[j]})$. Then it checks whether $z^T \star v_3$ is equal to $g_1^{\eta^T} \star (Y v_3)$ or not, then it computes $H = \prod e(z[i]; g_2^{\mu[i]})$. From there it computes $\vartheta = C \star v_4$, and it checks whether $\prod e(\vartheta[i]; g_2^{\varpi[i]})$ is equal to $e(g_1^{\delta \varpi^T \cdot V} \star (X v_4); g_2^\gamma)$. If all the previous tests have passed it performs a final check which is to know if $e(\zeta; g_2)$ is equal to $H \cdot D_1 \cdot D_2 \cdot e(Trace(C); g_2^\gamma)$ or not, if it passes it output y, but if any of the previous check has failed it outputs $\perp$.

Fig. 4. Proven publicly delegatable protocol for matrix-vector product

Apart from Freivalds's checks and vectorization, we need to use a masking of the form $u^T A + t^T$ (see Fig. 1) indistinguishable from a random distribution, but:

Prover	$A \in \mathbb{F}_p^{m \times n}$	Verifier

$$b_1, b_2, c_1, c_2, d_1, d_2 \text{ with } b_1 b_2 = m, c_1 c_2 = d_1 d_2 = n,$$

$$b_1 + b_2 = \mathcal{O}\left(m^{\frac{1}{2}}\right), c_1 + c_2 = \mathcal{O}\left(n^{\frac{1}{2}}\right), d_1 = \mathcal{O}\left(n^{\frac{1}{3}}\right), d_2 = \mathcal{O}\left(n^{\frac{2}{3}}\right)$$

$$\text{random } \mu \in \mathbb{F}_p^{b_1}, \eta \in \mathbb{F}_p^{b_2}, \sigma_{\{1;2\}} \in \mathbb{F}_p^{c_1}, \tau_{\{1;2\}} \in \mathbb{F}_p^{c_2}, \varpi \in \mathbb{F}_p^{d_1}$$

$$\text{random } \gamma \in \mathbb{F}_p, \delta \in \mathbb{F}_p, v \in \mathbb{F}_p^n \simeq V \in \mathbb{F}_p^{d_1 \times d_2}$$

$$U = \mu \cdot \eta^T \in \mathbb{F}_p^{b_1 \times b_2} \simeq u^T \in \mathbb{F}_p^m$$

$$T = \sigma_1 \cdot \tau_1^T + \sigma_2 \cdot \tau_2^T \in \mathbb{F}_p^{c_1 \times c_2} \simeq t^T \in \mathbb{F}_p^n$$

$$\omega^T = g_1^{u^T \cdot A + t^T + \gamma \delta \cdot v^T}$$

$$\text{publish } A, \omega, g_1^{\tau_1^T}, g_2^{\sigma_1}, g_1^{\tau_2^T}, g_2^{\sigma_2}, g_1^{\eta^T}, g_2^{\mu}$$

$$\text{publish } g_1^{\delta}, g_2^{\gamma}, (g_1^{\delta})^{V^T}, (g_2^{\gamma})^{\varpi^T}, (g_1^{\delta})^{\varpi^T V}$$

$$x \in \mathbb{F}_p^n \simeq \mathbb{F}_p^{c_2 \times c_1} \simeq \mathbb{F}_p^{d_2 \times d_1} \xleftarrow{\hspace{3cm}}$$

$$y = Ax \qquad (Fig.\,1)$$

$$\zeta = \omega^T \star x = \prod_{j=1}^{n} \omega_j^{x_j} \qquad (Fig.\,1)$$

$$s_1^T = g_1^{\tau_1^T} \star X \qquad (Fig.\,2)$$

$$s_2^T = g_1^{\tau_2^T} \star X \qquad (Fig.\,2)$$

$$z^T = g_1^{\eta^T} \star Y \qquad (Fig.\,2)$$

$$C = (g_1^{\delta})^V \star X \qquad (Fig.\,3)$$

$$\xrightarrow{\hspace{2cm} y, \zeta, s_1, s_2, z, C \hspace{2cm}}$$

$$\text{random } v_1 \in \mathbb{F}_p^{c_1}, v_2 \in \mathbb{F}_p^{c_1}, v_3 \in \mathbb{F}_p^{b_1}, v_4 \in \mathbb{F}_p^{d_1}$$

$$s_1^T \star v_1 \overset{?}{=} g_1^{\tau_1^T} \star (X \cdot v_1) \text{ and } s_2^T \star v_2 \overset{?}{=} g_1^{\tau_2^T} \star (X \cdot v_2)$$

$$D_1 = \left(\prod e(s_1[i]; g_2^{\sigma_1[i]})\right) \text{ and } D_2 = \left(\prod e(s_2[i]; g_2^{\sigma_2[i]})\right)$$

$$z^T \star v_3 \overset{?}{=} g_1^{\eta^T} \star (Y \cdot v_3)$$

$$H = \left(\prod e(z[i]; g_2^{\mu[i]})\right)$$

$$\vartheta = C \star v_4, \ \prod e(\vartheta[i]; g_2^{\gamma \varpi[i]}) \overset{?}{=} e(g_1^{\delta \varpi^T V} \star (X \cdot v_4); g_2^{\gamma})$$

$$e(\zeta; g_2) \overset{?}{=} H \cdot D_1 \cdot D_2 \cdot e(Trace(C); g_2^{\gamma})$$

Fig. 5. Exchanges in the proven publicly delegatable protocol with negligible cryptographic operations of Fig. 4.

1. We have to add an extra component $\gamma \delta v^T$ to $u^T A + t^T$ so that it is possible, when proving the reduction to co-CDH, to make up a random vector $\omega^T = g^{u^T A + t}$ where the components of $u^T A + t^T$ are canceled out. This component cannot be revealed to the Prover, nor the Verifier in the delegatable setting, otherwise its special structure could have been taken into account by the reduction. Also this component cannot have the rank-1 update structure as its has to be a multiple of $u^T A + t^T$. Therefore only the protocol of Fig. 3 can be used to check the dotproduct with g^{v^T}.
2. To be able to apply the analysis of [6, Theorem 3] while allowing fast computations with t, we use a special form for t, namely: $t^T = \rho_1 \tau_1^T + \rho_2 \tau_2^T$.

With these modifications we are able to prove the soundness of the protocol in Fig. 4.

Theorem 2. *Let $A \in \mathbb{F}_p^{m \times n}$ whose matrix-vector products costs $\mu(A)$ arithmetic operations. Protocol Fig. 4 is sound under the co-CDH assumption, perfectly complete and its number of performed operations is bounded as follows:*

	Preparation	Prover	Verifier
$\mathbb{F}_p$	$\mu(A) + \mathcal{O}(m+n)$	$\mu(A)$	$\mathcal{O}(m+n)$
$\mathbb{G}_i$	$\mathcal{O}(m+n)$	$\mathcal{O}\left(m + n^{4/3}\right)$	$\mathcal{O}\left(\sqrt{m} + n^{2/3}\right)$
Pairings	0	0	$\mathcal{O}(\sqrt{m} + \sqrt{n})$

Proof. Completeness stems again directly from Eq. (1).

For the complexity bounds, we fix $b_1 b_2 \geq m$ and $b_1 + b_2 = \Theta(\sqrt{m})$ (usually, pairing operations are costlier than group operations, therefore a good practice could be to take $b_1 < b_2$ and we, for instance, often have used $b_2 = 100 b_1$ with $b_1 b_2 \approx m$ which gave us a speed-up by a factor of 5), $c_1 c_2 \geq n$ and $c_1 + c_2 = \Theta(\sqrt{n})$, and finally $d_1 = \mathcal{O}\left(m^{1/3}\right)$ and $d_2 = \mathcal{O}\left(m^{2/3}\right)$. For the Prover, we then have that y obtained in $\mu(A)$ operations; ζ in $\mathcal{O}(n)$; s_1, s_2 and z computations are bounded by $\mathcal{O}(n+m)$ where C thus requires $\mathcal{O}\left(n^{4/3}\right)$ operations. The cost for the preparation is $\mathcal{O}(m+n)$ for U, T and $\varpi^T V$. ω requires $\mu(A) + 2m$ classical operations and $\mathcal{O}(m)$ group operations. $(g_2^\delta)^{V^T}$ requires $\mathcal{O}(n)$ group operations while $g_1^{\tau_i}$, $g_1^{\eta_i}$, $g_2^{\rho_i}$, and $g_2^{\mu_i}$, require $\Theta(\sqrt{m} + \sqrt{n})$ operations, more than for $(g_2^\gamma)^{\varpi^T}$ and $(g_1^\delta)^{\varpi^T V}$. The complexity for the Verifier is then dominated by $\mathcal{O}\left(n^{2/3}\right)$ operations to check C, $\mathcal{O}(n)$ classical operations for $Y \cdot v_3$ and $\mathcal{O}(\sqrt{n})$ pairing operations.

Finally for the soundness, assume that there is an adversary $\mathcal{A}$ that breaks the soundness of our protocol with non-negligible advantage ϵ for a matrix $A \in \mathbb{F}_p^{m \times n}$. In the following we will prove how an adversary $\mathcal{B}$ can use adversary $\mathcal{A}$ to break the co-CDH assumption with non-negligible advantage $\epsilon' \simeq \epsilon$. Let assume that $\mathcal{B}$ was given a co-CDH sample $(L = g_1^a, R = g_2^b)$. First $\mathcal{B}$ simulates the soundness experiment to adversary $\mathcal{A}$ in the following manner: when $\mathcal{A}$ calls the oracle $\mathcal{O}_{KeyGen}$, adversary $\mathcal{B}$ first chooses integers, b_1, b_2, c_1, c_2, d_1, and d_2 such that $m = b_1 b_2$ and $n = b_1 b_2 = d_1 d_2$. Then it generates random vectors $\mu_0 \in \mathbb{F}_p^{b_1}, \eta_0 \in \mathbb{F}_p^{b_2}, \rho_{01} \in \mathbb{F}_p^{c_1}, \tau_{01} \in \mathbb{F}_p^{c_2}, \rho_{02} \in \mathbb{F}_p^{c_1}, \tau_{02} \in \mathbb{F}_p^{c_2}, \varpi \in \mathbb{F}_p^{d_1}$ and a value $r \in \mathbb{F}_p$. We let u_0 be the vector representation of $\mu_0 \cdot \eta_0^T$ and t_0 that of $\rho_{01} \cdot \tau_{01}^T + \rho_{02} \cdot \tau_{02}^T$. We also let $v = -(A^T u_0 + t_0) \in \mathbb{F}_p^n$. Finally, $\mathcal{B}$ forms $\omega^T = L^{r \cdot v^T}$; $g_1^\eta = L^{\eta_0}$, $g_2^\mu = R^{\mu_0}$; $g_1^{\tau_1} = L^{\tau_{01}}$, $g_2^{\rho_1} = R^{\rho_{01}}$; $g_1^{\tau_2} = L^{\tau_{02}}$, $g_2^{\rho_2} = R^{\rho_{02}}$; $g_1^\delta = L$, $g_2^\gamma = g_2^r$; $g_1^{\delta V} = L^V$, $(g_2^\mu)^{\varpi^T} = (g_2^\gamma)^{\varpi^T}$ and $(g_1^\delta)^{\varpi^T * V} = (g_1^\gamma)^{\varpi^T V}$ and outputs:

param $= (m, n, b_1, b_2, c_1, c_2, d_1, d_2, p, e, \mathbb{G}_1, \mathbb{G}_2, \mathbb{G}_T, g_1, g_2, g_T)$.

$EK_f = \{A, \omega^T, (g_1^{\tau_1^T}), (g_1^{\tau_2^T}), (g_1^{\eta^T}), (g_1^{\delta \cdot V})\}$

$VK_f = \{(g_1^{\tau_1^T}), (g_1^{\tau_2^T}), (g_2^{\rho_1}), (g_2^{\rho_2}), (g_1^{\eta^T}), (g_2^\mu), (g_1^{\delta \varpi^T \cdot V}), (g_2^{\gamma \varpi}), g_2^\gamma\}$.

Thanks to the randomness and the decisional Diffie-Hellman assumption (DDH) in each group G_i, as well as [6, Theorem 3] for $\omega^T = (L^r)^{v^T}$, these public values are indistinguishable from randomly generated inputs. Further, we have $\omega^T = g_1^{arv^T} = g_1^{ab(u_0^T A + t_0^T + v^T) + arv^T} = g_1^{abu_0^T A + abt_0^T + a(b+r)v^T}$.

When adversary $\mathcal{A}$ calls the oracle $\mathcal{O}_{ProbGen}$ on input x, adversary $\mathcal{B}$ returns $\sigma_x = x$. Therefore, if $y = Ax$ and $\zeta = \omega^T \star x$, then the verification will pass: indeed the first two checks will ensure that $s_1^T = g_1^{\tau_1^T} \star X$ and $s_2^T = g_1^{\tau_2^T} \star X$ when the third check ensures that $z^T = g_1^{\eta^T} \star Y$. This shows that:

$$H = \left(\prod e(z[i]; g_1^{\mu[i]}) \right) = e(g_1; g_2)^{abu_0^T y},$$

and that:

$$D_j = \left(\prod e(s_j[i]; g_2^{\rho_j[i]}) \right) \text{ for } j = 1, 2.$$

Finally, the last check is that these two parts, as well as the last one, which is $e(g_1^\delta; g_2^\gamma)^{v^T \cdot x} = e(g_1; g_2)^{a(b+r)v^T \cdot x} = e(Trace(g_1^{\delta \cdot VX}); g_2^\gamma)$, are coherent with the definitions of ω and ζ above. Now, with a non-negligible probability ϵ, adversary $\mathcal{A}$ can pass the check for another $y' \neq y$, by providing an adequate ζ'. First, z^T, s_1^T, s_2^T and C must be correct, as they are checked directly and independently by the Freivalds first four checks. Second, we have that $e(\zeta'; g_2) = e(g_1; g_2)^{abu_0^T y' + abt_0^T x}(g_2^\delta; g_2^\gamma)^{v^T \cdot x}$ and therefore, we must also have $e(\zeta(\zeta')^{-1}; g_2) = e(g_1; g_2)^{abu_0^T(y-y')}$. As u_0 is a secret unknown to adversary $\mathcal{A}$, for a random y' the probability that $u_0^T(y - y') = 0$ is bounded by $1/|\mathbb{G}_1|$ and thus negligible. Thus adversary $\mathcal{B}$ can compute $c \equiv (u_0^T(y' - y))^{-1}$ mod $|\mathbb{G}_1|$ and $(\zeta/\zeta')^c = g_1^{ab}$. Therefore it breaks the co-CDH assumption with non-negligible probability $\epsilon' \simeq \epsilon$. The only other possibility is that adversary $\mathcal{A}$ was able to recover u_0^T. But that would directly implies that it has an advantage in the co-CDH: $g_1^\eta = L^{\eta_0}$, $g_2^\mu = R^{\mu_0}$.

Remark 1. Fast matrix multiplication can be used for the computation of C in the protocol of Fig. 4. This decreases the $\mathcal{O}(n^{4/3})$ factor of the Prover to $\mathcal{O}(n^{(1+\omega)/3})$ where ω is the exponent of matrix-matrix multiplication. The currently best known exponent, given in [9], is $\omega \leq 2.3728639$. This immediately yields a reduced bound for the Prover of $\mu(A) + \mathcal{O}(m + n^{1.12428797})$.

7   Conclusion and Experiments

We first recall in Table 1 the leading terms of the complexity bounds for our protocols and those of [4,6,16] (that is each value x in a cell is such that the actual cost is bounded by $x + o(x)$). There, we denote the base field operations by $\cdot\mathcal{F}$, the cryptographic group exponentiations or pairing operations by $\cdot\mathcal{G}$, and the cost of a product of the matrix $A \in \mathbb{F}_p^{m \times n}$ by a vector is $\mu(A)$. We see that our protocols are suitable to sparse or structured matrix-vector multiplication as they never require $\mathcal{O}(mn)$ operations but rather $\mu(A)$. Moreover, we see that most of the Verifier's work is now in base field operations where it was cryptographic operations for previously known protocols. As shown in Table 2 and in Fig. 6, this is very useful in practice, even for dense matrices. For these experiments we compare with our own implementations of the protocols of [4,6,16] over the PBC library[1] [10] for the pairings and the FFLAS-FFPACK library[2] [3] for the exact linear algebra over finite fields (C++ source files are available there: smc-vc.forge.imag.fr). We used randomly generated dense matrices and vectors and to optimize the costs (pairings are more expensive than exponentiations), we also chose the following parameters for the vectorizations: $b_1 = \lceil \sqrt{m}/10 \rceil$; $b_2 = \lceil 10\sqrt{m} \rceil$; $c_1 = \lceil \sqrt{n}/10 \rceil$; $c_2 = \lceil 10\sqrt{n} \rceil$; $d_1 = \lceil n^{1/3}/3 \rceil$; $d_2 = \lceil 3n^{2/3} \rceil$. We indeed chose a type 3 pairing over a Barreto-Naehrig curve [1] based on a 256-bits prime field, which should guarantee 128 bits of security. First, with $\mathbb{F}_p$ the

Table 1. Leading terms for the time and memory complexity bounds (exchange of A, x and y excluded).

Scheme	[6]	[16]	[4]
Mode	Public verif.	Public deleg.	Public deleg.
Preparator (KeyGen)	$2mn \cdot \mathcal{F} + mn \cdot \mathcal{G}$	$-$	$2mn \cdot \mathcal{F} + 2mn \cdot \mathcal{G}$
Trustee (ProbGen)	$2(m+n) \cdot \mathcal{F} + 2m \cdot \mathcal{G}$	$mn \cdot \mathcal{F} + (2m+n) \cdot \mathcal{G}$	$n \cdot \mathcal{G}$
Prover (Compute)	$\mu(A) \cdot \mathcal{F} + 2mn \cdot \mathcal{G}$	$\mu(A) \cdot \mathcal{F} + 2mn \cdot \mathcal{G}$	$\mu(A) \cdot \mathcal{F} + 2mn \cdot \mathcal{G}$
Verifier	$2m \cdot \mathcal{G}$	$2m \cdot \mathcal{G}$	$m \cdot \mathcal{G}$
Extra storage	$\mathcal{O}(mn)$	$\mathcal{O}(mn)$	$\mathcal{O}(mn)$
Extra communications	$\mathcal{O}(m)$	$\mathcal{O}(m)$	$\mathcal{O}(1)$
Scheme	Fig. 1	Fig. 4	
Mode	Public verif.	Public deleg.	
Preparator (KeyGen)	$(\mu(A)+n) \cdot \mathcal{F} + n \cdot \mathcal{G}$	$(\mu(A)+m+5n) \cdot \mathcal{F} + 2n \cdot \mathcal{G}$	
Trustee (ProbGen)	$2(m+n+1) \cdot \mathcal{F} + 1 \cdot \mathcal{G}$	0	
Prover (Compute)	$\mu(A) \cdot \mathcal{F} + 2n \cdot \mathcal{G}$	$\mu(A) \cdot \mathcal{F} + (2n^{4/3}+m) \cdot \mathcal{G}$	
Verifier	$1 \cdot \mathcal{G}$	$(2m+4n) \cdot \mathcal{F} + (6\sqrt{m}+2n^{2/3}) \cdot \mathcal{G}$	
Extra storage	$\mathcal{O}(m+n)$	$\mathcal{O}(n)$	
Extra communications	$\mathcal{O}(1)$	$\mathcal{O}(n^{2/3} + \sqrt{m})$	

---

[1] https://crypto.stanford.edu/pbc, version 0.5.14.
[2] http://linbox-team.github.io/fflas-ffpack, version 2.2.2.

Table 2. Matrix-vector multiplication public verification over a 256-bit finite field with different protocols on a i7 @3.4 GHz.

	1000 × 1000					2000 × 2000			
	[14]	[6]	[16]	[4]	Fig. 4	[6]	[16]	[4]	Fig. 4
KeyGen	141.68 s	152.62 s	-	154.27 s	**0.80 s**	615.81 s	-	612.72 s	**1.75 s**
ProbGen	-	1.25 s	2.28 s	2.30 s	-	2.13 s	4.98 s	4.56 s	-
$Ax = y$	20.14 s	**0.19 s**	**0.19 s**	**0.19 s**	**0.19 s**	**0.78 s**	**0.78 s**	**0.78 s**	**0.78 s**
Compute	188.60 s	273.06 s	433.88 s	271.03 s	**2.26 s**	1097.96 s	1715.46 s	1079.71 s	**5.37 s**
Verify	2.06 s	26.62 s	27.56 s	**0.33 s**	0.90 s	52.60 s	55.79 s	**0.62 s**	1.19 s
	4000 × 4000				8000 × 8000				
	[6]	[16]	[4]	Fig. 4	[6]	[16]	[4]	Fig. 4	
KeyGen	2433.10 s	-	2452.98 s	**4.89 s**	9800.42 s	-	9839.26 s	**15.64 s**	
ProbGen	3.81 s	13.29 s	9.24 s	-	7.41 s	43.44 s	18.46 s	-	
$Ax = y$	**3.28 s**	**3.28 s**	**3.28 s**	**3.28 s**	**13.30 s**	**13.30 s**	**13.30 s**	**13.30 s**	
Compute	4360.43 s	6815.40 s	4329.46 s	**13.76 s**	17688.69 s	27850.90 s	17416.38 s	**37.00 s**	
Verify	103.14 s	107.99 s	**1.20 s**	1.65 s	211.07 s	220.69 s	2.37 s	**2.25 s**	

256-bits prime field[3], $\mathbb{G}_1$ is the group of $\mathbb{F}_p$-rational points $E(\mathbb{F}_p)$ with parameters: $\mathbb{G}_1$ $(E): y^2 = x^3 + 6$, modulo p. Second, $\mathbb{G}_2$ is a subgroup of a sextic twist of E defined over $\mathbb{F}_{p^2}$ denoted $E'(\mathbb{F}_{p^2})$ with parameters[4]: $\mathbb{G}_2$ $(E'): y^2 = x^3 + 6e$, $\mathbb{F}_{p^2} \cong \mathbb{F}_p[X]/(X^2 - 2)$, $e = a_0 + a_1 X \in \mathbb{F}_{p^2}$. The third group $\mathbb{G}_T$ is then a subgroup of the multiplicative group of the field $\mathbb{F}_{p^{12}}$. This curve is reasonably well-suited to our needs and is supported by the PBC library.

In the first set of timings of Table 2, we also compare the latter protocols with a compiled verifiable version obtained via the Pepper software[5] [14]. This software uses a completely different strategy, namely that of compiling a C program into a verifiable one. We added the timings for $n = 1000$ as a comparison, but the Pepper compilation thrashed on our 64 GB machine for $n \geq 2000$.

In terms of Prover time, we see that our protocols are between two to three orders of magnitude faster than existing ones. Further evidence is given in Table 3, where we present more timings for the comparison between our protocol and, to our knowledge and according to Table 2, the best previously known from [4]. The associated speed-ups supports our claim of a *Prover efficient* protocol with a gain of two orders of magnitude.

Moreover, overall we see that with the new protocol, the data preparation (KeyGen) is now very close to a single non-verified computation and that the work of the Prover can be less than three times that of a non-verified computation (note first, that in both Table 2 and Fig. 6, the "Compute" fields include the computation of $y = Ax$, and, second, that the Prover overhead being asymptotically faster than the compute time, this latter overhead is rapidly amortized). Finally, only the protocol of [4] did exhibit a verification step faster than the

---

[3] $p = 57896044618658115533954196422662521694340972374557265300857239534749215487669.$

[4] $a_0 = 52725052272451289818299123952167568817548215037303638731097808561703910178375,$
$a_1 = 39030262586549355304602811636399374839758981514400742761920075403736570919488.$

[5] https://github.com/pepper-project/pepper, git: fe3bf04.

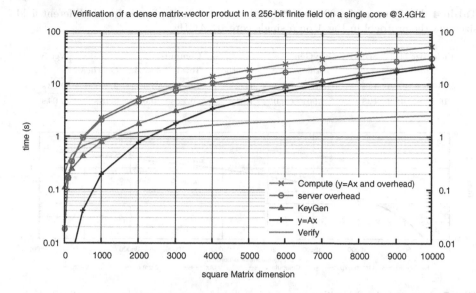

Fig. 6. Protocol Fig. 4 performance.

Table 3. Speed-up of our novel Protocol over a 256-bit finite field on a i7 @3.4 GHz.

Size	100	200	500	1000	2000	3000	4000
[4]	2.77 s	10.93 s	67.93 s	271.03 s	1079.71 s	2430.05 s	4329.46 s
Fig. 4	0.17 s	0.34 s	0.98 s	2.26 s	5.37 s	9.16 s	13.76 s
Speed-up	17	32	69	120	201	265	315
Size	5000	6000	7000	8000	9000	10000	
[4]	6790.15 s	9780.24 s	13309.61 s	17416.38 s	22002.51 s	27175.12s	
Fig. 4	18.55 s	24.03 s	29.93 s	37.00 s	44.00 s	51.97 s	
Speed-up	366	407	445	471	500	523	

computation itself for size 2000×2000 whereas, as shown in Fig. 6, our protocol achieves this only from size 3000×3000. However, we see that we are competitive for larger matrices. Moreover, as shown by the asymptotics of Theorem 2, our overall performance outperforms all previously known protocols also in practice, while keeping an order of magnitude faster Verification time.

A   Small Fields

The protocol of Fig. 1 is quite efficient. We have made experiments with randomly generated dense matrices and vectors with the PBC library (see Footnote 1) for the pairings and the FFLAS-FFPACK library (see Footnote 2) for the exact linear algebra over finite fields. For instance, it is shown in Table 4, that for a 8000×8000 matrix over a field of size 256 bits, the protocol is highly practical:

Table 4. Verification of a 8000 × 8000 matrix-vector multiplication with different field sizes via the protocol in Fig. 1 on a single core @3.4 GHz.

Field size	$|G|$	Security	KeyGen			Compute			Verify
			Total	$u^T A$	Overhead	Total	$y = Ax$	Overhead	
256	256	128	13.65 s	12.34 s	1.22 s	15.72 s	13.46 s	2.26 s	0.03 s
10	322	128	1.96 s	0.05 s	1.81 s	0.22 s	0.09 s	0.13 s	0.04 s

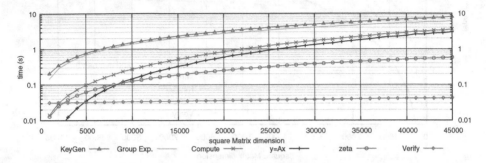

Fig. 7. Trustee-helped Verification of a dense matrix-vector product in a 10-bits finite field on a single core @3.4 GHz.

first, if the base field and the group orders are of similar sizes, the verification phase is very efficient; second, the overhead of computing ζ for the server is quite negligible and third, the key generation is dominated by the computation of one matrix-vector product.

Differently, if the base field is small, say machine word-size, then having to use cryptographic sizes for the group orders can be penalizing for the Key Generation: multiplying a small field matrix A with a large field vector u^T is much slower than $y = Ax$ with x and A small. First of all, the computations must be compatible. For this, one possibility is to ask and verify instead for $y = Ax$ over $\mathbb{Z}$ and then to let the Verifier compute $y \mod p$ for himself. There, to reduce the overhead of computing $u^T A$, one can instead select the m values of the vector u as $u_\ell = \alpha r_i s_j$ with $\ell = i\lceil \sqrt{m} \rceil + j$ for α a randomly chosen large value and r_i, s_j some randomly chosen small values. Indeed then $u^T A$ can be computed by first performing $(rs^T)A$ via $\mathcal{O}(\sqrt{m})$ matrix-vector computations with s (or a $\sqrt{m} \times n \sqrt{m}$ matrix-vector multiplication) followed by $\mathcal{O}(n\sqrt{m})$ multiplications by r (or a $n \times \sqrt{m}$ matrix-vector multiplication) where s_j and r_i are small values. Then it remains only to multiply a vector of small values by α. We have traded $\mathcal{O}(mn)$ operations with large values for $\mathcal{O}(\sqrt{m}n\sqrt{m} + n\sqrt{m})$ operations with small values and $\mathcal{O}(n)$ with large values.

Now, in order for the values to remain correct over $\mathbb{Z}$, the value of $(u^T A + t^T)x$ must not overflow. For this, one must choose a group order larger than mnp^4 (for $(rs^T)Ax$). Now the security is not anymore half the size of the group order but potentially half the size of the set from which t^T is selected, that is at most the group order size minus that of np (for $t^T x$). To be conservative we even propose, as an estimated security of the obtained protocol, to consider only half the size of α (that is the size of the group order minus that of mnp^4). In terms of efficiency, the improvement is shown in Table 4, last row. On the one hand, the key generation is now dominant and can be amortized only after about 10 matrix-vector multiplications. On the other hand, the verification time starts to be faster than the computation time. This is also shown in Fig. 7 where the equivalent of the last row in Table 4 is shown for different matrix dimensions.

References

1. Barreto, P.S.L.M., Naehrig, M.: Pairing-friendly elliptic curves of prime order. In: Preneel, B., Tavares, S. (eds.) SAC 2005. LNCS, vol. 3897, pp. 319–331. Springer, Heidelberg (2006). doi:10.1007/11693383_22
2. Bertoni, G., Daemen, J., Peeters, M., Assche, G.: Sponge-based pseudo-random number generators. In: Mangard, S., Standaert, F.-X. (eds.) CHES 2010. LNCS, vol. 6225, pp. 33–47. Springer, Heidelberg (2010). doi:10.1007/978-3-642-15031-9_3
3. Dumas, J.G., Giorgi, P., Pernet, C.: Dense linear algebra over prime fields: the FFLAS and FFPACK packages. ACM Trans. Math. Softw. **35**(3), 1–42 (2008)
4. Elkhiyaoui, K., Önen, M., Azraoui, M., Molva, R.: Efficient techniques for publicly verifiable delegation of computation. In: Proceedings of the 11th ACM on Asia Conference on Computer and Communications Security, ASIA CCS 2016, pp. 119–128. ACM, New York (2016)
5. Fiat, A., Shamir, A.: How to prove yourself: practical solutions to identification and signature problems. In: Odlyzko, A.M. (ed.) CRYPTO 1986. LNCS, vol. 263, pp. 186–194. Springer, Heidelberg (1987). doi:10.1007/3-540-47721-7_12
6. Fiore, D., Gennaro, R.: Publicly verifiable delegation of large polynomials and matrix computations, with applications. In: Proceedings of the 2012 ACM Conference on Computer and Communications Security, CCS 2012, pp. 501–512. ACM, New York (2012)
7. Freivalds, R.: Fast probabilistic algorithms. In: Bečvář, J. (ed.) MFCS 1979, vol. 74, pp. 57–69. Springer, Heidelberg (1979)
8. Goldwasser, S., Kalai, Y.T., Rothblum, G.N.: Delegating computation: interactive proofs for muggles. In: Dwork, C. (ed.) STOC 2008, pp. 113–122. ACM Press, May 2008
9. Le Gall, F.: Powers of tensors and fast matrix multiplication. In: Proceedings of the 39th International Symposium on Symbolic and Algebraic Computation, ISSAC 2014, pp. 296–303. ACM, New York (2014)
10. Lynn, B.: The pairing-based cryptography (PBC) library (2010). https://crypto.stanford.edu/pbc
11. NIST: FIPS publication 202: SHA-3 standard: permutation-based hash and extendable-output functions, August 2015
12. Parno, B., Howell, J., Gentry, C., Raykova, M.: Pinocchio: Nearly practical verifiable computation. In: 2013 IEEE Symposium on Security and Privacy, SP 2013, Berkeley, CA, USA, 19–22 May 2013, pp. 238–252. IEEE Computer Society (2013). http://dx.doi.org/10.1109/SP.2013.47
13. Parno, B., Raykova, M., Vaikuntanathan, V.: How to delegate and verify in public: verifiable computation from attribute-based encryption. In: Cramer, R. (ed.) TCC 2012. LNCS, vol. 7194, pp. 422–439. Springer, Heidelberg (2012). doi:10.1007/978-3-642-28914-9_24

14. Setty, S.T.V., McPherson, R., Blumberg, A.J., Walfish, M.: Making argument systems for outsourced computation practical (sometimes). In: 19th Annual Network and Distributed System Security Symposium, NDSS 2012, San Diego, California, USA, 5–8 February 2012. The Internet Society (2012). http://www.internetsociety.org/sites/default/files/04_3.pdf
15. Walfish, M., Blumberg, A.J.: Verifying computations without reexecuting them. Commun. ACM **58**(2), 74–84 (2015)
16. Zhang, Y., Blanton, M.: Efficient secure and verifiable outsourcing of matrix multiplications. In: Chow, S.S.M., Camenisch, J., Hui, L.C.K., Yiu, S.M. (eds.) ISC 2014. LNCS, vol. 8783, pp. 158–178. Springer, Cham (2014). doi:10.1007/978-3-319-13257-0_10

JSFfox: Run-Timely Confining JavaScript for Firefox

Weizhong Qiang(✉), JiaZhen Guo, Hai Jin, and Weifeng Li

Services Computing Technology and System Lab,
Cluster and Grid Computing Lab, Big Data Technology and System Lab,
School of Computer Science and Technology,
Huazhong University of Science and Technology, Wuhan 430074, China
wzqiang@hust.edu.cn

Abstract. Current web applications incorporate third-party content hosted at different origins that offer a series of online services, as well as a suit of reusable libraries. Since those services and libraries constantly demand access to privacy-sensitive data for implementing normal operations, web developers and users must trust them not to induce privacy exfiltration. However, due to a common feature of all-or-nothing fashion, the security mechanisms of present web browsers are essentially insufficient for mitigating the risks caused by third-party code.

This paper presents JSFfox, a JavaScript confinement system which enforces flexible information-flow policies for Firefox. Under JSFfox, not only the compartments but also the transferred message that contains the sensitive data are associated with information-flow labels, which can be tracked for enforcing substantial policies. We characterize a wide range of web applications for demonstrating the motivations and requirements of JSFfox's design and implement the secure versions of those applications, which guarantees flexibility for developers as well as privacy for users. We develop a functional prototype of JSFfox built on top of Firefox, and the experimental results show that JSFfox has a fully backward-compatibility with current web and introduces a negligible overhead compared with the legacy Firefox.

1 Introduction

Modern web applications incorporate a large number of third-party content from a variety of origins that are not equally trustworthy. Previous research [16] has indicated that 88.45% of the Alexa top 10,000 web sites include at least one third-party and remotely-hosted content, and such inclusions will request JavaScript from a total of 20,225 uniquely-addressed remote hosts. That content, in the form of the markup and executable script, can interact with the web environment through a collection of powerful API, including issuing requests to remote servers, communicating with other scripts loaded in the browser, and accessing users' confidential data (e.g., passwords, geographical location, banking account, and emails). Especially, the emerging HTML5 standards [24] have sufficiently expanded the API available to scripts.

© Springer International Publishing AG 2017
J. Pieprzyk and S. Suriadi (Eds.): ACISP 2017, Part II, LNCS 10343, pp. 135–150, 2017.
DOI: 10.1007/978-3-319-59870-3_8

Such untrusted content can cause a series of damaging consequences including users' browsing histories being tracked [7], users' input in web forms being obtained [11], cookies and confidential data from web page content being stolen [6], and even forgery requests being injected into an ongoing session on behalf of the user [3,17].

To impose restrictions on the untrusted content, present browsers rely on numerous security mechanisms, such as the *Same Origin Policy* (SOP), *Content Security Police* (CSP) [22], and *Cross-Origin Resource Sharing* (CORS) [23]. These mechanisms, however, have a notable feature of either denying or granting complete access to the untrusted scripts. Obviously, this all-or-nothing manner is not suitable for such a flexible and constantly changing web environment.

Recently, information-flow control has been applied as a promising and effective approach that can mitigate the misbehavior of the untrusted content, and, therefore, make up for the current browser security mechanisms [4,9,12,20,27]. Some of the solutions enforce per-object granularity policies, and, therefore, lead to a heavy overhead. Moreover, they require the modification of the existing JavaScript interpreter [9], or the implementation of a new one [12]. In contrast, other solutions [5,20,27] built on existing JavaScript engines, compartmentalize scripts into compartments that encapsulate content from a single origin, enforce policies at the granularity of compartments.

In this paper, we propose JSFfox, a novel information-flow control system that confines untrusted JavaScript for Firefox. JSFfox can implement general and flexible information flow control policies for interactions between web application components and the browser APIs, and prohibit untrusted code from leaking sensitive data (e.g., through an untrusted Internet channel).

More specifically, each component in a browser is specifically associated with an information-flow label which is identified by web origins. JSFfox offers two different granularities of information-flow labels. The *context label* is the one regrarding the granularity of a context (e.g., iframe, worker), which represents the privilege of all data within the relevant context. It can not only express secrecy and integrity but also precisely define the endorsement and declassification operations, permitting the controlled flow of data to untrusted contexts for realizing a specific functionality (e.g., a password manager can obtain or send the password from or to a relevant page).

The *message label* is the one specifically introduced in JSFfox and it can be assigned to a transferred message that contains sensitive data between contexts. Since some data (e.g., bank account, password) in a context can be considered as absolute private which cannot be disclosed from the browser by untrusted contexts, the *message label* enables JSFfox to track that kind of data and restrict the communication capability of the context which receives the data.

We characterize three motivating web applications; an application that incorporates third-party online services, a third-party mashup, and an application which imports untrusted third-party libraries. All of these are difficult to be deployed in a way that guarantees both privacy and flexibility in present browsers. By realizing secure versions of three mentioned applications under a JSFfox prototype, we concretely prove that JSFfox can enforce practical and efficient information-flow control policies to prevent the leakage of secrets from browsers.

In summary, this paper makes the following contributions:

- We describe the design of the JSFfox, a confine system for untrusted code which specifies and enforces fine-grained information-flow polices to prohibit secrets from leaving the browser.
- We introduce a feasible approach to track and secure the sensitive data, as well as to confine the insecure declassification.
- We present a case-study regarding web applications of enforcement of practically relevant policies enabled by JSFfox.
- We describe functional prototype implementation built on Firefox with a reasonable performance overhead.

The remainder of this paper is organized as follows. In Sect. 2, we describe background, and give motivation examples. Section 3 gives a high-level overview of the design of JSFfox, and Sect. 4 details the secure versions of our motivation examples mentioned in Sect. 2.2. In Sect. 5, we discuss key implementation aspects and we evaluate JSFfox with respect to compatibility, security, and performance in Sect. 6. Section 7 discusses related work, and Sect. 8 gives the conclusion.

2 Background and Motivation

In this section, we first review the security mechanisms in today's browsers, and then give several motivating applications that indicate the requirements which JSFfox needs to satisfy.

2.1 Browser Security Mechanisms

Same Origin Policy (SOP) simply requires that dynamic content can only read the resources (e.g., cookies, DOM, http response) of content from the same origin[1], rather than access content from a different origin. Typically, browsers isolate content retrieved from different origins to prevent malicious web site operators from interfering with the operation of benign web sites.

Today's browsers offer several approaches to bypass SOP for developers. The *postMessage* [24] allows data to be sent between two contexts across domains. For safety reasons, a sender always specifies an exact target origin, meanwhile a receiver always verifies the sender's identity using the origin and possibly source properties. However, recent research [19] illustrates the potential risk of privacy disclosure due to incorrect or nonexistent origin check in *postMessage*. *Cross-Origin Resource Sharing* (CORS) [23] introduces a standard mechanism that

---

[1] An origin is a source of authority encoded by the protocol (e.g., *http*), domain name (e.g., *a.com*), and port (e.g., *80*) of a resource URL.

can be used by browsers for the support of issuing cross-domain requests to remote servers.

Moreover, *Content Security Policy* (CSP) [22] enforced by browsers is technically a whitelist-style tool which web developers can leverage to lock down their applications in various ways, mitigating the risk of content injection vulnerabilities, and reducing the privilege that their applications execute.

Note that all of the aforementioned security mechanisms are purely all-or-nothing style in nature. At runtime, those mechanisms maintain static and constant access control policies but do not confine a receiving compartment which can deal with the obtained data at will. Therefore, if a privacy-fixated web developer needs to deliver secret information to a context of foreign origin then the receiving context must be completely trustworthy and benign.

2.2 Motivations

After a brief review of the security mechanisms in the status-quo browsers, we introduce three typical motivating application examples which demonstrate the imperfections of those security mechanisms and indicate the important requirements that JSFfox needs to satisfy.

Third-party service. An online service, like a cloud note, can help users ubiquitously organize cross-platform data. Accordingly, developers are willing to offer this service in the form of an extension or library. We suppose a cloud note extension wants to capture the document from a web site, say *a.com*, and upload the obtained data. The existing browser security mechanisms allow the cloud note to access all data from *a.com* and then write to the network. Therefore, the cloud note which might encompass privacy-disclosure vulnerabilities or be injected with malicious code, is allowed to access the sensitive data from *a.com*, and then exfiltrate it from the browser. That situation, thus, demands that JSFfox tracks the flow of sensitive data, and whenever such unexpected access appears, prohibits the receiving context from communicating with untrusted origins.

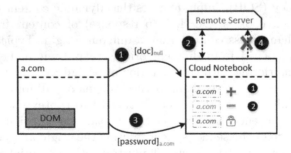

Fig. 1. Third-party cloud note architecture under JSFfox

Figure 1 shows how such a design might look. In this, and subsequent examples, compartments are represented by rectangular frames, communication operations are denoted as arrows, and the execution sequence of events is numbered. Each compartment could be labeled (Sect. 3.1, Context label) with the origins to whose sensitive data they have been exposed, and also be granted with the capability of raising or reducing that label. A compartment's initial label is denoted as its own origin; if a compartment wishes to send/receive data, it has to reduce/raise its label at the cost of becoming more restricted in the capability of reading/writing. Moreover, a compartment can impose a restriction on another compartment by labeling the transferred message (Sect. 3.1, Message label), and then the receiving compartment cannot reduce the origins in the message label from its own label even with relevant declassifying capability. We use the "addition" or "subtraction" operators to indicate the operation of raising or reducing the label and the "lock" symbol to represent the origin that cannot be removed because of the imposed *message label*.

As shown in Fig. 1, the initial label of the loaded *a.com* simply holds its own origin. In step 1, the cloud note raises its label to obtain the document (whose label is null) from *a.com*. In step 2, with reduction of the label, the cloud note can freely communicate with the remote server to upload the document. In step 3, malicious code in the cloud note wants to steal the user's password using *postMessage*; the password is labeled *a.com* to indicate that the data is sensitive to this origin and cannot be leaked from a browser by third-party contexts. Once receiving the labeled message, the cloud note cannot reduce the origin *a.com* from its label. Therefore, JSFfox can automatically deny the cloud note's further access to the network in step 4.

Third-party mashup. Mashup applications use content from more than one origins to create a single new service. For instance, there is a shopping guide platform which needs to reunite a user's purchase data hosted by *taobao.com* with a user's bank account statement hosted by *unionpay.com*. Apparently, both types of data are sensitive for a privacy-fixated user. However, the mashup increases the privacy disclosure risk, because the data from *taobao.com* might be exposed to *unionpay.com*, and vice-verse, and to any other remote origins.

Currently, to implement the mashup, the application code must bypass SOP to allow the sharing of data across domains by configured CORS policy. Note that when an origin receives sensitive data from another through XHR, it can freely do anything including exfiltrate that data from the browser. The key requirement of confinement for mashup is that untrusted code can make requests to multiple origins but once the sensitive data from those origins flows to it, then its privilege of communicating with untrusted origins must be restricted.

Untrusted third-party library. To conveniently build applications, third-party libraries such as *jQuery*, make a great difference for developers. If a developer purely imports a third-party library into a page that possesses sensitive data, there is no confinement to the untrusted library because of the absence of isolation. However, we cannot isolate third-party library into the isolated compartment, as we can do so in the cloud note example, since a library generally possesses the privilege of sensitive operations of the entire page such as DOM manipulation, event handling, and XHR.

The critical requirement is to achieve the isolation of an untrusted library without affecting functional operations. Besides, JSFfox needs to support the capability of granting and restricting privilege. For example, a page should be able to create a compartment, confer its privilege (e.g., importing *jQuery* code into an untrusted page, sending network requests to a wider web) on that compartment, and then, be confined, resulting in the loss of that privilege.

Currently, a library generally imports another untrusted library to reuse provided functionality. Therefore, JSFfox needs to support the multi-level compartment confinement (i.e., one trusted context confines an untrusted one which in turn confines a further untrusted one).

3   System Design

In this section, we first detail JSFfox's label-based policies, and then, outline how to assign and enforce policies.

3.1   Policy Specification

In JSFfox, each browser component is associated with an information-flow label, which specifies the allowed flows of information between components. JSFfox introduces two different granularities of information-flow labels, both of which appear in the third-party service example in Fig. 1. A *context label* consists of basic labels and a capability label, representing the privilege of all data within the context. When a context sends sensitive data to another, it can use a *message label* to track that data and confine the potentially untrusted receiving context.

Basic label. Each context possesses two kinds of basic labels: secrecy (S) and integrity (I). If a secrecy tag, for example, identified as $a.com^2$, belongs to S, then JSFfox supposes that the context has observed the data from the origin *a.com*. For integrity, if I contains an integrity tag written with `localStorage`, then the privilege of accessing *localStorage* has been granted to that context.

Capability label. To make up for the static nature of the basic label, JSFfox introduces the capability label, denoted as O, which has three kinds of special tags; $t+$ for endorsement; $t-$ for declassification; and $t_1 \rightarrow t_2$ for reclassification.

A context with the endorsement capability as $t+ \in O$ enables itself to add tag t to its basic labels. For secrecy, endorsement lets a context expand its secrecy label to enhance the privilege receiving data from other origins. For integrity, it lets a context access the sensitive resource relevant to the tag t.

Declassification is a powerful (and dangerous) operation, which gives a context the capability of subtracting the relevant tags from its secrecy label.

---

[2] For clarity, we use `a.com` as the hostname-based tag; while the complete tag certainly include the scheme and port.

A context holding the declassification capability might narrow its secrecy label to communicate with wider contexts and servers. Meanwhile, declassification is necessary because some provided services need to transfer the obtained secrets to arbitrary web pages to achieve specific functionality.

We describe the third-party service application as a typical example, in Sect. 2.2. This application should have the a.com- capability for uploading the document obtained from a.com. Without declassification, the tag a.com in the cloud note's label would cause the label check to fail since that tag is not in secrecy label of network channel to the remote server. With declassification, however, the cloud note can freely deal with the sensitive data from a.com (e.g., password, cookies, etc.), including disclosing the data to untrusted origins. Therefore, the declassification must be judiciously assigned, and even when necessary, it must be confined. However, such confinement is not supplied in the existing coarse-grained systems [5,20].

Reclassification is a weaker form of declassification. The $t_1 \rightarrow t_2$ reclassification tag only enables the context to transform tag t_1 into t_2 in secrecy label.

Context label. In JSFfox, labeled contexts directly extend browsing contexts in form of iframes, pages, etc. A context label specifies the security policy for all data within the context, which JSFfox enforces by tracking the information flow to and from other contexts and servers. In general, a *context label*, written with *(S,I,O)*, consists of a secrecy label *S*, an integrity label *I*, and a capability label *O*. To realize label-based policies, JSFfox's enforcement only permits interactions between contexts and servers whose labels are, at least, restricted. Ignoring capability labels, a sender can communicate with a receiver only when $S_{sender} \subseteq S_{receiver}$ (i.e., the receiver should at least know all secrets of the sender) and $I_{sender} \supseteq I_{receiver}$ (i.e., the sender should at least have all permissions of the receiver).

A context can voluntarily raise and reduce its basic labels based only on its capability label. To achieve an information transmission, the receiver raises it secrecy label with corresponding endorsement tags, while the sender narrows its secrecy label by declassification and expands its integrity label by endorsement. Naturally, the receiver becomes more restricted in its capability of sending messages and the sender's capability of accepting information is limited as well.

To support the multi-level contexts confinement discussed in Sect. 2.2, a labeled context can create additional labeled sub-contexts in the form of iframes, workers, etc. Thus this permits developers to isolate the code of different levels of trustworthiness within the same page into isolated compartments. Certainly, child contexts should not exceed the privilege of their parent, otherwise they can probably reveal secret data. Therefore, when a child context is created, its initial label should either be specified by the parent and must be more limiting or directly inherit the current label of parent.

Web developers can create two categories of labeled contexts. The first one is for the standard compartments in the form of pages, workers, iframes, etc. Inspired by TreeHouse [14], the second category of labeled context is in the form of a lightweight worker (*LWorker*), which we use in the untrusted third-party library example for isolating the trusted code, from the untrusted jQuery library. Different from normal workers [25], *LWorker* runs in the same thread as the parent, sharing its event loop. JSFfox benefits from that sharing which permits the child worker to freely access the DOM of the parent.

Message label. To track the flow of sensitive data and guarantee the secure declassification, we introduce the *message label*, which is bound with the payload of an individual inter-context message. The payload takes the form of a serialized immutable object of type Blob [24]. JSFfox allows the developers to specify the message label which will be attached to a message Blob being transferred between contexts.

A *message label* simply in the form of a secrecy label indicates that the encapsulated data is sensitive to the origins in the label, and cannot be disclosed by any other untrusted third-party context. To prevent overuse of the message label, any message label should be as or more limiting than the current secrecy label of the sending context.

A sender can impose a *message label* on a receiver by utilizing provided *labeledMessage* API. When the labeled message is accepted, the tags in receiver's secrecy label that belong to the message label is locked, which means those tags cannot be removed by de- or reclassification operations. In the third-party service example as discussed in Sect. 2.2, after receiving the password labeled with `a.com`, the third-party context even with relevant declassification `a.com-`, cannot remove that tag to issue network requests.

3.2 Policy Assignment

JSFfox provides two methods, of different priorities, to allocate labels. The high priority method is the API offered by JSFfox, which can help developers freely customize the security policies for their applications.

JSFfox also provides the second method, with low priority, in which labels are automatically derived from the annotated policy (e.g., CSP, permissions). For example, if the browser loads *a.com*, and its annotated CSP permits third-party content only from *trust.com*, then *a.com*'s label might be:

$$S = \{\texttt{a.com}\}, \quad I = \{\}, \quad O = \{\texttt{a.com+}, \texttt{ network+}, \texttt{ a.com} \rightarrow \texttt{trust.com}\}$$

It is worth mentioning that JSFfox automatically formulates the labels for the static and passive components that have no attached capability labels, such as the APIs for accessing browser storage and network channels. Their secrecy labels might rely on the parameters of the API invocation (e.g., hostname of accessing site), while their integrity labels might correspond to the permissions with which they are protected. For example, the label of the API for accessing the network of origin *a.com* might be $S = \{\texttt{a.com}\}$, $I = \{\texttt{network}\}$.

3.3 Policy Enforcement

Whenever a cross-compartment communication occurs, all relevant labels will be checked by the policy enforcement functionality. Consider the example that a sender wants to send message to a receiver. We assume the sender's label as (S_1, I_1, O_1), the receiver's label as (S_2, I_2, O_2), and the transferred message's label as (S_m). The communication should be permitted only if all the following conditions are satisfied; (1) the sender holds an S_1' which is obtained by applying declassification to S_1 as permitted by O_1, and the receiver holds an S_2' which is obtained by raising S_2 through endorsement defined by O_2, such that $S_1' \subseteq S_2'$; S_m should belong to S_1'; (2) the sender holds an I_1' which is obtained by applying endorsement capabilities to I_1 in O_1, and $I_1' \supseteq I_2$. After the success of communication, the receiver's secrecy label will become S_2' and all the tags in the subset (which is equivalent to S_m) of S_2', as discussed before, will be locked.

4   Applications

In this section, we demonstrate how to implement secure versions of the applications discussed in Sect. 2.2.

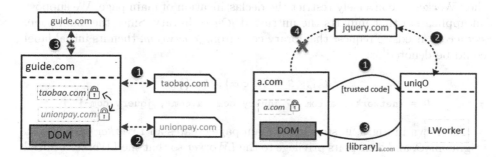

Fig. 2. Third-party mashup under JSFfox

Fig. 3. Untrusted third-party library under JSFfox

Third-party mashup. Due to the requirement of sharing data across domains, mashup applications rely on CORS for issuing cross-origin requests. However, the whitelist-based confinement provided by CORS is insufficient, because once the data is received, the requesting mashup can disclose that data at will. Unlike the all-or-nothing fashion in CORS, reclassification enables a context to bypass the SOP by providing a more sophisticated way to restrict the communication privilege of that context. We assume a shopping guide website, say *guide.com*, utilizing the authorized read-only API, separately exposed by *guide.com* and *unionpay.com* to access a user's purchase data and bank account. Since *guide.com* requires issuing cross-domain network requests, its initial label is denoted as:

$$S = \{\texttt{guide.com}\}, \quad I = \{\}, \quad O = \{\texttt{network+},$$
$$\texttt{taobao.com+, unionpay.com+, guide.com-, unionpay.com} \rightleftharpoons \texttt{taobao.com}\}$$

As shown in Fig. 2, in step 1, as the declassification `guide.com-`, and endorsement `network+` and `taobao.com+`, are assigned to *guide.com*, it can make a network request to origin *taobao.com* via XHR. In step 2, after receiving the response from *taobao.com*, the mashup can convert the secrecy label by using the reclassification `taobao.com → unionpay.com`, and then, communicate with the origin *unionpay.com*. Due to the restriction of reclassification, the mashup cannot subtract both tags `taobao.com` and `unionpay.com` simultaneously from its secrecy label. Thus, any message being sent from this mashup to any origin other than *taobao.com* and *unionpay.com* will not succeed (as shown in step 3).

In contrast to simply applying CORS in the all-or-nothing fashion, in JSFfox, the *guide.com* and *unionpay.com* do not need to trust the mashup—even if the mashup has already seen the secrets, it cannot arbitrarily leak the secrets.

Untrusted third-party library. To support the confinement for an untrusted third-party library, JSFfox enables the page being protected to create a specific compartment called LWorker, to isolate the trusted code from that page which is tightly coupled with the library. Then, the message label is utilized to enable the LWorker to conversely restrict the declassification of main page. We suppose an application that imports the untrusted *jQuery* library. Since the main page, say *a.com*, needs to request the library code from *jquery.com*, then its initial label could be denoted as:

$$L_{mp}: \ S = \{\texttt{a.com}\}, \ I = \{\}$$
$$O = \{\texttt{network+}, \ \texttt{a.com} \rightarrow \texttt{jquery.com}, \ \texttt{a.com+}, \ \texttt{jquery.com-}\}$$

As shown in Fig. 3, in step 1, the main page creates an *LWorker* with a fresh origin *uniqO*, and confers its privilege to the *LWorker* so that the *LWorker*'s initial label equals to L_{mp}. In step 2, the trusted *LWorker* transforms its basic label with the reclassification `a.com → jquery.com` and endorsement `network+`, and then, requests to *jquery.com* to download the untrusted *jQuery* code. In step 3, the *LWorker* then uses the declassification `jquery.com-` and endorsement `a.com+` to inject into the main page with the untrusted *jQuery* code encapsulated in the message labeled with `a.com`. After the labeled message is received, the tag `a.com` in secrecy label of the main page is locked, and then that secrecy label cannot be transformed into `jquery.com` by using the reclassification `a.com → jquery.com`, which prohibits the untrusted jQuery library in main page to send the data to the untrusted origins (as shown in step 4).

Note that after loading the untrusted library which is associated with the *message label* `a.com`, the main page becomes untrusted but completely confined, while the *LWorker* containing the trusted code can still access the DOM of the main page, as well as communicate with the wider web.

5   Implementation

We implement JSFfox based on Firefox version 36.0a1. As we have discussed in Sect. 3, the implementation of JSFfox demands to modify Firefox in order to support two main mechanisms: (1) assignment of labels; (2) enforcement for protect access to sensitive API and communication.

Assignment of labels. Since enforcement granularity of JSFfox works at the context lever, we can develop a new DOM-level API to specify and assign labels for the Gecko, without any modifications to the browser's JavaScript engine.

Table 1. Existing browser mechanisms modified for enforcement

Channel	Mechanism
Intra-browser communication	Cross-compartment wrappers
XHR	CSP + DOM interception
Content loading	CSP
Browser storage	SOP + sandbox (CSP)

Intra-browser enforcement. Compartments are the foundation for Gecko's existing isolation model [26]. Gecko guarantees that JavaScript code running in a given compartment is only allowed to access objects in the same compartment. When code in compartment A tries to access an object in compartment B, Gecko gives it a cross-compartment wrapper, which is a real Proxy-Object with access-methods needed for security restrictions.

Table 1 shows existing browser mechanisms modified for enforcement of JSF-fox. Since JSFfox's implementation shares many features with existing isolation model, we depend upon cross-compartment wrappers to mediate the intra-browser communication. We modify all wrappers and give priority to JSFfox for enforcing relevant labels, which guarantees that all cross-compartment communication is prioritized when it is confined by JSFfox's policies.

Browser-server enforcement. As shown in Table 1, CSP is the main confinement mechanism for browser-server communication. While CSP helps mediate external communication by restricting the source and destination of web content, its whitelist-style is insufficient for supporting our flexible policies. To adapt to the dynamically changing labels, whenever a compartment wants to issue a network request, we customize a new CSP policy for that compartment according to its present label. For example, we assume an active compartment with origin *a.com* holds the secrecy label S = {a.com, ad.com}, while it has no capability of declassifying the tag a.com. If that compartment makes a network request to *ad.com*, JSFfox will automatically set the CSP directives to "none", Thus, preventing this network communication.

Browser storage enforcement. As shown in Table 1, we rely on the sandbox directive to restrict access to browser storage (e.g., cookies, localStorage).

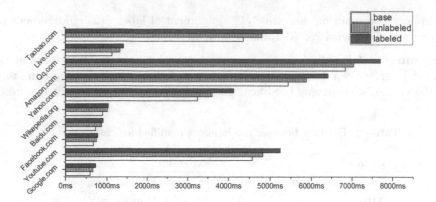

Fig. 4. Macro-benchmark for page loads of the main pages of the top 10 Alexa

6   Evaluation

We conduct all experiments on three setups; Firefox without JSFfox (base); Firefox with disabled JSFfox (unlabeled); and Firefox with enabled JSFfox (labeled). Our evaluation comprises macro-benchmark for page loads, micro-benchmark of API functions, and benchmarks of motivating examples, all of which are measured on a 4-core i7-6700HQ with 8 GB of RAM, running Linux 3.10.

6.1   Macro-Benchmark of Page Loads

We evaluate the page loads for Alexa's global top-10 sites [2] to measure the latency of page loads, as well as to verify the compatibility of JSFfox. Since we cannot modify those web applications to assign labels through JSFfox's API, we manually generate CSPs for the sites that are not configured with the underlying CSP to allow them to completely load. To simulate a typical browsing environment, caching is enabled during browsing but cleared between different runs. Figure 4 shows that, by setting Firefox with JSFfox enabled, the overhead added by JSFfox to the page loads at an average of 19.9%, and the main cost drives from the label checking that occurs when a page is loaded. Note

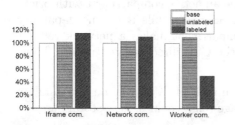

Fig. 5. Latency for communication

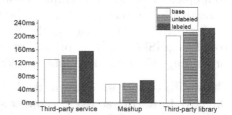

Fig. 6. Benchmarks of applications

that popular web sites constantly modify the content, which brings in inevitable imprecision on the measurements.

6.2   Micro-Benchmark of API Functions

Operations of label. We measure the latency of setting/getting the current label and checking the labels, respectively. The results show that the cost of setting/getting the label is on the magnitude of one microsecond, while the operation of checking labels is slower with 7 ms on average.

Communications. We evaluate the round-trip communication latency across iframes, workers, as well to the network. As shown in Fig. 5, compared with legacy Firefox (base), for the iframe communication, JSFfox incurs a slowdown of 15.3%; for the network communication, it incurs a slowdown of 9.6%. However, *LWorker* runs faster than the normal worker on legacy Firefox (base), with 48.3%, which is because the LWorker shares an OS thread and event loop with its parent.

DOM. We also measure the performance of core functionalities of DOM, such as querying, traversing the DOM, by executing the Dromaeo benchmark suite [18]. The result shows the overhead added by JSFfox averages 4%, and the maximum is less than 7%.

6.3   Benchmarks of Applications

Figure 6 shows the performance of applications, and we detail it as follows.

Third-party service. We implement an application which incorporates a third-party service. This third-party service being isolated into an iframe, simulates the main functions of the cloud note service, including capturing the content, and uploading obtained data. On JSFfox (labeled), the workload completes in 156 ms; on the legacy Firefox (base), it completes in 131 ms. The slowdown mainly derives from the processing of the labeled message.

Third-party mashup. We implement a simple third-party mashup application which issues AJAX requests to two separate origins, each of which produces a response containing a 36-byte JSON object. The average execution time is 68 ms on JSFfox (labeled), which is 11 ms slower than the unconfined version running on legacy Firefox (base). The slowdown is caused by the operation for changing the current label which requires re-computing CSP.

Untrusted third-party Library. We evaluate the load time of a shopping application which separately imports a *jQuery* library and a library which traverses the DOM to add dynamic effects to buttons. The latter library attempts to disclose the page's content via XHR. We use an *LWorker* to encapsulate the trusted code of the application, and consider the rest code staying in the main page as untrusted. The average latency on JSFfox (labeled) is 226 ms, 23 ms slower than that on the legacy Firefox (base). In summary, JSFfox prevents the privacy leakage with negligible overhead.

7   Related Work

The existing JavaScript confinement systems based on information flow control can be classified as fine-grained and coarse-grained. We compare JSFfox with these two categories of related systems.

Coarse-grained IFC. JSFfox shares many features with existing coarse-grained IFC systems. COWL [20] proposes a label-based mandatory access control model for today's browsers. Aside from the differences in the policy language, JSFfox additionally specifies the least privilege for each compartment by defining its capability label, and explores the confinement for browser extensions.

Recently, Lujo Bauer et al. proposed an approach for enforcing flexible information flow policies on the Chromium [5], which can encompass a wide range of browser features. However, that approach cannot confine the declassification which the authors mentioned is dangerous, while JSFfox introduces the message label to guarantee the secure declassification. In addition to assigning labels based on annotated policies as that approach did, JSFfox provides substantial APIs for developers to customize the security policy for their applications. Besides, JSFfox supports the confinements for a wider range of applications, due to the distinctive confinement to third-party libraries.

Fine-grained IFC. These approaches investigate prevention of privacy leakage at per-object granularity, which is easier to confine misbehavior of untrusted libraries. FlowFox [9] implements a fine-grained information flow control mechanism based on the technique of secure multi-execution (SME) [10]. SME operates the program at different security levels and strictly manages communication between them, which ensures that no secret from a high level context can flow into a low-level context. JSFlow [12] tracks fine-grained information flow by executing JavaScript in an interpreter written in JavaScript, which makes JSFlow slower by two orders of magnitude on average than a fully JITed JavaScript engine.

While fine-grained IFC systems operate at much finer granularity than JSFfox, they need to track every piece of JavaScript instructions and require massive modifications to the JavaScript interpreter. JSFfox only enforces label-based policies when cross-compartment operations are made, so it needs to make no modifications to the JavaScript engine and only adds negligible overhead to cross-compartment operations. Consequently, JSFfox is not only more efficient, but also relatively more straightforward to be added to the legacy browsers.

Isolation and safe sub-languages. Many systems based on isolation and safe sub-languages have been implemented to offer web security, including Caja [8], ConScript [15], WebJail [21], TreeHouse [14], JSand [1], and Embassies [13].

These systems generally aim at mediating security-sensitive operations of JavaScript, such as accessing the DOM, and issuing the network request. Compared to JSFfox, they generally impose the most restrictions in an all-or-nothing fashion, and are thus not suitable for building some of the applications which rely on more flexible policies (e.g., the third-party mashup example).

8 Conclusion

Web applications currently incorporate third-party content from multiple origins which are not equally trustworthy. The confinement for untrusted code in the status-quo browser security mechanisms is insufficient, thus, putting users' privacy at risk.

In this paper, we propose JSFfox, a novel information-flow control system that confines untrusted JavaScript in web browsers. JSFfox provides developers with flexibility in constructing applications which incorporate untrusted third-party code, while preserving the privacy of users. Moreover, our positive experience of implementing secure versions of three types of typical web applications which cannot be enhanced by current web browsers by keeping enough privacy for users at negligible cost in performance, suggests that JSFfox holds potential to be a practical IFC system for preserving privacy of users in web environment.

Acknowledgement. This work is supported by National Natural Science Foundation of China under grant No.61370106, and National High-tech R&D Program of China (863 Program) under grant No.2015AA016001.

References

1. Agten, P., Van Acker, S., Brondsema, Y., Phung, P.H., Desmet, L., Piessens, F.: JSand: complete client-side sandboxing of third-party JavaScript without browser modifications. In: Proceedings of the 28th Annual Computer Security Applications Conference, pp. 1–10. ACM (2012)
2. Alexa: The alexa top 500 sites on the web (2016). http://www.alexa.com/topsites
3. Barth, A., Jackson, C., Mitchell, J.C.: Robust defenses for cross-site request forgery. In: Proceedings of the 15th ACM Conference on Computer and Communications Security, pp. 75–88. ACM (2008)
4. Bashir, M.A., Arshad, S., Robertson, W., Wilson, C.: Tracing information flows between ad exchanges using retargeted ads. In: Proceedings of the 25th USENIX Security Symposium, pp. 481–496 (2016)
5. Bauer, L., Cai, S., Jia, L., Passaro, T., Stroucken, M., Tian, Y.: Run-time monitoring and formal analysis of information flows in chromium. In: Proceedings of the 22nd Annual Network and Distributed System Security Symposium (2015)
6. Bauer, L., Cai, S., Jia, L., Passaro, T., Tian, Y.: Analyzing the dangers posed by chrome extensions. In: Proceedings of the 2nd IEEE Conference on Communications and Network Security, pp. 184–192. IEEE (2014)
7. Boda, K., Földes, Á.M., Gulyás, G.G., Imre, S.: User tracking on the web via cross-browser fingerprinting. In: Laud, P. (ed.) NordSec 2011. LNCS, vol. 7161, pp. 31–46. Springer, Heidelberg (2012). doi:10.1007/978-3-642-29615-4_4
8. Caja, G.: A source-to-source translator for securing javascript- based web content (2014). http://code.google.com/p/google-caja/
9. De Groef, W., Devriese, D., Nikiforakis, N., Piessens, F.: Flowfox: a web browser with flexible and precise information flow control. In: Proceedings of the 19th ACM Conference on Computer and Communications Security, pp. 748–759. ACM (2012)
10. Devriese, D., Piessens, F.: Noninterference through secure multi-execution. In: Proceedings of the 31st IEEE Symposium on Security and Privacy, pp. 109–124 (2010)

11. Martani, F.: XSS, passwords theft using JavaScript (2015). http://www.martani.net/2009/08/xss-steal-passwords-using-javascript.html
12. Hedin, D., Birgisson, A., Bello, L., Sabelfeld, A.: JSFlow: tracking information flow in JavaScript and its APIs. In: Proceedings of the 29th Annual ACM Symposium on Applied Computing, pp. 1663–1671. ACM (2014)
13. Howell, J., Parno, B., Douceur, J.R.: Embassies: radically refactoring the web. In: Proceedings of the 10th USENIX Symposium on Networked Systems Design and Implementation, pp. 529–545 (2013)
14. Ingram, L., Walfish, M.: Treehouse: JavaScript sandboxes to help web developers help themselves. In: Proceedings of the 23rd USENIX Conference on Annual Technical Conference, pp. 13–13. USENIX Association (2012)
15. Meyerovich, L.A., Livshits, B.: Conscript: specifying and enforcing fine-grained security policies for JavaScript in the browser. In: Proceedings of the 31st IEEE Symposium on Security and Privacy, pp. 481–496. IEEE (2010)
16. Nikiforakis, N., Invernizzi, L., Kapravelos, A., Van Acker, S., Joosen, W., Kruegel, C., Piessens, F., Vigna, G.: You are what you include: large-scale evaluation of remote JavaScript inclusions. In: Proceedings of the 19th ACM Conference on Computer and Communications Security, pp. 736–747. ACM (2012)
17. Nikiforakis, N., Meert, W., Younan, Y., Johns, M., Joosen, W.: SessionShield: lightweight protection against session hijacking. In: Erlingsson, Ú., Wieringa, R., Zannone, N. (eds.) ESSoS 2011. LNCS, vol. 6542, pp. 87–100. Springer, Heidelberg (2011). doi:10.1007/978-3-642-19125-1_7
18. Resig, J.: Dromaeo JavaScript performance test suite (2016). http://dromaeo.com/
19. Son, S., Shmatikov, V.: The postman always rings twice: attacking and defending postmessage in html5 websites. In: Proceedings of the 20th Annual Network and Distributed System Security Symposium (2013)
20. Stefan, D., Yang, E.Z., Marchenko, P., Russo, A., Herman, D., Karp, B., Mazieres, D.: Protecting users by confining JavaScript with cowl. In: Proceedings of the 11th USENIX Symposium on Operating Systems Design and Implementation, pp. 131–146 (2014)
21. Van Acker, S., De Ryck, P., Desmet, L., Piessens, F., Joosen, W.: WebJail: least-privilege integration of third-party components in web mashups. In: Proceedings of the 27th Annual Computer Security Applications Conference, pp. 307–316. ACM (2011)
22. W3C: Content security policy level 3 (2016). http://www.w3.org/TR/CSP/
23. W3C: Cross-origin resource sharing (2014). http://www.w3.org/TR/cors/
24. W3C: HTML5 web messaging. http://www.w3.org/TR/webmessaging/. Accessed 4 Apr 2015
25. W3C: Web workers (2015). http://www.w3.org/TR/workers/
26. Wagner, G., Gal, A., Wimmer, C., Eich, B., Franz, M.: Compartmental memory management in a modern web browser. ACM SIGPLAN Notices 46(11), 119–128 (2011)
27. Yip, A., Narula, N., Krohn, M., Morris, R.: Privacy-preserving browser-side scripting with BFlow. In: Proceedings of the 4th ACM European Conference on Computer Systems, pp. 233–246. ACM (2009)

Malware Detection

PriMal: Cloud-Based Privacy-Preserving Malware Detection

Hao Sun[1], Jinshu Su[1,2(✉)], Xiaofeng Wang[1], Rongmao Chen[1],
Yujing Liu[1], and Qiaolin Hu[3]

[1] College of Computer, National University of Defense Technology, Changsha, China
haosunlight@163.com, sjs@nudt.edu.cn
[2] Science and Technology on Parallel and Distributed Laboratory,
National University of Defense Technology, Changsha, China
[3] Air Force Early Warning Academy, Wuhan, China

Abstract. The ongoing threat of malware has raised significant security and privacy concerns. Motivated by these issues, the cloud-based detection system is of increasing interest to detect large-scale malware as it releases the burden of client and improves the detection efficiency. However, most existing cloud-based detection systems overlook the data privacy protection during the malware detection. In this paper, we propose a cloud-based anti-malware system named PriMal, which protects the data privacy of both the cloud server and the client, while still achieves usable detection performance. In the PriMal, a newly designed private malware signature set intersection (PMSSI) protocol is involved to enable both the cloud server and client to achieve malware confirmation without revealing the data privacy in semi-honest model. Moreover, we propose the relevant signature engine to reduce the detection range and overhead. The experimental results show that PriMal offers a practical approach to achieve both usable malware detection and strong data privacy preservation.

Keywords: Privacy preservation · Oblivious transfer · Cloud-based · Malware detection

1 Introduction

In recent years, the prevalence of malicious software (a.k.a. malware) is a growing threat to the security and privacy of our computers and networks. Statistical analysis from Symantec shows that the total volume of malware in 2015 was around 2.1 billion, and was 25.3% more than that in the preceding year [1]. This explosive growth indicates that it is of significant interest to provide a scalable and efficient approach to detect the large-scale malware.

Signature-based detections have been de facto most widely used solutions against malware for decades [16]. Many anti-malware systems still rely primarily on pattern matching for screening and analyzing suspicious contents [5]. Due

© Springer International Publishing AG 2017
J. Pieprzyk and S. Suriadi (Eds.): ACISP 2017, Part II, LNCS 10343, pp. 153–172, 2017.
DOI: 10.1007/978-3-319-59870-3_9

to the quantity of signatures growing with the volume of malware, current prevalent anti-malware solutions [4,14,19] adopt the cloud services to achieve high-performance service and lightweight engine. In these cloud-based systems, different types of detection agents are centralized into the cloud server to provide the security detection as a service. To detect the suspicious files, the client generally needs to upload certain information about the files, such as bare contents or hash checksums (e.g., MD5, SHA-1), and receives an assessment indicating that whether the file is infected or not.

Unfortunately, most existing cloud-based detection systems overlook the data privacy protection, which is a critical issue due to the untrustworthy cloud environment. Apparently, uploading bare contents will result in some important information(location, password) directly exposed. Moreover, the security of MD5 and SHA-1 hashes have been compromised by feasible collision attacks [18,20].

For cloud-based malware detection, we focus on the privacy requirements of two traditional parties: **cloud server** and **client**. Four different levels are listed to indicate the gradually increasing strength of data privacy protection:

- **Level I: One-Party Protection (OPP).** In this level, only one party's privacy is protected. The other party without protection is designed to expose its privacy information (signatures or file contents) in the system. We consider this level as the lowest requirement for privacy protection.
- **Level II: Two-Party Weak Protection (TPWP).** In this level, both parties are considered to be trusted to each other. The private information can be transmitted between two parties but should not be exposed to the third party. Certain mechanisms, such as encryption or transformation, are needed to prevent the eavesdropping.
- **Level III: Two-Party Strong Protection (TPSP).** In this level, the privacy requirements are considered in semi-honest model[1]. It means the parties are honest but curious, i.e., they honestly follow the system specification, but try to learn additional information from the communication [10]. Therefore, the secure system in this level should be resistant to the curious attempts from either party.
- **Level IV: Two-Party Complete Protection (TPCP).** In this level, the privacy of both parties is protected in malicious model. It means the parties run any arbitrary strategy in an attempt to break the protocol and dig the privacy information.

Motivations of This Work. To well address the aforementioned security and privacy concerns, an ideal cloud-based system should perform well with respect to both the malware detection and the data privacy protection for both server and client. Hence, there are two main motivations which inspire our design:

(1) Privacy preservation. Most related cloud-based anti-malware systems focus on the detection performance and their privacy preservation need to be

---

[1] In the field of secure computation, the semi-honest model is not the strongest model but it is widely accepted and used in many applications. Hence, we conclude the protection is strong as compared to Level II.

strengthened. In SplitScreen [4], the client does not need to upload their files but the cloud server is designed to deliver parts of the signature database to the client which also induces disclosing of server privacy. As defined above, SplitScreen meets the requirement of Level I. RScam [19] satisfies Level II because only hash locations of suspicious information, rather than bare contents, are transmitted between two parties. However, a curious server could retrieve the file contents via detection results without the permission or awareness of client.

Our proposed design should meet the privacy requirements of Level III. The privacy concerns should be considered for both client and cloud server. The important data of client should not be exposed as reported in [2,12] and the signature databases are proprietary assets which should not be known by untrusted clients [12]. It is worth mentioning that the commercial cooperations which many security vendors voluntarily share the signature databases with each other to improve detection do not belong to the issues of privacy leakage.

(2) Scalability. Recently, several similar kinds of research [12,13,17] are trying to provide secure and usable cloud-based middlebox services (network intrusion detection, web firewall application and so on) by applying privacy-preserving mechanisms over untrusted cloud environment. Nevertheless, they all encounter non-trivial challenges of practical performance when taking the data privacy protection into consideration [21]. It may indicate that there is a strong tension between the efficiency and privacy of cloud-based services.

Our design aims at secure cloud-based malware detection and encounters more serious obstacles. Similar with prevalent cloud-based middlebox services [5,21], the scale of signature set we apply is also large (details are listed in Table 2). Moreover, the data to be detected are irregular in our application. There are no fixed tuples or offsets in file contents which mean the states to be checked are complicated and randomized. Hence, the detection range must be narrowed and the application of privacy-preserving mechanisms should be targeted.

Our Contributions. To achieve our design goals, we propose PriMal to provide cloud-based malware detection service with privacy preservation. Our central principle is *achieving practical and secure malware detection over unencrypted data*. In the following, we detail our contributions.

- Firstly, we adopt oblivious transfer (OT) [3,11], which is an important foundation for secure computation, as the crypto building block to assure privacy preservation. The core challenge of privacy-preserving malware detection is achieving exact pattern matching between the signatures from cloud server and the file contents from client without revealing any information (except that the client receives detection results[2]) about them to either party. Fortunately, OT is an appropriate and powerful tool for dealing with such challenge in secure computation. Based on the latest improvement of OT, we propose a novel privacy-preserving detection mechanism PMSSI, short for private mal-

---

[2] The cloud server has to ask for the permission of client if the detection results are needed to improve the security service.

Table 1. Comparison with existing malware detection systems

Systems	Privacy requirements			
	Level I: One-Party Protection	Level II: Two-Party Weak Protection	Level III: Two-Party Strong Protection	Level IV: Two-Party Complete Protection
ClamAV[a]	×	×	×	×
SplitScreen [4]	√	×	×	×
RScam [19]	√	√	×	×
PriMal	√	√	√	×

[a] ClamAV is a widely used open-source and host-based system for malware detection [6]. We implement a cloud version of it in our evaluation and set it as the baseline of our comparison.

ware signature set intersection. To the best of our knowledge, no previous work has implemented similar endeavor.

- Secondly, we construct an efficient filtering engine to achieve scalability with large-scale signatures and file contents. The engine extracts representative information to avoid directly encrypting and exposing the original data (signatures and file contents). The results contribute to the reduction of scanning range and detection consumption.
- Finally, we analyze PriMal theoretically and experimentally to demonstrate that it is practical to achieve both usable malware detection and strong privacy preservation in semi-honest model. Moreover, the detailed comparison in privacy requirements with existing malware detection systems is listed in Table 1.

2   Related Work

Malware detection based on signature remains important and technically reliable after decades of development in anti-malware industry. It is always utilized as a filter to rapidly distinguish the suspicion from large-scale contents. Nowadays, the cloud-based anti-malware systems become more and more widespread. They place different types of detection agents over the cloud server and offer security as a service. The cloud environment provides high-performance computation support to reduce the match consumption in malware scanning and largely lighten the resource burden on the client.

CloudAV [14] first puts forward the notion of cloud-based malware scanning in academic research and the authors apply their strategy to a mobile environment. It runs a local cloud service consists of heterogeneous anti-virus engines running in parallel virtual machines and uses an end-user agent to transfer suspicious files to the cloud server to be checked by all anti-virus engines. CloudAV

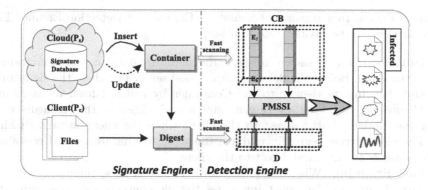

Fig. 1. The system architecture of PriMal

achieves high detection rate, yet obviously, exposes the sensitive data which compromise the privacy of users.

SplitScreen [4] implements a distributed anti-malware system to speed up the malware scanning. SplitScreen designs its first scanning mechanism based on bloom filter to perform slight comparisons with file data and reduce the size to be accurately matched. However, the server is designed to deliver parts of the signature database to the client which will cause the privacy leakage of the server. RScam [19] is a cloud-based anti-malware system which provides efficient security service and data privacy protection for resource-constrained devices. However, the untrusted of the cloud server has not been considered. Or rather, RScam can prevent the eavesdropping from the third party but cannot deal with the curious or malicious server, because the cloud server will know the file contents of client if the signature segments successfully match.

Recently, privacy-preserving mechanism starts to be applied to the untrusted cloud to solve the privacy issue of cloud-based services. The core challenge is how to achieve practical performance and strong security simultaneously. BlindBox [17] tries to enable deep packet inspection (DPI) services over encrypted HTTPS traffic. It protects the data by a strong privacy-preserving scheme but with limited application scenarios and prohibitive performance. An improved design [12] is proposed to extend BlindBox to support wider middlebox functionalities with the privacy-preserving premise. Several designs that aim at other middlebox applications, such as IDS [21] and Web Application Firewall [13], are proposed to guarantee the secure cloud-based services. Our proposed design which aims at malware detection encounters the homologous but more serious challenge (discussed in Sect. 1) as compared to these middlebox designs.

3   Overview of System Architecture

In this paper, we propose PriMal, a new cloud-based privacy-preserving anti-malware system to provide malware detection service and assure strong data privacy protection for both the cloud server and client. Figure 1 shows the overall design of PriMal that consists of Signature Engine and Detection Engine. The entire process can be divided into four steps:

(1) **Initialization.** As shown in Fig. 1, the signature databases are maintained in the cloud. Before the detection, the cloud server initializes the signatures and then inserts them into the Container by tailored hash mechanisms. Meanwhile, the cloud server generates a hash digest of the signature container and sends the digest to the client when the client installs PriMal. The cloud server regularly updates the signature databases and container and sends the updated digest to the client.

(2) **Fast Scanning.** When the client needs to detect files, three substeps are carried out. (1) The client initializes the file contents into the segments. (2) The client maps the file segments into bit vectors by the same hash mechanisms in **Initialization** and makes the comparison with the digest. It is noteworthy that the client considers each matched segment as the suspicious one and sifts out the unmatched segments. (3) The coordinates of suspicious segments in the digest are sent to the cloud server.

(3) **PMSSI.** Once the cloud server receives the suspicious coordinates, it will find the corresponding signature segments in Container. Then the PMSSI mechanism is called to offer exact matching between the signature segments and suspicious file segments in a privacy-preserving manner. After PMSSI, the client gets the matching results while the cloud server gets nothing.

(4) **Verification.** If the files are compromised by malware, the client will get the right results which mean the suspicious file segments successfully match with the signature segments. Otherwise, the client gets random and meaningless contents. Subsequent measures, such as deletion or isolation, can be taken according to the results.

4   Signature Engine

In this section, we introduce the details about signature engine based on ClamAV signature database which consists of MD5 signatures and string signatures. These signatures are unpacked and uncompressed by ClamAV engine before inserted into signature engine. Hence, the file contents in the client also need to be unpacked before malware detection.

Let DB be the signature databases managed in the cloud server P_S, F_C be the normal files stored in the client P_C. We describe the initialization method using the signatures in DB as a general example. The file contents should be initialized by the same method and parameters.

Considering signatures do not have a uniform length generally, we set a sliding window with the size of w to scan the signatures in DB. For an arbitrary signature X of length l, there will be a set of segments of length w-*byte* after initial scanning, namely, $X \rightarrow \{X_1, X_2, \ldots, X_{l-w+1}\}$. The value of w should be set deliberately and practically to reduce the false negative. According to statistics, for the databases of ClamAV (from 2009 to 2015), an average of 96%

signatures are MD5 signatures with constant 16 bytes and the rest are string signatures. Hence, we set $w = 16$ in the implementation and consider the signature whose length is less than 16 bytes as the short signature. The proportion of short signatures is at most 0.048% after initialization and it is evaluated as the false negative in Table 4.

Based on the latest efficient hash table design [7], we construct the signature engine which consists of a Container and a Digest (shown in Fig. 1) to improve efficiency and scalability. The basic infrastructure of the container is the H-way associated hash table with the size of M. Each element of the hash table is indicated by the bucket (CB) which contains b entries to store the hash of a signature segment. Meanwhile, the hash digest (D) is a bit vector which stands for the buckets are empty or not, with the value 0 or 1 respectively. Generally, each segment has two candidate buckets determined by two hash functions in the container, which means $H = 2$. In PriMal, we use one 2-universal hash function h and modulo(q) hash[3] function mh to generate two candidate locations for the segments. For instance, the first bucket location of X_1 is $l_1(X_1) = h(X_1) \in [M]$, the second one is $l_2(X_1) = (l_1 \oplus h(mh(X_1))) \in [M]$, and the value stored in either bucket is $mh(X_1)$.

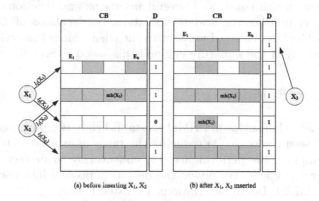

(a) before inserting X_1, X_2 (b) after X_1, X_2 inserted

Fig. 2. Illustration of insertion operation in signature engine

The basic operations of the engine are similar with the partial-key cuckoo hashing in [7], and the insertion operation is illustrated in Fig. 2. For X_1 that has not been inserted, firstly the two candidate bucket locations are computed, then if either l_1 or l_2 has vacant entries, $mh(X_1)$ will be added randomly to that bucket. If both candidate buckets of X_2 are full (all the entries are occupied, gray in Fig. 2), then one existing segment must be relocated. The victim segment X_3 is chosen randomly from the $2b$ entries and kicked out or displaced by X_2. Then X_3 will repeat the insertion operation and may kick out other victim segments until

---

[3] Modulo(q) hash function [9] randomly maps a byte to a class between 0 to $q - 1$, q is the power of 2 and smaller than 256.

a vacant entry is found or a maximum number of displacements is reached (e.g., displacement times $dt = 50$ in our implementation). If no vacant entry is found, then the engine is too full to insert and the insertion is considered as a failure. In the evaluation of PriMal, we adjust reasonable parameters of the signature engine to generate fewest failures. In addition, the digest D is maintained along with the operations in CB. Initially, CB contains no element and all the bits in D are 0. After a successful insertion in an empty bucket, the value of the corresponding bit in D is set to be 1. Any subsequent insertions to that bucket will not change the bit value.

The lookup process is simple and efficient. Given a segment X, the two candidate bucket locations are firstly computed, then $2b$ corresponding entries are matched with $mh(X)$ to check if X has been inserted. Moreover, the signature engine also supports efficient deletion operations. For the signature segment X that is proved to be incorrect or reduplicate for malware description, the cloud server call delete operation to get rid of X from the engine. The lookup process is executed and if any entry matches in any bucket, $mh(X)$ will be deleted from that entry. If the deletion makes the bucket empty, the corresponding bit in D should be set to 0. The cloud server needs to periodically update the signature database with the increment of signature quantity. The update is a set of operations which consists of several insertions and deletions. When the cloud server accomplishes the update operation, the locations of D where the corresponding bits have changed are sent to the client. More theoretical analysis about the accuracy of the signature engine is discussed in Sect. 6.

5   Detection Engine

The design of detection engine in PriMal is established in two purposes we desired for usable and secure service: (1) reducing the range of exact match in malware detection to improve the performance; (2) endeavoring to protect the privacy of cloud server and client. We divide the detection process into two steps: fast scanning and PMSSI. Detail descriptions are listed below.

5.1   Fast Scanning

In the PriMal system, the signature engine, which consists of the CB and D, is designed to store the hash value of signatures and serve for detection. The digest D is the crux of fast scanning process which is stored in the client when the system is firstly installed. As aforementioned in Sect. 4, the files of client need to be initialized with the sliding window with length w as same as the signatures. Let F_{seg} be the set of file segments after initialization, fast scanning is executed on the client side, and the purpose is picking out the suspicious set of segments F_{sus} and the corresponding location set L_{sus} by the digest D.

Algorithm 1 presents details of fast scanning. At the beginning, we divide the F_{seg} into several regular subsets of size n. It means that the detection engine detects at most n file segments one time. For each segment f in F_i, we calculate

---

Algorithm 1. Fast Scanning

Input: file segments set F_{seg}, digest D
Output: suspicious segment set F_{sus} and bucket location set L_{sus}
1: $F_{sus}, L_{sus} = \emptyset$
2: The size of F_{seg} is various, so we divide F_{seg} into set $\{F_1, \cdots, F_i, \cdots\}$, n is the uniform size of F_i.
3: **while** each $f \in F_i$ **do**
4:     calculate $mh(f)$, $l_1(f)$ and $l_2(f)$;
5:     **if** $D[l_1(f)] == 1$ or $D[l_2(f)] == 1$ **then**
6:         insert $mh(f)$ into F_{sus};
7:         insert $l_\alpha(f)$ into L_{sus}; //α is the matched location, can be 1 or 2 or both
8:     **end if**
9: **end while**
10: send L_{sus} to the cloud server

---

its modular hash and the two candidate bucket locations, and then we check the corresponding bits value in D. The hash functions which are utilized to generate D bring no false negative [7], so if the bit value is 0, it means the segment is trustworthy. However, any match (value is 1) means the segment is suspicious because we cannot confirm which candidate bucket the segment is finally inserted into. Both the matched location and the modular hash stored in it should be inserted into the corresponding suspicious set.

When the scanning of all segments finishes, we randomly permute the elements in F_{sus} and L_{sus} simultaneously to prevent the matched segments from leaking information about the other segments in F_{seg}. It is noteworthy that the client can privately maintenance the mapping relationship of file names and segments in order to easily find the victim files after the whole detection. Fast scanning is easy to be applied in the client due to its lightweight and it can largely reduce the number of file segments to be further confirmed. After fast scanning, the client sends the L_{sus} to the cloud server which can also cut down the communication overhead. Figure 3 illustrates the process of fast scanning.

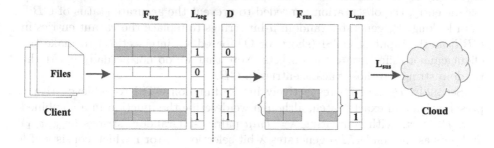

Fig. 3. Illustration of fast scanning

5.2   PMSSI Mechanism

Before we present the PMSSI mechanism, let us briefly introduce our crypto building block: oblivious transfer (OT) [3,11] which is an extremely powerful tool in privacy-preserving computation. In a classical OT, a sender with a pair of input strings (x_0, x_1) communicates with a receiver with the input of a choice bit $\alpha \in \{0, 1\}$. The result is the receiver gets x_α without getting anything about $x_{1-\alpha}$, and the sender gets nothing about α. Generally, an OT protocol is denoted as OT_l^m which means the sender has m pairs l-bit strings $(x_{j,0}, x_{j,1})(j \in [m])$ and the receive has an m-bit selection vector $\mathbf{r} = (r_1, \cdots, r_m)$. After protocol execution, the receiver gets x_{j,r_j}.

The first efficient OT-extension [11] is proposed to solve the inefficiency problem of OT. It can reduce OT_l^m to OT_κ^κ, κ is a security parameter which is always equal to l but smaller than m, and OT_κ^κ can be further reduced by invoking OT_κ^1 κ times. We adopt [3], which is the latest improvement of OT-extensions in semi-honest model, to assure the security of basic interaction.

The intuitive heuristic to ensure comprehensive privacy preservation is stipulating both the cloud server and client to participate the OT extension protocol. The input of cloud server would be CB and that of the client would be F_{seg}. However, communication and computation overhead of the client will be inevitably high in most OT-based protocols if strong privacy protection is provided [15]. Therefore applying the OT directly is unsuitable for the client and the purpose of cloud-based malware detection.

We design the fast scanning process to decrease the volume of segments that need to be scanned in the client. After fast scanning, we utilize PMSSI mechanism to serve as the exact match in malware detection. The detection results in this process are cryptic to semi-honest cloud server because the safe OT-extension [3] adapted in PMSSI.

Algorithm 2 shows the process of PMSSI which can be divided into two substeps. Firstly, for each suspicious bucket location l in the L_{sus}, the client P_C gets the corresponding modular hash $mh(f_l) \in F_{sus}$, and the cloud server P_S check each entry E of $CB[l]$. Because $D[l] == 1$ is confirmed in fast scanning, there will be at least one entry occupied in $CB[l]$. If the bucket contains any vacant entry, the obscuration is needed to prevent the accurate status of $CB[l]$ from leaking. P_S generates random μ-bit strings to replace the vacant entries in $CB[l]$ as the input of OTSI (short for OT-based set intersection) to make the client cannot differentiate the buckets. Note that we do not actually insert the random strings to those vacant entries in CB.

Secondly, P_C and P_S respectively invoke function OTSI to achieve privacy preservation and exact match, although we describe the function in a combined way. P_S starts with generating $\lambda = bm\mu$ pairs κ-bit random strings $(x_{i,0}, x_{i,1})$ and acts as the sender. P_C generates λ-bit selection vector $\mathbf{r}$ which consists of b copies of each $mh(f_l) \in F_{sus}$ and acts as the receiver. Then P_C and P_S invoke OT_κ^λ based on [3] with their respective inputs. The OT_κ^λ will be reduced to OT_κ^κ where P_C and P_S play reversed roles (P_C acts as the sender, P_S acts as the

---

Algorithm 2. PMSSI Mechanism

Input: Suspicious bucket location set L_{sus}, P_S: CB, P_C: F_{sus}

Output: P_C gets the result set R_{mal}, P_S gets $\perp$

1: $R_{mal} = \emptyset$, κ is a security parameter, m is the size of L_{sus} and F_{sus}, μ is the bit length of modular hash result mh;

2: **while** each $l \in L_{sus}$ **do**

3:     **if** $CB[l]$ in P_S has d vacant entries E **then**

4:         P_S generates d random μ-bit strings

5:     **end if**

6: **end while**

7: P_C gets modular hash set $F_{sus} = \bigcup_1^m \{mh(f_l)\}$;

8: P_S gets entry set $E_{bm} = \bigcup_1^{bm} \{E\}$;

9: P_S: OTSI(E_{bm}), P_C:OTSI(F_{sus});

10: **Verification:** P_C compares bm pairs (XRS_k, XRC_k). if any pair matches, add f_l into R_{mal};

11: **return** $P_C \leftarrow R_{mal}$

12:

13: **function** OTSI(E_{bm}, F_{sus}) //*combined description*;

14:     P_S initializes $\lambda = b * m * \mu$ pairs of κ-bit random strings $(x_{i,0}, x_{i,1})$, $i \in [\lambda]$;

15:     P_C initializes λ-bit selection vector $\mathbf{r} = \{r_1, \cdots, r_m\}$, and $r_j = \{mh(f_l^j, \cdots, f_l^j)\}, 1 \leq j \leq m$, means r_j consists of b copies of each $mh(f_l) \in F_{sus}$;

16:     P_S and P_C invoke the OT_κ^λ protocol, input of P_S is the random strings, input of P_C is the selection vector $\mathbf{r}$;

17:     P_S calculate bm xor results. let $E_k = mh(X_{l,k}) = \{mh_k^1, \cdots, mh_k^\mu\}, mh_k^t \in \{0,1\}$, $XRS_k = \bigoplus_{(k-1)\mu+1}^{k\mu} x_{p,mh_k^t}, k \in [1,bm], t \in [1,\mu], p \in [1+(k-1)\mu, k\mu]$. Send $XRS = \{XRS_1, \cdots, XRS_{bm}\}$ to P_C;

18:     P_C gets λ strings x_{i,r_i}, calculates bm xor results XRC_k according to $\mathbf{r}$;

19: **end function**

---

receiver), then further to κ invocations of basic OT_κ^1 extensions. In this way, the computational and communication overheads are reduced.

After the OTSI, P_C gets λ strings $x_{i,r_i}, i \in [\lambda]$ while P_S gets nothing about the selection vector $\mathbf{r}$. However, the x_{i,r_i} are randomly generated by P_S which contains no information about the signatures. Hence P_S calculates bm XOR results $XRS = \{XRS_1, \cdots, XRS_{bm}\}$ according to the modular hash value of signature segments E_{bm} as depicted in Algorithm 2. For instance, $t \in [1,\mu], XRS_1 = \bigoplus_1^\mu x_{p,mh_1^t}, p \in [1,\mu], XRS_2 = \bigoplus_{\mu+1}^{2\mu} x_{p,mh_2^t}, p \in [\mu+1, 2\mu], \cdots, XRS_b = \bigoplus_{(b-1)\mu+1}^{b\mu} x_{p,mh_b^t}, p \in [(b-1)\mu+1, b\mu], \cdots$. Each XRS_k is the XOR result of μ random strings which are selected according to the $mh(X_{l,k})$, and XRS will be sent to the client after calculating all the XOR results.

Similarly, P_C calculates the bm XOR results XRC and compares with XRS. If and only if the $mh(f_l)$ is exactly same with $mh(X_{l,k})$, the XRC_k matches XRS_k successfully. Otherwise, the XRS_k are random to P_C. At last, if any pair of (XRC_k, XRS_k) matches, f_l should be added to R_{mal}. Otherwise, f_l can be confirmed as clean segment. The workflow of PMSSI is depicted in Fig. 4.

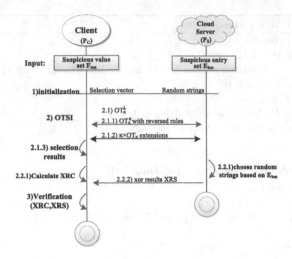

Fig. 4. Workflow of PMSSI

In PriMal, the public key operations in OT extension protocols [3] are implemented based on elliptic curve (EC) groups over $\mathbb{F}_p$ in OpenSSL (1.0.2a), other implementation parameters will be specified in Sect. 6. The main computational complexity of PMSSI is determined by the OTSI function which invokes OT_κ^λ based on [3]. Before invoking the OTSI function, the operation cost focuses on d times generation of random μ-bit in P_S which is negligible. In one execution of OTSI function in P_C, the detail computational cost includes: generating κ pairs of κ-bit seeds, basic OT_κ^κ based on EC, generating 2κ random λ-bit, calculating bm XOR results and comparing them. The computational cost of P_S is proportional to that of P_C. The communication cost between the cloud server and client is $(3\lambda + bm + 2\kappa)\kappa$ bits which mainly comes from [3]. The execution times of OTSI function are determined by the quantity of file segment n. For the powerful cloud server, these costs listed above are very slight; for the client, the costs would be acceptable given that their privacy is protected.

6 Discussion

In this section, we discuss the security and accuracy of PriMal from the theoretical perspective to show the balance between the intensity of privacy preservation and detection performance.

6.1 Security

Following the most of related privacy-preserving researches, we hypothesize the untrusted behaviors of both parties based on the semi-honest model [8]. In this model, the cloud server offers malware detection services faithfully, but intends to exploit the sensitive information from the interactive communication and tries to infer the file contents of client. Likewise, the client honestly follows the protocol specification but is curious about the signatures. In the following section, we briefly analyze the security of PriMal in semi-honest model. The main theorem is stated below:

Theorem 1. *Let the OTSI (E_{bm}, F_{sus}) in Algorithm 2 be indicated as $\pi_\cap$. If the underlying OT_κ^λ protocol is secure, then the $\pi_\cap$ is secure in the presence of semi-honest adversaries.*

Server's view: Assuming the cloud server is corrupted. The view of cloud server simulator during the protocol contains the message OT_{srv} from the OT_κ^λ protocol, λ pairs of κ-bit random strings $(x_{i,0}, x_{i,1})$ and the XRS. The XRS can be seen as the function $\oplus$ which inputs $\{E_k, (x_{i,0}, x_{i,1})\}$ and outputs random results. So the simulator Sim_{srv} outputs the simulated view: $(E_k, x_{i,0}, x_{i,1}, \oplus, OT_{srv})$. A view of the real protocol execution contains the message from OT protocol, the λ pairs of random strings and XOR operation results. In the simulated view, the random strings are distributed uniformly as in a real execution, so the distribution of XRS is also same as in the real execution. The protocol meets the requirements of TPSP (Level III): (1) If the file segments is confirmed to be malicious, the client gets $XRS \cap XRC$ but cannot reveal X_l because of modular hash; (2) if the file segment is trustworthy, the XRS is randomly distributed to the client. As the OT protocol is secure, then the message OT_{srv} should be indistinguishable from the view in a real execution. Thus we conclude the simulated view is indistinguishable from a real view.

Client's view: Assuming the client is corrupted. The view of client simulator during the protocol only contains the message OT_{cli} from OT_κ^λ protocol and the selection vector $\mathbf{r}$. The view of a real execution contains the same. In the simulated view, $\mathbf{r}$ is set to be same as in the real execution according to the security definitions of secure computation [8]. As the OT protocol is secure, the message OT_{cli} should be indistinguishable from the view in a real execution. Thus we conclude the simulated view is indistinguishable from a real view.

6.2   Accuracy

The accuracy is measured based on the false negative and false positive caused by the hashing scheme adopted in PriMal. A false negative occurs when a segment has been inserted into the signature engine earlier but is asserted as clean when matching. While the false positive occurs when a query segment not inserted into the signature engine is incorrectly stated as present. In what follows we will conduct the theoretical analysis of these measurements.

False Negative. The false negative is caused by two main factors. The first one is the initialization based on fixed-size slide window. For instance, suppose the signature *"abcdefg"* has been inserted with $w = 6$, which means two signature fragments are constructed and inserted into the engine: *"abcdef"* and *"bcdefg"*. Now if we scan the file content *"bcdef"* will get the incorrect response that the file is clean. However, it is remarkable that false negative in PriMal would occur only for the short file content whose length is less than w bytes. This situation seldom takes place and is hard to be evaluated in prevalent security detection because sizes of files to be scanned are always larger than w bytes.

The second one is the insertion failures of cuckoo hashing. It is noteworthy that this factor is not treated as a false negative in [7] because the failure segments can be maintained for further lookup. In our paper, it is incompatible that maintaining these segments for exact matching and satisfying the requirements of Level III. The number of insertion failures is impacted by the bucket size b, hash table size m and the displacement times dt. The detailed false negatives are evaluated in Table 4.

False Positive. There are two types of false positives in PriMal. The first one is caused by the hash functions employed in the signature engine, which is called *hashing false positive*. Secondly, the modular arithmetic adopted in the initialization brings the possibility of collision between two different segments and the modular hash of signature segments adopted in the storage mechanism. Here we call it *segment false positive*.

Hashing false positive: The hash functions we use above are 2-universal which make the hash results are nearly randomized and the process of modular hash serves similarly as the fingerprint of [7]. This type of false positive comes from the hash collisions which may lead to the conclusion that a specific segment is suspicious when it is not. In the worst case of looking up a non-existent item, the $2b$ candidate entries are checked. The upper bound of the total probability of a false modular hash hit is:

$$\varepsilon = 1 - (1 - \frac{1}{2^{w \cdot \log_2 q}})^{2b} \approx \frac{2b}{q^w} \tag{1}$$

Let N_S be the number of signatures in DB, $\bar{l}$ be the average length of signatures be queried at a time in DB. Then the number of segments after being incised by the window w is $(\bar{l} - w + 1) \cdot N_S$. According to the relation (1), let FP_h be the hashing false positive of an arbitrary signature in DB that is:

$$FP_h = 1 - (1 - \varepsilon)^{(\bar{l} - w + 1) \cdot N_S} \tag{2}$$

Segment false positive: As we described in Sect. 4, the PriMal system adopts the modulo(q) hash function mh to generate candidate locations in CB. However, this will introduce collisions between different segments. Specifically, there are two distinct situations lead to segment collisions.

The first situation happens when two uninserted segments whose modular hash values are equal. Suppose that S and S' are two different strings (signatures or files) with the same length of $\bar{l}$-byte. The collision happens if each byte of string belongs to same class after the modular hash. The second situation happens when the uninserted file segments is wrongly matched. Suppose that $S = s_1 s_2 \ldots s_{\bar{l}}$ is initialized into $(\bar{l} - w + 1)$ segments with w-byte. The collision happens when all these fragment are wrongly resulted in suspicion. Let F_1 be the false positive before inserting, F_2 be the false positive after inserting, we can conclude the relations below:

$$F_1 = (\frac{\lceil\frac{256}{q}\rceil}{256})^{\bar{l}}, \qquad F_2 = (\frac{\lceil\frac{256}{q}\rceil}{256})^{w\cdot(\bar{l}-w+1)} \qquad (3)$$

Consequently the probability of collisions are the sum of F_1 and F_2. However, we should negate the situation that all the bytes in the string are really equal. Let FP_s be the segment false positive rate, then we have:

$$FP_s = [F_1 + F_2 - (\frac{1}{256})^{\bar{l}}] \cdot N_S \leq \\ [(\frac{1}{q} + \frac{1}{256})^{\bar{l}} + (\frac{1}{q} + \frac{1}{256})^{w\cdot(\bar{l}-w+1)} - (\frac{1}{256})^{\bar{l}}] \cdot N_S \qquad (4)$$

In conclusion, the false positive of PriMal can be computed by the summation of relation (2) and (4). Figure 5 shows the detail values of FP_h and FP_s with two values of q. As observed, FP_h is much larger than FP_s with different numbers of signatures. So FP_s is negligible as compared to FP_h and the false positive of PriMal is mainly determined by FP_h. It is reasonable that FP_h mounts up with the growth of signatures because empty entries get rare. Meanwhile, the growth of q decreases FP_h and FP_s distinctly because larger q generates larger result space of modular hash which dilutes the probabilities of collisions.

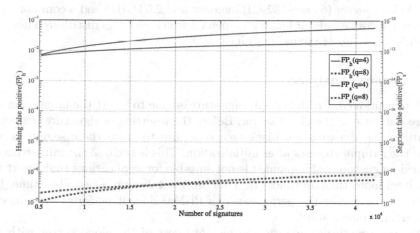

Fig. 5. Two types of false positive in PriMal with different values of q. (Parameters: $\bar{l} = 30, w = 16, b = 2$ and different numbers of signatures range from 530000 to 4200000.)

7   Performance Evaluation

In this section, we evaluate the performance of PriMal system and make some comparisons with related works. Our system is constructed based on ClamAV(engine version 0.96) as detection infrastructure and EC groups over $\mathbb{F}_p$

Table 2. Signature segment distribution with different numbers of signature

Segments	The number of signature						
	530 K	830 K	1 M	2 M	3 M	3.7 M	4.2 M
MD5	429,422	739,290	956,952	1,835,112	2,808,716	3,585,710	4,072,748
String	7,287,854	7,495,898	7,682,817	7,732,660	7,924,836	8,332,140	8,081,249

in OpenSSL (1.0.2a) for basic OT protocols. We implement PriMal with additional 3 K lines of C code and the cloud version of ClamAV, SplitScreen, and RScam for comparison. The signature databases we adopt originate from the ClamAV open source platform. Several versions from Feb 2009 to Dec 2015 are employed, the numbers of signatures range from 530000 to 4200000, respectively. The vast majority of signatures are MD5 with uniform size of 16 bytes each which means one MD5 signature can be treated as a signature segment directly. The residual signatures are string signatures. Table 2 lists the specific distribution of two different types (MD5 and string) of signatures after initialization.

If unspecified, we use $w = 16, q = 4, b = 2, \kappa = 80, n = 2^{17}$ for the evaluations with the latest database (main v.55 and daily v.21187) and show the average results over 10 runs. Our total 12 GB suspicious traffic set consists of about 100000 unique samples named by MD5 hashes, which are captured by specific IDS from the campus network. Experiments are performed on a CentOS 5.6 virtual cloud server (8 cores, 32-GB memory and 2.53 GHz) and a common open research network emulator based on OpenVZ which provides distributed network and different types of virtual machines.

7.1   Memory Analysis

As aforementioned, PriMal adopts signature engine to insert the large-scale signature database in the cloud server. Before the inserting of signature segments, we utilize the dynamic red-black tree structure to store these segments and prune the reduplicate ones after initialization. This is because the infrastructure is based on cuckoo hashing and it is not suitable for applications that insert the same item more than $2b$ times [7]. This process takes up a period of time, but we do not count it in the performance of PriMal since it performs only once at the starting of evaluation.

We first practically analyze the memory cost of the cloud server with ten different versions of signature databases. Moreover, we compare our statistic with the memory cost of the cloud server in Clamav, SplitScreen and RScam. Figure 6 shows the details when $M = 2^{24}$. As observed, the memory costs of the cloud server in PriMal increase slowly with the growth of signature volume which benefits from the efficient infrastructure and modular hashing mechanism. The RScam costs the most memory footprint because the server needs to maintain the statements of signature segments to achieve accurate orientation and exact matching. The growth of SplitScreen is faster than PriMal which induces the total memory cost of SplitScreen is larger than that of PriMal when the number

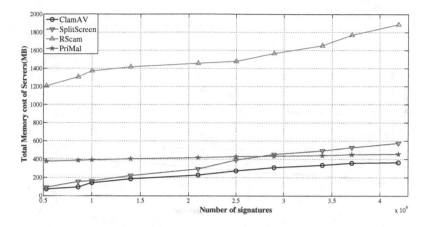

Fig. 6. Memory cost comparison with different numbers of signatures

of signatures exceeds 3 million. Hence, we can conclude that our signature engine achieves high space efficiency in dealing with large-scale signature databases.

7.2   Time and Communication Analysis

We evaluate the time performance of PriMal in the virtual machine as a client with 1 GB memory, 256 KB L2 cache, 2.53 GHz CPU, and the bandwidth between the cloud server and client is 10 Mbps. In PriMal, the cloud server and client invoke one execution of PMSSI for n file segments. To make it easier to understand, we randomly choose 200 suspicious samples with the average size of n bytes to evaluate the average time cost of one execution of PMSSI.

There are two parameters that impact the time performance. The first one is the size of signature engine(M). If M grows large, the digest D will become sparse and the collision probability of two different segments becomes low. Then the size of L_{sus} will decrease and the computation cost during the PMSSI will reduce. The second one is the number of signatures which impacts in the opposite way as M do. The more signatures are inserted into the signature engine, the less sparse D becomes.

Figure 7 depicts the detailed average time costs of one OTSI execution with the different number of signatures and M. Moreover, the time costs of SplitScreen ($M = 2^{28}$) scanning individual file are also showed in Fig. 7 as a comparison. As observed, the time performance can be approximate to SplitScreen when $M = 2^{28}$. The total time cost of scanning multiple files grows linearly with the times of PMSSI executions, but these executions can be processed independently and using multiple threads. It is noteworthy that larger M causes higher memory cost while brings lower time cost. When $M = 2^{28}$ with 4200000 signatures, the memory cost of P_S is 2.4 GB which is acceptable for the cloud server.

As described in PMSSI, the communication cost is $(3\lambda + bm + 2\kappa)\kappa$. In our evaluation, m is the major factor that impacts the cost, and it depends on the

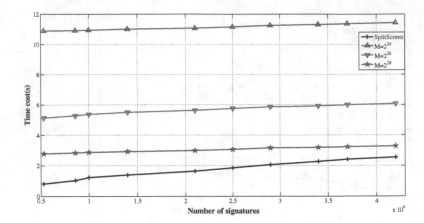

Fig. 7. Time cost of PriMal with different sizes of signature engine and SplitScreen

total number of file segments n. Hence, we evaluate the communication cost with the different number of file segments and signatures. Table 3 lists the details with $M = 2^{24}$. The cost is inevitably high to assure all the file segments are checked in the privacy-preserving manner. However, cost remains stable with the number of signatures grows because of the low false positive.

The practical statistics of time and communication prove that it is a real challenge to achieve both high-performance malware detection and strong privacy preservation. However, the time and communication costs are reasonable considering that we rely on the most efficient OT protocols and provide strong security in the semi-honest cloud environment. We conclude that PriMal is competent to protect the security and privacy of small but sensitive data.

Table 3. Average communication cost of PMSSI

Comm. (MB)	The number of signature				
	530 K	1 M	2 M	3 M	4.2 M
$n = 2^{13}$	9.8	10.2	10.3	10.5	10.6
$n = 2^{15}$	38.4	40.1	40.7	41.2	41.7
$n = 2^{17}$	109	114.7	116.1	117.6	119.5

7.3 False Negative

In this section, we give a practical evaluation of the false negative. As discussed in Sect. 6.2, it originates from the short signatures and insertion failures during initialization. The number of short signatures is determined by the length of sliding window w. As we set w to be 16 (length of standard MD5 signatures),

Table 4. False negative (FN) and corresponding number of negative segments. Entries in bold are the best choice among the column.

FN (Segments)	$b = 2, M = 2^{24}$	$b = 4, M = 2^{23}$	$b = 8, M = 2^{22}$
$dt = 10$	0.3493% (42454)	0.1932% (23477)	0.1081% (13135)
$dt = 20$	0.3449% (41913)	**0.1930% (23454)**	**0.1080% (13133)**
$dt = 30$	0.3448% (41904)	0.1930% (23454)	0.1080% (13133)
$dt = 50$	**0.3447% (41895)**	0.1930% (23454)	0.1080% (13133)

the number of short signatures is fixed. We mainly discuss the insertion failures in the case of different parameter settings.

Table 4 shows that the false negative decreases with the increase of dt and b. The total number of entries is fixed to be 2^{25} because this volume is sufficient to contain the latest signature database according to Table 2. The intuitive choice to ensure lowest false negative is setting $b = 8, M = 2^{22}$ and $dt = 20$. However, the increment of b increases the number of suspicious segments to be checked in PMSSI. As a result, the time and communication cost will increase greatly. Therefore, we conclude the most moderate setting is $b = 2, M = 2^{24}, dt = 50$ because the false negative and costs are acceptable.

8   Conclusion

In this paper, we have presented PriMal, a cloud-based anti-malware system with privacy preservation which is the first system to take the privacy into consideration in the malware detection. In PriMal, we propose a novel malware detection protocol, called PMSSI, which enables the cloud server and client to achieve malware confirmation with privacy preservation in semi-honest model. Meanwhile, we design the relevant signature engine to reduce the detection range and cut down the computation and communication costs. Theoretical analysis proves that PriMal achieves strong privacy preservation and extremely low false positive. Statistical results show that PriMal provides low-cost memory overhead with acceptable performance on computation and communication costs.

Acknowledgement. This research is supported in part by the project of Guangxi cooperative innovation center of cloud computing and big data No. YD16505. The authors gratefully thank the anonymous reviewers for their helpful comments.

References

1. Internet security threat report. https://www.symantec.com/about/newsroom
2. Radioshack sells customer data after settling with states. http://www.bloomberg.com/news/articles/2015-05-20/radioshack-receives-approval-to-sell-name-to-standard-general

3. Asharov, G., Lindell, Y., Schneider, T., Zohner, M.: More efficient oblivious transfer and extensions for faster secure computation. In: Proceedings of CCS, Berlin, Germany, pp. 535–548. ACM (2013)
4. Cha, S.K., Moraru, I., Jang, J., Truelove, J., Brumley, D., Andersen, D.G.: Splitscreen: enabling efficient, distributed malware detection. In: Proceedings of NSDI, pp. 12–25. USENIX Association (2010)
5. Choi, B., Chae, J., Jamshed, M., Park, K.: DFC: accelerating string pattern matching for network applications. In: Proceedings of NSDI, pp. 551–565. USENIX Association (2016)
6. ClamAV. Clamavnet (2016). http://www.clamav.net
7. Fan, B., Andersen, D.G., Kaminsky, M., Mitzenmacher, M.D.: Cuckoo filter: practically better than bloom. In: Proceedings of CoNEXT, pp. 75–87 (2014)
8. Goldreich, O.: The Foundations of Cryptography - vol. 2, Basic Applications, vol. 2. Cambridge University Press, New York (2004)
9. Haghighat, M.H., Tavakoli, M., Kharrazi, M.: Payload attribution via character dependent multi-bloom filters. IEEE Trans. Inf. Forensics Secur. 8(5), 705–716 (2013)
10. Henecka, W., Schneider, T.: Faster secure two-party computation with less memory. In: Proceedings of AsiaCCS, pp. 437–446. ACM (2013)
11. Ishai, Y., Kilian, J., Nissim, K., Petrank, E.: Extending oblivious transfers efficiently. In: Boneh, D. (ed.) CRYPTO 2003. LNCS, vol. 2729, pp. 145–161. Springer, Heidelberg (2003). doi:10.1007/978-3-540-45146-4_9
12. Lan, C., Sherry, J., Popa, R.A., Ratnasamy, S., Liu, Z.: Embark: Securely outsourcing middleboxes to the cloud. In: Proceedings of NSDI, pp. 255–273. USENIX (2016)
13. Melis, L., Asghar, H.J., Cristofaro, E.D., Kaafar, M.A.: Private processing of outsourced network functions: feasibility and constructions. In: Proceedings of SDN-NFV Security, pp. 39–44. ACM (2016)
14. Oberheide, J., Cooke, E., Jahanian, F.: Cloudav: N-version antivirus in the network cloud. In: Proceedings of USENIX Security Symposium, Berkeley, CA, USA, pp. 91–106. USENIX Association (2008)
15. Pinkas, B., Schneider, T., Segev, G., Zohner, M.: Phashing: private set intersection using permutation-based hashing. In: Proceedings of USENIX Security Symposium, pp. 515–530 (2015)
16. Santos, I., Brezo, F., Ugarte-Pedrero, X., Bringas, P.G.: Opcode sequences as representation of executables for data-mining-based unknown malware detection. Inf. Sci. 231, 64–82 (2013)
17. Sherry, J., Lan, C., Popa, R.A., Ratnasamy, S.: Blindbox: deep packet inspection over encrypted traffic. In: Proceedings of SIGCOMM, pp. 213–226. ACM (2015)
18. Stevens, M., Bursztein, E., Karpman, P., Albertini, A., Markov, Y.: The first collision for full sha-1. Technical report, Shattered, February 2017
19. Sun, H., Wang, X., Su, J., Chen, P.: RScam: cloud-based anti-malware via reversible sketch. In: Thuraisingham, B., Wang, X.F., Yegneswaran, V. (eds.) SecureComm 2015. LNICSSITE, vol. 164, pp. 157–174. Springer, Cham (2015). doi:10.1007/978-3-319-28865-9_9
20. Wang, X., Yu, H., Wang, W., Zhang, H., Zhan, T.: Cryptanalysis on HMAC/NMAC-MD5 and MD5-MAC. In: Joux, A. (ed.) EUROCRYPT 2009. LNCS, vol. 5479, pp. 121–133. Springer, Heidelberg (2009). doi:10.1007/978-3-642-01001-9_7
21. Yuan, X., Wang, X., Lin, J., Wang, C.: Privacy-preserving deep packet inspection in outsourced middleboxes. In: Proceedings of INFOCOM, pp. 1–9. IEEE (2016)

A New Malware Classification Approach Based on Malware Dynamic Analysis

Ying Fang[✉], Bo Yu, Yong Tang, Liu Liu, Zexin Lu, Yi Wang,
and Qiang Yang

National University of Defense Technology, Changsha 410073, China
fangying15@nudt.edu.cn

Abstract. Dynamic analysis plays an important role in analyzing malware variants which have used obfuscation, polymorphism and metamorphism techniques. Malware classification is an emerging approach for discriminating different malware families. However, existing malware classification methods have mediocre performance in small scale datasets and some machine learning algorithms have difficulties in handling imbalanced datasets. To solve these issues, we propose an ensemble learning based dynamic malware classification approach aiming at datasets of different scales. Additionally a novel feature selection method is presented to select features with strong discrimination power. In particular, we continue to explore issues in feature representation and feature selection. To verify the efficiency of our approach, we perform a series of comparative experiments with existing feature selection methods, commercial anti-malware tools and current malware classification techniques. The experimental results demonstrate that our approach can classify malware variants in high F1-score while imposing low classification time in datasets of different scales.

Keywords: Malware classification · Ensemble learning · Feature selection · TF-IDF

1 Introduction

Malware as a crucial security threat presents significant challenges to cybersecurity. The large number of variants and the sophisticated malware behavior can bring considerable difficulties in malware analysis.

Yet malware analysis tools have troubles in alleviating threats of malware variants [1], and the number of new malware variants remains high. As the unknown malware variants are largely from known malware families, existing dynamic analysis tools can be improved by classification studies. For the reason that characteristics of known malware families can be inferred and comprehended by studying malware classification, and such characteristics can be deployed in new malware analysis tools as heuristic rules. Therefore, it is necessary to conduct a research on malware classification.

© Springer International Publishing AG 2017
J. Pieprzyk and S. Suriadi (Eds.): ACISP 2017, Part II, LNCS 10343, pp. 173–189, 2017.
DOI: 10.1007/978-3-319-59870-3_10

Existing automated malware analysis techniques fall into two general categories: (1) static and (2) dynamic methods [2]. However, obfuscation and morphism techniques have developed a lot to evade static malware analysis tools [3]. In order to reduce the limitation of static analysis, researchers analyze malware in dynamic manner, which means executing malicious code in a virtual system environment and collecting dynamic information such as system call [4], network access [5] and memory modification [6]. The dynamic information can provide an intuitive comprehension of malware behaviors to further deduction of their intentions.

However, the results of traditional machine learning algorithms are easy to be limited by the raw data, and over-fitting is sometimes hard to be avoided [7], especially the imbalanced datasets are more likely to cause deviation. Meanwhile existing malware classification researches focus on large scale datasets [8], and few studies research on how to classify small scale datasets. Small scale datasets contain less information than the large one, and it is more difficult to decide which feature should be extracted and selected. Furthermore in reality, some malware families such as Regin and Flame own no more than 100 samples. Taking these facts into consideration, we present an ensemble learning based malware classification approach that uses a new feature selection method aiming at classifying malware variants in different scale datasets accurately and efficiently.

In this paper, we present a novel dynamic-based malware classification approach using ensemble learning algorithms, which can be used in datasets of different scales. The considered dynamic features include Application Program Interface (API) calls, return value and module name. In the feature selection phase, we propose a new method based on Term Frequency-Inverse Document Frequency (TF-IDF) [9]. Our approach is evaluated in different scale datasets and compared with existing malware classification approaches and anti-malware tools. Our feature selection method is compared with Chi-square test (CHI) [10] and Principal Component Analysis (PCA) [11,12].

The contributions of this paper are shown below:

- We present a new feature selection method based on TF-IDF. By using this method, our dynamic-based malware classification approach can generate higher accuracy than previous work.
- We explore the ideal representation of feature space and employ various popular ensemble learning techniques in malware classification.

The rest of the paper is organized as follows. Section 2 describes the framework of classification approach and the method of constructing the feature space. Section 3 presents the evaluation of our approach. Related works are reviewed in Sect. 4. Section 5 concludes our work.

2   Methodology

In this section, we firstly describe the framework of our approach, then we present the method of extracting, representing and selecting features, finally the ensemble learning algorithms we used are introduced.

2.1   Framework Overview

Figure 1 gives an overview of our framework for malware classification. Firstly a training dataset and a testing dataset are built, and then the malware variants are monitored in a SandBox [13] for obtaining the malicious traces. In the training phase, from dynamic execution traces, API calls, return value and module name are extracted as features and their number of occurrences are saved in a trace frequency information table (TFIT). According to TFIT, the weight of each feature is calculated and the feature with high weight is selected. After that, the selected features are weighted and normalized. Since the feature vectors have been obtained, malware variants are labeled with their families and the malware classification model can be constructed via ensemble learning algorithm. In the testing phase, at first the feature vectors are gained with the same method which is used in the training phase. Then the feature vectors are tested in our classification model and the evaluation results can be obtained.

2.2   Feature Extraction

To extract features from runtime malware variants, Pin (A dynamic binary instrumentation tool) is used to obtain the real-time dynamic execution traces. A real-world example of the trace is shown in Fig. 2:

From the dynamic execution trace of malware variants, several data types including function call names, action time, input and output parameters, execution results and other details are gathered. These trace types are analyzed preliminarily to assign which type in execution trace should be chosen. With twenty malware variants in two different malware families, each trace type is extracted respectively and Term Frequency (TF) is used as features. The feature space is constructed as a classification model using Random Forest (RF) algorithm. Table 1 shows the Accuracy of each trace type. Therefore, API calls, return value and module name are elected for further analysis. TFIT contains these features and their number of occurrences. In Table 2, an example of TFIT is listed.

Table 1. The Accuracy of each trace type

Trace Type	Function call names	Action time	Return	Module	Repeated	Details	Result
Accuracy	0.85	0.52	0.97	0.94	0.41	0.23	0.45

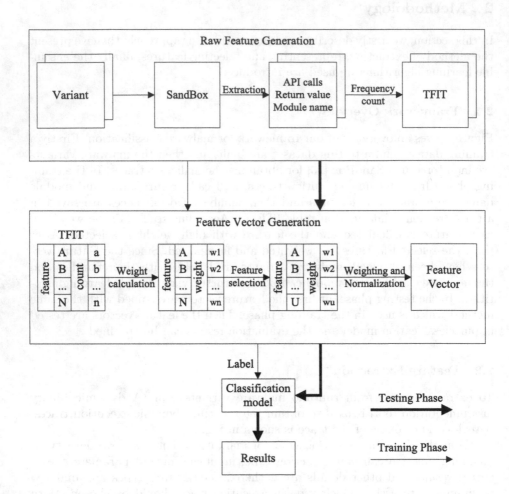

Fig. 1. The framework of malware classification approach

Table 2. An example of trace frequency information table

Execution trace	Frequency	Execution trace	Frequency
GetProcAddress	936	RegQueryValueExW	296
strncmp	0	ReadProcessMemory	0
VirtualAllocEx	0	VirtualAllocEx	16
RegSetValueExA	80	RegOpenKeyExA	0
RegQueryValueExA	0	WSAStartup	2

```
<function_call name="Process32NextW">
   <action time="2015-10-26 14:44:33:1229 +0800">
      <return>0x00000001</ return >
      <module>0x00404210@jusched.exe</ module >
      <repeated>0</ repeated >
      <details>{"cntThreads": "0x00000034", "cPriClassBase":
"0x00000008", "szExeFile": "System", "th32ParentProcessID":
"0", "th32ProcessID": "4", "th32DefaultHeapID": "0",
"th32ModuleID": "0", "hSnapshot": "0x00000054"}</details>
      <tid>228</ tid >
      <result>0</ result >
   </action>
</ function_call>
```

Fig. 2. An example of dynamic execution trace

2.3   Feature Representation

In our case, the dynamic execution traces are extracted as strings, and the feature representation choices are inspired from Sect. 4 and listed below:

1. Hash. A hash function can map data from arbitrary size to fixed size. A string is transformed into fixed size binary number via overlapping and mapping each element in the string. Finally, the output binary number is transformed into decimal number.
2. Binary. To simplify the extracted feature, TF of each string is used as raw features and a threshold T is set. Then we truncate the TF to either 0 or 1, which means that if $TF \geq T$, set it to 1, else if $TF < T$, set it to 0.

2.4   Feature Selection

As described previously, the malware classification task is treated as a feature-based classification problem [14]. The classifier can learn a model from the features that we have extracted and predict which malware family the candidate variants should be in. In this section, we describe our feature selection method.

The first step is to calculate the weight of each feature vector. The weight defines the importance of each feature. Therefore a lightweight and accurate classification model can be built through the strategy of weighting. The second step is to select features according to the calculated weight. The third step is to weight and normalize feature vectors. We choose Min-Max scaling in this step [15].

A. Weight calculation

Weight calculation is based on TF-IDF and used for feature selection, and the improved algorithm is proposed due to the limitations of TF-IDF algorithm itself. Let $l - (x_1, x_2, \cdots x_n)$ denotes the feature in malware variant a, its dimension is n; Num is the total number of malware variants in the training dataset; m is the total number of malware variants that include feature t; e indicates the number of

Table 3. An example of malware variants

Malware family	Malware variant	feature r (counts)	feature s (counts)	feature t (counts)
A	a	r_1	s_1	t_1
B	b_1	r_2	s_2	t_2
	b_2	r_3	s_3	t_3

malware families; $c_i(1 \leq i \leq e)$ defines each malware family. Table 3 exemplifies malware variants and their features to illustrate the weight calculation method. First the post-probability $P(c_i|t)$ is calculated.

$$P(c_i|t) = \frac{P(t|c_i)P(c_i)}{P(t)}$$

Some elements in Table 3 are acquired to illustrate the formula listed above.

$$P(A|t) = \frac{P(t|A)P(A)}{P(t)} = \frac{\frac{t_1}{r_1+s_1+t_1} * \frac{r_1+s_1+t_1}{r_1+\cdots+t_3}}{\frac{t_1+t_2+t_3}{r_1+\cdots+t_3}} = \frac{t_1}{t_1 + t_2 + t_3}$$

Namely, $P(c_i|t) = \frac{count_c}{count_t}$, $count_c$ is the number of occurrences of feature t in family c_i; $count_t$ is the number of occurrences of feature t in the training dataset.

Then, a formula is defined to confirm the distinguish ability $E[P(c|t)]$ of feature t.

$$E[P(c|t)] = \frac{\sum_{i=1}^{e} \sum_{j=1}^{e} [P(c_i|t) - P(c_j|t)]^2}{2}$$

TF of feature t in malware variant a is calculated as follows:

$$TF(t,a) = \frac{count_a}{countall_a}$$

$count_a$ is the number of feature t in malware variant a, $countall_a$ is the total number of features in malware variant a.

The weight of feature t is computed the following:

$$w(t,a) = \frac{TF(t,a) \times E[P(c|t)]}{\sqrt{\sum_{t \in a} [TF(t,a) \times E[P(c|t)]]^2}}$$

B. Feature selection and normalization

Since the weights of features have been gained, the feature with strong discrimination power can be selected, namely, the feature with high weight value. Top u features are elected and the weighted formula is shown as follows:

$$t^w = t \times w(t,a)$$

Namely,

$$(x_1^w, x_2^w, \cdots x_u^w) = (x_1, x_2, \cdots x_u) \times w(t, a)$$

The weighted features have different value ranges, while normalization can reduce its influences in constructing classification model. Min-Max scaling is chosen for normalization, the value domain of each element in the weighted feature vector is adjusted to [0.0, 1.0]. The formula is shown as the following:

$$x_j^{norm} = \frac{x_j^w - x_{min}}{x_{max} - x_{min}}$$

In a weighted feature vector, x_j^w indicates the j_{th} element, x_{min} is the minimum value and x_{max} is the maximum value. x_j^{norm} indicates the j_{th} element in the normalized feature vector. After normalization, our feature space can be gained.

2.5 Ensemble Machine Learning Algorithms

Ensemble learning builds a prediction model by combining the strengths of a collection of simpler-base models [16]. In our malware classification approach, ensemble machine learning algorithms are applied in training the obtained feature space and building the classification model. Figure 3 illustrates how to build the model. We choose RF [17], Gradient Boosted Regression Trees (GBRT) [18] and Voting Classifier (VC) [19] in our experiments for their high efficiency. GBRT is a generalization of boosting to arbitrary differentiable loss functions [16]. VC combines different machine learning classifiers, which can predict the label of each class and balance out their individual weaknesses. In our case, the machine learning algorithms in Voting Classifier are SVM, DT and KNN.

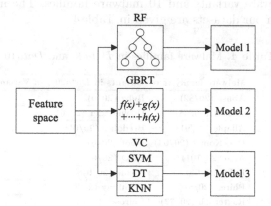

Fig. 3. Building a classification model

3   Experiments and Discussion

In this section, we describe our datasets and a series of experiments in our classification approach. Our approach will be investigated in many aspects, each of which is used to answer one of the questions listed below:

(1) How to represent feature for better malware classification? (Sect. 3.2)
(2) Can proposed feature selection method help? Selecting features for constructing feature space and comparing with other feature selection methods (Sect. 3.3).
(3) How is the performance of presented approach on our datasets? (Sect. 3.4)
(4) How is the performance of our approach compared to commercial tools and other existing classification approaches? (Sect. 3.5)

The experiments are performed on Intel Core i7 2.00 GHz with 8.00 GB RAM, running on Ubuntu 15.10 operating system. Malware variants are monitored in Windows XP via Sandbox for obtaining the dynamic execution traces.

We evaluate the performance of our approach in terms of popular evaluation metrics [20], Accuracy and F1-score. Accuracy is the fraction of variants that are correctly detected; F1-score is a weighted harmonic average between Precision and Recall [21]; Precision is the fraction of detected malware variants that are correctly detected out of the total detected dataset, and Recall is the fraction of the detected malware variants out of the total malware dataset.

3.1   Dataset

In this research, our work only aims at Windows malware. We collected two different scale malware datasets from our previous work. The first dataset $Data20$ is a small scale dataset, which includes 400 malware variants and 20 malware families. The second dataset $Data10$ is a large and imbalanced dataset, which includes 760 malware variants and 10 malware families. The malware families and their types in our datasets are given in Table 4.

Table 4. Malware families in $Data20$ and $Data10$

Type	Malware family (♯ of Variants in $Data20$/♯ of Variants in $Data10$)	
Worm	Abuse (20/82)	Bybz (20/0)
	Clisbot (20/68)	Downloader (20/0)
Backdoor	Allaple (20/91)	Bredolab (20/0)
	DarkKomet (20/54)	Gbot (20/0)
Trojan	Arto (20/101)	BHO (20/0)
	Boht (20/65)	Buzus (20/0)
	Phires (20/81)	Pirminay (20/0)
	Ragterneb (20/77)	Refroso (20/0)
Trojan-Downloader	Adnur (20/65)	BHO (20/0)
	BrainInst (20/76)	Calipr (20/0)

3.2   Experiments for Feature Representation

Two types of feature representations introduced in Sect. 2.3 are tested in $Data20$ using our classification approach. RF is used in this section to build the classification model. Firstly, the Accuracy of API calls, return value, module name and the combined feature are evaluated to choose the threshold in Binary method. Table 5 shows the Accuracy of different threshold T in different feature types. Our approach achieves the highest Accuracy of 0.83 at $T = 0.3$. Therefore, $T = 0.3$ is the threshold.

Table 5. The Accuracy of different threshold T

T	API calls	Return value	Module name	Combined
0.10	0.31	0.37	0.53	0.48
0.20	0.52	0.63	0.58	0.66
0.25	0.60	0.71	0.71	0.68
0.3	**0.71**	**0.81**	**0.81**	**0.83**
0.35	0.62	0.66	0.66	0.66
0.40	0.47	0.56	0.54	0.56
0.45	0.40	0.53	0.50	0.49
0.50	0.28	0.26	0.37	0.30

Then, the classification Accuracy of each feature representation method is illustrated in Table 6. Therefore the better choice of feature representation is Hash.

Table 6. The classification Accuracy of Hash and Binary

Feature	Hash	Binary
API calls	0.90	0.71
Return value	0.94	0.81
Module name	0.97	0.81
combined	0.96	0.83

3.3   Experiments for Feature Selection

To assess our presented feature selection method, our method is compared to CHI and PCA in $Data20$ and $Data10$ respectively. Firstly, we evaluate how many features in our method should be selected. The dimension of API calls is relatively small, which is 67, so the experiments of feature selection are only performed on return value and module name. The feature space gained from

$Data20$ is fed to RF classifier. The feature number $u = \{100, 200, 300, 400, 500\}$ is evaluated, the Accuracy and time overhead of different u are presented in Table 7. Therefore, in follow-up experiments, top 300 features in return value and top 200 features in module name are selected for constructing feature space, namely, the dimension of combined feature space we selected is 567.

Table 7. The Accuracy and overhead of u

Feature number	100	200	300	400	500
Return value	0.63	0.84	**0.94**	0.94	0.94
Overhead(s)	0.89	1.23	**1.76**	1.88	2.03
Module name	0.90	**0.97**	0.97	0.97	0.97
Overhead(s)	2.47	**2.67**	3.06	3.11	3.23

Figure 4 compares the Accuracy of three feature selection methods in $Data20$ and $Data10$. The classification models are built via RF, GBRT and VC respectively. Meanwhile, the results we recorded of CHI and PCA are the best classification results they have got by reducing the combined features. We can find that our feature selection method perform better in datasets with different scales, especially in the small ones.

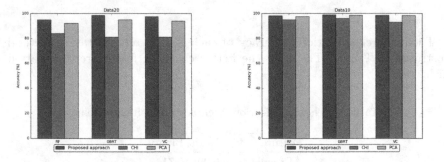

Fig. 4. Comparison with existing feature selection methods

3.4   Experiments for Feature Selection

For $Data20$ in our evaluation, Table 8 summarizes the Accuracy, F1-score and classification overhead with different kinds of features from three classification models built via RF, GBRT and VC. It can be easily inferred from the table statistics that our constructed model has the ability to classify malware variants in small scale datasets into correct categories. For malware classification, Precision and Recall should be high as a low value shall result in a wrong classification of malware. However, Precision and Recall are contradictory in some case. Therefore, F1-score is used to evaluate our approach. F1-score combines Precision and

Recall, and it should be as high as possible. As can be seen from Table 8, we achieve 0.98 of Accuracy and F1-score respectively, which means the features we extracted have high recognition, and the approach is suitable for malware classification. It also demonstrates that the model built by GBRT algorithm can achieve the best Accuracy and the model built by VC algorithm can classify the most rapidly. Additionally, the time of building feature space in *Data*20 is shown in Table 9 which indicates the efficiency of our classification approach.

Table 8. Classification results of *Data*20

RF	API calls	Return value	Module name	Combined
Accuracy	0.92	0.94	0.97	0.96
F1-score	0.91	0.93	0.97	0.95
Overhead(s)	2.41	1.76	2.67	2.31
GBRT	API calls	Return value	Module name	Combined
Accuracy	0.91	0.94	0.98	**0.98**
F1-score	0.90	0.93	0.98	**0.98**
Overhead(s)	1.18	0.61	**1.58**	1.21
VC	API calls	Return value	Module name	Combined
Accuracy	0.95	0.96	0.97	0.98
F1-score	0.95	0.95	0.97	0.97
Overhead(s)	**0.25**	**0.21**	3.93	**0.24**

Table 9. Runtime overhead of feature processing

Feature	API calls	Return value	Module name	Combined
Feature processing(s)	371.72	415.41	440.41	1227.24

To further evaluate the robustness of our approach, we compare receiver operating characteristic (ROC) curves via the combined feature in *Data*10 and *Data*20. ROC curve is a graphical plot that illustrates the performance of a binary classifier system. In our evaluation, we calculate the ROC curve of each malware family and compute the average curve as the ROC curve in our multi-classifier. Figure 5 depicts the ROC curves of RF, GBRT and VC in *Data*10 and *Data*20. Each dataset shows great performance on malware classification, which demonstrates that our approach can be used in different scale datasets.

3.5   Experiments for Comparison

In the previous section, we have evaluated our proposed malware classification approach. To adequately assess the quality of our results, we perform two comparative experiments with commercial anti-malware tools (Kaspersky and 360) and other malware classification approaches.

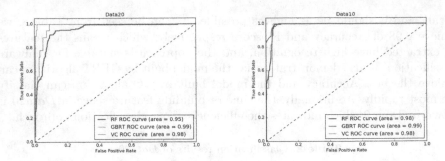

Fig. 5. ROC curves of RF, GBRT and VC

In this section, our classification model is constructed by GBRT algorithm and the combined features extracted from $Data20$ are used to train the model.

A. Commercial tools

Kaspersky and 360 are two universal anti-malware commercial tools. Confusion matrix used in this section to illustrate the classification results of our approach and these two tools. Confusion matrix is a specific table layout the performance of an algorithm, each column of the matrix represents the variants in a predicted class while each row represents the variants in an actual class [22]. The confusion matrices are presented in Fig. 6. From the figure, our approach is outperformed other tools.

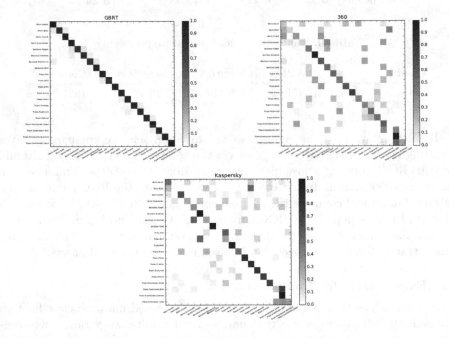

Fig. 6. The confusion matrices of GBRT, 360 and Kaspersky

From statistical analysis, 360 and Kaspersky can detect malware accurately, however, the ability of classifying malware variants is not as good as we supposed. It may due to the differences in designing the anti-malware tools and the proposed classification method. In fact, 360 only classified 37% malware variants into our offered families, and Kaspersky only classified 38.5%. The rest malware variants are assigned into other malware families, which we did not mention in Fig. 6. Especially in Kaspersky, 31.25% malware variants are considered as HEUR:Trojan.Win32.Generic. Therefore, we observe that existing anti-malware tools cannot classify malware variants into their real malware families.

B. Existing approaches

In this section, our classification approach is compared with previous work [23, 24]. Figure 7 indicates the Accuracy and F1-score of each approach. From the figure, our proposed approach achieves the highest Accuracy and F1-score for the reason that the extraction and representation method in our approach can cover the most useful features.

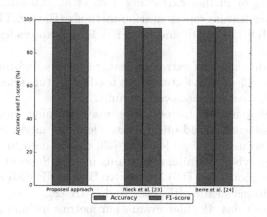

Fig. 7. Comparison with existing malware classification approaches

4   Related Work

Existing machine learning based malware analysis techniques can result in better outcomes such as [25]. In this section, we review the machine learning based malware analysis approaches by the following steps.

(1) Data collection and feature extraction. Features are extracted and converted into a multi-dimensional vector space which aims at distinguishing malware families or malicious and benign programs. The transformation techniques include N-gram, TF, etc.

(2) Model construction and training. The model for analyzing malware can be constructed through training machine learning algorithms with feature space.

(3) Evaluation. The model is tested for evaluating the results and improving itself.

Feature extraction and feature representation play an important role in machine learning based malware analysis works, and excellent feature space is necessary for analyzing malware. Features can be extracted from opcode sequences [11,26] or quantitative data flow graphs [27] via n-gram method. Cesare et al. [12] have decomposed control flow graphs and obtained fixed size k-subgraphs, or n-gram strings as features. Graphs such as machine-domain behavior graph [28], annotated control flow graph [29], triggering relation graph [30], API dependency graph [31] and ordered system-call graph [32] also can be extracted for representing malware variants. These graphs are pruned to boost performance and reduce noise, as well as it can be used to analyze malware via image matching or further extracting. Cen et al. [14] and Zhao et al. [33] have listed total five feature representation methods (Binary, TF, Inverse Document Frequency (IDF), TF-IDF and $\log(TF + 1)$) to express feature, which has inspired our work.

To reduce the dimension of extracted feature vectors, Information Gain (IG) [34], CHI, PCA and TF-IDF [33] etc. can be used for feature selection and feature reduction. Thus the feature space can be built.

Machine learning models include supervised learning model for malware detection and classification, and unsupervised learning model for malware clustering. Moreover, semi-supervised learning [23] can be used to analyze malware incrementally. Supervised learning algorithms include Support Vector Machine (SVM) [35,36], Decision Tree (DT) [26], Naive Bayes (NB) [37] and some ensemble learning algorithms such as RF, etc., and KNN [26] is common in unsupervised learning algorithms. Popular evaluation metrics include Precision, Recall and F-measure and ROC [22] etc.

However, it is possible that these malware analysis methods may not be suitable for malware variants in datasets of small scales or imbalance. Meanwhile traditional machine learning algorithms are sometimes too sensitive and not as robustness as enough. As introduced previously, ensemble learning algorithms can be used to balance out shortages of machine learning, and a new malware classification approach is demanded for tackling datasets of different scales.

5   Conclusion

In this paper, we propose a new dynamic-based malware classification approach using ensemble learning algorithms which is able to handle datasets of different scales. To carry out this objective, we capture the execution traces of malware variants and extract features from these traces. Then, we presented a novel TF-IDF based feature selection method which can elect high discriminative features in different scale datasets. The feature space is formed from the reduced feature vectors, and it can be used to build classification model via ensemble learning algorithms. Our experimental results demonstrate that our approach can be used to classify malware variants and achieves a high F1-score and a low time overhead. In addition, the presented feature selection method and our classification approach are compared with other related solutions, the results show that our approach performs better. Our future work aims at ameliorating the feature processing method to achieve more rapidly processing.

Acknowledgement. Project supported by the National Natural Science Foundation of China (No. 61472437 and No. 61379148)

References

1. Rieck, K., Holz, T., Willems, C., Düssel, P., Laskov, P.: Learning and classification of malware behavior. In: Zamboni, D. (ed.) DIMVA 2008. LNCS, vol. 5137, pp. 108–125. Springer, Heidelberg (2008). doi:10.1007/978-3-540-70542-0_6
2. Liu L., Wang, B.-S., Yu, B., Zhong, Q.-X.: Automatic malware classification and new malware detection using machine learning. Frontiers of Information Technology & Electronic Engineering, pp. 1–12 (2016)
3. Damodaran, A., Di Troia, F., Visaggio, C.A., Austin, T.H., Stamp, M.: A comparison of static, dynamic, and hybrid analysis for malware detection. J. Comput. Virol. Hacking Tech. **13**(1), 1–12 (2017)
4. Kolosnjaji, B., Zarras, A., Webster, G., Eckert, C.: Deep learning for classification of malware system call sequences. In: Kang, B.H., Bai, Q. (eds.) AI 2016. LNCS, vol. 9992, pp. 137–149. Springer, Cham (2016). doi:10.1007/978-3-319-50127-7_11
5. Chouhan, P.K., Hagan, M., McWilliams, G., Sezer, S.: Network based malware detection within virtualised environments. In: Lopes, L., et al. (eds.) Euro-Par 2014. LNCS, vol. 8805, pp. 335–346. Springer, Cham (2014). doi:10.1007/978-3-319-14325-5_29
6. Rhee, J., Riley, R., Dongyan, X., Jiang, X.: Kernel malware analysis with untampered and temporal views of dynamic kernel memory. In: Recent Advances in Intrusion Detection, International Symposium, pp. 178–197 (2010)
7. Witten, L.H., Frank, E., Hall, M.A., Pal, C.J., Mining, D.: Practical machine learning tools and techniques. Elsevier Ltd. (2011)
8. Shehata, H., Yousef, G., Mahdy, B., Ali, M.: Behavior-based features model for malware detection. J. Comput. Virol. Hacking Tech. **12**(2), 59–67 (2016)
9. Roelleke, T., Wang, J.: TFIDF uncovered: a study of theories and probabilities. In: International ACM SIGIR Conference on Research and Development in Information Retrieval, pp. 435–442 (2008)
10. Aoyama, H.: On the chi-square test for weighted samples. Ann. Inst. Stat. Math. **5**(1), 25–28 (1953)
11. Okane, P., Sezer, S., McLaughlin, K., Im, E.G.: SVM training phase reduction using dataset feature filtering for malware detection. IEEE Trans. Inf. Forensics Secur. **8**(3), 500–509 (2013)
12. Cesare, S., Xiang, Y., Member, S.: Control flow-based malware variant detection. IEEE Trans. Dependable Secure Comput. **11**(4), 304–317 (2014)

13. Liu, K., Shuai, L., Liu, C.: POSTER: fingerprinting the publicly available sandboxes. In: ACM SIGSAC Conference on Computer and Communications Security, pp. 1469–1471 (2014)
14. Cen, L., Gates, C.S., Si, L., Li, N.: A probabilistic discriminative model for android malware detection with decompiled source code. IEEE Trans. Dependable Secure Comput. **12**(4), 400–412 (2015)
15. Jain, Y.K., Bhandare, S.K.: Min max normalization based data perturbation method for privacy protection. Int. J. Comput. Commun. Technol. **2**(8), 45–50 (2011)
16. Hastie, T., Tibshirani, R., Friedman, J.: The Elements of Statistical Learning. SSS. Springer, New York (2009)
17. Breiman, L.E.O.: Random forests. Mach. Learn. **45**(1), 5–32 (2001)
18. Friedman, J.H.: Greedy function approximation: a gradient boosting machine 1 function estimation 2 numerical optimization in function space. Ann. Stat. **29**(5), 1189–1232 (2000)
19. Ruta, D., Gabrys, B.: A theoretical analysis of the limits of majority voting errors for multiple classifier systems. Pattern Anal. Appl. **5**(4), 333–350 (2002)
20. Gunawardana, A., Shani, G.: A survey of accuracy evaluation metrics of recommendation tasks. J. Mach. Learn. Res. **10**, 2935–2962 (2009)
21. Yang, Y., Liu, X.: A re-examination of text categorization methods. In: International ACM SIGIR Conference on Research and Development in Information Retrieval, pp. 42–49 (1999)
22. Martin, D., Powers, W.: Evaluation: from precision, recall and F-measure to ROC, informendness, markendness & correlation. J. Mach. Learn. Technol. **2**(1), 37–63 (2011)
23. Rieck, K., Trinius, P., Willems, C., Holz, T.: Automatic analysis of malware behavior using machine learning. J. Comput. Secur. **19**(4), 639–668 (2011)
24. Le Berre, S., Chevalier, A., Pourcelot, T.: Démarche d'analyse collaborative de codes malveillants. In: Symposium sur la sécurité des technologies de l'information et des communications, pp. 3–19 (2016)
25. Bayer, U., Comparetti, P.M., Hlauschek, C., Kruegel, C., Kirda, E.: Scalable, behavior-based malware clustering. In: Network and Distributed System Security Symposium, pp. 1–18 (2009)
26. Ding, Y., Dai, W., Yan, S., Zhang, Y.: Control flow-based opcode behavior analysis for Malware detection. Comput. Secur. **44**(2), 65–74 (2014)
27. Wuchner, T., Ochoa, M., Pretschner, A.: Robust and effective malware detection through quantitative data flow graph metrics. Comput. Sci. **9148**, 98–118 (2015)
28. Rahbarinia, B.: Efficient and accurate behavior-based tracking of malware-control domains in large ISP networks. ACM Trans. Priv. Secur. **19**(2), 1–31 (2016)
29. Alam, S., Horspool, R.N., Traore, I., Sogukpinar, I.: A framework for metamorphic malware analysis and real-time detection. Comput. Secur. **48**, 212–233 (2015)
30. Zhang, H., Yao, D.D., Ramakrishnan, N., Zhang, Z.: Causality reasoning about network events for detecting stealthy malware activities. Comput. Secur. **58**(C), 180–198 (2016)
31. Zhang, M., Duan, Y., Yin, H., Zhao, Z.: Semantics-aware android malware classification using weighted contextual API dependency graphs. In: ACM SIGSAC Conference on Computer and Communications Security, pp. 1105–1116 (2014)
32. Naval, S., Laxmi, V., Rajarajan, M., Member, S.: Employing program semantics for malware detection. IEEE Trans. Inf. Forensics Secur. **10**(12), 2591–2604 (2015)
33. Zhao, Z., Wang, J., Bai, J.: Malware detection method based on the control-flow construct feature of software. IET Inf. Secur. **8**(1), 18–24 (2014)

34. Moonsamy, V., Tian, R., Batten, L.: Feature reduction to speed up malware classification. In: Nordic Conference on Secure IT Systems, pp. 176–188 (2011)
35. Watson, M.R., Marnerides, A.K., Shirazi, N., Mauthe, A., Hutchison, D.: Malware detection in cloud computing infrastructures. IEEE Trans. Dependable Secure Comput. **13**(2), 192–205 (2016)
36. Mohaisen, A., Alrawi, O.: AMAL: high-fidelity, behavior-based automated malware analysis and classification. In: Rhee, K.-H., Yi, J.H. (eds.) WISA 2014. LNCS, vol. 8909, pp. 107–121. Springer, Cham (2015). doi:10.1007/978-3-319-15087-1_9
37. Yerima, S., Sezer, S., Muttik, I.: High accuracy android malware detection using ensemble learning. IET Inf. Secur. **9**(6), 313–320 (2015)

Privacy

Privacy-Preserving Aggregation of Time-Series Data with Public Verifiability from Simple Assumptions

Keita Emura[(⊠)]

National Institute of Information and Communications Technology (NICT),
Tokyo, Japan
k-emura@nict.go.jp

Abstract. Aggregator oblivious encryption was proposed by Shi et al. (NDSS 2011), where an aggregator can compute an aggregated sum of data and is unable to learn anything else (aggregator obliviousness). Since the aggregator does not learn individual data that may reveal users' habits and behaviors, several applications, such as privacy-preserving smart metering, have been considered. In this paper, we propose aggregator oblivious encryption schemes with public verifiability where the aggregator is required to generate a proof of an aggregated sum and anyone can verify whether the aggregated sum has been correctly computed by the aggregator. Though Leontiadis et al. (CANS 2015) considered the verifiability, their scheme requires an interactive complexity assumption to provide the unforgeability of the proof. Our schemes are proven to be unforgeable under a static and simple assumption (a variant of the Computational Diffie-Hellman assumption). Moreover, our schemes inherit the tightness of the reduction of the Benhamouda et al. scheme (ACM TISSEC 2016) for proving aggregator obliviousness. This tight reduction allows us to employ elliptic curves of a smaller order and leads to efficient implementation.

1 Introduction

1.1 Aggregator Oblivious Encryption

Aggregator oblivious encryption was proposed by Shi et al. [44], where an aggregated sum of n users' data (such as energy consumption from smart meters) can be computed in a privacy-preserving manner. In brief, an honest dealer generates secret keys for users and an aggregator. A user i encrypts data $x_{i,t}$ at time t, and sends the ciphertext $c_{i,t}$ to the aggregator. The aggregator can compute the aggregated sum $X_t = \sum_{i=1}^{n} x_{i,t}$ from $\{c_{i,t}\}_{i\in[1,n]}$ and sends X_t to a data analyzer (such as an energy provider). It is particularly worth noting that the aggregator learns X_t and nothing else and this security notion has been formalized as aggregator obliviousness. Note that if homomorphic encryption [19,41] is simply employed, then the aggregator has the capability to decrypt each $c_{i,t}$ and can obtain $x_{i,t}$. Since $x_{i,t}$ may reveal consumer habits and behaviors, e.g.,

© Springer International Publishing AG 2017
J. Pieprzyk and S. Suriadi (Eds.): ACISP 2017, Part II, LNCS 10343, pp. 193–213, 2017.
DOI: 10.1007/978-3-319-59870-3_11

when a certain consumer turns the air conditioner on, it may appear when the consumer returns home, aggregator oblivious encryption is better to preserve the privacy of users. Moreover, the aggregator is not required to be a fully trusted authority and is modeled as honest-but-curious. That is, the data analyzer can collect the aggregated sum of $x_{i,t}$ via the aggregator in a privacy-preserving manner. In addition, only a unidirectional channel is required from each user to the aggregator. This could be an advantage compared to the schemes that require bidirectional channels between the smart meters and the aggregator [18,42]. Though the Shi et al. scheme is not tolerant of user failures (i.e., if even a single user fails to respond in a certain aggregation round, the aggregation algorithm does not work), Chan et al. [11] proposed a fault-tolerant solution such that the aggregator can still compute the aggregated sum from the remaining users.

The Shi et al. scheme is aggregator obliviousness under the Decisional Diffie-Hellman (DDH) assumption in the random oracle model. They employed the lifted ElGamal encryption approach [12] and therefore $X_t = \sum_{i=1}^{n} x_{i,t}$ needs to be suitably small since the aggregator is required to solve the discrete logarithm g^{X_t} with respect to basis g. Later, Joye and Libert [27] proposed an aggregator oblivious encryption scheme with large plaintext spaces by employing the Paillier-type homomorphic operation [41]. The Joye-Libert scheme is aggregator obliviousness under the Decision Composite Residuosity (DCR) assumption in the random oracle model. Both schemes [27,44] were generalized by Benhamouda, Joye, and Libert (BJL) [8]. They gave a generic construction of aggregator oblivious encryption from smooth projective hash functions [13] with an extra additively homomorphic property over the key space, with both DDH and DCR-based instantiations. An attractive point of the BJL construction is its tight reduction. Namely, the reduction loss is $O(t_{\mathsf{max}})$ whereas that of the Shi et al. scheme [44] is $O(t_{\mathsf{max}}n^3)$ where t_{max} is the maximum time to be supported by the system and n is the number of users. If we consider the exact security [7,37], then tight reduction is important. As in Benhamouda et al. [8], we set that $n = t_{\mathsf{max}} = 2^{20} \approx 10^6$ which approximately allows the computation of an aggregation every 15 min for 30 years throughout a city like Paris. Then, the security loss of the Shi et al. scheme is approximately 2^{80}. That is, That is, for achieving 112-bit security, the Shi et al. scheme requires approximately 7,680-bit public key or elliptic curves with 384–511-bit order, which is recommended by NIST [4] for achieving 192-bit security. On the other hand, the security loss of the Benhamouda et al. scheme is approximately 2^{20}, and to achieve 112-bit security, approximately 3,072-bit public key or elliptic curves with 256–383-bit order is required.[1]

1.2 Aggregator Oblivious Encryption with Public Verifiability

As mentioned above, the aggregator is modeled as honest-but-curious and is assumed to output X_t correctly. For stronger security, Leontiadis et al. [31]

---

[1] This key-length is recommended by NIST [4] for achieving 128-bit security. To be precise, the Benhamouda et al. scheme archives 108-bit security under this key length. Thus, a slightly longer key is required to achieve 112-bit security.

considered a new model: a user i produces a tag $\sigma_{i,t}$ in addition to $c_{i,t}$, and sends $(c_{i,t}, \sigma_{i,t})$ to the aggregator, and the aggregator is required to generate a publicly verifiable proof σ_t that proves the decryption result of $\{c_{i,t}\}_{i \in [1,n]}$ is exactly X_t. Of course, it is required that the aggregator cannot produce a forged σ_t for some $X_t \neq \sum_{i=1}^{n} x_{i,t}$, and this security notion is formalized as aggregator unforgeability. Since the data analyzer can recognize whether the aggregator correctly computed the aggregated sum, this functionality can be seen as a kind of verifiable computation [2, 17].

Though the Leontiadis et al. approach is interesting, one drawback of their construction is the underlying complexity assumption. They introduced an interactive assumption called the LEOM assumption for proving aggregator unforgeability. The LEOM assumption is defined as follows.

Definition 1 (LEOM Assumption [31]). *Let $D = (p, e, g_1, g_2, \mathbb{G}_1, \mathbb{G}_2, \mathbb{G}_T)$ be bilinear groups. Choose $\alpha \xleftarrow{\$} \mathbb{G}_1$ and $\delta, \gamma_1, \ldots, \gamma_n \xleftarrow{\$} \mathbb{Z}_p$ and set $\Gamma = g_2^\gamma$ and $\Delta = g_2^{\sum_{i=1}^{n} \gamma_i}$. The LEOM oracle $\mathcal{O}_{\mathsf{LEOM}}$ takes as input $(t, \{x_{i,t}\}_{i=1}^{n})$, chooses $\beta_t \xleftarrow{\$} \mathbb{G}_1$, and returns $(\alpha, \beta_t, \{\beta_t^{\gamma_i} \alpha^{\delta x_{i,t}}\}_{i=1}^{n})$. If a query at t contains $i' \in [1,n]$ such that $x_{i,t} \neq x'_{i,t}$, then $\mathcal{O}_{\mathsf{LEOM}}$ returns $\perp$. Assume that $\mathcal{O}_{\mathsf{LEOM}}$ is called once at each t. We say that the LEOM assumption holds if for any probabilistic polynomial time (PPT) adversary $\mathcal{A}$, the advantage $\mathrm{Adv}_{LEOM}(\lambda) := \Pr[\mathcal{A}^{\mathcal{O}_{\mathsf{LEOM}}(\cdot,\cdot)}(D, \Gamma, \Delta) \rightarrow (t, z, c)]$ is negligible where $\mathcal{A}$ has queried $(t, \{x_{i,t}\}_{i=1}^{n})$ and $z \neq \sum_{i=1}^{n} x_{i,t}$ and $c = \beta_t^{\sum_{i=1}^{n} \gamma_i} \alpha^{z\delta}$ holds.*

However, as explained by Naor [38], it is better to avoid interactive assumptions as much as possible to prevent circular arguments. Making cryptographic primitives secure under weak assumptions is one of the important topics of cryptography. To name a few, verifiable random functions [23, 24], group signatures [33, 34], structure-preserving signatures [1], identity-based encryption [46], attribute-based encryption [40, 45], oblivious transfer [21] and so on, and constructing an aggregator oblivious encryption scheme with public verifiability from static and simple assumptions are still left as open problems.

1.3 Our Contribution

In this paper, we propose two aggregator oblivious encryption schemes with public verifiability from static and simple assumptions (a variant of the Computational Diffie-Hellman (CDH) assumption). See Table 1 for detailed comparisons. For aggregator obliviousness, both schemes are tightly reduced to the BJL scheme. That is, our schemes inherit the tightness of the reduction of the Benhamouda et al. scheme. This tight reduction allows us to employ elliptic curves with a smaller order and leads to efficient implementation. On the other hand, the Leontiadis et al. scheme is reduced to the Shi et al. scheme and has a loose reduction.

The first scheme provides weak aggregator unforgeability, where an adversary can obtain ciphertexts and tags $\{(c_{i,t}, \sigma_{i,t})\}_{i=1}^{n}$ of $x_{i,t}$ chosen by the

Table 1. Comparison of DL-based aggregator oblivious encryption

Scheme	Ciphertext size ($c_{i,t}$)	Tag size ($\sigma_{i,t}$)	Secret key size	Public parameter size (params + vk)
BJL (DDH) [8]	$|\mathbb{G}_1|$	-	$2|\mathbb{Z}_p|$	$|\mathbb{G}_1|+$ 2 hash
LEOM [31]	$|\mathbb{G}_1|$	$|\mathbb{G}_1|$	$2|\mathbb{Z}_p| + |\mathbb{G}_1|$	$|\mathbb{G}_1|+|\mathbb{G}_2|+$ 1 hash
Ours 1	$|\mathbb{G}_1|$	$|\mathbb{G}_1|$	$3|\mathbb{Z}_p| + |\mathbb{G}_1|$	$|\mathbb{G}_1| + (1 + t_{max})|\mathbb{G}_2| + |\mathbb{G}_T|$+6 hash[c]
Ours 2	$|\mathbb{G}_1|$	$|\mathbb{G}_1|$	$2|\mathbb{Z}_p| + |\mathbb{G}_1|$	$|\mathbb{G}_1| + |\mathbb{G}_2| + |\mathbb{G}_T|$+5 hash

Scheme	$|p|$[b]	Encryption algorithm	Aggregator unforgeability	Complexity assumptions for proving AO/AU[d]	Bulletin board
BJL (DDH) [8]	256	Deterministic	-	DDH/-	-
LEOM [31]	1031	Deterministic	Full	DDH/LEOM[e]	-
Ours 1	383	Deterministic	Weak	DDH/mCDH[f]	-
Ours 2	383	Probabilistic	Full	DDH/mCDH[f]	Required

[a] $\mathbb{Z}_p$, $|\mathbb{G}_1|$, $|\mathbb{G}_2|$, and $|\mathbb{G}_T|$ denote the bit-length of an element of $\mathbb{Z}_p$, $\mathbb{G}_1$, $\mathbb{G}_2$, and $\mathbb{G}_T$, respectively.
[b] $|p|$ denotes the bit-length of p for 112-bit security. Here, we set $n = t_{max} = 2^{20}$ [8]. For the BJL scheme, we refer the NIST recommendation [4] since the BJL scheme is pairing-free. For the LEOM scheme and ours, we refer the result by Menezes, Sarkar, and Singh [36] who re-evaluated parameters of pairing-friendly elliptic curves by considering the result by Kim and Barbulescu [29].
[c] Remark that no user is required to have the large-size verification key.
[d] AO/AU: Aggregator Obliviousness/Aggregator Unforgeability
[e] LEOM: Leontiadis-Elkhiyaoui-Önen-Molva. An interactive complexity assumption.
[f] mCDH: modified Computational Diffie-Hellman. A static complexity assumption.

encryption oracle. Note that in the smart meter setting, $x_{i,t}$ (such as power consumption) is measured by the meter. Thus, we believe that weak aggregator unforgeability is still meaningful in the actual usage. One drawback to the first scheme, beside weak aggregator unforgeability, is the large-size verification key vk = $\{vk_t := g_2^{\sum_{i=1}^{n} v_{i,t}}\}_{t\in[1,t_{max}]}$ where t_{max} is the maximum time to be supported by the system. If we employ Barreto-Naehrig (BN) curves [5] with a 383-bit order, then approximately 100 MByte-sized verification keys need to be published when $t_{max} = 2^{20} \approx 10^6$ [8]. Note that no user is required to have the large-size verification key. Moreover, verification keys for past times can be removed. In addition, if we can assume that these keys are updated by the dealer every time over a certain time period (i.e., periodic inspection of meters every one to two years), or if we can set a relatively small t_{max}, then we can significantly reduce the size of the keys to be stored. Remark that, if a user manages all $v_{i,t}$ as its secret key, then the secret key size also depends on t_{max}. To avoid such a large-size secret key, we additionally introduce a hash function H and a time-independent secret key v_i, and we compute $v_{i,t} = H(v_i, t)$. This helps us to reduce the secret key size.

Though we can reduce the verification key size according to the t_{max} settings, it would be better to support constant-size keys. Our second scheme solves the large-size key problem by choosing $v_{i,t}$ on the fly. That is, in the second scheme a user i chooses $v_{i,t}$ in the encryption phase, whereas in the first scheme all keys are generated by an honest dealer, as in previous works [8,27,31,44]. Though the Enc algorithm becomes probabilistic, this strategy allows us to prove that the scheme provides aggregator unforgeability where an adversary can obtain ciphertexts and tags $\{(c_{i,t}, \sigma_{i,t})\}_{i=1}^{n}$ of $x_{i,t}$ chosen by the adversary. Moreover, vk can be removed from the public value. A drawback of the second scheme is that a malicious aggregator could modify vk. Thus, we additionally need to introduce public channels equipped with memory, such as a bulletin board [22] that is publicly readable and that every user can write to, but nobody can delete from. See Sect. 4 for a more detailed explanation.

1.4   Related Work

Aggregator oblivious encryption considers collecting the aggregated sum of users (e.g., the total consumption of customers) in a certain region for each time period. This could be employed for privacy-preserving energy management systems. On the other hand, collecting the aggregated sum of a particular user might be desired for a certain reason. For example, if an energy provider would like to send an invoice to a customer and would like to know the total amount of the consumption of the customer. This could be employed for privacy-preserving supplier billing systems [25,43]. Some schemes support both billing and energy management functionality [6,15,39]. Ohara et al. [39] in particular proposed such a smart metering scheme with verifiability of the integrity of the total amount of consumption or the billing price.

In our setting (as in [8,27,31,44]), the number of users n is selected and fixed during the setup phase. Some papers considered dynamic joins and leaves [11,26, 30,32]. Chan et al. [11] proposed a binary interval tree technique that reduces the communication cost for joins and leaves, and Jawurek et al. [26] further improved the communication overhead of the Chan et al. scheme. Although the Chan et al. and Jawurek et al. schemes require public key settings, Li and Cao [32] proposed a more efficient scheme that only requires symmetric key settings. Though these schemes assume an honest dealer that issues keys to the users and the aggregator via a secure channel, Leontiadis et al. [30] proposed a key update mechanism that does not require any trusted dealer. They introduced an additional semi-trusted party called the collector that collects partial key information from users via a secure channel.

Some schemes employ bilinear groups with composite order $N = pq$ [16,35]. This could be a bottleneck since we need to assume that N is difficult to be factorized and is selected as sufficiently large. In the meantime, our schemes are constructed over bilinear groups with a prime order.

Benhamouda et al. [8] mentioned that multi-input functional encryption [20] implies aggregator oblivious encryption. Since Badrinarayanan et al. [3] proposed verifiable functional encryption and also considered its multi-input setting, we might be able to construct verifiable aggregator oblivious encryption from verifiable multi-input functional encryption. Though, as in Benhamouda et al., we leave this attempt in this paper due to the efficiency point of view.

2   Preliminaries

Let p is a λ-bit prime, $\mathbb{G}_1, \mathbb{G}_2$ and $\mathbb{G}_T$ are groups of order p, $e : \mathbb{G}_1 \times \mathbb{G}_2 \to \mathbb{G}_T$ is a bilinear map, and g_1 and g_2 are generators of $\mathbb{G}_1$ and $\mathbb{G}_2$, respectively. We use the (type 3) asymmetric setting, i.e., $\mathbb{G}_1 \neq \mathbb{G}_2$, and no efficient isomorphism between $\mathbb{G}_1$ and $\mathbb{G}_2$ is known.

Next, we define the Decisional Diffie-Hellman (DDH) assumption on $\mathbb{G}_1$ as follows.

Definition 2 (DDH Assumption). *Let* $D := (p, e, g_1, g_2, \mathbb{G}_1, \mathbb{G}_2, \mathbb{G}_T)$, $g_1' \xleftarrow{\$}$ $\mathbb{G}_1$ *and* $r_1, r_2 \xleftarrow{\$} \mathbb{Z}_p^*$ *where* $r_1 \neq r_2$. *We say that the DDH assumption holds on* $\mathbb{G}_1$ *if for any PPT adversary* $\mathcal{A}$, *the advantage* $\mathrm{Adv}_{DDH}(\lambda) :=$ $|\Pr[\mathcal{A}(D, g_1', g_1^{r_1}, g_1'^{r_1}) \rightarrow true] - \Pr[\mathcal{A}(D, g_1', g_1^{r_1}, g_1'^{r_2}) \rightarrow true]|$ *is negligible.*

Next, we define a new complexity assumption. This is a variant of the Computational Diffie-Hellman (CDH) assumption. We call this assumption the modified CDH (mCDH) assumption.[2]

Definition 3 (Modified CDH Assumption). *Let* $D := (p, e, g_1, g_2, \mathbb{G}_1,$ $\mathbb{G}_2, \mathbb{G}_T)$, *and* $a, b \xleftarrow{\$} \mathbb{Z}_p^*$. *We say that the Modified CDH assumption holds if for any PPT adversary* $\mathcal{A}$, *the advantage* $\mathrm{Adv}_{mCDH}(\lambda) :=$ $\Pr[\mathcal{A}(D, g_1^a, g_1^{1/a}, g_1^b, g_2^a) \rightarrow g_1^{ab}]$ *is negligible.*

We can check that the mCDH assumption holds in the generic bilinear group model by reducing the mCDH problem to the following problem: given $(g_1, g_1^a, g_1^{a^2}, g_1^b, g_2, g_2^a) \in \mathbb{G}_1^4 \times \mathbb{G}_2^2$ for random $a, b \in \mathbb{Z}_p$, compute $e(g_1, g_2)^{a^2 b}$. We can assume that the problem is difficult to be solved since it belongs to the Uber assumption family [10]. This reduction can be easily done by setting $g_1' := g_1^{1/a}$ and $B := ab$. Then, an instance of the mCDH problem $(g_1, g_1^a, g_1^{1/a}, g_1^b, g_2, g_2^a)$ is represented as: given $(g_1'^a, g_1'^{a^2}, g_1', g_1'^B, g_2, g_2^a)$, compute $g_1^{ab} = g_1'^{a^2 b} = g_1'^{aB}$. We rewrite it: given $(g_1, g_1^a, g_1^{a^2}, g_1^b, g_2, g_2^a)$, compute g_1^{ab}. That is, if the mCDH problem can be solved, then we can compute $e(g_1^{ab}, g_2^a) = e(g_1, g_2)^{a^2 b}$.

3   Definitions of Verifiable Aggregator Oblivious Encryption

In this section, we give the syntax of verifiable aggregator oblivious encryption and its security definitions (aggregator obliviousness and aggregator unforgeability), and introduce the DDH-based BJL scheme [8]. As in Shi et al. we consider encrypt-once security where each user only encrypts once at each time t.

---

[2] Kiltz and Vahlis [28] defined the modified Decisional Bilinear Diffie-Hellman (mDBDH) assumption where given $(g, g^x, g^y, g^{y^2}, g^z, Z)$ decide whether $Z = e(g, g)^{xyz}$ or not. That is, compared to the original DBDH assumption, the element g^{y^2} is additionally given to the adversary. In our assumption, if we set $g_1^{1/a} := g_1'$ then $(g_1^{1/a}, g_1, g_1^a)$ can be seen as $(g_1', g_1'^a, g_1'^{a^2})$. That is, the element $g_1'^{a^2}$ is added to an instance of the CDH assumption. Hence, we call the assumption mCDH.

3.1 Syntax of Verifiable Aggregator Oblivious Encryption

Definition 4 (Verifiable Aggregator Oblivious Encryption [31])

Setup: *The setup algorithm takes as input a security parameter λ, and outputs a public parameter* param *and a secret key of aggregator* sk_A, *a set of user secret keys* $\{\mathsf{sk}_i\}_{i=1}^n$, *and the aggregate verification key* vk. *We assume that the maximum time* $t_{\max}$ *is contained in* param, *and* $t_{\max}$ *is a polynomial of the security parameter. We assume that* $t \in [1, t_{\max}]$ *and the verification key at* t *vk_t is contained in* vk.

Enc: *The encryption algorithm takes as input* param, t, *a value* $x_{i,t}$, *and* sk_i, *and outputs a ciphertext* $c_{i,t}$ *and a tag* $\sigma_{i,t}$.

AggrDec: *The aggregation and decryption algorithm takes as input* param, t, *and a set of ciphertexts and tags* $\{(c_{i,t}, \sigma_{i,t})\}_{i=1}^n$, *and* sk_A, *and outputs* $X_t :=$ $\sum_{i=1}^n x_{i,t} \bmod M$, *and the proof* σ_t *where M is some fixed integer contained in* param.

VerifySum: *The verification of aggregation algorithm takes as input* param, t, *vk_t, and (X_t, σ_t), and outputs 1 or 0.*

We require the following correctness. For all $(\mathsf{param}, \mathsf{sk}_A, \{\mathsf{sk}_i\}_{i=1}^n, \mathsf{vk}) \leftarrow$ $\mathsf{Setup}(1^\lambda)$, and $(c_{i,t}, \sigma_{i,t}) \leftarrow \mathsf{Enc}(\mathsf{param}, t, x_{i,t}, \mathsf{sk}_i)$, and $(X_t, \sigma_t) \leftarrow$ $\mathsf{AggrDec}(\mathsf{param}, t, \{(c_{i,t}, \sigma_{i,t})\}_{i=1}^n, \mathsf{sk}_A)$, $\mathsf{VerifySum}(\mathsf{param}, t, X_t, \sigma_t, \mathsf{vk}_t) = 1$, and $X_t = \sum_{i=1}^n x_{i,t} \bmod M$ hold.

Let us introduce the entities of the system and how to run the algorithms above as follows. We consider four entities, a trusted dealer, an aggregator, users, and a data analyzer. First, the dealer runs $(\mathsf{param}, \mathsf{sk}_A, \{\mathsf{sk}_i\}_{i=1}^n, \mathsf{vk}) \leftarrow$ $\mathsf{Setup}(1^\lambda)$, and issues sk_A to the aggregator and sk_i to the user i, respectively, and publishes $(\mathsf{param}, \mathsf{vk})$.[3] At time t, each user i encrypts $x_{i,t}$ such that $(c_{i,t}, \sigma_{i,t}) \leftarrow$ $\mathsf{Enc}(\mathsf{param}, t, x_{i,t}, \mathsf{sk}_i)$, and sends $(c_{i,t}, \sigma_{i,t})$ to the aggregator. The aggregator runs $(X_t, \sigma_t) \leftarrow \mathsf{AggrDec}(\mathsf{param}, t, \{(c_{i,t}, \sigma_{i,t})\}_{i=1}^n, \mathsf{sk}_A)$, and sends (X_t, σ_t) to the data analyzer. The data analyzer checks whether the computed aggregated sum X_t is correct by running $1/0 \leftarrow \mathsf{VerifySum}(\mathsf{param}, t, X_t, \sigma_t, \mathsf{vk}_t)$.

3.2 Security Definitions

Next, we define aggregator obliviousness. This requires that the aggregator cannot learn anything more than the aggregate value X_t for each time t. We additionally require that tags $\sigma_{i,t}$ do not affect the security. Let st be state information that $\mathcal{A}$ can preserve any information, and st is used for transferring state information to the other stage. Let $\mathbb{U}$ be the whole set of users for which, at the end of the game, no encryption queries have been made on t^* and no corruption queries

---

[3] In the definition of Leontiadis et al. [31], each user i chooses a tag value tk_i, and sends its encoding value to the dealer in the Setup phase. The dealer computes vk from all tk_i. Here we simply assume that vk is generated by the dealer since the dealer is modeled as a trusted entity. Later, we consider the case that vk is generated by users in the encryption phase.

have been made. The adversary indicates $\mathbb{S}_{t^*} \subseteq \mathbb{U}$ and obtains $(c_{i,t^*}, \sigma_{i,t^*})$ for all $i \in \mathbb{S}_{t^*}$. Remark that the AggrDec algorithm works only when all ciphertexts are collected. That is, if $\mathbb{S}_{t^*}$ is a proper subset of $\mathbb{U}$ ($\mathbb{S}_{t^*} \subsetneq \mathbb{U}$), then there exist at least one ciphertext c_{i,t^*} such that $i \in \mathbb{U} \backslash \mathbb{S}_{t^*}$. In this case, the adversary cannot run the AggrDec algorithm. Thus, as in the definition of Benhamouda et al. [8] and Shi et al. [44], we require that $\sum_{i \in \mathbb{S}_{t^*}} x_{i,t^*}^{(0)} \bmod M = \sum_{i \in \mathbb{S}_{t^*}} x_{i,t^*}^{(1)} \bmod M$ must be hold if sk_A is compromised by the adversary and $\mathbb{S}_{t^*} = \mathbb{U}$. Though in the definition of Leontiadis et al. [31], sk_A is always given to the adversary and always the condition $\sum_{i \in \mathbb{S}_{t^*}} x_{i,t^*}^{(0)} \bmod M = \sum_{i \in \mathbb{S}_{t^*}} x_{i,t^*}^{(1)} \bmod M$ is required, we follow the definition given in [8,44] where the adversary is allowed to select whether the adversary compromises sk_A or not.

Definition 5 (Aggregator Obliviousness [8,31]). *For any PPT adversary $\mathcal{A}$ and a security parameter $\lambda \in \mathbb{N}$, we define the experiment $\mathrm{Exp}_{\mathcal{A}}^{AO}(\lambda)$ as follows. If sk_A is compromised at the end of the game and $\mathbb{S}_{t^*} = \mathbb{U}$, then it is required that $\sum_{i \in \mathbb{S}_{t^*}} x_{i,t^*}^{(0)} \bmod M = \sum_{i \in \mathbb{S}_{t^*}} x_{i,t^*}^{(1)} \bmod M$.*

$\mathrm{Exp}_{\mathcal{A}}^{AO}(\lambda)$:

   $(\mathsf{param}, \mathsf{sk}_A, \{\mathsf{sk}_i\}_{i=1}^{n}, \mathsf{vk}) \leftarrow \mathsf{Setup}(1^{\lambda})$

   $(\mathbb{S}_{t^*}, t^*, \{(x_{i,t^*}^{(0)}, x_{i,t^*}^{(1)})\}_{i \in \mathbb{S}_{t^*}}) \leftarrow \mathcal{A}^{\mathcal{O}_{\mathsf{enc}}, \mathcal{O}_{\mathsf{corrupt}}}(\mathsf{param}, \mathsf{vk}, st); \ \mathbb{S}_{t^*} \subseteq \mathbb{U}; \ b \xleftarrow{\$} \{0,1\}$

   For all $i \in \mathbb{S}_{t^*}$

   $\qquad (c_{i,t^*}, \sigma_{i,t^*}) \leftarrow \mathsf{Enc}(\mathsf{param}, t, x_{i,t^*}^{(b)}, \mathsf{sk}_i)$

   $b' \leftarrow \mathcal{A}^{\mathcal{O}_{\mathsf{enc}}, \mathcal{O}_{\mathsf{corrupt}}}(\{(c_{i,t^*}, \sigma_{i,t^*})\}_{i \in \mathbb{S}_{t^*}}, st)$

   If $b = b'$, then return 1 and 0 otherwise

- $\mathcal{O}_{\mathsf{enc}}$: *This encryption oracle takes as input a tuple $(i, t, x_{i,t})$, and returns $(c_{i,t}, \sigma_{i,t}) \leftarrow \mathsf{Enc}(\mathsf{param}, t, x_{i,t}, \mathsf{sk}_i)$. Note that $\mathcal{A}$ is not allowed to input $(i, t^*, \cdot)$ where $i \in \mathbb{S}_{t^*}$ to this oracle.*
- $\mathcal{O}_{\mathsf{corrupt}}$: *This corruption oracle takes as input $i \in [0, n]$, and returns sk_i. If $i = 0$, then the oracle returns sk_A. Note that $\mathcal{A}$ is not allowed to input $i \in \mathbb{S}_{t^*}$ to this oracle.*

We say that an encryption scheme is aggregator obliviousness if the advantage $\mathrm{Adv}_{\mathcal{A}}^{AO}(\lambda) := 2|\Pr[\mathrm{Exp}_{\mathcal{A}}^{AO}(\lambda) = 1] - 1/2|$ is negligible for any PPT adversary $\mathcal{A}$.

Next, we define aggregator unforgeability. This requires that an adversary (modeled as the malicious aggregator) cannot produce a forged tag σ_t that is accepted by the VerifySum algorithm. As in the definition of unforgeability given by Leontiadis et al. [31], we consider two cases: an adversary is required either the adversary does not obtain ciphertexts and tags at the challenge time t^* (type I forgery) or the adversary has obtained all ciphertexts and tags $\{(c_{i,t^*}, \sigma_{i,t^*})\}_{i=1}^{n}$ (type II forgery). In the type II forgery case, it is assumed that ciphertexts and tags are honestly generated, and $\mathcal{A}$ obtains ciphertexts and tags of all users in the system. Type I adversary captures the case that the aggregator tries to generate a forged tag σ_t at a future time t (i.e., users have not generated $(c_{i,t}, \sigma_{i,t})$). Type II adversary captures the case that the aggregator tries to generate a forged tag σ_t at a past/current time t (i.e., users have generated $(c_{i,t}, \sigma_{i,t})$).

Definition 6 (Aggregator Unforgeability [31]). *For any PPT adversary $\mathcal{A}$ and a security parameter $\lambda \in \mathbb{N}$, we define the experiment $\mathrm{Exp}_{\mathcal{A}}^{AU}(\lambda)$ as follows.*

$\mathrm{Exp}_{\mathcal{A}}^{AU}(\lambda)$:

$\quad (\mathsf{param}, \mathsf{sk}_A, \{\mathsf{sk}_i\}_{i=1}^{n}, \mathsf{vk}) \leftarrow \mathsf{Setup}(1^\lambda)$

$\quad (t^*, X_{t^*}, \sigma_{t^*}) \leftarrow \mathcal{A}^{\mathcal{O}_{\mathsf{enc}}}(\mathsf{param}, \mathsf{sk}_A, \mathsf{vk})$

$\quad$ *If one of the followings hold, then return 1 and 0 otherwise*

$\quad\quad$ *(Type I)* : $\mathsf{VerifySum}(\mathsf{param}, t^*, X_{t^*}, \sigma_{t^*}, \mathsf{vk}_{t^*}) = 1$

$\quad\quad\quad \wedge$ *No encryption oracle is called at t^**

$\quad\quad$ *(Type II)* : $\mathsf{VerifySum}(\mathsf{param}, t^*, X_{t^*}, \sigma_{t^*}, \mathsf{vk}_{t^*}) = 1$

$$\wedge\, X_{t^*} \neq \sum_{i=1}^{n} x_{i,t^*} \bmod M$$

– $\mathcal{O}_{\mathsf{enc}}$: *This encryption oracle takes as input a tuple $(i, t, x_{i,t})$, and returns* $(c_{i,t}, \sigma_{i,t}) \leftarrow \mathsf{Enc}(\mathsf{param}, t, x_{i,t}, \mathsf{sk}_i)$.

We say that an encryption scheme is aggregator unforgeable if the advantage $\mathrm{Adv}_{\mathcal{A}}^{AU}(\lambda) := \Pr[\mathrm{Exp}_{\mathcal{A}}^{AU}(\lambda) = 1]$ is negligible for any PPT adversary $\mathcal{A}$.

Next, we slightly weaken the definition of Leontiadis et al. in the following. In their definition, the adversary (modeled as the malicious aggregator) can choose $x_{i,t}$ and can obtain the corresponding $(c_{i,t}, \sigma_{i,t})$ from the encryption oracle. This definition is an analogy of Existential Unforgeability against Chosen Message Attack (EUF-CMA) in the signature context where an adversary is allowed to obtain signatures on messages which are (adaptively) chosen by the adversary. However, in the actual situation, the aggregator does not decide $x_{i,t}$, and just receives $c_{i,t}$ sent from users. Actually, in the smart meter setting, $x_{i,t}$ (such as power consumption) is measured by the meter. Thus, it seems reasonable to propose that the adversary just queries (i, t) to the encryption oracle, and the oracle chooses $x_{i,t}$ and returns the corresponding $(c_{i,t}, \sigma_{i,t})$ to the adversary. Our definition is an analogy of Existential Unforgeability against Random Message Attack (EUF-RMA) in the signature context where an adversary is given signatures on randomly chosen messages.

Definition 7 (Weak Aggregator Unforgeability). *For any PPT adversary $\mathcal{A}$ and a security parameter $\lambda \in \mathbb{N}$, the experiment $\mathrm{Exp}_{\mathcal{A}}^{wAU}(\lambda)$ is the same as $\mathrm{Exp}_{\mathcal{A}}^{AU}(\lambda)$ except $\mathcal{O}_{\mathsf{enc}}$.*

– $\mathcal{O}_{\mathsf{enc}}$: *This encryption oracle takes as input a tuple (i, t). The oracle chooses $x_{i,t}$ and returns $(c_{i,t}, \sigma_{i,t}) \leftarrow \mathsf{Enc}(\mathsf{param}, t, x_{i,t}, \mathsf{sk}_i)$.*

We say that an encryption scheme is weakly aggregator unforgeable if the advantage $\mathrm{Adv}_{\mathcal{A}}^{wAU}(\lambda) := \Pr[\mathrm{Exp}_{\mathcal{A}}^{wAU}(\lambda) = 1]$ is negligible for any PPT adversary $\mathcal{A}$.

3.3 The DDH-based BJL Scheme

Benhamouda, Joye, and Libert (BJL) [8] gave a generic construction of aggregator oblivious encryption from smooth projective hash functions [13]. Here, we introduce its DDH instantiation. The underlying idea is essentially the same as that of the She et al. aggregator oblivious encryption. The aggregator has keys (s_0, t_0) where $s_0 + \sum_{i=1}^{n} s_i = 0$ and $t_0 + \sum_{i=1}^{n} t_i = 0$, and this structure allows the aggregator to cancel out a part of ciphertext $H_1(t)^{\sum_{i=1}^{n} s_i}$ and $H_2(t)^{\sum_{i=1}^{n} t_i}$.

Setup: Let $\mathbb{G}_1$ be a DDH-hard group with λ-bit prime order $p = M$ and g_1 be a generator of $\mathbb{G}_1$.

Let $H_i : \mathbb{Z} \to \mathbb{G}_1$ $(i = 1, 2)$ be hash functions. Choose $s_1, \ldots, s_n, t_1, \ldots, t_n \xleftarrow{\$} \mathbb{Z}_p$, set $s_0 = -\sum_{i=1}^{n} s_i$ and $t_0 = -\sum_{i=1}^{n} t_i$. Output param $= ((p, g_1, \mathbb{G}_1), H_1, H_2)$, $\mathsf{sk}_A = (s_0, t_0)$ and $\mathsf{sk}_i = (s_i, t_i)$.

Enc: Parse $\mathsf{sk}_i = (s_i, t_i)$. Compute $c_{i,t} = g_1^{x_{i,t}} H_1(t)^{s_i} H_2(t)^{t_i}$ and output $c_{i,t}$.

AggrDec: Parse $\mathsf{sk}_A = (s_0, t_0)$. Compute $V_t = H_1(t)^{s_0} H_2(t)^{t_0} \prod_{i=1}^{n} c_{i,t} = g_1^{X_t}$ where $X_t = \sum_{i=1}^{n} x_{i,t}$, and solve the discrete logarithm V_t with respect to basis g_1. Output X_t.

4 Proposed Constructions

In this section, we propose two schemes. For aggregator obliviousness, both schemes are tightly reduced to the DDH-based BJL scheme. The first scheme only provides weak aggregator unforgeability, whereas the second scheme provides aggregator unforgeability. The unforgeability of both schemes relies on the mCDH assumption and the second scheme additionally requires public channels with memory, such as a bulletin board [22] (which is publicly readable, and every user can write to, but nobody can delete from). Moreover, users are required to generate random numbers in the Enc algorithm. Thus, the Enc algorithm in the second scheme is probabilistic whereas that of the first scheme is deterministic.

4.1 High-Level Description

Aggregator Obliviousness: We employ (type 3) elliptic curves where $\mathbb{G}_1 \neq \mathbb{G}_2$ and no efficient isomorphism between $\mathbb{G}_1$ and $\mathbb{G}_2$ is known. Then, we run the BJL scheme [8] over the DDH-hard group $\mathbb{G}_1$, and borrow the ciphertext form $c_{i,t}$ and secret keys sk_A and sk_i. Since the BJL scheme is aggregator obliviousness under the DDH assumption, we can expect that our scheme is also aggregator obliviousness. In order to directly reduce the aggregator obliviousness of our scheme to that of the BJL scheme, we independently prepare the verification part. That is, we introduce $v_{i,t}$ for each user i and in the security proof, $v_{i,t}$ can be chosen independently from the BJL scheme. This setting allows us to compute the tag $\sigma_{i,t}$ from $c_{i,t}$ and $v_{i,t}$ in the security proof. More precisely, the challenge ciphertexts and tags of our scheme $\{(c_{i,t^*}, \sigma_{i,t^*})\}_{i \in \mathbb{S}_{t^*}}$ can be constructed from the challenge ciphertext of the BJL scheme $\{c_{i,t^*}\}_{i \in \mathbb{S}_{t^*}}$ and the corresponding $v_{i,t}$. Thus, we can construct an algorithm that breaks the aggregator obliviousness of the BJL scheme by using an adversary of our scheme. Remark that $\sigma_{i,t}$ has the similar form of $c_{i,t}$ in our scheme due to this reason. This strategy has been considered by Leontiadis et al. [31]. They provided a reduction of their scheme to the Shi et al. scheme [44]. However, as mentioned by Benhamouda et al. [8], the security loss is $O(t_{\max} n^3)$ in the Shi et al. scheme, whereas it is $O(t_{\max})$ in the BJL scheme. Thus, we have chosen the BJL scheme as the underlying scheme in this paper.

Aggregator Unforgeability: For public verification, we pay attention to that the form of the ciphertext $c_{i,t}$ of the BJL scheme is similar to a decryption key of the Boneh-Boyen identity-based encryption (IBE) scheme [9].[4] Due to the above reason, the tag $\sigma_{i,t}$ has the similar form of $c_{i,t}$ in our schemes. Since secure IBE implies a signature [14] (informally, ID is regarded as a message to be signed, and its decryption key is regarded as a signature), we can expect that $\sigma_{i,t}$ is unforgeable. However, to utilize the Boneh-Boyen technique, X_t needs to be embedded into vk in the security proof. Here, we have two choices: whether vk is fixed in the setup phase or not. If vk is chosen by the honest dealer and is fixed in the setup phase, X_t is also required to be fixed in the setup phase (to utilize the security proof technique of selective-ID security of Boney-Boyen IBE), and therefore only weak aggregator unforgeability is provided. Moreover, since one X_t is embedded with one vk, long verification keys is also required where the size lineally depends on $t_{\max}$. We set vk $= \{vk_t\}_{t \in [1, t_{\max}]}$ and vk$_t := g_2^{\sum_{i=1}^{n} v_{i,t}}$ for $t \in [1, t_{\max}]$. We remark that no user is required to have the large-size verification key. Moreover, if a user i manages all $v_{i,t}$ for $t \in [1, t_{\max}]$ as its secret key sk$_i$, the secret key size also depends on $t_{\max}$. To avoid such a large-size secret key, we additionally introduce a hash function H and a time-independent secret key v_i, and we compute $v_{i,t} = H(v_i, t)$. That is, in the scheme $v_{i,t}$ is computed by $H(v_i, t)$ whereas in the security proof, $v_{i,t}$ is selected so as to utilize the Boneh-Boyen technique, and set $H(v_i, t) := v_{i,t}$. This helps us to reduce the secret key size.

4.2 The Proposed Scheme 1: Providing Weak Aggregator Unforgeability

We give the first scheme as follows. As mentioned above, vk is chosen in the setup phase.

Setup(1^λ): Choose $(p, e, g_1, g_2, \mathbb{G}_1, \mathbb{G}_2, \mathbb{G}_T)$ where $\mathbb{G}_1$, $\mathbb{G}_2$ and $\mathbb{G}_T$ are groups of λ-bit prime order $p = M$, $g_1 \in \mathbb{G}_1$ and $g_2 \in \mathbb{G}_2$ are generators, and $e : \mathbb{G}_1 \times$

---

[4] A decryption key of the Boneh-Boyen IBE scheme is informally described as $(g^\alpha H_{\mathsf{BB}}(ID)^r, g^r)$ for a master key α and a random r, the Boneh-Boyen hash H_{BB}. In our first construction, α, ID, and r are regarded as $x_{i,t}$, t, and $v_{i,t}$ respectively. Thus, the number of verification keys depends on $t_{\max}$.

$\mathbb{G}_2 \to \mathbb{G}_T$ is a bilinear map. Let $H : \mathbb{Z}_p \times [1, t_{\max}] \to \mathbb{Z}_p$ and $H_i : \mathbb{Z} \to \mathbb{G}_1$ ($i = 1, 2, 3, 4, 5$) be hash functions. Choose $\gamma, s_1, \ldots, s_n, t_1, \ldots, t_n, v_1, \ldots, v_n \xleftarrow{\$} \mathbb{Z}_p$, compute $v_{i,t} = H(v_i, t)$ for all $i \in [1, n]$ and $t \in [1, t_{\max}]$ and set $s_0 = -\sum_{i=1}^{n} s_i$, $t_0 = -\sum_{i=1}^{n} t_i$, $h = g_1^{\gamma}$, and $Z = e(h, g_2)$. Output $\mathsf{param} = ((p, e, g_1, g_2, \mathbb{G}_1, \mathbb{G}_2, \mathbb{G}_T), Z, H, H_1, H_2, H_3, H_4, H_5)$, $\mathsf{sk}_A = (s_0, t_0)$, $\mathsf{sk}_i = (s_i, t_i, v_i, h)$, and $\mathsf{vk} = \{\mathsf{vk}_t\}_{t \in [1, t_{\max}]}$ where $\mathsf{vk}_t = g_2^{\sum_{i=1}^{n} v_{i,t}}$.

$\mathsf{Enc}(\mathsf{param}, t, x_{i,t}, \mathsf{sk}_i)$: Parse $\mathsf{sk}_i = (s_i, t_i, v_i, h)$. Compute

$$v_{i,t} = H(v_i, t), \quad c_{i,t} = g_1^{x_{i,t}} H_1(t)^{s_i} H_2(t)^{t_i}, \text{ and } \sigma_{i,t} = h^{x_{i,t}} H_3(t)^{s_i} H_4(t)^{t_i} H_5(t)^{v_{i,t}}$$

and output $(c_{i,t}, \sigma_{i,t})$.

$\mathsf{AggrDec}(\mathsf{param}, t, \{(c_{i,t}, \sigma_{i,t})\}_{i=1}^{n}, \mathsf{sk}_A)$: Parse $\mathsf{sk}_A = (s_0, t_0)$. Compute

$$V_t = H_1(t)^{s_0} H_2(t)^{t_0} \prod_{i=1}^{n} c_{i,t} = g_1^{X_t}$$

where $X_t = \sum_{i=1}^{n} x_{i,t}$, and solve the discrete logarithm V_t with respect to basis g_1. Moreover, compute

$$\sigma_t = H_3(t)^{s_0} H_4(t)^{t_0} \prod_{i=1}^{n} \sigma_{i,t}$$

Output (X_t, σ_t).

$\mathsf{VerifySum}(\mathsf{param}, t, X_t, \sigma_t, \mathsf{vk}_t)$: Output 1 if

$$\frac{e(\sigma_t, g_2)}{e(H_5(t), \mathsf{vk}_t)} = Z^{X_t}$$

holds. Otherwise, output 0.

The correctness cleary holds from the following equations.

$$H_1(t)^{s_0} H_2(t)^{t_0} \prod_{i=1}^{n} c_{i,t} = H_1(t)^{s_0} H_2(t)^{t_0} \prod_{i=1}^{n} g_1^{x_{i,t}} H_1(t)^{s_i} H_2(t)^{t_i}$$

$$= H_1(t)^{s_0 - \sum_{i=1}^{n} s_i} H_2(t)^{t_0 - \sum_{i=1}^{n} t_i} g_1^{\sum_{i=1}^{n} x_{i,t}}$$

$$= g_1^{X_t}$$

$$\sigma_t = H_3(t)^{s_0} H_4(t)^{t_0} \prod_{i=1}^{n} \sigma_{i,t}$$

$$= H_3(t)^{s_0} H_4(t)^{t_0} \prod_{i=1}^{n} h^{x_{i,t}} H_3(t)^{s_i} H_4(t)^{t_i} H_5(t)^{v_{i,t}}$$

$$= h^{X_t} H_5(t)^{\sum_{i=1}^{n} v_{i,t}}$$

$$e(\sigma_t, g_2) = e(h^{X_t} H_5(t)^{\sum_{i=1}^{n} v_{i,t}}, g_2) = e(h, g_2)^{X_t} e(H_5(t), g_2^{\sum_{i=1}^{n} v_{i,t}})$$

$$= Z^{X_t} e(H_5(t), \mathsf{vk}_t)$$

Theorem 1. *Our scheme 1 is aggregator obliviousness under the DDH assumption on $\mathbb{G}_1$ in the random oracle model.*

We consider the following two games. Game 0 is the original game. Game 1 is the same as Game 0 except that H_3 and H_4 are computed as $H_3(t) = H_1(t)^\gamma$ and $H_4(t) = H_2(t)^\gamma$ for some $\gamma \in \mathbb{Z}_p$. Since $(H_1(t), H_2(t), H_3(t), H_4(t))$ is a DDH tuple, this modification does not affect the security under the DDH assumption on $\mathbb{G}_1$. Briefly, let $(g_1, g_1', g_1^{r_1}, g_1'^{r_2}) \in \mathbb{G}_1^4$ be an DDH instance on $\mathbb{G}_1$. For $t \in [1, t_{\max}]$, choose $\tilde{t}_1, \tilde{t}_2 \overset{\$}{\leftarrow} \mathbb{Z}_p$, and set $H_1(t) := g_1^{\tilde{t}_1}$, $H_2(t) := g_1'^{\tilde{t}_2}$, $H_3(t) := (g_1^{r_1})^{\tilde{t}_1}$, and $H_4(t) := (g_1'^{r_2})^{\tilde{t}_2}$. Clearly, if the instance is not a DDH tuple, i.e., $r_1 \neq r_2$, then we simulate Game 0, and if the instance is a DDH tuple, i.e., $r_1 = r_2$, then we simulate Game 1. In Game 1, we construct an algorithm $\mathcal{B}$ that breaks aggregator obliviousness of the BJL scheme as follows.

Proof: Let $\mathcal{A}$ be the adversary of our scheme, and $\mathcal{C}$ be the challenger of the BJL scheme. We construct an algorithm $\mathcal{B}$ that breaks aggregator obliviousness of the BJL scheme as follows. First, $\mathcal{C}$ prepares $(p, e, g_1, g_2, \mathbb{G}_1, \mathbb{G}_2, \mathbb{G}_T, H_1, H_2)$ and sends it to $\mathcal{B}$. $\mathcal{B}$ chooses $\gamma, v_1, \ldots, v_n, v_{1,1}, \ldots, v_{n,t_{\max}} \overset{\$}{\leftarrow} \mathbb{Z}_p$. $\mathcal{B}$ computes $h = g_1^\gamma$, $Z = e(h, g_2)$, $\mathsf{vk}_{i,t} = g_2^{v_{i,t}}$ for $i \in [1, n]$ and $t \in [1, t_{\max}]$, and $\mathsf{vk}_t = g_2^{\sum_{i=1}^n v_{i,t}}$. $\mathcal{B}$ sets $H(v_i, t) := v_{i,t}$ for $i \in [1, n]$ and $t \in [1, t_{\max}]$. Remark that if $\mathcal{A}$ sends a hash query t, then $\mathcal{B}$ forwards it to $\mathcal{C}$ when $\mathcal{A}$ requests $H_1(t)$ or $H_2(t)$. For H_3 and H_4, $\mathcal{B}$ sets $H_3(t) = H_1(t)^\gamma$ and $H_4(t) = H_2(t)^\gamma$, and returns the hash values. For H_5, $\mathcal{B}$ just returns a random value. $\mathcal{B}$ sends $\mathsf{param} = ((p, e, g_1, g_2, \mathbb{G}_1, \mathbb{G}_2, \mathbb{G}_T), Z, H, H_1, H_2, H_3, H_4, H_5)$, $\{\mathsf{vk}_t\}_{t \in [1, t_{\max}]}$, and vk to $\mathcal{A}$.

If $\mathcal{A}$ sends an encryption query $(i, t, x_{i,t})$ to $\mathcal{B}$, then $\mathcal{B}$ forwards it to $\mathcal{C}$ as an encryption oracle, and obtains $c_{i,t}$. $\mathcal{B}$ computes $c_{i,t}^\gamma H_5(t)^{v_{i,t}} = h^{x_{i,t}} H_3(t)^{s_i} H_4(t)^{t_i} H_5(t)^{v_{i,t}}$, and returns $(c_{i,t}, \sigma_{i,t})$ to $\mathcal{A}$. If $\mathcal{A}$ sends a corruption query $i \in [0, n]$ to $\mathcal{B}$, $\mathcal{B}$ forwards it to $\mathcal{C}$ as a corruption query, and obtains $\mathsf{sk}_\mathcal{A}$ (if $i = 0$) or (s_i, t_i) (if $i \in [1, n]$). If $i = 0$, then $\mathcal{B}$ returns $\mathsf{sk}_\mathcal{A}$ to $\mathcal{A}$. If $i \in [1, n]$, then $\mathcal{B}$ sets $\mathsf{sk}_i = (s_i, t_i, v_i, h)$, and returns sk_i to $\mathcal{A}$. We remark that if $\mathcal{A}$ sends a hash query (v_i, t), then $\mathcal{B}$ responds $v_{i,t}$ to $\mathcal{A}$.

In the challenge phase, $\mathcal{A}$ sends $(\mathbb{S}_{t^*}, t^*, \{(x_{i,t^*}^{(0)}, x_{i,t^*}^{(1)})\}_{i \in \mathbb{S}_{t^*}})$ to $\mathcal{B}$. Then, $\mathcal{B}$ forwards it to $\mathcal{C}$ as the challenge, and obtains $\{c_{i,t^*}\}_{i \in \mathbb{S}_{t^*}}$. As in the response of encryption queries, $\mathcal{B}$ computes $\sigma_{i,t^*} = c_{i,t^*}^\gamma H_5(t)^{v_{i,t^*}}$ for $i \in \mathbb{S}_{t^*}$, and returns $\{(c_{i,t^*}, \sigma_{i,t^*})\}_{i \in \mathbb{S}_{t^*}}$ to $\mathcal{A}$.

$\mathcal{B}$ responds queries sent from $\mathcal{A}$ as in the previous phase. Finally, $\mathcal{A}$ outputs a bit b'. $\mathcal{B}$ outputs b' and then $\mathcal{B}$ can break aggregator obliviousness of the BJL scheme with the same advantage of $\mathcal{A}$. This concludes the proof since the BJL scheme is aggregator obliviousness under the DDH assumption on $\mathbb{G}_1$ in the random oracle model. $\square$

Theorem 2. *Our scheme 1 is weakly aggregator unforgeable under the mCDH assumption in the random oracle model.*

For the proof of Type I forgery, we employ the following assumption: given (g_1^a, g_1^b, g_2^a) compute g_1^{ab}. Since this is equivalent to the CDH assumption if the symmetric pairing setting is employed, we simply call the assumption the CDH assumption in this paper. Remark that this is weaker than mCDH since $g_1^{1/a}$ is not contained in the instance. Since no encryption oracle is called at t^*, the proof is relatively easy. We embed the instance g_1^a to $v_{i,t}$ and g_1^b to the response of the random oracle H_5 respectively. At time t^*, $\mathcal{A}$ outputs (σ_{t^*}, X_{t^*}). From the verification equation, (σ_{t^*}, X_{t^*}) must satisfy $\sigma_{t^*} = H_5(t^*)^{\sum_{i=1}^n v_{i,t}} h^{X_{t^*}}$. Since $H_5(t^*)^{\sum_{i=1}^n v_{i,t}}$ contains g_1^{ab}, we can solve the CDH problem. Remark that this proof strategy requires $O(t_{\max})$ reduction loss from the advantage of the CDH problem. However, we can achieve a tight reduction (i.e., $O(1)$ reduction loss) from the advantage of the mCDH problem (see below).

For the proof of Type II forgery, our proof strategy is explained as follows. Again, (σ_{t^*}, X_{t^*}) must satisfy $\sigma_{t^*} = H_5(t^*)^{\sum_{i=1}^n v_{i,t}} h^{X_{t^*}}$. Though $Z = e(h, g_2)$ is published, h itself is not published (contained in sk_i). Thus, we set $h = g_1^{ab}$ and simulate the encryption oracle by using the Boneh-Boyen technique. We embed $1/a$ to $x_{i,t}$ such that $x_{i,t} := x'_{i,t}/a$ for $x'_{i,t} \in \mathbb{Z}_p$. This setting helps us to compute $h^{x_{i,t}} = (g_1^{ab})^{x'_{i,t}/a} = (g_1^b)^{x'_{i,t}}$ without knowing $h = g_1^{ab}$. Remark that ciphertexts $\{c_{i,t}\}$ must be decryptable by the adversary, i.e., the discrete logarithm $\log_{g_1} V_t$ must be sufficiently small. If all $x_{i,t}$ are related to $1/a$ as above, then $\log_{g_1} V_{t^*} = (\sum_{i=1}^n x'_{i,t})/a$ is not computable. Thus, for relatively small X'_t, we set $x_{i,t} := x'_{i,t}/a$ for $i \in [1, n-1]$ and set $x_{n,t} := X'_t - \sum_{i=1}^{n-1} x'_{i,t}/a$. Then, $\sum_{i=1}^n x_{i,t} = X'_t$ holds and $\log_{g_1} V_t = X'_t$ is computable by the adversary as in the scheme. For simulation, we need to decide each X'_t in the setup phase, and embed it to $v_{n,t}$ for utilizing the Boneh-Boyen technique. This is the reason why our scheme is weak aggregator unforgeable ($x_{i,t}$ is chosen by the oracle), and the size of verification keys linearly depend on $t_{\max}$. Remark that we can achieve a tight reduction (i.e., $O(1)$ reduction loss) from the advantage of the mCDH problem, and this proof also works well for Type I forgery (simply we assume that the encryption oracle at t^* is not sent from $\mathcal{A}$, choose X'_{t^*} randomly, and $X_{t^*} \neq X'_{t^*}$ holds with overwhelming probability $1 - 1/p$).

Proof

Type I Forgery: Let $(p, e, g_1, g_2, \mathbb{G}_1, \mathbb{G}_2, \mathbb{G}_T, (g_1^a, g_1^b, g_2^a))$ be an instance of the CDH problem. We construct an algorithm $\mathcal{B}$ that computes g_1^{ab} by using an adversary $\mathcal{A}$ that breaks aggregator unforgeability of our scheme as follows. $\mathcal{B}$ sets $\mathsf{param} = (p, e, g_1, g_2, \mathbb{G}_1, \mathbb{G}_2, \mathbb{G}_T)$, chooses γ, s_i, t_i, and sk_A as usual, chooses $v'_{i,t} \xleftarrow{\$} \mathbb{Z}_p$ for $i \in [1, n]$ such that $\sum_{i=1}^n v'_{i,t} \neq 0$, and chooses $t \in [1, t_{\max}]$, and implicitly sets $v_{i,t} := v'_{i,t}a$. $\mathcal{B}$ computes $\mathsf{vk}_t = (g_2^a)^{\sum_{i=1}^n v'_{i,t}}$. $\mathcal{B}$ sends $(\mathsf{params}, \mathsf{sk}_A, \mathsf{vk} = \{\mathsf{vk}_t\}_{t \in [1, t_{\max}]})$ to $\mathcal{A}$.

Moreover, $\mathcal{B}$ guesses t^* (with success probability $1/t_{\max}$). For a time t, $\mathcal{B}$ chooses $\tilde{t} \xleftarrow{\$} \mathbb{Z}_p$ and sets $H_5(t)$ as

$$H_5(t) = \begin{cases} g_1^{\tilde{t}} & (t \neq t^*) \\ (g_1^b)^{\tilde{t}^*} & (t = t^*) \end{cases}$$

For other hash functions, $\mathcal{B}$ just returns a random value. For responding an encryption query (i, t) where $t \neq t^*$, $\mathcal{B}$ chooses $x_{i,t}$ and computes $\sigma_{i,t} = h^{x_{i,t}} H_3(t)^{s_i} H_4(t)^{t_i} (g_1^a)^{v_{i,t}'\tilde{t}} = h^{x_{i,t}} H_3(t)^{s_i} H_4(t)^{t_i} (g_1^{\tilde{t}})^{a v_{i,t}'} = h^{x_{i,t}} H_3(t)^{s_i} H_4(t)^{t_i} H_5(t)^{v_{i,t}}$. Remark that $\mathcal{A}$ does not send an encryption query at time t^* in this type.

Finally, at time t^*, $\mathcal{A}$ outputs (σ_{t^*}, X_{t^*}). From the verification equation, (σ_{t^*}, X_{t^*}) must satisfy $\sigma_{t^*} = H_5(t^*)^{\sum_{i=1}^{n} v_{i,t}} h^{X_{t^*}}$. That is,

$$\sigma_{t^*} h^{-X_{t^*}} = H_5(t^*)^{\sum_{i=1}^{n} v_{i,t^*}} = ((g_1^b)^{\tilde{t}^*})^{a \sum_{i=1}^{n} v_{i,t^*}'}$$

holds. $\mathcal{B}$ solves the CDH problem by computing $(\sigma_{t^*} h^{-X_{t^*}})^{1/\tilde{t}^* \sum_{i=1}^{n} v_{i,t^*}'} = g_1^{ab}$.

Type II Forgery: Let $(p, e, g_1, g_2, \mathbb{G}_1, \mathbb{G}_2, \mathbb{G}_T, (g_1^a, g_1^b, g_1^{1/a}, g_2^a))$ be an instance of the Modified CDH problem. We construct an algorithm $\mathcal{B}$ that computes g_1^{ab} by using an adversary $\mathcal{A}$ that breaks aggregator unforgeability of our scheme as follows. $\mathcal{B}$ sets $\mathsf{param} = (p, e, g_1, g_2, \mathbb{G}_1, \mathbb{G}_2, \mathbb{G}_T)$, chooses γ, s_i, t_i, sk_A, and $v_{i,t}$ for $i = [1, n-1]$ and $t \in [1, t_{\mathsf{max}}]$ as usual. For $t \in [1, t_{\mathsf{max}}]$, $\mathcal{B}$ chooses $v_{n,t}' \xleftarrow{\$} \mathbb{Z}_p$, and also chooses $X_t' \xleftarrow{\$} \mathbb{Z}_p$ such that the size of X_t' is sufficiently small where the discrete logarithm problem $g_1^{X_t}$ with respect to basis g_1 can be solved. This is the necessary condition that ciphertexts can be decrypted by the adversary as in the scheme. For $t \in [1, t_{\mathsf{max}}]$, $\mathcal{B}$ chooses $\tilde{t} \xleftarrow{\$} \mathbb{Z}_p$ and sets $H_5(t)$ as $(g_1^b)^{\tilde{t}}$. $\mathcal{B}$ implicitly sets $v_{n,t} = v_{n,t}' + (-aX_t')/\tilde{t}$. $\mathcal{B}$ computes $\mathsf{vk}_t = (g_2^a)^{-X_t'/\tilde{t}} g_2^{v_{n,t}' + \sum_{i=1}^{n-1} v_{i,t}}$. $\mathcal{B}$ implicitly sets $h = g_1^{ab}$ and computes $Z = e(g_1^b, g_2^a) = e(h, g_2)$. $\mathcal{B}$ sends $(\mathsf{params}, \mathsf{sk}_A, \mathsf{vk} = \{\mathsf{vk}_t\}_{t \in [1, t_{\mathsf{max}}]})$ to $\mathcal{A}$.

For responding an encryption query (i, t), $\mathcal{B}$ computes $(c_{i,t}, \sigma_{i,t})$ as follows. $\mathcal{B}$ chooses $x_{i,t}' \xleftarrow{\$} \mathbb{Z}_p$ for $i \in [1, n-1]$ and implicitly sets $x_{i,t}$ as

$$x_{i,t} = \begin{cases} x_{i,t}'/a & (i \in [1, n-1]) \\ X_t' - \sum_{i=1}^{n-1} x_{i,t}'/a & (i = n) \end{cases}$$

and computes

$$i \in [1, n-1] : c_{i,t} = (g_1^{1/a})^{x_{i,t}'} H_1(t)^{s_i} H_2(t)^{t_i}$$
$$= g_1^{x_{i,t}'/a} H_1(t)^{s_i} H_2(t)^{t_i} = g_1^{x_{i,t}} H_1(t)^{s_i} H_2(t)^{t_i}$$
$$i = n : c_{i,t} = g_1^{X_t'} (g_1^{1/a})^{-\sum_{i=1}^{n-1} x_{i,t}'} H_1(t)^{s_i} H_2(t)^{t_i}$$
$$= g_1^{X_t' - \sum_{i=1}^{n-1} x_{i,t}'/a} H_1(t)^{s_i} H_2(t)^{t_i}$$
$$= g_1^{x_{i,t}} H_1(t)^{s_i} H_2(t)^{t_i}$$

and

$$i \in [1, n-1]: \quad \sigma_{i,t} = (g_1^b)^{x'_{i,t}} H_3(t)^{s_i} H_4(t)^{t_i} H_5(t)^{v_{i,t}}$$
$$= (g_1^{ab})^{x'_{i,t}/a} H_3(t)^{s_i} H_4(t)^{t_i} H_5(t)^{v_{i,t}}$$
$$= h^{x_{i,t}} H_3(t)^{s_i} H_4(t)^{t_i} H_5(t)^{v_{i,t}}$$

$$i = n: \quad \sigma_{i,t} = (g_1^b)^{-\sum_{i=1}^{n-1} x'_{i,t} + \tilde{t} v'_{n,t}} H_3(t)^{s_i} H_4(t)^{t_i}$$
$$= (g_1^{ab})^{X'_t} (g_1^b)^{-\sum_{i=1}^{n-1} x'_{i,t}} (g_1^{-ab})^{X'_t} (g_1^b)^{\tilde{t} v'_{n,t}} H_3(t)^{s_i} H_4(t)^{t_i}$$
$$= (g_1^{ab})^{X'_t} (g_1^{ab})^{-\sum_{i=1}^{n-1} x'_{i,t}/a} (g_1^{-ab})^{X'_t} (g_1^b)^{\tilde{t} v'_{n,t}} H_3(t)^{s_i} H_4(t)^{t_i}$$
$$= (g_1^{ab})^{X'_t - \sum_{i=1}^{n-1} x'_{i,t}/a} H_3(t)^{s_i} H_4(t)^{t_i} ((g_1^b)^{\tilde{t}})^{v'_{n,t} + (-aX'_t)/\tilde{t}}$$
$$= h^{x_{i,t}} H_3(t)^{s_i} H_4(t)^{t_i} H_5(t)^{v_{i,t}}$$

Remark that $\sum_{i=1}^{n} x_{i,t} = X'_t$ and $\{c_{i,t}\}_{i \in [1,n]}$ can be decrypted by the adversary who has sk_A.

Finally, $\mathcal{A}$ outputs $(t^*, X_{t^*}, \sigma_{t^*})$ where $t^* \in [1, t_{\max}]$ and $X_{t^*} \neq X'_{t^*}$. From the verification equation, (σ_{t^*}, X_{t^*}) must satisfy $\sigma_{t^*} = H_5(t^*)^{\sum_{i=1}^{n} v_{i,t^*}} h^{X_{t^*}}$. Here, $\sigma_{t^*} = H_5(t^*)^{\sum_{i=1}^{n} v_{i,t^*}} h^{X_{t^*}} = ((g_1^b)^{\tilde{t}^*})^{v'_{n,t^*} + (-aX'_{t^*}/\tilde{t}^*) + \sum_{i=1}^{n-1} v_{i,t^*}} (g_1^{ab})^{X_{t^*}} = (g_1^{ab})^{X_{t^*} - X'_{t^*}} (g_1^b)^{\tilde{t}^* (v'_{n,t^*} + \sum_{i=1}^{n-1} v_{i,t^*})}$ holds. $\mathcal{B}$ computes

$$(\sigma_{t^*} / (g_1^b)^{\tilde{t}^* (v'_{n,t^*} + \sum_{i=1}^{n-1} v_{i,t^*})})^{1/(X_{t^*} - X'_{t^*})} = g_1^{ab}$$

and solves the mCDH problem. □

4.3 The Proposed Scheme 2: Providing Aggregator Unforgeability

In the first scheme, $v_{i,t}$ is chosen in the setup phase. This leads to large-size verification keys, and is the reason why the first scheme provides weak aggregator unforgeability. As mentioned before, as another choice, a user i chooses $v_{i,t} \xleftarrow{\$} \mathbb{Z}_p$ at time t on the fly (i.e., in the encryption phase), computes $\mathsf{vk}_{i,t} := g_1^{v_{i,t}}$, and sends $\mathsf{vk}_{i,t}$ to the aggregator together with $(c_{i,t}, \sigma_{i,t})$. Then $\mathsf{vk}_t = \prod_{i=1}^{n} \mathsf{vk}_{i,t}$ is used in the VerifySum algorithm. In this case, X_t, chosen by the adversary in the security proof, can be embedded to vk_t on the fly in the encryption oracle, and therefore we can provide aggregator unforgeability. Moreover, one hash function H and vk can be removed from the public value, and v_i can also be removed from sk_i.

One problem with this strategy is that the Enc algorithm becomes probabilistic. That is, a user is required to generate a random number $v_{i,t}$ for each time t. This could be problematic if users have limited computational power. Another problem is that the aggregator (which is an adversary of the aggregator unforgeability game) could modify vk_t, and the VerifySum algorithm is run by a maliciously generated vk_t. Then, no security is guaranteed. One solution is to use a bulletin board [22] which is publicly readable and every user can write to, but nobody can delete from. The bulletin board can be considered a public channel with memory. That is, a user i writes $\mathsf{vk}_{i,t}$ to the bulletin board BB. Remark that the computation cost of $\mathsf{vk}_t = \prod_{i=1}^{n} \mathsf{vk}_{i,t}$ is almost similar to that of $V_t = H_1(t)^{s_0} H_2(t)^{t_0} \prod_{i=1}^{n} c_{i,t}$. That is, if a data analyzer who runs the VerifySum algorithm computes vk_t, then the data analyzer does not need to delegate the computation of the aggregated sum to the aggregator, and this leads to a wag-the-dog situation. So, we assume that the aggregator computes vk_t, and $\mathsf{vk}_{i,t}$ written in BB acts as a deterrent against the aggregator that modifies vk_t, since the data analyzer can check anytime whether vk_t provided by the aggregator is computed by $\{\mathsf{vk}_{i,t}\}_{i=1}^{n}$ or not. In summary, we slightly modify the syntax such that the bulletin board BB is added as an input of the Enc algorithm, and the AggrDec algorithm outputs vk_t together with (X_t, σ_t).

We give the second scheme as follows.

Setup(1^λ): Choose $(p, e, g_1, g_2, \mathbb{G}_1, \mathbb{G}_2, \mathbb{G}_T)$ where $\mathbb{G}_1$, $\mathbb{G}_2$ and $\mathbb{G}_T$ are groups of λ-bit prime order $p = M$, $g_1 \in \mathbb{G}_1$ and $g_2 \in \mathbb{G}_2$ are genera-tors, and $e : \mathbb{G}_1 \times \mathbb{G}_2 \to \mathbb{G}_T$ is a bilinear map. Let $H_i : \mathbb{Z} \to \mathbb{G}_1$ ($i = 1,2,3,4,5$) be hash functions. Choose $\gamma, s_1, \ldots, s_n, t_1, \ldots, t_n \xleftarrow{\$} \mathbb{Z}_p$, set $s_0 = -\sum_{i=1}^{n} s_i$, $t_0 = -\sum_{i=1}^{n} t_i$, $h = g_1^\gamma$, and $Z = e(h, g_2)$. Out-put param $= ((p, e, g_1, g_2, \mathbb{G}_1, \mathbb{G}_2, \mathbb{G}_T), Z, H_1, H_2, H_3, H_4, H_5)$, $\mathsf{sk}_A = (s_0, t_0)$, $\mathsf{sk}_i = (s_i, t_i, h)$, and $\mathsf{vk} = \emptyset$.

Enc(param, $t, x_{i,t}, \mathsf{sk}_i, \mathsf{BB}$): Parse $\mathsf{sk}_i = (s_i, t_i, h)$. Choose $v_{i,t} \xleftarrow{\$} \mathbb{Z}_p$, compute $\mathsf{vk}_{i,t} := g_1^{v_{i,t}}$, and compute

$$c_{i,t} = g_1^{x_{i,t}} H_1(t)^{s_i} H_2(t)^{t_i} \text{ and } \sigma_{i,t} = h^{x_{i,t}} H_3(t)^{s_i} H_4(t)^{t_i} H_5(t)^{v_{i,t}}$$

and output $(c_{i,t}, \sigma_{i,t}, \mathsf{vk}_{i,t})$. Moreover, write $\mathsf{vk}_{i,t}$ to the bulletin board BB.
AggrDec(param, $t, \{(c_{i,t}, \sigma_{i,t}, \mathsf{vk}_{i,t})\}_{i=1}^{n}, \mathsf{sk}_A$): Parse $\mathsf{sk}_A = (s_0, t_0)$. Compute

$$V_t = H_1(t)^{s_0} H_2(t)^{t_0} \prod_{i=1}^{n} c_{i,t} = g_1^{X_t}$$

where $X_t = \sum_{i=1}^{n} x_{i,t}$, and solve the discrete logarithm V_t with respect to basis g_1. Moreover, compute

$$\sigma_t = H_3(t)^{s_0} H_4(t)^{t_0} \prod_{i=1}^{n} \sigma_{i,t} \text{ and } \mathsf{vk}_t = \prod_{i=1}^{n} \mathsf{vk}_{i,t}$$

Output $(X_t, \sigma_t, \mathsf{vk}_t)$.
VerifySum(param, $t, X_t, \sigma_t, \mathsf{vk}_t$): Output 1 if

$$\frac{e(\sigma_t, g_2)}{e(H_5(t), \mathsf{vk}_t)} = Z^{X_t}$$

holds. Otherwise, output 0.

Theorem 3. *Our scheme 2 is aggregator obliviousness under the DDH assump-tion on $\mathbb{G}_1$ in the random oracle model.*

This is essentially the same as that of the first scheme. We omit it.

Theorem 4. *Our scheme 2 is aggregator unforgeable under the mCDH assumption in the random oracle model.*

Proof (Sketch): The proof is almost similar to that of the first scheme. The difference is the response of the encryption query $(i, t, x_{i,t})$ for Type II forgery. Let $(i_n, t, x_{i_n,t})$ where $i_n \in [1, n]$ be the last encryption query at t. Without loss of generality, we set $i_n = n$. If $i \in [1, n-1]$, then choose $x'_{i,t} \xleftarrow{\$} \mathbb{Z}_p$ (regardless of $x_{i,t}$) and $v_{i,t} \xleftarrow{\$} \mathbb{Z}_p$, compute $c_{i,t} = (g_1^{1/a})^{x'_{i,t}} H_1(t)^{s_i} H_2(t)^{t_i}$ and $\sigma_{i,t} = (g_1^b)^{x'_{i,t}} H_3(t)^{s_i} H_4(t)^{t_i} H_5(t)^{v_{i,t}}$. Return $(c_{i,t}, \sigma_{i,t})$ to $\mathcal{A}$, and write $\mathsf{vk}_{i,t} = g_2^{v_{i,t}}$ to BB. If $i = n$, then choose $v'_{i,t} \xleftarrow{\$} \mathbb{Z}_p$, compute $X'_t = \sum_{i=1}^{n-1} x_{i,t}$ from queries $\{(i, t, x_{i,t})\}_{i \in [1,n-1]}$, and compute

$$c_{i,t} = g_1^{X'_t}(g_1^{1/a})^{-\sum_{i=1}^{n-1} x'_{i,t}} H_1(t)^{s_i} H_2(t)^{t_i} \text{ and } \sigma_{i,t} = (g_1^b)^{-\sum_{i=1}^{n-1} x'_{i,t} + \tilde{t} v'_{n,t}} H_3(t)^{s_i} H_4(t)^{t_i}$$

Here, $H_5(t)$ is set as $(g_1^b)^{\tilde{t}}$ as in the proof of the first scheme. Return $(c_{i,t}, \sigma_{i,t}, \mathsf{vk}_{i,t})$ to $\mathcal{A}$, and write $\mathsf{vk}_{i,t} = (g_2^a)^{-X'_t/\tilde{t}} g_2^{v'_{n,t}}$ to BB. We note that $\{c_{i,t}\}_{i \in [1,n]}$ can be decrypted by the adversary, and the decryption result is exactly $\sum_{i=1}^n x_{i,t}$ that the adversary queried. We conclude the proof. $\square$

5   Conclusion and Open Problem

In this paper, we propose two aggregator oblivious encryption schemes with public verifiability from static and simple assumptions. The first scheme just provides weak aggregator unforgeability, and it seems still meaningful in the smart meter settings since power consumption is measured by the meter. Though the scheme requires $O(t_{\mathsf{max}})$-size verification keys, and it could be a bottleneck for supporting long-term period, the scheme still efficiently works for a relatively short-term period. The second scheme provides aggregator unforgeability and constant-size verification keys, whereas we need to additionally assume the existence of public channels with memory, such as bulletin board [22]. Thus, removing the bulletin board assumption (without increasing the size of verification keys) could be an interesting future work. Moreover, as in [8], proposing a generic construction of aggregator oblivious encryption with public verifiability (containing a Paillier-type instantiation) also could be an interesting open problem.

Acknowledgement. The author would like to thank Dr. Miyako Ohkubo for her invaluable comments against the bulletin board assumption, and thank Dr. Takuya Hayashi for his invaluable suggestions against elliptic curve parameters.

References

1. Abe, M., Chase, M., David, B., Kohlweiss, M., Nishimaki, R., Ohkubo, M.: Constant-size structure-preserving signatures: Generic constructions and simple assumptions. J. Cryptology **29**(4), 833–878 (2016)
2. Backes, M., Fiore, D., Reischuk, R.M.: Verifiable delegation of computation on outsourced data. In: ACM CCS, pp. 863–874 (2013)
3. Badrinarayanan, S., Goyal, V., Jain, A., Sahai, A.: Verifiable functional encryption. In: Cheon, J.H., Takagi, T. (eds.) ASIACRYPT 2016. LNCS, vol. 10032, pp. 557–587. Springer, Heidelberg (2016). doi:10.1007/978-3-662-53890-6_19
4. Barker, E.: NIST Special Publication 800-57 Part 1, Revision 4. http://dx.doi.org/10.6028/NIST.Spp.800--57pt1r4
5. Barreto, P., Naehrig, M.: Pairing-friendly elliptic curves of prime order. In: Selected Areas in Cryptography, pp. 319–331 (2005)
6. Barthe, G., Danezis, G., Grégoire, B., Kunz, C., Béguelin, S.Z.: Verified computational differential privacy with applications to smart metering. In: IEEE Computer Security Foundations Symposium, pp. 287–301 (2013)
7. Bellare, M., Rogaway, P.: The exact security of digital signatures-how to sign with RSA and Rabin. In: Maurer, U. (ed.) EUROCRYPT 1996. LNCS, vol. 1070, pp. 399–416. Springer, Heidelberg (1996). doi:10.1007/3-540-68339-9_34
8. Benhamouda, F., Joye, M., Libert, B.: A new framework for privacy-preserving aggregation of time-series data. ACM Trans. Inf. Syst. Secur. **18**(3), 10 (2016)
9. Boneh, D., Boyen, X.: Efficient selective-ID secure identity-based encryption without random Oracles. In: Cachin, C., Camenisch, J.L. (eds.) EUROCRYPT 2004. LNCS, vol. 3027, pp. 223–238. Springer, Heidelberg (2004). doi:10.1007/978-3-540-24676-3_14
10. Boyen, X.: The Uber-assumption family. In: Galbraith, S.D., Paterson, K.G. (eds.) Pairing 2008. LNCS, vol. 5209, pp. 39–56. Springer, Heidelberg (2008). doi:10.1007/978-3-540-85538-5_3
11. Chan, T.H., Shi, E., Song, D.: Privacy-preserving stream aggregation with fault tolerance. In: Financial Cryptography, pp. 200–214 (2012)
12. Cramer, R., Gennaro, R., Schoenmakers, B.: A secure and optimally efficient multi-authority election scheme. In: Fumy, W. (ed.) EUROCRYPT 1997. LNCS, vol. 1233, pp. 103–118. Springer, Heidelberg (1997). doi:10.1007/3-540-69053-0_9
13. Cramer, R., Shoup, V.: Universal hash proofs and a paradigm for adaptive chosen ciphertext secure public-key encryption. In: Knudsen, L.R. (ed.) EUROCRYPT 2002. LNCS, vol. 2332, pp. 45–64. Springer, Heidelberg (2002). doi:10.1007/3-540-46035-7_4
14. Cui, Y., Fujisaki, E., Hanaoka, G., Imai, H., Zhang, R.: Formal security treatments for IBE-to-signature transformation: relations among security notions. IEICE Trans. **92–A**(1), 53–66 (2009)
15. Danezis, G., Fournet, C., Kohlweiss, M., Béguelin, S.Z.: Smart meter aggregation via secret-sharing. In: ACM Workshop on Smart Energy Grid Security, pp. 75–80 (2013)
16. Fan, C., Huang, S., Lai, Y.: Privacy-enhanced data aggregation scheme against internal attackers in smart grid. IEEE Trans. Industr. Inf. **10**(1), 666–675 (2014)
17. Fiore, D., Gennaro, R., Pastro, V.: Efficiently verifiable computation on encrypted data. In: ACM CCS, pp. 844–855 (2014)
18. Garcia, F.D., Jacobs, B.: Privacy-friendly energy-metering via homomorphic encryption. In: Security and Trust Management, pp. 226–238 (2010)

19. Gentry, C.: Fully homomorphic encryption using ideal lattices. In: STOC, pp. 169–178 (2009)
20. Goldwasser, S., et al.: Multi-input functional encryption. In: Nguyen, P.Q., Oswald, E. (eds.) EUROCRYPT 2014. LNCS, vol. 8441, pp. 578–602. Springer, Heidelberg (2014). doi:10.1007/978-3-642-55220-5_32
21. Green, M., Hohenberger, S.: Practical adaptive oblivious transfer from simple assumptions. In: Ishai, Y. (ed.) TCC 2011. LNCS, vol. 6597, pp. 347–363. Springer, Heidelberg (2011). doi:10.1007/978-3-642-19571-6_21
22. Hirt, M., Sako, K.: Efficient receipt-free voting based on homomorphic encryption. In: Preneel, B. (ed.) EUROCRYPT 2000. LNCS, vol. 1807, pp. 539–556. Springer, Heidelberg (2000). doi:10.1007/3-540-45539-6_38
23. Hofheinz, D., Jager, T.: Verifiable random functions from standard assumptions. In: Kushilevitz, E., Malkin, T. (eds.) TCC 2016. LNCS, vol. 9562, pp. 336–362. Springer, Heidelberg (2016). doi:10.1007/978-3-662-49096-9_14
24. Jager, T.: Verifiable random functions from weaker assumptions. In: Dodis, Y., Nielsen, J.B. (eds.) TCC 2015. LNCS, vol. 9015, pp. 121–143. Springer, Heidelberg (2015). doi:10.1007/978-3-662-46497-7_5
25. Jawurek, M., Johns, M., Kerschbaum, F.: Plug-in privacy for smart metering billing. In: Privacy Enhancing Technologies, pp. 192–210 (2011)
26. Jawurek, M., Kerschbaum, F.: Fault-tolerant privacy-preserving statistics. In: Privacy Enhancing Technologies, pp. 221–238 (2012)
27. Joye, M., Libert, B.: A scalable scheme for privacy-preserving aggregation of time-series data. In: Financial Cryptography, pp. 111–125 (2013)
28. Kiltz, E., Vahlis, Y.: CCA2 secure IBE: standard model efficiency through authenticated symmetric encryption. In: CT-RSA, pp. 221–238 (2008)
29. Kim, T., Barbulescu, R.: Extended tower number field sieve: a new complexity for the medium prime case. In: Robshaw, M., Katz, J. (eds.) CRYPTO 2016. LNCS, vol. 9814, pp. 543–571. Springer, Heidelberg (2016). doi:10.1007/978-3-662-53018-4_20
30. Leontiadis, I., Elkhiyaoui, K., Molva, R.: Private and dynamic time-series data aggregation with trust relaxation. In: Gritzalis, D., Kiayias, A., Askoxylakis, I. (eds.) CANS 2014. LNCS, vol. 8813, pp. 305–320. Springer, Cham (2014). doi:10.1007/978-3-319-12280-9_20
31. Leontiadis, I., Elkhiyaoui, K., Önen, M., Molva, R.: PUDA - privacy and unforgeability for data aggregation. In: CANS, pp. 3–18 (2015)
32. Li, Q., Cao, G.: Efficient privacy-preserving stream aggregation in mobile sensing with low aggregation error. In: Privacy Enhancing Technologies, pp. 60–81 (2013)
33. Libert, B., Mouhartem, F., Peters, T., Yung, M.: Practical "signatures with efficient protocols" from simple assumptions. In: AsiaCCS, pp. 511–522 (2016)
34. Libert, B., Peters, T., Yung, M.: Short group signatures via structure-preserving signatures: standard model security from simple assumptions. In: Gennaro, R., Robshaw, M. (eds.) CRYPTO 2015. LNCS, vol. 9216, pp. 296–316. Springer, Heidelberg (2015). doi:10.1007/978-3-662-48000-7_15
35. Lu, R., Liang, X., Li, X., Lin, X., Shen, X.: EPPA: an efficient and privacy-preserving aggregation scheme for secure smart grid communications. IEEE Trans. Parallel Distrib. Syst. **23**(9), 1621–1631 (2012)
36. Menezes, A., Sarkar, P., Singh, S.: Challenges with assessing the impact of NFS advances on the security of pairing-based cryptography. IACR Cryptology ePrint Archive 2016:1102 (2016)
37. Micali, S., Reyzin, L.: Improving the exact security of digital signature schemes. J. Cryptology **15**(1), 1–18 (2002)

38. Naor, M.: On cryptographic assumptions and challenges. In: Boneh, D. (ed.) CRYPTO 2003. LNCS, vol. 2729, pp. 96–109. Springer, Heidelberg (2003). doi:10.1007/978-3-540-45146-4_6

39. Ohara, K., Sakai, Y., Yoshida, F., Iwamoto, M., Ohta, K.: Privacy-preserving smart metering with verifiability for both billing and energy management. In: ASIAPKC, pp. 23–32 (2014)

40. Okamoto, T., Takashima, K.: Fully secure functional encryption with general relations from the decisional linear assumption. In: Rabin, T. (ed.) CRYPTO 2010. LNCS, vol. 6223, pp. 191–208. Springer, Heidelberg (2010). doi:10.1007/978-3-642-14623-7_11

41. Paillier, P.: Public-key cryptosystems based on composite degree residuosity classes. In: Stern, J. (ed.) EUROCRYPT 1999. LNCS, vol. 1592, pp. 223–238. Springer, Heidelberg (1999). doi:10.1007/3-540-48910-X_16

42. Rastogi, V., Nath, S.: Differentially private aggregation of distributed time-series with transformation and encryption. In: ACM SIGMOD, pp. 735–746 (2010)

43. Rial, A., Danezis, G.: Privacy-preserving smart metering. In: WPES, pp. 49–60 (2011)

44. Shi, E., Chan, T.H., Rieffel, E.G., Chow, R., Song, D.: Privacy-preserving aggregation of time-series data. In: NDSS (2011)

45. Takashima, K.: Expressive attribute-based encryption with constant-size ciphertexts from the decisional linear assumption. In: Abdalla, M., Prisco, R. (eds.) SCN 2014. LNCS, vol. 8642, pp. 298–317. Springer, Cham (2014). doi:10.1007/978-3-319-10879-7_17

46. Waters, B.: Dual system encryption: realizing fully secure IBE and HIBE under simple assumptions. In: Halevi, S. (ed.) CRYPTO 2009. LNCS, vol. 5677, pp. 619–636. Springer, Heidelberg (2009). doi:10.1007/978-3-642-03356-8_36

Privacy-Utility Tradeoff for Applications Using Energy Disaggregation of Smart-Meter Data

Mitsuhiro Hattori[1][✉], Takato Hirano[1], Nori Matsuda[1], Rina Shimizu[1], and Ye Wang[2]

[1] Mitsubishi Electric Corporation, Kamakura, Kanagawa, Japan
Hattori.Mitsuhiro@eb.MitsubishiElectric.co.jp
[2] Mitsubishi Electric Research Laboratories, Cambridge, MA, USA

Abstract. Privacy-preserving data mining technologies have been studied extensively, and as a general approach, du Pin Calmon and Fawaz have proposed a data distortion mechanism based on a statistical inference attack framework. This theory has been extended by Erdogdu et al. to time-series data and been applied to energy disaggregation of smart-meter data. However, their theory assumes both smart-meter data and sensitive appliance state information are available when applying the privacy-preserving mechanism, which is impractical in typical smart-meter systems where only the total power usage is available. In this paper, we extend their approach to enable the application of a privacy-utility tradeoff mechanism to such practical applications. Firstly, we define a system model which captures both the architecture of the smart-meter system and the practical constraints that the power usage of each appliance cannot be measured individually. This enables us to formalize the tradeoff problem more rigorously. Secondly, we propose a privacy-utility tradeoff mechanism for that system. We apply a linear Gaussian model assumption to the system and thereby reduce the problem of obtaining unobservable information to that of learning the system parameters. Finally, we conduct experiments of applying the proposed mechanism to the power usage data of an actual household. The experimental results show that the proposed mechanism works partly effectively; i.e., it prevents usage analysis of certain types of sensitive appliances while at the same time preserving that of non-sensitive appliances.

Keywords: Privacy-preserving data mining · Statistical inference · Non-intrusive appliance load monitoring · Convex optimization

1 Introduction

1.1 Background

The proliferation of personal devices capable of Internet connectivity has enabled new applications and services [3]. Examples include healthcare advice service based on the user's activity data captured by fitness tracking devices, navigation services based on the GPS data from the user's smart phone, and demand

© Springer International Publishing AG 2017
J. Pieprzyk and S. Suriadi (Eds.): ACISP 2017, Part II, LNCS 10343, pp. 214–234, 2017.
DOI: 10.1007/978-3-319-59870-3_12

response services based on the power consumption data of household smart-meters. Such new services will definitely enrich our everyday life.

At the same time, however, these services will collect users' personal data intentionally or unintentionally, which may in some cases violate their privacy [30]. In a well-known case, a retail company identified a teenage girl as pregnant based on her shopping habits [7], which can be thought of as illegal acquisition of sensitive information. The primary target of the paper is smart-meter data, which has been shown to potentially reveal the behavior of individuals [24,26].

These privacy concerns in the era of Internet of Things have triggered re-examination of privacy regulation around the world. For instance, the EU Parliament passed the General Data Protection Regulation (GDPR) in 2016 which will be enforced in 2018. Most of the new privacy regulations, including the GDPR, now require explicitly that "natural persons should have control of their own personal data."[1] It is therefore required for any service providers to treat users' personal data solicitously according to the demands of each individual. This social trend motivates the rapid development of privacy-preserving data mining technologies.

1.2   Related Work

A prominent line of privacy-preserving techniques is k-anonymity [29,32] and its derivatives such as ℓ-diversity [21], t-closeness [19] and m-invariance [34]. Their primary goal is to convert an aggregation of personal data into a non-personal (anonymous) dataset while preserving information as much as possible. Although their privacy metrics are intuitive and easy to evaluate, it is difficult or almost impossible to protect users' privacy according to the detailed demands of each individual. Indeed, their basic strategy is to anonymize individuals by bundling similar records into indistinguishable bunches via generalization and omission of data. However, by nature of these metrics, privacy on an individual basis cannot be addressed.

Differential privacy [8,9] is in another line of research. Unlike k-anonymity and its derivatives, differential privacy defines the privacy metrics based on a rigorous mathematical framework. The privacy definition of differential privacy is such that an adversary querying the database, which contains personal data of many individuals, should face difficulty in determining whether the data record of any specific individual is even in the database. Anonymity is their primary concern and accommodating users' specific privacy demands is therefore almost outside of their scope.

The most relevant work to ours is the consideration of privacy within a statistical inference attack framework [4,11,12,25,28]. In this framework, privacy is modeled as the amount of information obtained about the sensitive data when observing the released data. It is therefore possible to evaluate privacy on an individual basis by modeling the system with an appropriate definition of the

---

[1] In Recital 7 of the GDPR.

sensitive and useful data. The primary goal of this framework is to find an optimal balance between privacy of an individual and utility of the service, and the problem of finding an optimal balance is formalized as an optimization problem where the objective function and constraint functions represent the privacy and utility. A solution of the optimization problem gives an optimal privacy mapping which distorts the useful data to obtain privacy while still proving utility.

The theoretical aspect of this framework is proposed and analyzed by du Pin Calmon and Fawaz [25]. Salamatian et al. applied the theory to a Census dataset and TV rating dataset, and showed that it is indeed possible to reduce the revelation of political affiliation while enabling TV program recommendation services [28]. Erdogdu et al. extended the theory to time-series datasets and applied the extended theory to energy disaggregation of smart-meter data [11,12]. They showed that it is possible to modify power data to conceal the usage of a sensitive appliance while still allowing detection of the usage of a useful appliance, where the useful and sensitive appliances in their experiments were the washer-dryer and microwave, respectively.

Although Erdogdu et al. [11,12] made a significant step towards applying the theory to real systems, there is still much room for improvement. For example, they considered only the case where both the smart-meter data and usage data of the sensitive appliances are directly observable. However, in actual use cases such as ordinary smart-meter systems, individual appliance usage data may not be directly observable. Therefore, it is desirable to achieve the optimal privacy mapping even in the case where usage of sensitive appliances is not available.

Privacy on smart-meter systems has been considered and tackled by many researchers [16,20,33,35,37]. Most of the privacy preservation techniques they use are introduction of additional batteries and disturbance of the power usage data with the batteries. However, introducing additional devices may be undesirable due to cost.

1.3 Contribution

In this paper, we extend the approach of Erdogdu et al. [11,12] to apply a privacy-utility tradeoff mechanism to practical applications and thereby close the academic-industry gap. As an example of practical applications, we consider in this paper an anomaly detection service of elderly residents living alone. The detection of anomalies with the residents can be based on the states of household appliances inferred via energy disaggregation. Using a smart-meter as a sensor device for anomaly detection is attractive because it requires no additional devices. This motivates many research efforts [1,2,31], but most of them pay little attention to privacy.

Firstly, we define a system model which captures both the architecture of the smart-meter system and the practical constraints that the power usage of each appliance cannot be measured individually. In our system model, modified smart-meter data is sent to a service provider who then conducts energy disaggregation of the smart-meter data to infer the appliance states. The energy disaggregation is conducted by a provider rather than on the user side since energy disaggregation often requires significant computational effort which may be impractical for the limited processing power of a smart-meter. The privacy issue here is that the provider may infer states of appliances that the user thinks of as sensitive. We capture this privacy issue by defining an adversary model and specifying adversary's goal as well as his prior knowledge.

Secondly, we modify the optimization problem of Erdogdu et al. [11,12] in such a way that individual appliance energy usage data is not required. As we have noted, their privacy-utility tradeoff mechanism takes as input both the smart-meter data and usage data of the sensitive appliances. In our system model, however, the latter information is unavailable. We apply a linear Gaussian model to the system and thereby reduce the problem of determining an unknown system model to that of learning the model parameters such as the mean power consumption of each appliance and the stationary distribution of appliance states. These system parameters are, in some cases, available without conducting supervised learning on each household, because the mean power is often listed on a specification document of the appliance and the stationary distribution can be simulated based on typical usage pattern of the residents. Therefore, our mechanism is considered to be applicable to practical smart-meter systems.

Thirdly, we conduct several experiments of applying the proposed mechanism to the power usage data of an actual household. We collected power usage data for nine days, and we also manually collected the ground truth appliance usage for the same period to compute the system parameters that the adversary would possess a priori. Optimal privacy-utility tradeoffs are computed for two use cases, and the raw power data is distorted according to the optimized mechanism. We evaluate the privacy and utility aspects by examining the degradation of appliance usage inference performance. It is shown quantitatively that our mechanism is reasonable and effective, especially when high-power appliances such as the oven toaster are designated as sensitive. We elaborate in this paper the steps we conducted, the parameters we computed and the inference results we obtained in detail, so that interested researchers can follow our work.

1.4 Organization of the Paper

The rest of the paper is organized as follows. Section 2 elaborates our target application and defines a system model and an adversary model. Our theoretical analysis and proposition is given in Sect. 3, and experimental results and discussions are described in Sect. 4. Section 5 concludes the paper with future directions. Where necessary, detailed discussions are provided in the appendices.

2   Target Application: System and Adversarial Models

In this section, we first elaborate our target application and its privacy issue. Then we define a system model of the application and an adversary model of an "honest-but-curious" service provider.

2.1   Target Application and Privacy Issue

The target application we consider in this paper is an anomaly detection service of elderly residents living alone. More concretely, we consider an application where smart meter data, which is the aggregated power usage of all the appliances in a household, is collected from the house and disaggregated on a remote monitoring site, and appliance states are inferred whereby anomalies of the residents are detected. This service is proposed by Alcalá et al. [1,2] and implemented by Song et al. [31].

The use of smart-meter for an anomaly detection is preferable in that unlike anomaly detection using additional sensors such as wearable medical devices, we need no extra devices since smart-meters have already been installed in many countries and are ready for use. The rapid development of energy disaggregation technologies, also known as non-intrusive appliance load monitoring (NILM) [15,17,18,22,23], also motivates the use of smart-meter as a sensor device for anomaly detection.

A straightforward way of implementing this service will be to disaggregate and detect the anomaly state on the user side and notify it to the service provider. However, energy disaggregation and anomaly detection could be too computationally intensive to be performed efficiently in a typical smart-meter with limited processing and memory capabilities. Besides, the correctness of anomaly detection can be improved by comparing the smart-meter data of a user with that of other users, which is easily conducted on the provider side but difficult on the user side.

The privacy issue we need to resolve in this application is that the service provider may infer states of the appliances that the user think of as sensitive, as well as those required for anomaly detection. For example, the kettle is ideal for anomaly detection because many people, especially those in the UK, use it regularly and also they often think of it as a non-sensitive appliance. The hairdryer, on the other hand, is useful but many people (especially women) would think of it as sensitive because usage of the dryer implies that the user must have taken a bath. The difficulty of this issue lies in the fact that appliances in a household differ from person to person and the sensitivity to each appliance also differ. It is therefore required to develop a privacy technology that can prevent the service provider from inferring states of the appliances that the user thinks of as sensitive while allowing inference of states of the non-sensitive appliances, based on the preference of each user.

From the cryptography perspective, the service provider can be thought of as so-called "honest-but-curious" adversary, because he basically obeys the protocol (providing anomaly detection service to the user) but at the same time he tries to extract as much sensitive information as possible (inferring states of the appliances that the user think of as sensitive). We capture this adversarial situation with our adversary model in Sect. 2.2.

2.2   System and Adversary Models

System Model. Our system model is depicted in Fig. 1.

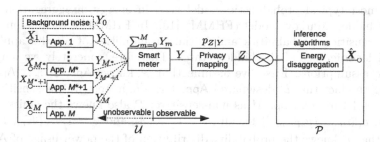

Fig. 1. Our system model. We assume App. 1 through App. M^* are the appliances that a user $\mathcal{U}$ designated as sensitive, and App. $M^* + 1$ through App. M are those that $\mathcal{U}$ designated as non-sensitive. Solid lines represent observable data and dotted lines represent unobservable data.

Suppose there are M appliances in the house of a user $\mathcal{U}$. Each appliance App. m ($m = 1, \ldots, M$) has several operating states denoted by $1, \ldots, K_m$, where $X_m \in \{1, \ldots, K_m\}$ denotes the realization of its operating state, and Y_m denotes its energy consumption. Note however that we cannot directly measure either X_m or Y_m, and can only measure the aggregated power usage $Y = \sum_{m=0}^{M} Y_m$ at the smart-meter, where Y_0 is the background noise. The smart-meter data Y is then passed to the privacy mapping module which takes as input Y and maps it into the distorted data Z. Here the mapping from Y to Z is according to the conditional probability distribution $p_{Z|Y}$ which is computed beforehand by solving the privacy-utility tradeoff problem proposed in Sect. 3. The distorted data Z is then sent to a service provider $\mathcal{P}$, and $\mathcal{P}$ will conduct energy disaggregation with Z and infer the appliance states $\hat{\boldsymbol{X}} = (\hat{X}_1, \ldots, \hat{X}_M)$ using some inference algorithms.

The smart-meter measures the power usage Y regularly (typically every one minute), and the distorted data Z is sent to $\mathcal{P}$ successively. $\mathcal{P}$ may store all the time-series $Z^{(1)}, \ldots, Z^{(T)}$ for some time period T (typically one day; we used nine days for our experiment in Sect. 4) and use them for inference of $\hat{\boldsymbol{X}}^{(1)}, \ldots, \hat{\boldsymbol{X}}^{(T)}$.

We should note here that although we modeled in Fig. 1 that the privacy mapping module is on the outside of the smart-meter, this is only for clarity and in practice it can be integrated into the smart-meter. Indeed, the privacy mapping operation is lightweight and can be executed with limited processing power and memory.

Adversary Model. The goal of an adversarial service provider $\mathcal{P}$ is to infer states of the appliances that $\mathcal{U}$ thinks of as sensitive. Suppose that $\mathcal{U}$ designated appliances App. 1 through App. M^* as sensitive and App. $M^* + 1$ through App. M

as non-sensitive. In this case, the adversarial goal of $\mathcal{P}$ is to infer $X_1, \ldots, X_{M^*}$ from Z.

We assume that $\mathcal{P}$ knows all the appliances in $\mathcal{U}$'s house. Also, we assume $\mathcal{P}$ knows the statistical distribution of each appliance.

The most typical probabilistic model used in energy disaggregation is the factorial hidden Markov model (FHMM) [13]. In FHMM, the emission distribution, transition probabilities and initial probabilities of all the appliances are used for inference of the hidden states. Therefore, concretely we make the following assumptions. First, we assume that $\mathcal{P}$ knows App. 1, ..., App. M, including the fact that $\mathcal{U}$ designated App. 1 through App. M^* as sensitive and App. $M^* + 1$ through App. M as non-sensitive. $\mathcal{P}$ also knows the emission distribution $p_{Y_m^{(t)}|X_m^{(t)}}(y_m|x_{m,k})$ for all $m = 1, \ldots, M$ and $k = 1, \ldots, K_m$. I.e., we assume that $\mathcal{P}$ knows the probability distribution of the power usage of App. m at the state $x_{m,k}$, for all m and k. $\mathcal{P}$ additionally knows the transition probabilities $P_{X_m^{(t+1)}|X_m^{(t)}}(x_{m,k'}|x_{m,k})$ and the initial probabilities $P_{X_m^{(1)}}(x_{m,k})$ for all $m = 1, \ldots, M$ and $k, k' = 1, \ldots, K_m$, i.e., the probability with which App. m transits the state from $x_{m,k}$ to $x_{m,k'}$ when the time steps from t to $t+1$.

We now elaborate the justification of these assumptions. In actual use cases, $\mathcal{P}$ does not necessarily need to know the parameters for the sensitive appliances App. 1, ..., App. M^*. Namely, $\mathcal{P}$ does not need to know $p_{Y_m^{(t)}|X_m^{(t)}}(y_m|x_{m,k})$ and $P_{X_m^{(t+1)}|X_m^{(t)}}(x_{m,k'}|x_{m,k})$ for $m = 1, \ldots, M^*$. However, we make this assumption to consider a more adversarial $\mathcal{P}$.

3   A Proposed Privacy-Utility Tradeoff Mechanism

In this section, we modify the optimization problem of Erdogdu et al. [11,12] in such a way that appliance usage data is not required. We formalize the optimization problem with definitions of privacy and utility in Sect. 3.1. Then in Sect. 3.2 we modify the problem by applying the linear Gaussian model assumption.

3.1   Formalization of the Problem

Here we formalize the privacy-utility tradeoff problem in a rigorous way.

Notation. Suppose $X \in \mathcal{X}$ is a discrete random variable and $Y \in \mathcal{Y}$ is a continuous random variable, where $\mathcal{X}$ and $\mathcal{Y}$ are some (possibly infinite) sets. We use capital $P_X(x)$ for the probability mass function of X and small $p_Y(y)$ for the probability density function of Y. $E_Y[f(Y)]$ denotes the expected value of function $f(Y)$, i.e., $E_Y[f(Y)] = \int_{\mathcal{Y}} p_Y(y)f(y)dy$. We use $\mathcal{N}(\mu, \sigma^2)$ to denote the Gaussian distribution with mean μ and variance σ^2, and $p_{Y|X=x} \sim \mathcal{N}(\mu, \sigma^2)$ denotes that given that $X = x$, Y is conditionally distributed according to the Gaussian distribution with mean μ and variance σ^2.

Let $\boldsymbol{X} = (\boldsymbol{X}^*, \bar{\boldsymbol{X}})$ be a vector of discrete random variables representing the appliance states, where $\boldsymbol{X}^* = (X_1, X_2, \ldots, X_{M^*})$ are discrete random variables of the sensitive appliance states and $\bar{X} = (X_{M^*+1}, X_{M^*+2}, \ldots, X_M)$ are those of the non-sensitive appliance states, both of which are designated by $\mathcal{U}$.

Definitions of Privacy and Utility. The privacy metric we consider in this paper is as follows.

Definition 1 (Privacy metric). *The privacy metric is the mutual information of sensitive appliance states X^* and distorted smart-meter data Z; i.e.,*

$$I(X^*; Z) = \sum_{x^* \in \mathcal{X}^*} P_{X^*}(x^*) \int_{\mathcal{Z}} p_{Z|X^*}(z|x^*) \log \frac{p_{Z|X^*}(z|x^*)}{p_Z(z)} dz. \tag{1}$$

The mutual information $I(X^*; Z)$ represents the quantity of information one can obtain about X^* from the observed Z. It is therefore used extensively in the literature as a privacy metric [11,12,25,27,36]. Note however that X^* is a vector of discrete random variables while Z is a continuous random variable, which is different from the situation considered in the literature where all the random variables were discrete. We therefore extended the theory.

Utility is measured by the following distortion metric.

Definition 2 (Distortion metric). *Let $d : \mathcal{Y} \times \mathcal{Z} \to \mathbb{R}^+$ be some distortion function.[2] The distortion metric is the expectation of $d(Y, Z)$; i.e.,*

$$E_{Y,Z}[d(Y, Z)] = \iint_{\mathcal{Y} \times \mathcal{Z}} p_{Z|Y}(z|y) p_Y(y) d(y, z) dy dz. \tag{2}$$

Lower distortion intuitively corresponds to better utility.

However, the distortion metric in Definition 2 may appear slightly different from what we should deal with in this paper. Indeed, the ideal distortion metric would be the one that directly captures the degradation of the results of appliance usage analysis. However, the outcome of the appliance usage analysis depends heavily on the algorithms used for the analysis and therefore it is infeasible to estimate the degradation in general. Also, empirically the distortion metric in Definition 2 is effective, as shown in Sect. 4.

The Privacy-Utility Tradeoff Problem. Suppose for now that the joint distribution $p_{X^*,Y}$ is already known. Then given $p_{X^*,Y}$, a distortion function d and a distortion constraint δ, the privacy mapping $p_{Z|Y}$ that minimizes the privacy information leakage can be found by solving the following optimization problem:

$$\inf_{p_{Z|Y}} I(X^*; Z) \quad \text{subject to } E_{Y,Z}[d(Y, Z)] \leq \delta. \tag{3}$$

We show in Appendix A that (3) is computable and has a desirable property that is convexity.

---

[2] Examples of distortion function include the L_1 norm, L_2 norm and more generally L_p norm.

3.2 Gaussian Model Assumption

We assumed in Sect. 3.1 that $p_{X^*,Y}$ is already known. In practical smart-meter systems, however, this assumption does not hold and we need to substitute $p_{X^*,Y}$ with other known parameters. We propose here the substitution method.

First, observe that from the law of total probability,

$$
\begin{aligned}
p_{X^*,Y}(x^*, y) = \sum_{\bar{x} \in \bar{X}} p_{X^*,\bar{X},Y}(x^*, \bar{x}, y) &= \sum_{\bar{x} \in \bar{X}} p_{X,Y}(x, y) \\
&= \sum_{\bar{x} \in \bar{X}} P_X(x) p_{Y|X}(y|x).
\end{aligned}
\tag{4}
$$

Now, computing $p_{X^*,Y}(x^*, y)$ boils down to computing $P_X(x)$ and $p_{Y|X}(y|x)$.

In order to compute $p_{Y|X}(y|x)$, we apply a linear Gaussian model. This model has been used extensively to simulate the emission of home appliances in the energy disaggregation literature [14,18,22].

Let Y_0 be a random variable of the background noise and Y_m be that of the emission of appliance m. Then,

$$
Y = Y_0 + \sum_{m=1}^{M} Y_m,
\tag{5}
$$

$$
p_{Y_0} \sim \mathcal{N}(\mu_0, \sigma_0^2),
\tag{6}
$$

$$
p_{Y_m|X_m=x_{m,k}} \sim \mathcal{N}(\mu_{m,k}, \sigma_{m,k}^2),
\tag{7}
$$

where μ_0 and σ_0^2 are the mean and variance of the Gaussian distribution of the background noise, and $\mu_{m,k}$ and $\sigma_{m,k}^2$ are those of appliance m in state k. Then, according to the standard probability theory [10],

$$
p_{Y|X=x} \sim \mathcal{N}\left(\mu_0 + \sum_{m=1}^{M} \mu_{m,k}, \ \sigma_0^2 + \sum_{m=1}^{M} \sigma_{m,k}^2\right).
\tag{8}
$$

Equation (8) implies that computing $p_{Y|X}$ is now reduced to obtaining the parameters $\Theta = \{\mu_0, \sigma_0^2, \{\mu_{m,k}, \sigma_{m,k}^2\}\}$. These parameters can be obtained either from the specification documents or reference models of the appliances, or by doing preliminary training activities.

Assuming that the variance of the total power data Y is independent of states of the appliances, (8) can further be simplified as

$$
p_{Y|X=x} \sim \mathcal{N}\left(\mu_0 + \sum_{m=1}^{M} \mu_{m,k}, \ \sigma^2\right),
\tag{9}
$$

where σ^2 is the variance of Y. In this case, computing $p_{Y|X}$ can be reduced to obtaining the parameters $\Theta' = \{\mu_0, \{\mu_{m,k}\}, \sigma^2\}$. We use this simplified model in Sect. 4.

$P_X(x)$ can also be obtained from the reference models of the appliances or by doing preliminary training activities.

Now, it is easy to see that $p_{X^*,Y}$ can be obtained from Θ' and P_X and therefore the optimization problem is solvable.

4   Experiments on Household Power Usage Data

This section exhibits our experimental results of applying the proposed mechanism to the power usage data of an actual household. We give an overview of our experiments in Sect. 4.1, and we discuss in Sect. 4.2 the electric power meter and the home appliances that we used for the experiments. Section 4.3 shows the datasets and parameters that we obtained in the experiments. The optimization problem is solved and the privacy mapping is applied in Sect. 4.4. Section 4.5 evaluates the privacy and utility aspects of our mechanism quantitatively, and the implications of the results are discussed in Sect. 4.6.

4.1   Overview

Our goal is to examine whether the theory we propose in Sect. 3 is effective in an actual situation (i.e., in natural daily life), not in an artificial environment or in a special circumstance. To this end, we collected the power usage data of an actual household using a commercially available power meter device for nine days. As our proposed theory requires estimation of Θ' and P_X for the assumed model distribution, and as our adversary model assumes that the adversarial $\mathcal{P}$ has full knowledge of the emission, transition and initial probabilities, we also manually collected the ground truth of the appliance usage in the household for the same nine days, and then applied a supervised learning algorithm to estimate those parameters.

Then, we considered two use cases: (1) oven toaster is designated as sensitive; and (2) television is designated as sensitive. For each case, we chose an appropriate distortion constraint δ by trial-and-error, and with Θ', P_X and δ, we solved the convex optimization problem (3) and obtained a privacy mapping $p_{Z|Y}$. We then distorted the power usage data according to $p_{Z|Y}$, and obtained distorted power usage data. In order to evaluate the privacy and utility of our mechanism, we applied an inference algorithm to the distorted data to infer the appliance usage of the sensitive and non-sensitive appliances, and compared the performance with that of the original data.

Since the power meter we used outputs discrete values, in the experiments we regard Y and Z as discrete random variables $\tilde{Y}$ and $\tilde{Z}$ respectively, and compute and apply a conditional probability mass function $P_{\tilde{Z}|\tilde{Y}}$. Discussion on the optimization problem with discrete random variables can be found in Appendix B.

4.2   Devices

The electric power meter we used is the $OWL\ +USB$[3] which records the electric power used in a household every minute. This power meter is attached to the

---

[3] http://www.theowl.com/index.php/energy-monitors/standalone-monitors/owl-usb/.

circuit-breaker of the target household, and the total power usage of the household is recorded. Due to limitations of the A/D converter used in the power meter, the resolution of the power recorded is 7 W.

All the appliances in the target household are listed in Table 1. As Table 1 shows, a total of 17 appliances are present.[4]

Table 1. Appliances used in the target household and the parameters obtained from the supervised learning. $\mu_{m,\text{ON}}$ is the estimated mean power of appliance m. a_m and b_m are the estimated transition probabilities of transiting from OFF to ON and from ON to OFF, respectively.

m	Appliance	$\mu_{m,\text{ON}}$	a_m	b_m
0	Background + refrigerator	103.44		
1	Bathroom light	12.73	0.000404	0.0219
2	Hairdryer	380.02	0.000159	0.667
3	Electric heater	350.37	0.000161	0.0148
4	Entrance light	90.90	0.000318	0.222
5	Kitchen light	175.63	0.00257	0.0321
6	Kotatsu	168.77	0.000652	0.0246
7	Laundry machine	57.00	0.00408	0.0142
8	Lavatory light	51.95	0.00408	0.505
9	Living room light	84.69	0.00194	0.00544
10	Microwave	1115.80	0.000159	0.333
11	Oven toaster	1133.40	0.000957	0.245
12	Personal computer	111.85	0.000663	0.0152
13	Reading room light	72.24	0.00219	0.0366
14	Rice steamer	323.62	0.000322	0.0230
15	Television	123.16	0.00366	0.00335
16	Vacuum cleaner	1057.90	0.000159	0.182
17	Washstand light	34.89	0.000637	0.216

$\sigma^2 = 5436.5$

4.3 Datasets and Parameters

Power Usage and Appliance Usage Datasets. We collected the power usage data for nine days. Samples are shown in Fig. 2 and the histogram is shown in Fig. 3. The minimum power is 35 W, the maximum power is 2093 W and the average power is 232.78 W.

---

[4] Strictly speaking, the number of appliances used in the household is 18 because a refrigerator is also used. However, it was always ON throughout the data collection and therefore we regarded it as a part of the background noise.

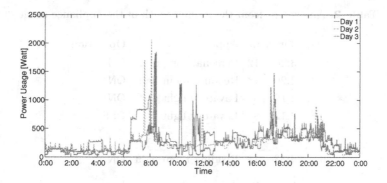

Fig. 2. Samples of the power usage data

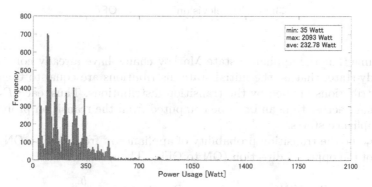

Fig. 3. Histogram of the power usage data

We also collected manually the ground truth of the appliance usage in the target household. Table 2 shows an excerpt from the ground truth.

Model Parameters. In order to obtain the model parameters Θ' and $P_{\mathbf{X}}$ from the power usage data and the ground truth, we used a supervised learning algorithm.

For simplicity, we employed a couple of simplification techniques. First, we modeled the hidden states of the appliances with the factorial hidden Markov model (FHMM) [13]. The FHMM assumes that the hidden states between appliances are independent, which reduces the computational complexity of learning and inference. This assumption is reasonable in our situation and therefore we used this model to simplify the computation of $\Theta' = \{\mu_0, \{\mu_{m,k}\}, \sigma^2\}$.

Second, we assumed each appliance has only two possible states: $\mathcal{X}_m = \{\mathsf{ON}, \mathsf{OFF}\}$ for all $m \in \{1, 2, \ldots, M = 17\}$. This two-state assumption simplifies the computation of $P_{\mathbf{X}}$. Note here that since we have assumed all the appliances behave independently from each other, we can compute $P_{\mathbf{X}}(\boldsymbol{x})$ as the product of probability of each appliance; i.e., $P_{\mathbf{X}}(\boldsymbol{x}) = \prod_{m=1}^{M} P_{X_m}(x_m)$. We

Table 2. An excerpt from the ground truth of the appliance usage

Day	Time	m	Appliance	Operation
1	3:20	12	Personal computer	ON
	3:20	13	Reading room light	ON
	4:16	8	Lavatory light	ON
	4:17	8	Lavatory light	OFF
	⋮	⋮	⋮	⋮
9	4:33	13	Reading room light	ON
	⋮	⋮	⋮	⋮
	23:18	9	Living room light	OFF
	23:20	15	Television	OFF

also assume that the appliance state Markov chains have already converged to the steady-state, that is, the initial state distributions are equal to the steady-state distributions implied by the transition distributions. Thus, each $P_{X_m}(x_m)$ is stationary across time and can be computed from the transition probabilities of the appliance states.

Let a_m be the transition probability of appliance m from OFF to ON and b_m be that of the opposite direction (ON to OFF). Then,

$$P_{X_m}(\text{ON}) = \frac{a_m}{a_m + b_m}, \quad P_{X_m}(\text{OFF}) = \frac{b_m}{a_m + b_m}. \tag{10}$$

Hence, P_X can be computed by $\{a_m, b_m\}$. In addition, we assumed that $\mu_{m,\text{OFF}} = 0$ for all m.

We used all of the nine day data of power usage and appliance usage for the supervised learning, and obtained $\Theta' = \{\mu_0, \{\mu_{m,\text{ON}}\}, \sigma^2\}$ and $\{a_m, b_m\}$. The results are shown in Table 1.

4.4 Optimization and Distortion

As we explained in Sect. 4.1, we considered the following two use cases:

Case 1. Oven toaster ($m = 11$) is designated as sensitive,
Case 2. Television ($m = 15$) is designated as sensitive.

For each case, we solved the convex optimization problem and obtained a discrete privacy mapping $P_{\tilde{Z}|\tilde{Y}}$. We used as a distortion metric the L_1 distance $d(\tilde{y}, \tilde{z}) = |\tilde{y} - \tilde{z}|$. The optimization problem was solved by the convex optimization software CVX,[5] where we used $\delta = 6$ for Case 1 and $\delta = 72$ for Case 2.

Then we distorted the power usage data according to $P_{\tilde{Z}|\tilde{Y}}(\tilde{z}|\tilde{y})$. A sample of the raw and distorted power usage data is shown in Figs. 4 and 5.

---

[5] http://cvxr.com/cvx/.

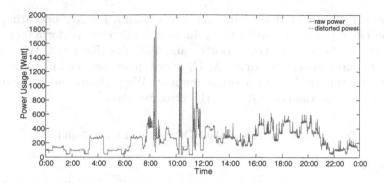

Fig. 4. A sample of the raw and distorted power usage data (sensitive appliance is oven toaster and $\delta = 6$)

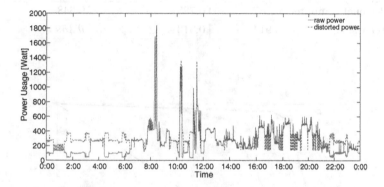

Fig. 5. A sample of the raw and distorted power usage data (sensitive appliance is television and $\delta = 72$)

4.5 Evaluation of Privacy and Utility

We now evaluate both the privacy and utility aspects of the distorted power usage data.

Since our goal of the privacy-utility tradeoff is to retain the inference of the non-sensitive appliance states while preventing that of the sensitive appliance states, we evaluate them by measuring the degradation of the appliance state inference. We therefore apply an inference algorithm to the raw data and the distorted data (for both Case 1 and 2) to infer the hidden states of the appliances, and evaluate the detection rates.

We again model the hidden states with the FHMM accompanied by the parameters we obtained in the supervised learning, and infer the hidden states for the nine days using an approximate inference algorithm called the completely factorized variational approximation (CFVA) [13]. CFVA is used to avoid the computational complexity of exact inference algorithms. For this binary (ON and OFF) classification, the CFVA algorithm provides marginal posterior likelihoods which we can threshold at custom values to obtain a receiver operating characteristic (ROC) curve in order to evaluate the inference performance across different tradeoffs between true positive and false positive rates. We can also compute the area under the curve (AUC) which quantifies the inference performance across this tradeoff in a single number. We perform and compare this evaluation between the raw data and the distorted data.

Table 3. AUC values of the ROC curves (Figs. 6, 7 and 8)

m	Appliance	AUC		
		Raw (Fig. 6)	Oven toaster (Fig. 7)	Television (Fig. 8)
3	Electric heater	0.904	0.902	0.889
11	Oven toaster	0.969	*0.551*	0.969
12	Personal computer	0.787	0.783	0.648
15	Television	0.914	0.913	*0.459*

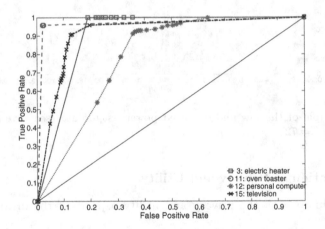

Fig. 6. ROC curves of the results of inference with raw data

Figure 6 shows the ROC curve of the inference results of several appliances, where the analysis was performed on the raw dataset. The AUC values are evaluated and shown in Table 3. As the AUC values tell, the states of the oven toaster are inferred almost correctly, the states of the electric heater and television are inferred with high accuracy, and the states of the personal computer are inferred with marginal accuracy.

Figure 7 gives ROC curves of the inference results with the distorted data for Case 1. The inference performance for the oven toaster is degraded severely while the inference performance for the other appliances are preserved, as desired.

Figure 8 gives ROC curves of the inference results with the distorted data for Case 2. The inference performance for the television is degraded severely. The inference performance for the oven toaster and electric heater are preserved almost completely. The inference performance for the personal computer is degraded to some extent, but still enables meaningful inference.

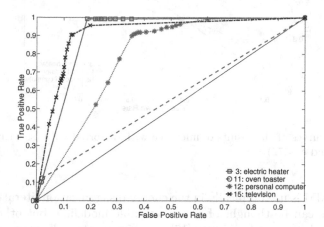

Fig. 7. ROC curves of the results of inference with distorted data (sensitive appliance is oven toaster and $\delta = 6$)

4.6 Discussion

As we have shown in Sect. 4.5, the distortion works highly effectively for the case where the sensitive appliance is the oven toaster. This may be due to the fact that the oven toaster is realistically modeled with only two states: {ON, OFF}, and therefore our simplified model fits well. Moreover, the consumed power is as high as 1,000 W, which enables us to compute an optimal privacy mapping $P_{\tilde{Z}|\tilde{Y}}$ that attains both small mutual information and small distortion such as $\delta = 6$. Note that 1,000 W or higher power consumption occurs rarely, as Fig. 3 shows, and thus the distortion of higher power values does not affect other low-power appliances.

On the other hand, for the case where the sensitive appliance is the television, the distortion renders inference of the sensitive appliance almost impossible but at the same time makes inference of the personal computer degraded to some extent. This may stem from the fact that the television consumes a relatively low power of 123 W and thus distortion of middle power values would affect other middle-power appliances including the personal computer. Another possibility is that the personal computer takes not only two but multiple states and the distortion to the middle-range power usage degrades the inference.

We should discuss the impact of the assumptions and approximations we made in the evaluation. We modeled the hidden states of the appliances with

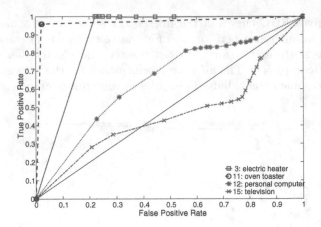

Fig. 8. ROC curves of the results of inference with distorted data (sensitive appliance is television and $\delta = 72$)

FHMM. FHMM is used typically in the energy disaggregation literature [18] and therefore this can be thought of as a reasonable modeling, but other inference algorithms such as neural networks [17] may give greater advantage to an adversarial $\mathcal{P}$. We used a binary-state (ON and OFF) assumption for all the appliances. This may fit to some appliances (e.g. electric heater) but not to others (e.g. personal computer). Multiple-state model will definitely give higher performance to both benign and adversarial $\mathcal{P}$. Use of an exact inference algorithm will make the performance better at the price of computational complexity.

5   Conclusion

We proposed in this paper a privacy-utility tradeoff mechanism which accommodates the situation where the sensitive appliance usage is not observable. We first described a target application and its privacy issue, and gave a system and adversary model. Then we formalized the tradeoff as a convex optimization problem that we show can be solved. Finally, we exhibited experimental results on smart-meter data and showed that the proposed mechanism is practical and effective.

Future work will be to extend this theory to the case where the service provider uses other inference algorithms such as neural networks.

Acknowledgments. We would like to thank the anonymous referees for their valuable comments.

A Computability and Convexity of the Optimization Problem

A.1 Computability

We show that both the objective function (1) and constraint function (2) can be computed respectively and therefore the optimization problem (3) is solvable, assuming $p_{\boldsymbol{X}^*,Y}$ is known.

We start with (1). First note that $\boldsymbol{X} \rightarrow Y \rightarrow Z$ forms the Markov chain because the smart-meter data Y depends on the appliance states $\boldsymbol{X}$ and the distorted data Z depends on the smart-meter data Y. Then,

$$p_{Z|\boldsymbol{X}^*}(z|\boldsymbol{x}^*) = \int_{\mathcal{Y}} p_{Z|Y}(z|y) p_{Y|\boldsymbol{X}^*}(y|\boldsymbol{x}^*) dy. \tag{11}$$

Here,

$$p_{Y|\boldsymbol{X}^*}(y|\boldsymbol{x}^*) = \frac{p_{\boldsymbol{X}^*,Y}(\boldsymbol{x}^*, y)}{P_{\boldsymbol{X}^*}(\boldsymbol{x}^*)}, \tag{12}$$

$$P_{\boldsymbol{X}^*}(\boldsymbol{x}^*) = \int_{\mathcal{Y}} p_{\boldsymbol{X}^*,Y}(\boldsymbol{x}^*, y) dy. \tag{13}$$

Also,

$$p_Z(z) = \sum_{\boldsymbol{x}^* \in \mathcal{X}^*} P_{\boldsymbol{X}^*}(\boldsymbol{x}^*) p_{Z|\boldsymbol{X}^*}(z|\boldsymbol{x}^*). \tag{14}$$

Therefore, we can confirm that all the members in (1) can be computed from $p_{\boldsymbol{X}^*,Y}$ and $p_{Z|Y}$.

As for (2), we can easily confirm the computability by seeing that

$$p_Y(y) = \sum_{\boldsymbol{x}^* \in \mathcal{X}^*} p_{\boldsymbol{X}^*,Y}(\boldsymbol{x}^*, y). \tag{15}$$

A.2 Convexity

We additionally note here that (3) is a convex optimization problem. This is because, as with [25], the objective function and the constraint function are convex functions of the optimization variable $p_{Z|Y}$.

Convex optimization has several desirable properties. From an analytical viewpoint, it is assured that any local minimum is a global minimum and finding a global minimum is therefore reduced to finding a local minimum [5]. From a practical viewpoint, efficient algorithms such as interior-point methods have been proposed, and software libraries are available [6].

B   Modification to Discrete Power Data

In Sect. 3.2 we considered the case where the smart-meter data and distorted data are continuous. In practical situations, however, it is possible that the smart-meter data is quantized to discrete levels. Indeed, as we describe in detail in Sect. 4, we use discrete power data in our experiment that has been quantized to a resolution of 7 W. It is therefore required to modify the optimization problem (3) to accommodate such cases. We describe here the discretized version of the optimization problem.

Let $\tilde{Y} \in \tilde{\mathcal{Y}}$ be a discrete random variable representing the quantized smart-meter data and $\tilde{Z} \in \tilde{\mathcal{Z}}$ represent the distorted data, where $\tilde{\mathcal{Y}}$ and $\tilde{\mathcal{Z}}$ are finite sets. Let $d : \tilde{Y} \times \tilde{Z} \to \mathbb{R}^+$ be some distortion function. Then the optimization problem in (3) becomes

$$\min_{p_{\tilde{Z}|\tilde{Y}}} I(\boldsymbol{X}^*; \tilde{Z}) \quad \text{subject to } E_{\tilde{Y},\tilde{Z}}[d(\tilde{Y}, \tilde{Z})] \leq \delta, \tag{16}$$

where

$$I(\boldsymbol{X}^*; \tilde{Z}) = \sum_{\boldsymbol{x}^* \in \mathcal{X}^*} \sum_{\tilde{z} \in \tilde{\mathcal{Z}}} P_{\mathcal{X}}(\boldsymbol{x}^*) P_{\tilde{Z}|\boldsymbol{X}^*}(\tilde{z}|\boldsymbol{x}^*) \log \frac{P_{\tilde{Z}|\boldsymbol{X}^*}(\tilde{z}|\boldsymbol{x}^*)}{P_{\tilde{Z}}(\tilde{z})}, \tag{17}$$

$$E_{\tilde{Y},\tilde{Z}}[d(\tilde{Y}, \tilde{Z})] = \sum_{\tilde{y} \in \tilde{\mathcal{Y}}} \sum_{\tilde{z} \in \tilde{\mathcal{Z}}} P_{\tilde{Z}|\tilde{Y}}(\tilde{z}|\tilde{y}) P_{\tilde{Y}}(\tilde{y}) d(\tilde{y}, \tilde{z}). \tag{18}$$

References

1. Alcalá, J., Parson, O., Rogers, A.: Detecting anomalies in activities of daily living of elderly residents via energy disaggregation and cox processes. In: BuildSys 2015. ACM (2015)
2. Alcalá, J., Ureña, J., Hernández, A.: Activity supervision tool using non-intrusive load monitoring systems. In: ETFA 2015. IEEE (2015)
3. Atzori, L., Iera, A., Morabito, G.: The internet of things: a survey. Comput. Netw. **54**(15), 2787–2805 (2010)
4. Basciftci, Y.O., Wang, Y., Ishwar, P.: On privacy-utility tradeoffs for constrained data release mechanisms. In: ITA 2016. IEEE (2016)
5. Boyd, S., Vandenberghe, L.: Convex Optimization. Cambridge University Press, Cambridge (2004)
6. Boyd, S., Vandenberghe, L., Grant, M.: Advances in convex optimization. In: Chinese Control Conference 2006. IEEE (2006)
7. Duhigg, C.: How companies learn your secrets. The New York Times Magazine (2012)
8. Dwork, C.: Differential privacy. In: Bugliesi, M., Preneel, B., Sassone, V., Wegener, I. (eds.) ICALP 2006. LNCS, vol. 4052, pp. 1–12. Springer, Heidelberg (2006). doi:10.1007/11787006_1
9. Dwork, C.: Differential privacy: a survey of results. In: Agrawal, M., Du, D., Duan, Z., Li, A. (eds.) TAMC 2008. LNCS, vol. 4978, pp. 1–19. Springer, Heidelberg (2008). doi:10.1007/978-3-540-79228-4_1

10. Eisenberg, B., Sullivan, R.: Why is the sum of independent normal random variables normal? Math. Mag. **81**(5), 362–366 (2008)
11. Erdogdu, M.A., Fawaz, N.: Privacy-utility trade-off under continual observation. In: ISIT 2015, pp. 1801–1805. IEEE (2015)
12. Erdogdu, M.A., Fawaz, N., Montanari, A.: Privacy-utility trade-off for time-series with application to smart-meter data. In: AAAI 2015 Workshop on Computational Sustainability (2015)
13. Ghahramani, Z., Jordan, M.I.: Factorial hidden Markov models. Mach. Learn. **29**(2/3), 245–273 (1997)
14. Guo, Z., Wang, Z.J., Kashani, A.: Home appliance load modmodel from aggregated smart meter data. IEEE Trans. Power Syst. **30**(1), 254–262 (2015)
15. Hart, G.: Nonintrusive appliance load monitoring. Proc. IEEE **80**(12), 1870–1891 (1992)
16. Kalogridis, G., Denic, S.Z.: Data mining and privacy of personal behaviour types in smart grid. In: ICDMW 2011. IEEE (2011)
17. Kelly, J., Knottenbelt, W.: Neural NILM: deep neural networks applied to energy disaggregation. In: BuildSys 2015. ACM (2015)
18. Kim, H., Marwah, M., Arlitt, M., Lyon, G., Han, J.: Unsupervised disaggregation of low frequency power measurements. In: SDM 2011, pp. 747–758. SIAM (2011)
19. Li, N., Li, T., Venkatasubramanian, S.: t-closeness: privacy beyond k-anonymity and l-diversity. In: ICDE 2007, pp. 106–115. IEEE (2007)
20. Li, S., Khisti, A., Mahajan, A.: Privacy-optimal strategies for smart metering systems with a rechargeable battery. In: ACC 2016. IEEE (2016)
21. Machanavajjhala, A., Gehrke, J., Kifer, D., Venkitasubramaniam, M.: L-diversity: privacy beyond k-anonymity. In: 22nd International Conference on Data Engineering, ICDE 2006, p. 24. IEEE (2006). doi:10.1109/icde.2006.1
22. Parson, O., Ghosh, S., Weal, M., Rogers, A.: Non-intrusive load monitoring using prior models of general appliance types. In: AAAI 2012, pp. 356–362 (2012)
23. Parson, O., Ghosh, S., Weal, M., Rogers, A.: An unsupervised training method for non-intrusive appliance load monitoring. Artif. Intell. **217**, 1–19 (2014)
24. Pillitteri, V.Y., Brewer, T.L.: Guidelines for smart grid cybersecurity. Internal Report NISTIR 7628 Revision 1, National Institute of Standards and Technology (2014)
25. du Pin Calmon, F., Fawaz, N.: Privacy against statistical inference. In: Allerton 2012. IEEE (2012)
26. Quinn, E.L.: Smart metering and privacy: Existing laws and competing policies. SSRN Electron. J. (2009). doi:10.2139/ssrn.1462285
27. Rajagopalan, S.R., Sankar, L., Mohajer, S., Poor, H.V.: Smart meter privacy: a utility-privacy framework. In: SmartGridComm 2011. IEEE (2011)
28. Salamatian, S., Zhang, A., du Pin Calmon, F., Bhamidipati, S., Fawaz, N., Kveton, B., Oliveira, P., Taft, N.: Managing your private and public data: Bringing down inference attacks against your privacy. IEEE J. Sel. Top. Sig. Proces. **9**(7), 1240–1255 (2015)
29. Samarati, P.: Protecting respondents identities in microdata release. IEEE Trans. Knowl. Data Eng. **13**(6), 1010–1027 (2001)
30. Schneier, B.: Data and goliath: The hidden battles to collect your data and control your world. W. W. Norton & Company (2015)
31. Song, H., Kalogridis, G., Fan, Z.: Short paper: time-dependent power load disaggregation with applications to daily activity monitoring. In: WF-IoT 2014. IEEE (2014)

32. Sweeney, L.: k-anonymity: A model for protecting privacy. Int. J. Uncertainty Fuzziness Knowl. Based Syst. **10**(05), 557–570 (2002)
33. Tan, O., Gunduz, D., Poor, H.V.: Increasing smart meter privacy through energy harvesting and storage devices. IEEE J. Sel. Areas Commun. **31**(7), 1331–1341 (2013)
34. Xiao, X., Tao, Y.: m-invariance: towards privacy preserving re-publication of dynamic datasets. In: SIGMOD 2007, pp. 689–700. ACM (2007)
35. Yang, L., Chen, X., Zhang, J., Poor, H.V.: Cost-effective and privacy-preserving energy management for smart meters. IEEE Trans. Smart Grid **6**(1), 486–495 (2015)
36. Yang, W., Li, N., Qi, Y., Qardaji, W., McLaughlin, S., McDaniel, P.: Minimizing private data disclosures in the smart grid. In: ACM CCS 2012, pp. 415–427. ACM (2012)
37. Yao, J., Venkitasubramaniam, P.: The privacy analysis of battery control mechanisms in demand response: revealing state approach and rate distortion bounds. IEEE Trans. Smart Grid **6**(5), 2417–2425 (2015)

Private Graph Intersection Protocol

Fucai Zhou$^{(\boxtimes)}$, Zifeng Xu, Yuxi Li, Jian Xu, and Su Peng

Software College, Northeastern University, Shenyang, China
fczhou@mail.neu.edu.cn, dk@tnimdk.com, eliyuxi@gmail.com,
xujian@swc.neu.edu.cn, supeng@stumail.neu.edu.cn

Abstract. A wide range of applications can benefit from storing and managing data as graph structures, and graph theory algorithms can be used to solve various computing problems. In this paper, we propose a secure two-party private graph intersection protocol against semi-honest servers. The protocol allows a server and a client, each holding a private graph, to jointly compute the intersection of their graphs. The protocol utilizes homomorphic encryptions and a private set intersection subprotocol to prevent information leakage during the process. At the end of the protocol, the server learns the graph intersection, and the client learns the vertex intersection.

Keywords: Graph encryption · Graph theory · Multi-party computation · Homomorphic encryption

1 Introduction

Graph data and graph processing have received increased interests, since they can help to solve many practical problems. Using graph structures to store and process web data has been extensively studied over the past decades [1–3]. Representing static pages as vertices and the links between the pages as edges naturally convert web data into directed graphs. Furthermore, various types of graph operations can be used to solve different web problems, including web searching [4–7], web crawling [8–10] and data mining [11–13].

Beyond web data, many other areas start to store data as graph structures in order to convert different computing problems into graph problems, such as social network [14–16], biological network [17–19] and communication network [20]. Graph intersection is one of the most common graph problems, and it can be used to solve various practical problems. In more details, graph intersection computes the intersected part, for both vertex and edge, between two input graphs.

Various database systems have been proposed to store, manage and query graph data [21]. However, along with the rapid growth in the size of the graph data in recent years, efficient processing of large graphs has becoming a challenging problem. For example, traditional methods and algorithms tend to fail for graphs with billions or trillions of vertices and edges. As a result, several solutions and systems for efficient processing of large-scale graphs have been studied [22,23].

Along with the development of cloud computing and remote storage, outsourcing data storage to third parties has become a common solution for both

© Springer International Publishing AG 2017
J. Pieprzyk and S. Suriadi (Eds.): ACISP 2017, Part II, LNCS 10343, pp. 235–248, 2017.
DOI: 10.1007/978-3-319-59870-3_13

corporations and individuals. However, outsourcing sensitive data to untrusted service providers remains at risk. For example, the cloud storage providers may dig into the private data themselves, or they may leak the data to other parties for profits. As a result, the study of privacy-preserving data storage, while remaining the ability to query and search, has become a popular research area in academia in the past years. The most well-studied solution so far is the searchable symmetric encryption (SSE) [24,25]. Briefly speaking, a searchable symmetric encryption scheme allows a client to outsource his data to a third party without losing confidentiality. In addition, the client can perform searches and queries on his data without leaking any useful information. A number of SSE schemes have been proposed with different features [26–28]. In 2010, Chase and Kamara introduced the notion of structured encryption and proposed a SSE scheme for graph data [29]. The scheme allows privacy-preserving storage for graph data, and supports neighbor queries and adjacency queries. In 2015, Meng, Kamara, Nissim and Kollios proposed a SSE scheme that supports approximate shortest distance queries for graph data [30].

1.1 Our Result

In this paper, we present the first private graph intersection protocol. As far as we can tell, only few graph intersection protocols have been proposed, and none of them concerns about the privacy protection for the input graphs.

The private graph intersection protocol involves two participants, a server S and a client C. Each of the participants holds a private graph, denoted as G_S and G_C, respectively. The protocol allows the two participants to interactively compute the intersection of their graphs. At the end of the protocol, the server learns the graph intersection, and the client learns the vertex intersection.

In the protocol, the vertex collection of a graph is represented as a sorted set, and the edge collection is represented as an adjacency matrix. The protocol utilizes a secure two-party private set intersection protocol as a sub-protocol for computing the vertex intersection. Furthermore, the protocol uses the homomorphic property of the Paillier encryption scheme to compute the edge intersection. During the protocol, neither the server nor the client can learn any information about the private graph of the other participant, beyond that can be deduced from the result of the protocol.

We give a security analysis about the protocol, and we proof that the protocol is secure against semi-honest adversarial servers. We also provide a discussion on the performance of the protocol.

2   Preliminaries

2.1   Paillier Encryption Scheme

The Paillier encryption scheme is a public key cryptosystem, proposed by Paillier in 1999 [31]. The scheme involves three algorithms, (KeyGen,Enc,Dec), defined below:

$(pk, sk) \leftarrow \text{KeyGen}(1^k)$ is the key generation algorithm. The input is a security parameter k. The outputs are a public key pk and a secret key sk. The public key contains a large number N which specifies the message space, the ciphertext space and the random space to be $\mathbb{Z}_N$, $\mathbb{Z}_{N^2}^*$ and $\mathbb{Z}_N^*$, respectively.

$m^{\oplus} \leftarrow \text{Enc}(pk, m; r)$ is the encryption algorithm. The input is the public key pk, a plaintext $m \in \mathbb{Z}_N$ and a random number $r \in \mathbb{Z}_N^*$. The output is the ciphertext $m^{\oplus} \in \mathbb{Z}_{N^2}^*$. For simplicity, we use the notion $m^{\oplus} = \text{Enc}(m)$.

$m \leftarrow \text{Dec}(sk, m^{\oplus})$ is the decryption algorithm. The input is the secret key sk and a ciphertext $m^{\oplus} \in \mathbb{Z}_{N^2}^*$. The output is the plaintext $m \in \mathbb{Z}_N$. For simplicity, we use the notion $m = \text{Dec}(m^{\oplus})$.

The Paillier encryption scheme has the following properties:

Correctness. For any $(pk, sk) \leftarrow \text{KeyGen}(1^k)$ and any $m \in \mathbb{Z}_N$, $\text{Dec}(\text{Enc}(m)) = m$ always holds.

IND-CPA Security. The ciphertexts of two plaintexts, $m_0^{\oplus}$ and $m_1^{\oplus}$, are indistinguishable for probabilistic polynomial-time adversaries that only have access to the public parameters.

Homomorphic Property. For any $m_0, m_1 \in \mathbb{Z}_N$, there exists an operation $\oplus$ in the ciphertext space, such that $\text{Dec}(\text{Enc}(m_0) \oplus \text{Enc}(m_1)) = m_0 + m_1$. Furthermore, there exists an operation $\odot$ in the ciphertext space, such that $\text{Dec}(\text{Enc}(m_0) \odot m_1) = m_0 \cdot m_1$.

2.2 Private Set Intersection

Private Set Intersection (PSI) is a cryptographic protocol that allows two parties, each holding a private set, to jointly compute the intersection of their sets without leaking any additional information. Private set intersection protocols have many important application areas in the real world, such as privacy-preserving data mining and sensitive database computation.

The first secure two-party private set intersection protocol is introduced by Freedman, Nissim and Pinkas (FNP) in 2004 [32]. The protocol utilizes homomorphic encryption and oblivious polynomial evaluation to ensure each party learns no information about the other party's private input during the computation. Later, several other protocols have been proposed with different features and security levels [33–35].

3 Problem Formation

3.1 Model and Definition

We formally describe the private graph intersection protocol (PGI). The protocol involves two participants, a server S and a client C. Each of the participants holds a private graph, which is intended to be kept secret from the other participant. We denote the graphs of the server and client as $G_S = (V_S, E_S)$ and $G_C = (V_C, E_C)$, respectively, where V and E are the vertex collection and edge collection of the graphs. The intersection of the two graphs is defined as $G_I = G_S \cap G_C = (V_I, E_I)$, where $V_I = V_S \cap V_C$ and $E_I = E_S \cap E_C$. The private graph intersection protocol allows the server and the client to jointly compute G_I. At the end of the protocol, the server learns G_I and the client learns V_I.

Definition 1 (Private Graph Intersection Protocol). Two probabilistic polynomial-time interactive Turing machines, S and C, define a Private Graph Intersection Protocol if the following properties hold:

Correctness: If both participants are honest, for any $G_S = (V_S, E_S)$ and any $G_C = (V_C, E_C)$, the private graph intersection protocol computes $G_I = (V_I, E_I) = G_S \cap G_C$. At the end of the protocol, S learns G_I and C learns V_I.

Server Zero-Knowledge: A semi-honest server learns nothing about the client's graph, beyond that can be deduced from G_I.

Client Zero-Knowledge: A semi-honest client learns nothing about the server's graph, beyond that can be deduced from V_I.

3.2   Graph Representation

In our protocol, we represent a graph as $G = (V, E)$, where V is the vertex collection and E is the edge collection. We represent the vertex collection as a sorted set with ascending order, $V = \{v_1, v_2, ..., v_m\}$, where m is the number of vertices, $v_i \in \mathbb{Z}$ and $v_i < v_{i+1}$ for $1 \leq i \leq m-1$. We represent the edge collection as an adjacency matrix,

$$E = \begin{pmatrix} e_{1,1} & \cdots & e_{1,m} \\ \vdots & \ddots & \vdots \\ e_{m,1} & \cdots & e_{m,m} \end{pmatrix},$$

where $e_{i,j}$ is the adjacency relation between the vertices v_i and v_j, and $e_{i,j} \in \{0, 1\}$. If vertices v_i and v_j are adjacent, i.e. there is at least one edge that connects them, $e_{i,j} = 1$, otherwise $e_{i,j} = 0$. Note that, E is a square matrix with m rows and m columns. For an undirected graph, E is a symmetric matrix, since the edges are two-way.

For example, we represent the directed graph illustrated in Fig. 1 as $G = (V, E)$, where $V = \{1, 5, 23, 50, 74\}$ and

$$E = \begin{pmatrix} 0 & 1 & 0 & 1 & 0 \\ 0 & 1 & 0 & 0 & 0 \\ 1 & 0 & 0 & 0 & 1 \\ 0 & 0 & 0 & 0 & 1 \\ 0 & 0 & 1 & 1 & 1 \end{pmatrix}.$$

Furthermore, we define a notion of sub-edge, denoted as A. For a graph $G = (V, E)$ and a vertex collection $V' \subseteq V$, the sub-edge is a sub matrix of E,

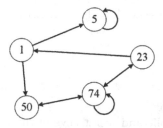

Fig. 1. Example graph

such that it only contains the adjacency relations between the vertices in V'. In more details, let $V = \{v_1, v_2, ..., v_m\}$ and $V' = \{v'_1, v'_2, ..., v'_n\}$, where $v'_i \in V$ and $n \leq m$. A is defined as:

$$A = \begin{pmatrix} a_{1,1} & \cdots & a_{1,n} \\ \vdots & \ddots & \vdots \\ a_{n,1} & \cdots & a_{n,n} \end{pmatrix},$$

where $a_{i,j}$ is the adjacency relation between the vertices v'_i and v'_j in graph G, and $a_{i,j} \in \{0, 1\}$.

For example, for the graph illustrated in Fig. 1, let $V' = \{1, 5, 74\}$. The sub-edge A is calculated as:

$$A = \begin{pmatrix} 0 & 1 & 0 \\ 0 & 1 & 0 \\ 0 & 0 & 1 \end{pmatrix}.$$

4   Private Graph Intersection Protocol

In this section, we propose a construction of the private graph intersection protocol. In the construction, the server and the client use the Paillier encryption scheme to achieve homomorphic multiplication, and use the FNP protocol as a sub-protocol for private set intersection (PSI).

4.1   Building Block: Private Set Intersection Protocol

In our construction, we use the FNP protocol as a sub-protocol to compute the vertex intersection. The FNP protocol is a construction of the private set intersection (PSI), and is proposed by Freedman, Nissim and Pinkas [32]. The protocol has two participants, a server S and a client C. Each of the participants hold a private set, and they wish to compute the intersection of their sets. The FNP protocol allows the server and the client to interactively compute the intersection without leaking any information, and only the server learns the result.

The FNP protocol is described as below:

Input: S and C hold the sets $A = \{a_1, a_2, ..., a_m\}$ and $B = \{b_1, b_2, ..., b_n\}$, respectively.

Output: S learns $I = A \bigcap B$.

Protocol:

1. S performs the following:
    (a) S generates the public and secret keys of the Paillier encryption scheme, and publishes the public key.
    (b) S constructs a polynomial $P(x) = \sum_{u=0}^{m} \alpha_u x^u$, such that all the roots are exactly the elements in A. In other words, $P(x) = 0$ if and only if $x \in A$.
    (c) S encrypts each α_i, for $0 \le i \le m$, under the Paillier encryption scheme, and sends the ciphertexts to C.
2. C performs the following:
    (a) By using the homomorphic properties of the Paillier encryption scheme, C evaluates $\text{Enc}(P(x))$ using the elements in B as inputs. In other words, C computes $\text{Enc}(P(b_i)) = \text{Enc}(\sum_{u=0}^{m} \alpha_u b_i^u)$, for $1 \le i \le n$.
    (b) For each $b_i \in B$, C chooses a random value r and computes $\text{Enc}(rP(b_i) + b_i)$. Then C sends all the resulting ciphertexts to S.
3. S decrypts all the ciphertexts received, and compares the decrypted values with his set A. If a decrypted value d has a corresponding element in A, it is an element of the intersection of A and B. In other words, if $d \in A$, $d \in I = A \bigcap B$.

The FNP protocol has the following properties:

Correctness: If both the participants are honest, the FNP protocol evaluates the intersection of the two input sets with high probability, and only the server obtains the result.

Zero-Knowledge: If the Paillier encryption scheme is semantically secure, the client learns nothing about the server's set, and the server learns nothing about the client's set, beyond that can be deduced from the result.

4.2   Protocol Construction

In our construction, the Paillier encryption scheme is denoted as a collection of algorithms (KeyGen, Enc, Dec). $(pk, sk) \leftarrow \text{KeyGen}(1^k)$ is the key generation algorithm, $m^{\oplus} \leftarrow \text{Enc}(m)$ is the encryption algorithm and $m \leftarrow \text{Dec}(m^{\oplus})$ is the decryption algorithm. The homomorphic multiplication operation between a ciphertext and a constant is denoted as $\odot$.

Furthermore, the FNP sub-protocol is denoted as $V_I \leftarrow \text{PSI}(V_S, V_C, pk, sk)$. The inputs are the vertex collections of the server and the client, V_S and V_C, and the public and secret keys of the Paillier encryption scheme, pk and sk. The output is the vertex intersection, $V_I = V_S \cap V_C$, which is only obtained by the server.

The server's graph is represented as $G_S = (V_S, E_S)$, where $V_S = \{v_{S,1}, v_{S,2}, ..., v_{S,m}\}$ and

$$E_S = \begin{pmatrix} s_{1,1} & \cdots & s_{1,m} \\ \vdots & \ddots & \vdots \\ s_{m,1} & \cdots & s_{m,m} \end{pmatrix}.$$

The client's graph is represented as $G_C = (V_C, E_C)$, where $V_C = \{v_{C,1}, v_{C,2}, ..., v_{C,n}\}$ and

$$E_C = \begin{pmatrix} c_{1,1} & \cdots & c_{1,n} \\ \vdots & \ddots & \vdots \\ c_{n,1} & \cdots & c_{n,n} \end{pmatrix}.$$

Note that, $v_{S,i}, v_{C,j} \in \mathbb{Z}_N$ for $1 \le i \le m$ and $1 \le j \le n$, where N is generated by the KeyGen algorithm of the Paillier encryption scheme as a part of the public key.

The private graph intersection protocol is described below:

Input: S and C hold the graphs $G_S = (V_S, E_S)$ and $G_C = (V_C, E_C)$, respectively.

Output: S learns $G_I = (V_I, E_I) = G_S \cap G_C$, and C learns $V_I = V_S \cap V_C$.

Protocol:

Step 1: S runs the $(pk, sk) \leftarrow \text{KeyGen}(1^k)$ algorithm, and obtains the public key and the secret key of the Paillier encryption scheme. Then S publishes pk.

Step 2: S and C jointly run the $V_I \leftarrow \text{PSI}(V_S, V_C, pk, sk)$ sub-protocol, and S obtains $V_I = V_S \cap V_C = \{v_{I,1}, v_{I,2}, ...v_{I,t}\}$.

Step 3:

(a) By using V_I, S constructs the sub-edge A_S from E_S:

$$A_S = \begin{pmatrix} a_{1,1} & \cdots & a_{1,t} \\ \vdots & \ddots & \vdots \\ a_{t,1} & \cdots & a_{t,t} \end{pmatrix}.$$

(b) S runs the Enc() algorithm to encrypt each element in A_S, and obtains an encrypted matrix $A_S^{\oplus} = \text{Enc}(A_S)$.

(c) S sends $A_S^{\oplus}$ and V_I to C.

Step 4:

(a) By using V_I, C constructs the sub-edge A_C from E_C:

$$A_C = \begin{pmatrix} b_{1,1} & \cdots & b_{1,t} \\ \vdots & \ddots & \vdots \\ b_{t,1} & \cdots & b_{t,t} \end{pmatrix}.$$

(b) C computes

$$
E_I^\oplus = A_S^\oplus \odot A_C = \begin{pmatrix} a_{1,1}^\oplus & \cdots & a_{1,t}^\oplus \\ \vdots & \ddots & \vdots \\ a_{t,1}^\oplus & \cdots & a_{t,t}^\oplus \end{pmatrix} \odot \begin{pmatrix} b_{1,1} & \cdots & b_{1,t} \\ \vdots & \ddots & \vdots \\ b_{t,1} & \cdots & b_{t,t} \end{pmatrix}
$$
$$
= \begin{pmatrix} a_{1,1}^\oplus \odot b_{1,1} & \cdots & a_{1,t}^\oplus \odot b_{1,t} \\ \vdots & \ddots & \vdots \\ a_{t,1}^\oplus \odot b_{t,1} & \cdots & a_{t,t}^\oplus \odot b_{t,t} \end{pmatrix}.
$$

(c) C sends $E_I^\oplus$ to S.

Step 5: S uses the Dec() algorithm to decrypt each element in $E_I^\oplus$, and obtains $E_I = \text{Dec}(E_I^\oplus)$. At last, S obtains $G_I = (V_I, E_I)$.

5   Analysis

5.1   Security Analysis

Lemma 1 (Correctness). If both participants are honest, for any $G_S = (V_S, E_S)$ and any $G_C = (V_C, E_C)$, the private graph intersection protocol computes $G_I = (V_I, E_I) = G_S \bigcap G_C$. At the end of the protocol, S learns G_I and C learns V_I.

Proof. The correctness of our protocol is ensured by the correctness of the FNP sub-protocol and the homomorphic property of the Paillier encryption scheme.

During the **Step 2** of the protocol, the client and the server jointly perform a FNP sub-protocol using their vertex collections as inputs. At the end of the sub-protocol, the server learns the vertex intersection V_I. At the end of **Step 3** of the protocol, the client receives V_I from the server.

During **Step 3** and **Step 4** of the protocol, the client and the server construct the sub-edges A_C and A_S, respectively, by using V_I. Note that, A_C and A_S contain the adjacency relations between the vertices in V_I for graphs G_C and G_S, respectively. In other words, if an edge exists between two vertices in V_I, it will have to a value of 1 in the sub-edge, otherwise it will have a value of 0. Therefore, the dot product of A_C and A_S will produce the adjacency matrix for the edge intersection. The reason is, if and only if an edge exists in both A_C and A_S, i.e. it is a common edge, the dot product of the adjacency relations will be 1, otherwise it will be 0.

In **Step 4** of the protocol, the client receives the ciphertext of the server's sub-edge under the Paillier encryption scheme. If the Paillier encryption scheme has the homomorphic property, i.e. it supports multiplication between a ciphertext and a constant, the client can compute the dot product of the sub-edges, and the result is the ciphertext of the edge intersection. Finally, the server can learn the edge intersection after decryption.

As a result, if the FNP protocol is correct and the Paillier encryption scheme has the homomorphic property, the server learns the graph intersection $G_I = (V_I, E_I)$, and the client learns the vertex intersection V_I. Since the FNP sub-protocol used in our construction is proved to be correct [32] and the Paillier encryption scheme is proved to have the homomorphic property [31], the correctness property holds for our protocol.   □

Lemma 2 (Server Zero-knowledge). A semi-honest server learns nothing about the client's graph, beyond that can be deduced from G_I.

Proof. The proof of Server Zero-knowledge is trivial. During the protocol, there are two parts where the server receives information about the client's graph. The first part is during the FNP sub-protocol at **Step 2** of the protocol, and the second part is during **Step 4**.

For the first part, the Server Zero-knowledge relies on the zero-knowledge property of the FNP sub-protocol. In other words, if the FNP sub-protocol is zero-knowledge, the server cannot learn any information about the client's vertex collection, beyond the vertex intersection.

For the second part, the server receives $E_I^\oplus$ from the client, which is the ciphertext of the edge intersection. Upon decryption, the server only learns the edge intersection.

As a result, if the FNP sub-protocol is zero-knowledge, the server learns nothing about the client's graph, beyond the graph intersection. Since the FNP sub-protocol is proved to have the zero-knowledge property [32], the Server Zero-knowledge property holds for our protocol.   □

Lemma 3 (Client Zero-knowledge). A semi-honest client learns nothing about the server's graph, beyond that can be deduced from V_I.

Proof. There are two parts where the client receives information about the server's graph. The first part is the PSI sub-protocol during **Step 2** of the protocol, and the second part is during **Step 3**.

For the first part, similar to the proof of Lemma 2, the Client Zero-knowledge relies on the zero-knowledge property of the FNP sub-protocol. In other words, if the FNP sub-protocol is zero-knowledge, the client cannot learn any information about the server's the vertex collection.

For the second part, we need to show that the information which the client receives during **Step 3** does not reveal any information about the server's graph, beyond the vertex intersection. According to the protocol construction, the client receives an encrypted adjacency matrix $A_S^\oplus$ and the vertex intersection V_I during **Step 3**. Therefore, if the client cannot distinguish between the cases where the server has different input graphs given the knowledge of $A_S^\oplus$ and V_I, the zero-knowledge for the client holds. Consider the following experiment:

$$EXP_{\mathcal{A}}^{IND-CPA}(1^k):$$

$$(pk, sk) \leftarrow \text{KeyGen}(1^k)$$

$$(G_0, G_1) \leftarrow \mathcal{A}$$

$$b \xleftarrow{\$} \{0, 1\}$$

$$V_I \leftarrow \text{PSI}(G_b, G_C, pk, sk)$$

$$A_b \leftarrow \text{SubEdge}(E_b, V_I)$$

$$A_b^{\oplus} \leftarrow \text{Enc}(A_b)$$

$$\hat{b} \leftarrow \mathcal{A}(A_b^{\oplus}, V_I)$$

if $\hat{b} = b$, output 1

otherwise, output 0

In the above experiment, $\mathcal{A}$ is a probabilistic polynomial-time adversarial client with a private graph $G_C = (E_C, V_C)$. The server first runs the KeyGen algorithm to generate the public and secret keys of the Paillier encryption scheme (**Step 1**). Then $\mathcal{A}$ chooses two graphs $G_0 = (E_0, V_0)$ and $G_1 = (E_1, V_1)$, and sends them to the server. In addition, G_0 and G_1 have the property that $V_0 \cap V_C = V_1 \cap V_C$. Upon receiving the graphs, the server randomly picks a bit $b = \{0, 1\}$, then sets the graph G_b to be his private graph. After that, the server and $\mathcal{A}$ jointly perform a FNP sub-protocol to compute the vertex intersection V_I (**Step 2**). By using V_I, the server constructs the sub-edge A_b from E_b. Then the server encrypts A_b using the Enc() algorithm of the Paillier encryption scheme, and obtains $A_b^{\oplus}$ (**Step 3**). At last, given the knowledge of $A_b^{\oplus}$ and V_I, $\mathcal{A}$ guesses a bit $\hat{b}$. If $\hat{b} = b$, the experiment outputs 1, otherwise outputs 0. The advantage of the above experiment for $\mathcal{A}$ is defined as $Adv_{\mathcal{A}} = \left| \Pr[EXP_{\mathcal{A}}(1^k) = 1] - \frac{1}{2} \right|$.

Due to the condition $V_0 \cap V_C = V_1 \cap V_C$, the vertex intersection V_I gives no useful information since V_I will be the same for both G_0 and G_1. Therefore, for $\mathcal{A}$ to have a significant advantage in the above experiment, $\mathcal{A}$ needs to have the ability to distinguish between $A_0^{\oplus}$ and $A_1^{\oplus}$ without decryption. Note that, both $A_0^{\oplus}$ and $A_1^{\oplus}$ are matrices containing ciphertexts under the Paillier encryption scheme, with the size $|V_I| \times |V_I|$. As a result, if the Paillier encryption scheme is IND-CPA secure, there is no probabilistic polynomial-time algorithm that can distinguish between $A_0^{\oplus}$ and $A_1^{\oplus}$ without decryption. Hence the advantage of the above experiment for $\mathcal{A}$ is negligible, i.e. $Adv_{\mathcal{A}} = \left| \Pr[EXP_{\mathcal{A}}(1^k) = 1] - \frac{1}{2} \right| = \varepsilon$, where ε is negligible.

At last, we construct a simulator Sim_S to simulate the view of the client in the ideal model. Sim_S is given the knowledge of the vertex intersection V_I. In the ideal model, Sim_S sends V_I and a matrix with $|V_I| \times |V_I|$ random values in $\mathbb{Z}_{N^2}$ to the client during **Step 3** of the protocol. Since the client cannot distinguish between the ciphertexts under the Paillier encryption scheme and random values, the view of the client in the ideal model is computationally indistinguishable from the view in the real model, i.e. $View_C^{real}[S(G_S), C] \approx View_C^{ideal}[Sim_S(V_I), C]$.

As a result, if the FNP sub-protocol is zero-knowledge and the Paillier encryption scheme is IND-CPA secure, the client learns nothing about the server's graph, beyond the vertex intersection. Since the FNP protocol is proved to have the zero-knowledge property [32] and the Paillier encryption scheme is proved to have IND-CPA security [31], the Server Zero-knowledge property holds for our protocol.   □

5.2 Performance Analysis

In this section, we denote m as the number of vertices in the server's graph, n as the number of vertices in the client's graph and t as the number of vertices in the intersection of the graphs. The communication cost is in terms of number of ciphertexts been transferred between the server and the client. The computation cost is measured using modular additions, multiplications and exponentiations.

Communication Cost: The construction of the protocol is simple and only requires $O(1)$ rounds of communication. During the FNP sub-protocol, the server sends $m + 1$ ciphertexts to the client, and the client sends n ciphertexts to the server. During the **Step 3** of the protocol, the server sends t^2 ciphertexts to the client. During the **Step 4**, the client sends t^2 ciphertext to the client. As a result, the total communication cost of our protocol is $O(m+n+t^2)$ ciphertexts.

Server Computation Cost: During the FNP sub-protocol, constructing the polynomial requires $O(m^2)$ modular additions and multiplication. Encrypting the coefficients requires $O(m)$ modular exponentiations and multiplications, and decrypting the received ciphertexts requires $O(n)$ modular exponentiations. In **Step 3**, encrypting each element in A_S requires $O(t^2)$ modular exponentiations and multiplications. In **Step 5**, decrypting each element in $E_I^\oplus$ requires $O(t^2)$ exponentiations.

Client Computation Cost: During the FNP sub-protocol, obliviously evaluating the polynomial requires $O(mn)$ modular exponentiations and multiplications. If the balanced hash-bucket scheme is employed, as described in [32], the costs of polynomial evaluations can be reduced to $O(nlnlnm)$. In **step 4**, computing $E_I^\oplus$ requires $O(t^2)$ modular exponentiations.

5.3 Information Leakage

In our construction of the private graph intersection protocol, we assume that the vertex intersection is allowed to be revealed to the client. In some scenarios this assumption is reasonable. For example, two airline companies want to find out which flight routes they have in common within a certain region, and only one of the companies is allowed to have the result. They can represent all the cities within the region as vertices and their flight routes as edges. By using the protocol, they can obtain the result without losing any private information, since the vertex intersection (all the cities within the region) is assumed to be publicly known for both client and server.

However, for a stronger security assumption, the vertex intersection should be considered as private information as well. Therefore, it may cause information leakage if the client learns the vertex intersection. We will focus on this problem in further works.

6 Conclusion

In this work, we propose the first private graph intersection protocol. The protocol allows two participants, each holding a private graph, to jointly compute the graph intersection without leaking any private information. The security of the protocol is based on homomorphic encryptions and a secure private set intersection sub-protocol. The protocol has many application areas, such as sensitive online services and privacy-preserving data mining.

Acknowledgments. This work was supported in part by the National Science and Technology Major Project under Grant 2013ZX03002006, in part by the Liaoning Province Science and Technology Projects under Grant 2013217004, in part by the Fundamental Research Funds for the Central Universities under Grant N151704002, in part by the Liaoning Province Doctor Startup Fund under Grant 20141012, in part by the Fundamental Research Funds for the Central Universities under Grant N130317002, in part by the Shenyang Province Science and Technology Projects under Grant F14-231-1-08, and in part by the National Natural Science Foundation of China under Grant 61472184, Grant 61321491, and Grant 61272546.

References

1. Broder, A., Kumar, R., Maghoul, F., et al.: Graph structure in the web. Comput. Netw. **33**(1), 309–320 (2000)
2. Kleinberg, J.M., Kumar, R., Raghavan, P., Rajagopalan, S., Tomkins, A.S.: The web as a graph: measurements, models, and methods. In: Asano, T., Imai, H., Lee, D.T., Nakano, S., Tokuyama, T. (eds.) COCOON 1999. LNCS, vol. 1627, pp. 1–17. Springer, Heidelberg (1999). doi:10.1007/3-540-48686-0_1
3. Botafogo, R.A., Shneiderman, B.: Identifying aggregates in hypertext structures. In: Proceedings of the third Annual ACM Conference on Hypertext, pp. 63–74. ACM (1991)
4. Zhang, B., Li, H., Liu, Y., et al.: Improving web search results using affinity graph. In: Proceedings of the 28th Annual International ACM SIGIR Conference on Research and Development in Information Retrieval, pp. 504–511. ACM (2005)
5. Page, L., Brin, S., Motwani, R., et al.: The PageRank citation ranking: Bringing order to the web. Stanford InfoLab (1999)
6. Kacholia, V., Pandit, S., Chakrabarti, S., et al.: Bidirectional expansion for keyword search on graph databases. In: Proceedings of the 31st International Conference on Very Large Data Bases, pp. 505–516. VLDB Endowment (2005)
7. Wang, M., Li, H., Tao, D., et al.: Multimodal graph-based reranking for web image search. IEEE Trans. Image Process. **21**(11), 4649–4661 (2012)
8. Chakrabarti, S., Van den Berg, M., Dom, B.: Focused crawling: a new approach to topic-specific web resource discovery. Comput. Netw. **31**(11), 1623–1640 (1999)
9. Cothey, V.: Web-crawling reliability. J. Am. Soc. Inform. Sci. Technol. **55**(14), 1228–1238 (2004)

10. Pant, G., Srinivasan, P., Menczer, F.: Crawling the web. In: Web Dynamics, pp. 153–177. Springer, Berlin Heidelberg (2004)

11. Buehrer, G., Chellapilla, K.: A scalable pattern mining approach to web graph compression with communities. In: Proceedings of the 2008 International Conference on Web Search and Data Mining, pp. 95–106. ACM (2008)

12. Craven, M., Slattery, S., Nigam, K.: First-order learning for web mining. In: Nédellec, C., Rouveirol, C. (eds.) ECML 1998. LNCS, vol. 1398, pp. 250–255. Springer, Heidelberg (1998). doi:10.1007/BFb0026695

13. Sharma, K., Shrivastava, G., Kumar, V.: Web mining: today and tomorrow. In: 2011 3rd International Conference on Electronics Computer Technology (ICECT), vol. 1, pp. 399–403. IEEE (2011)

14. Pamnani, R., Web, C.P., Mining, U.: A research area in web mining. In: Proceedings of ISCET, pp. 73–77 (2010)

15. Cha, M., Mislove, A., Gummadi, K.P.: A measurement-driven analysis of information propagation in the flickr social network. In: Proceedings of the 18th International Conference on World Wide Web, pp. 721–730. ACM (2009)

16. Myers, S.A., Sharma, A., Gupta, P., et al.: Information network or social network?: the structure of the twitter follow graph. In: Proceedings of the 23rd International Conference on World Wide Web, pp. 493–498. ACM (2014)

17. Carletti, V., Foggia, P., Vento, M.: Performance comparison of five exact graph matching algorithms on biological databases. In: Petrosino, A., Maddalena, L., Pala, P. (eds.) ICIAP 2013. LNCS, vol. 8158, pp. 409–417. Springer, Heidelberg (2013). doi:10.1007/978-3-642-41190-8_44

18. Pavlopoulos, G.A., Secrier, M., Moschopoulos, C.N., et al.: Using graph theory to analyze biological networks. Biodata Mining 4(1), 10 (2011)

19. Tian, Y., Mceachin, R.C., Santos, C., et al.: SAGA: a subgraph matching tool for biological graphs. Bioinformatics 23(2), 232–239 (2007)

20. Ahlswede, R., Cai, N., Li, S.Y.R., et al.: Network information flow. IEEE Trans. Inf. Theory 46(4), 1204–1216 (2000)

21. Angles, R., Gutierrez, C.: Survey of graph database models. ACM Comput. Surv. (CSUR) 40(1), 1 (2008)

22. Malewicz, G., Austern, M.H., Bik, A.J.C., et al.: Pregel: a system for large-scale graph processing. In: Proceedings of the 2010 ACM SIGMOD International Conference on Management of Data, pp. 135–146. ACM (2010)

23. Kyrola, A., Blelloch, G.E., GraphChi, G.C.: Large-scale graph computation on just a PC. In: OSDI, vol. 12, pp. 31–46 (2012)

24. Song, D.X., Wagner, D., Perrig, A.: Practical techniques for searches on encrypted data. In: Proceedings of 2000 IEEE Symposium on Security and Privacy, S&P 2000, pp. 44–55. IEEE (2000)

25. Curtmola, R., Garay, J., Kamara, S., et al.: Searchable symmetric encryption: improved definitions and efficient constructions. J. Comput. Secur. 19(5), 895–934 (2011)

26. Kamara, S., Papamanthou, C., Roeder, T.: Dynamic searchable symmetric encryption. In: Proceedings of the 2012 ACM Conference on Computer and Communications Security, pp. 965–976. ACM (2012)

27. Cash, D., Jarecki, S., Jutla, C., Krawczyk, H., Roşu, M.-C., Steiner, M.: Highly-scalable searchable symmetric encryption with support for boolean queries. In: Canetti, R., Garay, J.A. (eds.) CRYPTO 2013. LNCS, vol. 8042, pp. 353–373. Springer, Heidelberg (2013). doi:10.1007/978-3-642-40041-4_20

28. Liesdonk, P., Sedghi, S., Doumen, J., Hartel, P., Jonker, W.: Computationally efficient searchable symmetric encryption. In: Jonker, W., Petković, M. (eds.) SDM 2010. LNCS, vol. 6358, pp. 87–100. Springer, Heidelberg (2010). doi:10.1007/978-3-642-15546-8_7

29. Chase, M., Kamara, S.: Structured encryption and controlled disclosure. In: Abe, M. (ed.) ASIACRYPT 2010. LNCS, vol. 6477, pp. 577–594. Springer, Heidelberg (2010). doi:10.1007/978-3-642-17373-8_33

30. Meng, X., Kamara, S., Nissim, K., et al.: GRECS: graph encryption for approximate shortest distance queries. In: Proceedings of the 22nd ACM SIGSAC Conference on Computer and Communications Security, pp. 504–517. ACM (2015)

31. Paillier, P.: Public-key cryptosystems based on composite degree residuosity classes. In: Stern, J. (ed.) EUROCRYPT 1999. LNCS, vol. 1592, pp. 223–238. Springer, Heidelberg (1999). doi:10.1007/3-540-48910-X_16

32. Freedman, M.J., Nissim, K., Pinkas, B.: Efficient Private Matching and Set Intersection. In: Cachin, C., Camenisch, J.L. (eds.) EUROCRYPT 2004. LNCS, vol. 3027, pp. 1–19. Springer, Heidelberg (2004). doi:10.1007/978-3-540-24676-3_1

33. Kissner, L., Song, D.: Privacy-preserving set operations. In: Shoup, V. (ed.) CRYPTO 2005. LNCS, vol. 3621, pp. 241–257. Springer, Heidelberg (2005). doi:10.1007/11535218_15

34. Cristofaro, E., Tsudik, G.: Practical private set intersection protocols with linear complexity. In: Sion, R. (ed.) FC 2010. LNCS, vol. 6052, pp. 143–159. Springer, Heidelberg (2010). doi:10.1007/978-3-642-14577-3_13

35. Dachman-Soled, D., Malkin, T., Raykova, M., Yung, M.: Efficient robust private set intersection. In: Abdalla, M., Pointcheval, D., Fouque, P.-A., Vergnaud, D. (eds.) ACNS 2009. LNCS, vol. 5536, pp. 125–142. Springer, Heidelberg (2009). doi:10.1007/978-3-642-01957-9_8

Computing Aggregates Over Numeric Data with Personalized Local Differential Privacy

Mousumi Akter$^{(\boxtimes)}$ and Tanzima Hashem

Department of Computer Science and Engineering,
Bangladesh University of Engineering and Technology, Dhaka, Bangladesh
mousumiakter22@gmail.com, tanzimahashem@cse.buet.ac.bd

Abstract. The advancement of technology and the widespread usage of smart phones have made the collection of data from users easy and cost-effective, which allows the government, urban planner, and researchers to envision novel analysis. Along with the benefits, the shared data can bring serious privacy concerns as they reveal sensitive information about a user. Differential privacy has become an effective model for sharing privacy protected data with others. To facilitate users to protect the privacy of data before it leaves their personal devices, the concept of personal local differential privacy (PLDP) has been introduced for counting queries. We formulate PLDP for computing aggregates over numeric data. We present an efficient approach, private estimation of numeric aggregates (PENA), that guarantees PLDP of numeric data while computing an aggregate (e.g., the average or the minimum). We perform extensive experiments over a real dataset to show the effectiveness of PENA.

1 Introduction

In this era of flourishing Internet and smart phones, data collection from users has become easier and cost-effective and opened the door for novel applications and analysis. Business models like Waze - GPS, Maps and Traffic[1] have already been established based on user data. Not only in business, data collection has a huge impact on research; agglomeration of data and its analysis help researchers to perceive answers of their research questions and hypotheses. On the other hand, to grasp the behavior of a community there is no substitute for the data collection. Thus, the collection of enormous amount of real-time and historical data from users allows the government, business, and researchers to contribute in different domains for the improvement of the quality of human lives.

Along with the benefits, sharing data with others may bring serious privacy concerns as a user's data can reveal sensitive and private information about the user's health, habit and preference. Considering the privacy issues, traditionally data is shared with trusted parties, who are responsible for ensuring the privacy of user data before sharing the data with others. However, unexpected leakage of

---

[1] https://www.waze.com.

J. Pieprzyk and S. Suriadi (Eds.): ACISP 2017, Part II, LNCS 10343, pp. 249–260, 2017.
DOI: 10.1007/978-3-319-59870-3_14

personal data from the trusted authority may also cause a massive devastation, which happened to *Netflix*[2] and *AOL*[3]. In this paper, we aim to develop a novel approach to ensure the personalized local differential privacy (PLDP) of numeric data before it leaves a user's device. We focus on computing aggregate statistics over private numeric data collected from users in a distributed manner.

Differential privacy [7] is a widely accepted framework developed for ensuring data privacy of a statistical database. Protecting differential privacy of time series and numeric data in the centralized setting has been studied in the literature [17,18]. In a centralized setting, users provide data to a central trusted authority, and the trusted authority protects user data from others by applying the concept of differential privacy. Differential privacy adds noise to the data to provide rigorous privacy guarantee with an accuracy bound. However, in the local setting, users do not even trust the central authority [3] and want their data to be protected before leaving their devices without knowing the data of other users. Therefore, the local differential privacy is rigid to achieve and also challenging. In case of the centralized differential privacy, data from all users need to be aggregated first and then the noise is added to the data using Laplace or exponential mechanism according to the sensitivity [5] so that a user's data is not identifiable with a certain confidence level in the computed aggregate statistics. In the local setting, data from all users are not aggregated at a single place and thus, the traditional definition of the differential privacy is not applicable and the concepts of using Laplace and exponential mechanisms do not apply as they failed to achieve the desired level of accuracy [3].

Differential privacy in the local setting is termed as Local Differential Privacy (LDP) [15]. LDP paves a better way to achieve privacy beyond trusting the central authority and other users. Few recent works [9,15] have been done to ensure LDP of numeric data. For LDP, a user shares a randomized value instead of the actual one for a numeric attribute with an accumulator such that no one can reverse engineer the actual value from the shared data with a certain confidence level. Specifically, the confidence level is expressed as the maximum ratio of the probabilities of computing the shared randomized values for any pair of values of the numeric attribute. A major limitation of LDP is that if the possible range of the values of a numeric attribute is large, the accuracy of the computed aggregates over shared randomized values degrades significantly. However, in reality, people may have background knowledge about the range of possible values for an attribute. For example, though a salary attribute can have any positive numeric value but in reality, people may know the range of salaries depending on the workplace where a user is employed. Furthermore, users may not need to have the same privacy in terms of the confidence level but LDP does not provide flexibility to users to set their privacy levels, i.e., LDP assumes all users have same privacy level [15].

To overcome the above limitations of LDP, recently, personalized local differential privacy (PLDP) [3] has been introduced that gives users the flexibility

---

to control their privacy levels. However, their work is limited to the counting query and can not be extended for an aggregate function as they use one bit protocol [2]. In one bit protocol, a random bit is sent using Bernoulli probability distribution from the user and by tracing this bit answers of different histogram queries are estimated (e.g., how many people in a community likes to go for shopping on Sunday?).

In our research problem, we compute statistical aggregates such as finding the summation or the minimum values over numeric data, where identities of users are revealed for the authorization purpose but the privacy of the data shared by the users is protected. The accumulator knows who are taking part in the system but does not know what is the actual data of a user. Hence, obscuring user data from the central authority and from other users while facilitating the computation of aggregate functions is our main challenge. To the best of our knowledge, there is no work that ensures PLDP of numeric data and can compute any aggregate function.

In this paper, we propose a novel approach, private estimation of numeric aggregates (PENA) to compute aggregates over numeric data while ensuring PLDP. The underlying idea of PENA is to collect random responses from users over a safe range, i.e., the range within which a user's data is not identified with a specified confidence level. We develop a Local Random Responser (LRR) that generates a random response while ensuring PLDP of a user's data using Bernoulli probability distribution [3]. Bernoulli probability distribution ensures both the utility of responses and privacy of users.

In summary, the contributions of the paper are as follows:

- We formulate PLDP for computing aggregate functions over numeric data.
- We present an efficient approach PENA that can guarantee PLDP of numeric data while computing an aggregate function.
- We present the theoretical proof of the correctness of our solution.
- We perform extensive experiments to show that the effectiveness of our proposed approach.

The remainder of this paper is organized as follows. Section 2 formulates the problem, discusses the threat model, and shows the system architecture. In Sect. 3, we present our approach, PENA. Section 4 presents the results of our evaluation of PENA using real datasets. In Sect. 5, we discuss the related work. Finally, Sect. 6 concludes the paper.

2   Problem Formulation

We first formally define the concepts of differential privacy (DP), local differential privacy (LDP), and personalized local differential privacy (PLDP), and then formulate the problem that we consider in this paper. We discuss our threat model in Sect. 2.1 and the system architecture in Sect. 2.2.

Differential Privacy (DP) [5,8]. A randomized function f provides ϵ-differential privacy if for two databases t, t' that differs from at most one row and for all $z \in Z$, $\frac{Pr[f(t) \in z]}{Pr[f(t') \in z]} \leq e^\epsilon$.

Local Differential Privacy (LDP) [15]. A randomized function f provides ϵ-local differential privacy, if and only if for any two values of an attribute t, t' $\in$ Dom (f) and for any possible output t^* of f, $\frac{Pr[f(t)=t^*]}{Pr[f(t')=t^*]} \leq e^\epsilon$.

Personalized Local Differential Privacy (PLDP) [3]. A randomized function f provides $(\mathcal{T}, \epsilon)$-personalized local differential privacy, if and only if for any two values of an attribute t, $t' \in \tau$ and for any possible output t^* of f, $\frac{Pr[f(t)=t^*]}{Pr[f(t')=t^*]} \leq e^\epsilon$.

In the case of PLDP, $\mathcal{T}$ defines a safe range for a user and each user can have her own privacy requirement in term of ϵ. For example, if the numeric data of any user u is \$700, the user may feel safe to share the data in the range $\mathcal{T} =$ \$0–\$10000. If $\epsilon = 0.2$, it means that the ratio of the probabilities of generating t^* is less than or equal to $e^{0.2}$.

In this paper, we address the problem of ensuring PLDP for numeric data of users while computing aggregate functions like the average or the minimum. Formally, given a group of n users $U = \{u_1, u_2, \ldots, u_n\}$, a numeric data $t \in \mathcal{T}$ of every user in the group transformed according to the privacy specification $(\mathcal{T}, \epsilon)$ of the user, the accumulator computes the aggregates over the shared private data of users.

2.1 Threat Model

We consider the accumulator, other users, and eavesdroppers as adversaries. Users do not want their numeric data to be identified in a safe range with more than the required confidence level. The target of adversaries is to identify the actual numeric data of users, refine the safe range and increase the confidence level of identifying the numeric data. We assume that users and the accumulator follow the protocol of the system while sharing their numeric data and computing aggregates.

2.2 System Architecture

Users are connected to an accumulator through the Internet or wireless adhoc networks. Figure 1 shows the system architecture of our proposed approach. Every user independently shares their data after ensuring their PLDP. The accumulator then generates the aggregates (e.g., the average or the minimum) and provides them to the government, researchers, urban planners, and others.

3   Private Estimation of Numeric Aggregates (PENA)

In this section, we present our approach, private estimation of numeric aggregates (PENA) to compute aggregates over numeric data while ensuring PLDP.

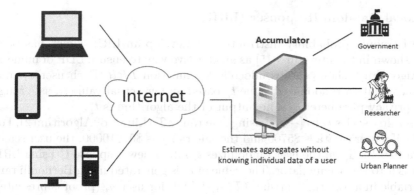

Users share private data to the accumulator   Collect aggregates from the accumulator

Fig. 1. System architecture.

PENA uses a local random responser (LRR) and exploits Bernoulli probability distribution [15] to achieve PLDP. Bernoulli probability distribution is initially designed to guarantee LDP in [15], where every user has same privacy level, i.e., same ϵ_i. In this paper, we extend it for ensuring PLDP, where users can have different ϵ_i.

Algorithm 1 shows the pseudocode for PENA. The general idea of our PENA framework is to collect random responses from users over a specified safe range $\mathcal{T}$. For different subsets of users $\mathcal{T}$ can be different. For simplicity, we assume here for a subset of users $\{u_1, u_2, \ldots, u_n\}$ have safe range $\mathcal{T}$. Every user u_i among n users responds with a random numeric value f_i that is generated using Bernoulli probability distribution using function LRR (Line 2). After receiving $f_1, f_2, \ldots, f_n$, the accumulator estimates the aggregate over the received values using Function $ComputeAggregate$ (Line 4). For example, if the aggregate is average then $ComputeAggregate$ estimates the aggregate as $(\mathcal{T}_{max} - \mathcal{T}_{min}) \times \frac{\sum_{i=1}^{n} f_i}{n}$, where $\mathcal{T}_{max}$ and $\mathcal{T}_{min}$ represent the maximum and minimum values of the safe range $\mathcal{T}$.

Algorithm 1. Private Estimation of Numeric Aggregates

Input: A group of n users $U = \{u_1, u_2, \ldots, u_n\}$
Output: Estimate numeric aggregates f over the random responses of users
1: **for** each user u_i **do**
2:     $f_i \leftarrow LRR(\mathcal{T}, t_i, \epsilon_i)$
3: **end for**
4: **return** $f \leftarrow ComputeAggregate(f_1, f_2, \ldots, f_n)$

In the next section, we develop a local random responser (LRR) to achieve PLDP over numeric data.

3.1   Local Random Responser (LRR)

We use Bernoulli probability distribution to develop an LRR, which has been already shown in the literature [15] as an effective way to ensure LDP of numeric data. Algorithm 2 shows the pseudocode for function LRR. Each user u_i runs LRR to compute a randomized value t_i^* based on her actual value t_i, safe range $\mathcal{T}$, and privacy parameter ϵ_i. The output of the algorithm is t_i^*.

A user first scales t_i to $[-1, 1]$ using safe range $\mathcal{T}$ (Line 1 of Algorithm 2). For example, if a user's data is \$5700 and the safe range is \$0–\$10000, the user scales the data to 0.14. Then the user randomizes t_i into a new response t_i^* using LRR and sends it to the accumulator. The value of t_i^* is generated using Bernoulli random variable in a way that satisfies $(\mathcal{T}, \epsilon_i)$-PLDP for user u_i (proof is presented in Sect. 3.2). LRR generates two types of random responses. The probability of generating a random response among two options is calculated using a Bernoulli random variable, and the calculation of the probability depends on the user's scaled value t_i and defined confidence level ϵ_i (Line 2). It can be compared with a coin flip. The probability of generating head is calculated by Bernoulli random variable. Then the coin is flipped with the computed probability. If head is found then the user responds with $\frac{e^{\epsilon_i}+1}{e^{\epsilon_i}-1}$ (Line 4). Otherwise, the user responds with $-\frac{e^{\epsilon_i}+1}{e^{\epsilon_i}-1}$ (Line 6).

Algorithm 2. Local Random Responser

Input: Safe range $\mathcal{T}$
Input: User u_i's numeric data t_i
Input: User u_i's privacy parameter ϵ_i
Output: Randomized response $t_i^* \in \{\frac{e^{\epsilon_i}+1}{e^{\epsilon_i}-1}, -\frac{e^{\epsilon_i}+1}{e^{\epsilon_i}-1}\}$
 1: Generate scaled $t_i \in [-1, 1]$ using $\mathcal{T}$
 2: Sample a Bernoulli variable b such that $\Pr[b = 1] = \frac{t_i \cdot (e^{\epsilon_i}-1)+e^{\epsilon_i}+1}{2e^{\epsilon_i}+2}$
 3: **if** $b = 1$ **then**
 4:    $t_i^* \leftarrow \frac{e^{\epsilon_i}+1}{e^{\epsilon_i}-1}$
 5: **else**
 6:    $t_i^* \leftarrow -\frac{e^{\epsilon_i}+1}{e^{\epsilon_i}-1}$
 7: **end if**
 8: **return** t_i^*

3.2   Theoretical Analysis

In this section, we present the theoretical analysis of privacy assurance of our proposed approach. We give the following theorem to prove that LRR guarantees PLDP for every user.

Theorem 1. *For any user u_i with privacy specification (τ, ϵ_i) and any $t_i^* \in \{\frac{e^{\epsilon_i}+1}{e^{\epsilon_i}-1}, -\frac{e^{\epsilon_i}+1}{e^{\epsilon_i}-1}\}$ LRR guarantees (τ, ϵ_i)-PLDP for u_i.*

Proof. By definition of PLDP, we have to prove that, for any t_i, $t'_i \in \tau$ and any $t_i^* \in \{\frac{e^{\epsilon_i}+1}{e^{\epsilon_i}-1}, \frac{Pr[LRR(\mathcal{T},t_i,\epsilon_i)=t_i^*]}{Pr[LRR(\mathcal{T},t'_i,\epsilon_i)=t_i^*]} \le e^{\epsilon_i}$.

LRR scales t_i to $[-1, 1]$ using safe range $\mathcal{T}$, and assume that t_i^* is $\frac{e^{\epsilon_i}+1}{e^{\epsilon_i}-1}$. For, the other case, i.e., $t_i^* = -\frac{e^{\epsilon_i}+1}{e^{\epsilon_i}-1}$, the proof can be done similarly.

According to Algorithm 2, the probabilities to compute $t_i^* = \frac{e^{\epsilon_i}+1}{e^{\epsilon_i}-1}$ for t_i and t'_i are $Pr[LRR(\mathcal{T}, t_i, \epsilon_i)=t_i^*] = \frac{t_i \cdot (e^{\epsilon_i}-1)+e^{\epsilon_i}+1}{2e^{\epsilon_i}+2}$ and $Pr[LRR(\mathcal{T}, t'_i, \epsilon_i)=t_i^*] = \frac{t'_i \cdot (e^{\epsilon_i}-1)+e^{\epsilon_i}+1}{2e^{\epsilon_i}+2}$, respectively.

Thus,

$$
\begin{aligned}
\frac{Pr[LRR(\mathcal{T},t_i,\epsilon_i)=t_i^*]}{Pr[LRR(\mathcal{T},t'_i,\epsilon_i)=t_i^*]} &= \frac{\frac{t_i \cdot (e^{\epsilon_i}-1)+e^{\epsilon_i}+1}{2e^{\epsilon_i}+2}}{\frac{t'_i \cdot (e^{\epsilon_i}-1)+e^{\epsilon_i}+1}{2e^{\epsilon_i}+2}} \\
&= \frac{t_i \cdot (e^{\epsilon_i}-1)+e^{\epsilon_i}+1}{t'_i \cdot (e^{\epsilon_i}-1)+e^{\epsilon_i}+1} \\
&\le \frac{max_{t_i \in [-1,1]}(t_i \cdot (e^{\epsilon_i}-1)+e^{\epsilon_i}+1)}{min_{t'_i \in [-1,1]}(t'_i \cdot (e^{\epsilon_i}-1)+e^{\epsilon_i}+1)} \\
&\le \frac{1 \cdot (e^{\epsilon_i}-1)+e^{\epsilon_i}+1}{-1 \cdot (e^{\epsilon_i}-1)+e^{\epsilon_i}+1} \\
&\le \frac{e^{\epsilon_i}-1+e^{\epsilon_i}+1}{-e^{\epsilon_i}+1+e^{\epsilon_i}+1} \\
&\le \frac{2e^{\epsilon_i}}{2} \\
&\le e^{\epsilon_i}
\end{aligned}
$$

We have $\frac{Pr[LRR(\mathcal{T},t_i,\epsilon_i)]}{Pr[LRR(\mathcal{T},t'_i,\epsilon_i)]} \le e^{\epsilon_i}$. Hence, LRR guarantees (τ, ϵ_i)-PLDP for u_i.

3.3 Simulation

In this section, we illustrate our proposed approach PENA with an example. Suppose the accumulator sets the safe range $\mathcal{T}$ as \$0–\$10000. Users scale their data to $[-1, 1]$ using the safe range $\mathcal{T}$, and generate random responses using local random responser (LRR). Without loss of generality, we show how a user computes her random response. Let the actual numeric data of a user is \$800 and ϵ is 0.2. The scaled numeric data of the user is $t = (\frac{800}{10000}) * 2 - 1 = -0.84$.

Since, $\frac{e^{\epsilon}+1}{e^{\epsilon}-1} = 10.03$ and $\frac{t \cdot (e^{\epsilon}-1)+e^{\epsilon}+1}{2e^{\epsilon}+2} = 0.46$, the user either sends 10.03 with probability 0.46 or sends -10.03 with probability 0.54 $(1 - 0.46)$ to the accumulator. Similarly, other users send their random responses to the accumulator.

The accumulator estimates the aggregate (e.g., the average or the minimum) over the received values from users and the safe range.

4 Experiments

In this section, we evaluate and compare the performance of our proposed approach PENA through extensive experiments. Since there is no existing work for PLDP over numeric data in the literature, we modify the work [15] that is proposed for ensuring LDP of numeric data while computing aggregates and compare it with PENA. For LDP, the safe range $\mathcal{T}$ does not exist and $\mathcal{T}$ is assumed to be the set of all possible values for numeric data and thus, the achieved level

Table 1. Parameter settings for experiments

Parameter	Values	Default
Privacy level ϵ	0.2, 0.4, 0.6, 0.8, 1	0.5
User participation (%)	20, 40, 60, 80, 100	50
Safe range $\mathcal{T}$	1.0, 1.1, 1.2, 1.3, 1.4, 1.5	1.0

of the accuracy for the computed aggregates is not satisfactory to apply in real scenarios. For our experiments, we incorporate $\mathcal{T}$ in [15]. However, we cannot extend [15] to support personalize privacy level ϵ. Note that we select [15] for our comparison because it has been shown in the literature that [15] outperforms other LDP based approaches for numeric data like [9].

We show our experiments for aggregate functions average and minimum. Our approach is also applicable for other types of aggregates (e.g., maximum). We validate our proposed solution using the dataset:IPUMS [1] that contains 3.15 M total family income records of United states. The whole data space is normalized to $[-1, 1]$ using safe range $\mathcal{T}$. We performed several sets of experiments by varying the following parameters: privacy level ϵ, the percentage of user participation over 3.1 M tuples, safe range $\mathcal{T}$.

Table 1 shows ranges and default values used for each parameter. To observe the effect of one parameter in an experiment others are kept in default values. For [15], $\epsilon = 0.5$ means we set ϵ to 0.5 for all users, and in PENA, $\epsilon = 0.5$ means users have the flexibility to generate any random privacy level from 0 to 0.5. All experiments are run on an Intel-CORE i3 Windows 7 machine. For each experiment, we perform 100 independent runs and take the average performance of this 100 independent runs. Experimental results show that PENA outperforms modified LDP based approach [15] in terms of accuracy while ensuring higher privacy levels for users for both aggregates average and minimum.

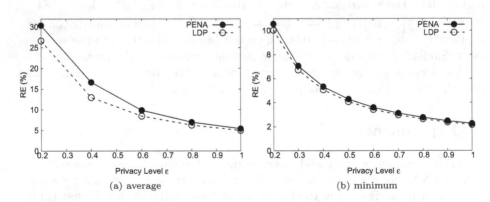

(a) average   (b) minimum

Fig. 2. Effect of privacy level (ϵ) on relative error (RE%)

Effect of Privacy Level (ϵ). Privacy level (ϵ) controls the privacy of a particular user. Figures 2(a) and (b) show that the relative error decreases with the
relaxation of privacy level for both LDP and PENA. This is because, with the
increase of ϵ, more accurate user data are used in the aggregation. On the other
hand, users can have higher privacy levels in PENA than the LDP-based app-
roach. For example, for $\epsilon = 0.5$, in PENA, values of ϵ for users are varied from 0 to
0.5, whereas in the LDP-based approach, all users have $\epsilon = 0.5$. Since a smaller
value of ϵ ensures higher privacy for a user, most of the users in PENA have
higher privacy levels than those in the LDP-based approach. In spite of ensuring the higher privacy level for users, both PENA and the LDP-based approach
show similar levels of accuracy as shown in Fig. 2.

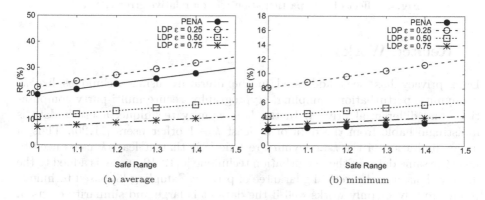

Fig. 3. Effect of safe range ($\mathcal{T}$) on relative error (RE%)

Effect of Safe Range ($\mathcal{T}$). A higher value of the safe range $\mathcal{T}$ ensures a
higher level of privacy. We scale the maximum numeric value of the dataset to
1. Figure 3(a) and (b) show that relative error increases slowly for every (10%)
increase of the safe range for average aggregation. For privacy level $\epsilon = 0.30$,
PENA outperforms the LDP-based approach for aggregate function average
(Fig. 3(a)) and for $\epsilon = 0.80$, PENA outperforms the LDP-based approach for
aggregate function minimum (Fig. 3(b)).

Effect of Percentage of User Participation. Figure 4(a) shows that the
relative error increases slightly with the increase of the percentage of user participation for aggregate function average. For 40% or less user participation (i.e.,
1.26 M users among 3.15 M), PENA generates error less than 20%. Figure 4(b)
shows that the relative error remains almost constant over large dataset to evaluate minimum aggregate function. This result shows the effectiveness of PENA to
handle large dataset to compute both aggregate functions average and minimum.

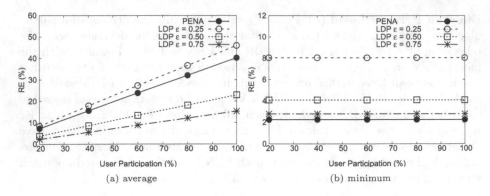

Fig. 4. Effect of user participation (%) on relative error (RE%)

5 Related Work

Data privacy has been addressed in the literature using techniques like k-anonymity, perturbation, sampling, cryptography, secure multi-party computations and differential privacy. In the k-anonymity technique, a user's data is indistinguishable from the data of at least $k - 1$ other users [11,20]. Thus, a major limitation of the k-anonymity technique is that at least k users need to have the same data. In the perturbation technique [6,12,19], noise is added to the data without any theoretical guarantee of privacy. Sampling [6] based technique to ensure privacy only works well if the dataset is large and similarity exists in the data. Though cryptographic techniques [16] ensure strong privacy, they are not feasible for real world applications because of their extremely high processing overhead. Secure multi-party protocols [13] involve a group of users to compute aggregates, where a user's data privacy is violated if all group members collude. In recent years, differential privacy (DP) [7] has become an effective model to protect data privacy of users because of its theoretical privacy guarantee and less processing overhead.

DP has been introduced in [4] and since then it has been applied to solve variant problems in computing statistics. However, the major limitation of DP is that users need to trust the data accumulator. The accumulator gathers actual data from users, and shares the statistics after ensuring the requirements of DP, i.e., no one can identify a user's data with a certain confidence level in the computed aggregate statistics. On the other hand, local differential privacy guarantees privacy of data without involving a trusted accumulator. There exist a number of approaches [9,10,15] to ensure LDP for computing histograms and ordinal queries. In [15], the authors developed a solution for protecting LDP of numeric data for computing aggregates (e.g., summation or minimum).

Both DP and LDP assume the same privacy levels for all users, which might not be always the case. In [14], the authors incorporated personalized settings for differential privacy, where a trusted accumulator is required but users can have different privacy levels. Recently, in [3], the authors applied the concept of personalized privacy in the local setting, and developed an approach to ensure personalized LDP (PLDP) of users. However, the approach has limited applicability only for counting queries. In this paper, we develop PENA that guarantees PLDP and can compute any aggregate like average, minimum or maximum.

6   Conclusion

We have developed the first approach, private estimation of numeric aggregates (PENA), to compute aggregates over numeric data while guaranteeing personalized local differential privacy (PLDP). PENA does not involve a central trusted authority and provides users the flexibility to control their privacy levels. Experiments using real datasets show that PENA outperforms modified LDP based approach in terms of accuracy while ensuring higher privacy levels for users for both aggregates average and minimum.

Acknowledgments. This research has been done in the department of Computer Science and Engineering, Bangladesh University of Engineering and Technology (BUET). The work is supported by BUET and United International University (UIU).

References

1. Ipums. Integrated public use microdata series: Version 6.0 (2015). https://www. ipums.org/
2. Bassily, R., Smith, A.: Local, private, efficient protocols for succinct histograms. In: STOC, pp. 127–135 (2015). doi:10.1145/2746539.2746632
3. Chen, R., Li, H., Qin, A., Kasiviswanathan, S.P., Jin, H.: Private spatial data aggregation in the local setting. In: ICDE, pp. 289–300 (2016). doi:10.1109/ICDE.2016. 7498248
4. Dinur, I., Nissim, K.: Revealing information while preserving privacy. In: PODS, pp. 202–210 (2003). doi:10.1145/773153.773173
5. Dwork, C.: Differential privacy. In: Bugliesi, M., Preneel, B., Sassone, V., Wegener, I. (eds.) ICALP 2006. LNCS, vol. 4052, pp. 1–12. Springer, Heidelberg (2006). doi:10.1007/11787006_1
6. Dwork, C.: A firm foundation for private data analysis. Commun. ACM **54**(1), 86–95 (2011). doi:10.1145/1866739.1866758
7. Dwork, C., McSherry, F., Nissim, K., Smith, A.: Calibrating noise to sensitivity in private data analysis. In: Halevi, S., Rabin, T. (eds.) TCC 2006. LNCS, vol. 3876, pp. 265–284. Springer, Heidelberg (2006). doi:10.1007/11681878_14
8. Dwork, C., Roth, A., et al.: The algorithmic foundations of differential privacy. Found. Trends® Theor. Comput. Sci. **9**(3–4), 211–407 (2014). doi:10.1561/ 0400000042
9. Erlingsson, Ú., Pihur, V., Korolova, A.: Randomized aggregatable privacy-preserving ordinal response. In: CCS, pp. 1054–1067 (2014). doi:10.1145/2660267. 2660348
10. Fanti, G.C., Pihur, V., Erlingsson, Ú.: Building a RAPPOR with the unknown: privacy-preserving learning of associations and data dictionaries. In: PoPETs, vol. 3, pp. 41–61 (2016)

11. Hashem, T., Kulik, L.: Safeguarding location privacy in wireless ad-hoc networks. In: Krumm, J., Abowd, G.D., Seneviratne, A., Strang, T. (eds.) UbiComp 2007. LNCS, vol. 4717, pp. 372–390. Springer, Heidelberg (2007). doi:10.1007/978-3-540-74853-3_22

12. Hashem, T., Kulik, L., Zhang, R.: Privacy preserving group nearest neighbor queries. In: EDBT, pp. 489–500 (2010). doi:10.1145/1739041.1739100

13. Hashem, T., Hashem, T., Iqbal, A.: Ensuring feedback data privacy in the context of developing countries. In: ACM DEV, pp. 18:1–18:4 (2016). doi:10.1145/3001913.3006627

14. Jorgensen, Z., Yu, T., Cormode, G.: Conservative or liberal? Personalized differential privacy. In: ICDE, pp. 1023–1034 (2015). doi:10.1109/ICDE.2015.7113353

15. Nguyên, T.T., Xiao, X., Yang, Y., Hui, S.C., Shin, H., Shin, J.: Collecting and analyzing data from smart device users with local differential privacy. arXiv preprint (2016). arXiv:160605053

16. Rastogi, V., Nath, S.: Differentially private aggregation of distributed time-series with transformation and encryption. In: Proceedings of the ACM SIGMOD International Conference on Management of Data (SIGMOD) (2010). doi:10.1145/1807167.1807247

17. Sarathy, R., Muralidhar, K.: Evaluating laplace noise addition to satisfy differential privacy for numeric data. Trans. Data Priv. 4(1), 1–17 (2011)

18. Shamir, A.: How to share a secret. Commun. ACM 22(11), 612–613 (1979)

19. Soma, S.C., Hashem, T., Cheema, M.A., Samrose, S.: Trip planning queries with location privacy in spatial databases. World Wide Web 20(2), 205–236 (2017)

20. Sweeney, L.: Achieving k-anonymity privacy protection using generalization and suppression. Int. J. Uncertain. Fuzziness Knowl. Based Syst. 10(5), 571–588 (2002). doi:10.1142/S021848850200165X

An Efficient Toolkit for Computing Private Set Operations

Alex Davidson[✉] and Carlos Cid

Royal Holloway, University of London, Egham TW20 0EX, UK
{alex.davidson.2014,carlos.cid}@rhul.ac.uk

Abstract. Private set operation (PSO) protocols provide a natural way of securely performing operations on data sets, such that crucial details of the input sets are not revealed. Such protocols have an ever-increasing number of practical applications, particularly when implementing privacy-preserving data mining schemes. Protocols for computing private set operations have been prevalent in multi-party computation literature over the past decade, and in the case of private set intersection (PSI), have become practically feasible to run in real applications. In contrast, other set operations such as union have received less attention from the research community, and the few existing designs are often limited in their feasibility. In this work we aim to fill this gap, and present a new technique using Bloom filter data structures and additive homomorphic encryption to develop the first private set union protocol with both linear computation and communication complexities. Moreover, we show how to adapt this protocol to give novel ways of computing PSI and private set intersection/union cardinality with only minor changes to the protocol computation. Our work resembles therefore a toolkit for scalable private set computation with linear complexities, and we provide a thorough experimental analysis that shows that the online phase of our designs is practical up to large set sizes.

Keywords: Private set operations · Bloom filters · Additively homomorphic encryption · Secure computation · Data mining

1 Introduction

The emergence of Big Data has resulted in an increasing need for analytical data mining techniques allowing entities to gain information from the large data sets that they own. Even more so can be learnt by combining internal data sets with private data from external entities. However, in order to safeguard incentives for combining data, participants require privacy-preserving measures to be put into place to stop secret information from being leaked to competitors or untrusted parties. Private set operation (PSO) protocols provide a natural way of securely performing operations on these combined data sets, such that only the output of the set operation is revealed. Numerous works in research in genetic data computations and information sharing have highlighted the importance of efficient private set operation computation [6,15].

© Springer International Publishing AG 2017
J. Pieprzyk and S. Suriadi (Eds.): ACISP 2017, Part II, LNCS 10343, pp. 261–278, 2017.
DOI: 10.1007/978-3-319-59870-3_15

Previous Work. Research into private set intersection (PSI) protocols has resulted in several designs that are practically feasible for real-world use. While pioneering work such as [12,20] brought the problem into the attention of the cryptographic research community, more recent research (e.g. [10,19,22–24]) has shown that certain techniques and data structures, such as oblivious transfer (OT) and Bloom filters, can be used to design protocols that scale and perform well even for very large data sets. These constructions play a crucial role in developing large-scale data mining applications where data privacy and efficient computation are both important. For example, computations over genetic data, as shown in [15], may require comparing records from databases with millions of elements.

In spite of recent progress in the design of PSI protocols, research into performing other set operations with similar security guarantees has not been as comprehensive. Current designs for computing private set union (PSU) include [4,13,25], while generic designs for computing multiple set operations are given in [1,14,18]. With a much smaller base of research, computational complexities for computing PSU remain super-linear in the size of the sets involved (e.g. $O(n \log \log n)$). Moreover, there has been relatively little work done in computing set cardinality (PSI/PSU-CA) operations where only the size of the output set is revealed. Dedicated techniques for computing these operations are given in [5,9,11] though designs are also given in the generic constructions of [1,18].

Consequently, implementations of PSOs such as union are unlikely to scale well as set sizes increase up to the dimensions being required for current applications. Furthermore, complex data mining can require a conjugation of several set operations. Without a way for computing scalable privacy-preserving protocols for *all* of the main operations it is not possible to carry out these procedures in an efficient manner. It is important that privacy-preserving methods for real-world problems remain almost as efficient as tools with non-cryptographic guarantees in order to motivate the uptake of these new solutions. Furthermore, it would be beneficial to have an efficient 'toolkit' for performing multiple PSO protocols, so that developers would no longer need to implement completely different designs for each set operation to achieve optimal efficiency.

Our Contributions. We first address the void in efficient PSU protocols by developing a new two-party construction, secure against semi-honest adversaries where only one participant (the client) learns the output. Our design makes use of similar design structures to previous works such as [9,10,13,17]: the efficient data structure provided by Bloom filter alongside partially homomorphic encryption to allow oblivious computation. However our PSU protocol is the first to demonstrate both linear computation and communication complexities, and as a result it is immediately more scalable than previous designs. Table 1 provides an asymptotic comparison of our design with the previous PSU work; we detail our protocol design in Sect. 3.

Our protocol for computing PSU is very simple, and we show that minor changes in the computation done by the server (non-output party) can be

Table 1. Complexities for previous PSU protocols.

	Communication	Computation	Multi-party?
Kissner and Song [18]	$O(N^2 n \log |E|)$	$O(n^2)$	Y
Brickell and Shmatikov [4]	$O((n+m) \log |E|)$	$O((n+m) \log |E|)$	N
Frikken [13]	$O(n)$	$O(n \log \log n)$	N
Blanton and Aguiar [1]	$O(N^3 n \log(Nn))$	$O(N^3 n \log(Nn))$	Y
Our work	$\boldsymbol{O(n)}$	$\boldsymbol{O(n)}$	N

leveraged to convert the protocol into a PSI or PSI/PSU-CA exchange. These constructions also have linear complexities putting them in line with current practical solutions in the wider research area. We give these adaptations in Sect. 4. Consequently, our work can be viewed as a toolkit for performing the *main* set operations that are required by conventional applications. The simplicity of the design means that developers only need to consider implementations for an additively homomorphic encryption scheme and a Bloom filter. We focus here on semi-honest adversaries only, but we could ensure security in the malicious setting using a trusted third party, based on similar methods to those of [8,17]; full details are provided in the extended version of this paper.

In Sect. 5, we demonstrate the concrete practicality of our design by performing a rigorous experimental analysis using an implementation written in Go. We show that our designs run with comparable communication overheads and runtimes relative to state-of-the-art PSI protocols. Observe that our construction provides a much more generic functionality than dedicated PSI protocols and so we balance out an expensive offline phase, slightly slower running times and high communication overheads with the ability to perform much more dynamic computations.

The main bottleneck of our design is provided by the encryption scheme that we use (Paillier's [21]). Our protocols are however agnostic to the encryption scheme used and so any improvements that can be made in this phase will directly translate to improvements in our PSO design. The simplicity of our design is highlighted in the small number of lines of code that we require for our implementation; we plan to make our code open-source in the near future.

2   Preliminaries and Notation

2.1   Notation

We will primarily consider two-party protocols with players P_1 and P_2 who own sets S_1 and S_2, respectively. We may commonly refer to P_1 as the 'client' and P_2 as the 'server' in the interaction. The client typically receives output from the computation while the server does not.[1]

---

[1] It is however possible to enforce bilateral output by running the protocol twice and swapping the roles.

We commonly denote the cardinalities of the sets by $n = |S_1|$ and $m = |S_2|$. We denote the domain of elements by E, the security parameter by λ and, when discussing multi-party protocols, the number of players by N, where $c < N$ denotes the number of corrupted players in a protocol instantiation. When discussing the use of homomorphic operations over ciphertexts, we use $+_H$ when invoking additions on underlying plaintext data. Section 2.3 fully describes our notation regarding partially homomorphic encryption (PHE) schemes. For a key pair (pk, sk) for a public-key encryption scheme, we denote generic encryption and decryption by E_{pk} and D_{sk}, respectively.

2.2 Bloom Filters

Bloom filters were first introduced by Bloom in [2] as a lightweight data structure that allows for the representation of data sets and checking of inclusion using only hash function evaluations. A Bloom filter is initially represented by a string of B bits that are all initialised to 0. There are k hash functions $h_l : \{0,1\}^\lambda \mapsto \{1, \ldots, B\}$ for $l \in \{1, \ldots, k\}$ published alongside the Bloom filter. We then represent set elements $x \in X$ in the Bloom filter by evaluating $h_1(x), \ldots, h_k(x)$ and changing each index that these hash functions point to from 0 to 1. If a value has already been changed to 1, it is left alone. Any party can use the hash functions to check if an element is stored in the Bloom filter.

Definition 1. (Represented elements). *We say that an element, e, is represented in the Bloom filter, **BF**, if we have that*

$$\mathbf{BF}[h_i(e)] = 1, \quad \forall i \in \{1, \ldots, k\}$$

*where $\{h_1, \ldots, h_k\}$ are the hash functions used in conjunction with **BF**. We say that the set S is represented by **BF** if every element $e \in S$ is represented in **BF**.*

Optimal Bloom filter parameters. One constraint on Bloom filters is that they can lead to false positives when checking membership: an element $y \notin X$ may appear to be in X after checking all hash outputs if all the values have been set to 1. However, as shown in [10], if $p = 1 - (1 - 1/B)^{kn}$ is the probability that any bit in the Bloom filter is set to 1, then the upper bound of the false-positive probability is given by

$$\epsilon = p^k \times \left(1 + O\left(\frac{k}{p} \sqrt{\frac{\ln B - k \ln p}{B}} \right) \right),$$

which is negligible in k, the number of hash functions. In practice one will select the values of k and B when building a Bloom filter for a set of size n such that ϵ is capped at a specific low value (e.g. 2^{-50}). In [10] it is claimed that performance optimality is achieved when

$$k = \frac{B}{n} \ln 2, \quad \text{and} \quad B \geq n \log_2 e \cdot \log_2 1/\epsilon, \tag{1}$$

where e is the base of the natural logarithm. By minimising B we get the optimal value of k to be

$$k = \log_2 1/\epsilon. \tag{2}$$

We will assume (as in [10]) that these parameters are always chosen in this way. The proofs that these values are optimal can be found in [3].

Inverting and Encrypting Bloom Filters. In this work, we use a non-standard representation of a Bloom filter by inverting each entry prior to encryption. Also, rather than treating each entry as a bit, we use 0 and 1 elements from the plaintext space of a given encryption scheme.

Definition 2. (Encrypted Bloom filters). *Let $\boldsymbol{BF}_i$ be the Bloom filter computed for the set S_i (using hash functions $h_1, \ldots, h_k$), with B entries. The corresponding encrypted Bloom filter is denoted by $\boldsymbol{EBF}_i$ and has B entries where each entry is defined in the following way:*

$$\boldsymbol{EBF}_i[b] = E_{pk}(\boldsymbol{BF}_i[b])$$

for some public key pk. In the following we define $\boldsymbol{EBF}_i = \{C[1], \ldots, C[B]\}$ and for $y_j \in S_i$, then $\boldsymbol{EBF}_i[h_u(y_j)] = C_u^{(j)}$ for $u = \{1, \ldots, k\}$ and where h_u is the uth hash function used in computing the original Bloom filter. In this case $C_u^{(j)}$ is the ciphertext obtained by querying the uth hash function for $\boldsymbol{EBF}_i$ on y_j.

Definition 3. (Inverted Bloom filters). *Let $\boldsymbol{BF}_i$ be a Bloom filter. We define the corresponding inverted Bloom filter to be $\boldsymbol{IBF}_i$ where*

$$\boldsymbol{IBF}_i[j] = \begin{cases} 1 \text{ if } \boldsymbol{BF}_i[j] = 0 \\ 0 \text{ otherwise.} \end{cases}$$

When referring to an encrypted, inverted Bloom filter we will write $\mathbf{EIBF}_i$.

2.3 Partially Homomorphic Encryption

Let (pk, sk) be a key pair for a public-key encryption scheme, and let $\tilde{x} = E_{pk}(x)$ and $\tilde{y} = E_{pk}(y)$. We say that the encryption scheme is *additively homomorphic* if we have the following properties:

- There is a homomorphic addition operation, $+_H$, over $\tilde{x}$ and $\tilde{y}$ such that $D_{sk}(\tilde{x} +_H \tilde{y}) = x + y$.
- It is possible to compute $\tilde{x} \cdot r$, where r is a scalar and $D_{sk}(\tilde{x} \cdot r) = x \cdot r$ (scalar multiplication)

Paillier's encryption scheme [21] is an example of a semantically secure public key encryption scheme that is additively homomorphic on operations over the ciphertexts.

We further define a final property of such a scheme, known as ReRand, which allows a party with knowledge of the public key to re-randomise ciphertexts. We use this property later in our protocols.

– ReRand(pk, c): an algorithm that takes the public key pk and a ciphertext c encrypted under pk as input. The algorithm encrypts the value 0 by computing $E_{pk}(0) = c_0$ and then outputs $\tilde{c} = c +_H c_0$.

Notice that ReRand does not change the value of the underlying plaintext.

2.4   Security Model

Definition 4. (Indistinguishability of distributions). *Let $X = \{\mathcal{X}_\lambda\}_{\lambda \in S}$ and $Y = \{\mathcal{Y}_\lambda\}_{\lambda \in S}$ be probability ensembles indexed by S. We say that these ensembles are computationally indistinguishable for all probabilistic polynomial time (PPT) algorithms, $\{\mathcal{D}_n\}_{n \in \mathbb{N}}$, if there exists a negligible function $\mathsf{negl} : \mathbb{N} \mapsto [0,1]$ where*

$$| \Pr[\mathcal{D}_n(\lambda, \mathcal{X}) = 1] - \Pr[\mathcal{D}_n(\lambda, \mathcal{Y}) = 1] | < \mathsf{negl}(n).$$

In this case we write $X \simeq Y$.

Let π be a protocol that represents a polynomial-time functionality f. Let S_i be the input set of a participant P_i for $i \in \{1, 2\}$ and let aux_i be a set of auxiliary information that P_i holds. Define the view of the protocol for P_i to be $\mathsf{view}_i^\pi(S_1, S_2) = (\mathsf{Inp}_i, r_i, \mathcal{T}_i, \pi(S_1, S_2)_i)$ where $\mathsf{Inp}_i = (S_i, aux_i)$ is the combined input of P_i to π, r_i represents internal coin tosses, $\mathcal{T}_i$ are the messages viewed by P_i and $\pi(S_1, S_2)_i$ is the output for P_i. We use the following to define security against semi-honest adversaries.

Definition 5. (Semi-honest security). *Protocol π securely computes the functionality f in the presence of static semi-honest adversaries if there exists polynomial-time simulators Sim_1, Sim_2 where*

$$\{Sim_1(\mathsf{Inp}_1, f(S_1, S_2))\} \simeq \{\mathsf{view}_1^\pi(S_1, S_2)\},$$

$$\{Sim_2(\mathsf{Inp}_2, f(S_1, S_2))\} \simeq \{\mathsf{view}_2^\pi(S_1, S_2)\}.$$

Intuitively, this states that each party's view of the protocol can be simulated using only the input they hold and the output that they receive from the protocol. Therefore a corrupted party is unable to learn any extra information that cannot be derived from the input and output explicitly.

3   PSU Protocol

In this section, we detail the construction of our PSU protocol using encrypted Bloom filters where encryption is performed via an IND-CPA secure AHE scheme. The homomorphic aspect allows the 'server' to evaluate functions over the ciphertexts without learning anything. Variations of this technique have been used previously for oblivious polynomial evaluation, for example [12,13].

3.1   Overview

Both parties receive the k hash functions which are chosen to evaluate the Bloom filter for elements in the corresponding sets. The elements $y_j \in S_2$ are assumed to be represented by elements in $\mathbb{Z}_N$.

Additionally, we assume that P_1 has a public key pk which is also made available to P_2. P_1 also has a secret key sk that they use for decryption. Both parties also have access to sources of internal randomness that they can use for computing any tasks that require to sample random values. The following is a description of how the protocol operates; we provide a diagrammatic overview of our PSU design in Fig. 1.

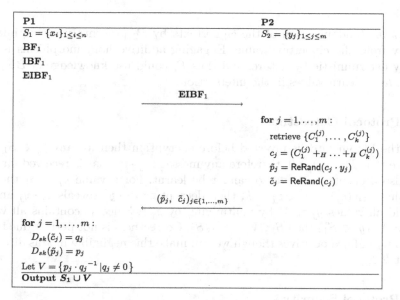

Fig. 1. An overview of our $\pi_\cup^{\mathrm{EBF}}$ protocol that uses encrypted, inverted Bloom filters

Protocol Steps. *Inputs* - P_1: $[\ (pk, sk),\ S_1,\ |S_2|\ ]$, P_2: $[\ pk,\ S_2,\ |S_1|\ ]$

1. P_1 calculates $\mathbf{BF_1}$ representing S_1 using the set of hash functions $h_1, \ldots, h_k$. They then invert each entry in $\mathbf{BF_1}$ to retrieve $\mathbf{IBF_1}$.
2. P_1 separately encrypts each element $\mathbf{IBF_1}[l]$ of the inverted Bloom filter, where $1 \leq l \leq B$, using pk. P_1 now possesses $\mathbf{EIBF_1}$, denote $\mathbf{EIBF_1}[l] = C[l]$. They send $\mathbf{EIBF_1}$ to P_2.
3. P_2 evaluates each element $y_j \in S_2$ using the k hash functions and retrieves $\{C_1^{(j)}, \ldots, C_k^{(j)}\}$ where $C_d^{(j)} = \mathbf{EIBF_1}[h_d(y_j)]$ for $j \in \{1, \ldots, m\}$.
4. P_2 computes $c_j = (C_1^{(j)} +_H \ldots +_H C_k^{(j)})$ and sends $(\tilde{p}_j, \tilde{c}_j) = (\mathsf{ReRand}(c_j \cdot y_j), \mathsf{ReRand}(c_j))$ to P_1 (in some randomly permuted order).
5. First P_1 checks the value of $\tilde{c}_j$ by computing $D_{sk}(\tilde{c}_j) = q_j$. If $q_j = 0$ then $D_{sk}(\tilde{p}_j) = 0$ so nothing can be learnt. Else $D_{sk}(\tilde{p}_j) = q_j \cdot y_j = p_j$.

6. P_1 computes q_j^{-1} for $q_j \neq 0$ and then calculates $p_j \cdot q_j^{-1} = y_j$.

7. P_1 adds all y_j to the set V where $q_j \neq 0$ and outputs the set $S_1 \cup V$.

Remark 1. We adopt the notation $c_j \cdot y_j$ for scalar multiplication between a ciphertext c_j and a scalar y_j. This preserves the generality of the protocol relative to the AHE scheme used. However for Paillier encryption this multiplication would usually be invoked via an exponentiation, i.e. $c_j^{y_j}$.

Remark 2. It should be noted that the protocol leaks the size of the intersection cardinality between the players P_1 and P_2. This is similar to the previous PSU designs of [1,13,14], and likewise we don't consider this as a drawback in our design.

Remark 3. Randomisation of the ciphertexts by P_2 prevents y_j being inferred directly from the ciphertext value. Engaging additive homomorphisms is necessarily deterministic by nature, and thus P_1 could use knowledge of $\mathbf{BF}_1$ and $h_1, \ldots, h_k$ to learn values in the intersection.

3.2 Protocol Correctness

Since the Bloom filter is inverted before encryption then for any $y_j \in S_1 \cap S_2$ we have that $D_{sk}(c_j) = 0$, therefore any message $c_j \cdot y_j$ that is received for such a y_j also decrypts to 0 and so cannot be learnt. For a value $y_j \notin S_1$ then we have that $D_{sk}(c_j) = 1 < z_j < k$, then decrypting $c_j \cdot y_j$ reveals $z_j \cdot y_j$ and P_1 can add all values y_j to V by multiplying by z_j^{-1}. Since V contains all values $(y_j \in S_2) \wedge (y_j \notin S_1)$ then $S_1 \cup V = S_1 \cup S_2$. Correctness is not perfect due to the possibility of false positives though we can make this negligible in k as discussed in Sect. 2.2.

3.3 Protocol Security

We show that this protocol is secure with respect to the ideal functionality of a PSU computation defined by $\mathcal{F}_\cup$ and the security model defined in Sect. 2.4. For two parties P_1 and P_2 with sets S_1, S_2 respectively, we define the functionality for the definition to be:

$$\mathcal{F}_\cup(S_1, S_2) = S_1 \cup S_2. \tag{3}$$

As the definition suggests we need to show that it is impossible to derive anything from the execution of the protocol that is not implied by possession of the input and output of the corrupted player in question.

Theorem 1. *Suppose that the protocol, $\pi_\cup^{EBF}$, is instantiated with an IND-CPA secure AHE scheme with re-randomised messages. Then $\pi_\cup^{EBF}$ securely realises $\mathcal{F}_\cup$, as in Eq. (3), in the presence of static semi-honest adversaries.*

Proof. We will show that the PSU protocol is secure when P_2 is corrupted first, due to the simplicity of the proof relative to the P_1 corruption case. Recall that the input for player P_1 is $\mathsf{Inp}_1 = (S_1, aux_1 = |S_2| = m)$ and for P_2 it is $\mathsf{Inp}_2 = (S_2, aux_2 = |S_1|)$.

Server corrupted. The simulator receives $\mathsf{Inp}_2 = (S_2, aux_2 = |S_1|)$ and the messages $(\mathcal{T}, \emptyset)$, where $\mathcal{T}$ is the entire message transcript that P_2 witnesses and $\emptyset$ denotes the empty output received. For P_2, $\mathcal{T}$ simply contains an encrypted Bloom filter sent by P_1. Therefore, the simulator is only tasked with constructing an encrypted Bloom filter that is indistinguishable from the one provided in the real execution. From knowledge of $(|S_1|, (h_1, \ldots, h_k))$ the simulator is able to construct an empty Bloom filter using the correct parameters and the same hash functions. The simulator encrypts each entry of the Bloom filter using the IND-CPA encryption scheme. Let $\mathcal{T}'$ denote the simulated transcript; both $\mathcal{T}$ and $\mathcal{T}'$ just contain IND-CPA encrypted Bloom filters. It is trivial to show that any adversary who can distinguish between these transcripts can break the IND-CPA security of the encryption scheme.

Client corrupted. The simulator receives $\mathsf{Inp}_1 = (S_1, aux_1 = |S_2|)$ and the messages $(\mathcal{T}, S_1 \cup S_2)$ where $\mathcal{T} = \{(\tilde{p}_j, \tilde{c}_j)\}_{j \in [1,m]}$. It derives $|S_1 \cap S_2| = I$ from S_1 and $|S_2|$, by calculating $|(S_1 \cup S_2) \backslash S_1| = U$ and subsequently $|S_2| - |(S_2 \backslash S_1)| = I$. It constructs I encryptions, c_g, of 0 and U encryptions $c_j = C_1^{(j)} +_H \ldots +_H C_k^{(j)}$ computed as in the original protocol using the elements $y_j \in (S_1 \cup S_2) \backslash S_1$ constructed via the output and the input set. Finally, it sends $m = I + U$ messages in total where I messages are two encryptions of zero and the remaining U messages are represented by $\{(\tilde{p}_j, \tilde{c}_j)\}$, let $\mathcal{T}'$ be the simulated transcript containing these messages.

It is clear that the adversary learns the same union output in the case of $\mathcal{T}'$ since messages are constructed identically as in the real-setting. Notice that in the real-world execution the ciphertexts $(\tilde{p}_j, \tilde{c}_j)$ are re-randomised after performing homomorphic additions and thus are indistinguishable from brand new encryptions. Since $\mathcal{T}'$ only differs in that each message is a fresh encryption, we can show that any adversary that can distinguish $\mathcal{T}$ with non-negligible advantage must break the security of the encryption scheme after re-randomisation. However, if an adversary is able to do this then they must break its IND-CPA security since re-randomising involves multiplying with a freshly encrypted ciphertext. As a consequence, the simulated transcript must be indistinguishable in its encrypted form from $\mathcal{T}$ by the IND-CPA security of the encryption scheme. Since the correctness of the simulation holds this means that no adversary that can distinguish between the two real and simulated cases must exist.   □

Malicious Security. It was shown in previous works [8,17] that it is possible to prove security against malicious adversaries relating to input privacy. Broadly speaking, P_1 presents their set to a trusted certificate authority who verifies that it is honestly generated before creating an encrypted Bloom filter and signing it. When P_2 receives the Bloom filter, they verify the signature before computing the functionality above. This prevents P_1 from creating an adversarially generated Bloom filter that would potentially reveal the entirety of S_2. Since this method requires a trusted third party, this enhanced protocol can be thought of as an authenticated PSU design. This argument also applies for the PSI and PSI/PSU-CA protocol variants. We do not provide the full details here but a discussion will appear in an extended edition of this paper.

3.4   Asymptotic Efficiency

Communication Complexity. In the first round of our protocol, P_1 sends B ciphertexts to P_2. By Eq. (1) we have that $B = nk \log e$. By choosing a constant false-positive probability for ϵ we also render k as a constant and so $O(n)$ total ciphertexts are sent.

In the second round, P_2 sends $2m$ ciphertexts to P_1 and so clearly we have communication $O(m)$ here. If we assume, as in previous works, that $n = m$ then the total communication complexity is given by $O(n)$.[2]

Computational Complexity. P_1 computes B encryptions and $2m$ decryptions (in the worst case). P_1 must also compute m inverses of group elements, though techniques for doing this are very efficient. In practice, we can also reduce the number of decryptions by not computing $D_{sk}(\tilde{p}_j)$ if $D_{sk}(\tilde{c}_j) = 0$. On average this will lead to savings that are proportional to the size of the intersection.

P_2 will compute $m(k + 1)$ homomorphic additions and so, by the choice of k, the work done by both parties is linear in m. Assuming that $n = m$ we get that computation comprises $O(n)$ operations. The protocols of [1,4,13,14,18] all exhibit computational complexities that are super-linear in n, by comparison.

4   Adaptations to PSI and PSI/PSU-CA

An attractive feature of our simple protocol construction is the ease that we can adapt the design to securely compute different set operations. Here we consider the widely used operations PSI and PSI/PSU-CA and how we can adapt our technique for securely computing PSU to compute these functionalities instead. We define the ideal functionalities for PSI ($\mathcal{F}_\cap$) and PSI-CA ($\mathcal{F}_{|\cap|}$) as:

$$\mathcal{F}_\cap(S_1, S_2) = S_1 \cap S_2, \quad \mathcal{F}_{|\cap|}(S_1, S_2) = |S_1 \cap S_2| \tag{4}$$

(with $\mathcal{F}_{|\cup|}$ defined analogously). We will prove the security of our designs with respect to these functionalities.

4.1   PSI Protocol

A PSI protocol can be constructed using the same inverted Bloom filter and AHE scheme that we use for the PSU variant, the only thing that change are

---

[2] This can be easily done by padding the smaller of the two sets up to the size of the larger one.

the messages that P_2 computes. First, P_2 computes $c_j = C_1^{(j)} +_H \ldots +_H C_k^{(j)}$ as before, for each $y_j \in S_2$ and thus:

$$c_j = \begin{cases} E_{pk}(0) & \text{if } y_j \in S_1 \\ E_{pk}(z_j) & \text{if } y_j \notin S_1 \end{cases}$$

where $1 \leq z_j \leq k$ is the number of encryptions of 1 corresponding to y_j. P_2 then sends the messages $(\mathsf{ReRand}((r_j \cdot c_j) +_H E_{pk}(y_j)), \mathsf{ReRand}(c_j))$ (for randomly sampled r_j) to P_1. Recall that P_1 should only learn those y_j that satisfy $y_j \in S_1$ since the operation is a set intersection. In the case where $y_j \notin S_1$, we have that P_1 receives encryptions of the pair $((r_j \cdot z_j) + y_j, z_j)$. Since r_j is a random mask, intuitively P_1 is unable to learn the value y_j. When $y_j \in S_1$ they receive encryptions of $(y_j, 0)$, where clearly they can learn y_j. Figure 2 gives an overview of this protocol.

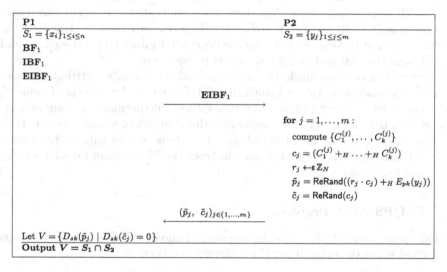

Fig. 2. A protocol that securely realises $\mathcal{F}_\cap$ in a similar way to $\pi_\cup^{\mathrm{EBF}}$.

Protocol Correctness. The correctness of the protocol follows since P_1 outputs those y_j such that c_j is an encryption of 0, since this allows for P_1 to decrypt $\tilde{p}_j$ to retrieve y_j. This only occurs when $y_j \in S_1$ (with respect tot he false-positive probability). Moreover, when $y_j \notin S_1$ they receive a randomly masked decryption and so y_j cannot be learnt.

Protocol Security.

Theorem 2. *Suppose that the protocol, $\pi_\cap^{EBF}$, is instantiated with an IND-CPA secure, AHE scheme with re-randomised messages. Then $\pi_\cap^{EBF}$ securely realises $\mathcal{F}_\cap$ in the presence of static semi-honest adversaries.*

Proof. The security argument when P_2 is corrupted is identical to the one shown in Theorem 1 since the encrypted Bloom filter is unchanged. For the corruption of P_1 we note that the security relies now on P_1 not being able to learn elements $y'_j \notin S_1 \cap S_2$ in order to realise $\mathcal{F}_\cap$ securely. The simulator receives the input $\mathsf{Inp}_1 = (S_1, aux_1 = |S_2|)$ and the messages $(\mathcal{T}, S_1 \cap S_2)$. The transcript contains m pairs of encryptions $\{(\tilde{p}_j, \tilde{c}_j)\}_j$ of the form $(r_j \cdot c_j +_H E_{pk}(y_j), \tilde{c}_j)$.

Let $I = |S_1 \cap S_2|$ and $J = |S_2| - I$. The simulator encrypts the I elements in $S_1 \cap S_2$ along with I encryptions of 0 for the messages that the adversary should learn. They then sample J random elements r'_i and random $1 \leq z'_i \leq k$ for $1 \leq i \leq J$ and compute their encryptions. They shuffle the order of the entire set of ciphertexts and submit pairs $(\tilde{p}'_j, \tilde{c}'_j)$ for $j \in [1, m]$ to P_1.

By a similar argument to the PSU security proof, the re-randomisation procedure means that P_1 cannot learn anything from the ciphertexts themselves. Therefore, the only situation where the adversary can distinguish is if they can learn a different output. Note that there are I encryptions of $(y_j, 0)$ which correspond exactly to those $y_j \in S_1 \cap S_2$. Therefore, we only have to show that the adversary cannot distinguish between the decrypted values $((r_j \cdot z_j) + y_j, z_j)$ and (r'_j, z'_j) from the real and simulated worlds respectively.

Since r_j is a random mask, $(r_j \cdot z_j) + y_j$ is also randomly distributed across the domain. Therefore, this is identically distributed to the decrypted value r'_j and thus P_1 cannot distinguish these two values. Furthermore, as long as z'_j is chosen such that it mirrors the probability distribution of values given in $\boldsymbol{BF}_1$ then this should also be indistinguishable. Finally note that this distribution is entirely public since the simulator can construct the Bloom filter from knowledge of S_1 and $h_1, \ldots, h_k$. □

4.2 PSI/PSU-CA Protocol

We can make use of the fact that by calculating one of PSI-CA or PSU-CA then we can calculate the other using the following relation:

$$|X \cap Y| = |X| + |Y| - |X \cup Y| \tag{5}$$

and thus we can concentrate on only computing one of the operations. We can create a secure protocol, $\pi_{|\cap|}^{\mathsf{EBF}}$, for calculating PSI-CA by adapting the protocol $\pi_{\cup}^{\mathsf{EBF}}$ to have P_2 to just send the message $(\tilde{c}_j)$ where c_j is calculated in the same way as the previous protocols and $\tilde{c}_j = \mathsf{ReRand}(c_j \cdot r_j)$. We compute $\tilde{c}_j$ using the ability to compute scalar multiplications on c_j and where r_j is some randomly chosen non-zero integer. We need to mask c_j in this way since only adding an encryption of zero as before would reveal extra information to P_1 on decryption.

The protocol proceeds in the same way except that P_1 only decrypts $\tilde{c}_j$. If $D_{sk}(\tilde{c}_j) = 0$ then they increment a counter c. Once all $\tilde{c}_j$ have been decrypted then P_1 outputs c as the answer. For PSU-CA they compute the count of $\tilde{c}_j$ that do not decrypt to 0 and then output $|S_1| + c$.

Protocol Correctness. Correctness is satisfied since $D_{sk}(\tilde{c}_j) = 0$ if and only if $y_j \in S_1$ (and thus $y_j \in S_1 \cap S_2$) with all but the negligible probability of a false positive occurring.

Protocol Security.

Theorem 3. *Suppose that the protocol, $\pi_{|\cap|}^{EBF}$, is instantiated with an IND-CPA secure AHE scheme and that ciphertexts are re-randomised. Then $\pi_{|\cap|}^{EBF}$ securely realises $\mathcal{F}_{|\cap|}$ in the presence of static semi-honest adversaries.*

Proof. The proof for security here is encompassed by the previous security arguments, we provide a sketch proof only due to space constraints. The case where P_2 is corrupted is covered as before. The simulator can construct the required number of encrypted values based on knowledge of the output. The adversary cannot distinguish the real and simulated encrypted formats due to the re-randomisation of ciphertexts. The decrypted values reveal nothing apart from the cardinality of the set (which holds by correctness) since the simulator applies an identical random mask to each concealed value. □

4.3 Asymptotic Evaluation

It is easily observable that the asymptotic performance of these two adaptations is essentially the same as the PSU variant. The cardinality variant is slightly more efficient since P_2 sends half as many ciphertexts and computes less homomorphic operations. Likewise the PSI variant requires that P_2 compute m fresh encryptions, on for each y_j. Fortunately this cost is absorbed into the $O(n)$ computation cost when taking $n = m$.

In Table 2, we provide a comparison of the asymptotic performance with the most efficient cardinality protocols. We do not provide the same analysis for our PSI protocol due to the relative density of results with similar complexities, though our design is asymptotically competitive with the most practical designs. We also provide a comparison of our toolkit with previous designs by Kissner and Song [18]. Our work improves demonstrably from their designs in both communication and computation. More recent attempts to provide multiple functionalities [1,14] also fall short of realising linear computational complexities and so our toolkit is asymptotically optimal in comparison with these previous works.

5 Experimental Evaluation

Parameter choices. To fully evaluate the practicality of our designs we present the results of an implementation of the proposed protocols. The implementations are written in Go and all experiments have been run on hardware with 256 gb RAM with an Intel(R) Xeon(R) CPU E5-2667 v2 @ 3.30 GHz and utilising a maximum of 8 cores (when parallel computation is required). We instantiate the

Table 2. Left: Comparison of our PSI/PSU-CA protocols with [5,11]. **Right:** Comparison of our complexities with the protocols of [18].

	Communication	Computation
[5]	$O(n)$	$O(n)$
[11]	$O(B)$	$O(B)$
$\pi_{\cap}^{EBF}/\pi_{\cup}^{EBF}$	$O(n)$	$O(n)$

		Communication	Computation
[18]	PSI	$O(cNn\log|E|)$	$O(n^2)$
	PSU	$O(N^2n\log|E|)$	$O(n^2)$
	PSI/PSU-CA	$O(N^2n\log|E|)$	$O(n^2)$
π^{EBF}	PSI	$2n+B$	$O(n)$
	PSU	$2n+B$	$O(n)$
	PSI/PSU-CA	$n+B$	$O(n)$

protocol with an open-source implementation of Paillier encryption in `Go`, known as `go-go-gadget-paillier`[3] with optimisations[4] to provide the homomorphic capability over ciphertexts. We provide our own implementation of the encrypted Bloom filter functionality. Our PSO implementation requires only 425 lines of code.

For the experiments, we examine running times for sets sizes ranging from 2^8 to 2^{18} elements; these sizes are used commonly in prior work. We choose a false positive probability of $\epsilon = 2^{-30}$ alongside the choice of optimal parameters for our Bloom filter as described in Sect. 2.2 – for example $k = 30$ and thus $B = kn\log e$ by Eq. (1) for sets of size n. For the Paillier encryption scheme we experiment with moduli N with bit-lengths 1024 and 2048 roughly equivalent to 80 and 116 bit security. We chose the domain of possible elements to be $5n$ where n is the set size and we choose the sets at random from this domain. This choice was made merely to guarantee that the size of the intersection is not too low, ensuring a realistic simulation. During our experimentation we make use of concurrency features in `Go` to make significant savings via parallel execution of operations. Times were ~3× quicker using parallel execution and thus we do not present our single-threaded results.

5.1 Results

In Table 3 we give the full runtimes for our PSO protocols. Table 5 provides the maximum amount of communication data[5] and in Table 4 we provide the time taken for the initial encryption. For reference, in Appendix A, we provide comparisons with efficient PSI designs [7,10,16]. The existing works of [19,22,23] provide even faster designs though these use inherently symmetric primitives which are not comparable with our work. It should be noted however that our designs represent a much more generic functionality since we can compute multiple set operations. These previous designs are only suitable for PSI computation. There are no current implementations of PSU designs for an experimental comparison.

---

[3] github.com/roasbeef/go-go-gadget-paillier.

[4] github.com/mcornejo/go-go-gadget-paillier.

[5] We do not provide estimates for the 2048 bit case since they are derivable by doubling the 1024 bit estimates.

Clearly, there is a large gap in efficiency between our protocols and those of state-of-the-art PSI designs. However, observe that the majority of our running times are spent on encrypting the initial Bloom filter that is sent to P_2. In fact, the homomorphic operations and output computation each take $<5\%$ of all operating runtime for all set sizes. Subsequently, we can see that the actual online phase of our protocol could be regarded as practical. As a consequence, the main bottleneck of our design appears to be the encryption phase and thus any optimisation in the underlying encryption scheme would drastically improve the practicality of our construction.

Table 3. Runtimes (secs) for increasing set sizes, **left** = 1024-bit moduli, **right** = 2048-bit. 'Hom. ops' refers to time taken for homomorphic operations; 'Out time' refers to time taken to compute output; 'Full time' includes time for encryption from Table 4.

Set size	Timings	PSU	PSI	CA	Set size	Timings	PSU	PSI	CA
2^8	Hom. ops	0.49	0.5	0.5	2^8	Hom. ops	3.33	3.36	3.33
	Out time	0.56	0.54	0.55		Out time	3.66	3.55	3.58
	Full time	11.78	11.76	11.75		Full time	78.02	77.76	77.76
2^{10}	Hom. ops	1.94	1.96	1.95	2^{10}	Hom. ops	13.45	13.33	13.44
	Out time	2.21	2.2	2.22		Out time	14.77	14.26	14.31
	Full time	44.73	44.68	44.7		Full time	312.44	311.61	311.76
2^{12}	Hom. ops	7.82	7.82	7.87	2^{12}	Hom. ops	52.97	53.41	53.15
	Out time	8.61	8.74	8.86		Out time	55.59	57.98	56.44
	Full time	175.7	175.79	175.96		Full time	1233.59	1235.69	1233.84
2^{14}	Hom. ops	31.37	31.32	31.59	2^{14}	Hom. ops	212.33	212	212.55
	Out time	35.78	34.9	35.48		Out time	228.13	223.31	225.11
	Full time	702.4	702.39	703.24		Full time	4952.94	4947.32	4949.66
2^{16}	Hom. ops	126.16	127.43	127.01	2^{16}	Hom. ops	856.27	859.67	857.9
	Out time	141.72	138.82	141.76		Out time	902.81	906.9	907.27
	Full time	2836.5	2834.68	2837.19		Full time	19881.51	19888.79	19887.17
2^{18}	Hom. ops	510.19	503.95	508.53	2^{18}	Hom. ops	3411.87	3416.9	3419.2
	Out time	536.48	556.72	556.05		Out time	3580.25	3595	3575.94
	Full time	11341.2	11327.78	11331.67		Full time	79272.48	79290.82	79274.15

Table 4. Encryption times (sec)

	2^8	2^{10}	2^{12}	2^{14}	2^{16}	2^{18}
1024 bits	10.7	40.53	159.23	636.17	2568.41	10267.03
2048 bits	70.85	284.02	1124.3	4512	18122	72278.95

Table 5. Maximum communication costs (mb) for our protocols for 1024 bit security.

Set sizes	2^8	2^{10}	2^{12}	2^{14}	2^{16}	2^{18}
Comms (mb)	2.83	11.32	45.28	181.12	724.49	2897.97

5.2   Amortising Bloom Filter Encryption

Importantly, we can think of the Bloom filter encryption phase as an offline cost. By encrypting with an additively homomorphic scheme, we are able to retain functionality of the Bloom filter even after encryption has took place. Notice that the encrypting party is only required to store new elements, and recall that it is impossible to remove elements even from a standard Bloom filter. After a Bloom filter has been encrypted elements can still be added to the set by adding '1' to any specified ciphertext that currently encrypts '0'.

Using this homomorphic property allows us to amortise the encryption operation over the natural life of a Bloom filter (i.e. until the underlying set has to be recomputed, or the maximum number of elements has been reached). Consequently, it is reasonable to suggest that the encryption phase of our protocol can be thought of as a one-time cost. The encrypted Bloom filter could then be used in multiple PSO instantiations, as long as re-randomisation of ciphertexts takes place. The 'online' phase of our protocol is very efficient to run and so it is an advantageous feature of our design that the main cost can be amortised across several instantiations.

6   Conclusion

In this paper we have devised a new method of computing the main private set operations with linear complexities. Our PSU protocol is the first construction that demonstrates both linear computation and communication. We have also shown that the design is easily adapted to support other private set functionalities. Finally, our experimental work shows the practicality of our protocols in the online phase. Our designs provides therefore an efficient toolkit for generic PSO computations.

Acknowledgements. The authors would like to thank Sumit Debnath, Mikkel Lambaek and Claudio Orlandi for their help in establishing problems with previous versions of this work. This work was supported by the EPSRC and the UK Government as part of the Centre for Doctoral Training in Cyber Security at Royal Holloway, University of London (EP/K035584/1).

A   Runtimes and Communication from Previous Work

See Tables 6 and 7.

Table 6. Runtimes (seconds) taken from [23]

Security level	80-bit					128-bit				
Set sizes	2^{10}	2^{12}	2^{14}	2^{16}	2^{18}	2^{10}	2^{12}	2^{14}	2^{16}	2^{18}
De Cristofaro and Tsudik [7]	0.5	2.0	7.9	31.3	124.9	7.7	31.0	124.3	497.2	1982.1
Huang et al. [16][a]	1.2	5.1	21.2	100.3	462.7	1.9	7.8	36.5	168.9	762.4
Dong et al. [10][a]	0.15	0.5	2.0	8.1	34.3	0.27	1.0	4.1	16.7	67.6

[a]With optimisations from [23]

Table 7. Communication costs (mb) taken from [23]

Security level	80-bit					128-bit				
Set sizes	2^{10}	2^{12}	2^{14}	2^{16}	2^{18}	2^{10}	2^{12}	2^{14}	2^{16}	2^{18}
De Cristofaro et al. [7]	0.3	1.1	4.3	17.3	69.0	0.8	3.1	12.5	50.0	200.0
Huang et al. [16][a]	18.8	90.0	420.0	1920.0	8640.0	30.0	144.0	672.0	3072.0	13824.0
Dong et al. [10][a]	1.1	4.5	18.1	72.6	290.4	2.9	11.6	46.2	184.9	739.7

[a]With optimisations from [23]

References

1. Blanton, M., Aguiar, E.: Private and oblivious set and multiset operations. In: Youm, H.Y., Won, Y. (eds.) ASIACCS 2012, pp. 40–41. ACM Press, May 2012
2. Bloom, B.H.: Space/time trade-offs in hash coding with allowable errors. Commun. ACM **13**(7), 422–426 (1970)
3. Bose, P., Guo, H., Kranakis, E., Maheshwari, A., Morin, P., Morrison, J., Smid, M.H.M., Tang, Y.: On the false-positive rate of bloom filters. Inf. Process. Lett. **108**(4), 210–213 (2008)
4. Brickell, J., Shmatikov, V.: Privacy-preserving graph algorithms in the semi-honest model. In: Roy, B. (ed.) ASIACRYPT 2005. LNCS, vol. 3788, pp. 236–252. Springer, Heidelberg (2005). doi:10.1007/11593447_13
5. De Cristofaro, E., Gasti, P., Tsudik, G.: Fast and private computation of cardinality of set intersection and union. In: Pieprzyk, J., Sadeghi, A.-R., Manulis, M. (eds.) CANS 2012. LNCS, vol. 7712, pp. 218–231. Springer, Heidelberg (2012). doi:10.1007/978-3-642-35404-5_17
6. Davidson, A., Fenn, G., Cid, C.: A model for secure and mutually beneficial software vulnerability sharing. In: Proceedings of the 2016 ACM on Workshop on Information Sharing and Collaborative Security (WISCS 2016), pp. 3–14, New York, NY, USA. ACM (2016)
7. De Cristofaro, E., Tsudik, G.: Practical private set intersection protocols with linear complexity. In: Sion, R. (ed.) FC 2010. LNCS, vol. 6052, pp. 143–159. Springer, Heidelberg (2010). doi:10.1007/978-3-642-14577-3_13
8. Debnath, S.K., Dutta, R.: Efficient private set intersection cardinality in the presence of malicious adversaries. In: Au, M.-H., Miyaji, A. (eds.) ProvSec 2015. LNCS, vol. 9451, pp. 326–330. Springer, Cham (2015). doi:10.1007/978-3-319-26059-4_18
9. Debnath, S.K., Dutta, R.: Secure and efficient private set intersection cardinality using bloom filter. In: Lopez, J., Mitchell, C.J. (eds.) ISC 2015. LNCS, vol. 9290, pp. 209–226. Springer, Cham (2015). doi:10.1007/978-3-319-23318-5_12

10. Dong, C., Chen, L., Wen, Z.: When private set intersection meets big data: an efficient and scalable protocol. In: Sadeghi, A.-R., Gligor, V.D., Yung, M. (eds.) ACM CCS 2013, pp. 789–800. ACM Press (2013)

11. Egert, R., Fischlin, M., Gens, D., Jacob, S., Senker, M., Tillmanns, J.: Privately computing set-union and set-intersection cardinality via bloom filters. In: Foo, E., Stebila, D. (eds.) ACISP 2015. LNCS, vol. 9144, pp. 413–430. Springer, Cham (2015). doi:10.1007/978-3-319-19962-7_24

12. Freedman, M.J., Nissim, K., Pinkas, B.: Efficient private matching and set intersection. In: Cachin, C., Camenisch, J.L. (eds.) EUROCRYPT 2004. LNCS, vol. 3027, pp. 1–19. Springer, Heidelberg (2004). doi:10.1007/978-3-540-24676-3_1

13. Frikken, K.: Privacy-preserving set union. In: Katz, J., Yung, M. (eds.) ACNS 2007. LNCS, vol. 4521, pp. 237–252. Springer, Heidelberg (2007). doi:10.1007/978-3-540-72738-5_16

14. Hazay, C., Nissim, K.: Efficient set operations in the presence of malicious adversaries. J. Cryptol. 25(3), 383–433 (2012)

15. Hormozdiari, F., Joo, J.W.J., Wadia, A., Guan, F., Ostrovsky, R., Sahai, A., Eskin, E.: Privacy preserving protocol for detecting genetic relatives using rare variants. Bioinformatics 30(12), 204–211 (2014)

16. Huang, Y., Evans, D., Katz, J.: Private set intersection: are garbled circuits better than custom protocols? In: NDSS 2012. The Internet Society, February 2012

17. Kerschbaum, F.: Outsourced private set intersection using homomorphic encryption. In: Youm, H.Y., Won, Y. (eds.) ASIACCS 2012, pp. 85–86. ACM Press, May 2012

18. Kissner, L., Song, D.: Privacy-preserving set operations. In: Shoup, V. (ed.) CRYPTO 2005. LNCS, vol. 3621, pp. 241–257. Springer, Heidelberg (2005). doi:10.1007/11535218_15

19. Kolesnikov, V., Kumaresan, R., Rosulek, M., Trieu, N.: Efficient batched oblivious PRF with applications to private set intersection. In: Weippl, E.R., Katzenbeisser, S., Kruegel, C., Myers, A.C., Halevi, S. (eds.) ACM CCS 2016, pp. 818–829. ACM Press (2016)

20. Meadows, C.A.: A more efficient cryptographic matchmaking protocol for use in the absence of a continuously available third party. In: Proceedings of the 1986 IEEE Symposium on Security and Privacy, Oakland, California, USA, April 7–9, 1986, pp. 134–137 (1986)

21. Paillier, P.: Public-key cryptosystems based on composite degree residuosity classes. In: Stern, J. (ed.) EUROCRYPT 1999. LNCS, vol. 1592, pp. 223–238. Springer, Heidelberg (1999). doi:10.1007/3-540-48910-X_16

22. Pinkas, B., Schneider, T., Segev, G., Zohner, M.: Phasing: private set intersection using permutation-based hashing. In: USENIX Security Symposium, pp. 515–530. USENIX Association (2015)

23. Pinkas, B., Schneider, T., Zohner, M.: Faster private set intersection based on OT extension. In: Proceedings of the 23rd USENIX Security Symposium, San Diego, CA, USA, 20–22 August, 2014, pp. 797–812 (2014)

24. Rindal, P., Rosulek, M.: Improved private set intersection against malicious adversaries. Cryptology ePrint Archive, Report 2016/746 (2016). http://eprint.iacr.org/2016/746

25. Seo, J.H., Cheon, J.H., Katz, J.: Constant-round multi-party private set union using reversed laurent series. In: Fischlin, M., Buchmann, J., Manulis, M. (eds.) PKC 2012. LNCS, vol. 7293, pp. 398–412. Springer, Heidelberg (2012). doi:10.1007/978-3-642-30057-8_24

Authentication

Privacy-Preserving k-time Authenticated Secret Handshakes

Yangguang Tian[1]([⊠]), Shiwei Zhang[1], Guomin Yang[1], Yi Mu[1], and Yong Yu[2]

[1] School of Computing and Information Technology,
Institute of Cybersecurity and Cryptology, University of Wollongong,
Wollongong, NSW 2522, Australia
{yt412,sz653,gyang,ymu}@uow.edu.au
[2] School of Computer Science, Shaanxi Normal University, Xi'an 710062, China
yuyong@snnu.edu.cn

Abstract. Secret handshake allows a group of authorized users to establish a shared secret key and at the same time authenticate each other anonymously. A straightforward approach to design an unlinkable secret handshake protocol is to use either long-term certificate or one-time certificate provided by a trusted authority. However, how to detect the misusing of certificates by an insider adversary is a challenging security issue when using those approaches for unlinkable secret handshake. In this paper, we propose a novel k-time authenticated secret handshake (k-ASH) protocol where each authorized user is only allowed to use the credential for k times. We formalize security models, including session key security and anonymity, for k-ASH, and prove the security of the proposed protocol under some computational problems which are proved hard in the generic bilinear group model. The proposed protocol also achieved public traceability property if a user misuses the k-time credential.

Keywords: Unlinkable secret handshake · Insider adversary · k-time authentication · Public traceability · Generic bilinear group model

1 Introduction

Secret handshake is a useful cryptographic primitive and has been extensively studied in the literature. It allows an authorized user to share a secret key with others without revealing their real identities. The following scenario can clarify its practicality. A FBI agent wants to contact with another agent, and both of them do not want to disclose their identity information during interaction. The only information they need to know is the peer belongs to the same agent system. There have been two types of unlinkable secret handshake system in the literature: one is based on the long-term certificate (e.g., [14,15]), and the other is based on one-time certificate (e.g., [16]). In the former type, the authorized user generates the shared secret value using the secret long-term certificate given by a trusted authority (TA) of the organization. In the latter type, the long-term

© Springer International Publishing AG 2017
J. Pieprzyk and S. Suriadi (Eds.): ACISP 2017, Part II, LNCS 10343, pp. 281–300, 2017.
DOI: 10.1007/978-3-319-59870-3_16

secret value will be replaced by a set of one-time certificates and the authorized user will use one of them for unlinkable secret handshake in each session.

For the long-term certificate, an authorized user is allowed to reuse the given certificate when establishing a secret value with another authorized user. For example, the given secret certificate is blended with Diffie-Hellman key exchange, in order to generate a secret key with forward secrecy (e.g., [14,15]). Since the same certificate is used everytime, how to ensure the unlinkability is the major challenge in the protocol design. On the other hand, the one-time certificate approach (e.g., [16]) can address the unlinkability easily since each certificate is supposed to be used only once. Nevertheless, none of the previous approaches has considered the issue of misusing of certificates. We should note that for the one-time certificate schemes, the user is supposed to use each certificate once. However, reusing the given one-time certificates is a security issue that has not been formally considered in the previous works.

We give an example where misusing of the certificates (or credentials) should be prevented in secret handshake in some scenarios. Suppose there are n players subscribed to a real-time gaming system. Each user will obtain a set of k credentials from the game server after paying a subscription fee that is proportional to k. The players can form ad-hoc groups to play the game and a player can join a gaming session using one credential at a time. In order to ensure that only registered players are eligible to communicate with the peers, the players should generate a common session key to protect the communication. Also, it is desirable that the players cannot recognize each other except the fact that they are all legitimate subscribers of the system. Therefore, we may use a multi-party secret handshake protocol to achieve the security and privacy goals. However, in this example, a malicious player may try to reuse his credentials to continue playing the game without topping up extra money after all the credentials are used up. Therefore, it is important to identify such cheating players who reuse their one-time credentials. However, we found that the misusing of credentials has not been formally addressed in the previous secret handshake schemes. In this paper, we focus on addressing the credential misusing problem under the one-time certificate setting, and leave the task of designing such a scheme under the long-term certificate setting as our future work.

1.1   This Work

In this paper, we introduce the notion of k-time authenticated secret handshake (k-ASH), allowing all authorized users in a system to agree on a common secret value anonymously while preventing them from misusing their credentials issued by a trusted party of the system. Our contributions can be summarized as follows:

1. We present the formal security definition for k-time ASH protocol. In particular, we extend the eCK model [21] to define session key security and a variant of Juels-Weis privacy model [17] to define user anonymity.

2. We present a new unlinkable k-time ASH using anonymized Schnorr signature [22] and tag bases [25] to trace the cheating users who reuse their one-time credentials.
3. We prove a variant of the Computational Diffie-Hellman problem (VoCDH) and an extension of Decisional Combined Bilinear Diffie-Hellman problem (EVoDCBDH) [27] in the generic bilinear group model, and prove the security of the new k-time ASH protocol under these assumptions.

1.2 Related Work

Key Exchange. Bellare and Rogaway [6] introduced the first complexity-theoretic security model for key exchange under the symmetric-key setting. The model was later extended and enhanced under different contexts [2,5,7]. Canetti and Krawczyk [11] later refined the previous models and proposed a new model, known as the CK model, which is widely used in the analysis of many well-known key exchange protocols. Some variants [20,21] of CK model were also proposed to allow an adversary to obtain either long-term secret key or ephemeral secret key of the challenge session. Burmester and Desmedt [10] (BD) introduced several key exchange protocols in the multi-party setting, including star-based, broadcast-based, tree-based, and cyclic-based protocols. Later, a few generic transformations [8,18,19] were proposed to convert passive-secure group key exchange protocols into active-secure ones.

Secret Handshakes. Balfanz et al. [1] introduced the concept of secret handshake that allows any users in the same group to generate a shared value secretly using the long-term certificate approach. Afterwards, Castelluccia et al. [12] constructed a more efficient scheme than [1] under the standard Computational Diffie-Hellman Assumption. But both schemes did not provide the unlinkability property. In [26], Xu and Yung provided an unlinkable scheme but with weaker anonymity, named k-unlinkability, which means in the worst case, an adversary can infer that a participant is one out of certain k users. For achieving the full anonymity, Jarecki et al. [16] proposed two group secret handshake protocols using the BD group key agreement protocol (e.g., [10]). In particular, the second construction in [16] used one-time certificate to achieve full anonymity under the Gap Diffie-Hellman Assumption. Meanwhile, several secret handshake protocols have been proposed in the literature (e.g., [14,15]) which achieved full anonymity without using one-time certificate. The protocol in [15] and the improvement protocol in [14] are long-time certificate based, and both of them are allowed to reuse the given certificate with unlimited number of times.

2 Security Model

In this section, we present the security models for k-ASH. As mentioned in the introduction, a secure k-ASH protocol should achieve both session key security and anonymity. Below we present the corresponding security models to capture the above requirements. Specifically, the session key security model is a *modified* version of eCK model [21], which is an extension of CK model [11] in the secret handshake setting, while the anonymity model is extended from the privacy models ([17, 24]) for RFID authentication protocols.

States. We define a system user set $\mathcal{U}$ with n users, i.e. $|\mathcal{U}| = n$. We say an oracle Π_U^i may be *used* or *unused*. The oracle is considered as unused if it has never been initialized. Each unused oracle Π_U^i can be initialized with a secret key x. The oracle is initialized as soon as it becomes part of a group. After the initialization the oracle is marked as used and turns into the *stand-by* state where it waits for an invocation to execute a protocol operation. Upon receiving such invocation the oracle Π_U^i learns its partner identifier pid_U^i and turns into a *processing* state where it sends, receives and processes messages according to the description of the protocol. During that stage, the internal state information $state_U^i$ is maintained by the oracle. The oracle Π_U^i remains in the processing state until it collects enough information to compute the session key K_U^i. As soon as K_U^i is computed Π_U^i *accepts* and *terminates* the protocol execution meaning that it would not send or receive further messages. If the protocol execution fails then Π_U^i terminates without having accepted.

Partnering. We denote the i-th session established by a user U by Π_U^i, and identities of all the users recognized by Π_U^i during the execution of that session by pid_U^i. We define sid_U^i as the unique session identifier belonging to the session i established by the user U. Specifically, $\mathsf{sid}_U^i = \{m_j\}_{j=1}^n$, where $m_j \in \{0, 1\}^*$ is the message transcript among users. We say two instance oracles Π_U^i and $\Pi_{U'}^j$ are *partners* if and only if $\mathsf{pid}_U^i = \mathsf{pid}_{U'}^j$, and $\mathsf{sid}_U^i = \mathsf{sid}_{U'}^j$.

2.1 System Model

We define a k-time authenticated secret handshake protocol consists of the following algorithms:

- Setup: The algorithm takes the security parameter λ as input, outputs the master public parameters mpk (including the k-time tag bases) and the master secret keys msk.
- KeyGen: The algorithm takes the master public key mpk as input, outputs a public/secret key pair (X, x).
- Register: This is an interactive algorithm that executed between the user and the TA. TA takes the master secret key msk and a public key X of one user as input, outputs a set of credentials $\{s_i\}_{i=1}^k$ on X. The user will become a registered user after interaction with TA.
- Handshake: This is an interactive algorithm that executed by registered users. Each user takes his/her secret key x, one of his/her credentials $\{s_i\}_{i=1}^k$ and mpk as input, outputs a shared secret key K if and only if his/her counterparts are registered users.
- Tracing: The algorithm takes two handshake transcripts of one user and one of tag bases as input, outputs the user's public key X.

2.2 Session Key Security

We define the session key security model for k-ASH protocols, in which each user obtains a set of credentials associated with his/her public key from the TA, and establishes a session key using one of the given secret credentials in one session. The model is defined via a game between a probabilistic polynomial time (PPT) adversary $\mathcal{A}$ and a simulator $\mathcal{S}$. $\mathcal{A}$ is an active attacker with full control of the communication channel among all the users.

- Setup: $\mathcal{S}$ first generates master public/secret key pair (mpk, msk) for the TA and long-term secret keys $\{x_i\}_{i=1}^n$ for n users by running the corresponding KeyGen algorithms, where x_i denotes the secret key of user i. In addition, $\mathcal{S}$ generates a set of secret credentials $\{s_{i,j}\}_{j=1}^k$ for user i by running the Register algorithm. $\mathcal{S}$ also tosses a random coin b which will be used later in the game. Let $\mathcal{U}$ denote all the registered users.
- Training: $\mathcal{A}$ can make the following queries in arbitrary sequence to simulator $\mathcal{S}$.
  - Establish: $\mathcal{A}$ is allowed to register a user U' with public key X_i'. If a user is registered by $\mathcal{A}$, then we call this user *dishonest*; Otherwise, it is *honest*.
  - Send: If $\mathcal{A}$ issues send query in the form of (U, i, m) to simulate a network message for the i-th session of user U, then $\mathcal{S}$ would simulate the reaction of instance oracle Π_U^i upon receiving message m, and returns to $\mathcal{A}$ the response that Π_U^i would generate; If $\mathcal{A}$ issues send query in the form of $(U,' start')$, then $\mathcal{S}$ creates a new instance oracle Π_U^i and returns to $\mathcal{A}$ the first protocol message.
  - Session key reveal: $\mathcal{A}$ can issue reveal query to an accepted instance oracle Π_U^i. If the session is accepted, then $\mathcal{S}$ will return the session key to $\mathcal{A}$; Otherwise, a special symbol '$\perp$' is returned to $\mathcal{A}$.
  - Ephemeral secret key reveal: If $\mathcal{A}$ issues an ephemeral secret key reveal query to (possibly unaccepted) instance oracle Π_U^i, then $\mathcal{S}$ will return all ephemeral secret values contained in Π_U^i at the moment the query is asked.
  - long term secret key reveal: If $\mathcal{A}$ issues a long term secret key reveal (or corrupt, for short) query to user i, then $\mathcal{S}$ will return both the long term secret key and the secret credential set $(x_i, \{s_{i,j}\}_{j=1}^k)$ to $\mathcal{A}$.
  - Master secret key reveal: If $\mathcal{A}$ issues a master secret key reveal query to TA, then $\mathcal{S}$ will return the master secret keys msk to $\mathcal{A}$.
  - Test: This query can only be made to an accepted and *fresh* (as defined below) session i of a user U. Then $\mathcal{S}$ does the following:
    * If the coin $b = 1$, $\mathcal{S}$ returns the real session key to the adversary;
      * Otherwise, a random session key is drawn from the session key space and returned to the adversary.

Note that $\mathcal{A}$ can generate a set of secret credentials $\{s_{i,j}\}_{j=1}^k$ of user i after issuing Master secret key reveal query to TA. It is also worth noting that $\mathcal{A}$ can continue to issue other queries after the Test query. However, the test session must maintain fresh throughout the entire game.

Finally, $\mathcal{A}$ outputs b' as its guess for b. If $b' = b$, then the simulator outputs 1; Otherwise, the simulator outputs 0.

Freshness. We say an *accepted* instance oracle Π_U^i is fresh if $\mathcal{A}$ does not perform any of the following actions during the game:

- $\mathcal{A}$ issues Session key reveal query to Π_U^i or its accepted partnered instance oracle $\Pi_{U'}^j$;
- $\mathcal{A}$ issues both Long term secret key reveal query to U' s.t. $U' \in \mathrm{pid}_U^i$ and Ephemeral secret key reveal query for an instance $\Pi_{U'}^j$ partnered with Π_U^i;
- $\mathcal{A}$ issues Long term secret key reveal query to user U' s.t. $U' \in \mathrm{pid}_U^i$ prior to the acceptance of instance Π_U^i and there exists no instance oracle $\Pi_{U'}^j$ partnered with Π_U^i.

  Note that the Master key reveal query to TA is equivalent to the Long term secret key reveal to all users in pid_U^i.

We define the advantage of an adversary $\mathcal{A}$ in the above game as

$$\mathrm{Adv}_{\mathcal{A}}(\lambda) = \Pr[\mathcal{S} \to 1] - 1/2. \tag{1}$$

Definition 1. *We say a k-ASH protocol has* session key security *if for any PPT $\mathcal{A}$, $\mathrm{Adv}_{\mathcal{A}}(\lambda)$ is a negligible function of the security parameter λ.*

2.3   Anonymity

Informally, an adversary is not allowed to identify who are the handshake users, with the condition that honest users authenticate with each other within k times. We define a game between an *insider* adversary $\mathcal{A}$ and a simulator $\mathcal{S}$ as follows:

- Setup: $\mathcal{S}$ generates master public/secret key pairs (mpk, msk) for the TA and long term secret keys $\{x_i\}_{i=1}^n$ for n users by running the corresponding KeyGen algorithms. In addition, $\mathcal{S}$ generates a set of secret credentials $\{s_{i,j}\}_{j=1}^k$ for user i by running the Register algorithm. $\mathcal{S}$ also tosses a random coin b which will be used later in the game. We denote the original n users set as $\mathcal{U}$.
- Training: $\mathcal{A}$ is allowed to issue Establish, Send, Ephemeral secret key reveal, Session key reveal and at most n-2 Long term secret key reveal queries to $\mathcal{S}$. We denote the honest (i.e., uncorrupted) user set as $\mathcal{U}'$.
- Challenge: $\mathcal{A}$ randomly selects two users $U_i, U_j \in \mathcal{U}'$ as challenge candidates, then $\mathcal{S}$ remove them from $\mathcal{U}'$ and simulates U_b^* to $\mathcal{A}$ by either $U_b^* = U_i$ if $b = 1$ or $U_b^* = U_j$ if $b = 0$.

  Let $\mathcal{A}$ interact with U_b^*. Note that $\mathcal{A}$ is allowed to activate at most k sessions for U_i, U_j throughout the entire game.

$$\mathcal{A} \Leftrightarrow U_b^* = \begin{cases} U_i & b = 1 \\ U_j & b = 0 \end{cases}$$

Finally, $\mathcal{A}$ outputs b' as its guess for b. If $b' = b$, then the simulator outputs 1; Otherwise, the simulator outputs 0.

We define the advantage of $\mathcal{A}$ in the above game as

$$\text{Adv}_{\mathcal{A}}(\lambda) = \Pr[\mathcal{S} \to 1] - 1/2. \tag{2}$$

Definition 2. *We say a k-ASH protocol has* anonymity *if for any PPT $\mathcal{A}$, $\text{Adv}_{\mathcal{A}}(\lambda)$ is a* negligible *function of the security parameter λ.*

3 Our Construction

3.1 Preliminaries

Bilinear Map. The bilinear map $\hat{e} : \mathbb{G} \times \mathbb{G} \to \mathbb{G}_1$ has the following properties:

1. Bilinearity: $\hat{e}(g^{\alpha_i}, g^{\alpha_j}) = \hat{e}(g, g)^{\alpha_i \cdot \alpha_j} : \forall \alpha_i, \alpha_j \in \mathbb{Z}_q, g \in \mathbb{G}$.
2. Non-degeneracy: $\hat{e}(g, g) \neq 1$.
3. Computable: There exists an efficient algorithm for computing the bilinear map.

Note that the map $\hat{e}$ is symmetric since $\hat{e}(g^{\alpha_i}, g^{\alpha_j}) = \hat{e}(g, g)^{\alpha_i \cdot \alpha_j} = \hat{e}(g^{\alpha_j}, g^{\alpha_i})$.

3.2 Modified Computational Diffie-Hellman Problem

Definition 3 *Computational Diffie-Hellman (CDH) Assumption [20]:* *Given $g, g^a, g^b \in \mathbb{G}$ where $a, b \in_R \mathbb{Z}_q$, we define the advantage of the adversary in solving the CDH problem as*

$$\text{Adv}_{\mathcal{A}}^{CDH}(\lambda) = \Pr[\mathcal{A}(g, g^a, g^b) = g^{ab} \in \mathbb{G}]$$

We say a CDH assumption holds in group $\mathbb{G}$ if for any PPT $\mathcal{A}$, $\text{Adv}_{\mathcal{A}}(\lambda)$ is a negligible *function of the security parameter λ.*

We propose a variant of computational diffie-hellman problem (VoCDH) below.

Definition 4. *Given $g, g^a, g^{1/a}, g^b \in \mathbb{G}$ where $a, b \in_R \mathbb{Z}_q$, we define the advantage of the adversary in solving the VoCDH problem as*

$$\text{Adv}_{\mathcal{A}}^{VoCDH}(\lambda) = \Pr[\mathcal{A}(g, g^a, g^{1/a}, g^b) = g^{ab} \in \mathbb{G}]$$

We prove the above VoCDH problem is hard in $\mathbb{G}$ with a bilinear map $\hat{e} : \mathbb{G} \times \mathbb{G} \to \mathbb{G}_1$ in the generic bilinear group model [9,23].

Theorem 1. *Let $\epsilon_1, \epsilon_2 : \mathbb{F}_p \to \{0, 1\}^*$ be two random encodings (injective functions) where $\mathbb{F}_p$ is a prime field and $\mathbb{G} = \{\epsilon_1(a) | a \in \mathbb{F}_p\}, \mathbb{G}_1 = \{\epsilon_2(a) | a \in \mathbb{F}_p\}$. If a, b are uniformly and independently chosen from $\mathbb{F}_p$ and encodings ϵ_1, ϵ_2 are randomly chosen, we then define the advantage of the adversary in solving the VoCDH with at most q, q_1 queries to the group operation oracles $\mathcal{O}, \mathcal{O}_1$ and $q_{\hat{e}}$ queries to the bilinear pairing oracle $\mathcal{O}_{\hat{e}} : \epsilon_1 \times \epsilon_1 \to \epsilon_2$ as*

$$\text{Adv}_{\mathcal{A}}^{VoCDH}(\lambda) = \Pr[\mathcal{A}(\epsilon_1(1), \epsilon_1(a), \epsilon_1(b), \epsilon_1(a^{-1}))$$
$$= \epsilon_1(a \cdot b)] \leq \frac{4(q + q_1 + q_{\hat{e}} + 4)^2}{p}$$

Proof. Let $\mathcal{S}$ be the simulator to simulate the entire game for $\mathcal{A}$. $\mathcal{S}$ maintains two polynomial sized dynamic lists: $L_1 = \{(p_i, \epsilon_{1,i})\}, L_2 = \{(q_i, \epsilon_{2,i})\}$, the $p_i \in \mathbb{F}_p[X_1, X_2]$ are 2-variate polynomials over $\mathbb{F}_p$, such that $p_0 = 1, p_1 = X_1, p_2 = X_2, p_3 = X_1^{p-2}$, and $\{\epsilon_{1,i}\}_{i=0}^3 \in_R \{0,1\}^*$ are corresponding arbitrary strings, $\mathcal{S}$ then sets those pairs $(p_i, \epsilon_{1,i})$ as L_1. Therefore, the two lists are initialised as $L_1 = \{(p_i, \epsilon_{1,i})\}_{i=0}^3, L_2 = \emptyset$.

At the beginning of the game, $\mathcal{S}$ sends $\{\epsilon_{1,i}\}_{i=0,\cdots,3}$ to $\mathcal{A}$. After this, $\mathcal{S}$ simulates the group operation oracle $\mathcal{O}, \mathcal{O}_1$ and the bilinear pairing oracle $\mathcal{O}_{\hat{e}}$ as follows. We assume that all requested operands are obtained from $\mathcal{S}$.

- $\mathcal{O}$: The group operation involves two operands $\epsilon_{1,i}, \epsilon_{1,j}$. Based on these operands, $\mathcal{S}$ searches the list L_1 for the corresponding polynomials p_i and p_j. Then $\mathcal{S}$ perform the polynomial addition or subtraction $p_l = p_i \pm p_j$ depending on whether multiplication or division is requested. If p_l is in the list L_1, then $\mathcal{S}$ returns the corresponding ϵ_l to $\mathcal{A}$. Otherwise, $\mathcal{S}$ uniformly chooses $\epsilon_{1,l} \in_R \{0,1\}^*$, where $\epsilon_{1,l}$ is unique in the encoding string L_1, and appends the pair $(p_l, \epsilon_{1,l})$ into the list L_1. Finally, $\mathcal{S}$ returns $\epsilon_{1,l}$ to $\mathcal{A}$ as the answer. Group operation queries in $\mathbb{G}_1$ (i.e., $\mathcal{O}_1$) is treated similarly.
- $\mathcal{O}_{\hat{e}}$: The group operation involves two operands $\epsilon_{1,i}, \epsilon_{1,j}$. Based on these operands, $\mathcal{S}$ searches the list L_1 for the corresponding polynomials p_i and p_j. Then $\mathcal{S}$ perform the polynomial multiplication $p_l = p_i \cdot p_j$. If p_l is in the list L_2, then $\mathcal{S}$ returns the corresponding $\epsilon_{2,l}$ to $\mathcal{A}$. Otherwise, $\mathcal{S}$ uniformly chooses $\epsilon_{2,l} \in_R \{0,1\}^*$, where $\epsilon_{2,l}$ is unique in the encoding string L_2, and appends the pair $(p_l, \epsilon_{2,l})$ into the list L_2. Finally, $\mathcal{S}$ returns $\epsilon_{2,l}$ to $\mathcal{A}$ as the answer.

After querying at most q, q_1, q_e times of corresponding oracles, $\mathcal{A}$ terminates and outputs $\epsilon_1(x_1 \cdot x_2)$. At this point, $\mathcal{S}$ chooses random $a, b \in_R \mathbb{F}_p$ and sets $X_1 = a, X_2 = b$. The simulation by $\mathcal{S}$ is perfect unless the **abort** event happens. Thus, we bound the probability of event **abort** by analyzing the following cases:

1. $p_i(a,b) = p_j(a,b)$: Since $p_i \neq p_j$ as the method of L_1 is generated, $p_i - p_j$ is a non-zero polynomial of degree 0, 1, or $p-2$ where $p-2$ is produced by X_1^{p-2}. Since $X_1 \cdot X_1^{p-2} = X_1^{p-1} \equiv 1 \pmod{p}$, we have $X_1(p_i - p_j)$ is a non-zero polynomial of degree 0, 1, or 2. Therefore, the maximum degree of $X_1(p_i - p_j)$ is 2. By using lemma 1 in [23], we have $\Pr[(X_1(p_i - p_j))(a,b) = 0] \leq \frac{2}{p}$ and thus $\Pr[p_i(a,b) = p_j(a,b)] \leq \frac{2}{p}$. As there are $\binom{q+4}{2}$ pairs of (p_i, p_j), we have the **abort** probability is $\Pr[\text{abort}_1] \leq \binom{q+4}{2} \cdot \frac{2}{p}$.

2. $q_i(a,b) = q_j(a,b)$: Since $q_i \neq q_j$ as the method of L_2 is generated and q_i, q_j are in the form of $\sum a_{k,l} p_k p_j$ for some constants $a_{k,l}$, $q_i - q_j$ is a non-zero polynomial of degree 0, 1, 2, $p-1$, $p-2$, or $2p-4$. Similar to above case, we have $X_1^2 \cdot X_1^{p-1} \equiv X_1^2, X_1^2 \cdot X_1^{p-2} \equiv X_1$, and $X_1^2 \cdot X_1^{2p-4} = (X_1^{p-1})^2 \equiv 1 \pmod{p}$. Therefore, $X_1^2(q_i - q_j)$ is a non-zero polynomial of degree ranging from 0 to 4. Since the maximum degree of $X_1^2(q_i - q_j)$ is 4, we have $\Pr[(X_1^2(q_i - q_j))(a,b) = 0] \leq \frac{4}{p}$ and thus $\Pr[q_i(a,b) = q_j(a,b)] \leq \frac{4}{p}$. As there are $\binom{q_1 + q_{\hat{e}}}{2}$ pairs of (q_i, q_j), we have the **abort** probability is $\Pr[\text{abort}_2] \leq \binom{q_1 + q_{\hat{e}}}{2} \cdot \frac{4}{p}$.

3. $p_i(a, b) = ab$: Since the degree of p_1 is 0, 1, or $p - 2$, and the degree of X_1X_2 is 2, we have that $p_i - X_1X_2$ is a non-zero polynomial of degree 2 or $p - 2$. Similar to the case 1, we have $X_1(p_i - X_1X_2)$ is a non-zero polynomial of maximum degree of 3. Therefore, we have $\Pr[(X_1(p_i - X_1X_2))(a, b) = 0] \leq \frac{3}{p}$ and thus $\Pr[p_i(a, b) = ab] \leq \frac{3}{p}$. As there are $q + 4$ polynomials in L_1, we have the abort probability is $\Pr[\text{abort}_3] \leq \frac{3(q+4)}{p}$.

By combining all above cases, we have the abort probability is

$$\Pr[\text{abort}] = \Pr[\text{abort}_1] + \Pr[\text{abort}_2] + \Pr[\text{abort}_3]$$
$$\leq \binom{q+4}{2} \cdot \frac{2}{p} + \binom{q_1 + q_{\hat{e}}}{2} \cdot \frac{4}{p} + \frac{3(q+4)}{p}$$
$$< \frac{(q+4)^2 + 2(q_1 + q_{\hat{e}})^2 + 3(q+4)}{p}$$
$$< \frac{4(q + q_1 + q_{\hat{e}} + 4)^2}{p}$$

3.3 Modified Decisional Combined Bilinear Diffie-Hellman Problem

Definition 5. *Variant of Decisional Combined Bilinear Diffie-Hellman Problem: Given $g, g^a, g^b, h^c, h^d, h^{1/d} \in \mathbb{G}$ where $a, b, c, d \in_R \mathbb{Z}_q$ and $h = g^e$, we define the advantage of the adversary in solving the VoDCBDH problem as*

$$\text{Adv}_{\mathcal{A}}^{VoDCBDH}(\lambda) = \Pr[w = \mathcal{A}(g, g^a, g^b, g^{ec}, g^{ed}, g^{e/d},$$
$$T_0, T_1, w \in_R \{0, 1\}) : T_w = g^{ab+ecd}, T_{w-1} = Z].$$

The VoDCBDH problem is a variant of Decisional Combined Bilinear Diffie-Hellman Problem [27]. We prove the VoDCBDH problem is hard in $\mathbb{G}$ with a bilinear map $\hat{e} : \mathbb{G} \times \mathbb{G} \to \mathbb{G}_1$ in the generic bilinear group model [9,23].

Theorem 2. *The lower bound of the complexity of the VoDCBDH problem is stated as follows, querying the group operations and bilinear pairing operations at most q times.*

$$\text{Adv}_{\mathcal{A}}^{VoDCBDH}(\lambda) \leq \frac{3(q+9)^2}{p}.$$

To prove this theorem, we introduce an intermediate problem (see Lemma 2), and we prove that the hardness of intermediate problem implies the hardness of the VoDCBDH problem. After that, we prove the intermediate problem is intractable (see Lemma 1) and then the theorem follows.

Definition 6. *Given $g, g^d, g^{cd}, g^{d^2}, g^e, g^{ae}, g^{be} \in \mathbb{G}$ where $a, b, c, d, e \in_R \mathbb{Z}_p$ and $g \in_R \mathbb{G}$, the modified problem is to distinguish g^{abe+cd^2} from a random element*

$Z \in_R \mathbb{G}$. *The advantage of an adversary $\mathcal{A}$ to solve the modified problem is defined as*

$$\text{Adv}_{\mathcal{A}}^{Modified}(\lambda) = \Pr[w = \mathcal{A}(g, g^d, g^{cd}, g^{d^2}, g^e, g^{ae}, g^{be},$$
$$T_0, T_1, w \in_R \{0,1\}) : T_w = g^{abe+cd^2}, T_{w-1} = Z]$$

Lemma 1. *If an algorithm $\mathcal{A}$ can solve the VoDCBDH problem with the advantage $\text{Adv}_{\mathcal{A}}^{VoDCBDH}(\lambda)$, then we can built an algorithm $\mathcal{S}$ to solve the modified problem with the advantage $\text{Adv}_{\mathcal{S}}^{Modified}(\lambda)$ such that*

$$\text{Adv}_{\mathcal{A}}^{VoDCBDH}(\lambda) \leq \text{Adv}_{\mathcal{S}}^{Modified}(\lambda).$$

Proof. The simulator $\mathcal{S}$ obtains an instance $\hat{\theta} = (\hat{g}, \hat{g}^{\hat{d}}, \hat{g}^{\hat{c}\hat{d}}, \hat{g}^{\hat{d}^2}, \hat{g}^{\hat{e}}, \hat{g}^{\hat{a}\hat{e}}, \hat{g}^{\hat{b}\hat{e}}, T_0, T_1)$. Then $\mathcal{S}$ checks whether $\hat{g}^{\hat{d}} = 1$ or not. If $\hat{g}^{\hat{d}} = 1$, that is $\hat{d} = 0$, the simulator $\mathcal{S}$ returns $w = 0$ if $e(\hat{g}^{\hat{a}\hat{e}}, \hat{g}^{\hat{b}\hat{e}}) = e(T_0, \hat{g}^{\hat{e}})$ or returns $w = 1$ otherwise, and solves $\hat{\theta}$ with the probability of 1. If $\hat{g}^{\hat{d}} \neq 1$, the simulator $\mathcal{S}$ continues and sets $\theta = (g, g^a, g^b, h, h^c, h^d, h^{\frac{1}{d}}, T_0, T_1) = (\hat{g}^{\hat{e}}, \hat{g}^{\hat{a}\hat{e}}, \hat{g}^{\hat{b}\hat{e}}, \hat{g}^{\hat{d}}, \hat{g}^{\hat{c}\hat{d}}, \hat{g}^{\hat{d}^2}, \hat{g}, T_0, T_1)$, it implicitly sets $g = \hat{g}^{\hat{e}}$, $h = \hat{g}^{\hat{d}}$, $a = \hat{a}$, $b = \hat{b}$, $c = \hat{c}$, and $d = \hat{d}$. After that, $\mathcal{S}$ sends θ to $\mathcal{A}$. At some point, the adversary $\mathcal{A}$ outputs a bit w, indicating $T_w = g^{ab}h^{cd}$. Since $T_w = g^{ab}h^{cd} = (\hat{g}^{\hat{e}})^{\hat{a}\hat{b}}(\hat{g}^{\hat{d}})^{\hat{c}\hat{d}} = \hat{g}^{\hat{a}\hat{b}\hat{e}+\hat{c}\hat{d}^2}$, the simulator $\mathcal{S}$ wins with the probability $\text{Adv}_{\mathcal{A}}^{VoDCBDH}(\lambda)$. Therefore, we have

$$\text{Adv}_{\mathcal{S}}^{Modified}(\lambda) \geq \Pr[\hat{g}^{\hat{d}} = 1] + \Pr[\hat{g}^{\hat{d}} \neq 1] \cdot \text{Adv}_{\mathcal{A}}^{VoDCBDH}(\lambda)$$
$$\geq \frac{1}{p} + \frac{p-1}{p}\text{Adv}_{\mathcal{A}}^{VoDCBDH}(\lambda) \geq \text{Adv}_{\mathcal{A}}^{VoDCBDH}(\lambda).$$

Lemma 2. *The lower bound of the complexity of the modified problem is stated as follows, querying the group operations and bilinear pairing operations at most q times.*

$$\text{Adv}_{\mathcal{S}}^{Modified}(\lambda) \leq \frac{3(q+9)^2}{p}.$$

Proof. The modified problem is an instance of Decisional Bilinear (P, f)-Diffie-Hellman problem family [27] where $P = (p_1, \ldots, p_7) = (1, d, cd, d^2, e, ae, be)$ and $f = abe + cd^2$. We show that f is not dependent on P by contradiction.

Assume f is dependent on P that by definition in [27] there exists 57 constants $a_{i,j}$, b_k, and c that

$$Q = cf^2 + \sum_{k=1}^{7} b_k p_k f + \sum_{i=1}^{7}\sum_{j=1}^{7} a_{i,j} p_i p_j = 0$$

where at least one of b_k or c is non-zero. We analyze the above equation in two cases.

1. $c \neq 0$: In this case, there is a term $f^2 = a^2b^2e^2 + 2abcd^2e + c^2d^4$ in Q. Furthermore, the term $a^2b^2e^2$ is not in any combination of $p_k f$ or $p_i p_j$, then f^2 cannot be canceled out. Hence, we have $Q \neq 0$ if $c \neq 0$.

2. $c = 0$: In this case, we have $Q = cf^2 + \sum_{k=1}^{7} b_k p_k f + \sum_{i=1}^{7} \sum_{j=1}^{7} a_{i,j} p_i p_j$ where at least one of b_k is non-zero. In other words, Q has at least a term $p_k f = p_k(abe + cd^2) = p_k abe + p_k cd^2$. As $Q = 0$, both two terms $p_k abe$ and $p_k cd^2$ should be canceled out. In the first step, we focus on the term $p_k abe$. There are two methods to cancel the term $p_k abe$.

(a) To cancel with $p_{k'} f = p_k abe + p_{k'} cd^2$ where $k \neq k'$, we have $p_k abe = p_{k'} cd^2$, that is, $p_k = \theta cd^2$ and $p_{k'} = \theta abe$ for some polynomial θ. Since no such pair of p_k and $p_{k'}$ in P, we cannot cancel $p_k abe$ via $p_{k'} f$.

(b) To cancel with $p_i p_j$, we have $p_k abe = p_i p_j$. By observing P, the only polynomial which has a is $p_6 = ae$. Thus we have $p_k abe = p_6 p_j \iff p_k b = p_j$. By observing P again, the only polynomial which has b is $p_7 = be$. Thus we have $p_k = e = p_5$.

Therefore, $p_k abe$ can be canceled out when $k = 5$. To further cancel out $p_5 f$, the term $p_5 cd^2 = cd^2 e$ has to be canceled out. As before, there are two methods to cancel the term $cd^2 e$.

(a) To cancel with $p_k f = p_k abe + p_k cd^2$ where $k \neq 5$, we have $p_k abe = cd^2 e$. Since the term $\frac{cd^2}{ab}$ is not in P, we cannot cancel out the term $cd^2 e$.

(b) To cancel with $p_i p_j$, we have $p_i p_j = cd^2 e$. By observing P, the only polynomial, which has c is $p_3 = cd$. Thus we have $p_i p_3 = cd^2 e \iff p_i = de$. Since the term de is not in P, we cannot cancel out the term $cd^2 e$.

Since it is impossible to cancel out any term $p_k f$, we have $Q \neq 0$ if $c = 0$.

To sum up, it is impossible to make $Q = 0$, which contradicts the assumption. Therefore, we have f is not dependent on P. By the theorem 1 in [27], we directly have the lemma.

By combining the Lemmas 1 and 2, we have

$$\mathrm{Adv}_{\mathcal{A}}^{\mathrm{VoDCBDH}}(\lambda) \leq \mathrm{Adv}_{\mathcal{S}}^{\mathrm{Modified}}(\lambda) \leq \frac{3(q+9)^2}{p}.$$

3.4 Extended Decisional Combined Bilinear Diffie-Hellman Problem

We propose an extension of variant of Decisional Combined Bilinear Diffie-Hellman Problem below.

Definition 7 Extended variant of Decisional Combined Bilinear Diffie-Hellman (EVoDCBDH) Assumption: Given $g, g^a, g^b, g^e, g^f, h^c, h^d, h^{1/d}, h^l \in \mathbb{G}$ where $a, b, c, d, e, f, l \in_R \mathbb{Z}_q$ and $h = g^e$, we define the advantage of the adversary in solving the EVoDCBDH problem as

$$\mathrm{Adv}_{\mathcal{A}}^{EVoDCBDH}(\lambda) = \Pr[w = \mathcal{A}(g, g^a, g^b, g^f, h^c, h^d, h^{1/d},$$
$$h^l, T_0, T_1, w \in_R \{0,1\}) : T_w = y^{ab+ecd}, T_{w-1} = g^{bf+edl}]$$

Theorem 3. *We say a EVoDCBDH assumption holds in group $\mathbb{G}$ if for any PPT $\mathcal{A}$, $\mathrm{Adv}_{\mathcal{A}}(\lambda)$ is a negligible function of the security parameter λ.*

Proof. Let $\mathcal{S}$ denote the VoDCBDH problem solver, who is given $(g^a, g^b, g^e, g^f, h^c, h^d, h^{1/d}, h^l)$, and aims to distinguish $T = g^{ab} \cdot h^{cd}$ from another value $g^{bf} \cdot h^{dl}$. $\mathcal{S}$ simulates the game for $\mathcal{A}$ as follows.

- Setup: $\mathcal{S}$ chooses $f, l \in_R \mathbb{Z}_q$ and computes g^f, h^l, then generates other public parameters using the given instances and sends them to $\mathcal{A}$. $\mathcal{S}$ also tosses a random coin w which will be used later in the game.
- Challenge stage: $\mathcal{S}$ returns the challenge T if $b = 0$; Otherwise, returns the value $g^{bf} \cdot h^{dl}$ to $\mathcal{A}$. Note that the value T comes from his own challenger. Finally, $\mathcal{A}$ outputs w' as its guess for w. If $w' = w$, then $\mathcal{S}$ outputs 1; Otherwise, $\mathcal{S}$ outputs 0.

  Probability analysis: Since the value T from its challenger can be either $g^{ab} \cdot h^{cd}$ or R, thus we have

$$\begin{aligned}
\mathrm{Adv}_{\mathcal{S}}^{VoDCBDH} &= \Pr[\mathcal{A} \to 1 \mid T = g^{ab} \cdot h^{cd}] - \Pr[\mathcal{A} \to 1 \mid T = R] \\
&= [\mathrm{Adv}_{\mathcal{A}}^{EVoDCBDH} + 1/2] - [\mathrm{Adv}_{\mathcal{S}}^{VoDCBDH} + 1/2] \\
&= \mathrm{Adv}_{\mathcal{A}}^{EVoDCBDH} - \mathrm{Adv}_{\mathcal{S}}^{VoDCBDH} \\
&\Rightarrow \mathrm{Adv}_{\mathcal{A}}^{EVoDCBDH} = 2 \cdot \mathrm{Adv}_{\mathcal{S}}^{VoDCBDH}.
\end{aligned}$$

3.5   Exponent Challenge Response Signature

We firstly review the Exponent Challenge-Response signature, which will be used in our k-ASH protocol.

Definition 8 *The Exponential Challenge-Response (XCR) signature scheme [20]: The signer possess a public/secret key pair (g^a, a) $(a \in \mathbb{Z}_q)$. A verifier provides a message m together with a challenge $g^{w'}$ $(w' \in \mathbb{Z}_q$ is chosen by verifier). The signature produced by signer using challenge $g^{w'}$ is defined as $(g^w, g^{w'(w+a \cdot H(g^w \| m))})$ $(w \in \mathbb{Z}_q$ is chosen by signer). Then the verifier accepts a signature pair (g^w, σ) as valid iff $g^w \neq 0$ and $\sigma = (g^w \cdot g^{a \cdot H(g^w \| m)})^{w'}$.*

3.6   Our k-ASH Protocol

Now we present our proposed unlinkable secret handshake with k-time authentication protocol in the two party setting (without loss of generality, we use user $\widehat{A}$ and user $\widehat{B}$ here). It works as follows:

- Setup: TA takes the security parameter λ and the number of handshakes k as input, outputs the master public key $mpk = (g, h, \{g^{t_i}\}_{i=1}^{i=k}, h^\alpha, h^{1/\alpha})$, and the master secret key $msk = (\{t_i\}_{i=1}^{i=k}, \alpha)$. TA also generates four hash functions $H_1 : \mathbb{G} \times \mathbb{G}_1 \to \mathbb{Z}_q, H_2 : \{0,1\}^* \to \mathbb{Z}_q, H_3 : \mathbb{G} \to \mathbb{Z}_q, H_4 : \mathbb{G} \to \mathbb{Z}_q$ and denotes the bilinear pairing $\hat{e} : \mathbb{G} \times \mathbb{G} \to \mathbb{G}_1$.
- KeyGen: User $\widehat{A}$ chooses $x_a \in \mathbb{Z}_q$ and computes g^{x_a} as his/her public key.

– Register: User $\widehat{A}$ submits his/her public key g^{x_a} to TA. TA then chooses $w_{a_i} \in \mathbb{Z}_q$ and computes $s_{a_i} = w_{a_i} + \alpha \cdot H_1(h^{w_{a_i}} || \hat{e}(g^{x_a}, h^\alpha)^{t_i})$ and returns a credential set $\{h^{w_{a_i}}\}_{i=1}^{i=k}, \{s_{a_i}\}_{i=1}^{i=k}$ to user $\widehat{A}$. While user $\widehat{A}$ can verify them using the following equations: $\{h^{s_{a_i}} \overset{?}{=} h^{w_{a_i}} \cdot h^{\alpha \cdot H_1(h^{w_{a_i}} || \hat{e}(h^\alpha, g^{t_i})^{x_a})}\}_{i=1}^{i=k}$.

– Handshake (Fig. 1):

- User $\widehat{A}$ chooses the ephemeral secret key $r_a \in_R \mathbb{Z}_q$, computes $R_a = h^{r_a'} = h^{H_2(r_a || x_a || s_{a_i})}$ and sends it to user $\widehat{B}$;
- User $\widehat{B}$ performs the following.

  * Choose the ephemeral secret key $r_b \in_R \mathbb{Z}_q$, computes $R_b = h^{r_b'} = h^{H_2(r_b || x_b || s_{b_i})}$;
  * Compute $C_{b_i} = \hat{e}(h^\alpha, g^{t_i})^{x_b}$;
  * Compute $\widehat{C_{b_i}} = g^{t_i \cdot x_b} \cdot h^{s_{b_i} \cdot e_b / \alpha}$, where $e_b = H_3(R_a^{r_b'})$;
  * Send $R_b, g^{t_i}, h^{w_{b_i}}, C_{b_i}, \widehat{C_{b_i}}, e_b$ to user $\widehat{A}$.

- User $\widehat{A}$ receives the incoming message from user $\widehat{B}$, then performs the following.

  * Verify $e_a = H_3(R_b^{r_a'}) \overset{?}{=} e_b$. If verification fails, reject the session; Otherwise, proceeds;
  * Verify $\hat{e}(\widehat{C_{b_i}}, h^\alpha) \overset{?}{=} C_{b_i} \cdot \hat{e}(h^{w_{b_i}} \cdot h^{\alpha \cdot e_{b_i}}, h^{e_a})$, where $e_{b_i} = H_1(h^{w_{b_i}} || C_{b_i})$. If verification fails, reject the session; Otherwise, proceed to the next step;
  * Compute the session key $K = H_4((h^{s_{b_i} \cdot e_b^*} \cdot R_b)^{s_a^*})$, where $e_b^* = H_3(R_b || e_{b_i}), s_a^* = s_{a_i} \cdot e_a^* + r_a', e_a^* = H_3(R_a || e_{a_i}), e_{a_i} = H_1(h^{w_{a_i}} || C_{a_i})$;
  * Send $g^{t_i}, h^{w_{a_i}}, C_{a_i}, \widehat{C_{a_i}}, e_a$ to user $\widehat{B}$. Note that the computation of $C_{a_i}, \widehat{C_{a_i}}$ by user $\widehat{A}$ follows the same procedures as above.

- User $\widehat{B}$ verifies the received message using the same method as user $\widehat{A}$, and computes the session key $K = H_4((h^{s_{a_i} \cdot e_a^*} \cdot R_a)^{s_b^*})$, where $e_a^* = H_3(R_a || e_{a_i}), s_b^* = s_{b_i} \cdot e_b^* + r_b', e_b^* = H_3(R_b || e_{b_i})$.

Note that the computation of session key used the XCR signature from [20].

– Tracing

If user $\widehat{A}$ used the same credential twice, e.g., $(\widehat{C_{a_i}}, e_{a_i})$ and $(\widehat{C'_{a_i}}, e'_{a_i})$, then anyone can compute $g^{t_i \cdot x_a} = [(g^{t_i \cdot x_a} \cdot h^{s_{a_i} \cdot e_{a_i}/\alpha})^{e'_{a_i}} / (g^{t_i \cdot x_a} \cdot h^{s_{a_i} \cdot e'_{a_i}/\alpha})^{e_{a_i}}]^{1/(e'_{a_i} - e_{a_i})}$, where $e_{a_i} = H_3(R^{r_a}), e'_{a_i} = H_3(R'^{r_a})$. That means if user $\widehat{A}$ reused a credential, then user $\widehat{A}$' identity can be revealed since $\hat{e}(g^{t_i \cdot x_a}, g) = \hat{e}(g^{t_i}, g^{x_a})$ for public key g^{x_a}.

4 Security Analysis

4.1 Session Key Security

Theorem 4. *The proposed k-ASH protocol achieves session key security (Definition 1) in the random oracle model if the VoCDH assumption is held in the underlying group $\mathbb{G}$.*

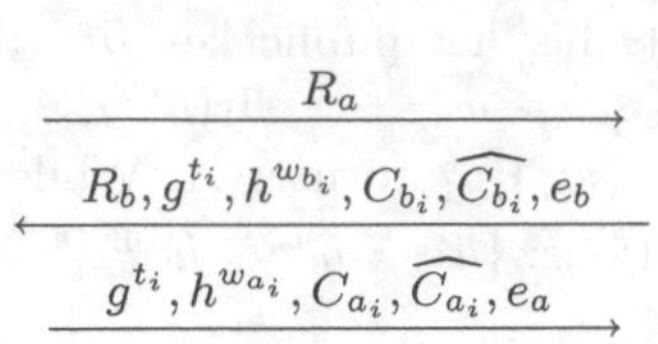

$$\widehat{A} \qquad\qquad\qquad\qquad \widehat{B}$$

$$\xrightarrow{\hspace{1cm} R_a \hspace{1cm}}$$

$$\xleftarrow{\hspace{0.3cm} R_b, g^{t_i}, h^{w_{b_i}}, C_{b_i}, \widehat{C_{b_i}}, e_b \hspace{0.3cm}}$$

$$\xrightarrow{\hspace{0.3cm} g^{t_i}, h^{w_{a_i}}, C_{a_i}, \widehat{C_{a_i}}, e_a \hspace{0.3cm}}$$

Fig. 1. Handshake

Proof. We define a sequence of games G_i, $i = 0, \cdots, 3$ and let $\mathtt{Adv}_i^{k-ASH}$ denote the advantage of the adversary in game G_i. Assume that $\mathcal{A}$ activates at most m (perhaps $m \geq k$) sessions in each game.

- G_0 This is original game for session key security.
- G_1 This game is identical to game G_0 except that $\mathcal{S}$ will output a random bit if the nonce R_i is used twice by two different instance oracles. Therefore, we have:

$$\left| \mathtt{Adv}_0^{k-ASH} - \mathtt{Adv}_1^{k-ASH} \right| \leq m^2/2^\lambda \tag{3}$$

- G_2 This game is identical to game G_1 except that $\mathcal{S}$ will output a random bit if **Forge** event happens where $\mathcal{A}$ made a send query in the form of $(h^{r_0}, g^{t_i}, h^{w_0}, \hat{\mathtt{e}}(h^\alpha, g^{t_i})^{x_i}, g^{t_i \cdot x_i} \cdot h^{s_0 \cdot \mathtt{H}_3(R^{*r_0})/\alpha}, \mathtt{H}_3(R^{*\cdot r_0}))$ and an $\mathtt{H}_4$ query with a valid forgery $\sigma = R^{*s_0^*} = R^{*[s_0 \cdot \mathtt{H}_3(h^{r_0}||\mathtt{H}_1(h^{w_0}||\hat{\mathtt{e}}(h^\alpha, g^{t_i})^{x_i})) + r_0]}$ for challenge R^*, such that user i is not corrupted (i.e., no **Long term secret key reveal** query to user i or **Master secret key reveal** query to TA) when the hash query is made. Then we have:

$$\left| \mathtt{Adv}_1^{k-ASH} - \mathtt{Adv}_2^{k-ASH} \right| \leq \Pr[\textbf{Forge}] \tag{4}$$

Lemma 3. *The **Forge** event happens only with a negligible probability when the VoCDH assumption is held in $\mathbb{G}$.*

Let $\mathcal{S}$ denote the VoCDH problem solver, who is given $h^a, h^{1/a}, h^b$, and aims to compute h^{ab}. $\mathcal{S}$ simulates the game for $\mathcal{A}$ as follows:

- Setup stage: $\mathcal{F}$ sets up the game for $\mathcal{A}$ by creating n users (set $\mathcal{U}$) with the corresponding public/secret key pairs $\{X_i, x_i\}_{i=1}^n$. $\mathcal{F}$ randomly selects an index i and guesses that the **Forge** event will happen with regard to user i and session i. $\mathcal{S}$ then sets the mpk as $h^\alpha = h^a, h^{1/\alpha} = h^{1/a}$ and generates other public parameters honestly. In addition, $\mathcal{S}$ sets the challenge as $R^* = h^b$ in the guessed session i, $\mathcal{S}$ simulates the game for $\mathcal{A}$ as follows.
- $\mathcal{S}$ answers $\mathcal{A}$'s queries as follows:
  * If $\mathcal{A}$ issues establish query in the form of (U', X'), such that $U' \notin \mathcal{U}$, then user U' with public key X' will be added to the system.
  * If $\mathcal{A}$ issues a send query in the form of $(h^{r'}, g^{t_i}, h^{w'}, \hat{\mathtt{e}}(h^a, g^{t_i})^{x'}, g^{t_i \cdot x'} \cdot h^{(s' \cdot e')/a})$ to user i, then $\mathcal{S}$ verifies it successfully (notice that $\mathcal{A}$ may corrupt a user with secret key x' and secret signature pair $(h^{w'}, s')$), and next to generating the signatures (h^{w_i}, s_i) as follows:

1. Chooses $s_i, e_i \in_R \mathbb{Z}_q$;
2. Sets $h^{w_i} = h^{s_i}/h^{a \cdot e_i}$;
3. Sets $H_1(h^{w_i}||C_i) = e_i$, where $C_i = \hat{e}(h^a, g^{t_i})^{x_i}$.

Then, S chooses $r'_i \in \mathbb{Z}_q$ and computes $e = H_3(h^{r' \cdot r_i})$. Eventually, S generates the message $(h^{r_i}, g^{t_i}, h^{w_i}, C_i, g^{t_i \cdot x_i} \cdot h^{(s_i \cdot e)/a}, e)$ and sends it to A.

* If A issues an ephemeral secret key reveal query to instance oracle $\Pi^i_{U_i}$, then S returns the ephemeral value r_i $(r'_i = H_2(r_i||x_i||s_i))$ to A.

* If A issues a long term secret key reveal query to user j $(\neq i)$, then S returns x_j and secret signatures $\{s_j\}^k_{j=1}$ to A. Note that S can simulate secret signatures (h^{w_j}, s_j) of user j $(\neq i)$ using the same method that described above. If A issues a long term secret key reveal key query to user i or a master secret key reveal key query to TA, then abort.

* Session key reveal query and Test query: S answers the session key reveal query and the test query by using the session key it has derived during the protocol simulation described above.

- When **Forge** event occurs (i.e., A outputs: $h^{r_0}, g^{t_i}, h^{w_0}, \hat{e}(h^a, g^{t_i})^{x_i}$, $g^{t_i \cdot x_i} \cdot h^{(s_0 \cdot H_3(h^{b \cdot r_0}))/a}, H_3(h^{b \cdot r_0}))$, S checks whether:

1. The **Forge** event with respect to user i on challenge h^b;
2. Verifies:

$$\hat{e}(g^{t_i \cdot x_i} \cdot h^{(s_0 \cdot H_3(h^{b \cdot r_0}))/a}, h^a) \overset{?}{=} \hat{e}(h^a, g^{t_i})^{x_i} \cdot \hat{e}(h^{s_0}, h^{e^*})$$

Note that $h^{s_0} = h^{w_0} \cdot h^{a \cdot e_1}$, $s_0 = w_0 + a \cdot e_1$, $e_1 = H_1(h^{w_0}||\hat{e}(h^a, g^{t_i})^{x_i})$, $e^* = H_3(h^{b \cdot r_0})$.

3. Verifies:

$$\hat{e}(D, h) = \hat{e}((h^{s_i \cdot H_3(h^b||e_i)} \cdot h^b)^{s_0 \cdot H_3(h^{r_0}||e_1)+r_0}, h)$$
$$\overset{?}{=} \hat{e}(h^{s_i \cdot H_3(h^b||e_i)} \cdot h^b, h^{s_0 \cdot e_0} \cdot h^{r_0})$$

Note that the value D is used to compute session key $K(= H_4(D))$, $e_0 = H_3(h^{r_0}||e_1)$.

If all the above conditions hold, S confirms it as a successful forgery from H_4 and proceeds:

$$\sigma_1 = \frac{D}{(h^{s_0 \cdot e_0} \cdot h^{r_0})^{s_i \cdot H_3(h^b||e_i)}}$$
$$= (h^b)^{s_0 \cdot e_0 + r_0} = h^{b[(w_0 + a \cdot e_1)e_0 + r_0]}$$

According to the forking lemma [4], by rewinding the adversary twice, S would obtain four forgeries from H_4, which will be listed below.

$$\sigma_1 = h^{b[(w_0 + a \cdot e_1)e_0 + r_0]}, e_0 = H_3(h^{r_0}||e_1);$$
$$\sigma_2 = h^{b[(w_0 + a \cdot e_1)e'_0 + r_0]}, e'_0 = H_3(h^{r_0}||e_1);$$
$$\sigma_3 = h^{b[(w_0 + a \cdot e'_1)\widehat{e_0} + r'_0]}, \widehat{e_0} = H_3(h^{r'_0}||e'_1);$$
$$\sigma_4 = h^{b[(w_0 + a \cdot e'_1)\widehat{e'_0} + r'_0]}, \widehat{e'_0} = H_3(h^{r'_0}||e'_1);$$

Therefore, $\mathcal{S}$ can perform the computation below to obtain a solution to VoCDH.

$$D_1 = (\frac{\sigma_1}{\sigma_2})^{1/(e_0-e_0')} = h^{b \cdot w_0} \cdot h^{ab \cdot e_1}$$

$$D_2 = (\frac{\sigma_3}{\sigma_4})^{1/(\widehat{e}_0-\widehat{e_0'})} = h^{b \cdot w_0} \cdot h^{ab \cdot e_1'}$$

$$h^{ab} = (\frac{D_1}{D_2})^{1/(e_1-e_1')}.$$

The simulation performed by $\mathcal{S}$ is perfect. Since at most n users and m sessions in the game, we have:

$$\Pr[\mathbf{Forge}] \leq n \cdot m \cdot \mathsf{Adv}_{\mathcal{S}}^{VoCDH}(\lambda) \tag{5}$$

– G_3: This game is identical to game G_2 except that in the test session, we replace the session key $K = \mathsf{H}_4(h^{s_i^* \cdot s_j^*})$ by a random value $r \in \mathbb{Z}_q$. Since we model H_4 as a random oracle, if the event **Forge** does not happen, then we have

$$\mathsf{Adv}_2^{k-ASH} = \mathsf{Adv}_3^{k-ASH} \tag{6}$$

It is easy to see that in game G_3, $\mathcal{A}$ has no advantage, i.e.,

$$\mathsf{Adv}_3^{k-ASH} = 0 \tag{7}$$

Combining the above results together, we have

$$\mathsf{Adv}_{\mathcal{A}}^{k-ASH}(\lambda) \leq m^2/2^{\lambda} + n \cdot m \cdot \mathsf{Adv}_{\mathcal{A}}^{VoCDH}(\lambda)$$

4.2   Anonymity

Theorem 5. *The proposed k-ASH protocol achieves* anonymity (Definition 2) *in the random oracle model if the EVoDCBDH Assumption is held in the underlying group* $\mathbb{G}$.

Proof. Let $\mathcal{S}$ denote a EVoDCBDH problem distinguisher, who is given $(g, h, g^a, g^b, g^f, h^c, h^d, \mathsf{H}^{1/d}, h^l)$, and aims to distinguish $g^{ab} \cdot h^{cd}$ and $g^{bf} \cdot h^{dl}$. $\mathcal{S}$ simulates the game for $\mathcal{A}$ as follows.

– Setup: $\mathcal{S}$ sets up the game for $\mathcal{A}$ by creating n users. $\mathcal{S}$ sets $h^{\alpha} = h^{1/d}, h^{1/\alpha} = h^d$ (the $msk = (\alpha, 1/\alpha)$ are implicitly set as $(1/d, d)$ respectively), and randomly selects one tag base $g^{t^*} = g^b$ and generates other tag bases honestly (i.e., g^{t_i}, $t_i \in \mathbb{Z}_q$ is chosen by $\mathcal{S}$). In addition, $\mathcal{S}$ randomly chooses users i, j from user set $\mathcal{U}$ and sets $g^{x_i} = g^a, g^{x_j} = g^f$ (the secret keys (x_i, x_j) are implicitly set as (a, f) respectively), and generates public/secret key pair for other users honestly.
– If $\mathcal{A}$ issues a send query in the form of $(R', g^{t_i}, h^{w'}, C_{b'}, \widehat{C_{b'}})$ to user i, then $\mathcal{S}$ performs the simulation as follows.

- S simulates the signature pair (h^{w_i}, s_i) using the same method that described in Lemma 3;
- S computes $\widehat{C_i} = g^{a \cdot t_i} \cdot h^{d \cdot s_i \cdot e_i'}$, and $C_i = \hat{e}(h^{1/d}, g^a)^{t_i}$, where $e_i' = \mathtt{H}_3(R'^{r_i})$, $r_i \in \mathbb{Z}_q$;
- S generates $R_i = h^{r_i}$ and sets $e_i = \mathtt{H}_1(h^{w_i} \| C_i)$;
- S returns $(R_i, g^{t_i}, h^{w_i}, C_i, \widehat{C_i}, e_i')$ to user A as the response. Note that S can simulate the response of user j using the same method as above.

- It is easy to see that all queries to other users can be simulated perfectly using the user secret keys, and S can simulate secret credentials using the same method as described in Lemma 3.
- Challenge: If A issues a send query in the form of $(R, g^{t_i}, h^{w'}, C_i', \widehat{C_i'})$ to user i, then S computes $\widehat{C_i} = (g^{ba} \cdot h^{dc})^{e^*}$ and $C_i = \hat{e}(\widehat{C_i}, h^{1/d})/\hat{e}(h^c, h^{e^*})$, where $e^* = \mathtt{H}_3(R^{r^*})$. Eventually, S returns $(R^*, g^b, h^{w_i}, C_i, \widehat{C_i}, e^*)$ to A as the response. Similarly, if A issues a send query to user j, then S computes $\widehat{C_j} = (g^{bf} \cdot h^{dl})^{e^*}$ and $C_j = \hat{e}(\widehat{C_j}, h^{1/d})/\hat{e}(h^l, h^{e^*})$, where $e^* = \mathtt{H}_3(R^{r^*})$. Eventually, S returns $(R^*, g^b, h^{w_j}, C_j, \widehat{C_j}, e^*)$ to A as the response. Note that S can perfectly simulate the value $h^{w_i} = h^c/h^{e_i/d}$, and sets $e_i = \mathtt{H}_1(h^{w_i} \| C_i)$ for user i, S also can simulate the value h^{w_j} of user j using the same method.

Finally, S outputs whatever A outputs. If A guesses the random bit correctly, then S can break the EVoDCBDH problem. Hence, we have

$$\mathsf{Adv}_A^{k-ASH} \leq \mathsf{Adv}_S^{EVoDCBDH}(\lambda) \tag{8}$$

5 Extension

We can extend the above k-time ASH protocol in the two party setting to the multiple party setting using the classic BD broadcasting protocol [10]. The Setup, KeyGen, Register and Tracing algorithms are same as the two party setting, except the Handshake algorithm, which will be described below. Note that we suppose at most n users in the multiple party setting.

- **Round 1:** User i computes $R_i = h^{r_i'} = h^{\mathtt{H}_2(r_i \| x_i \| s_i)}, r_i \in_R \mathbb{Z}_q$ and **broadcasts** $(R_i, g^{t_i}, h^{w_i}, C_i)$. Note that x_i, s_i denote the secret key and the secret credential value of user i, and $C_i = \hat{e}(h^\alpha, g^{t_i})^{x_i}$. Also notice that the indices are taken module n so that user 0 is user n and user $i{+}1$ is user 1.
- **Round 2:** After receiving $n{-}1$ messages in Round 1, then user i computes $\{\widehat{C_j} = g^{t_i \cdot x_i} \cdot h^{s_i \cdot e_j/\alpha}, e_j = \mathtt{H}_3(R_j^{r_i'})\}_{j=1, j \neq i}^{n-1}$ and $\{h^{s_j} = h^{w_j} \cdot h^{\alpha \cdot \mathtt{H}_1(h^{w_j} \| C_j)}\}_{j=1, j \neq i}^{n-1}$. Eventually, user i computes the intermediate key $K_i = \dfrac{\mathtt{H}_4(h^{s_{i+1}^* \cdot s_i^*})}{\mathtt{H}_4(h^{s_{i-1}^* \cdot s_i^*})}$ and **broadcasts** $(K_i, \{\widehat{C_j}, e_j\}_{j=1, j \neq i}^{n-1})$.
  Note that $s_i^* = s_i \cdot e^* + r_i', e^* = \mathtt{H}_3(R_i \| \mathtt{H}_1(h^{w_i} \| C_i))$,
  $h^{s_{i+1}^*} = (h^{w_{i+1}} \cdot h^{\alpha \cdot \mathtt{H}_1(h^{w_{i+1}} \| C_{i+1})})^{e_{i+1}^*} \cdot R_{i+1}, e_{i+1}^* = \mathtt{H}_3(R_{i+1} \| \mathtt{H}_1(h^{w_{i+1}} \| C_{i+1})),$
  $h^{s_{i-1}^*} = (h^{w_{i-1}} \cdot h^{\alpha \cdot \mathtt{H}_1(h^{w_{i-1}} \| C_{i-1})})^{e_{i-1}^*} \cdot R_{i-1}, e_{i-1}^* = \mathtt{H}_3(R_{i-1} \| \mathtt{H}_1(h^{w_{i-1}} \| C_{i-1})).$

- **Key Derivation:** User i verifies the received messages $\{\widehat{C_j}\}_{j \neq i}$ from $n-1$ users (it supports batch verification, see below), if either of them fail, then abort; Otherwise, computes the final session key $sk_i = H_4(h^{s^*_{i-1} \cdot s^*_i})^n \oplus K_i^{n-1} \oplus K_{i+1}^{n-2} \cdots \oplus K_{i-2})$.

1. Batch Verification. User i is able to batch verify the received n-1 messages from n-1 users using the small exponents test in [3,13].

$$\hat{e}(\prod_{j=1}^{n-1} \widehat{C_j}^{\delta_j}, h^\alpha) = \hat{e}(\prod_{j=1}^{n-1} g^{t_i \cdot x_j \cdot \delta_j} \cdot h^{s_j \cdot e_j \cdot \delta_j / \alpha}, h^\alpha)$$

$$= \prod_{j=1}^{n-1} \hat{e}(g^{t_i \cdot x_j \cdot \delta_j}, h^\alpha) \cdot \hat{e}(\prod_{j=1}^{n-1} h^{s_j \cdot e_j \cdot \delta_j}, h)$$

$$\stackrel{?}{=} \prod_{j=1}^{n-1} C_j^{\delta_j} \cdot \hat{e}(\prod_{j=1}^{n-1} h^{s_j \cdot \delta_j}, h^{e_j}).$$

where $\delta_j \in \mathbb{Z}_q, e_j = H_3(R_j^{r'_i})$ and $j \in [1, j \neq i, \cdots, n-1]$. If batch verification fail, then abort; Otherwise, proceeds.

2. Correctness Check.

$$sk_i = H_4(h^{s^*_{i-1} \cdot s^*_i})^n \oplus K_i^{n-1} \oplus K_{i+1}^{n-2} \cdots \oplus K_{i-2}$$

$$= H_4(h^{s^*_{i-1} \cdot s^*_i})^n \oplus \frac{H_4(h^{s^*_{i+1} \cdot s^*_i})^{n-1}}{H_4(h^{s^*_{i-1} \cdot s^*_i})^{n-1}}$$

$$\oplus \frac{H_4(h^{s^*_{i+2} \cdot s^*_{i+1}})^{n-2}}{H_4(h^{s^*_i \cdot s^*_{i+1}})^{n-2}} \cdots \oplus \frac{H_4(h^{s^*_{i-1} \cdot s^*_{i-2}})}{H_4((h^{s^*_{i-3} \cdot s^*_{i-2}})}$$

$$= H_4(h^{s^*_{i-1} \cdot s^*_i}) \oplus H_4((h^{s^*_i \cdot s^*_{i+1}}) \cdots \oplus H_4((h^{s^*_{i-2} \oplus s^*_{i-1}}).$$

It is easy to see that all users compute the same key.

The k-time ASH protocol in the multiple party setting also achieved session key security, anonymity and public traceability. In particular, the security analysis (including session key security and anonymity) in the two party setting can be extended to the multiple party setting.

6 Conclusion

In this paper, we proposed a k-time authenticated secret handshake protocol based on the k-time tag bases and anonymized Schnorr signature. We also defined the formal security models for session key security and (full) anonymity, and proved the security of the proposed k-ASK protocol under our proposed complexity assumptions which have been proved hard in the generic bilinear group model.

Acknowledgements. This work is supported by the National Natural Science Foundation of China (61602396, 61572303), the Fundamental Research Funds for the Central Universities under Grant GK201702004.

References

1. Balfanz, D., Durfee, G., Shankar, N., Smetters, D.K., Staddon, J., Wong, J.: Secret handshakes from pairing-based key agreements. In: 2003 IEEE Symposium on Security and Privacy (S&P 2003), 11–14, Berkeley, CA, USA, pp. 180–196, May 2003
2. Bellare, M., Canetti, R., Krawczyk, H.: A modular approach to the design and analysis of authentication and key exchange protocols (extended abstract). In: Proceedings of the Thirtieth Annual ACM Symposium on the Theory of Computing, pp. 419–428 (1998)
3. Bellare, M., Garay, J.A., Rabin, T.: Fast batch verification for modular exponentiation and digital signatures. In: Nyberg, K. (ed.) EUROCRYPT 1998. LNCS, vol. 1403, pp. 236–250. Springer, Heidelberg (1998). doi:10.1007/BFb0054130
4. Bellare, M., Neven, G.: Multi-signatures in the plain public-key model and a general forking lemma. In: ACM, CCS 2006, pp. 390–399 (2006)
5. Park, S.B., Kang, M.S., Lee, S.J.: Authenticated key exchange protocol secure against offline dictionary attack and server compromise. In: Li, M., Sun, X.-H., Deng, Q., Ni, J. (eds.) GCC 2003. LNCS, vol. 3032, pp. 924–931. Springer, Heidelberg (2004). doi:10.1007/978-3-540-24679-4_154
6. Bellare, M., Rogaway, P.: Entity authentication and key distribution. In: Stinson, D.R. (ed.) CRYPTO 1993. LNCS, vol. 773, pp. 232–249. Springer, Heidelberg (1994). doi:10.1007/3-540-48329-2_21
7. Bellare, M., Rogaway, P.: Provably secure session key distribution: the three party case. In: Proceedings of the Twenty-Seventh Annual ACM Symposium on Theory of Computing, pp. 57–66 (1995)
8. Bohli, J., Vasco, M.I.G., Steinwandt, R.: Secure group key establishment revisited. Int. J. Inf. Sec. 6(4), 243–254 (2007)
9. Boneh, D., Boyen, X., Goh, E.-J.: Hierarchical identity based encryption with constant size ciphertext. In: Cramer, R. (ed.) EUROCRYPT 2005. LNCS, vol. 3494, pp. 440–456. Springer, Heidelberg (2005). doi:10.1007/11426639_26
10. Burmester, M., Desmedt, Y.G.: Efficient and secure conference-key distribution. In: Lomas, M. (ed.) Security Protocols 1996. LNCS, vol. 1189, pp. 119–129. Springer, Heidelberg (1997). doi:10.1007/3-540-62494-5_12
11. Canetti, R., Krawczyk, H.: Analysis of key-exchange protocols and their use for building secure channels. In: Pfitzmann, B. (ed.) EUROCRYPT 2001. LNCS, vol. 2045, pp. 453–474. Springer, Heidelberg (2001). doi:10.1007/3-540-44987-6_28
12. Castelluccia, C., Jarecki, S., Tsudik, G.: Secret handshakes from CA-oblivious encryption. In: Lee, P.J. (ed.) ASIACRYPT 2004. LNCS, vol. 3329, pp. 293–307. Springer, Heidelberg (2004). doi:10.1007/978-3-540-30539-2_21
13. Ferrara, A.L., Green, M., Hohenberger, S., Pedersen, M.Ø.: Practical short signature batch verification. In: Fischlin, M. (ed.) CT-RSA 2009. LNCS, vol. 5473, pp. 309–324. Springer, Heidelberg (2009). doi:10.1007/978-3-642-00862-7_21
14. Gu, J., Xue, Z.: An improved efficient secret handshakes scheme with unlinkability. IEEE Commun. Lett. 15(2), 259–261 (2011)
15. Huang, H., Cao, Z.: A novel and efficient unlinkable secret handshakes scheme. IEEE Commun. Lett. 13(5), 363–365 (2009)
16. Jarecki, S., Kim, J., Tsudik, G.: Group secret handshakes or affiliation-hiding authenticated group key agreement. In: Abe, M. (ed.) CT-RSA 2007. LNCS, vol. 4377, pp. 287–308. Springer, Heidelberg (2006). doi:10.1007/11967668_19

17. Juels, A., Weis, S.A.: Defining strong privacy for RFID. ACM Trans. Inf. Syst. Secur. **13**(1), 7 (2009)

18. Katz, J., Shin, J.S.: Modeling insider attacks on group key-exchange protocols. In: ACM, CCS 2005, pp. 180–189 (2005)

19. Katz, J., Yung, M.: Scalable protocols for authenticated group key exchange. In: Boneh, D. (ed.) CRYPTO 2003. LNCS, vol. 2729, pp. 110–125. Springer, Heidelberg (2003). doi:10.1007/978-3-540-45146-4_7

20. Krawczyk, H.: HMQV: a high-performance secure Diffie-Hellman protocol. In: Shoup, V. (ed.) CRYPTO 2005. LNCS, vol. 3621, pp. 546–566. Springer, Heidelberg (2005). doi:10.1007/11535218_33

21. LaMacchia, B., Lauter, K., Mityagin, A.: Stronger security of authenticated key exchange. In: Susilo, W., Liu, J.K., Mu, Y. (eds.) ProvSec 2007. LNCS, vol. 4784, pp. 1–16. Springer, Heidelberg (2007). doi:10.1007/978-3-540-75670-5_1

22. Schnorr, C.P.: Efficient identification and signatures for smart cards. In: Brassard, G. (ed.) CRYPTO 1989. LNCS, vol. 435, pp. 239–252. Springer, New York (1990). doi:10.1007/0-387-34805-0_22

23. Shoup, V.: Lower bounds for discrete logarithms and related problems. In: Fumy, W. (ed.) EUROCRYPT 1997. LNCS, vol. 1233, pp. 256–266. Springer, Heidelberg (1997). doi:10.1007/3-540-69053-0_18

24. Sun, D., Cao, Z.: On the privacy of Khan et al.'s dynamic id-based remote authentication scheme with user anonymity. Cryptologia **37**(4), 345–355 (2013)

25. Teranishi, I., Furukawa, J., Sako, K.: k-times anonymous authentication (extended abstract). In: Lee, P.J. (ed.) ASIACRYPT 2004. LNCS, vol. 3329, pp. 308–322. Springer, Heidelberg (2004). doi:10.1007/978-3-540-30539-2_22

26. Xu, S., Yung, M.: k-anonymous secret handshakes with reusable credentials. In: ACM, CCS 2004, pp. 158–167 (2004)

27. Zhang, S., Yang, G., Mu, Y.: Linear encryption with keyword search. In: Liu, J.K., Steinfeld, R. (eds.) ACISP 2016. LNCS, vol. 9723, pp. 187–203. Springer, Cham (2016). doi:10.1007/978-3-319-40367-0_12

Exploring Effect of Location Number on Map-Based Graphical Password Authentication

Weizhi Meng[1](✉), Wang Hao Lee[2], Man Ho Au[3], and Zhe Liu[4]

[1] Department of Applied Mathematics and Computer Science,
Technical University of Denmark, Copenhagen, Denmark
weme@dtu.dk
[2] Infocomm Security Department,
Institute for Infocomm Research, Singapore, Singapore
whlee@i2r.a-star.edu.sg
[3] Department of Computing, The Hong Kong Polytechnic University,
Kowloon, Hong Kong
[4] Interdisciplinary Centre for Security, Reliability and Trust,
University of Luxembourg, Luxembourg, Luxembourg

Abstract. Graphical passwords (GPs) that authenticate users using images are considered as one potential alternative to overcome the issues of traditional textual passwords. Based on the idea of utilizing an extremely large image, map-based GPs like PassMap and GeoPass have been developed, where users can select their secrets (geographical points) on a world map. In particular, PassMap allows users to select two locations on a map, while GeoPass reduces the number of locations to only one. At first glance, selecting one location is more vulnerable to attacks, while increasing the location number may add burden on users. In the literature, there is no research exploring this issue. Motivated by this, our purpose in this work is to explore the effect of location number (the number of geographical points) and compare two schemes of PassMap and GeoPass in terms of users' performance and feedback. In this work, we develop a generic and open platform for realizing map-based schemes, and conduct a user study with 60 participants. The study reveals that selecting two locations would not degrade the scheme performance. Our effort aims to complement exiting research studies in this area.

Keywords: User authentication · Graphical passwords · Map-based password authentication · Geographical location · Security and usability

1 Introduction

Over the past few decades, textual passwords are the most widely adopted method for user authentication, in which users have to recall and input the correct textual strings for authentication [32]. However, it has long been recognized

---

W. Meng is previously known as Yuxin Meng.

© Springer International Publishing AG 2017
J. Pieprzyk and S. Suriadi (Eds.): ACISP 2017, Part II, LNCS 10343, pp. 301–313, 2017.
DOI: 10.1007/978-3-319-59870-3_17

that traditional textual passwords have many serious issues associated with their security and usability [11,33]. For example, users are not good at remembering their passwords for a long time, especially complex and random passwords. As a result, they are very likely to choose simple strings or recycle passwords. The recent study showed that this situation might be even worse than previously believed (i.e., little variation in guessing difficulty) [1].

To improve memorability and security, graphical passwords (GPs) have been developed as a potential alternative to textual passwords. It is known that people generally have better memory and recognition for images than textual strings [22, 24]. Based on this observation, various graphical password schemes have been proposed. For example, Wiedenbeck *et al.* [31] designed PassPoints, a system that allows users to click several places on an image as their passwords. Chiasson *et al.* [2] then proposed a click-based GP scheme, named Cued Click Points (CCP), which allows users to click on one point for a sequence of images, and the next image displayed is based on the previous click-point.

To enhance password space, map-based graphical password authentication has recently attracted more attention like PassMap [28] and GeoPass [30], based on the idea of using an extremely large image. More specifically, PassMap allows users to select two sequenced locations on a large world map, whereas GeoPass reduces the number of locations to only one (while users can only choose a location at zoom level 16). The use of a map-image is believed to provide much more memorable points for users.

Motivations. We advocate that map-based GPs can be deployed as a second-factor authentication method, which improves users' memorability while requiring more login time. Intuitively, selecting one geographical location is more vulnerable to shoulder surfing attacks, but increasing the number of locations may add unexpected burden on users. With the development of graphical passwords, a large amount of map-based schemes have been proposed. However, there is no study aiming to explore the effect of location number on scheme performance. In this work, our purpose is thus to investigate this issue in terms of users' performance and feedback.

Our work aims to complement existing research results in this area and benefit the future design for map-based GPs. As PassMap and GeoPass are two typical schemes in the literature, we choose them in our user study. The contributions of this work can be summarized as follows.

- We develop an open and generic platform for implementing map-based GP schemes, which can realize both PassMap (i.e., selecting two locations) and GeoPass (i.e., selecting one location). This platform provides a unified environment for usability comparison. According to the observations from both schemes, a click-point is set to be valid at zoom level 16. More details can be referred to Sect. 3.
- We conduct a user study with 60 participants to compare the scheme performance between PassMap and GeoPass, in terms of users' performance and feedback. It is found that users could perform similarly for these two schemes.

Our results reveal that increasing the number of locations from one to two would not degrade the performance of users' memorability.

The remaining parts of this paper are organized as follows. In Sect. 2, we review related studies in relation to the classification of graphical passwords and map-based graphical passwords. Section 3 describes our platform implementation, presents a user study with 60 participants, and analyzes the results in terms of users' performance and feedback. We make a further discussion about security and usability in Sect. 4 and conclude our work in Sect. 5.

2   Related Work

This section introduces a typical classification of graphical password schemes (e.g., recognition-based, pure recall-based and cued recall-based scheme) and details the evolution of map-based GP schemes.

2.1   GP Classification

Typically, graphical password systems can be classified into three categories [3, 27]: recognition-based scheme (i.e., recognizing images), pure recall-based scheme (i.e., reproducing a drawing without a hint) and cued recall-based scheme (i.e., reproducing a drawing with hints).

- **Recognition-based GPs.** Such schemes demand users to select one or more images from an image pool for authentication. For example, *PassFaces* [23] requires users to recognize a set of human faces for authentication. *Story* [5] requires users to recognize a set of sequenced images (e.g., people, food) from a large image pool.
- **Pure recall-based GPs.** These GP schemes usually ask users to draw something on an image as their passwords. *DAS* [12] is one typical pure recall scheme, which requires users to draw on a grid. In addition, *Pass-Go* [29] allows users to select intersections on a grid as a way to input a password. Based on this idea, unlock patterns have been developed as a tuned version of *Pass-Go* on Android phones, which requires users to unlock their phones by inputting correct patterns.[1] More analyses and similar schemes can be referred to [7,13,19,20].
- **Cued recall-based GPs.** This kind of GP scheme demands users to click on a sequence of points on one or multiple background images to construct their secrets. *PassPoints* [31] is an example, which requires users to recall a sequence of five selected points on a single background image. Another variant is developed by Chiasson *et al.* [4], called Persuasive Cued Click-Points (PCCP), which requires users to select a point on each of a sequence of background images.

---

[1] https://www.berkeleychurchill.com/software/android-pwgen/pwgen.php.

The existing GP schemes are mostly based on the actions of choice, click and draw, so that some combined schemes have also been developed. For example, Meng [14] proposed a click-draw based graphical password scheme (*CD-GPS*) aiming to improve the image-based authentication in the aspects of both security and usability, through combining the above three actions. More specifically, their scheme contains two operational steps: image selection and secret drawing. That is, users first choose an ordered sequence of images and then select some of them to click-draw their secrets. More analyses and studies on *CD-GPS* and generic graphical passwords can be referred to [6,10,15–17,21]

2.2   Map-Based Graphical Passwords

The initial idea of using digital map in graphical password first appeared in [8], but not much details were given. Spitzer *et al.* [25] then proposed an implementation of *CCP* that combined the graphical approach with user's navigating familiarity through Google maps. In their settings, users were presented with an image of the United States and could simply click some defined key destination through identifying zooming levels.

In 2012, Georgakakis *et al.* [9] proposed *NAVI*, in which the credentials of a user are his/her username and a password formulated by drawing a route on a pre-defined map image. They provided an analysis about the password strength, but did not give any user study. Later, Sun *et al.* [28] proposed a map-based GP authentication system called *PassMap*, in which a password consists of a sequence of two locations on a world map. They performed a user study and showed that participants could be easy to remember *PassMap* passwords in practice. Similar to *PassMap*, Thorpe *et al.* [30] developed *GeoPass*, where a user chooses only one location as the secret. They reported that up to 97% participants were able to remember their selected locations over a span of 8–9 days and most without any failed login attempts. It is worth noting that *PassMap* and *GeoPass* are very similar schemes in that secrets are constructed by clicking one or two places on a world map (e.g., Google map). Meng [18] then designed *RouteMap*, which allows users to draw a route on a map as their passwords. Shin et al. [26] further implemented a modified version of *GeoPass* on a mobile device. These studies prove that users can have a better memorability with map-based graphical password schemes.

Generally, *PassMap* and *GeoPass* have been discussed more often than other map-based GPs. One big difference between them is the number of locations, where *PassMap* requires users to select two locations while *GeoPass* only needs to choose one location. Intuitively, selecting one location is vulnerable to shoulder surfing attacks, while selecting two locations may add burden on users' memory. In the literature, Meng [18] previously compared the multiple password memory between *PassMap* and *GeoPass*. However, there is no study to explore the effect of the number of locations on scheme performance, which can benefit the future design of map-based GPs.

3   Implementation and User Study

3.1   Platform and Scheme Implementation

As most map-based GP research did not release their source, we developed a Python-based generic platform to realize map-based schemes. The platform interface was implemented in our lab computers with a 17-inch screen, which can set up the required number of locations and zoom levels. In this case, our platform can realize most existing map-based GPs including *PassMap* and *GeoPass*. Two interface examples are shown in Figs. 1 and 2. In particular, Fig. 1 shows an interface for registering username and geographical locations. There is a search bar that can help users locate their preferred area in a quick manner. Figure 2(a) shows a login page for inputting username and location, and Fig. 2(b) presents a selected location.

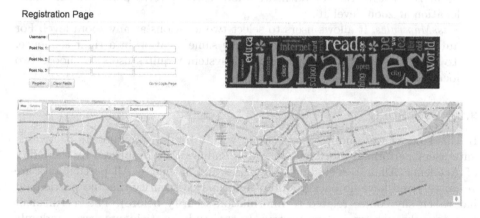

Fig. 1. The registration interface for map-based GP schemes.

(a)   (b)

Fig. 2. The login interface for map-based GP schemes.

Platform Implementation. To develop the GP platform, we utilized the JavaScript based Google Maps API, which provides an extensive move-by-dragging, zooming and search functions. As shown in Fig. 1, when users zoom in/out on the map, our system reports and records the zoom levels. The search function allows users to shift to a specific part of the map quickly and further zoom in to locate a specific area. Similar to [28], our system embedded a 640×420 pixel frame block for displaying the world map in a web page and road map instead of satellite-type map is used by default. The tolerance areas are 21×21 pixels, which is reasonable according to the results in [28,30].

Scheme Implementation. Through applying different rules, our platform can realize various existing map-based GPs. To implement PassMap and GeoPass, we follow the same rules from [28,30] as below.

- *GeoPass rules.* It requires users to choose only one location, which should be at zoom level 16. For authentication, users have to point out the same location at zoom level 16.
- *PassMap rules.* It allows users to select two locations at any zoom level. For authentication, users have to choose the same location in a right sequence. To avoid the effect of zoom levels, our system requires users to choose two locations at zoom level 16.

3.2   User Study

In this section, we conduct a user study with a total of 60 students to investigate users' performance between PassMap and GeoPass (approved by the Office of Academic Affairs), including 25 females and 35 males. All participants are volunteers and have no background of information security (i.e., no participant has taken any course related to information security before). The recruitment was done through emails and posters. In the study, participants were randomly divided into two groups (where each group contains 30 participants).

Methodology. Both PassMap and GeoPass are implemented on the same computer settings. Before the study, we introduced our objectives to all participants in advance. To avoid any bias, we presented a demo video and gave a detailed description to all the participants according to the same steps (i.e., how to use the prototype system).

Before the experiment, each participant could have three trials to get familiar with the authentication system. In the study, we require all participants to create five passwords for each scheme and each password corresponds to a scenario. This study involves five scenarios: the first password is created for an email account (personal use), the second one is created for a bank account, the third one is created for another email account (commercial use), the fourth one is created for a library account (see Fig. 1) and the last one is created for a social networking account. The detailed steps in each experiment are shown as below:

- *Experiment1.* This experiment requires each participant to create five *PassMap* passwords.

- Step 1. Creation: creating a password for *PassMap*.
- Step 2. Confirmation: confirming the password by selecting the same secrets in the correct place. If users incorrectly confirmed their password, they could retry the confirmation or return to Step 1.
- Step 3. Login: logging into the system with the created passwords. Users could cancel an attempt if they noticed an error.
- Step 4. Feedback: All participants were required to complete a *feedback form* about the password creation and confirmation.

In the second day, all participants were required to complete a login session and gave their feedback.

- Step 4. Login: Logging into the prototype system with all created *PassMap* passwords. Users can cancel an attempted login if they noticed an error and try again.
- Step 5. Feedback: All participants should complete a *feedback form* about the password login.

- *Experiment2*. This experiment requires each participant to create five *GeoPass* passwords.
  - Step 1. Creation: creating a password for *GeoPass*.
  - Step 2. Confirmation: confirming the password by selecting the same secrets in the correct place. If users incorrectly confirmed their password, they could retry the confirmation or return to Step 1.
  - Step 3. Login: logging into the prototype system with the created passwords. Users could cancel an attempted login if they noticed an error.
  - Step 4. Feedback: All participants were required to complete a *feedback form* about the password creation and confirmation.

In the second day, all participants were required to complete a login session and gave their feedback.

- Step 4. Login: Logging into the system with all created *GeoPass* passwords. Users could cancel an attempted login if they noticed an error and try again.
- Step 5. Feedback: All participants should complete a *feedback form* about the password login.

Ten-point Likert scales were used in each feedback question where 1-score indicates strong disagreement and 10-score indicates strong agreement. These collected questions and scores are mainly used to reflect participants' performance and explore their attitude towards these two schemes. As a result, 150 real trials were recorded for *Experiment1* and *Experiment2* respectively.

Results. As shown in Table 1, *success rate* and *average completion time* are used for evaluating user's performance regarding the step of creation, confirmation and login in *Experiment1* and *Experiment2*. More specifically, *success rate* in the step of *Creation* means that participants created their passwords without restarting; *success rate* in the step of *Confirmation* means that participants confirmed their passwords without restarting and failed attempts for the first time; and *success rate* in the step of *Login* means that participants, for the first

Table 1. Success rate and average completion time for the step of creation, confirmation and login in *Experiment1* and *Experiment2*.

Experiment1 (PassMap)	Creation	Confirmation	Login
Success rate (the first time)	120/150 (80.0%)	123/150 (82.0%)	127/150 (84.7%)
Completion time (average in seconds)	32.6	19.7	26.3
Standard deviation (SD in seconds)	10.1	7.3	8.3
Experiment2 (GeoPass)	Creation	Confirmation	Login
Success rate (the first time)	125/150 (83.3%)	128/150 (85.3%)	133/150 (88.7%)
Completion time (average in seconds)	28.2	17.1	20.6
Standard deviation (SD in seconds)	8.7	6.5	7.2

time, pressed the login button and entered into the example system successfully. *Average completion time* is an average value computed by all participants.

We also apply chi-squared (χ^2) tests for the collected data to compare non-ordered categorical or nominal data. In all cases, we regard a value of $\rho < 0.05$ as indicating that the groups being tested are different from each other, making the results statistically significant. The results of *success rate* and *completion time* are discussed as below.

-Success rate. In *Experiment1*, success rate is 80.0% and 82.0% for Creation and Confirmation respectively. Some participants restarted the password creation, as they changed their selected map area (i.e., from Singapore to Beijing city). On the other hand, some participants restarted or made failed attempts due to a wrong click, or incorrect zoom levels. The Login step reaches a success rate of 84.7%, where some failed attempts were made due to incorrect zoom levels for the first time.

In *Experiment2*, success rate is 83.3%, 85.3% and 88.7% for Creation, Confirmation and Login, respectively. Similar to *Experiment1*, it is found that several participants restarted the creation step, selected a wrong location, and made an incorrect zoom level. The results of success rate in *Experiment2* are a bit better than those in *Experiment1*, but there are no statistically significant differences ($\chi^2 \approx 1.1$, $\rho > 0.05$; $\chi^2 \approx 1.2$, $\rho > 0.05$; $\chi^2 \approx 1.5$, $\rho > 0.05$).

-Completion time. Average completion time in *Experiment1* is 32.6, 19.7 and 26.3 s for Creation, Confirmation and Login, respectively. Some participants spent much more time in Creation by considering how to choose a good location. Then, they spent less time in Confirmation. The time consumption increased a bit in Login, as participants needed to recall their locations.

In *Experiment2*, average completion time is 28.2, 17.1 and 20.6 s for Creation, Confirmation and Login, respectively. The situation is similar to *Experiment1*, in which participants could perform fastest in Confirmation. It is found that there are no statistically significant differences in Creation and Confirmation ($\chi^2 \approx 2.1$, $\rho > 0.05$; $\chi^2 \approx 1.8$, $\rho > 0.05$), but the results are significant for Login ($\chi^2 \approx 4.1$, $\rho < 0.05$).

-Discussion. On the whole, based on the collected data, participants could perform a bit better in *Experiment2*. For example, participants in *Experiment2* could achieve higher success rate and less time consumption. However, these results are mostly no statistically significant differences. This indicates that participants did similar performance in both experiments, and there is no significant performance influence on selecting between one location and two locations.

It is worth noting that time consumption in Login is the only one significant result, which describes that participants could indeed perform a better login process in *Experiment2*. After informal interview with participants, it is found that selecting only one location is the main reason. In comparison, participants have to zoom-in/out map levels and select two locations in *Experiment1*.

Feedback. To validate our collected data, we analyze the feedback from participants. Ten-point Likert scales were used in each feedback question and we present main questions and corresponding scores in Table 2. The scores are simply average values calculated by all received scores.

Table 2. Several main questions and relevant scores in the user study.

Questions	Score (average)
1. I could easily create *PassMap* passwords	8.5
2. I could easily create *GeoPass* passwords	8.7
3. I could easily log in *PassMap* system	7.8
4. I could easily log in *GeoPass* system	8.2
5. The time consumption in the *Experiment1* is acceptable	7.4
6. The time consumption in the *Experiment2* is acceptable	7.8
7. Are you willing to use *PassMap* passwords in practice	8.1
8. Are you willing to use *GeoPass* passwords in practice	8.3

The scores in the first four questions indicate that most participants satisfied with the password creation and login in both passwords, while *GeoPass* received a bit higher score than *PassMap* (8.7 vs 8.5 and 8.2 vs 7.8). For time consumption, the scores of two schemes went below 8 (with a score of 7.4 and 7.8). At last, most participants were willing to use map-based GPs in their daily lives. In our informal interview, we aimed to validate the feedback. Up to 42 participants (20 from *Experiment1* and 22 from *Experiment2*) were satisfied with the use of map-based GPs and interested in applying such password schemes in their daily use. There are five participants (3 from *Experiment1*) showed no interest in daily use due to the time consumption.

Overall, most participants gave positive feedback for utilizing these two map-based passwords, where they considered it is easier for them to remember geographical locations than traditional textual passwords. They advocated that a world map can provide more memorable points, so that they could choose a secret based on their own knowledge.

4   Further Discussion

In order to design a strong graphical password scheme, there is a balance should be made between security and usability. This section briefly discusses and summarizes these two aspects for *PassMap* and *GeoPass*.

- *Security aspect.* Based on the results in [30], the most efficient attacker (i.e., has local knowledge) should have $2^{16.36}$ guessing attempts for *GeoPass* (with only one location). In the condition of two locations (like *PassMap*), the guessing attempts can be greatly increased. As stated early, selecting one location is more vulnerable to shoulder surfing attack, in which an attacker can infer the secret through direct observation. Increasing the number of locations can mitigate such attack by enhancing the password entropy. Our motivation in this work thus focuses on exploring the effect of location number on scheme performance. The detailed calculation of password space between *PassMap* and *GeoPass* can be referred to [28,30].
- *Usability aspect.* According to our study results, most participants gave positive feedback and were willing to use map-based passwords for authentication. It is found that there are no statistically significant differences between *PassMap* and *GeoPass* in the aspects of success rate and completion time, except for completion time in Login. This because selecting two locations is intuitively more time-consuming than selecting only one location. On the whole, this observation shows that selecting two locations would not degrade the scheme performance.

Overall, our study reveals that appropriately increasing the number of locations is feasible in designing future map-based graphical schemes, whilst we should make a balance between security and usability (i.e., how to decide a proper number of locations). To further investigate this issue, it is expected to have an even larger study with more diverse participants.

5   Conclusion

Map-based graphical passwords utilize an extremely large image and allow users to select their secrets on a world map. PassMap allows users to select two locations on a map, while GeoPass reduces the number of locations to only one. In this paper, our main purpose is to explore the effect of location number on scheme performance between PassMap and GeoPass, which are two typical map-based graphical schemes. We conduct a user study with 60 participants and analyze the results in terms of user's performance (e.g., success rate, completion time) and feedback. The study results demonstrate that participants could perform similarly for both schemes, and there is no significant performance influence on selecting between one location and two locations. That is, there is a potential to increase the number of locations in designing a map-based scheme. Our effort aims to complement existing research and provide useful guidelines for designing more secure map-based graphical passwords.

To the best of our knowledge, this is an early study aiming to explore this issue for map-based graphical schemes. Future work could include investigating the user's performance when increasing the number of locations to three or above, and exploring the effect of zoom levels on scheme performance.

Acknowledgments. We would like to thank all participants for their hard work and cooperation in the user study, and thank all anonymous reviewers for their helpful comments in improving the paper. Part of this work was supported by the National Natural Science Foundation of China (Grant No. 61602396).

References

1. Bonneau, J.: The science of guessing: analyzing an anonymized corpus of 70 million passwords. In: Proceedings of the 2012 IEEE Symposium on Security and Privacy, pp. 538–552 (2012)
2. Chiasson, S., Oorschot, P.C., Biddle, R.: Graphical password authentication using cued click points. In: Biskup, J., López, J. (eds.) ESORICS 2007. LNCS, vol. 4734, pp. 359–374. Springer, Heidelberg (2007). doi:10.1007/978-3-540-74835-9_24
3. Chiasson, S., Biddle, R., van Oorschot, P.C.: A second look at the usability of click-based graphical passwords. In: Proceedings of the 3rd Symposium on Usable Privacy and Security (SOUPS), pp. 1–12. ACM, New York (2007)
4. Chiasson, S., Stobert, E., Forget, A., Biddle, R.: Persuasive cued click-points: design, implementation, and evaluation of a knowledge-based authentication mechanism. IEEE Trans. Dependable Secur. Comput. 9(2), 222–235 (2012)
5. Davis, D., Monrose, F., Reiter, M.K.: On user choice in graphical password schemes. In: Proceedings of the 13th Conference on USENIX Security Symposium (SSYM), pp. 151–164. USENIX Association, Berkeley (2004)
6. Dirik, A.E., Memon, N., Birget, J.C.: Modeling user choice in the passpoints graphical password scheme. In: Proceedings of the 3rd Symposium on Usable Privacy and Security (SOUPS), pp. 20–28. ACM, New York (2007)
7. Dunphy, P., Yan, J.: Do background images improve "draw a secret" graphical passwords? In: Proceedings of the 14th ACM Conference on Computer and Communications Security (CCS), pp. 36–47 (2007)
8. Fox, S.: Future Online Password Could be a Map (2010). http://www.livescience.com/8622-future-online-password-map.html
9. Georgakakis, E., Komninos, N., Douligeris, C.: NAVI: novel authentication with visual information. In: Proceedings of the 2012 IEEE Symposium on Computers and Communications (ISCC), pp. 588–595 (2012)
10. Gołofit, K.: Click passwords under investigation. In: Biskup, J., López, J. (eds.) ESORICS 2007. LNCS, vol. 4734, pp. 343–358. Springer, Heidelberg (2007). doi:10.1007/978-3-540-74835-9_23
11. Inglesant, P.G., Sasse, M.A.: The true cost of unusable password policies: password use in the wild. In: Proceedings of ACM SIGCHI Conference on Human Factors in Computing Systems (CHI), pp. 383–392 (2010)
12. Jermyn, I., Mayer, A., Monrose, F., Reiter, M.K., Rubin, A.D.: The design and analysis of graphical passwords. In: Proceedings of the 8th Conference on USENIX Security Symposium, pp. 1–14. USENIX Association, Berkeley (1999)
13. Lin, D., Dunphy, P., Olivier, P., Yan, J.: Graphical passwords & qualitative spatial relations. In: Proceedings of the 3rd Symposium on Usable Privacy and Security (SOUPS), pp. 161–162 (2007)

14. Meng, Y.: Designing click-draw based graphical password scheme for better authentication. In: Proceedings of the 7th IEEE International Conference on Networking, Architecture, and Storage (NAS), pp. 39–48 (2012)

15. Meng, Y., Li, W.: Evaluating the effect of tolerance on click-draw based graphical password scheme. In: Chim, T.W., Yuen, T.H. (eds.) ICICS 2012. LNCS, vol. 7618, pp. 349–356. Springer, Heidelberg (2012). doi:10.1007/978-3-642-34129-8_32

16. Meng, Y., Li, W.: Evaluating the effect of user guidelines on creating click-draw based graphical passwords. In: Proceedings of the 2012 ACM Research in Applied Computation Symposium (RACS), pp. 322–327 (2012)

17. Meng, Y., Li, W., Kwok, L.-F.: Enhancing click-draw based graphical passwords using multi-touch on mobile phones. In: Janczewski, L.J., Wolfe, H.B., Shenoi, S. (eds.) SEC 2013. IAICT, vol. 405, pp. 55–68. Springer, Heidelberg (2013). doi:10.1007/978-3-642-39218-4_5

18. Meng, W.: RouteMap: a route and map based graphical password scheme for better multiple password memory. In: Qiu, M., Xu, S., Yung, M., Zhang, H. (eds.) NSS 2015. LNCS, vol. 9408, pp. 147–161. Springer, Cham (2015). doi:10.1007/978-3-319-25645-0_10

19. Meng, W.: Evaluating the effect of multi-touch behaviours on Android unlock patterns. Inf. Comput. Secur. 24(3), 277–287 (2016). Emerald

20. Meng, W., Li, W., Wong, D.S., Zhou, J.: TMGuard: a touch movement-based security mechanism for screen unlock patterns on smartphones. In: Manulis, M., Sadeghi, A.-R., Schneider, S. (eds.) ACNS 2016. LNCS, vol. 9696, pp. 629–647. Springer, Cham (2016). doi:10.1007/978-3-319-39555-5_34

21. Meng, W., Li, W., Kwok, L.-F., Choo, K.-K.R.: Towards enhancing click-draw based graphical passwords using multi-touch behaviours on smartphones. Comput. Secur. 65, 213–229 (2017)

22. Nelson, D.L., Reed, V.S., Walling, J.R.: Pictorial superiority effect. J. Exp. Psychol. Hum. Learn. Mem. 2(5), 523–528 (1976)

23. Passfaces. http://www.realuser.com/

24. Shepard, R.N.: Recognition memory for words, sentences, and pictures. J. Verbal Learn. Verbal Behav. 6(1), 156–163 (1967)

25. Spitzer, J., Singh, C., Schweitzer, D.: A security class project in graphical passwords. J. Comput. Sci. Coll. 26(2), 7–13 (2010)

26. Shin, J., Kancharlapalli, S., Farcasin, M., Chan-Tin, E.: SmartPass: a smarter geolocation-based authentication scheme. Secur. Commun. Netw. 8, 3927–3938 (2015)

27. Suo, X., Zhu, Y., Owen, G.S.: Graphical passwords: a survey. In: Proceedings of the 21st Annual Computer Security Applications Conference (ACSAC), pp. 463–472. IEEE Computer Society, USA (2005)

28. Sun, H., Chen, Y., Fang, C., Chang, S.: PassMap: a map based graphical-password authentication system. In: Proceedings of ASIACCS, pp. 99–100 (2012)

29. Tao, H., Adams, C.: Pass-Go: a proposal to improve the usability of graphical passwords. Int. J. Netw. Secur. 2(7), 273–292 (2008)

30. Thorpe, J., MacRae, B., Salehi-Abari, A.: Usability and security evaluation of GeoPass: a geographic location-password scheme. In: Proceedings of the 9th Symposium on Usable Privacy and Security (SOUPS), pp. 1–14 (2013)

31. Wiedenbeck, S., Waters, J., Birget, J.-C., Brodskiy, A., Memon, N.: Passpoints: design and longitudinal evaluation of a graphical password system. Int. J. Hum. Comput. Stud. **63**(1–2), 102–127 (2005)
32. Weir, M., Aggarwal, S., Collins, M., Stern, H.: Testing metrics for password creation policies by attacking large sets of revealed passwords. In: Proceedings of CCS, pp. 162–175 (2010)
33. Yan, J., Blackwell, A., Anderson, R., Grant, A.: Password memorability and security: empirical results. IEEE Secur. Priv. **2**, 25–31 (2004)

A QR Code Watermarking Approach
Based on the DWT-DCT Technique

Yang-Wai Chow[✉], Willy Susilo, Joseph Tonien, and Wei Zong

Institute of Cybersecurity and Cryptology,
School of Computing and Information Technology,
University of Wollongong, Wollongong, Australia
{caseyc,wsusilo,dong}@uow.edu.au, wz630@uowmail.edu.au

Abstract. The rapid growth in Internet and communication technology has facilitated an escalation in the exchange of digital multimedia content. This has resulted in an increase in copyright infringement, which has led to a greater demand for more robust copyright protection mechanisms. Digital watermarking is a means of detecting ownership and illegal use of digital products. This paper presents an approach to watermarking images by embedding QR code information in a digital image. The notion of the proposed scheme is to capitalize on the error correction mechanism that is inherent in the QR code structure, in order to increase the robustness of the watermark. By employing the QR code's error correction mechanism, watermark information contained within a watermarked image can potentially be decoded even if the image has been altered or distorted by an adversary. This paper studies the characteristics of the proposed scheme and presents experiment results examining the robustness and security of the QR code watermarking approach.

Keywords: Data hiding · Discrete Cosine Transform · Discrete Wavelet Transform · Error correction · QR code · Watermarking

1 Introduction

Advances in Internet and communication technology have given rise to an increase in the exchange and sharing of digital multimedia content. However, this has also facilitated the rise in copyright infringement, which has resulted in the demand for better and more robust copyright protection techniques.

Digital watermarking is an effective solution for detecting copyright infringement and the illegal usage of digital products. The notion of watermarking is to embed extra information in an original signal, and when needed, the watermark can be extracted [17]. The embedding of additional information in the original signal, also known as host data, must be done in a way that does not interfere with the normal usage of data [31]. Hence, to be a successful watermarking scheme, the difference between the watermarked and the original signal should be imperceptible. In addition, the watermark should be robust against

© Springer International Publishing AG 2017
J. Pieprzyk and S. Suriadi (Eds.): ACISP 2017, Part II, LNCS 10343, pp. 314–331, 2017.
DOI: 10.1007/978-3-319-59870-3_18

signal alteration, up to a point at which the host signal is damaged and loses its commercial value [32].

The field of digital watermarking is an area that has been studied extensively for many years [11]. Panah et al. [31] describe four main properties of any watermarking system; namely, invisibility, capacity, robustness and security. Invisibility is the property whereby the watermark should be imperceptible by a human; capacity refers to the amount of data that can be embedded; robustness is the ability of the watermarking scheme to withstand alterations or distortions to the signal; and security is the watermarking scheme's resistance against any intentional attempt by an adversary to impair the watermark [10,31].

Over the years, researchers have proposed various watermarking techniques for embedding information in various multimedia signals, including images, video and audio [35]. The work in this paper focuses on invisible watermarking for digital images. There are two main categories of invisible digital watermarking; namely, the spatial domain and the frequency domain. Spatial domain techniques work by altering the gray levels of some pixels. Whereas, the other category focuses on modifying coefficients in the frequency domain [19].

There are various advantages of operating in the frequency domain, such as, being able to incorporate features of the human visual system in watermarking more effectively, the ability spreading the energy of the embedded signal in the frequency domain over all pixels in the spatial domain, and being able to operate in the compressed domain since most image compression standards are based on the frequency domain [19]. For this reason, numerous researchers have proposed watermarking techniques in the frequency domain based on the Discrete Cosine Transform (DCT) and the Discrete Wavelet Transform (DWT) [4,25,28]. In recent years, the use of DWT-DCT hybrid techniques as a way of improving the robustness of the watermark has also received much attention [1–3,12,14,21,26,35].

This paper proposes a QR code watermarking technique that is based on the DWT-DCT approach. The QR code is a two-dimensional barcode that has seen widespread adoption in many different applications over the last few years, due to its convenience and ease of use, as any smartphone equipped with a camera and QR code reader can retrieve the information encoded within a QR code. The fundamental idea behind the technique proposed in this paper is to capitalize on the error correction mechanism that is inherent in the QR code structure. The purpose of this is to increase the robustness of the resulting watermark against alterations or distortions, as the information contained within the QR code can still be decoded as long as the corrupted data does not exceed the QR code's error correction capacity.

Our Contribution. In this paper, we present a watermarking technique for embedding QR code information in a host signal by adopting a combined DWT-DCT approach. This paper focuses on applying the proposed technique to digital images. We examine the scheme based on the key properties of a watermark, namely, invisibility, capacity, robustness and security. The capacity of the scheme is simply the data capacity of the embedded QR code, which depends on its version and error correction level. For the other properties, this paper shows results of our experiments demonstrating the invisibility characteristics of the scheme using conventional image quality metrics. In addition, we present results examining the proposed scheme's robustness and security properties under varying conditions and against common image alterations and attacks.

2   Background

This section provides a brief background to some of the key concepts and techniques used in this research.

2.1   The QR Code

The company Denso Wave [13] invented the Quick Response Code (QR code) in 1994 for the automotive industry in Japan. After its inception, the International Organization for Standardization (ISO) established a standard for the QR code [20]. Since then, QR codes have seen widespread adoption worldwide due to its ease of use, robustness, fast decoding, high data capacity and so on.

A QR code symbol is constructed as a two-dimensional array of light and dark squares, referred to as modules. There are forty sizes of QR code symbol versions ranging from versions 1 to 40, each consisting of a different number of modules, resulting in different data capacities. A QR code can encode different types of data (i.e. alphanumeric, binary, Kanji or a combination of these) and has support for four error correction levels (i.e. L, M, Q and H). The error correction mechanism provides a means for data recovery even when a certain amount of modules in a QR code are corrupted. The four error correction levels correspond to error tolerances of approximately 7%, 15%, 25% and 30% respectively. The QR code error recovery capability increases at the expense of message length. Figure 1 shows an example of a QR code version 1 with error correction level H; it encodes the word "message".

Fig. 1. QR code version 1, error correction level H.

2.2   Discrete Cosine Transform (DCT)

The Discrete Cosine Transform (DCT) converts a signal into the frequency domain and is often used in image processing, especially in JPEG compression

[19,33]. Given an input image, x, the computation of the DCT coefficients for the transformed output image, y, is obtained using the equation shown in Eq. 1. Once transformed, the original image can be recovered using the inverse DCT, as given by Eq. 2 [2,33].

$$y(u,v) = \sqrt{\frac{2}{M}}\sqrt{\frac{2}{N}}\alpha_u\alpha_v \sum_{u=0}^{M-1}\sum_{v=0}^{N-1} x(m,n)\cos\frac{(2m+1)u\prod}{2M}\cos\frac{(2n+1)u\prod}{2N} \quad (1)$$

where

$$\alpha_u = \begin{cases} \frac{1}{\sqrt{2}} & u = 0 \\ 1 & u = 1,2,...,N-1 \end{cases}$$

$$\alpha_v = \begin{cases} \frac{1}{\sqrt{2}} & v = 0 \\ 1 & v = 1,2,...,N-1 \end{cases}$$

$$x(m,n) = \sqrt{\frac{2}{M}}\sqrt{\frac{2}{N}}\alpha_u\alpha_v \sum_{u=0}^{M-1}\sum_{v=0}^{N-1} y(u,v)\cos\frac{(2m+1)u\prod}{2M}\cos\frac{(2n+1)u\prod}{2N}$$

$$(2)$$

The blocked based DCT approach separates an image into non-overlapping blocks, before applying the DCT to each block [22]. Watermark data is typically embedded in the mid-band coefficients of each DCT transformed block in order to keep visual alteration of an image to a minimum [4].

2.3 Discrete Wavelet Transform (DWT)

The Discrete Wavelet Transform (DWT) is another technique that is widely used in image and signal processing. The DWT technique for images involves the decomposition of an image into frequency channels of constant bandwidth on a logarithmic scale [25,30]. A 2D image is decomposed into four sub-bands, which are denoted as LL, LH, HL and HH at level 1 in the DWT domain. The LL sub-band represents the coarse-level coefficients, whereas the LH, HL and HH sub-bands represent the finest scale wavelet coefficients. Each sub-band can be decomposed further until the desired number of levels is reached. The human visual system is more sensitive to the LL sub-band (i.e. the low frequency component), watermarking is typically embedded in one or more of the other three sub-bands to maintain better image quality [25].

2.4 Arnold Transform

The Arnold transform is a invertible method that can be used for pixel scrambling, and has been adopted in various watermarking schemes [22]. The purpose of applying this transform is due to the fact that adjacent pixels in image data have strong correlation to each other. By using the Arnold transform, this high pixel correlation can be disrupted. The Arnold transform is shown in Eq. 3 [16], where p and q are positive integers, $\det(A) = 1$, and (x',y') are the new coordinates of the pixel after Arnold transform is applied to a pixel at position (x,y).

The period of the Arnold transform depends on p, q and the size N of the image. After several iterations of applying the transform, the correlation among adjacent pixels can be disturbed completely.

$$\begin{bmatrix} x' \\ y' \end{bmatrix} = A \begin{bmatrix} x \\ y \end{bmatrix} \mod N = \begin{bmatrix} 1 & p \\ q & pq+1 \end{bmatrix} \begin{bmatrix} x \\ y \end{bmatrix} \mod N \tag{3}$$

The Arnold Transform has also been used for image encryption [16]. The underlying notion for this is that the shuffling the pixels in the spatial domain confuses the relationship between the cipher image and the plain image. For image encryption, the parameters p, q and the number of iterations of applying the transform, can all be used as the secret keys.

3   Related Work

The QR code has seen a variety of applications in the area of information security. For example, QR codes have been used for secret sharing [8], authentication and transaction verification [7], authenticating visual cryptography shares [36] as well as for e-voting authentication [15].

Researchers have also proposed schemes for using the QR code in the area of data hiding and steganography. Among the work conducted in this area, Wu et al. [37] proposed a data embedding approach for hiding a QR code in a digital image. Their purpose was to camouflage the appearance of a QR code in an image so as not to degrade the visual quality of the picture. Huang et al. [18] developed a reversible data hiding approach for images with QR codes. The purpose of their method was to be able to restore a portion of an image that was covered by a QR code. A nested image steganography scheme was proposed by Chen and Wang [5] using QR codes, where two types of secret data, i.e. text (lossless) and image (lossy), are embedded in a cover image. The text portion was embedded in the form of a QR code. A similar approach was reported in Chung et al. [9].

In addition, QR codes have been used in a number of recent digital watermarking schemes. A method of embedding a QR code in the HH component at the first level of the DWT domain of a cover image was previously proposed [34]. The objective of this approach was to be able to detect malicious interference by an attacker based on a unique image registry code. A digital watermarking scheme using a Just Noticeable Difference (JND) model for embedding QR codes in images was described by Lee et al. [27]. The aim of their approach was to improve the imperceptibility of a watermark based on JND, which is the maximum difference at which the human visual system is not able to detect a difference. Kim et al. [24] studied a method of using 2D barcodes, e.g., QR codes, to insert a digital object identifier tag in digital content without degrading its quality. Kang et al. [22] proposed a watermarking approach based on the combination of DCT, QR codes and chaotic theory. In their approach, a QR code image is encrypted with a chaotic system to enhance the security of the watermark. Others have also proposed different QR code watermarking approaches [6,38].

The motivation behind the QR code watermarking technique proposed in this paper is to increase the robustness of the watermark against image alteration and/or distortion. The proposed approach capitalizes on the error correction mechanism that is inherent in the QR code structure. By embedding a QR code watermark into a digital image, the QR code can be decoded correctly as long as the data in the QR code has not been corrupted above its error correction capacity. As such, this approach attempts to increase the resulting robustness of the invisible watermarking scheme against watermarking attacks where an adversary tries to remove the watermark by altering or distorting the image.

4   Proposed QR Code Watermarking Scheme

4.1   The Embedding Process

The proposed QR code watermarking scheme takes a QR code, which contains the watermark information, and embeds it in a cover image. An overview of the process for embedding the QR code in the cover image is depicted in Fig. 2.

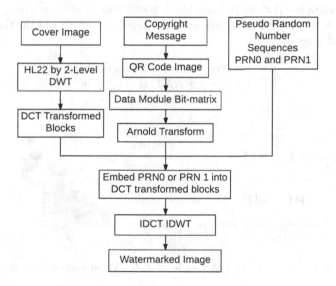

Fig. 2. Overview of the QR code watermark embedding process.

For generating the QR code, the QR code's mask pattern and error correction level are predetermined beforehand. This is so that the QR code's format information can be omitted in the embedding process, and only the data modules will be embedded in the cover image. The reason for this is to ensure that the format information cannot be corrupted even if the resulting watermarked image undergoes alteration or distortion. In that manner, when the QR code is extracted from the watermarked image, it can be correctly decoded with the predetermined format information as long as the data modules have not been corrupted beyond the QR code's error correction capacity. The QR code's data modules are extracted into a binary matrix, which is scrambled using Arnold transform to increase its robustness against alteration or distortion. This produces the data matrix that will be use for embedding the QR code data in the cover image.

The cover image will be decomposed using DWT into four sub-bands as depicted in Fig. 3(a). This can be continued to the desired level. In our experiments, we decomposed the HL sub-band to level 2, as shown in Fig. 3(b), and used the HL22 sub-band for embedding the watermark. The contents of this sub-band are then separated into non-overlapping blocks where the DCT is applied to each block. Only the mid-band coefficients of the DCT transformed blocks are modified to keep the visual alteration to a minimum, as depicted in Fig. 3(c). In addition, two non-correlated Pseudo-Random Number (PRN) sequences, are generated to represent bit '0' and bit '1' (i.e. PRN0 and PRN1). The length of each PRN sequence matches the number of mid-band DCT coefficients. The data matrix containing the QR code data is then embedded in the DCT coefficient blocks using the PRN sequences, according to Eq. 4, where x is the respective mid-band coefficient, x' is the modified coefficient and α is the gain factor. Finally, the inverse DCT and inverse DWT are applied to obtain the resulting watermarked image.

$$x' = \begin{cases} x + \alpha \times PRN0, \text{ if the bit is '0'} \\ x + \alpha \times PRN1, \text{ if the bit is '1'} \end{cases} \tag{4}$$

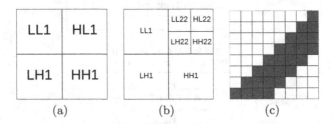

(a)   (b)   (c)

Fig. 3. (a) DWT at level 1; (b) DWT at level 2; (c) Mid-band coefficients of an 8 × 8 DCT block.

4.2   The Extraction Process

Image pre-filtering techniques have been used to improve watermark extraction results [29]. Therefore, we first apply a sharpening and the Gaussian of Laplacian filters to the watermarked image to increase the contrast between the watermark and the cover image related sections [23]. The resulting pre-filtered image then undergoes the same DWT and DCT procedure as the embedding process to decompose the image into sub-bands and non-overlapping blocks.

The data matrix can be extracted based on the correlation between the known PRN sequences and the mid-band coefficients of each DCT transformed block. The inverse Arnold transform is then applied to the data matrix using the known transform parameters to obtain the QR code data, which can be decoded based on the format information to obtain the encoded message. This process is shown in Fig. 4.

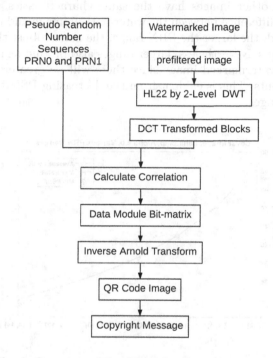

Fig. 4. Overview of the QR code extraction process.

5   Results and Discussion

To evaluate the proposed watermarking scheme, experiments implementing the watermarking process in MATLAB were conducted on three well know cover images; namely Lena, Peppers and Baboon. These images are shown in Fig. 6. The choice of these images was due to the varying degrees of variance in the images. These were 8-bit gray scale images with the dimensions of 512 × 512. The QR code that was previously shown in Fig. 1 was used as the watermark in the experiments. It was constructed with the error correction level H, which means that data corruption of below approximately 30% can still be decoded correctly. In the experiments, the range of PRN values were varied between a range of values that were centered on zero.

5.1 Invisibility

Quantitative measurements to ascertain the degree of imperceptibility of the watermark were conducted using the Peak Signal-to-Noise Ratio (PSNR), which is a commonly used image quality metric, between the original image and the watermarked image. Figure 5 shows a plot of the PSNR values for Lena that were obtained by varying the PRN range, with $\alpha = 4$, using different pseudo-random seed values. The other images have the same characteristics. Greater PSNR values mean less difference between the watermarked image and the cover image. On the other hand, the larger the PRN range, the more robust the watermark is to image alterations. Nevertheless, larger ranges also produces greater distortion in the resulting watermarked image since there will be greater modification of the DCT coefficients. This is evident from the decreasing PSNR values in Fig. 5 at larger PRN ranges.

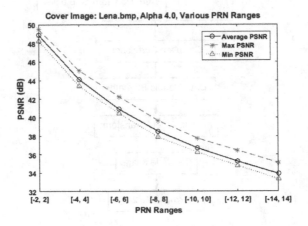

Fig. 5. Characteristic PSNR values.

Figures 6(a) to (e) gives a visual comparison of the watermarked image based on different watermark parameters. The stronger the watermark (i.e. more robust and higher chance of successful watermark extraction), the higher the distortion in the resulting watermarked image. The original cover images are shown in Fig. 6(a). Figure 6(b) show watermarked images with very low distortion obtained from a PRN range of ± 4 and $\alpha = 2$; in Fig. 6(c) the parameters where PRN: ± 6, $\alpha = 4$; in Fig. 6(d) the parameters where PRN: ± 10, $\alpha = 6$; Fig. 6(e) in turn shows an example of a watermarked image with very distortion with PRN: ± 14, $\alpha = 14$. It can be seen that the watermark is imperceptible from the perspective of the human visual system when the watermarked images were generated with lower parameters, while the distortion can clearly be seen with high parameter values. When the distortion is perceptible in the watermarked image, it looses its commercial value.

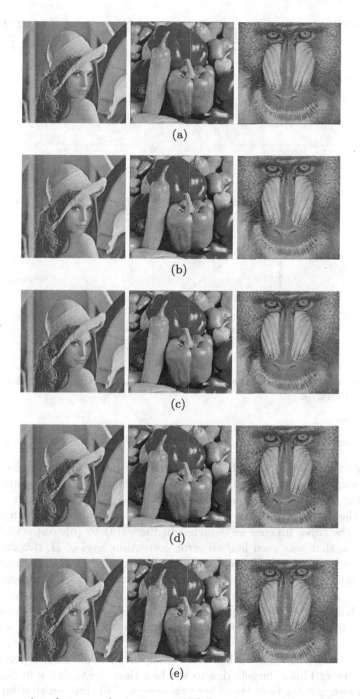

Fig. 6. Comparison between the images with different watermark strengths and levels of distortion; (a) very low distortion; (b) low distortion; (c) mid distortion; (d) high distortion; (e) very high distortion.

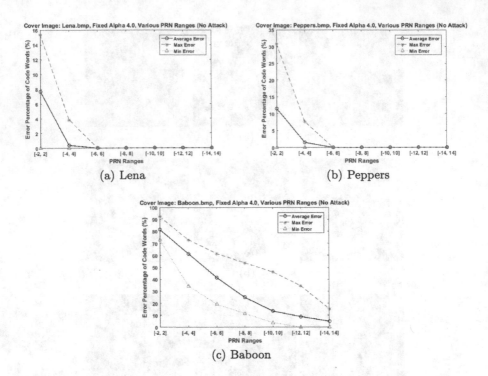

(a) Lena   (b) Peppers

(c) Baboon

Fig. 7. Percentage of codeword errors based on various PRN ranges for the respective watermarked images.

5.2   Robustness and Security

To evaluate the robustness and security of the proposed scheme, some common distortions and attacks were applied to the watermarked images; namely, JPEG compression, salt-and-pepper noise and cropping.

First, the robustness of the proposed scheme was evaluated by varying PRN ranges for the three images, as depicted in Figs. 7(a) to (c), respectively. Since the QR code that was used had an error correction level of H, this means that codeword errors below 30% gives rise to a high probability that the extracted QR code can be decoded correctly. It can be seen that the percentage of codeword errors in the watermarked Lena image, Fig. 7(a), is very much below the 30% threshold. While the watermarked Peppers image, Fig. 7(b), shows similar characteristics, note that the percentage of codeword errors are higher. Nevertheless, the errors are still below the threshold. On the other hand, Fig. 7(c), which shows the watermarked Baboon image, has a much higher percentage of codeword error. This is largely due to the fact that the variance in the Baboon image is much greater than the other two images. This implies that larger PRN ranges have to be used in the proposed scheme for images with large variances.

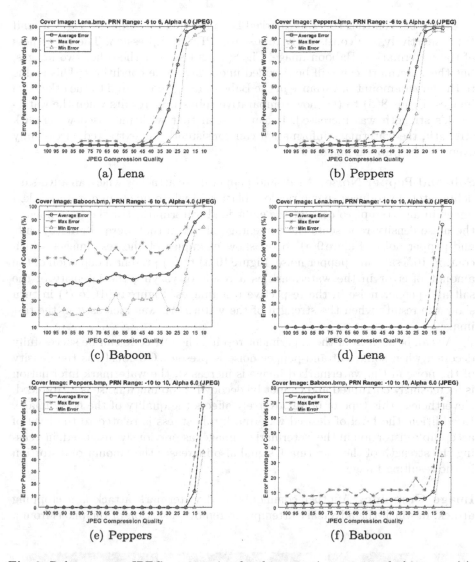

Fig. 8. Robustness to JPEG compression for the respective watermarked images; (a) to (c) medium strength watermark; (d) to (f) high strength watermark.

JPEG Compression. Figure 8 provides a depiction of the scheme's robustness to JPEG compression. JPEG compression is one of the commonly used attacks for watermark removal. MATLAB's inbuilt JPEG compression function was used for the experiments. The function accepts parameters ranging from 0 (i.e. low quality compression) to 100 (i.e. high quality compression), inclusive. It should be noted that once the JPEG compression quality is above a certain threshold the image quality significantly degrades to the point of having no commercial value.

It can be seen that the watermarked Lena and Peppers images, Fig. 8(a) and (b) respectively, are consistently robust to JPEG compression. The robustness of the watermarked Baboon image, Fig. 8(c), is less that the other two images, but the watermark can still be decoded under favorable conditions. This is due to the larger amount of variance in the Baboon image compared to the other two images. Figure 8(d) to (f) show comparative robustness results when the watermark's strength was increased. It can be seen that with increased watermark strength, the watermark information can consistently be extracted successfully even for the Baboon image.

Salt-and-Pepper Noise. A salt-and-pepper noise attack is where an adversary deliberately introduces sparse random black and white pixels in a watermarked image in an attempt to corrupt the embedded watermark. For the experiments, the noise density represents the percentage of pixels that were altered by salt-and-pepper noise. Figure 9(a) to (c) show examples of the test images which contain 10% salt-and-pepper noise. Figure 10(a) to (c) present a depiction of the amount of error in the watermark as a result of varying the intensity of the salt-and-pepper noise in the respective test images. Figure 10(d) to (f) in turn show the results when the strength of the watermark was increased in the test images.

As can be seen from the experiment results, the QR code can be successfully decoded when some salt-and-pepper noise is present. Obviously as the density of the noise in the watermarked image is increased, the watermark information is increasingly corrupted and cannot be decoded if too much noise is introduced. Nevertheless, this type of noise adversely affects the quality of the noisy image. In addition, the level of desired watermark robustness is related to the level of acceptable distortion in the watermarked image, as previously discussed, increasing the strength of the watermark signal also increases the amount of distortion in the resulting image.

Image Cropping. Another commonly used watermark attack is a cropping attack, in which the adversary attempts to remove a section of the pixels from a

(a) Lena   (b) Peppers   (c) Baboon

Fig. 9. Watermarked images containing 10% salt-and-pepper noise.

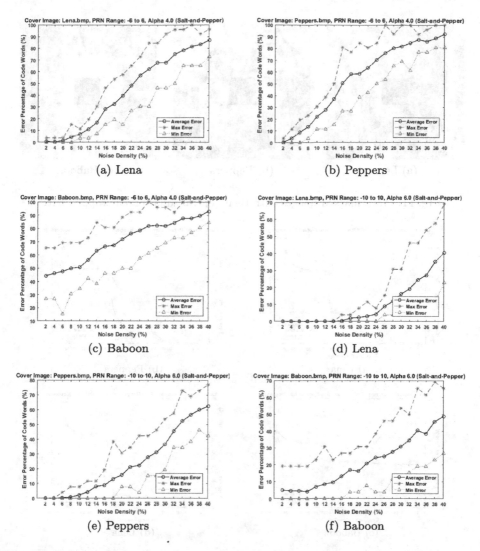

Fig. 10. Robustness to salt-and-pepper noise for the respective watermarked images; (a) to (c) medium strength watermark; (d) to (f) high strength watermark.

watermarked image with the intention of removing embedded watermark information. Examples of the respective test watermarked images that were used in the experiment are provided in Fig. 11(a) to (c). In these images, it can be seen that a central square area of the image has been cropped out. For the experiments, the size of the cropped area was varied.

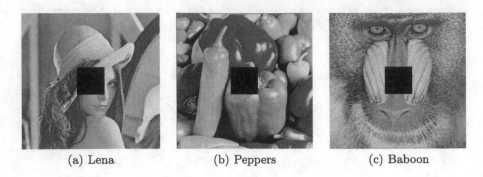

(a) Lena   (b) Peppers   (c) Baboon

Fig. 11. Watermarked images with their central square area cropped out.

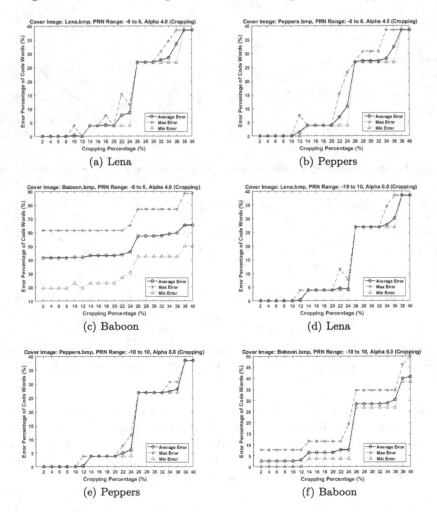

(a) Lena   (b) Peppers

(c) Baboon   (d) Lena

(e) Peppers   (f) Baboon

Fig. 12. Robustness to cropping for the respective watermarked images; (a) to (c) medium strength watermark; (d) to (f) high strength watermark.

Figure 12(a) to (c) show the robustness of the watermark scheme against an increasing percentage of the image being cropped out, and Fig. 12(d) to (f) in turn show the results with increased watermark strength. It can be seen that the proposed scheme is robust against cropping below a certain threshold. In practice, cropping an image by too much will adversely affect the commercial viability of the resulting cropped image.

6 Conclusion and Future Work

This paper presents an approach to QR code watermarking for digital images. The proposed approach involves the use of a hybrid DWT-DCT technique in conjunction with the error correction mechanism this is inherent as part of the QR code structure. The aim of embedding QR code information within an image lies behind that fact that the QR code can be correctly decoded even if the watermarked image is distorted, as long as the QR code's error tolerance capacity has not been overwhelmed. The quality of the resulting watermarked image is examined and experiment results demonstrating the robustness and security characteristics of the proposed scheme are presented in this paper against a number of commonly used watermark attacks. Future work will focus on determining an acceptable level of distortion from the human visual perspective, the use of color images, and methods of using different types of two-dimensional barcodes in the proposed scheme.

References

1. Akter, A., Nur-E-Tajnina, Ullah, M.A.: Digital image watermarking based on DWT-DCT: evaluate for a new embedding algorithm. In: 2014 International Conference on Informatics, Electronics Vision (ICIEV), pp. 1–6, May 2014
2. Al-Haj, A.: Combined DWT-DCT digital image watermarking. J. Comput. Sci. 3(9), 740–746 (2007)
3. Amirgholipour, S.K., Naghsh-Nilchi, A.R.: Robust digital image watermarking based on joint DWT-DCT. JDCTA 3(2), 42–54 (2009)
4. Barni, M., Bartolini, F., Cappellini, V., Piva, A.: A DCT-domain system for robust image watermarking. Signal Process. 66(3), 357–372 (1998)
5. Chen, W.-Y., Wang, J.-W.: Nested image steganography scheme using QR-barcode technique. Opt. Eng. 48(5), 057004–057004 (2009)
6. Cho, D.: Study on method of new digital watermark generation using QR-code. In: 2013 Eighth International Conference on Broadband and Wireless Computing, Communication and Applications, Compiegne, France, 28–30 October 2013, pp. 585–588. IEEE (2013)
7. Chow, Y.-W., Susilo, W., Yang, G., Au, M.H., Wang, C.: Authentication and transaction verification using QR codes with a mobile device. In: Wang, G., Ray, I., Alcaraz Calero, J.M., Thampi, S.M. (eds.) SpaCCS 2016. LNCS, vol. 10066, pp. 437–451. Springer, Cham (2016). doi:10.1007/978-3-319-49148-6_36
8. Chow, Y. W., Susilo, W., Yang, G., Phillips, J.G., Pranata, I., Barmawi, A.M.: Exploiting the error correction mechanism in QR codes for secret sharing. In: Liu, J.K.K., Steinfeld, R. (eds.) ACISP 2016. LNCS, vol. 9722, pp. 409–425. Springer, Cham (2016). doi:10.1007/978-3-319-40253-6_25

9. Chung, C.-H., Chen, W.-Y., Tu, C.-M.: Image hidden technique using QR-barcode. In: Fifth International Conference on Intelligent Information Hiding and Multimedia Signal Processing, 2009. IIH-MSP 2009, pp. 522–525. IEEE (2009)

10. Cox, I., Miller, M.L., Bloom, J.A.: Digital Watermarking. Morgan Kaufmann Publishers Inc., San Francisco (2002)

11. Cox, I.J., Miller, M.L.: The first 50 years of electronic watermarking. EURASIP J. Adv. Signal Process. **2002**(2), 820936 (2002)

12. Deb, K., Al-Seraj, M.S., Hoque, M.M., Sarkar, M.I.H.: Combined DWT-DCT based digital image watermarking technique for copyright protection. In: 2012 7th International Conference on Electrical and Computer Engineering, pp. 458–461, December 2012

13. Denso Wave Incorporated. QRcode.com. http://www.qrcode.com/en/

14. Emek, S., Pazarci, M.: Additive vs. image dependent DWT-DCT based watermarking. In: Gunsel, B., Jain, A.K., Tekalp, A.M., Sankur, B. (eds.) MRCS 2006. LNCS, vol. 4105, pp. 98–105. Springer, Heidelberg (2006). doi:10.1007/11848035_15

15. Falkner, S., Kieseberg, P., Simos, D.E., Traxler, C., Weippl, E.: E-voting authentication with QR-codes. In: Tryfonas, T., Askoxylakis, I. (eds.) HAS 2014. LNCS, vol. 8533, pp. 149–159. Springer, Cham (2014). doi:10.1007/978-3-319-07620-1_14

16. Guan, Z.-H., Huang, F., Guan, W.: Chaos-based image encryption algorithm. Phys. Lett. A **346**(1–3), 153–157 (2005)

17. Hartung, F., Kutter, M.: Multimedia watermarking techniques. Proc. IEEE **87**(7), 1079–1107 (1999)

18. Huang, H.-C., Chang, F.-C., Fang, W.-C.: Reversible data hiding with histogram-based difference expansion for QR code applications. IEEE Trans. Consum. Electron. **57**(2), 779–787 (2011)

19. Huang, J., Shi, Y.Q., Shi, Y.: Embedding image watermarks in DC components. IEEE Trans. Circuits Syst. Video Technol. **10**(6), 974–979 (2000)

20. International Organization for Standardization. Informationtechnology – automatic identification and data capture techniques – QR code 2005 bar code symbology specification. ISO/IEC18004:2006 (2006)

21. Joshi, A.M., Gupta, S., Girdhar, M., Agarwal, P., Sarker, R.: Combined DWT–DCT-based video watermarking algorithm using Arnold transform technique. In: Satapathy, S.C., Bhateja, V., Joshi, A. (eds.) ICDECT 2016. AISC, vol. 468, pp. 455–463. Springer, Singapore (2017). doi:10.1007/978-981-10-1675-2_45

22. Kang, Q., Li, K., Yang, J.: A digital watermarking approach based on DCT domain combining QR code and chaotic theory. In: 2014 Eleventh International Conference on Wireless and Optical Communications Networks (WOCN), pp. 1–7, September 2014

23. Kasmani, S.A., Sharifi, A.M.: A pre-filtering method to improve watermark detection rate in DCT based watermarking. Int. Arab J. Inf. Technol. **11**(2), 178–185 (2014)

24. Kim, J., Kim, N., Lee, D., Park, S., Lee, S.: Watermarking two dimensional data object identifier for authenticated distribution of digital multimedia contents. Signal Process. Image Commun. **25**(8), 559–576 (2010)

25. Lai, C.C., Tsai, C.C.: Digital image watermarking using discrete wavelet transform and singular value decomposition. IEEE Trans. Instrum. Meas. **59**(11), 3060–3063 (2010)

26. Laskar, R.H., Choudhury, M., Chakraborty, K., Chakraborty, S.: A joint DWT-DCT based robust digital watermarking algorithm for ownership verification of digital images. In: Venugopal, K.R., Patnaik, L.M. (eds.) ICIP 2011. CCIS, vol. 157, pp. 482–491. Springer, Heidelberg (2011). doi:10.1007/978-3-642-22786-8_61

27. Lee, H.-C., Dong, C.-R., Lin, T.-M.: Digital watermarking based on JND model and QR code features. In: Pan, J.-S., et al. (eds.) SIST. SIST, vol. 21, pp. 141–148. Springer, Heidelberg (2013). doi:10.1007/978-3-642-35473-1_15
28. Lin, S.D., Chen, C.-F.: A robust DCT-based watermarking for copyright protection. In: 2000 Digest of Technical Papers. International Conference on Consumer Electronics. Nineteenth in the Series (Cat. No.00CH37102), pp. 10–11, June 2000
29. Ling, C., Ur-Rehman, O.: Watermarking for image authentication. In: Živić, N. (ed.) Robust Image Authentication in the Presence of Noise, pp. 43–73. Springer, Cham (2015). doi:10.1007/978-3-319-13156-6_2
30. Mallat, S.: A theory for multiresolution signal decomposition: the wavelet representation. IEEE Trans. Pattern Anal. Mach. Intell. **11**(7), 674–693 (1989)
31. Panah, A.S., Schyndel, R.V., Sellis, T., Bertino, E.: On the properties of non-media digital watermarking: a review of state of the art techniques. IEEE Access **4**, 2670–2704 (2016)
32. Podilchuk, C.I., Delp, E.J.: Digital watermarking: algorithms and applications. IEEE Signal Process. Mag. **18**(4), 33–46 (2001)
33. Rao, K.R., Yip, P.: Discrete Cosine Transform: Algorithms, Advantages. Applications. Academic Press Professional Inc., San Diego (1990)
34. Thulasidharan, P.P., Nair, M.S.: QR code based blind digital image watermarking with attack detection code. AEU Int. J. Electron. Commun. **69**(7), 1074–1084 (2015)
35. Wang, X.Y., Zhao, H.: A novel synchronization invariant audio watermarking scheme based on DWT and DCT. IEEE Trans. Signal Process. **54**(12), 4835–4840 (2006)
36. Weir, J., Yan, W.Q.: Authenticating visual cryptography shares using 2D barcodes. In: Shi, Y.Q., Kim, H.-J., Perez-Gonzalez, F. (eds.) IWDW 2011. LNCS, vol. 7128, pp. 196–210. Springer, Heidelberg (2012). doi:10.1007/978-3-642-32205-1_17
37. Wu, W.-C., Lin, Z.-W., Wong, W.-T.: Application of QR-code steganography using data embedding technique. In: Park, J.J.J.H., Barolli, L., Xhafa, F., Jeong, H.Y. (eds.) Information Technology Convergence. LNEE, vol. 253, pp. 597–605. Springer, Dordrecht (2013). doi:10.1007/978-94-007-6996-0_63
38. Zhang, W., Meng, X.: An improved digital watermarking technology based on QR code. In: 2015 4th International Conference on Computer Science and Network Technology (ICCSNT), vol. 01, pp. 1004–1007, December 2015

Elliptic Curve Cryptography

Generating Complete Edwards Curves

Theo Fanuela Prabowo[(✉)] and Chik How Tan

Temasek Laboratories, National University of Singapore,
5A Engineering Drive 1, #09-02, Singapore 117411, Singapore
{tsltfp,tsltch}@nus.edu.sg

Abstract. Twisted Edwards curves are elliptic curves of the form $ax^2 + y^2 = 1 + dx^2y^2$ for some constants a and d. The curves are called complete Edwards curves for the special case when $a = 1$ and d is not a square. Using complete Edwards curves for elliptic curve cryptography has many advantages as they have very efficient, complete, and unified point addition formula. In order to use complete Edwards curves for elliptic curve cryptography, we need to specify the curve as well as a point on the curve (typically of prime order). In this paper, we introduce some algorithms for generating complete Edwards curves over $\mathbb{F}_p$ with $4p_0$ number of points, where p_0 is a prime and p is a prime of user-specified bit length. These algorithms are able to generate a complete Edwards curve over $\mathbb{F}_p$ and a point of prime order on the curve in less than 3 (resp. 15, 35) minutes when p is a 256 (resp. 384, 512)-bit prime. These are much faster than the running time of the twisted Edwards curves generation algorithm proposed by Costello et al. in [4].

Keywords: Elliptic curve cryptography · Elliptic curves generator · Edwards curves · Twisted Edwards curves

1 Introduction

Elliptic curve cryptography (ECC) was introduced independently by Koblitz [7] and Miller [9] in the late 1980s. It is based on the elliptic curve discrete logarithm problem (ECDLP) as the underlying hard problem. ECC is now a popular area of public key cryptography due to the many advantages it offers. It requires smaller key size to achieve the same level of security (as compared to RSA-based cryptosystem). This results in cheaper computational cost and memory requirement. It also facilitates faster key generation. It is for these reasons that ECC is now more widely used.

Elliptic curve can be expressed in a few different forms. The most popular form is the short Weierstrass form: $y^2 = x^3 + ax + b$ as it is the most general form (for fields of characteristic $\neq 2, 3$). Montgomery [10] later introduced what is now called the Montgomery form: $by^2 = x^3 + ax + x$. The Montgomery form is less general than the short Weierstrass form, in the sense that not all elliptic curves can be expressed in Montgomery form. However, the computations in elliptic curves in Montgomery form are more efficient than those in short Weierstrass

© Springer International Publishing AG 2017
J. Pieprzyk and S. Suriadi (Eds.): ACISP 2017, Part II, LNCS 10343, pp. 335–348, 2017.
DOI: 10.1007/978-3-319-59870-3_19

form. Moreover, elliptic curves in Montgomery form are resistant against timing attacks [12]. Other than short Weierstrass and Montgomery forms, there are still a number of other different forms, such as extended Jacobi quartic form, twisted Hessian form, etc. [8]. However, these forms are less commonly used in cryptography.

More recently, a new form of elliptic curves called twisted Edwards form was introduced. Elliptic curves in twisted Edwards form are defined by equation of the form: $ax^2 + y^2 = 1 + dx^2y^2$. Edwards form was first introduced by Edwards in [6]. Bernstein and Lange then considered using the Edwards form for elliptic curve cryptography in [2] and introduced the twisted Edwards form in [3]. Twisted Edwards form has a lot of advantages compared to other forms. The computations in twisted Edwards form can be performed very efficiently. The point addition formulas in twisted Edwards form is currently more efficient than any other point addition formulas in other forms of elliptic curves. Another benefit of twisted Edwards form is that it has a *complete* and *unified* point addition formula for certain classes of curves, which means that the formula works for any pair of points on the curves without any exception. This is not the case for elliptic curves in short Weierstrass form and Montgomery form. Having complete and unified point addition formula, elliptic curves in twisted Edwards form (or twisted Edwards curves for short) are more resistant against side-channel attacks.

In order to use twisted Edwards curves for elliptic curve cryptography, we need to specify the curve as well as a point on the curve (typically of prime order). In this paper, we introduce an algorithm for generating complete Edwards curves over the finite field $\mathbb{F}_p$ of p elements, where p is a prime of user-specified bit length b. Our algorithm takes an integer b as input. It then generates a complete Edwards curve $E : x^2 + y^2 = 1 + dx^2y^2$ over $\mathbb{F}_p$, where p is a b-bit prime and the number of points on the curve E is $4p_0$ for some odd prime p_0. We also present another algorithm for generating a point of prime order p_0 on the curve E. The rest of this paper is organized as follows. In Sect. 2, a quick review on twisted Edwards curves is given. In Sect. 3, we present our algorithm for generating complete Edwards curves over $\mathbb{F}_p$ and another algorithm for generating a point of prime order on the curves. The main significance of our algorithms is that they are much faster than the current state-of-the-art method of generating twisted Edwards curves. To illustrate this, in Sect. 4, we review the algorithm proposed by Costello et al. in [4] for generating twisted Edwards curves over $\mathbb{F}_p$, where p is a user-specified prime. We then compare this algorithm with our algorithms. Finally, the paper is concluded in Sect. 5.

2   Preliminaries

2.1   Twisted Edwards Curves

Let p be an odd prime and $\mathbb{F}_p$ be the finite field of p elements. A twisted Edwards curve $E_{E,a,d}$ over $\mathbb{F}_p$ is an elliptic curve over $\mathbb{F}_p$ defined by

$$ax^2 + y^2 = 1 + dx^2y^2,$$

where a and d are distinct elements of $\mathbb{F}_p^\times$. Edwards curve is a special case of twisted Edwards curve where we set $a = 1$.

Twisted Edwards curves support more efficient and unified point addition formula. The addition law on twisted Edwards curves $E_{E,a,d}$ is given by

$$(x_1, y_1) + (x_2, y_2) := \left(\frac{x_1 y_2 + x_2 y_1}{1 + d x_1 x_2 y_1 y_2}, \frac{y_1 y_2 - a x_1 x_2}{1 - d x_1 x_2 y_1 y_2} \right).$$

With the above addition law, the points on twisted Edwards curves form a group, with $(0, 1)$ as the identity element. One may check that $-(x_1, y_1) = (-x_1, y_1)$ and that the point $(0, -1)$ has order 2. In [3], it was shown that the above addition formula holds for any pair of points (without any exception) if a is a square and d is not a square in the field $\mathbb{F}_p$. Twisted Edwards curves satisfying these conditions are called *complete* twisted Edwards curves.

2.2 CM Method

CM method is a powerful method to generate an elliptic curve (in short Weierstrass form) over $\mathbb{F}_p$ with a specified number of points. More precisely, given a prime p and an integer N satisfying certain conditions, the CM method will output $a, b \in \mathbb{F}_p$ such that the number of points in the elliptic curve $y^2 = x^3 + ax + b$ over $\mathbb{F}_p$ equals to N. The conditions that must be satisfied by N and p are the following Diophantine equations:

$$4p = u^2 + |D|v^2, \qquad N = p + 1 \pm u,$$

for some integers u, v and some discriminant D. The CM method will then generate two curves, which are quadratic twist of each other. One is of order $p + 1 + u$ and the other one is of order $p + 1 - u$. For more details on the CM method, the reader is referred to Sect. 7.5.3 of [5].

3 Method to Generate Complete Edwards Curves

In this section, we present our method to generate complete Edwards curves. Our strategy is to use the CM method to generate elliptic curves in short Weierstrass form. We then convert it to complete Edwards curves. We remark that not all elliptic curves (in short Weierstrass form) are birationally equivalent to complete Edwards curves. Note that the point $(1, 0)$ in an Edwards curve $E_{E,1,d}$ is of order 4. This implies that we cannot have a complete Edwards curve having prime order. Thus, we look for complete Edwards curve of order $N = 4p_0$ for some prime p_0 instead. We need some additional conditions to ensure that the elliptic curves generated by the CM method can be expressed as complete Edwards curves. These conditions are given by the following theorem.

Theorem 1. (Part of Theorem 20 of [11]). *Let v be an odd integer and D be a discriminant with $D \equiv 0, 4 \pmod{16}$. Then the elliptic curve generated by the CM method has exactly one point of order two. Moreover, this elliptic curve can be converted to a complete Edwards curve.*

Thus, in order to generate complete Edwards curves using the CM method, we need to solve

$$4p = u^2 + |D|v^2, \qquad N = p + 1 \pm u, \qquad (1)$$

where p, p_0 are odd primes, $u, v \in \mathbb{Z}$ with $v \equiv 1 \pmod 2$, and D is a discriminant with $D \equiv 0, 4 \pmod{16}$.

In Subsect. 3.1, we give an algorithm to solve (1). We then address the problem of converting the elliptic curves produced by the CM method to a complete Edwards curve in Subsect. 3.2. The complete algorithm is presented in Subsect. 3.3.

3.1 Solving Diophantine Equations

The main tool that we need to solve (1) is the Cornacchia-Smith algorithm. It is an algorithm to solve Diophantine equation of the form $u^2 + dv^2 = p$ for u and v.

Algorithm 1. Cornacchia-Smith algorithm (Algorithm 2.3.12 of [5])

Input : a prime p and a positive integer d
Output: $[u, v]$, where $p = u^2 + dv^2$; or $[0,0]$ if such u and v do not exist

1. **if** $\left(\frac{-d}{p}\right) \neq 1$, **then return** $[0,0]$
2. Set $x_0 := \sqrt{-d} \pmod p$
3. **if** $2 \cdot x_0 < p$, **then** $x_0 := p - x_0$
4. Set $(a, b) := (p, x_0)$
5. Set $c := \lfloor \sqrt{p} \rfloor$
6. **while** $(b > c)$ **do** $(a, b) := (b, a \pmod b)$
7. Set $t := p - b^2$
8. **if** $\sqrt{t/d}$ is not an integer, **then return** $[0,0]$
9. **return** $[b, \sqrt{t/d}]$

As an application of Cornacchia-Smith algorithm, we give an algorithm called GenerateP0 to solve (1) for u, v, and p_0. Given an odd prime p and a discriminant $D \equiv 0, 4 \pmod{16}$, the algorithm will find u, v, p_0 satisfying (1). However, as we are only interested in the value of p_0, the algorithm will only return the value of p_0 as its output. In the algorithm, we basically use the Cornacchia-Smith algorithm to find integers u, v such that $p = \left(\frac{u}{2}\right)^2 + \frac{|D|}{4}v^2$, or equivalently $4p = u^2 + |D|v^2$. Once the value of u and v are known, the value of p_0 is automatically determined by $p_0 = \frac{p+1\pm u}{4}$. We then check whether v is odd and p_0 is a prime. If these conditions are not satisfied, the algorithm simply reports that there is no solution by returning 0. Otherwise, the algorithm will return the value of p_0. The algorithm is summarized in Algorithm 2.

Algorithm 2. GenerateP0

Input : an odd prime p and a discriminant D with $D \equiv 0,4 \pmod{16}$
Output: a prime p_0 such that $4p_0 = p + 1 \pm u$ and $4p = u^2 + |D|v^2$ for some
  integer u and odd integer v; or 0 if there is no such p_0.
1. Use Algorithm 1 to find u_0, v such that $4p = 4u_0^2 + |D| \cdot v^2$
2. **if** there is no u_0, v satisfying the above equation **or** v is even, **then return** 0
3. Set $u := 2u_0$ (so that $4p = u^2 + |D| \cdot v^2$)
4. Check whether $\frac{p+1-u}{4}$ or $\frac{p+1+u}{4}$ is a prime,
   if both of them are not prime, **then return** 0
5. Set $p_0 := \frac{p+1\pm u}{4}$ (whichever is prime)
6. **return** p_0

3.2   Conversion to Edwards Curves

Theorem 1 says that the elliptic curves produced by the CM method can be expressed as complete Edwards curves. However, it does not tell us how to convert the curves into complete Edwards curves. In this subsection, we give a method to convert some elliptic curves in short Weierstrass form into complete Edwards curves.

Lemma 1. *Suppose (u, v) is a point of order 4 on the elliptic curve $E : y^2 = x^3 + Ax^2 + Bx$ such that $2 \cdot (u, v) = (0,0)$. Then $A = \frac{v^2}{u^2} - 2u$ and $B = u^2$.*

Proof. Let μ be the slope of the tangent line to E at (u, v). Then $\mu = \frac{3u^2 + 2Au + B}{2v}$. As $2 \cdot (u, v) = (0, 0)$, the tangent line to E at (u, v) passes through $(0, 0)$. Being the slope of the line connecting (u, v) and $(0, 0)$, we have $\mu = \frac{v-0}{u-0} = \frac{v}{u}$. Equating the two expressions for μ gives $2v^2 = 3u^3 + 2Au^2 + Bu$. Moreover, as $(u, v) \in E$, we have $2v^2 = 2u^3 + 2Au^2 + 2Bu$. Subtracting these two equations, we have $u^3 = Bu$, which implies that $B = u^2$ (note that $u \neq 0$ as (u, v) is not of order two). We also note that $A = \frac{v^2 - u^3 - Bu}{u^2} = \frac{v^2}{u^2} - 2u$. $\square$

Theorem 2. *Suppose the elliptic curve $E_0 : y^2 = x^3 + ax + b$ over $\mathbb{F}_p$ has a point of order 4 and exactly one point of order 2. Let $(x_2, 0) \in E_0$ be the unique point of order two and (x_4, y_4) be a point of order 4 in the elliptic curve $E_1 : y^2 = x^3 + (3x_2)x^2 + (3x_2^2 + a)x$. Then $x_2^3 + ax_2 + b = 0$ and $x_4^2 = 3x_2^2 + a$. Moreover, E_0 is birationally equivalent to E_1 and they are birationally equivalent to $E_{E,1,d}$, where $d = 1 - \frac{4x_4}{2x_4 + 3x_2}$.*

Proof. It is clear that E_0 is birationally equivalent to E_1 via the map $(x, y) \mapsto (x - x_2, y)$. As (x_4, y_4) is a point of order 4 in E_1 and E_1 has exactly one point of order two, we must have $2 \cdot (x_4, y_4) = (0, 0)$. We then apply Lemma 1 to conclude that $3x_2 = \frac{y_4^2}{x_4^2} - 2x_4$ and $3x_2^2 + a = x_4^2$, i.e. E_1 is $y^2 = x^3 + \left(\frac{y_4^2}{x_4^2} - 2x_4\right)x^2 + x_4^2 x$. At this point, we have shown that $x_2^3 + ax_2 + b = 0$ and $x_4^2 = 3x_2^2 + a$.

Let $d = 1 - \frac{4x_4^3}{y_4^2}$. Then the map $E_1 \rightarrow E_{E,1,d}$ defined by $(u, v) \mapsto (x, y) :=$ $\left(\frac{y_4 u}{x_4 v}, \frac{u - x_4}{u + x_4} \right)$ is a birational equivalence with inverse given by $(x, y) \mapsto (u, v) :=$ $\left(\frac{x_4(1+y)}{1-y}, \frac{y_4(1+y)}{(1-y)x} \right)$. Therefore, E_1 is birationally equivalent to $E_{E,1,d}$, where $d =$ $1 - \frac{4x_4^3}{y_4^2} = 1 - \frac{4x_4^3}{x_4^3 + 3x_2 x_4^2 + (3x_2^2 + a)x_4} = 1 - \frac{4x_4^3}{2x_4^3 + 3x_2 x_4^2} = 1 - \frac{4x_4}{2x_4 + 3x_2}.$ □

Theorem 2 above gives a way to convert some elliptic curves in short Weierstrass form into complete Edwards curves. We end this subsection by proving the following simple but useful lemma.

Lemma 2. *Let $a, b, g \in \mathbb{F}_p$. Suppose at least one of $E : y^2 = x^3 + ax + b$ and $E' : y^2 = x^3 + ag^2 x + bg^3$ has a point of order 4 and exactly one point of order 2. Then there exist x_2, x_4, u_2, u_4 such that*

$$x_2^3 + ax_2 + b = 0, \qquad x_4^2 = 3x_2^2 + a, \tag{2}$$

$$u_2^3 + ag^2 u_2 + bg^3 = 0, \qquad u_4^2 = 3u_2^2 + ag^2, \tag{3}$$

$$u_2 = gx_2, \qquad u_4 = gx_4. \tag{4}$$

Proof. Suppose E has a point of order 4 and exactly one point of order 2. Then by Theorem 2, there exist $x_2, x_4 \in \mathbb{F}_p$ satisfying (2). Defining u_2 and u_4 by (4), we can check that (3) (and hence all of the equations) is satisfied.

Similarly, suppose E' has a point of order 4 and exactly one point of order 2. Then by Theorem 2, there exist $u_2, u_4 \in \mathbb{F}_p$ satisfying (3). Defining x_2 and x_4 by (4), one can check that all of the equations are satisfied.   □

3.3   The Algorithm

In this subsection, we combine the tools developed in previous subsections by presenting our algorithm (Algorithm 4) to generate complete Edwards curves over $\mathbb{F}_p$, where p is a prime of user-specified bit length. We will also give another algorithm to generate points of prime order on the complete Edwards curves produced by Algorithm 4. We start this subsection by introducing the following Algorithm 3.

Algorithm 3 consists of 4 phases: the Setup phase, the CM Method phase, the Conversion phase, and the Final phase. The Setup phase consists of the first three steps of the algorithm. In this phase, we solve (1) for p_0 by using Algorithm 2 discussed in Subsect. 3.1. We let D to run through a list of discriminants and check (using Algorithm 2) whether with the given value of p and D, we are able to solve (1). Once (1) is successfully solved, we simply break the loop, and set $N = 4p_0$.

The CM Method phase consists of Step 4, 5, and 6. In this phase, we use the CM Method (see Subsect. 2.2) to generate two elliptic curves of order $p + 1 + u$ and $p + 1 - u$ respectively. The two elliptic curves are $E : y^2 = x^3 + rx + s$ and $E' : y^2 = x^3 + rg^2 x + bg^3$, where g is some quadratic non-residue modulo p. However, these curves are in short Weierstrass form.

Algorithm 3. Main

Input : an odd prime p

Output: $[p, N, d]$, where the Edwards curve $x^2 + y^2 = 1 + dx^2y^2$ over $\mathbb{F}_p$ has cardinality $N = 4p_0$ for some prime p_0; or $[0,0,0]$ if such curve failed to be generated

1. **for** D_0 in [list of discriminants D with $D \equiv 0, 4 \pmod{16}$] **do**:
    (a) $p_0 := GenerateP0(p, D_0)$
    (b) **if** $p_0 \neq 0$, **then**
        i. Set $D := D_0$
        ii. **break**
2. **if** $p_0 = 0$ (meaning there is no p_0 satisfying the Diophantine equations required in GenerateP0), **then return** [0,0,0]
3. Set $N := 4p_0$
4. Set $T := HilbertClassPolynomial(D)$ and $S := T \pmod{p}$
5. Compute the root $j \in \mathbb{F}_p$ of S
6. Set $c := \frac{j}{j-1728} \pmod{p}$, $r := -3c \pmod{p}$, $s := 2c \pmod{p}$
7. Compute the root $t_1 \in \mathbb{F}_p$ of $y^3 + ry + s = 0$
8. Set $t_2 := \sqrt{3t_1^2 + r}$ in $\mathbb{F}_p$
9. Set $d := 1 - (4t_2) \cdot (3t_1 + 2t_2)^{-1}$ and $d_2 := 1 + (4t_2) \cdot (3t_1 - 2t_2)^{-1}$
10. Check whether the curve $x^2 + y^2 = 1 + dx^2y^2$ or $x^2 + y^2 = 1 + d_2x^2y^2$ over $\mathbb{F}_p$ has cardinality N
11. **return** $[p, N, d]$ or $[p, N, d_2]$ correspondingly

We then convert them to complete Edwards curves in the Conversion phase (Step 7, 8, 9). By Theorem 1, we know that the elliptic curve produced in the CM Method phase has a point of order 4 and a unique point of order 2. We then may apply Lemma 2 to check that there exist $t_1, t_2 \in \mathbb{F}_p$ such that $t_1^3 + rt_1 + s = 0$ and $t_2 = \sqrt{3t_1^2 + r}$ (these are computed in Step 7 and 8). By Theorem 2, if (x_4, y_4) is a point of order 4 in E, then $x_4^2 = 3t_1^2 + r$. Thus, we must have $x_4 = \pm t_2$. Theorem 2 also states that E is birationally equivalent to the Edwards curve $E_{E,1,d}$, where $d = 1 - \frac{4x_4}{2x_4 + 3t_1} = 1 - \frac{\pm 4t_2}{3t_1 \pm 2t_2}$. Similarly, we may apply Theorem 2 to E'. Let (u_4, v_4) be a point of order 4 in E'. By Lemma 2, we have $u_4 = \pm gt_2$. We then note that E' is birationally equivalent to $E_{E,1,d}$, where $d = 1 - \frac{4u_4}{2u_4 + 3gt_1} = 1 - \frac{\pm 4gt_2}{3gt_1 \pm 2gt_2} = 1 - \frac{\pm 4t_2}{3t_1 \pm 2t_2}$.

At the end of the Conversion phase, we have two candidate Edwards curves $E_{E,1,d}$ and $E_{E,1,d'}$, where $d = 1 - \frac{4t_2}{3t_1 + 2t_2}$ and $d' = 1 - \frac{4(-t_2)}{3t_1 - 2t_2}$. One of these Edwards curves is the desired curve, i.e. it is a complete Edwards curves with N number of points. In the Final phase, we determine which of these two candidates is the desired curve. In order to find the desired curve, we choose a random point P on $E_{E,1,d}$ and compute $N \cdot P$. As the number of points in the desired curve is N, we must have $N \cdot P = (0, 1)$ if $E_{E,1,d}$ is the desired curve. In other words, if $N \cdot P \neq (0, 1)$, then $E_{E,1,d}$ is not the desired curve and consequently $E_{E,1,d'}$ is the desired curve.

In practice, we only work with a finite list of discriminants. For computational purpose, it is suggested to use discriminants with class number ≤ 4. This is so that the computation to find a root of the (reduced) Hilbert class polynomial (in step 5 of Algorithm 3) is not difficult. In Appendix A, we list the discriminants D with $D \equiv 0, 4 \pmod{16}$ of class number at most 4. We exclude those discriminants D with $D \equiv 4 \pmod{32}$ due to the following lemma.

Lemma 3. *Let p, p_0, u, v, D be integers such that p and p_0 are prime, v is odd, and $D < 0$. Suppose $4p = u^2 + |D|v^2$ and $4p_0 = p + 1 \pm u$. Then $D \not\equiv 4 \pmod{32}$.*

Proof. Suppose $D \equiv 4 \pmod{32}$. As $4p = u^2 + |D|v^2$, we note that u is even, say $u = 2u_0$ for some integer u_0. So, $p = u_0^2 + (|D|/4)v^2$. Note that $|D|/4 \equiv -1 \pmod 8$, in particular it is odd. So, u_0 is even, say $u_0 = 2u_1$ for some integer u_1. Then $p = 4u_1^2 + (|D|/4)v^2$. Now $p_0 = \frac{p+1\pm u}{4} = u_1(u_1 \pm 1) + \frac{(|D|/4)v^2+1}{4}$. Note that $(|D|/4)v^2 + 1 \equiv 0 \pmod 8$. Thus, $\frac{(|D|/4)v^2+1}{4}$ is even. As, $u_1(u_1 \pm 1)$ is also even, we then have p_0 is even (and greater than 2). Thus, p_0 is not a prime, a contradiction. Hence, $D \not\equiv 4 \pmod{32}$. $\qquad\square$

We also list the Hilbert class polynomial of these discriminants in Appendix A. The Hilbert class polynomial of any discriminant can be computed using Algorithm 7.5.8 of [5]. Alternatively, it can also be obtained using a pre-defined command in Magma or Sage.

As we are working with a finite list of discriminants, it is possible that for a fixed value of p and any value of discriminants D on the finite list, there is no solution for (1). In that case, Algorithm 3 will simply terminate without producing the desired curve. To overcome this issue, we present the following final algorithm.

Algorithm 4. GenerateCurve

Input : an integer b (the bit-length of p)
Output: $[p, N, d]$, where p is a b-bit prime and the Edwards curve $E_{E,1,d}$ over
$\qquad\qquad \mathbb{F}_p$ has cardinality $N = 4p_0$ for some prime p_0
1. Set p to be a random b-bit prime
2. Set $O := \text{Main}(p)$
3. **if** $O = [0, 0, 0]$ (meaning there is no solution for (1) for the given value of p),
   then go to 1
4. **return** O

In this algorithm, we simply repeat the process with different value of p if there is no solution for (1) for the given value of p (and any value of discriminants D on the list). One may modify Algorithm 4 by imposing the condition that the prime chosen in Step 1 must be of certain forms (e.g. pseudo-Mersenne prime or Montgomery-friendly prime).[1]

Algorithm 4 is an algorithm to generate complete Edwards curves over the finite field $\mathbb{F}_p$ where p is a prime of specified bit-length. The number of points on these curves is $4p_0$ for some prime p_0. We end this section by presenting an algorithm that will generate a point of prime order p_0 on these complete Edwards curves. The algorithm basically generates a random point P on the Edwards curve $E_{E,1,d}$ and returns $4P$ as an output. This point $4P$ is of order dividing p_0 for the following reason. Recall that if g is an element of finite order in a group G and k is an integer, then $\mathrm{ord}(g^k) = \frac{\mathrm{ord}(g)}{\gcd(k,\mathrm{ord}(g))}$. Thus, we have $\mathrm{ord}(4P) = \frac{\mathrm{ord}(P)}{\gcd(4,\mathrm{ord}P)}$, and so $4P$ is a point of odd order. Hence, the order of $4P$ is either 1 or p_0. In the case that $\mathrm{ord}(4P) = 1$ (i.e. $4P = (0,1)$), we simply repeat the process with different P. The algorithm is summarized in Algorithm 5. Some sample output of Algorithms 4 and 5 are given in Appendix B.

Algorithm 5. PrimeOrderPoint

> **Input** : the output of Algorithm 4, i.e. $[p, N, d]$, where p and $N/4$ are prime, and the number of points on the Edwards curve $E_{E,1,d}$ over $\mathbb{F}_p$ is N
>
> **Output**: $[x, y]$, where (x, y) is a point on $E_{E,1,d}$ over $\mathbb{F}_p$ of prime order $p_0 = \frac{N}{4}$
>
> 1. Choose y_0 randomly from the interval $[1, p-1]$
> 2. Set $x_0' := \frac{y_0^2 - 1}{dy_0^2 - 1} \pmod{p}$
> 3. **if** $\left(\frac{x_0'}{p}\right) \neq 1$, **then** go to 1
> 4. Set $x_0 := \sqrt{x_0'} \pmod{p}$
> 5. Set $(x, y) := 4 \cdot (x_0, y_0)$
> 6. **if** $(x, y) = (0, 1)$, **then** go to 1
> 7. **return** (x, y)

---

4   Comparison with Twisted Edwards Curves Generation Method Proposed by Costello et al.

In this section, we review the twisted Edwards curves generation method introduced by Costello et al. in [4] and compare it with our method described in Sect. 3. While for Algorithm 4 the user can only specify the bit length of the prime p, for the algorithm introduced in [4] the user may specify the prime p. With a prime p as input, the algorithm will generate a twisted Edwards curve $E_{E,a,d}$ over $\mathbb{F}_p$.

---

[1] Pseudo-Mersenne primes are primes of the form $2^\alpha - \gamma$, while Montgomery-friendly primes are primes of the form $2^\alpha(2^\beta - \gamma) - 1$, where α, β, γ are integers. Primes of these forms are usually preferred for efficiency consideration [1].

In their algorithm, a is chosen to be either 1 or -1 depending on the prime p used. More precisely, they use

$$a := \begin{cases} 1 & \text{if } p \equiv 3 \pmod 4, \\ -1 & \text{if } p \equiv 1 \pmod 4. \end{cases}$$

Once the parameter a is fixed, it remains to determine the value of the parameter d. This algorithm simply tests the values of d in the sequence $\pm1, 2, -2, 3, -3, \cdots$ until it finds d with the smallest absolute value such that $E_{E,a,d}$ and its quadratic twist have optimal cofactors (i.e. the number of points in these curves is either $4 \times (prime)$ or $8 \times (prime)$). Counting the number of points on $E_{E,a,d}$ and its quadratic twist can be done at the same time by computing the trace of Frobenius $t_{a,d} = p+1 - \#E_{E,a,d}(\mathbb{F}_p)$ of the twisted Edwards curve $E_{E,a,d}$. After the trace of Frobenius $t_{a,d}$ is computed, the number of points in $E_{E,a,d}$ is given by $p + 1 - t_{a,d}$, while the number of points in its quadratic twist is $p + 1 + t_{a,d}$. The following is their algorithm for determining d when $p \equiv 3 \pmod 4$.

for $d \in [-1, 2, -2, 3, -3, \cdots]$ **do**

- Compute $t_{1,d}$.
- Set $(p + 1 - t_{1,d}) = hr$ and $(p + 1 + t_{1,d}) = h'r'$, where $h = 2^e$, $h' = 2^{e'}$ for some integers e, e'; and r and r' are odd.
- **if** $h = h' = 4$ **and** r is prime **and** r' is prime **then return** d.

end for

In [4], Costello et al. used the above algorithm with three different inputs $p = 2^{256} - 189, 2^{384} - 317, 2^{512} - 569$. The result is tabulated in Table 1 below.

Table 1. Edwards curves generated by Costello et al. [4]

Security level	Input: prime p	Bit-length of p	Output: parameter d ($x^2 + y^2 = 1 + dx^2y^2$)
128	$2^{256} - 189$	256	-15342
192	$2^{384} - 317$	384	-11556
256	$2^{512} - 569$	512	-78296

The running time of the algorithm is not mentioned in [4]. In the following, we shall give a rough estimate on the running time of the algorithm. We take the input $p = 2^{256} - 189$ as an example. For this input, the output is $d = -15342$. To produce this output, the algorithm has to run through 30683 iterations. The most expensive operation in each iteration is the computation of the trace of Frobenius. The best known algorithm to compute the trace of Frobenius is the SEA algorithm [13,14]. In Magma, running the SEA algorithm on elliptic curves over $\mathbb{F}_p$ takes 9 s on average. Thus, to produce the output of $d = -15342$, the algorithm would take about $30683 \times 9 = 276147$ seconds ≈ 76.7 h.

Table 2. Running time comparison

Bit-length of p	Algorithm 4	Algorithm in [4] (estimated)
256	≤ 3 min	76 h
384	≤ 15 min	$\gg 58$ h
512	≤ 35 min	$\gg 391$ h

For the input $p = 2^{384} - 317$ and $p = 2^{512} - 569$, the numbers of iterations needed to produce the output are 23111 and 156591 respectively. So, the running time would be at least 207999 s ≈ 58 h for $p = 2^{384} - 317$ and 1409319 s ≈ 391 h for $p = 2^{512} - 569$, assuming that each iteration takes 9 s on average. However, as the bit length of p is bigger, it takes much longer to execute the SEA algorithm. Thus, the actual running time is expected to be much longer than our estimates.

On the other hand, we run Algorithm 4 (as well as its pseudo-Mersenne and Montgomery-friendly variants) in Magma numerous times and noted the running time. The running time of our algorithm is tabulated in Table 2. We remark that the running time mentioned in Table 2 is the worst case running time out of the numerous executions of the algorithm. We also put the running time estimates of Costello et al.'s algorithm in the table as comparison. It is clear that our algorithm is much faster than that of [4].

5   Conclusion

Twisted Edwards curves are elliptic curves which are defined by equation of the form $ax^2 + y^2 = 1 + dx^2 y^2$ for some constant a and d. When $a = 1$, the curves are called Edwards curves. When a is a square and d is not a square in the underlying field, point additions on the twisted Edwards curves can be evaluated using a single unified formula that holds for any pair of points on the curves. In this case, we say that the twisted Edwards curves is complete.

In this paper, we introduced an algorithm (Algorithm 4) for generating complete Edwards curves over $\mathbb{F}_p$, where p is a prime of user-specified bit length, and the number of points on the curve is $4 \times (prime)$. We remarked that the algorithm can be modified by specifying that the prime p must be a prime of special form (e.g. pseudo-Mersenne or Montgomery-friendly prime). We also presented another algorithm (Algorithm 5) to produce a point of prime order on the curve generated by Algorithm 4.

We then compared our algorithms with the algorithm for generating twisted Edwards curve given by Costello et al. in [4]. We noted that for our algorithm the user inputs the bit length of the prime p, while for the algorithm in [4], the user enters the prime p as the input. We observed that our algorithms are able to generate a complete Edwards curve, along with a point of prime order on the curve in less than 3 (resp. 15, 35) minutes when the bit length of the prime p is 256 (resp. 384, 512) bits. These are much faster than the estimated running time of the algorithm proposed by Costello et al. in [4].

Appendix

A List of Discriminants and Their Hilbert Class Polynomials

No.	D	HilbertClassPolynomial(D)
1	-12	$X - 54000$
2	-16	$X - 287496$
3	-32	$X^2 - 52250000X + 12167000000$
4	-48	$X^2 - 2835810000X + 6549518250000$
5	-64	$X^2 - 82226316240X - 7367066619912$
6	-112	$X^2 - 274917323970000X + 1337635747140890625$
7	-44	$X^3 - 1122662608X^2 + 270413882112X - 653249011576832$
8	-76	$X^3 - 784074438864X^2 + 1128678666363648X - 827237892283232256$
9	-108	$X^3 - 151013228706000X^2 + 224179462188000000X - 187999470568800000000$
10	-172	$X^3 - 7827591061833300000X^2 + 1164707517403692000000X - 69266081032623900000000000000$
11	-268	$X^3 - 2166723729202485673800 00X^2 + 322408427628582369720000 00X - 318937643273692956938421600 0000000000$
12	-652	$X^3 - 68925893036109279891085639286946000X^2 + 1025617288377193226459213254129080000 00X - 18095625621665522953693950872675200892692248000000000$
13	-80	$X^4 - 1597177172000X^3 - 13028555239824000X^2 - 171263969177632000000X + 4222868839705267840000 00$
14	-96	$X^4 - 23340144296736X^3 + 6704210551921156288X^2 + 4478053641119672094 72X - 984163224549635621646336$
15	-128	$X^4 - 2729960418308000X^3 - 395258439243352250000X^2 - 55499520477163915000000 00X - 3453636562266580267656250000 00$
16	-144	$X^4 - 23578503968570400X^3 + 26949918540608794252 8X^2 + 490453856866850787293184X + 5717513212333286375791042 56$
17	-160	$X^4 - 18119551982464080 00X^3 - 2940735389875294896000X^2 + 1320822153677970138240 0000X - 29383505396043298041600 0000$
18	-192	$X^4 - 8041801037378436000X^3 + 157055216359097350507500 00X^2 + 8263355561881786154745000 00000X - 10800608861131599376493085 93750000$
19	-208	$X^4 - 47568078792050004000X^3 + 403237241218125526000000X^2 - 39086684948887089480000 00000X + 146359284147782763300 0000000000$
20	-240	$X^4 - 137033763558484836240 0X^3 + 1551063662363722598553024 3375X^2 - 3213137488352330508627918491550 000X + 51848746810441819437662737568196 890625$
21	-256	$X^4 - 6761166974781862161312X^3 - 182659267350620720090417 2752X^2 + 26925623396630083113758909667 84X - 10644106811181869521037208 505239142408$
22	-288	$X^4 - 14263776505846851077200 0X^3 - 8733000825595539913108600 0000X^2 + 1364781430446574260765640 0000000X + 40994594700208456153393000000000000$
23	-352	$X^4 - 396250122567179915333640 00X^3 - 99328134588221245548396654000 000X^2 + 14968574555823233750718997200 0000000X + 2338148636622354657578109930000 00000000$
24	-400	$X^4 - 19387735083548727178453842 24X^3 - 1286928686316186418463627944 3710336X^2 - 1907506145576788940647797499460 7212544X + 8744887373829579045094827612354450 117376$
25	-448	$X^4 - 755795350157415880885518 0200 00X^3 - 125199547498575939262869747778 41250000X^2 - 18314847446238545696830716579562 500000000X - 89644242822733628905053390445240 81787109375$
26	-592	$X^4 - 157293019493123985192760519611 6000X^3 + 3132504321611229483521632487251792 38000000X^2 - 466359042858849293316032894138251092 00000000X + 624329944132650345552467574294664755 69000000000000$
27	-928	$X^4 - 365698321891389219219142531076614125108000X^3 - 8992980876865725569995845414882451608653638542000000X^2 + 1339056499821629098407314617923975190564285928400000 0000X + 2211472872958406310091553782159198962412349932936170000000 00000$

B Sample Output of Algorithms 4 and 5

The sample output of Algorithms 4 and 5 are given in Tables 3, 4 and 5 below.

Table 3. Input (bit-length of p) = 256

Prime p	2^{256} - 90437671211985546874316358605566976675
Parameter d	22329574029308889626901538482037378195116564557043652036138893384155517544966
# $E_{E,1,d}$	4 × 28948022309329048855892746252171976963294556678555688323048256808032754388119
Point of prime order	(38827631816508813273841327893835794280440756912139095629484251847080307749332, 45829116834518642034200069292195310273647442070782884666574460125768495421042)

Table 4. Input (bit-length of p) = 384

Prime p	2^{384} - 1431712715302249176153463591222786594736847634233865480307
Parameter d	19701003098197239606139520050071806902539869635232723333973430845765209761160528573911521734145089396586197062413255
# $E_{E,1,d}$	4 × 9850501549098619803069760025035903451269934817616361666988912724620851618416199716515265055521363641980466510748829
Point of prime order	(20276696977617322881192514937581822781269464734275003364979120493216471108092676421739531805311493757613371809813335, 20177608000332933836528309688591293759937886040186443658471691078279871203594520696578763107668549007555074473299435)

Table 5. Input (bit-length of p) = 512

Prime p	2^{512} - 9236884931966751641228310144316961954531808116793136270160199561113067518679
Parameter d	8338373405875649770857518942505743213703027606162372210898580979163305305328223695986850324431265351430266149215962893734385441401397014004945963621838618
# $E_{E,1,d}$	4 × 3351951982485649274893506249551461531869841455148098344430890360930441007518439998561692274611542134986503267678569602506179958498860373550699760692315387
Point of prime order	(4221176987664061988834477481798535838679628228953622593354872274681074377661272412205621206287722762297218626276294075053564148168996099225259593206694004, 7997462079241487776422481985426302583630543829861538697758456830296460477778644049664970989485873761325036499067164466584007358797257459370337450680946804)

References

1. Bos, J.W., Costello, C., Longa, P., Naehrig, M.: Selecting elliptic curves for cryptography: an efficiency and security analysis. J. Cryptol. Eng. **6**, 259–286 (2016). doi:10.1007/s13389-015-0097-y

2. Bernstein, D.J., Lange, T.: Faster addition and doubling on elliptic curves. In: Kurosawa, K. (ed.) ASIACRYPT 2007. LNCS, vol. 4833, pp. 29–50. Springer, Heidelberg (2007). doi:10.1007/978-3-540-76900-2_3

3. Bernstein, D.J., Birkner, P., Joye, M., Lange, T., Peters, C.: Twisted Edwards curves. In: Vaudenay, S. (ed.) AFRICACRYPT 2008. LNCS, vol. 5023, pp. 389–405. Springer, Heidelberg (2008). doi:10.1007/978-3-540-68164-9_26

4. Costello, C., Longa, P., Naehrig, M.: A brief discussion on selecting new elliptic curves. Microsoft Research, Technical report MSR-TR-2015-46 (2015). http://research.microsoft.com/apps/pubs/default.aspx?id=246915

5. Crandall, R., Pomerance, C.: Prime Numbers: A Computational Perspective. Springer, New York (2005)

6. Edwards, H.M.: A normal form for elliptic curves. Bull. Am. Math. Soc. **44**(3), 393–422 (2007). doi:10.1090/S0273-0979-07-01153-6

7. Koblitz, N.: Elliptic curve cryptosystems. Math. Comput. **48**, 203–209 (1987). doi:10.1090/S0025-5718-1987-0866109-5

8. Hisil, H.: Elliptic curves, group law, and efficient computation, Ph.D. thesis, Queensland University of Technology (2010)

9. Miller, V.S.: Use of elliptic curves in cryptography. In: Williams, H.C. (ed.) CRYPTO 1985. LNCS, vol. 218, pp. 417–426. Springer, Heidelberg (1986). doi:10.1007/3-540-39799-X_31

10. Montgomery, P.L.: Speeding the Pollard and elliptic curve methods of factorization. Math. Comput. **48**, 243–264 (1987). doi:10.1090/S0025-5718-1987-0866113-7
11. Morain, F.: Edwards curves and CM curves. Technical report (2009). https://hal. inria.fr/inria-00375427
12. Okeya, K., Kurumatani, H., Sakurai, K.: Elliptic curves with the montgomery-form and their cryptographic applications. In: Imai, H., Zheng, Y. (eds.) PKC 2000. LNCS, vol. 1751, pp. 238–257. Springer, Heidelberg (2000). doi:10.1007/978-3-540-46588-1_17
13. Schoof, R.: Elliptic curves over finite fields and the computation of square roots mod p. Math. Comput. **44**, 483–494 (1985).
doi:10.1090/S0025-5718-1985-0777280-6
14. Schoof, R.: Counting points on elliptic curves over finite fields. J. Theor. Nombres Bordx. **7**, 219–254 (1995)

Secure GLS Recomposition
for Sum-of-Square Cofactors

Eunkyung Kim[1] and Mehdi Tibouchi[2(✉)]

[1] Department of Mathematics, Ewha Womans University, Seoul, Republic of Korea
ekkim0410@ewhain.net
[2] NTT Secure Platform Laboratories, Tokyo, Japan
tibouchi.mehdi@lab.ntt.co.jp

Abstract. The GLV/GLS technique speeds up scalar multiplications on elliptic curves endowed with an efficiently computable endomorphism: a scalar multiplication by a full-size scalar becomes a double scalar multiplication by half-size scalars, which is significantly faster. However, this requires to first decompose the original scalar into an appropriate linear combination of half-size scalars using reduction in a low-dimensional lattice. Since a reduced basis of the lattice can be precomputed, this is typically fast, but it tends to leak a lot of side-channel information about the scalar.

To avoid this issue, Aranha et al. (ASIACRYPT 2014) proposed to use "recomposition" instead, i.e. choose the two half-sized scalars at random in a suitable interval, defining a corresponding full-size scalar implicitly. If the statistical distance to uniform of the distribution of that scalar is negligible, the recomposition method is secure and avoids any of the leakage of GLV/GLS decomposition. The original paper obtained the statistical distance result for GLS curves of prime order. In this work, we extend their proof to GLS curves having a cofactor which can be written as a sum of two squares. This shows in particular how to obtain secure recomposition for (twisted) Edwards GLS curves and the fast binary curve GLS254 of Oliveira et al. (CHES 2013), as these curves have cofactor 4 and 2 respectively.

1 Introduction

The GLV/GLS Technique. In recent years, most of the record-breaking implementations of elliptic curve cryptography have been achieved using special elliptic curves endowed with fast endomorphisms: this includes [5,7,8,13] and more. These implementations rely on the methods introduced by Gallant–Lambert–Vanstone (GLV) [11], Galbraith–Lin–Scott (GLS) [9], and generalizations thereof. One can roughly describe these techniques as follows.

Consider an elliptic curve E over a finite field $\mathbb{F}_q$, and an endomorphism ψ of E over $\mathbb{F}_q$ which is assumed to be fast to evaluate. Suppose also, as is always the case in elliptic curve cryptography, that $E(\mathbb{F}_q)$ contains a unique subgroup G of large prime order ℓ. Then, since ψ sends points of order ℓ to points of order

© Springer International Publishing AG 2017
J. Pieprzyk and S. Suriadi (Eds.): ACISP 2017, Part II, LNCS 10343, pp. 349–365, 2017.
DOI: 10.1007/978-3-319-59870-3_20

(dividing) ℓ, it must leave G stable, and hence act on G by multiplication by some scalar λ, which is typically of full size (i.e. the bit size of λ is roughly the same as that of ℓ). Therefore, in order to compute a scalar multiplication $[k]P$ in G by a full-size scalar $k \in \mathbb{Z}/\ell\mathbb{Z}$, one can first write k in the form $k = k_1 + k_2\lambda \bmod \ell$ (where k_1, k_2 can be chosen as roughly *half-size* scalar), and then compute the *double* half-size scalar multiplication $[k_1]P + [k_2]\psi(P)$. Since operations such as doublings are shared in a double scalar multiplication, this is significantly faster than carrying out the single full-size scalar multiplication $[k]P$ directly.

This approach was first considered by Gallant, Lambert and Vanstone over prime finite fields, but constructing curves with efficient endomorphisms in that setting is not easy, and the corresponding curves tend to be quite special (e.g. have low CM discriminant). Galbraith, Lin and Scott later showed how to obtain a much larger class of elliptic curves with fast endomorphisms by moving to quadratic extension fields. Their strategy (or at least its most important special case) is as follows: from an elliptic curve E over $\mathbb{F}_q$ for a prime q, take its quadratic twist E' over $\mathbb{F}_{q^2}$; E' has an efficient endomorphism ψ induced from the Frobenius map of $E/\mathbb{F}_{q^2}$. If $E'(\mathbb{F}_{q^2})$ has a unique subgroup of a large prime order ℓ, the endomorphism ψ acts on that subgroup by multiplication by an integer λ, which can be shown to satisfy $\lambda^2 \equiv -1 \pmod{\ell}$. Thus, the fast scalar multiplication technique above applies to E' using ψ as the fast endomorphism. Elliptic curves constructed in this way are the main focus of the present paper, and what we will henceforth call *GLS curves*.

In their original paper, Galbraith, Lin and Scott had considered GLS curves E' obtained as twists of curves E defined over large prime fields: in particular, they applied their technique to construct a particularly efficient twisted Edwards curve [3] with fast endomorphism defined over $\mathbb{F}_{(2^{127}-1)^2}$. As observed by Hankerson, Karabina and Menezes [12], however, the construction extends naturally to fields of characteristic 2. This was used by Oliveira et al. [13] to obtain one of the fastest software implementation of elliptic curve cryptography, on a GLS curve over $\mathbb{F}_{2^{254}}$ called GLS254.

Decomposition vs. Recomposition. To obtain the half-size scalars k_1 and k_2 involved in the GLV/GLS double scalar multiplication, two competing approaches have been suggested in the literature (including in some of the earliest presentations of the GLV technique, like Gallant's talk at ECC'99 [10]).

A very natural approach is to start from a given scalar k, and *decompose* it in the form $k = k_1 + k_2\lambda \bmod \ell$ using lattice reduction in dimension 2 (or equivalently, continued fractions, a generalized Euclidean algorithm, etc.). Such a decomposition algorithm is described in the original GLV paper [11], and has received various improvements and simplifications (such as [14]). Since λ is typically fixed, one can precompute a short basis of the corresponding lattice, and the decomposition algorithm mostly boils down to a few multiplications by known constants, so it is quite fast in practice.

However, in contexts where side-channel attacks are a concern, Aranha et al. [1] have shown that the decomposition technique could be a security liability: because it involves the multiplication of the secret k by known constants (in a machine word by machine word fashion), it can very easily be targeted using standard side-channel attacks (such as correlation power analysis, correlation EM analysis, template attacks, etc.) to reveal partial or complete information about k. As a result, Aranha et al. were able to mount a key recovery against an 8-bit AVR smart card implementation of ECDSA on a GLS curve by targeting the decomposition phase alone.

These concerns regarding side-channel leakage can be alleviated by *avoiding computation* in the generation of k_1 and k_2. Instead of starting from k and deriving k_1 and k_2 from there, a simpler approach is to simply pick k_1 and k_2 at random, which defines the scalar $k = k_1 + k_2\lambda \bmod \ell$ only implicitly. Aranha et al. call that method the *recomposition technique*, because k is "recomposed" as a linear combination of k_1 and k_2. Gallant did mention that technique in his ECC'99 presentation, but expressed concerns about possible biases in the resulting scalar k. Such biases are not very serious for protocols like elliptic curve Diffie–Hellman, but they are a grave security issue in other settings like ECDSA signatures. Indeed, Aranha et al. demonstrated that when k_1 and k_2 are chosen in a naive way, the resulting bias on the distribution of k is sufficient to completely recover the signing key using statistical techniques.

More generally, it is not clear in general that even a non-naive way of sampling k_1 and k_2 will result in a recomposed scalar k with close to uniform distribution in $\mathbb{Z}/\ell\mathbb{Z}$. In fact, some numerical evidence provided by Brumley and Nyberg [6] suggested that in many specific settings, natural choices of sampling intervals for k_1 and k_2 failed to yield a uniform k. In contrast to their results, however, Aranha et al. proved that, in the specific case of GLS curves of *prime order*, choosing k_1 and k_2 uniformly at random in $[0, \sqrt{\ell})$ did yield a close-to-uniform distribution for k. In that specific case, the recomposition method is thus almost always preferable to decomposition: it is very simple and efficient (since it requires essentially no computation), and it offers a very desirable protection against side-channels.

Unfortunately, the proof given by Aranha et al. uses arithmetic properties of the number of points on GLS curves of prime order in a crucial way, and thus does not generalize directly to other settings. It is therefore unclear in general how to carry out secure recomposition (in the sense that k will be close to uniform), even on GLS curves of non-prime order.

Our Contribution. In this paper, we revisit the uniformity proof of Aranha et al., and show that it can be extended using slightly more advanced algebraic number theoretic techniques. More precisely, we show how to obtain secure recomposition on GLS curves not just of prime order, but also with *any* cofactor of the form $h = a^2 + b^2$ with $a, b \in \mathbb{Z}$.

This captures in particular the case of cofactors $2 = 1^2 + 1^2$ and $4 = 2^2 + 0^2$, which are of singular importance, because they cover twisted Edwards GLS curves as well as GLS curves over binary fields such as GLS254. Side-channel security is one of the major design goals of these curves, and it is thus especially desirable to ensure that the generation of k_1 and k_2 does not leak all of our secrets on a power or EM trace.

The rest of this paper is organized as follows: In Sect. 2, we provide background material about Gaussian integers and the notion of statistical distance, and review GLS curves and the result of [1] that describes secure GLS recomposition on prime order curves. In Sect. 3, we present our first result about secure GLS recomposition method for curves with cofactor 4 and 2. In Sect. 4, we extend our result to curves with an arbitrary cofactor that is the sum of two squares.

2   Preliminaries

2.1   Gaussian Integers

We denote by $\mathbb{Z}[i]$ the ring of Gaussian integers: $\mathbb{Z}[i] = \{a+bi : a, b \in \mathbb{Z}, i^2 = -1\}$. For a Gaussian integer $\zeta = a + bi$, we denote its conjugate by $\overline{\zeta} = a - bi$, and we define its norm by $N(\zeta) = \zeta\overline{\zeta} = a^2 + b^2$. Note that the norm N is multiplicative, i.e. $N(\zeta\omega) = N(\zeta)N(\omega)$ for any $\zeta, \omega \in \mathbb{Z}[i]$. The units of $\mathbb{Z}[i]$ are $\{\pm 1, \pm i\}$, which are all elements with norm 1, and we call $\pm\zeta, \pm i\zeta$ the associates of ζ.

In this paper, we often consider the existence of Gaussian integers having a given norm, so we define a function $f_N(n) = \#N^{-1}(n) = \#\{\zeta \in \mathbb{Z}[i]|N(\zeta) = n\}$, the number of Gaussian integers having norm n, for any positive integer n. If $f_N(n) > 0$, then there is a Gaussian integer ζ with $N(\zeta) = n$.

Lemma 1 (Theorem 3.2.1 [2]). *For a positive integer n,*

$$f_N(n) = 4(d_{1,4}(n) - d_{3,4}(n))$$

where $d_{j,k}(n)$ denotes the number of positive divisors d of n such that $d \equiv j \,(mod\ k)$. In particular, for an odd prime integer r, $f_N(r) = 8$ if $r \equiv 1\,(mod\ 4)$ and 0 otherwise.

It is easy to check that if $f_N(n) = 8$ and $N(a + bi) = a^2 + b^2 = n$, then $a \neq b$ and $ab \neq 0$ and $N^{-1}(n) = \{\pm(a + bi), \pm(a + bi)i, \pm(a - bi), \pm(a - bi)i\} = \{a + bi, -a - bi, -b + ai, b - ai, a - bi, -a + bi, b + ai, -b - ai\}$. Thus, all the Gaussian integers having norm n are associates of $a+bi$ or those of its conjugate $a - bi$, and we can say the Gaussian integer having norm n is unique up to order and up to sign.

The following lemma describes how $f_N(mn)$ is related to $f_N(m)$ and $f_N(n)$ when m and n are relatively prime.

Lemma 2. *For any two relatively prime integers m and n, $4f_N(mn) = f_N(m)f_N(n)$.*

Proof. Since $\gcd(m, n) = 1$, for any divisor g of mn, there exists the unique pair (d, e) such that $d \mid m, e \mid n$ and $g = de$.

$g \equiv 1\,(mod\ 4)$ if and only if $d \equiv e \equiv 1\,(mod\ 4)$ or $d \equiv e \equiv 3\,(mod\ 4)$. Thus, we have $d_{1,4}(mn) = d_{1,4}(m)d_{1,4}(n) + d_{3,4}(m)d_{3,4}(n)$. Similarly, $d_{3,4}(mn) = d_{1,4}(m)d_{3,4}(n) + d_{3,4}(m)d_{1,4}(n)$. Therefore,

$$f_N(mn) = 4(d_{1,4}(mn) - d_{3,4}(mn))$$
$$= 4(d_{1,4}(m) - d_{3,4}(m))(d_{1,4}(n) - d_{3,4}(n)) = \frac{1}{4}f_N(m)f_N(n). \quad \square$$

$\mathbb{Z}[i]$ is a unique factorization domain (UFD), in which every non-zero non-unit element can be written as a product of prime elements, uniquely up to units. A Gaussian integer ζ is a Gaussian prime (a prime elements of $\mathbb{Z}[i]$) if and only if either $N(\zeta)$ is a prime integer, or ζ is an associate of a prime integer congruent to 3 modulo 4. Let $\pi_2 = 1 + i \in \mathbb{Z}[i]$ with $N(\pi) = 2$, and let $\pi_p = a + bi \in \mathbb{Z}[i]$ with $N(\pi) = a^2 + b^2 = p$ for all prime integers p with $p \equiv 1 \pmod 4$, then π_2 and π_p's are Gaussian primes. For $\pi_p = a + bi$ and $N(\pi_p) = a^2 + b^2 = p$, since p is prime, both a, b are nonzero, $|a| \neq |b|$, and $\gcd(a, b) = 1$ over $\mathbb{Z}$. Thus, $\overline{\pi_p} = a - bi$ is not an associate of π_p, and hence $\overline{\pi_p}$'s are also Gaussian primes different from π_2 and π_p's. Note that if $p \equiv 1 \pmod 4$ is prime, then $f_N(p) = 8$ by Lemma 1, and $\pm\pi_p, \pm i\pi_p, \pm\overline{\pi_p}, \pm i\overline{\pi_p}$ are all Gaussian integers of the norm p. Finally, let $\pi_q \in \mathbb{Z}[i]$ be the prime integer q for all q with $q \equiv 3 \pmod 4$, then π_q's are Gaussian primes and hence the set of all Gaussian primes, up to units, is

$$\{\pi_2\} \cup \{\pi_p, \overline{\pi_p} \,|\, p \equiv 1 \pmod 4, \text{ prime}\} \cup \{\pi_q \,|\, q \equiv 3 \pmod 4, \text{ prime}\}.$$

For two Gaussian integers α, β, we say that α divides β, denoted by $\alpha \mid \beta$, if there exists $\gamma \in \mathbb{Z}[i]$ such that $\beta = \alpha\gamma$. By the multiplicative property of the norm, if $\alpha \mid \beta$, then $N(\alpha) \mid N(\beta)$ in $\mathbb{Z}$ and $N(\frac{\beta}{\alpha}) = \frac{N(\beta)}{N(\alpha)}$.

2.2 Statistical Distance, Pushforward

For $\mathscr{D}$ a probability distribution on a finite set S, we write $\Pr[s \leftarrow \mathscr{D}]$ for the probability assigned to the singleton $\{s\} \subset S$ by $\mathscr{D}$. The uniform distribution on S is denoted by $\mathscr{U}_S$ (or just $\mathscr{U}$ if the context is clear).

Definition 1 (Statistical distance). *Let $\mathscr{D}$ and $\mathscr{D}'$ be two probability distributions on a finite set S. The statistical distance between them is defined as the ℓ_1 norm:*

$$\Delta_1(\mathscr{D}, \mathscr{D}') = \sum_{s \in S} \left| \Pr[s \leftarrow \mathscr{D}] - \Pr[s \leftarrow \mathscr{D}'] \right|.$$

We simply denote by $\Delta_1(\mathscr{D})$ the statistical distance between $\mathscr{D}$ and $\mathscr{U}_S$:

$$\Delta_1(\mathscr{D}) = \sum_{s \in S} \left| \Pr[s \leftarrow \mathscr{D}] - \frac{1}{\#S} \right|,$$

and say that $\mathscr{D}$ is ε-statistically close to uniform when $\Delta_1(\mathscr{D}) \leq \varepsilon$. When $\Delta_1(\mathscr{D})$ is negligible, we simply say than $\mathscr{D}$ is statistically close to uniform.[1]

---

[1] For this to be well-defined, we of course need a family of random variables on increasingly large sets S. Usual abuses of language apply.

Definition 2 (Pushforward). *Let S, T be two finite sets and F any mapping from S to T. For any probability distribution $\mathscr{D}_S$ on S, we can define the pushforward $F_*\mathscr{D}_S$ of $\mathscr{D}_S$ by F as the probability distribution on T such that sampling from $F_*\mathscr{D}_S$ is proportional to sampling a value $s \leftarrow \mathscr{D}_S$ and returning $F(s)$. In other words:*

$$\Pr\left[t \leftarrow F_*\mathscr{D}_S\right] = \Pr\left[s \leftarrow \mathscr{D}_S;\ t = F(s)\right] = \mu_S\left(F^{-1}(t)\right) = \sum_{s \in F^{-1}(t)} \Pr[s \leftarrow \mathscr{D}_S],$$

where μ_S is the probability measure defined by $\mathscr{D}_S$.

Lemma 3. *Let S, T be two finite sets and F any mapping from S to T. For the uniform distribution $\mathscr{U}_S$ on S, if $F : S \to T$ is injective, then $\Delta_1(F_*\mathscr{U}_S) = 2\left(1 - \frac{\#S}{\#T}\right)$.*

Proof. For the uniform distribution $\mathscr{U}_S$ on S, $\Pr[s \leftarrow \mathscr{U}_S] = \frac{1}{\#S}$. By the definition of the pushforward of $\mathscr{U}_S$ by F, we have

$$\Delta_1(F_*\mathscr{U}_S) = \sum_{t \in T}\left|\left(\sum_{s \in F^{-1}(t)} \Pr[s \leftarrow \mathscr{U}_S]\right) - \frac{1}{\#T}\right| = \sum_{t \in T}\left|\left(\sum_{s \in F^{-1}(t)} \frac{1}{\#S}\right) - \frac{1}{\#T}\right|.$$

Since F is injective, $\#F^{-1}(t) = 1$ if $t \in F(S)$ and 0 otherwise where $F(S)$ is the image of F. Then, $\Delta_1(F_*\mathscr{D}_S)$ is $\sum_{t \in F(S)}|\frac{1}{\#S} - \frac{1}{\#T}| + \sum_{t \in T\setminus F(S)}|0 - \frac{1}{\#T}|$. Again, by the injectivity of F, $\#S \le \#T$ and $\#F(S) = \#S$, and therefore

$$\Delta_1(F_*\mathscr{D}_S) = \#S\left(\frac{1}{\#S} - \frac{1}{\#T}\right) + (\#T - \#S)\frac{1}{\#T} = 2\left(1 - \frac{\#S}{\#T}\right). \qquad \square$$

2.3   GLS Curves and Scalar Multiplications

In general, we call an elliptic curve a GLS curve if it is the quadratic twist over $\mathbb{F}_{q^2}$ of an elliptic curve defined over $\mathbb{F}_q$. Throughout the paper, we use the following notation for GLS curves: For an elliptic curve $E/\mathbb{F}_q$ with $\#E(\mathbb{F}_q) = q + 1 - t$, take its quadratic twist E' over $\mathbb{F}_{q^2}$, then E' is a GLS curve. Then $\psi = \phi\pi_q\phi^{-1}$ is an efficiently computable endomorphism on E' where $\phi : E \to E'$ is the twisting isomorphism and $\pi_q : E \to E$ is the q-th power Frobenius map of E. We can write $\#E'(\mathbb{F}_{q^2}) = (q - 1)^2 + t^2 = h\ell$ with cofactor h and ℓ a large prime integer. Then $E'(\mathbb{F}_{q^2})$ has the unique subgroup G of prime order ℓ provided $h < \ell$, and ψ acts on G by a multiplication by $\lambda \in \mathbb{Z}$ such that $\lambda^2 \equiv -1 \pmod{\ell}$. See [9] for more details.

For $P \in G$, if $k = k_1 + k_2\lambda \pmod{\ell}$, then $[k]P$ can be computed by $[k_1]P + [k_2]\psi(P) = [k_1]P + [k_2][\lambda]P = [k_1 + k_2\lambda]P$ as $\psi(P) = [\lambda]P$. Since k_1 and k_2 have size roughly half of the size of k, it is more advantageous to compute a double scalar multiplication $[k_1]P + [k_2]\psi(P)$ than to compute $[k]P$ directly.

Example 1 (Twisted Edwards GLS curves). A twisted Edwards curve [3] over a finite field $\mathbb{F}_q$ with $char(\mathbb{F}_q) \neq 2$ is defined by

$$E_{E,a,d} : ax^2 + y^2 = 1 + dx^2 y^2$$

where $a, d \in \mathbb{F}_q$ with $a, d \neq 0$ and $a \neq d$.

A twisted Edwards GLS curve is a GLS curve obtained from a twisted Edwards curve. It is also a twisted Edwards curve, so it has very efficient *unified* addition formula, as well as the fast endomorphism ψ like any other GLS curves. Note that twisted Edward GLS curves have order divisible by 4: indeed, their order is of the form $(q-1)^2 + t^2$ with q odd, so it is congruent to $t^2 \bmod 4$; but since all twisted Edwards curves have even order, t must be even and hence 4 divides $(q-1)^2 + t^2$.

In practice, one typically chooses curves with the optimal cofactor 4. One such curve, with particularly efficient arithmetic, is constructed in [9, Sect. 8], over the finite field $\mathbb{F}_{(2^{127}-1)^2}$, together with 8-bit and 64-bit implementations that outperform prime field Edwards curve arithmetic by a significant margin.

Example 2 (GLS254). GLS254 is the record-breaking GLS curve over $\mathbb{F}_{2^{254}}$ introduced by Oliveira et al. in [13]. Its cofactor is even (as for all ordinary curves in characteristic 2), and in fact exactly equal to 2. It also has an efficiently computable endomorphism ψ which acts on the prime order ℓ subgroup by a scalar multiplication by λ with $\lambda^2 \equiv -1 \pmod{\ell}$. See [13, Sect. 3.2] for details.

2.4 Recomposition Method for Prime Order

Recall that a GLS curve E' with cofactor h is an elliptic curve defined over $\mathbb{F}_{q^2}$ endowed with an efficiently computable endomorphism ψ. We can write $\#E'(\mathbb{F}_{q^2}) = (q-1)^2 + t^2 = h\ell$ where $\ell > h$ is prime and $|t| \leq \sqrt{q}$. On the large prime order subgroup G of $E'(\mathbb{F}_{q^2})$ with $\#G = \ell$, $\psi(P) = [\lambda]P$ for all $P \in G$ where $\lambda^2 \equiv -1 \pmod{\ell}$.

When computing $[k]P$ for a random $k \in \mathbb{Z}/\ell\mathbb{Z}$ and $P \in G$, we can apply the GLS recomposition method to speed up scalar multiplications: choose k_1, k_2 with $|k_1| = \Theta(\sqrt{\ell})$ and $|k_2| = \Theta(\sqrt{\ell})$, and compute $[k_1]P + [k_2]\psi(P)$. Let $k = k_1 + k_2\lambda \bmod \ell$, then $[k]P = [k_1]P + [k_2]\psi(P)$, and thus a scalar multiplication $[k]P$ by a full-size scalar k becomes a double scalar multiplication $[k_1]P + [k_2]\psi(P)$ by half-size scalars k_1 and k_2, which is significantly faster and easy to implement. If k is random enough, then we have achieved our goal, computing $[k]P$ with k random, without introducing any side-channel information about the scalar unlike decomposition technique. If these conditions are satisfied, then we say the GLS recomposition method is secure. Let us define this notion more formally:

Definition 3 (Secure GLS recomposition). *For $c_1, c_2 > 0$, the recomposition map $F : [0, c_1) \times [0, c_2) \rightarrow \mathbb{Z}/\ell\mathbb{Z}$ on the domain $[0, c_1) \times [0, c_2)$ is defined by*

$$F(x, y) = x + y\lambda \pmod{\ell},$$

where we denote $[a, b) := \{n \in \mathbb{Z} | a \leq n < b\}$ for simplicity.

We say that the GLS recomposition method is secure for (c_1, c_2) if $c_1 = \Theta(\sqrt{\ell})$ and $c_2 = \Theta(\sqrt{\ell})$, and the distribution $\mathscr{D}_{\lambda,\ell}(c_1, c_2)$ of the images of F

$$\mathscr{D}_{\lambda,\ell}(c_1, c_2) = \{choose \ (k_1, k_2) \xleftarrow{\$} [0, c_1) \times [0, c_2) : output \ k = k_1 + k_2\lambda \ (\bmod \ell)\}$$

is statistically close to the uniform distribution $\mathscr{U}_{\mathbb{Z}/\ell\mathbb{Z}}$.

Recall that $c_1 = \Theta(\sqrt{\ell})$ means c_1 is both $O(\sqrt{\ell})$ and $\Omega(\sqrt{\ell})$, and the same is true for $c_2 = \Theta(\sqrt{\ell})$. The condition that $c_1 = \Theta(\sqrt{\ell})$ and $c_2 = \Theta(\sqrt{\ell})$ is essential, otherwise we cannot take any advantage, in terms of speed, from recomposition method computing $[k_1]P + [k_2]\psi(P)$ instead of $[k]P$. Note that the distribution $\mathscr{D}_{\lambda,\ell}(c_1, c_2)$ is the pushforward $F_*\mathscr{U}_{[0,c_1)\times[0,c_2)}$ by F, in the sense of Sect. 2.2.

In 2015, Aranha et al. [1] proved that the GLS recomposition method is secure when $\#E'(\mathbb{F}_{q^2}) = (q-1)^2 + t^2$ is prime ℓ. They first showed that $F : [0, q-1) \times [0, q-1) \to \mathbb{Z}/\ell\mathbb{Z}$ is injective, and then, using that injective, that the statistical distance to uniform is negligible.

Proposition 1 (Lemma 3 [1]). *The recomposition map $F : [0, q-1) \times [0, q-1) \to \mathbb{Z}/\ell\mathbb{Z}$ defined by $F(x, y) = x + y\lambda(\bmod \ell)$ is injective where $\lambda \in \mathbb{Z}$ satisfies $\lambda^2 \equiv -1(\bmod \ell)$.*

Since we have $q - 1 = \Theta(\sqrt{\ell})$ from $(q-1)^2 \leq \ell = (q-1)^2 + t^2 \leq (q-1)^2 + 4q$, we can conclude that the GLS recomposition method for prime order GLS curve is secure.

Proposition 2 (Theorem 1 [1]). *Let E' be a GLS curve over $\mathbb{F}_{q^2}$ of prime order, namely, $\#E'(\mathbb{F}_{q^2}) = (q-1)^2 + t^2 = \ell$ with ℓ prime and $|t| \leq \sqrt{q}$. Then GLS recomposition method on E' is secure for $(q-1, q-1)$.*

3   Secure Recomposition Method for Cofactor 4 and 2

In this section, we prove that the GLS recomposition method is secure for the cases that cofactor of GLS curves is 4 or 2.

If a GLS curve $E'/\mathbb{F}_{q^2}$ has cofactor 4, namely, $\#E'(\mathbb{F}_{q^2}) = (q-1)^2 + t^2 = 4\ell$ with ℓ prime, then we first show that the recomposition map F is injective on the domain $[0, \frac{q-1}{2}) \times [0, \frac{q-1}{2})$. If F is injective, then it becomes easy to compute the statistical distance to uniform of the distribution of recomposed scalars.

Proposition 3. *Let E' be a GLS curve over $\mathbb{F}_{q^2}$ with cofactor 4, namely, $\#E'(\mathbb{F}_{q^2}) = (q-1)^2 + t^2 = 4\ell$ with ℓ prime and $|t| \leq 2\sqrt{q}$. Then the recomposition map $F : [0, \frac{q-1}{2}) \times [0, \frac{q-1}{2}) \to \mathbb{Z}/\ell\mathbb{Z}$ is injective.*

Proof. At first, we note that since $f_N(4), f_N(4\ell) \neq 0$ and $4f_N(4\ell) = f_N(4)f_N(\ell)$ by Lemma 2, we have $f_N(\ell) \neq 0$ and hence $f_N(\ell) = 8$ as ℓ is prime.

If F is not injective, then there exist $(x, y) \neq (x'y')$ such that $F(x, y) = F(x', y')$. As $\lambda^2 \equiv -1(\bmod \ell)$, we have $(x - x')^2 + (y - y')^2 \equiv 0(\bmod \ell)$. Since

$0 \leq |x-x'|, |y-y'| < \frac{q-1}{2}$ and $(q-1)^2 \leq 4\ell$, we have $(x-x')^2+(y-y')^2 < \frac{(q-1)^2}{2} \leq 2\ell$. Since (x, y) and (x', y') were distinct as points, we have $(x-x')^2+(y-y')^2 \neq 0$ and therefore we can conclude that $(x - x')^2 + (y - y')^2 = \ell$ over $\mathbb{Z}$.

On the other hand, we can write $4\ell = (q-1)^2 + t^2 = N(q-1+ti)$ and $4 = 2^2 + 0^2 = N(2)$. Note that q must be odd, otherwise we would have $(q-1)^2+t^2 \equiv 1+t^2 \equiv 0 \pmod 4$, but -1 is not a square mod 4. Thus, q is odd, and in particular $4 \mid (q-1)^2$ and hence $4 \mid t^2 = 4\ell - (q-1)^2$. Thus, both $q-1$ and t are both even integers and $\frac{q-1}{2}, \frac{t}{2} \in \mathbb{Z}$. Therefore, we have $\frac{q-1+ti}{2} = \frac{q-1}{2} + \frac{t}{2}i \in \mathbb{Z}[i]$ and $N(\frac{q-1}{2} + \frac{t}{2}i) = \frac{N(q-1+ti)}{N(2)} = (\frac{q-1}{2})^2 + (\frac{t}{2})^2 = \ell$.

And now, we can say that $N((x - x') + (y - y')i) = N(\frac{q-1}{2} + \frac{t}{2}i) = \ell$. Since $f_N(\ell) = 8$, by the arguments in Sect. 2.1, $(x - x') + (y - y')i$ is an associate of $\frac{q-1}{2} \pm \frac{t}{2}i$. Therefore, either $|x - x'|$ or $|y - y'|$ is $\frac{q-1}{2}$, which is a contradiction to the fact that $|x - x'|, |y - y'| < \frac{q-1}{2}$. $\square$

Corollary 4. *Let E' be a GLS curve over $\mathbb{F}_{q^2}$ with cofactor 4 with q odd, namely, $\#E'(\mathbb{F}_{q^2}) = (q - 1)^2 + t^2 = 4\ell$ with ℓ prime and $|t| \leq 2\sqrt{q}$. Then GLS recomposition method on E' is secure for $(\frac{q-1}{2}, \frac{q-1}{2})$.*

Proof. From $4\ell = (q-1)^2+t^2$ and $t^2 \leq 4q$, we have $(q-1)^2 \leq 4\ell \leq (q-1)^2+4q = (q + 1)^2$, or equivalently,

$$\frac{q - 1}{2} \leq \sqrt{\ell} \leq \frac{q + 1}{2}.$$

Thus, $\frac{q-1}{2} = \Theta(\sqrt{\ell})$. By Proposition 3, F is injective and so we can apply Lemma 3. The statistical distance to uniform is $\Delta_1(\mathscr{D}_{\lambda,\ell}(\frac{q-1}{2}, \frac{q-1}{2})) = 2(1 - \frac{(q-1)^2}{4\ell}) = \frac{t^2}{2\ell}$. Finally, as $t^2 \leq 4q$ and $4\ell \geq (q-1)^2$, $\Delta_1(\mathscr{D}_{\lambda,\ell}(\frac{q-1}{2}, \frac{q-1}{2})) \leq \frac{8q}{(q-1)^2}$, which is negligible. $\square$

Since twisted Edwards GLS curves (see Example 1) are typically chosen to have cofactor exactly 4, this result applies to those curves. It does apply, in particular, to the curve of Galbraith et al. in [9, Sect. 8]. That we can obtain secure GLS recomposition on twisted Edwards GLS curves is particularly interesting in the sense that those curves are designed with side-channel protection in mind (thanks to their unified arithmetic formulas), and thus a side-channel protected method to obtain the GLS scalars is also important.

Similarly, if a GLS curve $E'/\mathbb{F}_{q^2}$ has cofactor 2, namely, $\#E'(\mathbb{F}_{q^2}) = (q - 1)^2 + t^2 = 2\ell$ with ℓ prime, then we can show that F is injective on the domain $[0, \frac{q-1-|t|}{2}) \times [0, q - 1)$, and conclude that the recomposition method is secure for GLS curves with cofactor 2.

Proposition 5. *Let E' be a GLS curve over $\mathbb{F}_{q^2}$ with cofactor 2, namely, $\#E'(\mathbb{F}_{q^2}) = (q-1)^2+t^2 = 2\ell$ with ℓ prime and $|t| \leq 2\sqrt{q}$. Then the recomposition map $F : [0, \frac{q-1-|t|}{2}) \times [0, q - 1) \to \mathbb{Z}/\ell\mathbb{Z}$ injective.*

Proof. The proof will go similarly to Proposition 3. Note that $f_N(2)$ and $f_N(2\ell)$ are positive, and so $f_N(\ell)$ is also positive and $f_N(\ell) = 8$ as ℓ is prime.

If F is not injective, then we can find $(x, y) \neq (x', y')$ such that $(x - x')^2 + (y - y')^2 \equiv 0 \pmod{\ell}$. Since $(x - x')^2 + (y - y')^2 < \frac{(q-1)^2}{4} + (q-1)^2 < 3\ell$, there are two possibilities for values of $(x - x')^2 + (y - y')^2$, namely 2ℓ or ℓ.

Note that since $\gcd(2, \ell) = 1$ and $f_N(2) = 4$, $f_N(2\ell) = \frac{1}{4} f_N(2) f_N(\ell) = 8$ by Lemma 2. If $(x - x')^2 + (y - y')^2 = 2\ell = (q-1)^2 + t^2$, then $N((x - x') + (y - y')i) = N(q - 1 + ti) = 2\ell$. Since $f_N(2\ell) = 8$, we also can conclude that $(x - x') + (y - y')i$ is an associate of $q - 1 \pm ti$. Therefore, either $|x - x'|$ or $|y - y'|$ is $q - 1$. This is a contradiction to the fact that $|x - x'|, |y - y'| < q - 1$.

On the other hand, if $(x - x')^2 + (y - y')^2 = \ell$, we can write $2\ell = N(q - 1 + ti)$ and $2 = N(1 + i)$. From $\frac{q-1+ti}{1+i} = \frac{q-1+t}{2} + \frac{q-1-t}{2}i$, since $(q-1)^2 + t^2 = 2\ell$ is even, $q - 1$ and t have the same parity, i.e. $q - 1 \pm t \equiv 0 \pmod 2$. Hence $\frac{q-1+t}{2} + \frac{q-1-t}{2}i \in \mathbb{Z}[i]$ and $N(\frac{q-1+t}{2} + \frac{q-1-t}{2}i) = \frac{N(q-1+ti)}{N(1+i)} = (\frac{q-1+t}{2})^2 + (\frac{q-1-t}{2})^2 = \ell$. Thus, $N((x - x') + (y - y')i) = N(\frac{q-1+t}{2} + \frac{q-1-t}{2}i) = \ell$. Since $f_N(\ell) = 8$, $(x - x') + (y - y')i$ is an associate of $\frac{q-1+t}{2} \pm \frac{q-1-t}{2}i$. Therefore, $|x - x'|$ is either $\frac{q-1+t}{2}$ or $\frac{q-1-t}{2}$, which is a contradiction to the fact that $|x - x'| < \frac{q-1-|t|}{2}$. □

Corollary 6. *Let E' be a GLS curve over $\mathbb{F}_{q^2}$ with cofactor 2, namely, $\#E'(\mathbb{F}_{q^2}) = (q - 1)^2 + t^2 = 2\ell$ with ℓ prime and $|t| \leq 2\sqrt{q}$. Then GLS recomposition method on E' is secure for $(\frac{q-1-|t|}{2}, q - 1)$.*

Proof. From $2\ell = (q - 1)^2 + t^2$ and $t^2 \leq 4q$, we have

$$\frac{q - 1}{\sqrt{2}} \leq \sqrt{\ell} \leq \frac{q + 1}{\sqrt{2}},$$

and thus, $\frac{q-1-|t|}{2} = \Theta(\sqrt{\ell})$ and $q - 1 = \Theta(\sqrt{\ell})$.

We have seen that F is injective in Proposition 5, so we can apply Lemma 3 again. The statistical distance to uniform is $\Delta_1(\mathscr{D}_{\lambda,\ell}(\frac{q-1-|t|}{2}, q - 1)) = 2(1 - \frac{(q-1-|t|)(q-1)}{2\ell}) = \frac{t^2 + (q-1)|t|}{\ell}$. Since $|t| \leq 2\sqrt{q}$ and $2\ell \geq (q - 1)^2$, $\Delta_1(\mathscr{D}_{\lambda,\ell}(\frac{q-1-|t|}{2}, q - 1)) \leq \frac{8q + 4\sqrt{q}}{(q-1)^2}$, which is negligible. □

Thus, we have secure GLS recomposition over cofactor 2 curves, which includes most interesting GLS curves over binary fields. In particular, our results apply to Oliveira et al.'s GLS254 [13], which is of cofactor 2 over $\mathbb{F}_{q^2}$ with $q = 2^{127}$. Note however that, contrary to cofactor 1 and 4, the intervals in which we have to choose k_1 and k_2 to get security are *not the same*. This is not an issue for a performance or security standpoint, but it is important to keep in mind to achieve security.

Interestingly, the GLS254 paper does mention recomposition as a possible approach to generate the scalars k_1 and k_2, but it is quite vague as to how the authors propose to choose these scalars. The most natural interpretation of the relevant section is that they suggest taking them uniformly at random in $[0, q/\sqrt{2})$, which is inadvisable: it would yield a biased value of k, and would also be less efficient than using the intervals of Corollary 6 (which are of length essentially a power of 2). It turns out that the publicly available implementations of GLS254 (submitted to eBATS [4]) use the decomposition technique, however, so it is difficult to say for sure.

In any case, the result above seems to be the first proof that GLS recomposition can in fact be used securely with GLS254 (or any other cofactor 2 curve), provided that one chooses the intervals for k_1 and k_2 appropriately.

4 Secure Recomposition Method for Cofactor $h = a^2 + b^2$

In this section, we extend our result from Sect. 3 to GLS curves with any cofactor of the form $h = a^2 + b^2$.

4.1 Technical Lemma: Existence of α' Dividing $q - 1 + ti$

Until now, our strategy for proving that GLS recomposition is secure is as follows:

(i) F is injective on $[0, c_1) \times [0, c_2)$ with $c_1 = \Theta(\sqrt{\ell}), c_2 = \Theta(\sqrt{\ell})$
(ii) $\Delta_1(\mathscr{D}_{\lambda, \ell}(c_1, c_2))$ is negligible

For example, in order to prove that F is injective in Sect. 3, we wrote $h = N(\alpha)$ and $h\ell = N(q - 1 + ti)$ for $h \in \{2, 4\}$ and saw that α divides $q - 1 + ti$. It is crucial to have that $\alpha \mid q - 1 + ti$ in $\mathbb{Z}[i]$ since we compared the Gaussian integer $(x - x') + (y - y')i$, obtained by assuming F is not injective, with Gaussian integers related to $\frac{q-1+ti}{\alpha}$ to derive a contradiction.

If a GLS curve $E'/\mathbb{F}_{q^2}$ has cofactor $h = a^2 + b^2$, i.e. $\#E'(\mathbb{F}_{q^2}) = (q-1)^2 + t^2 = h\ell$ with $h = a^2 + b^2$, then both h and $h\ell$ can be seen as:

$$h = N(a + bi), \text{ and } h\ell = N(q - 1 + ti)$$

If $a + bi$ divides $q - 1 + ti$ in $\mathbb{Z}[i]$, then we can also prove the injectivity of F in the same way. However, we can't guarantee that $a + bi \mid q - 1 + ti$ in $\mathbb{Z}[i]$ only from the condition $N(a + bi) \mid N(q - 1 + ti)$ in $\mathbb{Z}$. Although it holds that $\alpha \mid \beta$ in $\mathbb{Z}[i]$ then $N(\alpha) \mid N(\beta)$ in $\mathbb{Z}$, the converse does not hold in general. Namely, $N(\alpha)|N(\beta)$ in $\mathbb{Z}$ does not means that $\alpha|\beta$ in $\mathbb{Z}[i]$.

Instead, in Theorem 7, we show that a partial converse holds: if $N(\alpha) \mid N(\beta)$ and $N(\beta) = N(\alpha)\ell$ in $\mathbb{Z}$ with ℓ prime, then we can always find α' such that $\alpha' \mid \beta$ in $\mathbb{Z}[i]$, $N(\alpha') = N(\alpha)$, and hence $N(\alpha')$ divides $N(\beta)$. Using this result, we will show that GLS recomposition method is secure for GLS curves with any cofactor of the form $h = a^2 + b^2$ in the next section.

Theorem 7. *For two Gaussian integers $\alpha, \beta \in \mathbb{Z}[i]$, if $N(\alpha) = h$ and $N(\beta) = h\ell$ with $\ell > h$ prime, then $\alpha' = \gcd(N(\alpha), \beta)$ over $\mathbb{Z}[i]$ has norm $N(\alpha') = N(\alpha) = h$. In particular, α' divides β in $\mathbb{Z}[i]$ and $N(\frac{\beta}{\alpha'}) = \ell$.*

Proof. Note that since $f_N(h\ell)$ and $f_N(h)$ are positive, so is $f(\ell)$ and $N^{-1}(\ell) \neq \emptyset$ where $f_N(n) = \#N^{-1}(n)$. Thus, $\ell \equiv 1 \pmod{\ell}$.

Since $\mathbb{Z}[i]$ is a UFD, the factorizations of α and β over $\mathbb{Z}[i]$ are unique, up to units. With the notation of Gaussian primes in Sect. 2.1,

$$\alpha = u\pi_2^{e_2} \prod_{p \equiv 1 \ (\text{mod } 4)} \pi_p^{e_p} \overline{\pi}_p^{e'_p} \prod_{q \equiv 3 \ (\text{mod } 4)} \pi_q^{e_q},$$

$$\beta = u'\pi_2^{d_2} \prod_{p \equiv 1 \ (\text{mod } 4)} \pi_p^{d_p} \overline{\pi}_p^{d'_p} \prod_{q \equiv 3 \ (\text{mod } 4)} \pi_q^{d_q},$$

where u, u' are units, $N(\pi_2) = \pi_2\overline{\pi}_2 = 2$, $N(\pi_p) = \pi_p\overline{\pi}_p = p$ with $p \equiv 1 \pmod 4$ prime, $\pi_q = q$ with $q \equiv 3 \pmod 4$ prime, and all exponents $e_r, d_r \geq 0$ for any prime r. Note that all but finitely many of exponents are zero. Then

$$N(\alpha) = 2^{e_2} \prod_{p \equiv 1 \ (\text{mod } 4)} p^{e_p + e'_p} \prod_{q \equiv 3 \ (\text{mod } 4)} q^{2e_q},$$

$$N(\beta) = 2^{e_2} \prod_{p \equiv 1 \ (\text{mod } 4)} p^{d_p + d'_p} \prod_{q \equiv 3 \ (\text{mod } 4)} q^{2d_q}.$$

Since $h = N(\alpha)$ divides $h\ell = N(\beta)$, we have $e_2 \leq d_2$, $e_p + e'_p \leq d_p + d'_p$, $e_q \leq d_q$ for all p and q. However, since $\frac{N(\beta)}{N(\alpha)} = \frac{h\ell}{h} = \ell$ prime and $\ell \equiv 1 \pmod 4$, we have

$$\frac{N(\beta)}{N(\alpha)} = 2^{d_2 - e_2} \ell^{(d_\ell + d'_\ell) - (e_\ell + e'_\ell)} \prod_{\substack{p \equiv 1 \ (\text{mod } 4) \\ p \neq \ell}} p^{(d_p + d'_p) - (e_p + e'_p)} \prod_{q \equiv 3 \ (\text{mod } 4)} q^{2(d_q - e_q)} = \ell.$$

Therefore, by comparing both sides, we can conclude that $e_2 = d_2$, $(d_\ell + d'_\ell) - (e_\ell + e'_\ell) = 1$, $e_p + e'_p = d_p + d'_p$ for all $p \neq \ell$, and $e_q = d_q$ for all q. Note that, since ℓ never divides $h = N(\alpha)$ as $h < \ell$, $e_\ell + e'_\ell = 0$ and $d_\ell + d'_\ell = 1$.

With these relations, the GCD of $N(\alpha)$ and β in $\mathbb{Z}[i]$ is

$$\alpha' = \gcd(N(\alpha), \beta) = \pi_2^{d_2} \prod_{\substack{p \equiv 1 \ (\text{mod } 4) \\ p \neq \ell}} \pi_p^{d_p} \overline{\pi}_p^{d'_p} \prod_{q \equiv 3 \ (\text{mod } 4)} \pi_q^{d_q}.$$

Then $\alpha' = \gcd(N(\alpha), \beta)$ has norm

$$N(\alpha') = 2^{d_2} \prod_{\substack{p \equiv 1 \ (\text{mod } 4) \\ p \neq \ell}} p^{d_p + d'_p} \prod_{q \equiv 3 \ (\text{mod } 4)} q^{2d_q} = N(\alpha). \qquad \square$$

4.2 Injectivity of the Recomposition Map

In this section, we give secure GLS recomposition for sum-of-square cofactor. As in Sect. 3, we will first show that F is injective on a reasonable domain (Theorem 8), then show the statistical distance is negligible and conclude that the GLS recomposition is secure (Corollary 9). Once F becomes injective, the statistical distance is easy to compute by Lemma 3.

Our method to prove that F is injective on a given domain $[0, c_1) \times [0, c_2)$ with $c_1 = \Theta(\sqrt{\ell}), c_2 = \Theta(\sqrt{\ell})$ is as follows: if there is a collision, which means that there exist $(x, y) \neq (x', y')$ with $F(x, y) = F(x', y')$, then $x + y\lambda \equiv x' + y'\lambda \pmod{\ell}$ and $(x - x')^2 \equiv (y - y')^2\lambda^2 \pmod{\ell}$. As $\lambda^2 \equiv -1 \pmod{\ell}$, we obtain a congruent relation $(x - x')^2 + (y - y')^2 \equiv 0 \pmod{\ell}$. Since c_1, c_2 are proportional to $\sqrt{\ell}$, we can bound $(x - x')^2 + (y - y')^2$ from above by a multiple of ℓ, say it bounded above by $B\ell$. Obviously, $(x - x')^2 + (y - y')^2 > 0$ by $(x, y) \neq (x', y')$, so $(x - x')^2 + (y - y')^2$ should be $z\ell$ for some z with $1 \leq z \leq B$.

On the other hand, we can interpret $(x - x')^2 + (y - y')^2$ as the norm of the Gaussian integer $(x - x') + (y - y')i$. Then we will show that $(x - x') + (y - y')i$ is different from all Gaussian integers having norm $z\ell$ for all z with $1 \leq z \leq B$, which gives a contradiction.

To generate all Gaussian integers of the norm $z\ell$, we use $\gamma \in \mathbb{Z}[i]$ having norm ℓ. As we explain in Sect. 4.1, one can efficiently find γ by computing $\frac{q-1+ti}{\gcd(h, q-1+ti)}$ from the known information of h and $q - 1 + ti$ as $N(q - 1 + ti) = h\ell$ and $N(\alpha) = h$. It is easy to find all $\zeta_z \in \mathbb{Z}[i]$ with $N(\zeta_z) = z$ since z is a small integer less than or equal to B. Then, we can find all Gaussian integers having norm $z\ell$ by multiplying ζ_z by γ in $\mathbb{Z}[i]$, and we have $N(\zeta_z\gamma) = N(\zeta_z)N(\gamma) = z\ell$.

From now on, we give our result of secure GLS recomposition for cofactor $h = a^2 + b^2$. Let us fix notation first. For a GLS curve $E'/\mathbb{F}_{q^2}$ with cofactor $h = a^2 + b^2$, i.e. $\#E'(\mathbb{F}_{q^2}) = (q - 1)^2 + t^2 = h\ell$ with $\ell > h$ prime. Let $\alpha = a + bi$ and $\beta = p - 1 + ti$, then $N(\alpha) = a^2 + b^2 = h$ and $N(\beta) = (q - 1)^2 + t^2 = h\ell$. By Theorem 7, there exists $\alpha' = \gcd(h, \beta) \in \mathbb{Z}[i]$ such that $\alpha' \mid \beta$ in $\mathbb{Z}[i]$ and $N(\alpha') = h$. Let $\alpha' = a' + b'i \in \mathbb{Z}[i]$, then for $\gamma := \frac{\beta}{\alpha'} \in \mathbb{Z}[i]$, we have

$$\gamma = \frac{q - 1 + ti}{a' + b'i} = \frac{a'(q-1) + b't}{h} + \frac{-b'(q-1) + a't}{h}i \in \mathbb{Z}[i]$$

and

$$\ell = N(\gamma) = \left(\frac{a'(q-1) + b't}{h}\right)^2 + \left(\frac{b'(q-1) - a't}{h}\right)^2.$$

Let $d = \gcd(a', b')$ over $\mathbb{Z}$ and write $a' = dm$, $b' = dn$ and $h' = m^2 + n^2$. Then $h = a'^2 + b'^2 = d^2(m^2 + n^2) = h'd^2$. We may assume $a' \geq 0$ and $b' \geq 0$ by multiplying units.

Theorem 8. *Let E' be a GLS curve over $\mathbb{F}_{q^2}$ with cofactor $h = a^2 + b^2$, namely, $\#E'(\mathbb{F}_{q^2}) = (q - 1)^2 + t^2 = h\ell$ with $\ell > h$ prime and $|t| \leq 2\sqrt{q}$. Then, with the notation above, the recomposition map $F : [0, \frac{(q-1)-2h'd|t|}{h'd}) \times [0, \frac{q-1}{d}) \to \mathbb{Z}/\ell\mathbb{Z}$ is injective.*

Proof. Note that $f_N(\ell) > 0$ as $f_N(h) > 0$ and $f_N(h\ell) > 0$.

If F is not injective, then there exist $(x, y) \neq (x', y')$ such that $F(x, y) = F(x', y')$ and hence $(x-x')^2 + (y-y')^2 \equiv 0 (\text{mod } \ell)$. From the domain intervals of F, we have $(x-x')^2 + (y-y')^2 < \left(\frac{q-1}{h'd}\right)^2 + \left(\frac{q-1}{d}\right)^2 = \left(\frac{1+h'^2}{h'h}\right)(q-1)^2 \leq \left(h' + \frac{1}{h'}\right)\ell$ as $h'd^2 = h$ and $(q-1)^2 \leq h\ell$. Thus, $(x-x')^2 + (y-y')^2 \leq h'\ell$ and $(x, y) \neq (x', y')$, we have

$$0 < (x - x')^2 + (y - y')^2 \leq h'\ell.$$

(i) If $a' = 0$ or $b' = 0$, say $b' = 0$, then $h = a'^2$, $d = \gcd(a', b') = a'$ and $h' = 1$. From the description above, we can conclude that $(x - x')^2 + (y - y')^2 \leq \ell$, and hence it holds over $\mathbb{Z}$ that $(x - x')^2 + (y - y')^2 = \ell = \left(\frac{q-1}{a'}\right)^2 + \left(\frac{t}{a'}\right)^2$, in other words, $N((x - x') + (y - y')i) = N\left(\frac{q-1}{a'} + \frac{t}{a'}i\right) = \ell$. Since $f_N(\ell) = 8$, $(x - x') + (y - y')i$ is an associate of $\frac{q-1}{a'} \pm \frac{t}{a'}i$. In any cases, either $|x - x'|$ or $|y - y'|$ is $\frac{q-1}{a'} = \frac{q-1}{d}$, which is a contradiction to the fact that $|x - x'|, |y - y'| < \frac{q-1}{d}$.

(ii) If $a'b' \neq 0$ and $a' = b'$, then $h = 2a'^2$, $d = \gcd(a', b') = a'$, $h' = 2$ and $(x - x')^2 + (y - y')^2 \leq 2\ell$. If $(x - x')^2 + (y - y')^2 = 2\ell$, then it holds that $2\ell = N((1+i)\gamma) = N\left((1+i)\left(\frac{q-1+t}{2a'} + \frac{-(q-1)+t}{2a'}i\right)\right) = N\left(\frac{q-1}{a'} + \frac{t}{a'}i\right) = \left(\frac{q-1}{a'}\right)^2 + \left(\frac{t}{a'}\right)^2$ where $\gamma = \frac{a'(q-1)+a't}{2a'^2} + \frac{-a'(q-1)+a't}{2a'^2}i = \frac{q-1+t}{2a'} + \frac{-(q-1)+t}{2a'}i$. Thus, $(x-x')^2 + (y-y')^2 = \left(\frac{q-1}{a'}\right)^2 + \left(\frac{t}{a'}\right)^2 = 2\ell$. Since $f_N(2\ell) = \frac{1}{4}f_N(2)f_N(\ell) = 8$, $(x-x') + (y-y')i$ is an associate of $\frac{q-1}{a'} \pm \frac{t}{a'}i$. We can say that either $|x-x'|$ or $|y - y'|$ is $\frac{q-1}{a'}$, and at the same time, $|x - x'|, |y - y'| < \frac{q-1}{a'}$, which is not possible. The only possibility that remains is $(x - x')^2 + (y - y')^2 = \ell = \left(\frac{q-1+t}{2a'}\right)^2 + \left(\frac{q-1-t}{2a'}\right)^2$ over $\mathbb{Z}$. Again, $(x - x') + (y - y')i$ is an associate of $\frac{q-1+t}{2a'} \pm \frac{q-1-t}{2a'}i$ as $f_N(\ell) = 8$. Then $|x - x'|$ should coincide with $\frac{q-1+t}{2a'}$ or $\frac{q-1+t}{2a'}$, but $|x - x'| < \frac{q-1-|t|}{2a'}$ and this is a contradiction.

(iii) If $a'b' \neq 0$ and $a' \neq b'$, then from $\ell \mid (x - x')^2 + (y - y')^2 \leq h'\ell$, it suffices to prove that $(x - x') + (y - y')i$ is different from ζ for all $\zeta \in \mathbb{Z}[i]$ with $N(\zeta) = z\ell$, and for all z such that $1 \leq z \leq h'$ and $f_N(z) > 0$.

If $(x - x')^2 + (y - y')^2 = \ell$, then since $N(\gamma) = \ell$ and $f_N(\ell) = 8$ for prime ℓ, $(x - x') + (y - y')i$ is an associate of γ or $\overline{\gamma}$. Thus, $|x - x'|$ should be either $\frac{a'(q-1)+b't}{h}$ or $\frac{b'(q-1)-a't}{h}$. However, $a'(q-1)+b't \geq a'(q-1)-b'|t| \geq d(q-1)-2h|t|$ by $a' \geq d$ and $2h \geq b'$, and similarly, $b'(q-1) - a't \geq d(q-1) - 2h|t|$. Therefore, $|x-x'| = \frac{a'(q-1)+b't}{h}$ or $\frac{b'(q-1)-a't}{h}$, where both of them are greater than or equal to $\frac{d(q-1)-2h|t|}{h} = \frac{(q-1)-2h'd|t|}{h'd}$. This is contradiction to the fact that $|x - x'| < \frac{(q-1)-2h'd|t|}{h'd}$.

Consider the case $(x - x')^2 + (y - y')^2 = z\ell$ for some z such that $1 < z \leq h'$. Note that there must exist a pair (z_1, z_2) such that $z = z_1^2 + z_2^2 = N(z_1 + z_2i)$: otherwise, $f_N(z) = 0$ and hence $f_N(z\ell) = 0$, a contradiction. We also emphasize that we do not fix in advance a specific choice of (z_1, z_2) for z. Then $z\ell = N((z_1 + z_2i)\gamma) = \left(\frac{(z_1a'+z_2b')(q-1)+(z_1b'-z_2a')t}{h}\right)^2 + \left(\frac{(z_2a'-z_1b')(q-1)+(z_2b'+z_1a')t}{h}\right)^2$. For simplicity, let $Z_1 = z_1a' + z_2b'$, $Z_2 = z_1b' - z_2a'$, $Z_1' = z_2a' - z_1b'$, and

$Z'_2 = z_2 b' + z_1 a'$, then $z\ell = (\frac{Z_1(q-1)+Z_2 t}{h})^2 + (\frac{Z'_1(q-1)+Z'_2 t}{h})^2$. Note that since $z = z_1^2 + z_2^2 \leq h' = \frac{h}{d^2}$, we have $|z_1|, |z_2| \leq \frac{\sqrt{h}}{d}$, and furthermore $|Z_1|, |Z_2|, |Z'_1|, |Z'_2| \leq \frac{2h}{d} = 2h'd$ by definition.

Claim. *If either $1 < z < h'$, or $z_1 + z_2 i$ has norm $z = N(z_1 + z_2 i) = m^2 + n^2 = h'$, but not an associate of $m \pm ni$, then $|Z_1| \geq d$ and $|Z'_1| \geq d$.*

Since $Z_1 = z_1 a' + z_2 b' = d(z_1 m + z_2 n)$, it suffices to show that $|z_1 m + z_2 n| \neq 0$. If $|z_1 m + z_2 n| = 0$, then $m \mid z_1 m = -z_2 n$ and hence m divides z_2 as $\gcd(m, n) = 1$, say $z_2 = m z_0$. Thus, $z_1 m = -z_2 n = -z_0 mn$, and so $z_1 = -z_0 n$. In any cases, $z \leq h'$, so we have $z = z_1^2 + z_2^2 = z_0^2(m^2 + n^2) = z_0^2 h' \leq h'$ and $z_0 = 0, \pm 1$. However, if z_0 is zero, then z is also zero, which contradicts to $z > 1$. If $z_0 = \pm 1$, then $z_1 = \mp n$, $z_2 = \pm m$, and thus $z_1 + z_2 i$ is an associate of $m \pm ni$, which we will treat later.

Back to the story, if $(x - x')^2 + (y - y')^2 = z\ell$, then we can say that $(x - x') + (y - y')i$ is an associate of $\frac{Z_1(q-1)+Z_2 t}{h} \pm \frac{Z'_1(q-1)+Z'_2 t}{h} i$. Thus, $|x - x'|$ is either $\frac{|Z_1(q-1)+Z_2 t|}{h}$ or $\frac{|Z'_1(q-1)+Z'_2 t|}{h}$. However, $|Z_1(q-1) + Z_2 t| \geq |Z_1|(q-1) - |Z_2||t| \geq d(q-1) - |Z_2||t| \geq d(q-1) - 2h|t|$ by $2h \geq 2h'd \geq |Z_2|$, and similarly, $|Z'_1(q-1) + Z'_2 t| \geq d(q-1) - 2h|t|$. Therefore, $|x - x'| = \frac{|Z_1(q-1)+Z_2 t|}{h}$ or $\frac{|Z'_1(q-1)+Z'_2 t|}{h}$, where both of them are $\geq \frac{d(q-1)-2h|t|}{h} = \frac{(q-1)-2h'd|t|}{h'd}$. This is contradiction to the fact that $|x - x'| < \frac{(q-1)-2h'd|t|}{h'd}$.

At last, if $z_1 + z_2 i$ has norm h' and is an associate of $m \pm ni$, then $z = N(z_1 + z_2 i) = m^2 + n^2 = h'$ and $h'\ell = N((z_1 + z_2 i)\gamma) = N((m + ni)\gamma) = (\frac{(m'a'+n'b')(q-1)+(m'b'-n'a')t}{h})^2 + (\frac{-(m'b'-n'a')(q-1)+(m'a'+n'b')t}{h})^2$. From the definition of m, n, we have $ma' + nb' = d(m^2 + n^2) = dh'$, $mb' - na' = dmn - dmn = 0$ and hence $h'\ell = (\frac{q-1}{d})^2 + (\frac{t}{d})^2$. By combining both equation, we can say that either $|x - x'|$ or $|y - y'|$ is $\frac{q-1}{d}$, but both are less than $\frac{q-1}{d}$, and this is a contradiction. This completes our proof. $\square$

Using the injectivity of F, it is easy to compute the statistical distance. Then in the following corollary, we can conclude that if a GLS curves has cofactor of the form $h = a^2 + b^2$, then we can have secure GLS recomposition method.

Corollary 9. *Let E' be a GLS curve over $\mathbb{F}_{q^2}$ with cofactor $h = a^2 + b^2$, namely, $\#E'(\mathbb{F}_{q^2}) = (q - 1)^2 + t^2 = h\ell$ with $\ell > h$ prime and $|t| \leq 2\sqrt{q}$. Then, with the notation in Proposition 8, the GLS recomposition method on E' is secure for $(\frac{(q-1)-2h'd|t|}{h'd}, \frac{q-1}{d})$.*

Proof. From $h\ell = (q - 1)^2 + t^2$ and $t^2 \leq 4q$, we have

$$\frac{q-1}{\sqrt{h}} \leq \sqrt{\ell} \leq \frac{q+1}{\sqrt{h}}.$$

Both $h'd$ and d are constants bounded by $h = h'd^2$. Since the cofactor h is usually much smaller than the prime factor ℓ, we can say that $\frac{(q-1)-2h'd|t|}{h'd} = \Theta(\sqrt{\ell})$ and $\frac{q-1}{d} = \Theta(\sqrt{\ell})$.

In Theorem 8, we see that F is injective. By Lemma 3, the statistical distance to uniform is $\Delta_1(\mathscr{D}_{\lambda,\ell}(\frac{(q-1)-2h'd|t|}{h'd}, \frac{q-1}{d})) = 2(1 - \frac{(q-1)^2 - 2h'd|t|(q-1)}{h\ell})$ which is less than $2(\frac{t^2 + 2h'd|t|(q-1)}{h\ell}) \leq 2(\frac{4q + 2h'd\sqrt{q}(q-1)}{(q-1)^2})$ since $|t| \leq 2\sqrt{q}$ and $h\ell \geq (q-1)^2$. Thus, the statistical distance is negligible.   □

Example 3. As a result of our work, we can have secure GLS recomposition method for cofactor $5 = 1^2 + 2^2$ or $13 = 2^2 + 3^2$.

Furthermore, just as we have secure GLS recomposition for cofactor 4 and 2 as special cases, we can have secure GLS recomposition for any powers of 2 cofactor. For a positive integer n, $2^{2n+1} = (2^n)^2 + (2^n)^2$ and $2^{2n} = (2^n)^2 + 0^2$ have the forms of sum of two squares, and hence we can apply our result. For example, $8 = 2^2 + 2^2$ or $16 = 4^2 + 0^2$, and so on.

References

1. Aranha, D.F., Fouque, P.-A., Gérard, B., Kammerer, J.-G., Tibouchi, M., Zapalowicz, J.-C.: GLV/GLS decomposition, power analysis, and attacks on ECDSA signatures with single-bit nonce bias. In: Sarkar, P., Iwata, T. (eds.) ASIACRYPT 2014. LNCS, vol. 8873, pp. 262–281. Springer, Heidelberg (2014). doi:10.1007/978-3-662-45611-8_14

2. Berndt, B.C.: Number Theory in the Sprit of Ramanujan. American Mathematical Society (2006)

3. Bernstein, D.J., Birkner, P., Joye, M., Lange, T., Peters, C.: Twisted Edwards curves. In: Vaudenay, S. (ed.) AFRICACRYPT 2008. LNCS, vol. 5023, pp. 389–405. Springer, Heidelberg (2008). doi:10.1007/978-3-540-68164-9_26

4. Bernstein, D.J., Lange, T.: eBACS: ECRYPT benchmarking of cryptographic systems. https://bench.cr.yp.to. Accessed 24 Mar 2017

5. Bos, J.W., Costello, C., Hisil, H., Lauter, K.: High-performance scalar multiplication using 8-dimensional GLV/GLS decomposition. In: Bertoni, G., Coron, J.-S. (eds.) CHES 2013. LNCS, vol. 8086, pp. 331–348. Springer, Heidelberg (2013). doi:10.1007/978-3-642-40349-1_19

6. Brumley, B.B., Nyberg, K.: On modular decomposition of integers. In: Preneel, B. (ed.) AFRICACRYPT 2009. LNCS, vol. 5580, pp. 386–402. Springer, Heidelberg (2009). doi:10.1007/978-3-642-02384-2_24

7. Costello, C., Hisil, H., Smith, B.: Faster compact Diffie–Hellman: endomorphisms on the x-line. In: Nguyen, P.Q., Oswald, E. (eds.) EUROCRYPT 2014. LNCS, vol. 8441, pp. 183–200. Springer, Heidelberg (2014). doi:10.1007/978-3-642-55220-5_11

8. Costello, C., Longa, P.: FourQ: four-dimensional decompositions on a Q-curve over the Mersenne prime. In: Iwata, T., Cheon, J.H. (eds.) ASIACRYPT 2015. LNCS, vol. 9452, pp. 214–235. Springer, Heidelberg (2015). doi:10.1007/978-3-662-48797-6_10

9. Galbraith, S.D., Lin, X., Scott, M.: Endomorphisms for faster elliptic curve cryptography on a large class of curves. J. Cryptol. **24**(3), 446–469 (2011)

10. Gallant, R.: Efficient multiplication on curves having an endomorphism of norm 1. Workshop on Elliptic Curve Cryptography (1999)

11. Gallant, R.P., Lambert, R.J., Vanstone, S.A.: Faster point multiplication on elliptic curves with efficient endomorphisms. In: Kilian, J. (ed.) CRYPTO 2001. LNCS, vol. 2139, pp. 190–200. Springer, Heidelberg (2001). doi:10.1007/3-540-44647-8_11

12. Hankerson, D., Karabina, K., Menezes, A.: Analyzing the Galbraith-Lin-Scott point multiplication method for elliptic curves over binary fields. Cryptology ePrint Archive, Report 2008/334 (2008). http://eprint.iacr.org/2008/334
13. Oliveira, T., López, J., Aranha, D.F., Rodríguez-Henríquez, F.: Two is the fastest prime: lambda coordinates for binary elliptic curves. J. Cryptogr. Eng. 4(1), 3–17 (2014)
14. Park, Y.-H., Jeong, S., Kim, C.H., Lim, J.: An alternate decomposition of an integer for faster point multiplication on certain elliptic curves. In: Naccache, D., Paillier, P. (eds.) PKC 2002. LNCS, vol. 2274, pp. 323–334. Springer, Heidelberg (2002). doi:10.1007/3-540-45664-3_23

Differential Addition on Twisted Edwards Curves

Reza Rezaeian Farashahi[1,2(✉)] and Seyed Gholamhossein Hosseini[1]

[1] Department of Mathematical Sciences, Isfahan University of Technology,
84156-83111, Isfahan, Iran
farashahi@cc.iut.ac.ir, g.hoseini@math.iut.ac.ir
[2] School of Mathematics, Institute for Research in Fundamental Sciences (IPM),
P.O. Box 19395-5746, Tehran, Iran

Abstract. This paper presents new differential addition (i.e., the addition of two points with the known difference) and doubling formulas, as the core step in Montgomery scalar multiplication, for twisted Edwards curves. The formulas are provided with cost of $5\mathbf{M} + 4\mathbf{S} + 1\mathbf{D}$, $3\mathbf{M} + 7\mathbf{S} + 1\mathbf{D}$ and $3\mathbf{M} + 6\mathbf{S} + 3\mathbf{D}$ when the given difference point is in affine form. Here, $\mathbf{M}, \mathbf{S}, \mathbf{D}$ denote the costs of a field multiplication, a field squaring and a field multiplication by a constant, respectively.

Keywords: Elliptic curves · Twisted Edwards curves · Montgomery ladder · Differential addition

1 Introduction

An elliptic curve E over a field $\mathbb{F}$ is given by the Weiersrasß equation

$$y^2 + a_1 xy + a_3 y = x^3 + a_2 x^2 + a_4 x + a_6$$

where coefficients a_1, a_2, a_3, a_4 and a_6 are in $\mathbb{F}$. Elliptic curves are represented in other forms such as Legendre equation, cubic equations, quartic equations and intersection of two quadratic surfaces [16,17]. Koblitz [13] and Miler [14] independently proposed the use of elliptic curves over finite fields in cryptography. Since the introduction of elliptic curve cryptography (ECC) elliptic curves over finite fields have been studied intensively and in particular, many proposals have been made to speed up their group arithmetic. ECC is one of the attractive asymmetric key cryptosystems with the main advantage of achieving smaller key sizes under the same security level compare to that of other existing asymmetric systems such as RSA. This makes ECC suitable for software and hardware implementation in constrained environments including RFID tags, mobiles, sensors, and smart cards.

The scalar multiplication is the main important operation of ECC which is implemented based on the basic operations in finite fields. That is to compute kP for a given point P on elliptic curve E defined over a finite field $\mathbb{F}_q$ and a given

© Springer International Publishing AG 2017
J. Pieprzyk and S. Suriadi (Eds.): ACISP 2017, Part II, LNCS 10343, pp. 366–378, 2017.
DOI: 10.1007/978-3-319-59870-3_21

integer k. The scalar multiplication is performed recursively by point addition and point doubling operations. One of the key factor in implementation of these basic curve operations is to reduce the number of field operations. This is why different forms of elliptic curves with several coordinates systems have been studied to improve the efficiency and to speed up the point multiplication. The well known recent form is Edwards curves [7] and their variants (see [1–3,12]) with great impact to ECC.

Side channel attacks use the time or power differences between implementing point addition and point doubling to reveal information about the bits of the secret k. Montgomery [15] introduced a technique for scalar multiplication of points for a special type of curves in large characteristic that is known as Montgomery ladder. In each step of the Montgomery scalar multiplication algorithm both the addition and the doubling are used which makes this method resistant against simple side-channel attacks. For Montgomery curves, the basic formulas in each step of the Montgomery ladder is differential addition and doubling expressed only by the x-coordinates of the points. For the fixed point P on the curve, this method computes the x-coordinate of the point kP recursively by computing the x-coordinates of the points $P + 2Q$ and $2Q$ from the x-coordinates of the points $P + Q$, Q. To avoid the costly field inversion operation, the computations are performed where points are represented in projective coordinates and the cost of projective x-coordinate formulas for Montgomery curves is $6\mathbf{M} + 4\mathbf{S} + 1\mathbf{D}$. Here a multiplication in $\mathbb{F}_q$ costs one $\mathbf{M}$, a squaring costs one $\mathbf{S}$ and the cost of field multiplication by a parameter (as a constant) is denoted by $\mathbf{D}$. The x-coordinate of the fixed base point P can be represented in affine form, then the differential mixed addition and doubling formulas are computed using $5\mathbf{M} + 4\mathbf{S} + 1\mathbf{D}$.

The Montgomery method is extended to other forms of elliptic curves, where the basic operation in each step of the ladder is differential addition and doubling expressed only by suitable w-coordinates of the points. That is to compute the w-coordinates of the addition and doubling from the w-coordinates of given points and their difference. The Montgomery-like formulas for Edwards and binary Edwards curves are presented in [3,6,8]. Gaudry and Lubicz [9] presents a very efficient Montgomery-like formulas for Kummer line the cost of $4\mathbf{M} + 6\mathbf{S} + 3\mathbf{D}$, and $3\mathbf{M} + 6\mathbf{S} + 3\mathbf{D}$ if the base point is affine. Bernstein and Lange [5] extends the Kummer-line formulas for incomplete Edwards curves with the same costs.

From the literature, the mixed differential addition and doubling formulas with the cost of $3\mathbf{M} + 6\mathbf{S} + 3\mathbf{D}$ are only given for elliptic curves with 3 points of order 2. Notice, complete twisted Edwards are suitable for cryptographic applications because of their fast complete addition law. A complete twisted Edwards curve has two points of order 4 and one single point of order 2. The main contribution of this paper is to provide faster Montgomery-like formulas for complete twisted Edwards curves, which covers all elliptic curves over finite fields with a point of order 4 and a single point of order 2. This paper presents new differential addition and doubling formulas for twisted Edwards curves with cost of $5\mathbf{M}+4\mathbf{S}+1\mathbf{D}$, $3\mathbf{M}+7\mathbf{S}+1\mathbf{D}$ and $3\mathbf{M}+6\mathbf{S}+3\mathbf{D}$ when the given difference point is in affine form.

The rest of the paper is organized as follows. In Sect. 2 we review twisted Edwards curves, and in Sect. 3 we briefly describe differential addition on elliptic curves. The proposed new differential addition and doubling formulas are provided in Sect. 4 and finally, Sect. 5 concludes the paper with a comparison between our work and other previously related work.

Throughout the paper, the letter p always denotes an odd prime number and q denotes a prime power of p. A field is denoted by $\mathbb{F}$ and a finite field of size q is denoted by $\mathbb{F}_q$. Let χ denote the quadratic character in $\mathbb{F}_q$, where $p \geq 3$. Then, for any q where $p \geq 3$, we have $u = w^2$ for some $w \in \mathbb{F}_q^*$ if and only if $\chi(u) = 1$.

2   Twisted Edwards Curve

In 2007, Edwards introduced a new normal form for elliptic curves [7]. An original *Edwards curve*, defined over a field $\mathbb{F}$ with characteristic $p \neq 2$, by the equation

$$\mathbf{E}_{\mathrm{E},c} : \quad X^2 + Y^2 = c^2(1 + X^2 Y^2),$$

with $c \in \mathbb{F}$ and $c^5 \neq c$. Bernstein and Lange [2] considered the use of Edwards curves over finite fields for elliptic curve cryptography. They extended the original curves to the family of so called *Edwards curves*

$$\mathbf{E}_{\mathrm{BL},d} : \quad X^2 + Y^2 = 1 + dX^2 Y^2,$$

where $d \in \mathbb{F}$ with $d \neq 0, 1$. The family of Edwards curves over a finite field $\mathbb{F}_q$ with odd characteristic is equivalent (up to $\mathbb{F}_q$ isomorphism) to the family of all elliptic curves over $\mathbb{F}_q$ with a $\mathbb{F}_q$-rational point of order 4 [1]. In other words, $\mathbf{E}_{\mathrm{BL},d}(\mathbb{F}_q)$, the group of $\mathbb{F}_q$-rational points of the Edwards curve $\mathbf{E}_{\mathrm{BL},d}$, has a $\mathbb{F}_q$-rational point of order 4 and in the other way around, every elliptic curve E over $\mathbb{F}_q$ with a point of order 4 can be represented as an Edwards curve. In addition, $\mathbf{E}_{\mathrm{BL},d}(\mathbb{F}_q)$ has a single point of order 2 if and only if $\chi(d) = -1$, i.e., the group $\mathbf{E}_{\mathrm{BL},d}(\mathbb{F}_q)$ has three points of order 2 if and only if $\chi(d) = 1$.

Edwards curves and their extensions have attracted great interest in elliptic curve cryptography (see [1–3,12]). Bernstein et al. proposed the family of so-called *twisted Edwards*, [1], given by

$$\mathbf{E}_{\mathrm{TE},a,d} : \quad aX^2 + Y^2 = 1 + dX^2 Y^2,$$

where a, d are distinct nonzero elements of $\mathbb{F}_q$. The addition and doubling law for $\mathbf{E}_{\mathrm{TE},a,d}$ are given by

$$
\begin{aligned}
(x_1, y_1),\ (x_2, y_2) &\mapsto \left(\frac{x_1 y_2 + x_2 y_1}{1 + dx_1 x_2 y_1 y_2},\ \frac{y_1 y_2 - a x_1 x_2}{1 - dx_1 x_2 y_1 y_2} \right), \\
(x_1, y_1) &\mapsto \left(\frac{2 x_1 y_1}{1 + dx_1^2 y_1^2},\ \frac{y_1^2 - a x_1^2}{1 - dx_1^2 y_1^2} \right).
\end{aligned}
\tag{1}
$$

The identity point of the addition law is $(0, 1)$ and the additive negation of a point (x, y) is $(-x, y)$. The point $(0, -1)$ is a point of order 2. If $\chi(a) = 1$ then the points $(\pm 1/\sqrt{a}, 0)$ are of order 4.

The projective closure of the twisted Edwards curve $\mathbf{E}_{TE,a,d}$ in $\mathbb{P}^2$ includes the projective points $(X : Y : Z)$ in $\mathbb{P}^2(\mathbb{F}_q)$ satisfying the curve equation

$$aX^2Z^2 + Y^2Z^2 = Z^4 + dX^2Y^2,$$

with the points at infinity $\infty_1 = (1 : 0 : 0)$ and $\infty_2 = (0 : 1 : 0)$. These points are singular. In the nonsingular model of $\mathbf{E}_{TE,a,d}$ the point ∞_1 splits into two distinct $\mathbb{F}_q$-rational points if $\chi(ad) = 1$ and is removed if $\chi(ad) = -1$. Similarly, above the point ∞_2 there exists exactly two distinct points if $\chi(d) = 1$ and no point if $\chi(d) = -1$. So, if $\chi(d) = \chi(ad) = -1$ then the set of $\mathbb{F}_q$-rational projective points of $\mathbf{E}_{TE,a,d}$ is the set of $\mathbb{F}_q$-rational affine points which form a group. To represent the points above the points at infinity, the projective closures of $\mathbf{E}_{TE,a,d}$ in $\mathbb{P}^3$ or in $\mathbb{P} \times \mathbb{P}$ are considered [4,12]. The twisted Edwards curve $\mathbf{E}_{TE,a,d}$ over $\mathbb{F}_q$ is represented by the set of points $(X : Y : T : Z)$ in $\mathbb{P}^3(\mathbb{F}_q)$ satisfying the equations

$$aX^2 + Y^2 = Z^2 + dT^2, \qquad XY = ZT.$$

Here, the $\mathbb{F}_q$-rational points above ∞_1 are $(1 : 0 : \pm\sqrt{a/d} : 0)$ if $\chi(ad) = 1$, and the points above ∞_2 are $(0 : \pm\sqrt{d} : 1 : 0)$ if $\chi(d) = 1$. Hisil et al. [12] gave the addition laws for the projective closure of $\mathbf{E}_{TE,a,d}$ embedded in $\mathbb{P}^3$ as follows.

$$
\begin{aligned}
&(X_1 : Y_1 : T_1 : Z_1) + (X_2 : Y_2 : T_2 : Z_2) \\
= \ &((X_1Y_2 + Y_1X_2)(Z_1Z_2 - dT_1T_2) : (Y_1Y_2 - aX_1X_2)(Z_1Z_2 + dT_1T_2) \\
&: (Y_1Y_2 - aX_1X_2)(X_1Y_2 + Y_1X_2) : (Z_1Z_2 - dT_1T_2)(Z_1Z_2 + dT_1T_2)).
\end{aligned} \tag{2}
$$

Here the identity point is $(0 : 1 : 0 : 1)$ and the additive negation of a point $(X : Y : T : Z)$ is $(-X : Y : -T : Z))$. The point $(0 : -1 : 0 : 1)$ is a point of order 2 and the points $(1 : 0 : \pm\sqrt{a/d} : 1)$ are the points of order 2 if $\chi(ad) = 1$. The points $(\pm 1/\sqrt{a} : 0 : 0 : 1)$ and $(0 : \pm\sqrt{d} : 1 : 0)$ are of order 4 if $\chi(a) = 1$ and $\chi(d) = 1$, respectively. Other points of order 4 are $(\alpha : \beta : \alpha\beta : 1)$ where $\alpha^4 = 1/ad$ and $\beta^4 = a/d$.

Notice, that the family of twisted Edwards curves is the extension of the family of Edwards curves. Clearly, every Edwards curve $\mathbf{E}_{BL,d}$ is the twisted Edwards $\mathbf{E}_{TE,1,d}$. Furthermore, a twisted Edwards curve $\mathbf{E}_{TE,a,d}$ is a twist of the Edwards curve $\mathbf{E}_{BL,\frac{d}{a}}$. Therefore, the family of twisted Edwards includes Edwards curves and their twists.

The addition law in twisted Edwards curve $\mathbf{E}_{TE,a,d}$ is complete if $\chi(d) = \chi(ad) = -1$. In other words, the projective formulas (2) have no exceptional cases if $\chi(a) = 1$ and $\chi(d) = -1$ [1,12]. Here, we show that the addition law in twisted Edwards curve $\mathbf{E}_{TE,a,d}$ is also complete if $\chi(a) = \chi(ad) = -1$.

Theorem 1. *Let a, d be elements of $\mathbb{F}_q$ such that $ad(a - d) \neq 0$. Let $\mathbf{E}_{TE,a,d}$ be a twisted Edwards curve over $\mathbb{F}_q$. Then, $\mathbf{E}_{TE,a,d}$ has a complete projective formulas over $\mathbb{F}_q$ if $\chi(ad) = -1$.*

Proof. If $\chi(d) = \chi(ad) = -1$, then the projective formulas (2) are complete formulas for $\mathbf{E}_{TE,a,d}$ [1,12]. If $\chi(a) = \chi(ad) = -1$, then the twisted Edwards curve $\mathbf{E}_{\text{TE},a,d}$ is birationally equivalent to $\mathbf{E}_{\text{TE},d,a}$ via the map $(x,y) \rightarrow (x,1/y)$. In other words, the projective points of the projective closures of $\mathbf{E}_{\text{TE},a,d}$ and $\mathbf{E}_{\text{TE},d,a}$ in $\mathbb{P}^3(\mathbb{F}_q)$ are corresponded to each other via the map $(X:Y:T:Z) \rightarrow (T:Z:X:Y)$. From (2) and using the exchange of variables, we obtain the projective formulas for the curve $\mathbf{E}_{\text{TE},a,d}$ as follows.

$$
\begin{aligned}
&(X_1:Y_1:T_1:Z_1) + (X_2:Y_2:T_2:Z_2) \\
=\ &((Z_1Z_2 - dT_1T_2)(T_1Z_2 + Z_1T_2) : (Y_1Y_2 - aX_1X_2)(Y_1Y_2 + aX_1X_2) \\
&: (T_1Z_2 + Z_1T_2)(Y_1Y_2 - aX_1X_2) : (Z_1Z_2 - dT_1T_2)(Y_1Y_2 + aX_1X_2)).
\end{aligned} \tag{3}
$$

Therefore, the projective formulas (3) are complete formulas for $\mathbf{E}_{\text{TE},a,d}$ over $\mathbb{F}_q$ where $\chi(a) = -1$ and $\chi(d) = 1$ which concludes the proof.

It is shown in [1], that a twisted Edwards curve $\mathbf{E}_{\text{TE},a,d}$ over a field $\mathbb{F}$ is birationally equivalent to a *Montgomery curve* [15] given by the equation

$$
\mathbf{E}_{\text{M},A,B}: \quad BY^2 = X^3 + AX^2 + X, \tag{4}
$$

where $A, B \in \mathbb{F}$ with $A \neq \pm 2$ and $B \neq 0$. In more details a twisted Edwards curve $\mathbf{E}_{\text{TE},a,d}$ is birationally equivalent to the Montgomery curve $\mathbf{E}_{\text{M},A,B}$ by the map $\psi : \mathbf{E}_{\text{TE},a,d} \rightarrow \mathbf{E}_{\text{M},A,B}$

$$
\psi(x,y) = \left(\frac{1+y}{1-y}, \frac{1+y}{x(1-y)} \right). \tag{5}
$$

where $A = 2(a+d)/(a-d)$, $B = 4/(a-d)$. Also, the Montgomery curve $\mathbf{E}_{\text{M},A,B}$ is birationally equivalent to the twisted Edwards curve $\mathbf{E}_{\text{TE},a,d}$ by the inverse map

$$
\psi^{-1}(x,y) = \left(\frac{x}{y}, \frac{x-1}{x+1} \right),
$$

where $a = (A+2)/B$, $d = (A-2)/B$.

3   Differential Addition

The main computational core for elliptic curve cryptography is performing scalar multiplication in an efficient and secure way. The computation of kP, for a given point P on elliptic curve E defined over a finite field $\mathbb{F}_q$ and a given integer k, is performed recursively by point addition (PA) and point doubling (PD) formulas. The time or power differences between implementing point addition (PA) and point doubling (PD) can reveal information about the bits of the secret k which makes the system insecure against side channel attacks.

In Montgomery curves [15], the special formulas for addition and doubling is done with the X and Z coordinates of a point in projective form. In each step of Montgomery ladder both addition and doubling are performed, which makes this method resistant against simple side-channel attacks. Recovering the

Algorithm 1. Projective x-coordinate dADD for Montgomery curves

> **Input :** $\mathbf{E}_{M,A,B}/\mathbb{F}_q : BY^2 = X^3 + AX^2 + X$ ▷ The Montgomery curve $\mathbf{E}_{M,A,B}$
> $(X_i : Z_i) = x(P_i)$, $i = 0, 1, 2$.   ▷ $x(P_0) = x(P_1 - P_2)$
> **Output :** $(X_i : Z_i) = x(P_i)$, $i = 3, 4$.   ▷ $x(P_3) = x(P_1 + P_2)$, $x(P_4) = x(2P_1)$

1: **function** DADD$((X_0 : Z_0), (X_1 : Z_1), (X_2 : Z_2))$
2:    $X_3 = Z_0 (X_1 X_2 - Z_1 Z_2)^2$
3:    $Z_3 = X_0 (X_1 Z_2 - X_2 Z_1)^2$
4:    $X_4 = (X_1^2 - Z_1^2)^2$
5:    $Z_4 = 4X_1 Z_1 ((X_1 + Z_1)^2 + (A - 2)X_1 Z_1)$
6:    **return** $((X_4 : Z_4), (X_3 : Z_3))$ ▷ The differential addition and doubling
7: **end function**

Y coordinate of the output point is done in the last step from the X and Z coordinates. Algorithm 1 provides the differential x-coordinate formulas for Montgomery curves $\mathbf{E}_{M,A,B}$ over $\mathbb{F}_q$ [15].

We note, that $\mathcal{O} = (0 : 1 : 0)$ is the point at infinity on the Montgomery curve $\mathbf{E}_{M,A,B}$ over $\mathbb{F}_q$ and $x(\mathcal{O})$ in $\mathbb{P}(\mathbb{F}_q)$ is represented by $(1 : 0)$. Also, $x((0,0))$ is given by $(0 : 1)$. We can easily check, that the projective x-coordinate differential addition formulas in Algorithm 1 work for all inputs except for the case where $x(P_0)$ equals $(1 : 0)$ or $(0 : 1)$, i.e., where the point P_0 equals $\mathcal{O}$ or $(0,0)$. In other words, the Montgomery ladder works for all inputs if the base point is not a point at infinity or the point $(0,0)$. The Montgomery ladder is given by the Algorithm 2, that for any integer k and any point P (not equal $\mathcal{O}$ and $(0,0)$) computes $x(kP)$ correctly. In particular, the ladder works properly even if the integer k is bigger than the order of the base point P. Therefore, one can use random scalar k as a countermeasure to protect against differential power analysis attack.

Algorithm 2. The modified Montgomery scalar multiplication

> **Input :** $\mathbf{E}_{M,A,B}/\mathbb{F}_q : BY^2 = X^3 + AX^2 + X$ ▷ The Montgomery curve $\mathbf{E}_{M,A,B}$
> $P = (x : y : z) \in \mathbf{E}_{M,A,B}(\mathbb{F}_q)$ ▷ $P \neq \mathcal{O} = (0 : 1 : 0)$, $P \neq (0 : 0 : 1)$
> $k = (k_{m-1}, \cdots, k_1, k_0)$ ▷ $0 \leq k \in \mathbb{Z}$
> $(X_0 : Z_0) := (x : z)$, $(X_1 : Z_1) := (1 : 0)$, $(X_2 : Z_2) := (x : z)$.
> **Output :** $x(kP)$

1: **for** $i := m - 1$ **down to** 0 **do**
2:    **if** $k_i = 0$ **then**
3:        $((X_1 : Z_1), (X_2 : Z_2)) := \text{dADD}((X_0 : Z_0), (X_1 : Z_1), (X_2 : Z_2))$
4:    **else**
5:        $((X_2 : Z_2), (X_1 : Z_1)) := \text{dADD}((X_0 : Z_0), (X_2 : Z_2), (X_1 : Z_1))$
6:    **end if**
7: **end for**
8: **return** $(X_1 : Z_1)$, $(X_2 : Z_2)$ ▷ The differential addition and doubling

The Montgomery method is extended to other forms of elliptic curves with a suitable rational function. Let w be a rational function in the coordinate ring of the elliptic curve E over $\mathbb{F}_q$ where $w(P) = w(-P)$ for every point P in $E(\mathbb{F}_q)$. The w-coordinate *differential addition* and *doubling* means to compute $w(P+Q)$ and $w(2Q)$ from given values $w(P)$, $w(Q)$ and $w(P-Q)$, where P, Q are points on $E(\mathbb{F}_q)$. If w is regular at the point P then $w(P)$ is represented by $(w(P) : 1)$ in the projective line $\mathbb{P}(\mathbb{F}_q)$. Otherwise, it is represented by $(1 : 0)$. For the fixed point P on the curve and a positive integer k, the w-coordinate of the point kP is performed recursively by differential addition and doubling formulas expressed only by w-coordinates of the points.

A projective w-coordinate differential addition is *complete* if it works for all inputs. Also, it is *almost complete* if the w-coordinate differential formulas work for all inputs except for the case where $w(P_0)$ equals $w(\mathcal{O})$, where $\mathcal{O}$ is the neutral element of the group of points $E(\mathbb{F}_q)$. Note that, the projective x-coordinate differential addition for Montgomery curves given in Algorithm 1 works for all inputs except for the case where $w(P_0)$ equals $(1 : 0)$ or $(0 : 1)$. The fast and complete differential addition formulas are very interesting for implementations. But, if the base point P_0 has large prime order then with suitable w-function $w(P_0) \neq w(\mathcal{O})$ and $w(P_0) \neq (1 : 0), (0 : 1)$. Therefore, the almost complete and Montgomery-like formulas are usable for cryptographic applications.

The cost of projective x-coordinate differential addition and doubling formulas for Montgomery curves $\mathbf{E}_{M,A,B}$ over $\mathbb{F}_q$ given by Algorithm 1 is $6\mathbf{M}+4\mathbf{S}+1\mathbf{D}$. The x-coordinate of the fixed base point P can be represented by $x(P) = (X_0 : Z_0)$, where $Z_0 = 1$, then the differential addition and doubling formulas are computed using $5\mathbf{M} + 4\mathbf{S} + 1\mathbf{D}$.

Castryck, Galbraith and Farashahi [6] give the y-coordinate differential addition Montgomery-like formulas for Edwards curves. They use the quasi free projective map between twisted Edwards and Montgomery curves which provides the Montgomery formulas for twisted Edwards curves with the cost of $6\mathbf{M} + 4\mathbf{S} + 1\mathbf{D}$, and $5\mathbf{M} + 4\mathbf{S} + 1\mathbf{D}$ if the base point is affine. They also give a doubling formulas with cost of $1\mathbf{M} + 3\mathbf{S} + 3\mathbf{D}$ assuming d is a square element. Gaudry and Lubicz [9] obtained a very efficient differential addition Montgomery-like formulas for Kummer line with the cost of $4\mathbf{M} + 6\mathbf{S} + 3\mathbf{D}$, and $3\mathbf{M} + 6\mathbf{S} + 3\mathbf{D}$ if the base point is affine. The Kummer line behaves very similar to the Montgomery form. Compare to the Montgomery form, the Kummer line formulas saves $2\mathbf{M} - 2\mathbf{S}$, but have extra 2 multiplication by constants. The Kummer line is linked to the Legendre curve $\mathbf{E}_\lambda : Y^2 = X(X-1)(X-\lambda)$, where $\lambda = a^4/(a^4 - b^4)$ and $(a : b)$ defines the Kummer line. The group order of the corresponding curve E_λ over $\mathbb{F}_q$ is divisible by 4, and in particular it has 3 points of order 2. Bernstein and Lange [5] provides a Kummer-line formulas for Edwards curves $\mathbf{E}_{\mathrm{BL},d}$ where $d = r^2$ is a square element. They give the cost of w-coordinates mixed differential addition and doubling formulas for $w = ry$ and $w = ry^2$ by $3\mathbf{M} + 6\mathbf{S} + 5\mathbf{D}$ and $3\mathbf{M} + 6\mathbf{S} + 3\mathbf{D}$ respectively. Here, the Edwards curve $\mathbf{E}_{\mathrm{BL},d}$ over $\mathbb{F}_q$ with $\chi(d) = 1$ has 3 points of order 2 and the addition law is not complete. In the next section, we provide new Montgomery-like formulas for complete twisted Edwards curves.

4 New Differential Additions

In this section, we provide new differential addition and doubling formulas for twisted Edwards. The mixed formulas have the cost $5\mathbf{M}+4\mathbf{S}+1\mathbf{D}$, $3\mathbf{M}+7\mathbf{S}+1\mathbf{D}$. In addition, we give mixed formulas with cost of $3\mathbf{M}+6\mathbf{S}+3\mathbf{D}$ for subfamily of twisted Edwards curves. These efficient and fast formulas are applicable for complete twisted Edwards in this subfamily. From the birational map between the twisted Edwards and Montgomery curve, we can use similar formulas for Montgomery curves.

4.1 Twisted Edwards

Here, we consider *twisted Edwards curves* $\mathbf{E}_{TE,a,d}$ and present new w-coordinates differential formulas.

We define the rational function w by $w(x,y) = d(xy)^2$. This function is well computed for all affine points on a twisted Edwards curves. Since $-(x,y) = (-x,y)$, for all points P on the curve, we have $w(P) = w(-P)$. Also, we have $w(\mathcal{O}) = 0$. For $i = 0,1,2,3,4$, let $w_i = w(P_i)$, where $P_i \in E_{a,d}$ with $w_0 = w(P_1 - P_2)$, $w_3 = w(P_1 + P_2)$ and $w_4 = w(2P_1)$. From the addition and doubling formulas for $\mathbf{E}_{TE,a,d}$ (1) with a straightforward calculation, we obtain the following differential addition formulas.

$$w_4 = \frac{4w_1((w_1+1)^2 - ew_1)}{(w_1^2-1)^2}, \quad w_3 w_0 = \frac{(w_1-w_2)^2}{(w_1w_2-1)^2}. \tag{6}$$

where $e = 4a/d$.

Assume that w_0 is given as a field element, and the inputs w_1, w_2 are given as fractions W_1/Z_1, W_2/Z_2 and the outputs w_4, w_3 are given as fraction W_4/Z_4 and W_3/Z_3. From Eq. (6) the explicit projective formulas are given by

$$\frac{W_4}{Z_4} = \frac{4W_1Z_1((W_1+Z_1)^2 - eW_1Z_1)}{(W_1-Z_1)^2(W_1+Z_1)^2},$$
$$\frac{W_3}{Z_3} = \frac{Z_0(W_1Z_2 - W_2Z_1)^2}{W_0(W_1W_2 - Z_1Z_2)^2}. \tag{7}$$

From the Eqs. (7), the cost of projective w-coordinates addition and doubling formulas is $6\mathbf{M} + 4\mathbf{S} + 1\mathbf{D}$. If we set $Z_0 = 1$, then the mixed projective w-coordinates differential addition and doubling formulas have the total cost $5\mathbf{M} + 4\mathbf{S} + 1\mathbf{D}$ as follows:

$$A_1 = (W_1 + Z_1), \ B_1 = (W_1 - Z_1), \ A_2 = (W_2 + Z_2), \ B_2 = (W_2 - Z_2),$$
$$C = A_1B_2, \ D = A_2B_1, \ E = A_1^2 - B_1^2,$$
$$W_4 = E(A_1^2 - (e/4)E), \ Z_4 = A_1^2B_1^2,$$
$$W_3 = (C - D)^2, \ Z_3 = w_0(C + D)^2. \tag{8}$$

From (8), the costs of differential addition and doubling formulas are $3\mathbf{M} + 2\mathbf{S}$ and $2\mathbf{M} + 2\mathbf{S} + 1\mathbf{D}$, respectively. And, the total cost of the mixed differential addition and doubling is $5\mathbf{M} + 4\mathbf{S} + 1\mathbf{D}$. In addition, the cost of following mixed differential addition and doubling formulas is $3\mathbf{M} + 7\mathbf{S} + 1\mathbf{D}$.

$$
\begin{aligned}
&A_1 = (W_1 + Z_1), \ B_1 = (W_1 - Z_1), \ A_2 = (W_2 + Z_2), \ B_2 = (W_2 - Z_2), \\
&\quad C = A_1 B_2, \ \ D = A_2 B_1, \ \ E = A_1^2 - B_1^2, \ \ F = (A_1^4 + B_1^4) - E^2, \\
&\qquad\qquad W_4 = 2(A_1^4 - (e/4)E^2) - F, \ Z_4 = F, \\
&\qquad\qquad W_3 = (C - D)^2, \ Z_3 = w_0(C + D)^2.
\end{aligned} \tag{9}
$$

Furthermore, for the twisted Edwards curves $\mathbf{E}_{\mathrm{TE},a,d}$ with $\chi(e(e - 4)) = \chi(a(a-d)) = 1$, the cost of the following mixed differential addition and doubling formulas is $3\mathbf{M} + 6\mathbf{S} + 3\mathbf{D}$. Here we let $r^2 = (e - 4)/e$.

$$
\begin{aligned}
&A_1 = (W_1 + Z_1), \ B_1 = (W_1 - Z_1), \ A_2 = (W_2 + Z_2), B_2 = (W_2 - Z_2), \\
&\quad C = A_1\,B_2, \ \ D = A_2\,B_1, \ \ H_1 = (rA_1^2 + B_1^2)^2, \ \ H_2 = (rA_1^2 - B_1^2)^2, \\
&\qquad G = (H_1 + H_2), \ K = (H_1 - H_2), \ S = \tfrac{1}{r}K, \ T = rK, \\
&\qquad\qquad W_4 = 2G - S - T, \ Z_4 = T - S, \\
&\qquad\qquad W_3 = (C - D)^2, \ Z_3 = w_0(C + D)^2.
\end{aligned} \tag{10}
$$

From differential addition and doubling formulas (10), the costs of differential addition and doubling are $3\mathbf{M} + 2\mathbf{S}$, $4\mathbf{S} + 3\mathbf{D}$ respectively. And, the total cost of the mixed differential addition and doubling formulas is $3\mathbf{M} + 6\mathbf{S} + 3\mathbf{D}$, where $2\mathbf{D}$ is the multiplication by the parameter r and one $\mathbf{D}$ is the multiplication by $1/r$. So, if the parameter r is chosen to be small then the cost of mixed differential formulas is $3\mathbf{M} + 6\mathbf{S} + 1\mathbf{D}$.

Example 1. Let $p = 2^{255} - 19$. Let $a = 1$ and $d = -204347024$. The twisted Edwards curve $\mathbf{E}_{\mathrm{TE},a,d}$ is a complete Edwards curve over $\mathbb{F}_p$ of order 8ℓ, where ℓ is the prime

$$
\begin{aligned}
\ell = {}&72370055773322622139731865630429942408 \\
&2316289981476462294766709361684665 3001.
\end{aligned}
$$

The cost of the mixed differential addition and doubling formulas (10) is $3\mathbf{M} + 6\mathbf{S} + 3\mathbf{D}$, where $2\mathbf{D}$ is the multiplication by the small constant $r = 14295$ and one $\mathbf{D}$ is the multiplication by $1/r$.

Remark 1. Let $\mathbf{E}_{\mathrm{TE},a,d}$ be a complete twisted Edwards curve over $\mathbb{F}_q$ with $\chi(d) = \chi(ad) = -1$. Then, $\mathbf{E}_{\mathrm{TE},a,d}$ has the four torsion subgroup as

$$
\mathbf{E}_{\mathrm{TE},a,d}(\mathbb{F}_q)[4] = \{(0,1),(0,-1),(1/\sqrt{a},0),(-1/\sqrt{a},0)\}.
$$

Then the coset of the point $P = (x,y)$ on the curve up to this subgroup equals

$$
P + \mathbf{E}_{\mathrm{TE},a,d}(\mathbb{F}_q)[4] = \{(x,y),(-x,-y),(y\sqrt{a},-x\sqrt{a}),(-y/\sqrt{a},x\sqrt{a})\}.
$$

We note that the proposed w-function has the property that $w(Q) = w(P)$ for all points Q in the coset of P.

As an alternative w-coordinate differential addition formulas, we define the rational function w by $w(x, y) = a(x/y)^2$. From the addition and doubling formulas for $\mathbf{E}_{TE,a,d}$ (1), we obtain the following differential addition formulas.

$$w_4 = \frac{4w_1((w_1 + 1)^2 - ew_1)}{(w_1^2 - 1)^2}, \quad w_3w_0 = \frac{(w_1 - w_2)^2}{(w_1w_2 - 1)^2},$$

where $e = 4d/a$. Similarly, we obtain the same projective and mixed w-coordinates formulas as (7), (8), (9) and (10). This w-function is also invariant for the coset of a point up to the 4-torsion subgroup of the complete twisted Edwards curve $\mathbf{E}_{TE,a,d}$ over $\mathbb{F}_q$ with $\chi(a) = \chi(ad) = -1$.

Furthermore, for twisted Edwards curves where $\chi(ad) = 1$, we define another differential formulas by the rational function w by $w(x, y) = \sqrt{ad}\left(\dfrac{2xy}{ax^2 + y^2}\right)^2$. Similarly, we obtain the following differential addition formulas.

$$w_4 = \frac{4w_1((w_1 + 1)^2 - ew_1)}{(w_1^2 - 1)^2}, \quad w_3w_0 = \frac{(w_1 - w_2)^2}{(w_1w_2 - 1)^2},$$

where $e = 2 + (a + d)/\sqrt{ad}$. So, we have the same results for this w-coordinates by formulas (7), (8), (9) and (10). Note that, this w-function is invariant for the coset of a point up to the full 2-torsion subgroup of the incomplete twisted Edwards curve $\mathbf{E}_{TE,a,d}$ over $\mathbb{F}_q$ with $\chi(ad) = 1$.

4.2   Montgomery Curves

Now, we consider the Montgomery curves. Note that above w-coordinates differential addition and doubling formulas for twisted Edwards curves can be applied for Montgomery curve using the birational maps between these two curves (5). Furthermore, from formulas (9) and (10), we give the mixed x-coordinates differential addition and doubling formulas for Montgomery curves with cost of $3\mathbf{M} + 7\mathbf{S} + 1\mathbf{D}$ and $3\mathbf{M} + 6\mathbf{S} + 3\mathbf{D}$.

We recall [15], that for the Montgomery curve $\mathbf{E}_{M,A,B}$ with the rational function $w(x, y) = x$, we have the following differential addition formulas.

$$w_4 = \frac{(w_1^2 - 1)^2}{4w_1((w_1 + 1)^2 - ew_1)}, \quad w_3w_0 = \frac{(w_1w_2 - 1)^2}{(w_1 - w_2)^2},$$

where $e = 2 - A$. In other words, the x-coordinates formulas for Montgomery curves and above w coordinates formulas (6) for twisted Edwards curves are inverse of each other. It means the projective formulas for Montgomery curves is obtained by the projective formulas (7) only by swapping the role of W and Z. Therefore, from formulas (9) we have the following formulas with cost of $3\mathbf{M} + 7\mathbf{S} + 1\mathbf{D}$

$$A_1 = (W_1 + Z_1), \ B_1 = (W_1 - Z_1), \ A_2 = (W_2 + Z_2), \ B_2 = (W_2 - Z_2),$$
$$C = A_1B_2, \ D = A_2B_1, \ E = A_1^2 - B_1^2, \ F = (A_1^4 + B_1^4) - E^2,$$
$$W_4 = F, \ Z_4 = 2(A_1^4 - (e/4)E^2) - F, \tag{11}$$
$$W_3 = w_0(C + D)^2, \ Z_3 = (C - D)^2.$$

and from formulas (10), we obtain the formulas with cost of $3\mathbf{M} + 6\mathbf{S} + 3\mathbf{D}$ as follows.

$$A_1 = (W_1 + Z_1),\ B_1 = (W_1 - Z_1),\ A_2 = (W_2 + Z_2), B_2 = (W_2 - Z_2),$$
$$C = A_1 B_2,\ D = A_2 B_1,\ H_1 = (rA_1^2 + B_1^2)^2,\ H_2 = (rA_1^2 - B_1^2)^2,$$
$$G = (H_1 + H_2),\ K = (H_1 - H_2),\ S = \tfrac{1}{r}K,\ T = rK, \tag{12}$$
$$W_4 = T - S,\ Z_4 = 2G - S - T,$$
$$W_3 = w_0(C + D)^2,\ Z_3 = (C - D)^2.$$

5 Concluding Remarks

The known Montgomery ladder differential addition formulas for elliptic curves over a finite field are not complete; they work for all input points P except for the case where $w(P)$ equals $(1:0)$ or $(0:1)$. However, the Montgomery ladder algorithm works perfectly in cryptographic applications, since the order of base point P should be a large prime number. The cost of the Montgomery-like formulas is $5\mathbf{M} + 4\mathbf{S} + 1\mathbf{D}$ if the base point P is affine. We believe, this record can be obtained for any form of elliptic curve with group order divisible by 4 by a suitable rational function. This includes the family of Jacobi curves.

Our proposed Montgomery-like formulas for twisted Edwards curves are improved in terms of efficiency and speed. They are almost complete formulas if the curve parameters are chosen carefully. The mixed formulas are provided for twisted Edwards curves with the cost of $3\mathbf{M} + 7\mathbf{S} + 1\mathbf{D}$. Also, faster mixed formulas are presented for a subfamily of twisted Edwards curves with the cost of $3\mathbf{M} + 6\mathbf{S} + 3\mathbf{D}$ which gives further speedup if the parameters are chosen to be small.

In Table 1, we compare our new differential addition formulas with the known formulas for other forms of elliptic curves. Notice, the fast and efficient presented

Table 1. Cost of differential addition and doubling for families of elliptic curves in odd characteristic

Model	Projective differential	Mixed differential
Montgomery [15]	$6\mathbf{M} + 4\mathbf{S} + 1\mathbf{D}$	$5\mathbf{M} + 4\mathbf{S} + 1\mathbf{D}$
This work (11)	$4\mathbf{M} + 7\mathbf{S} + 1\mathbf{D}$	$3\mathbf{M} + 7\mathbf{S} + 1\mathbf{D}$
This work (12)	$4\mathbf{M} + 6\mathbf{S} + 3\mathbf{D}$	$3\mathbf{M} + 6\mathbf{S} + 3\mathbf{D}$
Kummer curve [9]	$4\mathbf{M} + 6\mathbf{S} + 3\mathbf{D}$	$3\mathbf{M} + 6\mathbf{S} + 3\mathbf{D}$
Edwards curve $\mathbf{E}_{BL,d}$		
$(d = r^2, w = ry)$ [5]	$4\mathbf{M} + 6\mathbf{S} + 5\mathbf{D}$	$3\mathbf{M} + 6\mathbf{S} + 5\mathbf{D}$
$(d = r^2, w = ry^2)$ [5]	$4\mathbf{M} + 6\mathbf{S} + 3\mathbf{D}$	$3\mathbf{M} + 6\mathbf{S} + 3\mathbf{D}$
Jacobi quartic [10]	$6\mathbf{M} + 4\mathbf{S} + 1\mathbf{D}$	$5\mathbf{M} + 4\mathbf{S} + 1\mathbf{D}$
Twisted edwards		
This work (8)	$6\mathbf{M} + 4\mathbf{S} + 1\mathbf{D}$	$5\mathbf{M} + 4\mathbf{S} + 1\mathbf{D}$
This work (9)	$4\mathbf{M} + 7\mathbf{S} + 1\mathbf{D}$	$3\mathbf{M} + 7\mathbf{S} + 1\mathbf{D}$
This work (10)	$4\mathbf{M} + 6\mathbf{S} + 3\mathbf{D}$	$3\mathbf{M} + 6\mathbf{S} + 3\mathbf{D}$

formulas by Gaudry-Lubicz [9] and Bernstein-Lange [5] are given with the cost of $4\mathbf{M} + 6\mathbf{S} + 3\mathbf{D}$, and $3\mathbf{M} + 6\mathbf{S} + 3\mathbf{D}$ if the base point is affine, only for subfamily of elliptic curves with 3 points of order 2. Our formulas have the same costs and presented for a subfamily of twisted Edwards with a point of order 4 which includes the complete twisted Edwards curves therein.

For complete twisted Edwards curves, the proposed w functions are invariant in the coset of a point P with respect to the subgroup of $\mathbb{F}_q$-rational points with order 4. And, for incomplete twisted Edwards curves the suggested w function is invariant in the coset of a point P up to the subgroup of full 2-torsion points. For future works, we are going to investigate the use of these differential addition formulas along with the eliminating cofactors technique through point compression [11]. Computing the full point representation at the end of Montgomery ladder is an alternative question which is useful for cryptographic applications that need the full version of the scalar multiplication algorithm.

Acknowledgment. The authors would like to thank anonymous reviewers for their useful comments. This research was in part supported by a grant from IPM (No. 95050416).

References

1. Bernstein, D.J., Birkner, P., Joye, M., Lange, T., Peters, C.: Twisted edwards curves. In: Vaudenay, S. (ed.) AFRICACRYPT 2008. LNCS, vol. 5023, pp. 389–405. Springer, Heidelberg (2008). doi:10.1007/978-3-540-68164-9_26
2. Bernstein, D.J., Lange, T.: Faster addition and doubling on elliptic curves. In: Kurosawa, K. (ed.) ASIACRYPT 2007. LNCS, vol. 4833, pp. 29–50. Springer, Heidelberg (2007). doi:10.1007/978-3-540-76900-2_3
3. Bernstein, D.J., Lange, T., Rezaeian Farashahi, R.: Binary edwards curves. In: Oswald, E., Rohatgi, P. (eds.) CHES 2008. LNCS, vol. 5154, pp. 244–265. Springer, Heidelberg (2008). doi:10.1007/978-3-540-85053-3_16
4. Bernstein, D., Lange, T.: A complete set of addition laws for incomplete Edwards curves. J. Number Theory **131**, 858–872 (2011)
5. Bernstein, D., Lange, T.: Explicit-formulas database. http://www.hyperelliptic.org/EFD/
6. Castryck, W., Galbraith, S., Farashahi, R.: Efficient arithmetic on elliptic curves using a mixed Edwards Montgomery representation. https://eprint.iacr.org/2008/218.pdf
7. Edwards, H.M.: A normal form for elliptic curves. Bull. Amer. Math. Soc. **44**, 393–422 (2007)
8. Rezaeian Farashahi, R., Hosseini, S.G.: Differential addition on binary elliptic curves. In: Duquesne, S., Petkova-Nikova, S. (eds.) WAIFI 2016. LNCS, vol. 10064, pp. 21–35. Springer, Cham (2016). doi:10.1007/978-3-319-55227-9_2
9. Gaudry P. and Lubicz D.: The arithmetic of characteristic 2 Kummer surface. Finite Fields Appl. 15, 246–260 (2009)
10. Gu, H., Gu, D., Xie, W.: Differential addition on Jacobi quartic curves Conference: ICT and Energy Efficiency and Workshop on Information Theory and Security (CIICT 2012)

11. Hamburg, M.: Decaf: eliminating cofactors through point compression. In: Gennaro, R., Robshaw, M. (eds.) CRYPTO 2015. LNCS, vol. 9215, pp. 705–723. Springer, Heidelberg (2015). doi:10.1007/978-3-662-47989-6_34

12. Hisil, H., Wong, K.K.-H., Carter, G., Dawson, E.: Twisted edwards curves revisited. In: Pieprzyk, J. (ed.) ASIACRYPT 2008. LNCS, vol. 5350, pp. 326–343. Springer, Heidelberg (2008). doi:10.1007/978-3-540-89255-7_20

13. Koblitz, N.: Elliptic curve cryptosystems. Math. Comp. **48**(177), 203–209 (1987)

14. Miller, V.S.: Use of elliptic curves in cryptography. In: Williams, H.C. (ed.) CRYPTO 1985. LNCS, vol. 218, pp. 417–426. Springer, Heidelberg (1986). doi:10.1007/3-540-39799-X_31

15. Montgomery, P.L.: Speeding the Pollard and elliptic curve methods of factorization. Math. Comp. **48**(177), 243–264 (1987)

16. Silverman, J.H.: The Arithmetic of Elliptic Curves. Springer, Berlin (1995)

17. Washington, D.C.: Elliptic Curves: Number Theory and Cryptography, 2nd edn. CRC Press, Boca Raton (2008)

Short Papers

Certificate Transparency with Enhancements and Short Proofs

Abhishek Singh[1], Binanda Sengupta[2](✉), and Sushmita Ruj[2]

[1] IBM Research Laboratory, New Delhi, India
absingh0@in.ibm.com
[2] Indian Statistical Institute, Kolkata, India
{binanda_r,sush}@isical.ac.in

Abstract. Browsers can detect malicious websites that are provisioned with forged or fake TLS/SSL certificates. However, they are not so good at detecting these websites if they are provisioned with mistakenly (or maliciously) issued certificates. Google proposed certificate transparency which is an open framework to monitor and audit certificates in real time. Thereafter, a few other certificate transparency schemes have been proposed which can even handle revocation. All currently known constructions use Merkle hash trees and have proof size logarithmic in the number of certificates/domain owners. We present a new certificate transparency scheme with short (constant size) proofs. Our construction makes use of dynamic bilinear-map accumulators. The scheme has many desirable properties like efficient revocation, low verification cost and update costs comparable to the existing schemes. We provide proofs of security and evaluate the performance of our scheme.

Keywords: Certificate transparency · Revocation · Bilinear-map accumulator

1 Introduction

In public key cryptography, a web user should be able to verify the authenticity of public keys of different domains. For example, if a web browser uses the public key of some attacker instead of a bank's public key, then all the (possibly sensitive) information along with login credentials may be known to the attacker who can misuse them later. One solution to prevent such attacks is to rely on a third-party entity called *certificate authority* (CA) that issues digital certificates showing the association of public keys with the domain owners. The CA signs each of these certificates using its private key. However, this CA model suffers from two major problems [10]. Firstly, an untrusted CA may issue certificates for fake public keys [4]. Secondly, if the private key of a certificate owner is compromised, then the CA must revoke the certificate before its expiry date.

A. Singh—Work done while at Indian Statistical Institute, Kolkata, India.

J. Pieprzyk and S. Suriadi (Eds.): ACISP 2017, Part II, LNCS 10343, pp. 381–389, 2017.
DOI: 10.1007/978-3-319-59870-3_22

Certificate transparency (CT) [7,8], a technique proposed by Google, aims to make certificate issuance transparent by efficiently detecting fake certificates issued by malicious CAs. Public append-only log structures are maintained containing all the certificates. Domain owners can obtain proofs that their certificates are recorded in a log structure appropriately. Then, they provide the certificate along with a proof to their clients so that the clients can be convinced about the authenticity of the received certificate. Google's CT scheme provides *proof of presence* (if the issued certificate is present in the log structure) and *proof of extension* (if the log structure is maintained in an append-only mode). However, Google's CT does not handle revocation of a certificate. Ryan [10] extended Google's scheme to provide *proof of currency* (if the issued certificate is current or active) and *proof of absence of a domain owner* (if no certificates have been issued for a particular domain owner). These schemes have proofs of logarithmic size. We use bilinear-map accumulators [6] to have shorter proofs.

On the other hand, certificates can be revoked by CAs even before the expiry of the certificates (e.g., when the corresponding private key is known to be compromised). In this work, we introduce a proof of absence of a suspected certificate so that an auditor can ask for such proofs from the log maintainer for the certificates which belong to a certificate revocation list (CRL).

Our Contribution. Our contributions are summarized as follows.

- We have developed and extended the idea of enhanced certificate transparency proposed by Ryan [10]. We have designed a certificate transparency scheme (using bilinear-map accumulators and binary trees) that supports all the proofs found in the previous works. For the existing proofs, the parameters in our scheme are comparable to those proposed in the earlier schemes. Some of our proofs are shorter than those proposed in previous works.
- In addition to the proof of currency, we have introduced another proof (*proof of absence of a certificate*) related to certificate revocation. Both of these proofs are of constant size, and verification cost is also constant for them.
- We have analyzed the security and performance of our scheme.

2 Certificate Transparency

Certificate transparency (CT) [7,8] is a technique proposed by Google to efficiently detect certificates maliciously issued by certificate authorities. A certificate $c = cert(u, pk_u)$ is a signed (by a CA) pair (u, pk_u), where u is a domain owner and pk_u is a public key of u. The framework consists of the following main components. We refer the full version [11] for more details related to CT.

Certificate Log: All the certificates issued by CAs are stored in append-only log structures which are maintained by log maintainers in an authenticated fashion using Merkle hash trees [9].

Monitors: Monitors are publicly run servers that look for suspicious certificates by contacting the log maintainers periodically. Monitors also verify that all certificates in the log structures are visible. Domain owners or CAs can check the validity of a certificate with the help of monitors.

Auditors: Auditors are lightweight software components that can verify that logs are behaving correctly. They can also check whether a particular certificate is recorded in a log structure appropriately.

3   Our Construction

In our scheme, each certificate issued by a (possibly malicious) CA is associated with proofs showing the validity of that particular certificate. The certificates issued by various CAs are stored in public (and append-only) log structures maintained by *log maintainers*.

3.1   Data Structures Used in Our Construction

In our construction, the public log structure maintained by the log maintainer is organized by using the following tree data structures.

- **chronTree**: The chronTree is a Merkle hash tree where certificates are stored as the leaf-nodes of the tree (arranged in the chronological order in left-to-right manner). When a new certificate $c = cert(u, pk_u)$ is issued by a CA, it is added to the right of the chronTree. When a certificate $c = cert(u, pk_u)$ is revoked, a certificate $c' = cert(u, \texttt{null})$ is added to the right of the chronTree. The hash value of the root node (the root digest) is denoted by $digCT$.
- **accTree**: This tree is organized as a modified binary search tree in which active certificates are stored in the lexicographic order of the domain owners. Let X be the set of active (or current) certificates that is implemented as accTree. Each node in the accTree contains a certificate $c \in X$ and the corresponding membership witness w_c (using a bilinear-map accumulator).[1] The accumulation value $A(X)$ is linked to a leaf-node of the chronTree.
- **searchTree**: This tree is organized as a modified binary search tree where data items corresponding to the domain owners are stored in the lexicographic order (of the domain owners). A data item corresponding to a domain owner u is of the form $(u, List(pk_u))$, where $List(pk_u)$ is the list of N most recent public keys of u. So, the last certificate in the list is the current public key of the domain owner, and other keys are already revoked. The value of N is taken to be constant, and the list is maintained in a first-in-first-out (FIFO) fashion. The data items are stored in the nodes such that an in-order traversal of the searchTree provides the lexicographic ordering of the domain owners.

---

[1] A cryptographic accumulator [2] provides a *witness* to prove the membership of an element belonging to a set X without revealing the individual members of X. Damgård and Triandopoulos [6] proposed a dynamic bilinear-map accumulator that provides both *membership* and *non-membership* witnesses. We use this accumulator (described in the full version [11]) in our construction.

A collision-resistant function h is used to compute the hash values corresponding to the nodes of the searchTree. The hash value of a node is computed on the data item (of that node) and the hash values of its children. The hash value of the root node (the root digest) of the searchTree is denoted by $digST$ that is linked to a leaf-node of the chronTree.

3.2 Detailed Construction

In this section, we describe our construction in details. Our construction involves the following algorithms to achieve certificate transparency.

- **Setup(1^λ):** Let λ be the security parameter. The Setup algorithm generates (p, g, G, G_T, e) as the parameters of a bilinear map, where g is a generator of G. Let X be the set of active certificates issued by a certificate authority (CA), that is, $X = \{cert(u_i, pk_{u_i})\}$, where pk_{u_i} is the active public key issued by the CA for the domain owner u_i. The Setup algorithm selects a random element $s \xleftarrow{R} \mathbb{Z}_p^*$ as the secret trapdoor information. The set $\{g^{s^i} | 0 \leqslant i \leqslant q\}$ is made public, where q is an upper bound on $|X|$. The accumulation function $f_s(X) : 2^{\mathbb{Z}_p} \to G$ gives the accumulation value $A(X)$ defined as $f_s(X) = A = g^{\prod_{x_i \in X}(x_i+s)}$ [6].

  The algorithm constructs a chronTree by inserting certificates in the chronological (left-to-right) order and returns $digCT$ as the root digest. It also constructs a searchTree by inserting domain owners in the lexicographic order along with other relevant data associated with each domain owner and returns $digST$ as the root digest. The algorithm constructs an accTree by inserting (only) the active certificates (represented as the set X) along with their membership (in X) witnesses for different domain owners. For each active certificate $c \in X$, the membership witness $w_c = g^{\prod_{x_j \in X : x_j \neq c}(x_j+s)} = A^{\frac{1}{(c+s)}}$. We note that a *collision-resistant* hash function h is used to compute the hash values in the searchTree and the chronTree. Finally, $(p, g, G, G_T, e, \{g^{s^i} | 0 \leqslant i \leqslant q\}, h, A, digCT, digST)$ is set as the public parameters PP, and the secret key is the trapdoor value s.

- **Insert(c, sk, PP):** When a CA issues a new certificate $c = cert(u, pk_u)$, it asks the log maintainer to insert c in the log structure. The certificate c is added to the log structure as follows. The public parameters PP are updated accordingly.

  - Adding c to accTree: Compute the new accumulation value (corresponding to the new set $X' = X \cup \{c\}$) $A' = A^{(c+s)}$. The membership witness for c is A. For each $i \in X$, the updated membership witness is computed as $w_i' = w_i^{(c+s)}$. The accTree is updated accordingly.
  - Adding c to searchTree: Search for the node corresponding to the domain owner u (if it is present) and then append the new public key pk_u to the associated list of public keys for u. Otherwise, create a new node for u with the list containing only pk_u and insert it in the searchTree. Consequently, the root digest of the searchTree is updated as $digST'$.

- Adding c to chronTree: Add a new node containing $(c, A', digST')$ to the right of the chronTree. The root digest of the chronTree is updated as $digCT'$.
- **Revoke**(c, sk, PP): To revoke a certificate $c = cert(u, pk_u)$, the following operations are performed. The public parameters PP are updated accordingly.
  - Removing c from accTree: Compute the new accumulation value A' (corresponding to the new set $X' = X\backslash\{c\}$) as $A' = A^{\frac{1}{(c+s)}}$. Remove the node corresponding to the domain owner u of certificate c from the accTree. For each $i \in X'$, the updated membership witness is computed as $w_i' = w_i^{\frac{1}{(c+s)}}$. The accTree is updated accordingly.
  - There are no changes in the searchTree for the revocation of c.
  - Adding a new node for the domain owner u to chronTree: Add to the right of the existing chronTree a new node containing $(c', A', digST)$, where $c' = cert(u, \text{null})$. The new root digest of the chronTree is updated as $digCT'$.
- **Query**(PP): This algorithm is run by an auditor to output a query Q.
  - Proof of presence of a certificate (Type 1): The query Q asks for a proof of whether a certificate $c = cert(u, pk_u)$ is present in the log structure.
  - Proof of absence of a certificate (Type 2): The query Q asks for a proof of whether a certificate c is absent in the set of active certificates, that is, $c \notin X$.
  - Proof of absence of a domain owner (Type 3): The query Q asks for a proof of whether a domain owner u is absent (no certificates for u) in the log structure.
  - Proof of extension (Type 4): The query Q asks for a proof that if the chronTree corresponding to $digCT'$ is an extension of that corresponding to $digCT$.
  - Proof of currency (Type 5): The query Q asks for a proof of whether pk_u is the current public key of the domain owner u, that is, whether the certificate c is present in the set of active certificates ($c \in X$).
- **ProofGeneration**(Q, PP): Upon receiving the query Q, the log maintainer generates the corresponding proof $\Pi(Q)$ as follows.
  - Type 1 Proof: Search for the certificate c in the searchTree. If a node for the domain owner u is present in the searchTree, define h_1 and h_2 to be the hash values of the children of the node (they are taken to be null if the node is a leaf-node). Let the sequence of data items of the nodes along the search path be $dataseq_{type1} = (d_1, d_2, d_3, \ldots, d_r)$ for some $r \in \mathbb{N}$, where d_1 is the data item corresponding to the node for the domain owner u, d_r is the data item corresponding to the root node, and other data items correspond to the other intermediate nodes in the search path. Let the sequence of hash values of the nodes in the associated path (the path containing the siblings of the nodes along the search path mentioned above) along with h_1 and h_2 be $hashseq_{type1} = (h_1, h_2, h(v_1), h(v_2), h(v_3), \ldots)$. Send these sequences as Π.

- Type 2 Proof: Search for the certificate c in the accTree. If there is no node for u in the accTree, then send the non-membership witness $\hat{w}_c = (w_c, v_c)$ of c, where $v_c = -\prod_{x \in X}(x - c) \bmod p \in \mathbb{Z}_p^*$ and $w_c = g^{\frac{(\prod_{x \in X}(x+s))+v_c}{c+s}} \in G$.

- Type 3 Proof: The proof is similar to the Type 1 proof. Find the nodes in the searchTree corresponding to the domain owners u_1 and u_2 such that they were the neighbor (in the lexicographic ordering) nodes of the node corresponding to u if u were present in the searchTree, that is, $u_1 \leqslant u \leqslant u_2$ lexicographically. These nodes can be found by searching for the domain owner u in the searchTree, and the search ends at some leaf-node in the searchTree. The nodes corresponding to u_1 and u_2 reside on this search path itself, and one of them is the leaf-node (where the search ends). Let the sequence of data items of the nodes along the search path be $dataseq_{type3} = (d_1, d_2, \ldots, d_{r'})$ for some $r' \in \mathbb{N}$, where d_1 is the data item corresponding to the leaf-node, $d_{r'}$ is the data item corresponding to the root node, and other data items correspond to the other intermediate nodes in the search path. Let the sequence of hash values of the nodes in the associated path be $hashseq_{type3} = (h(v_1), h(v_2), \ldots)$. Send $(dataseq_{type3}, hashseq_{type3})$ as Π.

- Type 4 Proof: Compare the chronTree structures corresponding to $digCT$ and $digCT'$ and send one hash value per level of the latest chronTree as a proof Π. If the chronTree corresponding to $digCT'$ is an extension of the chronTree corresponding to $digCT$, then the latter chronTree is a subtree of the earlier chronTree. The proof $\Pi = (h_1, h_2, \ldots)$ is the sequence of hash values of the nodes required to compute the current root digest $digCT'$ from the previous root digest $digCT$. Here, h_1 is the hash value of the sibling node of node v whose hash value is $digCT$ (that is, v is the root of the previous chronTree), h_2 is the hash value of the sibling node of parent node of v, and so on.

- Type 5 Proof: Search for the certificate c in the accTree. If c is present in the node for u, then send the membership (in X) witness w_c stored at that node.

- **Verify**(Q, Π, PP): Given the query Q and the corresponding proof Π, the auditor $\mathcal{V}$ verifies Π in the following way depending on the type of the proof.

  - Type 1 Proof: $\mathcal{V}$ checks if $h(\cdots h(d_3, h(d_2, h(d_1, h_1, h_2), h(v_1)), h(v_2)) \ldots) \overset{?}{=} digST$ and outputs accept if the equation holds (or reject otherwise).

  - Type 2 Proof: $\mathcal{V}$ checks if $e(w_c, g^c \cdot g^s) \overset{?}{=} e(A \cdot g^{v_c}, g)$ and outputs accept if the equation holds (or reject otherwise).

  - Type 3 Proof: $\mathcal{V}$ checks if $h(\cdots h(d_3, h(d_2, h(d_1), h(v_1)), h(v_2)) \ldots) \overset{?}{=} digST$ and outputs accept if the equation holds (or reject otherwise).

  - Type 4 Proof: $\mathcal{V}$ checks if $h(\ldots (h(h(digCT, h_1), h_2) \ldots) \overset{?}{=} digCT'$ and outputs accept if the equation holds (or reject otherwise).

– Type 5 Proof: $\mathcal{V}$ checks if $e(w_c, g^c \cdot g^s) \overset{?}{=} e(A, g)$ and outputs accept if the equation holds (or reject otherwise).

4   Security Analysis

We assume that an auditor, a domain owner and a monitor are *honest* while a log maintainer and a certificate authority may be *dishonest*. We further assume that the log maintainer does *not* collude with the certificate authority. We analyze the security of our scheme in the following lemmas (see [11] for the proofs).

Lemma 1. *Let a certificate authority issue a fake certificate $c = cert(u, pk'_u)$ for a domain owned by u. If the certificate is not logged in the public log maintained by an honest log maintainer, then an auditor will reject the certificate.*

Lemma 2. *Let a certificate authority issue a fake certificate $c = cert(u, pk'_u)$ for a particular domain owned by u. If the certificate is present in the public log maintained by an honest log maintainer, then the domain owner will be able to immediately identify this certificate issued maliciously and to report this problem.*

Lemma 3. *Let a log maintainer be honest. Let a dishonest certificate authority issue a fake certificate $c = cert(u, pk'_u)$ for a particular domain owned by u. If the certificate c is not present in the log, then the certificate authority fails to produce a valid proof Π of any type, except with some probability negligible in λ.*

Lemma 4. *If a dishonest log maintainer maliciously provides a proof Π of any type for a certificate $c = cert(u, pk'_u)$, then an auditor or the domain owner u will be able to detect it.*

Table 1. Comparison among certificate transparency schemes.

Schemes for CT	Parameters	Proof of presence of a certificate (Type 1)	Proof of absence of a certificate (Type 2)	Proof absence of a domain owner (Type 3)	Proof of extension (Type 4)	Proof of currency (Type 5)
Google [8]	Proof size	$O(\log n)$	-	-	$O(\log n)$	-
	Cost of proof computation	$O(\log n)$	-	-	$O(\log n)$	-
	Cost of proof verification	$O(\log n)$	-	-	$O(\log n)$	-
Ryan [10]	Proof size	-	-	$O(\log t)$	$O(\log n)$	$O(\log t)$
	Cost of proof computation	-		$O(\log t)$	$O(\log n)$	$O(\log t)$
	Cost of proof verification	-	-	$O(\log t)$	$O(\log n)$	$O(\log t)$
Our scheme	Proof size	$O(\log t)$	$O(1)$	$O(\log t)$	$O(\log n)$	$O(1)$
	Cost of proof computation	$O(\log t)$	$O(m)$	$O(\log t)$	$O(\log n)$	$O(\log m)$
	Cost of proof verification	$O(\log t)$	$O(1)$	$O(\log t)$	$O(\log n)$	$O(1)$

5   Performance Analysis

Let n be the number of certificates present in the log structure, t be the number of domain owners and m be the number of active certificates ($n \geqslant t \geqslant m$). The asymptotic performance analysis is described in detail in the full version [11]. Table 1 shows a comparison among CT schemes. For performance evaluation, we take $\lambda = 128$ and $p = \Theta(2^{2\lambda})$. Barreto-Naehrig (BN) curves [1] are used for pairings. We take SHA-256 as the *collision-resistant* hash function h used in chronTree and searchTree. Timing analysis is done for a 2.5 GHz Intel Core i5-3210M processor using the software frameworks *PandA* [5] and *eBASH* [3].

Size and Verification Cost of a Proof. We mention the size (in bits) and the verification cost (in ms) of a proof as follows (see [11] for details).

- Type 1 Proof: The size of a proof is $\log t(256 + N \cdot pk_{size})$ bits, where N is the maximum size of the list of public keys stored corresponding to a domain owner and pk_{size} is the size of a public key. The verification of a proof takes around $(\log t \cdot hash_{in} \cdot (0.64) \cdot 10^{-6})$ ms, where $hash_{in} \approx (512 + N \cdot pk_{size})$.
- Type 2 Proof: The size of a proof is 512 bits. The verification of a proof takes around 3.06 ms.
- Type 3 Proof: The size of a proof is $\log t(256 + N \cdot pk_{size})$ bits. The verification of a proof takes around $(\log t \cdot hash_{in} \cdot (0.64) \cdot 10^{-6})$ ms.
- Type 4 Proof: The size of a proof is at most $256 \log n$ bits. The verification of a proof takes around $(\log n \cdot 64 \cdot (11.98) \cdot 10^{-6})$ ms.
- Type 5 Proof: The size of a proof is 256 bits. The verification of a proof takes around 3.06 ms.

6   Conclusion

We have developed a scheme which is an extended version of the existing certificate transparency schemes. Some of the proofs in our scheme enjoy constant proof-size and constant verification cost. We have also analyzed the security and performance of our scheme.

Acknowledgments. This project has been made possible in part by a gift from the NetApp University Research Fund, a corporate advised fund of Silicon Valley Community Foundation.

References

1. Barreto, P.S.L.M., Naehrig, M.: Pairing-friendly elliptic curves of prime order. In: Preneel, B., Tavares, S. (eds.) SAC 2005. LNCS, vol. 3897, pp. 319–331. Springer, Heidelberg (2006). doi:10.1007/11693383_22
2. Benaloh, J., Mare, M.: One-way accumulators: A decentralized alternative to digital signatures. In: Helleseth, T. (ed.) EUROCRYPT 1993. LNCS, vol. 765, pp. 274–285. Springer, Heidelberg (1994). doi:10.1007/3-540-48285-7_24

3. Bernstein, D.J., Lange, T.: eBASH: ECRYPT benchmarking of all submitted hashes. http://bench.cr.yp.to/ebash.html

4. Brewster, T.: Diginotar goes bankrupt after hack (2011). http://www.itpro.co.uk/636244/diginotar-goes-bankrupt-after-hack

5. Chuengsatiansup, C., Naehrig, M., Ribarski, P., Schwabe, P.: PandA: Pairings and arithmetic. In: Cao, Z., Zhang, F. (eds.) Pairing 2013. LNCS, vol. 8365, pp. 229–250. Springer, Cham (2014). doi:10.1007/978-3-319-04873-4_14

6. Damgård, I., Triandopoulos, N.: Supporting non-membership proofs with bilinear-map accumulators. IACR Cryptology ePrint Archive 2008, 538 (2008)

7. Google: Certificate transparency. https://www.certificate-transparency.org/

8. Laurie, B., Langley, A., Kasper, E.: Certificate transparency. https://tools.ietf.org/html/rfc6962

9. Merkle, R.C.: A certified digital signature. In: Brassard, G. (ed.) CRYPTO 1989. LNCS, vol. 435, pp. 218–238. Springer, New York (1990). doi:10.1007/0-387-34805-0_21

10. Ryan, M.D.: Enhanced certificate transparency and end-to-end encrypted mail. In: NDSS 2014 (2014). http://www.internetsociety.org/doc/enhanced-certificate-transparency-and-end-end-encrypted-mail

11. Singh, A., Sengupta, B., Ruj, S.: Certificate transparency with enhancements and short proofs. CoRR abs/1704.04937 (2017). https://arxiv.org/abs/1704.04937

Update-Tolerant and Revocable Password Backup

Moritz Horsch[✉], Johannes Braun[✉], Dominique Metz[✉],
and Johannes Buchmann[✉]

Technische Universität Darmstadt, Hochschulstraße 10, 64283 Darmstadt, Germany
{horsch,jbraun,metz,buchmann}@cdc.informatik.tu-darmstadt.de

Abstract. It is practically impossible for users to memorize a large
portfolio of strong and individual passwords for their online accounts.
A solution is to generate passwords randomly and store them. Yet, storing passwords instead of memorizing them bears the risk of loss, e.g., in
situations where the device on which the passwords are stored is damaged, lost, or stolen. This makes the creation of backups of the passwords
indispensable. However, placing such backups at secure locations to protect them as well from loss and unauthorized access and keeping them
up-to-date at the same time is an unsolved problem in practice.

We present PASCO, a backup solution for passwords that solves this
challenge. PASCO backups need not to be updated, even when the user's
password portfolio is changed. PASCO backups can be revoked without
having physical access to them. This prevents password leakage, even
when a user loses control over a backup. Additionally, we show how to
extend PASCO to enable a fully controllable emergency access. It allows
a user to give someone else access to his passwords in urgent situations.

1 Introduction

Online accounts are mainly protected by passwords. To resist the various known
attacks against passwords (e.g. [2]), users need to select a strong and different
password for each account. These two security conditions require a large portfolio of strong and individual passwords to be memorized, which is practically
impossible for users [3].

One solution is to create passwords randomly and store them on a user device,
such as done by password managers. However, this approach has the drawback
that the passwords are not available on all user devices [8]. The *PasswordLess
Password Synchronization* (PALPAS) scheme [6] solves this problem. It creates strong and individual passwords for accounts and makes them available on
all user devices. PALPAS does not store passwords, neither on devices nor on
servers. Thus, it is not vulnerable to security breaches at servers and inherent
offline brute-force attacks. PALPAS generates passwords only when needed. This
is done using a secret stored on all devices and some synchronization data stored
on a server. However, PALPAS is vulnerable to password loss. In case the secret
on the device is lost users cannot computer their passwords anymore.

J. Pieprzyk and S. Suriadi (Eds.): ACISP 2017, Part II, LNCS 10343, pp. 390–397, 2017.
DOI: 10.1007/978-3-319-59870-3_23

In this paper, we advance the PALPAS scheme with a secure and usable backup solution called PASCO (PALPAS RECOVERY). It allows users to recover their passwords in case their devices get lost. Additionally, our backup solution can be used to establish fully controllable emergency access to the passwords. Once a backup is created, it never needs to be updated even when the password portfolio changes.

Therefore, it can be kept completely offline in secure, different, and physical isolated locations which minimizes the risk of compromise and loss. Furthermore, the backup solution has an built-in revocation mechanism, which allows the user to completely invalidate a backup if he loses control over it. The revocation mechanism works without having access to the backup itself and guarantees that no passwords can be leaked from it once revoked.

The paper is organized as follows: In Sect. 2 we summarize related work and we present the background about PALPAS in Sect. 3. We describe PASCO in Sect. 4 and present its extension for emergency access in Sect. 5. We conclude the paper in Sect. 6.

2   Related Work

Beside many approaches to simplify the creation and memorization of passwords (e.g. [1,3,4,9,12]), storing passwords on user devices is the most common approach to solve the memorability problem of passwords. A prominent example are password managers. They store the user's passwords in a database, encrypted with a user-chosen master password. To synchronize the database between devices and prevent its loss, it is stored on a server. In emergency situations, a user can give someone else the master password, but then the person has access to all passwords. Moreover, a security breach at the server [10] allows adversaries to steal the database and to perform offline brute-force attacks [13]. Another approach is to only store data on servers that is independent from the passwords, as done by PALPAS [6], which we use in this paper. For a general model of such schemes we refer to Al Maqbali et al. [11].

3   Background: PALPAS

Our work is based on PALPAS [6] which we summarize in the following.

Password Generation. As illustrated in Fig. 1, PALPAS generates a password in two steps: First, a Pseudorandom Generator (PRG) generates a random value based on a *Seed* and a *Salt*. Second, a Password Generator (PG) derives a password from the random and ensures that it complies with a password policy (*PP*). The PRG and the PG are deterministic.

The *Seed* is a randomly generated secret that is used for the generation of all passwords. It is created when a user uses PALPAS for the first time and it does not change over time.

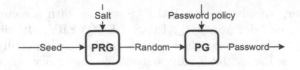

Fig. 1. PALPAS password generation [6].

The *Salt* is also a random value, but it differs for each account so that individual passwords for different accounts are created. Changing the *Salt* for an existing account allows to create a new password, e.g., during a regular password change. An initial salt is generated when PALPAS initially creates the password for an account, e.g., during account creation.

The *PP* specifies the password requirements of a service such as the password length and the allowed characters. By this, PALPAS ensures that the randomly created password is actually accepted by the service. The *PP* is created when a service is used for the first time. This can be done manually by the user or the *PP* is retrieved from a central service as presented by Horsch et al. [7]. During password change for an account (by changing the salt) it might also be necessary to update the *PP* in order to comply with the recent password requirements of a service.

Password Synchronization. PALPAS creates a password portfolio of strong and individual passwords using a fixed *Seed* and an individual *Salt* and a *PP* for each service, respectively. To enable the computation of the passwords on different devices, the *Seed* is shared by all user devices and the salts and policies are synchronized between them through a server, namely the Salt Synchronization Service (SSS).

When creating new or changing passwords, the corresponding salts and policies are added or updated at the SSS. Each time PALPAS recomputes a password, the corresponding *Salt* and *PP* for the account is retrieved from the SSS. In this way, any changes of the user's password portfolio are immediately available on all of his devices.

Moreover, the usernames of the user's accounts are synchronized between the devices through the SSS. For each user account A an account data object $Data_A = (Salt_A, PP_A, Username_A, url_A)$ is stored at the SSS, where url_A is the service's URL. Each $Data_A$ is encrypted with a key $K_{Data,Enc}$ by PALPAS before it is transferred to the SSS. To retrieve only the $Data_A$ for a specific account and not all of them, each $Data_A$ is associated with an identifier ID_A. It is generated by PALPAS by $ID_A = \mathrm{HMAC}(K_{Data,Mac}, url_A)$, where url_A is the service's URL. Both keys, $K_{Data,Enc}$ and $K_{Data,Mac}$, are derived from a key K_{Data} which is randomly created when a user uses PALPAS for the first time.

Moreover, the user's account at the SSS is protected from unauthorized access. Each user device has an individual key pair K_{Auth} for authentication, consisting of a private key SK_{Auth} and public key PK_{Auth}. The key pair is randomly created by the device when PALPAS is used for the first time and an account at the SSS is created. SK_{Auth} is stored on the device and PK_{Auth} is transferred to the SSS. To register multiple devices at the SSS, an regis- tered device requests an authentication token T_{Auth}. The new device creates its own key pair K_{Auth} and uses T_{Auth} to register its PK_{Auth} at the SSS. To set up PALPAS on all of his devices, a user needs to transfer the PALPAS secret $S = (Seed, K_{\text{Data}})$ to each device and register the device at the SSS using an authentication token. This has to be done only once. The data transfer can be easily achieved by a file transfer or a QR code.

Password Loss. The *Seed*, the salts, and the password policies are crucial for password generation. To retrieve the account data from the SSS, SK_{Auth} and K_{Data} are required. The availability of these five pieces of data must be guaranteed. Otherwise, the user's password portfolio is lost.

The account data is stored at the SSS. Their availability has to be guaranteed by the SSS. We assume that the SSS implements proper measures to restore the data at any time. We describe an alternative solution using multiple SSSs in the extended version of this paper (see [5]).

The PALPAS secret $S = (Seed, K_{\text{Data}})$ and the individual SK_{Auth} are exclu- sively stored on user devices and thus are at high risk of loss. Typical cases are lost, stolen, or damaged devices as well as malware.

4   PASCO

We now present PASCO (<u>PA</u>LPA<u>S</u> RE<u>CO</u>VERY). It ensures that users never lose their password portfolio by providing recoverability of the essential PALPAS data that is stored on the user device.

PASCO uses a separate backup device (BD) to store a backup of the PALPAS data. We consider the BD to be a tamper resistant device that provides secure storage, user authentication, and basic cryptographic algorithms. The BD stores the PALPAS secret $S = (Seed, K_{\text{Data}})$ encrypted by a one-time-pad (OTP). Furthermore, it has its own authentication key pair $K_{\text{Auth,BD}}$ for the SSS. The BD is protected by a user-chosen PIN. To prevent guessing attacks, it has a retry counter for the PIN. After five wrong PIN entries the BD erases all stored data. We provide a security evaluation and an implementation using a smart card of PASCO in [5].

Creating a Backup. We assume that the user already uses PALPAS and has registered a device at the SSS. The procedure to create a backup is described in the following. The data flow is illustrated in Fig. 2.

1. The user (U) initializes the BD with a PIN.
2. The user device (UD) connects to the SSS, authenticates itself with its $SK_{\text{Auth,UD}}$, and requests $T_{\text{Auth,DD}}$.
3. The UD sends $S = (Seed, K_{\text{Data}})$ and $T_{\text{Auth,BD}}$ to the BD.

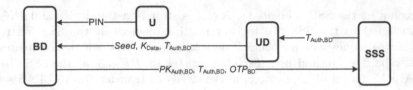

Fig. 2. Data flow of the PASCO backup procedure.

4. The BD randomly samples a one-time-pad key OTP_{BD} and computes S_{BD} $= S \oplus OTP_{BD}$. Then, it generates a key pair K_{Auth}. $SK_{Auth,BD}$ is stored at the BD and $PK_{Auth,BD}$, $T_{Auth,BD}$, and OTP_{BD} is send to the SSS. The SSS verifies $T_{Auth,BD}$ and stores $PK_{Auth,BD}$ and OTP_{BD}. Finally, BD stores S_{BD} and deletes OTP_{BD} and S.

An update of the BD is not necessary, even when the user's password portfolio is changed. Changing, adding, or deleting passwords only requires to update, store, or delete the related $Data_A$ at the SSS. This is already an integral part of PALPAS. As the SSS provides availability of the account data, PASCO itself does not need to take care of it.

Restoring Data from a Backup. To restore the PALPAS data on a device, the user needs to have the BD, the PIN, and a device with PALPAS. The restoring works as follows. The data flow is illustrated in Fig. 3.

1. The user (U) authenticates himself to the BD with his PIN.
2. The BD contacts the SSS, authenticates itself with its $SK_{Auth,BD}$, and requests $T_{Auth,UD}$ and OTP_{BD}.
3. The BD computes $S = S_{BD} \oplus OTP_{BD}$. Then, it transfers the $Seed$, K_{Data}, and $T_{Auth,UD}$ to the UD. The UD stores the $Seed$ and K_{Data}.
4. The UD creates a key pair K_{Auth}. $SK_{Auth,UD}$ is stored at the UD and $PK_{Auth,UD}$ and $T_{Auth,UD}$ is send to the SSS. The SSS verifies $T_{Auth,UD}$ and stores $PK_{Auth,UD}$. UD has now access to the user's account at the SSS and can retrieve the account data for generating the passwords.

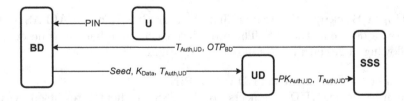

Fig. 3. Data flow of the PASCO restore procedure.

Revoking a Backup. All existing BDs are registered at the SSS with their individual $PK_{\text{Auth,BD}}$ and OTP_{BD}. To revoke a BD a user deletes the related $PK_{\text{Auth,BD}}$ and OTP_{BD} at the SSS. Now the BD can no longer retrieve any account data nor request new authentication tokens. Moreover, the deletion of the OTP_{BD} invalidates S_{BD} and it is impossible to recover the PALPAS secret S from the BD. Thus, the BD is useless and the passwords cannot get leaked.

5 PASCO Backups with Emergency Access

We now describe how a user can allow someone else to use a BD to access his accounts in urgent or emergency situations. In addition to storing the PALPAS data, the BD now implements the PALPAS password generation procedure. Furthermore, the SSS is equipped with a fine granular access control for the account data. For each PK_{Auth}, a user can specify different access rules. While, one $PK_{\text{Auth,BD}}$ may have access to all data, another $PK_{\text{Auth,BD'}}$ can only access the data for the user's mail account.

Creating and Managing a Backup. The procedure for creating a BD with emergency access is nearly the same. It only differs in the second step, where the UD requests $T_{\text{Auth,BD}}$. The request is supplemented by an access control list (ACL), which is basically a list of account data identifiers. The $PK_{\text{Auth,BD}}$ registered using $T_{\text{Auth,BD}}$ is later only granted access to the account data defined by the ACL. The ACL for each PK_{Auth} can be modified at any time without having physical access to a BD.

The BD can simultaneously act as a backup and password generation device. Thus, depositing a single BD at a friend's place is sufficient. To provide both features, the BD is equipped with multiple authentication keys. One $PK_{\text{Auth,BD}}$ is allowed to request an $T_{\text{Auth,UD}}$ as needed for the restoring procedure. Another $PK'_{\text{Auth,BD}}$ can only retrieve certain account data and is used for the emergency access. To equip a BD with multiple authentication keys, the creation procedure is performed multiple times with a different T_{Auth}, PK_{Auth}, ACL, and PIN. Depending on the PIN, the BD uses the corresponding $PK_{\text{Auth,BD}}$ for authentication at the SSS.

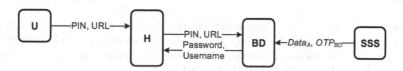

Fig. 4. Data flow of the PASCO emergency access procedure.

Accessing a Backup in Case of an Emergency. Allowing the friend (i.e. BD holder) to create the user's password for an account works as follows. The data flow is depicted in Fig. 4.

1. The user (U) tells the BD holder (H) the emergency PIN of the BD and the URL of the service where H should access the user's account.
2. H uses the PIN to authenticate himself to the BD and transfers the URL of the service to the BD.
3. The BD connects to the SSS and authenticates itself with $SK_{Auth,BD}$. It calculates ID_A for the URL and requests the corresponding $Data_A$.
4. The SSS checks the ACL for $PK_{Auth,BD}$ and, if the access is allowed, returns $Data_A$ and OTP_{BD}.
5. The BD computes $S = S_{BD} \oplus OTP_{BD}$ and then decrypts $Data_A$ with $K_{Data,Enc}$ to obtain $Salt_A$ and PP_A. Finally, it generates the password using the $Seed$, $Salt_A$, and PP_A (cf. Sect. 3).
6. The BD deletes S and hands the password and username over to H. H can now browse the service and log in to the user's account.

6   Conclusion

In this paper we presented PASCO, a backup solution for PALPAS. The combination of both is the first solution that provides the confidentiality, availability, and recoverability of the stored passwords. With the implementation we have shown that PASCO can be realized in practice. We have also presented a revocation mechanism that could additionally be integrated into PALPAS to enable the secure revocation of user devices. With the emergency access, we address a major concern of users regarding the storage of passwords. Moreover, this function can be used to generate passwords in general, which we will focus in our future work. Using the smart card as a password generator allows users to literally have their passwords in their wallet. With the two key features of PASCO, users need not update the card when their password portfolio is changed and they are able to revoke it in case of loss at any time.

References

1. Blocki, J., Komanduri, S., Cranor, L.F., Datta, A.: Spaced repetition and mnemonics enable recall of multiple strong passwords. In: Proceeding of NDSS (2015)
2. Bonneau, J.: The science of guessing: Analyzing an anonymized corpus of 70 million passwords. In: Proceeding of IEEE SP (2012)
3. Florêncio, D., Herley, C., van Oorschot, P.C.: Password portfolios and the finite-effort user: sustainably managing large numbers of accounts. In: Proceeding of USENIX Security Symposium (2014)
4. Halderman, J.A., Waters, B., Felten, E.W.: A convenient method for securely managing passwords. In: Proceeding of WWW (2005)
5. Horsch, M., Braun, J., Metz, D., Buchmann, J.: Update-tolerant and revocable password backup (extended version). CoRR, abs/1704.02883 (2017)

6. Horsch, M., Hülsing, A., Buchmann, J.: PALPAS - PAsswordLess PAssword synchronization. In: Proceeding of ARES (2015)
7. Horsch, M., Schlipf, M., Braun, J., Buchmann, J.: Password requirements markup language. In: Liu, J.K.K., Steinfeld, R. (eds.) ACISP 2016. LNCS, vol. 9722, pp. 426–439. Springer, Cham (2016). doi:10.1007/978-3-319-40253-6_26
8. Karole, A., Saxena, N., Christin, N.: A comparative usability evaluation of traditional password managers. In: Rhee, K.-H., Nyang, D.H. (eds.) ICISC 2010. LNCS, vol. 6829, pp. 233–251. Springer, Heidelberg (2011). doi:10.1007/978-3-642-24209-0_16
9. Kiesel, J., Stein, B., Lucks, S.: A large-scale analysis of the mnemonic password advice. In: Proceeding of NDSS (2017)
10. LastPass Corporate. LastPass Security Notification, June 2015. https://blog.lastpass.com/2015/06/lastpass-security-notice.html/
11. Al Maqbali, F., Mitchell, C.J.: Password generators: old ideas and new. In: Foresti, S., Lopez, J. (eds.) WISTP 2016. LNCS, vol. 9895, pp. 245–253. Springer, Cham (2016). doi:10.1007/978-3-319-45931-8_16
12. Shay, R., Bauer, L., Christin, N., Cranor, L.F., Forget, A., Komanduri, S., Mazurek, M.L., Melicher, W., Segreti, S.M., Ur, B.: A spoonful of sugar?: The impact of guidance and feedback on password-creation behavior. In: Proceeding of CHI (2015)
13. Ziegler, D., Rauter, M., Stromberger, C., Teufl, P., Hein, D.M.: Do you think your passwords are secure? In: Proceeding of PRISMS (2014)

Redactable Graph Hashing, Revisited

(Extended Abstract)

Andreas Erwig, Marc Fischlin[✉], Martin Hald, Dominik Helm, Robert Kiel,
Florian Kübler, Michael Kümmerlin, Jakob Laenge, and Felix Rohrbach

Technische Universität Darmstadt, Darmstadt, Germany
marc.fischlin@cryptoplexity.de

Abstract. We revisit the previous work of Arshad et al. (CODASPY
2014) about the security of redactable graph hashing schemes. Such
schemes, introduced in a series of works by Devanbu et al. (DBSec 2000,
CCS 2001, Algorithmica 2004), allow to hash graphs and to release sub
graphs which can be verified against the original hash value. Arshad
et al. introduce security notions for collision resistance and privacy of
graphs, where the latter should capture the infeasibility to reconstruct
the full graph from the hash value of a redacted one.

We discuss here that the original security notions of Arshad et al.
are too weak. Our argument is by virtue of intuitively insecure examples
which are deemed secure according to their notion. We therefore present
stronger security definitions. We also point out the differences in the privacy notions with respect to redactable and sanitizable schemes: In the
former case anyone can produce verifiable data from the graph, whereas
in the latter case only a designated party can. Sanitizable schemes allow
for stronger privacy guarantees. We finally discuss instantiation possibilities for the various security notions.

1 Introduction

Cryptographic primitives are often used to protect static data. But with the
growth of outsourcing computations and data maintenance, the need to have
primitives supporting operations on the secured data has also increased. For
instance, the breakthrough construction of fully homomorphic encryption [11]
allows in principle to run now computations on encrypted data, ensuring the
privacy of the data towards the evaluating party. Even earlier, for authenticity
and integrity the ideas of redactable or sanitizable signature schemes [2,12,14]
have introduced the possibility to sign data in such a way that external parties
can prove authenticity of partial data. This may require to protect the privacy
of the redacted data, e.g., when handing out partial medical data [3–5,15].

1.1 Redactable Graph Hashing

In this work we look at the notion of redactable graph hashing. The idea is that
one can create a hash value of a graph such that one can later verify the hash

© Springer International Publishing AG 2017
J. Pieprzyk and S. Suriadi (Eds.): ACISP 2017, Part II, LNCS 10343, pp. 398–405, 2017.
DOI: 10.1007/978-3-319-59870-3_24

against any (redacted) sub graph, yet possibly requiring some additional information for the verification. The idea has been introduced by Martel et al. [13] for (directed) acyclic graphs, with a focus on designing solutions. Recently, Arshad et al. [1] extended the approach to cyclic graphs and augmented the security considerations by more formal definitions and claims.

The approach of redactable graph hashing is highly convincing for designing functional cryptographic schemes. First, graphs are very general concepts such that devising constructions for graphs immediately gives solutions for a variety of other data structures. Second, redactable hash functions instantaneously yield redactable signature schemes. For this, one merely applies the common hash-then-sign paradigm, where the signer signs the graph hash value with a regular signature scheme. Redaction on the graph, which supposedly leaves the hash value untouched, then does not require to change the signature part for updating the cryptographic data.

1.2   Defining Security

Arshad et al. [1] present security definitions for collision-resistance and privacy of redactable graph hashing, as well as constructions and performance results. The former security property should guarantee that one cannot efficiently find distinct graphs with identical hash values, and the latter one should prevent leakage of information about the redacted parts. While Arshad et al. clearly deserve credit for putting forward the formal requirements of such schemes, our starting point is to note that their formal security notions do not seem to appropriately capture the desired properties. For instance, we point out that their definition of collision resistance only captures adversaries which faithfully create hash values and redactions according to the scheme. In general, however, adversaries may choose such data maliciously, and we indeed present a scheme which is intuitively insecure, but provides collision resistance according to their definition.

We therefore present new definitions for the security properties, following similar approaches for redactable and sanitizable signatures [6,7]. Our notion of collision resistance of graph hashing demands that the adversary cannot output a hash value and different graphs G, G' such that they both verify against the hash value. Of course, neither of the graphs can be a sub graph of the other one, since otherwise an adversary could simply redact G to G' to get different graphs for the same hash value. But the exact formalization is even a bit more tricky, since the adversary may derive both G and G' form a common super graph with the same hash value.

Another shortcoming in [1] refers to the privacy notion. If one adopts the common idea of privacy from the domain of redactable signatures, then privacy should guarantee that one cannot deduce any information about the original graph from the redacted version. In the full version we demonstrate that the privacy definition in [1] does not capture this property. That is, we present a scheme where redaction clearly leaks information about the original graph, but is deemed secure according to their notion. We therefore give a new definition of privacy in the spirit of redactable and sanitizable signatures.

1.3 Redactable Graph Hashes, or Sanitizable Graph Commitments?

An important conceptual observation we make here is that graph hashing may come in two flavors. One flavor follows the idea of hashing more closely, and assumes that anyone can re-hash the graph in question and check the graph against a given hash value. This usually assumes that the randomness in the hashing step, if any at all, is made public. Redaction can then be performed by anyone. The other option is to view the hash of a graph rather as a commitment, involving some secret randomness. This means that only a designated party, usually called the sanitizer, can use the secret randomness to provide a verifiable proof for redacted graphs.

Both approaches, redactable graph hashing and sanitizable graph commitments, are valid strategies in order to give out partial and authenticated information about the full graph. In both cases the owner of the graph may publish (a signed version of) the hash value or commitment, and subsequently give out sub graphs, whose correctness with respect to the initial value can be verified with the help of additional data. In the sanitization case, however, this step can be only done by a designated party holding some auxiliary secret data. Indeed, Martel et al. [13] implicitly consider this option when they speak of a publisher for the authenticated partial data, and made this even more explicit in a previous works [8–10]. We note that Arshad et al. [1] purely consider graph hashing schemes.

The terminology in our paper will be general enough to capture both cases simultaneously. Only for privacy we need to make a slight distinction. For sake of simplicity we will subsume both notions under the term redactable graph hashing.

1.4 Constructions

Finally, we show that our security properties can be met. Our construction follows the approach of Arshad et al. [1] by decomposing the graph into nodes and edges, and hashing all these components individually with a cryptographic hash function. Interestingly, our basic construction works for all of the aforementioned security properties by switching to a different component for the cryptographic hash function. For example, if one is only interested in collision resistance, but not privacy, for the redactable hashing scheme, then a common collision-resistant cryptographic hash function for the individual hashes suffices.

2 Preliminaries

Graphs. A directed labeled graph $G = (V, E, \text{CONTENT})$ is a set of nodes (or vertices) V and a set of edges $E \subseteq V \times V$, where each edge has a source and a destination node. The content (or labeling) function $\text{CONTENT} : V \cup E \to C$ maps the nodes and edges to some string in the content space $C \subseteq \{0,1\}^*$. In the following we sometimes write $e(u, v)$ to denote the edge e with source node u

and destination node v. We usually denote the number of nodes by $|V| = n$ and the number of edges by $|E| = m$. A sub graph $G_{\mathrm{sub}} = (V_{\mathrm{sub}}, E_{\mathrm{sub}}, \mathrm{CONTENT_{sub}})$ of G, written $G_{\mathrm{sub}} \subseteq G$, is itself a graph and satisfies $V_{\mathrm{sub}} \subseteq V$ and $E_{\mathrm{sub}} \subseteq E \cap V_{\mathrm{sub}} \times V_{\mathrm{sub}}$, as well as $\mathrm{CONTENT_{sub}}(x) = \mathrm{CONTENT}(x)$ for all $x \in V_{\mathrm{sub}} \cup E_{\mathrm{sub}}$.

For hashing the graph it is convenient to associate an absolute order on the nodes and edges. That is, we assume that there exists an implicit injective mapping $\mathrm{ORDER} : V \cup E \to \{1, 2, \ldots, m+n\}$. For example, for some order on the nodes $v_1, \ldots, v_n$ and the edges $e_1, \ldots, e_m$, e.g., according to their position in the digital representation, the function could be defined by $\mathrm{ORDER}(v_i) = i$ and $\mathrm{ORDER}(e_i) = n + i$. This ordering also allows us to identify each node and edge with a number between 1 and $m + n$. In addition, for privacy reasons we also use a random order in the sense that we introduce a random permutation $\pi : \{1, 2, \ldots, m+n\} \to \{1, 2, \ldots, m+n\}$. Composing this with the ordering ORDER this gives a bijection $\mathrm{ORDER}_\pi = \pi \circ \mathrm{ORDER}$ from $V \cup E$ to $\{1, 2, \ldots, m+n\}$.

Redactable Graph Hashing. Recall that we treat both redactable graph hashes as well as sanitizable graph commitments integratively, and only speak of redactable graph hashes. The difference between the two cases shows in the approach below when already the hashing algorithm outputs some secret information vo, called verification object in [1, 13], necessary to create verification data vo_{sub} for a sub graph G_{sub}.

The key generation and hashing algorithms HKGen and Hash follow the common approach for defining hash functions. In addition, we introduce a redaction algorithm HRedact. Since we consider randomized outputs for both hash values and commitments, we cannot necessarily recompute the hash value of some input and compare it to a given value. We therefore more abstractly introduce a verification algorithm HVf which checks the validity of a hash value. To define a reasonable notion of collision-resistance later, we need to distinguish the cases that the verification algorithm HVf checks for a full hash value or for a redacted value, and hence pass the operation mode $\mathsf{vfmode} \in \{\mathsf{hashed}, \mathsf{redacted}\}$ as additional input to HVf.

Definition 1 (Redactable Graph Hashing). *A redactable graph hashing scheme* $\mathcal{H}$ = (HKGen, Hash, HRedact, HVf) *consists of four probabilistic polynomial-time algorithms:*

Key Generation: *The key generation algorithm, on input the security parameter 1^n, outputs a public hash key, $hk \leftarrow_{\$} \mathsf{HKGen}(1^n)$.*

Hashing: *On input the hash key hk and a graph G, the (probabilistic) hashing algorithm returns a hash value, together with a (potentially empty) verification object, $(gh, vo) \leftarrow_{\$} \mathsf{Hash}(hk, G)$.*

Redaction: *On input the hash key hk, a hash value gh, a graph G, a sub graph $G_{sub} \subseteq G$, and possibly empty data vo, the (probabilistic) redaction algorithm returns a proof, $vo_{sub} \leftarrow_{\$} \mathsf{HRedact}(hk, gh, G, G_{sub}, vo)$.*

Verification: *On input the hash key hk, a hash value gh, a graph G, a (potentially empty) proof vo, and a mode identifier* **vfmode** ∈ {**hashed, redacted**}, *the verification algorithm returns a decision bit, d ←s* HVf(*hk, gh, G, vo,* **vfmode**).

We assume the usual correctness property that genuine hash values of graphs are accepted; a formal description is omitted from this extended abstract.

3   Security Properties

In this section we define our notion of collision resistance. The formal description of the privacy notions has been omitted from this version for space reasons.

The underlying idea behind defining collision resistance is that the adversary should neither be able to find different graphs which verify under the same hash value, nor to make the verifier accept a graph which is not a sub graph of the graph belonging to the hash value. The latter already includes the case of different graphs, such that there is no need to distinguish the two events below.

The redaction property introduces some additional complications with the above approach. Assume that the adversary creates the hash value gh for some graph G, and then redacts this graph with the hash value twice, for two distinct sub graphs G_{sub}, G'_{sub}. By construction both graphs would result in the same hash value gh, only the verification objects would differ, but they are a means to an end, similar to the randomizer for computing the hash value. We therefore ask the adversary to specify the super graph. That is, we let the adversary win if one of the graphs verifies as a full hash, and the other graph may either verify as a full hash or a redacted one. In any case, the second graph must not be a sub graph of the former one.

To given an argument for the appropriateness of our notion of collision resistance consider once more the setting where a party outputs the (signed) hash as a commitment to the full graph G. Then the party should not be able to later present a graph for the hash value which is not a sub graph of G. This is indeed captured by our notion of collision resistance.

$\mathbf{Exp}^{CR}_{\mathcal{H},\mathcal{A}}(1^n)$

---

1 : $hk \leftarrow_s \mathsf{HKGen}(1^n)$

2 : $(gh, G, G', vo, vo') \leftarrow_s \mathcal{A}(hk)$

3 :   **return** 1 **if**

4 : $G' \not\subseteq G$ **and** $\mathsf{HVf}(hk, gh, G, vo, \mathsf{hashed}) = 1$

5 :   **and** $\mathsf{HVf}(hk, gh, G', vo', \mathsf{vfmode'}) = 1$ for some $\mathsf{vfmode'} \in \{\mathsf{hashed, redacted}\}$

Fig. 1. Collision-resistance experiment for graph hashing

Definition 2 (Collision-Resistance). *A redactable graph hashing scheme $\mathcal{H}$ is collision-resistant if for any probabilistic polynomial-time algorithm $\mathcal{A}$ the probability*

$$\text{Prob}\left[\, \boldsymbol{Exp}_{\mathcal{H},\mathcal{A}}^{CR}(1^n)\,\right] \approx 0$$

for the experiment $\boldsymbol{Exp}_{\mathcal{H},\mathcal{A}}^{CR}(1^n)$ in Fig. 1 is negligible.

4   Constructions

In this section we describe our construction of a redactable graph hashing scheme. All security proofs are left out from this version. The basic construction is similar to the idea [1] and first hashes all nodes and edges individually. Then one can use advanced structures like iterated hash function evaluations or Merkle hash trees to combine these hash values into a shorter representation.

The hashing is based on a cryptographic hash function (for redactable graph hashing) or on a commitment (for sanitizable graph commitments). To capture all possibilities simultaneously, randomized hash functions, random oracle based solutions, and commitments, we abstractly speak of a cryptographic hash function $\mathsf{CHash} = (\mathsf{CHKGen}, \mathsf{CHash}, \mathsf{CHVf})$. This function consists of a key generation algorithm $chk \leftarrow \mathsf{CHKGen}(1^n)$, the (probabilistic) hash function $(ch, cvo) \leftarrow \mathsf{CHash}^{\mathsf{RO}}(chk, y)$, having possibly access to a random oracle $\mathsf{RO} : \{0,1\}^* \rightarrow \{0,1\}^n$ and possibly generating some additional verification object, as well as the verification algorithm $d \leftarrow \mathsf{CHVf}^{\mathsf{RO}}(chk, ch, cvo, y)$. Note that this also captures commitment schemes where cvo corresponds to the (initially secret) decommitment. We discuss the required security properties when considering the concrete instantiations for the different cases.

Key Generation $\mathsf{HKGen}(1^n)$: The key of our graph hashing scheme is given by the key of the cryptographic hash function $hk = chk \leftarrow \mathsf{CHKGen}(1^n)$.

Hashing $\mathsf{Hash}^{\mathsf{RO}}(hk, G)$: To hash a graph $G = (V, E, \text{CONTENT})$ we first pick a random permutation π over $\{1, 2, \ldots, m + n\}$ for the ordered entries in V and E. Then we go through the nodes and edges. For each node $v \in V$ we compute with the cryptographic hash function the value

$$(ch_v, cvo_v) \leftarrow \mathsf{CHash}^{\mathsf{RO}}(chk, 0||v||\text{CONTENT}(v)).$$

For each edge $e \in E$ we compute the hash value

$$(ch_e, cvo_e) \leftarrow \mathsf{CHash}^{\mathsf{RO}}(chk, 1||e||\text{CONTENT}(e)).$$

In both case we assume that the node or edge identifier is represented with some fixed-length encoding (in the sum of numbers n of nodes and m of edges).

The overall hash value gh and its verification object vo are given by

$$gh \leftarrow (ch_{\text{ORDER}_\pi^{-1}(1)}, \ldots, ch_{\text{ORDER}_\pi^{-1}(n+m)})$$
$$vo \leftarrow (\pi, cvo_{\text{ORDER}_\pi^{-1}(1)}, \ldots, cvo_{\text{ORDER}_\pi^{-1}(n+m)}).$$

Redaction $\mathsf{HRedact}^{\mathsf{RO}}(hk, gh, G, G_{\text{sub}}, vo)$: To redact a hash value gh, consisting of a sequence of hash values ch, first check that G_{sub} really is a sub graph of G and that the hash values ch for all nodes and edges in the sub graph are correct. If so, then replace all verification objects cvo in vo of nodes and edges which do *not* appear in G_{sub} by a special symbol $\perp$. Then, also redact the description of the permutation π by creating $\pi_{\text{sub}} : V_{\text{sub}} \cup E_{\text{sub}} \to \{1, 2, \ldots, m+n\}$ which coincides with the values of π for all elements x in the sub graph:

$$\pi(\text{ORDER}(x)) = \pi_{\text{sub}}(\text{ORDER}_{\text{sub}}(x))$$

for the implicit order $\text{ORDER}_{\text{sub}}$ for the sub graph. Let vo_{sub} be the redacted object.

Verification $\mathsf{HVf}^{\mathsf{RO}}(hk, gh, G, vo, \mathsf{vfmode})$: The algorithm first checks that G has at most the same number of nodes and edges as there are entries ch in $gh = (ch_1, \ldots, ch_{m+n})$. If so, then recover the order ORDER_π from the verification object $vo = (\pi, cvo_1, \cdots cvo_{m+n})$. For each node v in G check for the $\text{ORDER}_\pi(v)$-th entries $ch_{\text{ORDER}_\pi(v)}$ (in gh) and $cvo_{\text{ORDER}_\pi(v)}$ (in vo) that $cvo_{\text{ORDER}_\pi(v)} \neq \perp$ and

$$\mathsf{CHVf}^{\mathsf{RO}}(chk, ch_{\text{ORDER}_\pi(v)}, 0\|v\|\text{CONTENT}(v), cvo_{\text{ORDER}_\pi(v)}) = 1,$$

and accordingly for edges. Finally, for mode $\mathsf{vfmode} = \mathsf{hashed}$ also check that there is no entry $cvo = \perp$ in vo. If all these tests succeed, then output 1; else return 0.

5   Conclusion

Our solution poses some questions for further research. One of the most interesting aspects to be investigated is to improve the efficiency of such solutions. Alternatively, one may be able to show lower bounds for the size of hash values and verification objects for general redaction schemes. It would also be interesting to derive schemes with specific redaction procedures, such as the projection onto nodes (with edges being preserved). While such procedures can be easily implemented with our general approach, they pose additional security requirements, e.g., it must be guaranteed that edges for nodes cannot be dropped.

Acknowledgments. We thank the anonymous reviewers for comments. This work has been co-funded by the German Research Foundation DFG as part of project P2 within the CRC 1119 CROSSING and the SPP 1736 grant Fi 940/5-1.

References

1. Arshad, M.U., Kundu, A., Bertino, E., Madhavan, K., Ghafoor, A.: Security of graph data: hashing schemes and definitions. In: Proceedings of the 4th ACM Conference on Data and Application Security and Privacy, CODASPY 2014, NY, USA, pp. 223–234 (2014). http://doi.acm.org/10.1145/2557547.2557564
2. Ateniese, G., Chou, D.H., Medeiros, B., Tsudik, G.: Sanitizable signatures. In: Vimercati, S.C., Syverson, P., Gollmann, D. (eds.) ESORICS 2005. LNCS, vol. 3679, pp. 159–177. Springer, Heidelberg (2005). doi:10.1007/11555827_10
3. Bauer, D., Blough, D.M., Mohan, A.: Redactable signatures on data with dependencies and their application to personal health records. In: Proceedings of the 2009 ACM Workshop on Privacy in the Electronic Society, WPES 2009, Chicago, Illinois, USA, November 9, 2009, pp. 91–100. ACM (2009)
4. Brown, J., Ahamad, M., Ahmed, M., Blough, D.M., Kurc, T., Post, A., Saltz, J.: Redactable and auditable data access for bioinformatics research, pp. 21–25 (2013)
5. Brown, J., Blough, D.M.: Verifiable and redactable medical documents. In: American Medical Informatics Association Annual Symposium AMIA 2012, Chicago, Illinois, USA, November 3–7, 2012. AMIA (2012)
6. Brzuska, C., Fischlin, M., Freudenreich, T., Lehmann, A., Page, M., Schelbert, J., Schröder, D., Volk, F.: Security of sanitizable signatures revisited. In: Jarecki, S., Tsudik, G. (eds.) PKC 2009. LNCS, vol. 5443, pp. 317–336. Springer, Heidelberg (2009). doi:10.1007/978-3-642-00468-1_18
7. Brzuska, C., Fischlin, M., Lehmann, A., Schröder, D.: Unlinkability of sanitizable signatures. In: Nguyen, P.Q., Pointcheval, D. (eds.) PKC 2010. LNCS, vol. 6056, pp. 444–461. Springer, Heidelberg (2010). doi:10.1007/978-3-642-13013-7_26
8. Devanbu, P.T., Gertz, M., Kwong, A., Martel, C.U., Nuckolls, G., Stubblebine, S.G.: Flexible authentication of XML documents. In: Proceedings of the 8th ACM Conference on Computer and Communications Security, CCS 2001, Philadelphia, Pennsylvania, USA, November 6–8, 2001, pp. 136–145. ACM (2001)
9. Devanbu, P., Gertz, M., Martel, C., Stubblebine, S.G.: Authentic third-party data publication. In: Thuraisingham, B., Riet, R., Dittrich, K.R., Tari, Z. (eds.) DBSec 2000. IIFIP, vol. 73, pp. 101–112. Springer, Boston, MA (2002). doi:10.1007/0-306-47008-X_9
10. Devanbu, P.T., Gertz, M., Martel, C.U., Stubblebine, S.G.: Authentic data publication over the internet. J. Comput. Secur. **11**(3), 291–314 (2003)
11. Gentry, C.: Fully homomorphic encryption using ideal lattices. In: Mitzenmacher, M. (ed.) 41st Annual ACM Symposium on Theory of Computing, pp. 169–178. ACM Press, Bethesda, 31 May–2 Jun 2009
12. Johnson, R., Molnar, D., Song, D., Wagner, D.: Homomorphic signature schemes. In: Preneel, B. (ed.) CT-RSA 2002. LNCS, vol. 2271, pp. 244–262. Springer, Heidelberg (2002). doi:10.1007/3-540-45760-7_17
13. Martel, C.U., Nuckolls, G., Devanbu, P.T., Gertz, M., Kwong, A., Stubblebine, S.G.: A general model for authenticated data structures. Algorithmica **39**(1), 21–41 (2004)
14. Steinfeld, R., Bull, L., Zheng, Y.: Content extraction signatures. In: Kim, K. (ed.) ICISC 2001. LNCS, vol. 2288, pp. 285–304. Springer, Heidelberg (2002). doi:10.1007/3-540-45861-1_22
15. Wu, Z.Y., Hsueh, C., Tsai, C., Lai, F., Lee, H., Chung, Y.: Redactable signatures for signed CDA documents. J. Med. Syst. **36**(3), 1795–1808 (2012)

On the Security of Designing a Cellular Automata Based Stream Cipher

Swapan Maiti[1](✉), Shamit Ghosh[2](✉), and Dipanwita Roy Chowdhury[1](✉)

[1] Indian Institute of Technology Kharagpur, Kharagpur, India
swapankumar_maiti@yahoo.co.in, drc@cse.iitkgp.ernet.in
[2] Mentor Graphics, Noida, India
raaz714@gmail.com

Abstract. Over the years Cellular Automata (CA) have been getting importance as a better crypto-primitives in designing stream ciphers. Wolfram identified Rule 30 as a powerful nonlinear function for cryptographic applications. However, Rule 30 CA is vulnerable against Meier and Staffelbach (MS) attack. This paper analyzes maximum period nonlinear CA (M-NHCA) which is shown to be secure against MS attack. We present a new design construction of a stream cipher employing the maximum period nonlinear CA and linear CA in conjunction with a rotational symmetric bent function. The proposed cipher has also been analyzed in aspect of almost all the known attacks in particular, the fault attack against which most of the eStream candidates like Grain-128 are vulnerable.

Keywords: Stream cipher · Cellular automata · MS attack · Cryptanalysis of stream cipher

1 Introduction

Stream cipher is an important class in symmetric key cryptography. The eSTREAM project started in 2004, introduced a number of stream ciphers which are taken as standards in hardware and software efficient environments. However, most of the ciphers in the eStream portfolio are susceptible to fault attacks. To overcome these problems, Cellular Automata (CA) was proposed as one possible candidate to prevent attacks.

The 3-neighborhood nonlinear Rule 30 CA has long been considered a good pseudo-random generator and studied for cryptography [7]. It passed various statistical tests for pseudo-randomness with good results, untill Willi Meier and Othmar Staffelbach proposed an attack, called MS Attack [6]. Grain-like ciphers NOCAS [5], CAR30 [2] proposed are all CA based ciphers, but most of them are not strong against fault attack. Moreover, these works did not consider the MS attack, though it is a real threat against a CA based cipher.

In this work, we study nonlinear rules of M-NHCA and show that M-NHCA with multiple nonlinearity injections provide maximum length cycle as well as

© Springer International Publishing AG 2017
J. Pieprzyk and S. Suriadi (Eds.): ACISP 2017, Part II, LNCS 10343, pp. 406–413, 2017.
DOI: 10.1007/978-3-319-59870-3_25

better cryptographic primitives and they are also secure against MS attack. We propose a design of a stream cipher using the M-NHCA. The design of the cipher prevents almost all known attacks. The security of the proposed cipher is analyzed against in the light of related attacks. The main contribution of this work can be summarized as below:

- The first attempt to propose a scalable design architecture of CA based stream cipher.
- Security analysis of the nonlinear CA against MS attack.
- Detailed security analysis of the proposed stream cipher with a special emphasis to fault attacks.

The organization of the rest of the paper is as follows. The design architecture and working principle of the proposed cipher are shown in Sect. 2. Section 3 describes the design rationale of its each component. The detailed security analysis is furnished in Sect. 4. The robustness of the cipher against the existing cryptanalysis techniques with a special focus on MS attack is also studied in detail in this section. Finally, the paper is concluded in Sect. 5.

2   Design Architecture

The new cipher consists of three building blocks, namely Linear block which uses Linear Hybrid Cellular Automata (LHCA), Nonlinear block which uses Nonlinear Hybrid Cellular Automata (NHCA) and a final combiner function $h(\cdot)$. The overall structure can be found in Fig. 1.

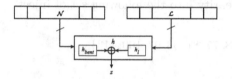
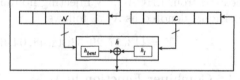

Fig. 1. Overview of the cipher design   **Fig. 2.** Initialization of the cipher

2.1   Linear Block

This block uses 128-bit maximum period LHCA $\mathcal{L}$ represented by $\{s_0, s_1, \cdots, ; s_{127}\}$ where s_i denotes the state of the i-th cell of $\mathcal{L}$. The state transition function of the i-th cell at time instant t can be expressed as: $s_i^{t+1} = s_{i-1}^t \oplus d_i . s_i^t \oplus s_{i+1}^t$, where $d_i = 0$(Rule 90)/ 1(Rule 150). Thus, an LHCA can be completely specified by a combination of rule 90 and 150, denoted as an n-tuple $[d_0, d_1, \cdots, d_{n-1}]$. An example of a 5-cell LHCA $\mathcal{L}'$ is shown in Fig. 3, specified by the rule vector $[1, 1, 1, 1, 0]$. Further details of CA can be found in [1]. The LHCA $\mathcal{L}$ used in the design is selected in a way to ensure maximum periodicity [1]. In our work, the characteristic polynomial of $\mathcal{L}$, is defined as: $f(x) = x^{128} + x^{29} + x^{27} + x^2 + 1$. which is primitive. The rule value of the LHCA $\mathcal{L}$ synthesized from $f(x)$, is given as $0x48882FBD67031A7A7A79C0E6BDF41112$.

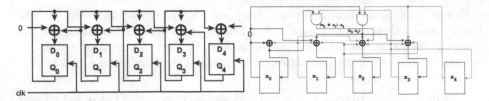

Fig. 3. Cellular automata $\mathcal{L}'$ with rule vector $[1, 1, 1, 1, 0]$

Fig. 4. NHCA $\mathcal{N}'$ synthesized from LHCA $\mathcal{L}'$

2.2 Nonlinear Block

This block uses maximum period Nonlinear Hybrid Cellular Automata (M-NHCA). An example of 5-cell M-NHCA $\mathcal{N}'$ (Fig. 4) is synthesized with non-linearity inject at single point from a 5-cell LHCA $\mathcal{L}'$ (Fig. 3) by the technique [3]. Here, we remove the restriction of single injection point and introduce multiple injection points to increase the nonlinearity of synthesized NHCA $\mathcal{N}'$. We consider an n-cell maximum period LHCA denoted by $\{x_0, x_1, \cdots, x_{n-2}, x_{n-1}\}$. For multiple nonlinearity injections, we follow the following criteria:

1. Non-linearity can be injected in cell position i, $2 \leq i \leq n - 3$ to form the nonlinear function $f_N(x_{i-2}^t, x_{i+2}^t) = (x_{i-2}^t \cdot x_{i+2}^t)$.
2. To retain the maximum length cycle, two nonlinearity inject positions i and j must satisfy $|i - j| \geq 4$.

In the proposed cipher, the NHCA $\mathcal{N}$ represented by $\{b_0, b_1, \cdots, b_{127}\}$, where b_i denotes the state of the i-th cell, is a 7-neighborhood 128-bit M-NHCA synthesized from LHCA $\mathcal{L}$ by injecting nonlinearity into the following set of inject positions, denoted as $\mathcal{X}$, as follows:

$$\mathcal{X} = \{13, 17, 29, 33, 44, 48, 64, 68, 77, 81, 93, 97, 109, 113\}$$

2.3 Combiner Function h(·)

The function $h(\cdot)$ can be expressed as a sum of two parts, a linear function $h_l(\cdot)$ and a nonlinear bent function $h_{bent}(\cdot)$, where $h(\cdot) = h_{bent}(\cdot) + h_l(\cdot)$. Before stating the specification of $h(\cdot)$ used in the proposed cipher, we furnish some basic concepts of a rotational symmetric Boolean function. Let $\{x_0, x_1, \cdots, x_n\}$ be the set of input bits to a Boolean function $f(\cdot)$. For $0 \leq j \leq n - 1$, we define the rotational shifting operation as: $\rho^j(x_i) = x_{(i+j)mod(n)}$. This definition can be extended for a Boolean function $f_s(\cdot)$ as follows:

$$\rho^j(f_s(x_0, x_1, \cdots, x_{n-1})) = f_s(\rho^j(x_0), \rho^j(x_1), \cdots, \rho^j(x_{n-1}))$$

A rotational symmetric function is defined as the summation of all the rotationally permuted terms of a base element which is called the short ANF and is denoted as

$$f(x_0, x_1, \cdots, x_{n-1}) = \sum_{j=0}^{n-1} \rho^j(f_s(x_0, x_1, \cdots, x_{n-1}))$$

where, $f_s(\cdot)$ is the short ANF of $f(\cdot)$. e.g. the function $f(x_0, x_1, x_2) = x_0 x_1 + x_1 x_2 + x_2 x_0$ can be denoted as

$$f(x_0, x_1, x_2) = \sum_{j=0}^{2} \rho^j (f_s(x_0, x_1, x_2))$$

where, $f_s(x_0, x_1, x_2) = x_0 x_1$. As mentioned earlier, the function $h_{bent}(\cdot)$ in the cipher is rotational symmetric. The short ANF form of $h_{bent}(\cdot)$ is denoted as $h_s(\cdot)$. The specifications of $h_l(\cdot)$ and $h_{bent}(\cdot)$ are shown in the following equations.

$$h_s(v_0, v_1, \cdots, v_7) = v_0 v_1 + v_0 v_2 + v_0 v_3 + v_0 v_1 v_2 + v_0 v_1 v_4 + v_0 v_1 v_6$$
$$+ v_0 v_2 v_4 + v_0 v_1 v_2 v_3 + v_0 v_1 v_3 v_4 + v_0 v_1 v_3 v_5$$

$$h_{bent}(v_0, v_1, \cdots, v_7) = \sum_{j=0}^{7} \rho^j (h_s(v_0, v_1, \cdots, v_7))$$

$$h_l(u_0, u_1, \cdots, u_4) = \sum_{i=0}^{4} u_i$$

The 256 memory elements in the two CA represent the state of the cipher. From this state, 13 variables are taken as input to the combiner function $h(\cdot)$. Six inputs are taken from $\mathcal{L}$ and seven inputs are taken from $\mathcal{N}$. The set of the input bits, also called tap bits, corresponds to the set denoted by $\mathcal{T}$ as follows:

$$\mathcal{T} = \{s_{12}, s_{35}, s_{58}, s_{78}, s_{97}, s_{119}, b_{16}, b_{32}, b_{47}, b_{67}, b_{80}, b_{96}, b_{112}\}$$

Hence, the output function (i.e. the combiner function $h(\cdot)$) is defined as

$$z = h(v_0, v_1, \cdots, v_7, u_0, u_1, \cdots, u_4) = h_{bent}(v_0, v_1, \cdots, v_7) + h_l(u_0, u_1, \cdots, u_4)$$

where, $v_0, v_1, v_2, v_3, v_4, v_5, v_6, v_7$ correspond to $b_{16}, s_{12}, s_{35}, s_{58}, s_{78}, s_{97}, s_{119}, b_{96}$ and u_0, u_1, u_2, u_3, u_4 correspond to $b_{32}, b_{47}, b_{67}, b_{80}, b_{112}$.

The number of tap points for the final combiner function, $h(\cdot)$, should be changed for different key lengths (e.g. 128, 192, 256). Moreover, the rotational symmetric bent function $h_{bent}(\cdot)$ should also be redesigned.

2.4   Initialization and Key Setup

Before generating any keystream, the cipher must be initialized with the key and IV. Here we have used a 128-bit key k and a 128-bit IV. To initialize the cipher, the key is loaded into $\mathcal{N}$ and the IV is loaded into $\mathcal{L}$. The LHCA used is synthesized from primitive polynomial and it provides maximum periodicity. Therefore, the LHCA state bits never contain all 0's while running the cipher and it ensures to resist the chosen IV attack. It overcomes the restriction of Grain of keeping 16 LSBs to be all 1's. The diffusion rate of NHCA evolution is much faster than that of nonlinear block of Grain-128. In 128 clock cycles, all 256 state bits (128 bits of nonlinear block and 128 bits of linear block) will be diffused in all 256 bits, which strengthens the security against attacks like algebraic attack and fault attack etc. Therefore, the cipher is clocked for 128 cycles without producing any keystream and the output of $h(\cdot)$ is fed back and XORed with the LSBs of both $\mathcal{L}$ and $\mathcal{N}$. The initialization phase is made 2 times faster than that of Grain-128 [4]. The initialization phase is depicted in Fig. 2.

3   Design Rationale

In this section, we give the logic behind the choices for the design parameters.

Maximum period LHCA: In the proposed cipher, the linear sequence generator is constructed from LHCA instead of LFSR. This design choice is attributed to the suitability of LHCA as a pseudorandom number generator (PRNG) due to its better randmoness property than that of the LFSR [1]. Further, having a maximum length cycle, an LHCA is considered as a cryptographically secure PRNG.

Maximum period NHCA: In case of ciphers like Grain, the faults injected into the nonlinear feedback shift register (NFSR) are directly transmitted to the output, enabling the attacker to form low degree equations by observing the output difference. Solving these set of equations facilitates the recovery of the internal state of the NFSR and subsequently the key. However, the presence of nonlinear hybrid cellular automata in the design of the cipher makes the formation of such equations almost infeasible. This claim is justified by the experimental results provided in the following section. Another notable difference of the NHCA from that of the NFSR in Grain is the absence of any feedback from the linear generator to the nonlinear one. This feedback is required to ensure large period length and to provide balancedness to the output of NFSR. However, as the NHCA $\mathcal{N}$ used here has maximum periodicity, such feedback is extraneous and subsequently discarded.

Choice of $h_l(\cdot)$ and $h_{bent}(\cdot)$: The function $h_l(\cdot)$ increases correlation immunity and resilliency whereas $h_{bent}(\cdot)$ provides high nonlinearity[1]. In addition, the function $h_{bent}(\cdot)$ is designed to be a rotational symmetric one. This ensures that the occurence of a fault is equiprobable for all the nonlinear terms in the bent function $h_{bent}(\cdot)$ in case of a faulty output. The lack of rotational symmetry of the filter function in Grain has already been exploited, therefore, it necessitates the use of such function to conceal the fault positions.

Choice of output function $h(\cdot)$: Recovery of the state bits by reverse engineering is prevented by the use of a combiner function. For this purpose, a Boolean function $h(\cdot)$ is selected as a sum of two parts, a nonlinear bent function $h_{bent}(\cdot)$ and a linear function $h_l(\cdot)$. The combiner function has nonlinearity 3840 and resiliency 4 that increase with iterations while expressed in terms of initial state bits. Because of incorporating rotational symmetric bent function $h_{bent}(\cdot)$, it strengthens the security of the cipher against attacks like algebraic attack and fault attack etc.

---

[1] Bent function possesses the highest possible nonlinearity.

4   Security Analysis

The following analyses show that the proposed cipher is secure against MS attack and as well as some general attacks on stream ciphers.

4.1   Analysis Against MS Attack

MS attack [6] is a known plaintext attack. Let us consider a 3-neighborhood n-bit maximum period null-boundary LHCA represented by $\{x_0, x_1, \cdots, x_{n-1}\}$ with rule vector $[d_0, d_1, \cdots, d_{n-1}]$, where, $d_i = 0$ (Rule 90) / 1 (Rule 150). Let nonlinearity be injected with the nonlinear functions $f_N(x_{j-2}^t, x_{j+2}^t) = (x_{j-2}^t \cdot x_{j+2}^t)$ at positions j and $f_N(x_{k-2}^t, x_{k+2}^t) = (x_{k-2}^t \cdot x_{k+2}^t)$ at positions k, where $k - j = 4$ as per criteria of multiple nonlinearity injections for producing M-NHCA $\mathcal{N}'$. The state transition functions (nonlinear) of neighboring cells of $\mathcal{N}'$ around the non-linearity positions j and k respectively, are as follows: for j^{th} position:

$$x_{j-1}^{t+1} = x_{j-2}^t \oplus d_{j-1} \cdot x_{j-1}^t \oplus x_j^t \oplus (x_{j-2}^t \cdot x_{j+2}^t) \tag{1}$$

$$x_j^{t+1} = x_{j-1}^t \oplus d_j \cdot x_j^t \oplus x_{j+1}^t \oplus d_j \cdot (x_{j-2}^t \cdot x_{j+2}^t)$$
$$\oplus ((x_{j-3}^t \oplus d_{j-2} \cdot x_{j-2}^t \oplus x_{j-1}^t) \cdot (x_{j+1}^t \oplus d_{j+2} \cdot x_{j+2}^t \oplus x_{j+3}^t)) \tag{2}$$

$$x_{j+1}^{t+1} = x_j^t \oplus d_{j+1} \cdot x_{j+1}^t \oplus x_{j+2}^t \oplus (x_{j-2}^t \cdot x_{j+2}^t) \tag{3}$$

Similarly, for k^{th} position (in terms of j with k=j+4), we can generate the expressions x_{j+i}^{t+1} for i=3,4,5 as 2nd rule set, where $(x_0^t, x_1^t, \cdots, x_{n-1}^t)$ is the site vector of M-NHCA $\mathcal{N}'$ at time step t.

Suppose, we are given the output sequence $\{x_i^t\}$ (i.e. the temporal sequence $\{x_{j+3}^t\}$) upto the unicity distance N as shown in Table 1, where $i = j + 3$ and $i = k - 1$ since $k - j = 4$. The site vector forms left and right triangle w.r.t the temporal sequence column. We choose a random seed $< x_{i+1}^t, \cdots, x_{n-1}^t >$ out of $2^{n-(i+1)}$ possibilities. In the completion forwards process, the right triangle can be determined using equations in the 2nd rule set and 90/150 rules. In completion backwards process, the left triangle can be formed using 90/150 rules and the 1st rule set and hence, the seed $< x_0^t, \cdots, x_{i-1}^t >$ can be determined. For the column $j+2$, $\frac{n-(i+1)}{2}$ values can be computed deterministically and other $\frac{n-(i+1)}{2}$ values can be chosen randomly with $2^{\frac{n-(i+1)}{2}}$ possibilities. The columns $j-2$ and $j-3$ are chosen as random out of 2^{j+1} and 2^j possibilities, respectively. The required time complexity is: $2^{n-(i+1)} \cdot 2^{\frac{n-(i+1)}{2}} \cdot 2^{j+1} \cdot 2^j = 2^{n+\frac{3}{4}(n-9)}$, where $j = i - 3$ and $i = \frac{n-1}{2}$, the middle cell position of the CA. The required time is greater than 2^n for $n > 9$.

Following
the similar approach, we can determine the seed $< x_{i+1}^t, \cdots, x_{n-1}^t >$ from the given output sequence $\{x_i^t\}$ by guessing the seed $< x_0^t, \cdots, x_{i-1}^t >$ with a time complexity of $2^{n+\frac{n-5}{2}}$, where $k = j + 4 = i + 1$ and $i = \frac{n-1}{2}$.

Table 1. Computing seed for NHCA $\mathcal{N}'$

x_0^t	...	x_{i-6}^t	x_{i-5}^t	...	x_{i-1}^t	x_i^t	x_{i+1}^t	...	x_{n-1}^t
		*	*				*	***	*
x_0^{t+1}	...	*	*	...	x_{i-1}^{t+1}	x_i^{t+1}	x_{i+1}^{t+1}	...	x_{n-1}^{t+1}
	...	*	*	...	x_{i-1}^{t+2}	x_i^{t+2}	x_{i+1}^{t+2}	...	
	...	*	*	...	x_{i-1}^{t+3}	x_i^{t+3}	x_{i+1}^{t+3}	...	
	:	:	:	:	:	:	:	:	
		*	*		.	.	.	...	
			*	...	.	.	.	...	
		...			.	.	.	...	
					x_{i-1}^{t+N-1}	.	x_{i+1}^{t+N-1}		
						x_i^{t+N}			

'*' represents "guess" value

Table 2. Cipher output for different characteristics

Itr#	Balancedness	Resiliency	Alg. Deg.	# of Vars.	Deg-1	Deg-2	Deg-3	Deg-4	Deg-5	Deg-6	Deg-7	Deg-8
0	Balanced	4	4	13	5	24	32	24	0	0	0	0
1	Balanced	7	6	40	13	154	519	1057	387	35	0	0
2	Balanced	14	5	50	16	335	1646	4528	531	0	0	0
3	Balanced	14	6	64	17	462	2734	9146	2964	250	0	0
4	Balanced	25	6	90	29	1056	9267	46644	9869	506	0	0
5	Balanced	29	6	99	35	1217	11542	62096	12432	578	0	0
6	Balanced	32	6	102	37	1250	12183	63930	8554	292	0	0
7	Balanced	36	6	126	41	2343	30881	230041	34172	1140	0	0
8	Balanced	34	6	128	45	2402	31832	239044	23386	537	0	0
9	Balanced	37	6	130	45	2521	34519	264520	26458	681	0	0
10	Balanced	33	8	152	50	4108	72617	775540	638331	808594	592230	21613

# of Deg-3 monomials at iteration #6: 12183

4.2 Algebraic Cryptanalysis

Algebraic cryptanalysis depends on constructing a probabilistic pattern of the outputs to distinguish the cipher from a random permutation and solving low degree equations from them. As LHCA involves only linear terms, a combiner Boolean function $h(\cdot)$ constructed out of it is immediately susceptible to algebraic attacks compromising its security. This can be prevented by introducing nonlinearity in the design along with the LHCA and $h(\cdot)$. This is achieved by the nonlinear transition function of the NHCA. Table 2 shows that the increase of number of nonlinear terms and the Algebraic degree of a cipher also increase the attack complexity. Therefore, from the result, it is expected that the recovery of the internal state from the output is beyond practical measure.

4.3 Linear Approximation and Correlation Attack

The linear cryptanalysis technique depends on approximating the output with an affine function. Nonlinearity is incorporated to prevent the affine approximation. This is accomplished with a nonlinear sequence generator $\mathcal{N}$ and a combiner function $h(\cdot)$. Table 3 shows the increase in nonlinearity of the injection points with number of iterations. Moreover, the number of linear terms in the combiner function $h(\cdot)$ increases during initialization. Hence, the resiliency of $h(\cdot)$ increases with iterations as shown in Table 2. Thus, due to the faster growth of resiliency of the output bit of the cipher, it is expected that this cipher is resistant against Correlation Attack.

Table 3. Nonlinearity of $\mathcal{N}$ for various iterations

Iteration #	Nonlinearity Injection Points													
	13	17	29	33	44	48	64	68	77	81	93	97	109	113
1	4	4	48	48	8	8	16	48	16	48	48	8	48	8
2	32	64	64	128	32	128	128	64	64	64	256	128	64	64
3	128	128	128	128	128	768	512	256	1536	512	512	256	256	1024
4	1536	768	3072	512	384	1024	1536	256	3072	512	512	512	768	2048

Table 4. Fault location vs. NHCA bits obtained

Fault location	Iteration No.	NHCA bits obtained	Fault location	Iteration No.	NHCA bits obtained	Fault location	Iteration No.	NHCA bits obtained
b_{37}	4	b_{33}	b_{46}	4	b_{43}	b_{75}	4	b_{90}
b_{91}	4	b_{28}	b_{90}	2	b_{47}	b_{79}	4	b_{76}
b_{91}	6	b_{96}	b_{93}	4	b_{47}	b_{88}	2	b_{80}
b_{33}	2	b_{33}	b_{96}	4	b_{63}	b_{107}	4	b_{112}
b_{43}	4	b_{47}	b_{98}	5	b_{71}	b_{111}	5	b_{108}
b_{46}	3	b_{51}	b_{70}	2	b_{97}	b_{118}	2	b_{112}

4.4   Analysis Against Fault Attack

In this work, we have studied the effects of injecting single-bit faults into various locations of $\mathcal{N}$ and $\mathcal{L}$. After the initialization phase, we run the cipher for a target cycle T to inject fault. We refer to this point as the *base point*. After injecting single-bit fault at the base point T, we have run the cipher for t cycles (say, t=10). As a result, only 13 bits of $\mathcal{N}$ at the base point T can be obtained and no bits of $\mathcal{L}$ can be obtained as shown in Table 4. The design of the cipher increases the degree, number of variables and number of non-linear terms in the output expression with iterations as shown in Table 2. Thus, the design is expected to be resistant against fault attack.

5   Conclusion

In this paper, we have introduced a new stream cipher using Cellular Automata. The design produces fast initialization in only 128 cycles. The cipher is secure against MS attack which is a real threat for CA based ciphers. The use of maximum period non-linear CA in place of NFSR, dropping of the feedback function from LFSR to NFSR and the rotational symmetric bent function make the cipher robust against fault attack.

References

1. Chaudhuri, P.P., Roy Chowdhury, D., Nandi, S., Chattopadhyay, S.: Additive Cellular Automata: Theory and Applications. IEEE Computer Socity Press, Los Alamitos (1997)
2. Das, S., Roy Chowdhury, D.: CAR30: a new scalable stream cipher with rule 30. Crypt. Commun. **5**(2), 137–162 (2013)
3. Ghosh, S., Sengupta, A., Saha, D., Chowdhury, D.R.: A scalable method for constructing non-linear cellular automata with period $2^n - 1$. In: Wąs, J., Sirakoulis, G.C., Bandini, S. (eds.) ACRI 2014. LNCS, vol. 8751, pp. 65–74. Springer, Cham (2014). doi:10.1007/978-3-319-11520-7_8
4. Hell, M., Johansson, T., Maximov, A., Meier, W.: A stream cipher proposal: grain-128. In: 2006 IEEE International Symposium Information Theory, pp. 1614–1618 (2006)
5. Karmakar, S., Roy Chowdhury, D.: NOCAS: a nonlinear cellular automata based stream cipher. In: 17th International Workshop on Cellular Automata and Discrete Complex Systems, Automata 2011, Center for Mathematical Modeling, University of Chile, Santiago, Chile, November 21–23, 2011, pp. 135–146 (2011)
6. Meier, W., Staffelbach, O.: Analysis of pseudo random sequences generated by cellular automata. In: Davies, D.W. (ed.) EUROCRYPT 1991. LNCS, vol. 547, pp. 186–199. Springer, Heidelberg (1991). doi:10.1007/3-540-46416-6_17
7. Wolfram, S.: Cryptography with cellular automata. In: Williams, H.C. (ed.) CRYPTO 1985. LNCS, vol. 218, pp. 429–432. Springer, Heidelberg (1986). doi:10.1007/3-540-39799-X_32

Stegogames

Clark Thomborson[1](✉) [iD] and Marc Jeanmougin[2] [iD]

[1] Computer Science Department, University of Auckland, Auckland, New Zealand
cthombor@cs.auckland.ac.nz
[2] GBA, Conservatoire National des Arts et Métiers, Paris, France
marc.jeanmougin@cnam.fr

Abstract. We explore the power of steganographic computation in an game-theoretic setting, where n stegocommunicants are attempting to complete a shared computation, and where a well-resourced censor is attempting to prevent the computation. For example, when collaboratively discovering the minimum value ($\min_i x_i$) in a public n-vector X, each stegocommunicant reads a randomly-selected element during each timestep. Each then transmits the index i of the smallest value they have seen to a randomly-selected collaborator. We prove that most stegocommunicants will learn the minimum value in $O(\log n)$ time, w.h.p., if at most 10% of their population is censored in any timestep. The censor in our model retains a copy of all intercepted messages, using this information to optimally select the targets of their censorship at the beginning of each timestep. Our model of stegocomputation is relevant to stegosystems in which: (1) the stegoencoding is determined by the address of the recipient, (2) the censor does not have sufficient computational resource to stegodecode more than a fixed fraction (nominally 10%) of the messages in flight, and (3) the censor cannot store any messages other than the ones it has stegodecoded.

Keywords: Steganography · Communication protocols · EREW PRAM

1 Introduction

Stegocommunication is similar to encrypted communication, because both involve the transmission and reception of messages under adversarial conditions.

Stegocommunication is distinguished from encrypted communication, because the former avoids revealing that messages are being transmitted, whereas the latter prevents an adversary from reading or falsifying messages.

Stegoencoding is sometimes deprecated as "weak encryption", because any stegoencoded message can be decoded, with a modest expenditure of computational resource, by an adversary who has contextual information about the message. By contrast, a strongly encrypted message can be read only by a skilled adversary who deploys massive computational resource. Furthermore, cryptographic techniques can be used to protect message integrity, whereas the integrity

J. Pieprzyk and S. Suriadi (Eds.): ACISP 2017, Part II, LNCS 10343, pp. 414–421, 2017.
DOI: 10.1007/978-3-319-59870-3_26

of a steganographic message can be attacked by any adversary who is able to decode it. However, a system's availability is adversely affected by its reliance on a cryptoprotocol, whenever a legitimate user has lost access to their key material, and whenever a cryptographic service is unavailable for an extended period of time. As we will show in this paper, a stegoprotocol can assure the successful completion of a shared computation for most of its participants; but this availability assurance comes at some expense in confidentiality. In this regard, our stegoprotocols are complementary to cryptoprotocols.

The Dolev-Yao model is widely accepted as the basis for cryptoprotocol design, because its axioms of strong cryptography and key-material secrecy are feasibly assured in many real-world situations, and because these axioms are sufficient to support a wide range of useful cryptoprotocols.

The primary contribution of this paper is an axiomatic model for stegoprotocol design. The adversary in our model is actively intercepting and interrupting, but is neither modifying nor impersonating.

We present and justify our model in Sect. 2. In Sect. 3, we illustrate our model by fully analysing a very small stegogame. In Sect. 4, we prove that stegocommunicants cannot conduct a secret ballot. In Sect. 5, we sketch a proof that stegocommunicants cannot be prevented from using a collaborative process to discover the minimum value in a public dataset of n values. In the concluding section, we summarise our findings and discuss some implications.

2   An Axiomatic Model of Stegocomputation

Axiom 1. *Each stegocommunicant can perform $O(1)$ randomized computations on $O(\log^{c_1} n)$-bit words, during each timestep, for some fixed constant c_1. Their multi-headed adversary, whom we name the Hydra, cannot predict the outputs of any stegocommunicant's private pseudorandom number generator.*

We strictly bound the computational power of stegocommunicants. We think it reasonable to assume that real-world stegocommunicants are able to take actions when cannot be predicted by their surveillants.

Axiom 2. *Each stegocommunicant has a unique name g_i, which is drawn at random from a set of size $O(n^{c_2})$ for some constant $c_2 > 3$.*

Randomly-selected names are sometimes called gensyms by LISP programmers, so our notation is mnemonic. For convenience when describing our stegoprotocols, we assume that the i-th stegocommunicant is named Gia, that the j-th is named Genji (when $j \neq i$), and that the k-th is named Ganika (when $k \neq i$ and $k \neq j$).

Axiom 3. *During each timestep, each stegocommunicant can send a stegomessage to one other stegocommunicant. If the destination of the stegomessage is unspecified, it is transmitted to a randomly selected stegocommunicant – and no one, not even the Hydra, can predict this random choice. Alternatively, the stegomessage may be addressed to someone already known (by gensym) to the stegotransmitter.*

We introduce this axiom to model a globally-accessible social network with millions or billions of participants. The participants in this network have agreed to accept a small number of messages per day from unknown sources, despite the risks of receiving objectionable messages, in order to participate in a public consensus-formation process which cannot effectively be censored by any government.

Random-introductions in social-networking systems are currently available in https://www.facebook.com/RandomFriendAdder/ and http://kikcontacts.com/random.

Axiom 4. *No stegocommunicant knows their index i in any compact range $1..c_3n$, for any constant $c_3 \geq 1$.*

We leave it as an open problem to develop a stegoprotocol for mapping gensyms onto $1..n$. We note that such a compact enumeration would allow stegocommunicants to map their names onto the nodes in a shuffle-exchange graph or other powerful structure for parallel computation. If it turns out to be infeasible for a compact indexing to be stegocomputed, then it would be interesting to explore the properties of a stegomodel in which gensyms are drawn at random from a set of size c_3n.

For analytic convenience, we assume the Hydra always defines (at least implicitly) a bijection of $1..n$ onto inboxes, as well as a bijection of $1..n$ onto gensyms. When we refer to the i-th stegocommunicant, we are using the Hydra's bijections. Each stegocommunicant Gia therefore knows her own name, but not her index i.

Axiom 5. *The Hydra censors at most αn of the stegocommunicants in each timestep.*

To assure this axiom in a real-world setting, stegocommunicants could make public postings on a popular, governmentally-sanctioned, social-networking system that supports random-sharing of public posts. Censors would be expected to block postings with abnormally high entropy, because these are likely to be encrypted. However messages which closely resemble normal traffic [5–8] would evade mass censorship: the censor must search each one, individually, for stegocontent.

In a practical implementation of a stegocommunication system that obeys Axiom 5, stegotransmitters could randomly-share ten of their public postings each day (or week), using the "share-to-random" facility of Axiom 3. One of these random-shares is the cover message for that day's stegotransmission, using a stegosystem that is keyed to some recent public postings by the sender. The recipient of each random-share must expend some computational resource to search through all possible stegokeyings to discover its stegocontent, if any. Note that this stegochannel is, essentially, employing a cryptographic system with a keyspace that is small enough to allow stegodecoding of individual messages by individual recipients, but is large enough to prevent the Hydra from stegodecoding more than αn messages per timestep.

Axiom 6. *The stegocommunications network delivers a stegomessage if and only if there is no contention for the recipient's inbox. The stegocommunicant associated with this inbox is unaware of the message delivery if they are currently being censored; in this case, the Hydra reads the message.*

This axiom could be assured by a communication-services provider which allocates one fixed-size inbox to each stegocommunicant. It is analytically attractive, because it makes our computational model very similar to the well-studied Exclusive Read Exclusive Write (EREW) Parallel Random Access Machine (PRAM) [3].

Axiom 7. *The case of no incoming messages is indistinguishable from the case of multiple incoming messages in an inbox, for the intended recipient and for the Hydra.*

We introduce this indistinguishability solely to simplify our analysis. In a real-world deployment, this axiom could be violated by a governmental censor who instrumented the communications fabric for traffic analysis, allowing it to know how many stegomessages were sent to each stegocommunicant in each time period. We leave it to future work to analyse the properties of our model without this simplifying assumption.

Axiom 8. *The stegocommunicants' goal is a computation of a randomised function $f(A, X)$ in polylog(n) time. The vector A has one private component per stegocommunicant. The vector X is a globally-accessible, uncensorable, write-once vector of length $O(n)$. The value of each component of the domain and range of $f()$ is encoded in a bitstring of length polylogarithmic in n. For any distribution on the domain (A, X), the stegocommunicants win the game if their computation is complete, accurate, and widely-dispersed (as defined immediately below) with high probability, i.e. with chance of failure $O(n^{-c})$ for fixed $c > 0$.*

1. Complete: *A value for each of the components of $f()$ is declared.*
2. Accurate: *No stegocommunicant declares an incorrect value for any component of $f()$.*
3. Widely dispersed: *At least half of the stegocommunicants declare a value for at least one component of $f()$.*

We introduce the vector A of private information to model information that is generated by individual stegocommunicants, and which they are attempting to share with other stegocommunicants.

Each element in the vector X is written only once per stegocomputation. Depending on the problem, X could be $O(n)$ words of randomly-generated data, data collected from $O(n)$ real-world sensors, or data written by stegocommunicants. For example, if Gia were initially provided with her index i, she could write her vote into cell x_i; and the problem to be solved might be to collate the votes. In an implementation, x_i could be a designated area on Gia's timeline or blog.

The completion conditions are complex. We think they are best understood by working through an illustrative example in the next section.

Axiom 9. *All stegocommunicants follow the same (randomized) stegoprotocol, and this stegoprotocol is known to the Hydra.*

This axiom distinguishes our model sharply from distributed computing models in which a fraction of the participants are untrustworthy. Furthermore, distributed computing models are usually analysed for their worst-case performance, rather than for the w.h.p. bounds of our Axiom 8.

No axiom can ever be fully assured in a real-world system. Trustworthiness axioms, such as this one, are especially problematic. The trustworthiness of any stegocommunicant may change over time, and no person or computer system is completely trustworthy – there is always some chance of faulty behaviour. In this respect, our model is inaccurate: it provides an upper-bound, rather than an unbiased estimate, of the likelihood that any real-world set of n stegocommunicants can successfully complete a stegocomputation over a censorious communication network.

We note that the result of any stegocomputation may be assessed for accuracy in a subsequent stegocomputation. We leave the development of such trustworthiness-assessment stegoprotocols to future work.

3   Private 3-Majority

In this section, we illustrate our model by analysing a stegogame on $n = 3$ stegocommunicants s_1, s_2, and s_3. Their adversary is a one-headed Hydra ($\alpha = 1/3$).

Each stegocommunicant has a private bit a_i. Their shared goal is to evaluate the majority predicate on their private bits, $f(A) = (\sum_i a_i > 1)$, after a single round ($T = 1$) of communication. Each stegocommunicant must either declare her answer, or remain silent, at the end of this round.

By our last axiom, the stegocommunicants win their game if a majority of stegocommunicants declare a correct answer, and if nobody declares an incorrect answer.

Below, we evaluate the stegocommunicants' winning probability under a plausibly-optimal stegoprotocol, when their private bits a_i are independent Bernoulli variates with $p = 0.5$. If this were a formal analysis rather than an illustration of our model, we would prove (or disprove!) our conjecture that this probability distribution is pessimal for the stegocommunicants.

In our exemplary stegoprotocol, each stegocommunicant Gia (s_i) chooses a target Genji (s_j) uniformly at random under the constraint that $j \neq i$. The body of Gia's message is her random value a_i. If Genji receives Gia's message, he reports the value $\max(a_i, a_j)$ at time $t = 1$. Otherwise Genji reports the value a_j.

In our model, a message is received by its intended recipient unless one or more of the following conditions arise:

– the sender is censored,
– the receiver is censored, or
– there are multiple message-arrivals in the receiver's inbox.

Informally: when Gia is censored, her outgoing message is routed to the Hydra rather than to Gia's intended recipient. Furthermore, a censored Gia is unable to access her own inbox – because one of the heads of the Hydra is accessing this exclusive-read memory. If multiple messages arrive in Gia's inbox during a single round, this write-contention causes this inbox to be unreadable. Accordingly, our computational model is essentially an adversarial EREW PRAM, with the inboxes taking the role of memory cells in the PRAM model. However there are only n cells of memory, memory cells have wordsize polylogarithmic in n [2], and every memory cell is "owned" [4] by exactly one stegocommunicant.

In our illustrative single-round stegogame, the Hydra has just one head, so it has only two possible strategies: it may censor nobody, or it may censor one stegocommunicant. We identify two subcases in the first strategy:

1. The stegocommunicant's randomly-chosen messaging pattern is a 3-cycle. In this subcase, every stegocommunicant receives a message.
2. The messaging pattern has a 2-cycle. In this subcase, one stegocommunicant receives a message, one stegocommunicant receives no message due to inbox contention, and one stegocommunicant has an empty inbox.

In both subcases, the stegocommunicants compute the correct value if their votes are unanimous: $\sum_i a_i \in \{0, 3\}$. This event occurs with probability $1/4$.

In both subcases, if $\sum_i a_i = 1$, the stegocommunicant with $a_j = 1$ reports an incorrect answer, causing the stegocommunicants to lose the game. This event occurs with probability $3/8$.

In the first subcase, if $\sum_i a_i = 2$ then the stegocommunicants compute the correct value. This event occurs with probability $3/8$, so the value of the game in the first subcase is $1(1/4) + 0(3/8) + 1(3/8) = 5/8$.

In the second subcase, if $\sum_i a_i = 2$ then the stegocommunicant with $a_j = 0$ reports a correct answer if and only if she receives a message. This event occurs with probability $1/3$, so the value of the game in the second subcase is $1(1/4) + 0(3/8) + (1/3)(3/8) = 3/8$.

Subcase 1 arises with probability $1/4$, independently of the values a_i, by the following argument. Without loss of generality s_1's target is s_2. With probability 0.5, s_2's target is s_3; and independently with probability 0.5, s_3's target is s_1.

We conclude that the stegocommunicants win the game against an uncensoring Hydra with probability $(5/8)(1/4) + (3/8)(1 - 1/4) = 14/32 = 7/16$.

We leave it to the reader to perform the (rather tedious) analysis of the Hydra's other possible strategy, of censoring one stegocommunicant, establishing the value of this game as $5/16$.

4   Majority Voting with Unpublished Ballots

A Hydra with $\Omega(n)$ heads can effectively prevent majority voting with secret ballots. Formally:

Theorem 1. *For any constant censorship rate $\alpha > 0$, the predicate $(\sum_i a_i \geq n/2)$ can not be reliably stegocomputed.*

Proof. A sufficient strategy for the Hydra is to choose αn stegocommunicants at random, and to censor these stegocommunicants at all times. A censored stego-communicant Gia does not communicate her a_i value to anyone. The uncensored stegocommunicants may estimate the total vote of the censored stegocommunicants, $\sum_{\{i:\exists k:C_k(1)=i\}} a_i$, by random sampling. However for an input ensemble in which a_i are independent Bernoulli variates with probability $p = 0.5$, the error in this estimate is $\Omega(\ln c \sqrt{\alpha n}) = \Omega((\ln(\alpha c)\sqrt{n})$ with probability $\Omega(n^{-c})$, implying that the stegocommunicants will not accurately compute the majority vote w.h.p.

5   Global Minimum-Finding on a Public Vector

A Hydra with n/10 heads cannot prevent n stegocommunicants from discovering the value of a smallest component in their globally-readable n vector X. A suitable stegoprotocol is easily described: each stegocommunicant probes the n-vector at random, retaining the index of the smallest value it has seen so far, and sending this index to a randomly-selected recipient.

Theorem 2. *If $\alpha \leq 0.1$, then $\min_i(x_i)$ can be reliably stegocomputed.*

Proof sketch. Every stegocommunicant probes at random into the n-vector X during each timestep, discovering a global minimum with probability $\geq 1/n$; this bound is tight when the global minimum is unique. Every stegocommunicant informs a randomly-selected stegocommunicant of the index of the minimal value it has seen to date. We use a discrete-state branching process [1] to model the spread of knowledge about the global minimum.

6   Discussion

We have exhibited a model of stegocommunication which supports proofs of reliable computation on a EREW PRAM model with adversarial message interceptions and interruptions.

We have proven that the adversary can prevent stegocommunicants from reliably computing the majority function on their private "votes". We note that an approximate private-vote could be stegocomputed by random-sampling. Furthermore, a majority public-vote could be stegodecided unless the voting is close.

We have also proven that the adversary cannot prevent stegocommunicants from discovering the minimum value in a public n-vector. This computational power would allow stegocommunicants to form a public consensus on the "best stegoprotocol" to be used in the next round of stegocomputation – if they had a prior agreement on the metric to be used when comparing two stegoprotocols.

We note that our model bears some resemblance to models of fault-tolerant distributed systems. However such models generally have a Byzantine trust model, such that any communicant may be untrustworthy. Furthermore the models generally lack a probabilistic support, but instead are analysed for worst-case behaviour: the algorithms are required to deliver correct results under a bounded-fault assumption e.g. that no more than $1/3$ of the Byzantine generals are untrustworthy. Under such models of distributed computation, runtimes are typically polynomial in n. By contrast, our model assumes n trustworthy stegocommunicants who have only polylog time to complete their computation.

Our primary contribution in this article is an axiomatised model of stegocomputation which is simple enough to be analytic, while remaining realistic enough to guide the design of reliable stegosystems of practical use. Some foreseeable practical uses of stegocomputation are "white-hat", for example the reliable distribution of digital certificates in a global public-key infrastructure – when one or more governments are actively attempting to prevent this distribution. Reliable stegocomputation would also be important to "black-hats", for example criminal gangs may someday use a stegogame to coordinate their criminal activity, if no crime-fighting agency has sufficient powers of censorship to prevent such coordination.

References

1. Allen, L.J.S.: Continuous-time and discrete-state branching processes. Stochastic Population and Epidemic Models. MBILS, vol. 1.3, pp. 1–12. Springer, Cham (2015). doi:10.1007/978-3-319-21554-9_1
2. Bellantoni, S.J.: Parallel random access machines with bounded memory wordsize. Inf. Comput. **91**(2), 259–273 (1991)
3. Borodin, A., von zur Gathen, J., Hopcroft, J.: Fast parallel matrix and GCD computations. Inf. Control **52**(3), 241–256 (1982)
4. Fernau, H., Lange, K.-J., Reinhardt, K.: Advocating ownership. In: Chandru, V., Vinay, V. (eds.) FSTTCS 1996. LNCS, vol. 1180, pp. 286–297. Springer, Heidelberg (1996). doi:10.1007/3-540-62034-6_57
5. Hopper, N., von Ahn, L., Langford, J.: Provably secure steganography. IEEE Trans. Comput. **58**(5), 662–676 (2009)
6. Liśkiewicz, M., Reischuk, R., Wölfel, U.: Grey-box steganography. Theoret. Comput. Sci. **505**, 27–41 (2013)
7. Takebe, H., Tanaka, K.: Grey-box public-key steganography. In: Chan, T.-H.H., Lau, L.C., Trevisan, L. (eds.) TAMC 2013. LNCS, vol. 7876, pp. 294–305. Springer, Heidelberg (2013). doi:10.1007/978-3-642-38236-9_27
8. Wayner, P.: Mimic functions. Cryptologia **XVI**(3), 193–214 (1992)

A Feasibility Evaluation of Fair
and Privacy-Enhanced Matchmaking
with Identity Linked Wishes

Dwight Horne[✉] and Suku Nair

Department of Computer Science and Engineering,
Southern Methodist University, Dallas, TX, USA
rhorne@smu.edu, nair@lyle.smu.edu

Abstract. The Prom Problem (TPP) represents a special class of matchmaking challenges that amplify the conflicting requirements of anonymity and authentication necessitating fair and privacy-enhanced matchmaking with identity-linked wishes (ILW). ILW are wishes that involve particular identities and are valid only if all associated parties have those same wishes. In this paper, we provide a feasibility evaluation of an implementation of a previously proposed algorithm for TPP along with a detailed characterization of its fairness, and present results from computation and communication specific performance testing. To quantify fairness, we propose the use of a fairness index that combines the concepts underlying Jain's index with previously established definitions of fair matchmaking and details of the protocol. We also delineate upper and lower bounds for the fairness index values in this context and discuss its relationship to the participants' confidence in the result. Finally, we present performance results that answer key questions thereby demonstrating the practicality of the solution both in terms of computational costs and communication overhead. The results quantify relative impacts of higher degrees of confidence and anonymity to guide identification of appropriate tradeoffs as the solution is applied to varying problem domains with security and privacy requirements comparable to TPP with ILW.

Keywords: Privacy-Enhanced Technology · Matchmaking · Prom Problem · Identity Linked Wishes

1 Introduction

Matchmaking scenarios attempting to match users with common wishes have provided opportunities for researchers to respond to a variety of challenges related to security and privacy [1–8]. Yet prior solutions are unsuitable in the case of *the Prom Problem* (TPP) which exemplifies a special class of matchmaking challenges involving *identity linked wishes* (ILW) – wishes that pertain to specific identities and are valid if and only if all involved parties have those same wishes [9]. TPP amplifies the conflicting matchmaking goals of anonymity and authentication necessitating fair and privacy-enhanced matchmaking with ILW. In TPP, Alice secretly wishes to attend the prom (a semi-formal dance of particular significance in high school) with Bob. She

© Springer International Publishing AG 2017
J. Pieprzyk and S. Suriadi (Eds.): ACISP 2017, Part II, LNCS 10343, pp. 422–434, 2017.
DOI: 10.1007/978-3-319-59870-3_27

desires a privacy-preserving method of determining whether Bob has the same wish but without the risk that someone else could find out. In fact, she does not even want Bob to know that she inquired about the secret if Bob does not feel the same way about her. The nature of ILW combined with a threat model in which no participants can be trusted results in susceptibility to a variety of attacks such as impersonation, false disclosure, database compromise, and inference. The Horne-Nair(HN) protocol has been put forth to provide privacy-enhanced matchmaking with ILW affording joint notification of wishes and equivalent exchange (i.e., fairness) using an untrusted matchmaker. A pseudo-code example of the solution has been disclosed in one of its simplest forms along with a security evaluation [9]. In this paper, we highlight notable aspects of an implementation of this privacy-enhanced technology (PET), quantify the fairness of the protocol, and present results from performance testing. The four fundamental questions for this study pertained to the real-world performance and practicality of the HN protocol for fair and privacy-enhanced matchmaking with ILW including computational performance, communication performance, a high degree of fairness, and a high degree of anonymity. In the remainder of this paper, Sects. 2 and 3 summarize related work and the HN protocol respectively. Section 4 characterizes fairness while Sects. 5 and 6 present results from performance testing and comment on results and future work.

2   Related Work

Modern matchmaking challenges date back to at least the Baldwin and Gramlich (BG) protocol for *trustable matchmaking* [1] that combined authentication, asymmetric cryptography, fake transactions, anonymous communication, and a query-response protocol with a trusted third party (TTP) to achieve a certain balance between authentication and anonymity. The protocol provided joint notification of equivalent, authenticated wishes which it equated with *fairness* in matchmaking but it failed to provide secrecy of wishes and relied on a TTP. Unfortunately, the protocol also stored wishes in a database posing a significant risk given frequent data breaches in modern times. Not long after the BG protocol, Meadows presented a matchmaking protocol to solve a different problem that used a TTP only for an initial phase and achieved secrecy of wishes [2]. However, the Meadows protocol relied on a high degree of trust between clients making it impractical for TPP.

After arguing that the BG and Meadows protocols are variants of mutual authentication protocols, and pointing out that the BG protocol is vulnerable to substitution attacks, Zhang and Needham proposed the notion of *private matchmaking* with additional privacy requirements [4]. The Zhang and Needham (ZN) protocol accomplished match authentication, anonymity, and secrecy of wishes using a public database as the matchmaker. In the ZN scheme, users would produce a key for encrypting wishes by applying a one-way function to their wishes. The ciphertext would be committed to the public database along with encrypted identity information and a session key to facilitate future communications. The ZN protocol was a clever way to locate others with common wishes in a private way. Yet when considered for TPP, the lack of fairness is a critical problem. The protocol is also vulnerable to dictionary attacks as mentioned in

[8] and that vulnerability is amplified by a small wish space. Hence, the ZN protocol is not well-suited to achieve privacy and security in the context of TPP and ILW.

Additional strides toward a solution to TPP with ILW were made with the introduction of the Shin and Gligor (SG) protocol [8]. The SG protocol was designed to support *privacy-enhanced matchmaking* which was described as requiring the additional goals of forward privacy of identities and wishes as well as online dictionary attack resistance. In the SG protocol, a user's wishes are used in place of the password in an existing protocol for password authenticated key exchange (PAKE) [10, 11]. Identities are also replaced with pseudonyms and authentication is achieved via digital signatures of execution transcripts. While the SG protocol satisfies the authors' properties of privacy-enhanced matchmaking, it lacks fairness in the context of TPP and it is unable to fully support security and privacy with ILW. As an example, suppose that Trudy impersonated Bob and executed the SG protocol with the wishes *Alice and Bob want to attend prom together*. In the end, Alice would compute the digital signature and learn that it was not Bob. Unfortunately, Alice's privacy would have already been compromised as Trudy would have learned her secret. The lack of fairness combined with simple, guessable wishes poses a fundamental problem when applying the SG protocol to TPP and ILW. Table 1 summarizes the most significant security and privacy related properties of the matchmaking protocols that readily lend themselves to direct comparison.

A number of other matchmaking protocols have also been proposed but they have more significant differences such as varying goals, problems they attempt to solve, and security properties that complicate direct comparison. In [3], Lee and Kim presented a protocol for matching registered users of a system using a TTP akin to the BG protocol but it also included public commitment, public verification, and non-repudiation. Atallah and Cho put forth a protocol to match registered users with common topics of interest (TOIs) [5]. It requires semantic hierarchies of TOIs and assumes both users and service providers are semi-honest. They also leverage *useless* messages that have a cost to the user to limit excessive message sending. In [7], a method was disclosed for verification of a shared secret. The approach combined asymmetric cryptography, random data, and one-way hashing to accomplish its goal but it has weaknesses when applied to TPP including vulnerability to inference, impersonation, and early termination attacks. Lastly, Patrick disclosed a method to confirm that two parties possess the same document [6]. It suffers from many of the same drawbacks. Even though these

Table 1. Comparison of matchmaking protocols [9]

Matchmaking protocol	Properties of matchmaking protocols						
	Third party	Wish secrecy	Anonymity	Fairness	Forward privacy	Dictionary attack resistance	ILW support
Baldwin/Gramlich	Trusted			✓			
Meadows	Trusted (init.)	✓					
Zhang/Needham	Untrusted	✓	✓				
Shin/Gligor	None	✓	✓		✓	✓	
Horne/Nair	Untrusted	✓	✓	✓	✓	✓	✓

matchmaking protocols do not lend themselves to direct comparison as in Table 1, they have many of the same vulnerabilities as the more closely related protocols in addition to disparate goals and security properties resulting in unsuitability for TPP with ILW.

3   The Prom Problem and Horne-Nair Protocol

There is a formal or semi-formal dance in high school in the USA called the prom. Comparable events in other countries go by names such as grad, debs, senior ball, or formal. In TPP, Alice wants to attend the prom with Bob and she would like a privacy preserving way of finding out if Bob feels the same way. However, if Bob does not share the same secret, she does not even want Bob to know that she inquired about it. TPP adds to the goals of privacy-enhanced matchmaking requirements for fairness and support for ILW. The involvement of ILW is a key factor that distinguishes TPP. Moreover, while we use matchmaking to frame the analysis and discussion, a solution to TPP can be applied in other contexts that require fairness and ILW such as voting negotiations in legislative bodies, corporate mergers and acquisitions, and executive recruiting. Consideration of threats highlighted in [9] may assist with appreciation of the challenges posed by TPP. Leading up to the prom, Eve might conduct an inference attack by observing fellow students interacting with the match-making protocol and inferring that they wish to attend the dance together, or Bob may observe Alice initiating a secret sharing protocol with him and infer her wishes. Impersonation attacks would also be commonplace if protocols that lack security and privacy with ILW were used. In cases where sensitive data such as individual's wishes are stored in a database, there is significant risk of data compromise. Furthermore, in matchmaking protocols that do not ensure fairness with ILW, early termination attacks pose a significant threat to privacy.

A detailed description of the HN protocol along with security analysis and pseudo-code examples representing one of the simplest embodiments appear in [9]. In essence, HN uses an untrusted matchmaker M, the essence of which is a publicly available database akin to M in the ZN protocol (also comparable to public broadcast). The protocol itself provides anonymity and privacy protections in that identities, pseudo-identities, or digital signatures of transcripts that could reveal participants' identities are never included in any messages exchanged or stored in the database. Despite that, the protocol assumes the use of anonymous communication to mitigate risks of traffic analysis attacks. Commonly used examples include anonymous proxies, virtual private networks (VPNs), and Onion routing networks like Tor [12]. If traffic analysis attacks were not a concern in certain contexts, then the anonymous commu-nications could be omitted. The concept of *groups* (e.g., *all members of Alice's senior class* or *all persons within a 20 mile radius*) was also incorporated as a convenience to avoid all-to-all communication problems of some prior protocols. Identities and groups can be managed by clients or entirely external to the application. Indeed, we expect commercial versions to use separate, commonly used systems for identity management (e.g., every Facebook® or LinkedIn® user is a *potential* user of the system). This is one of the properties of the protocol that helps to prevent ill effects from data breaches such as the Ashley Madison hack of 2015 [13]. The notation used includes $H(x)$ for application of a one-way hash function to input x, $E(PU_U, P)$ for encryption of plaintext P with user U's public key, $D(PR_U, C)$ for decryption of ciphertext C with U's private key, and R_U denoting random data (i.e., a nonce of appropriate length) selected by U. The protocol involves a challenge, counter-challenge, computation of verifier, and confirmation of said verifier in such a way as to provide anonymity, authentication, and joint notification of wishes anonymously via an untrusted matchmaker M. A sample execution of one embodiment of the protocol involves the following steps.

1. **Generate Challenge.** Alice selects a user (e.g., Bob), $G_i \in G | ID_U \in G_i$, and her nonce R_A. She then computes and sends $X := E(PU_B, w + E(PR_A, R_A))$ to M.
2. **Receive Challenge.** Bob receives challenge X (e.g., by anonymously querying M with G_i). Bob computes $\{w + F\} := D(PR_B, X)$ and chooses user U' with whom he may share generic wish w.
3. **Generate Counter-Challenge.** Assuming he chose Alice, Bob sends $Y := E(PU_A, E(PR_B, R_B))$ to M.
4. **Receive Counter-Challenge.** Alice queries M with X and receives counter-challenge Y.
5. **Compute Verifier.** Based on information available to each user, Alice computes verifier $V_{AB} := H(H(R_A) + H(D(PU_B, D(PR_A, Y))))$ and Bob computes verifier $V_{AB} := H(H(D(PU_A, F)) + H(R_B))$.
6. **Gradual Release of Verifier.** Aside from the first bit, $\forall b_i \in V_{AB} | 0 \equiv b_i \pmod 2$ Alice releases b_i after Bob releases $b_i - 1$ and $\forall b_j \in V_{AB} | 1 \equiv b_j \pmod 2$ Bob releases b_j after Alice releases $b_j - 1$.

Initially, Alice has generic wish w (e.g., want to attend prom together) that will be linked to her identity as well as Bob's indirectly via the protocol resulting in ILW. Anyone can guess such ILW, but their veracity would be unknown. In order for them to be validated, the goal is for precisely Alice and Bob to anonymously locate each other and authenticate the wishes in a fair and privacy-enhanced manner. Alice selects the G_i of a group of which Bob is a member and generates random data R_A. She encrypts R_A with PR_A and encrypts the result appended to generic wish w with PU_B yielding challenge value X which is sent to M. Note in step 1 that, although the idea of encrypting with one's private key may seem counter-intuitive or non-standard, in this context it can be considered a form of rudimentary signature with recovery and *key privacy* [14]. This step is an important contributor to satisfying the conflicting goals of anonymity and authentication with ILW. Subsequently, Bob may receive a push notification or poll the server using G_i to receive challenge X. Bob decrypts X with PR_B to reveal generic wish w and encrypted random data F (equivalent to Alice's E (PR_A, R_A)). Other members of G_i would also receive X and attempt decryption with their private keys but this would result in random data and the process would end. At this point, Bob chooses user U' with whom he may share secret w. To generate a counter-challenge for U', Bob selects R_B, encrypts it with PR_B, and encrypts the result using $PU_{U'}$ yielding Y. Note that w is an optional component of counter-challenge Y since it is associated with the original challenge that included w. Bob then sends Y to M as the counter-challenge associated with X. Subsequently, Alice receives counter-challenge Y. Now each participant has the data necessary to produce verifier

V_{AB} as described in step 5 so that it can be used for confirmation of the shared, secret ILW. Alternatively, if Y had included generic wish w, then Alice would compute $\{w, L\} := D(PR_A, Y)$ and $V_{AB} = H(H(R_A) + H(D(PU_B, L)))$. At this point, if Bob chose Alice as U', then they would have independently computed the same V_{AB}. Finally, step 6 involves confirmation of the verifier by gradually releasing bits of V_{AB} anonymously, in an alternating fashion, via public database M. The gradual release process could terminate upon the first non-matching bit and neither of the parties would have a sizeable advantage. But improved security can be achieved by completing the process with random bits and the use of decoy bits is assumed to be employed hereafter. A participant's confidence in the matching result increases with each correct bit that is gradually released. More precisely, for a number of bits released N, the confidence λ of the initiator and responder may be calculated as $\lambda = (1 - \varepsilon)$ where error ε is $(1/2)^{\lfloor N/2 \rfloor}$ and $(1/2)^{\lceil N/2 \rceil}$ respectively (note the difference of floor versus ceiling).

4   Fairness in Matchmaking

In the matchmaking literature, fairness was distinguished early on as being exemplified by the properties of joint notification of wishes and equivalent exchange [1]. Otherwise stated, for a matchmaking protocol to be considered fair, the probability that the participants compute the same correct result is approximately equal and no party can achieve a sizeable advantage. The fairness property in matchmaking was later more formally defined as follows [9]. Given users U_1 and U_2, the probability that a probabilistic polynomial time adversary A can cause either of the following is negligible:

1. U_1 receives answer b while U_2 receives ¬b
2. Only one of the users receives a response

In the HN protocol, given that all users see each bit that is released, the second property is trivially satisfied. Hence, attempts to quantify fairness concentrate on the first property. A significant amount of work has led to a number of respected approaches to quantifying fairness in resource allocation such as Jain's fairness index [15] and recent work has even sought a unifying theory or framework [16, 17] for incorporating other formulas. But it is not obvious at first whether the formulas for fairness in resource allocation are applicable to matchmaking.

A Matchmaking Fairness Index. One of Jain's key contributions was reduction of the notion of fairness to a combination of selecting an appropriate allocation metric and quantifying equality [15]. Consequently, consider the two ways that adversary A may attempt to prevent joint notification with equivalent exchange such that U_1 and U_2 might disagree as to the outcome. First, if A interacts with U_1 via the protocol, A may try to cause a false negative through early termination trying to achieve a non-negligible difference in their assessments of the result. In the second case, A might try to introduce a false positive result by attempting to correctly guess each bit that A is responsible for contributing thus falsely convincing U_1 of a match. In both attack scenarios, each participant's confidence in the result is the critical factor in determining fairness. Recall that, for a number of bits released N, the confidence λ of the initiator and responder may be calculated as $\lambda = (1-\varepsilon)$ where error ε is $(1/2)^{\lceil N/2 \rceil}$ and $(1/2)^{\lfloor N/2 \rfloor}$ for U_1 and U_2. This assumes matching bits because confidence drops to zero upon the first incorrect bit. It follows then that considering matchmaking to be a special case with one shared resource and selecting the aforementioned confidence value λ as the allocation metric in the context of Jain's fairness index yields (1).

$$Fairness\ Index\ f(x) = f(N) = \frac{[1 - 1/2^{\lfloor N/2 \rfloor}]^2}{[1 - 1/2^{\lceil N/2 \rceil}]^2} \tag{1}$$

Note that (1) has certain desirable qualities such as boundness and continuity. The bounds theoretically range from 0.0 (no fairness) to 1.0 (perfect fairness). Intuitively, the gradual release process achieves perfect fairness any time the participants have the same confidence in the matching result, which holds true when an even number of bits have been released. Indeed, in such cases the fairness index computation results in f (x) = 1.0. However, cases with an odd number of bits result in different confidence values and thus imperfect fairness. Initially it may appear that the worst case would be a single bit release resulting in f(x) = 0.0. But consider that for a single bit release, the odds of guessing the correct bit are 1/2 which is no better than the odds of randomly guessing either match or no match. It is logical then to consider the single bit case to have no true meaning when considering fairness. The more practical lower bound on fairness would be in the case of a three bit release resulting in f(x) = 0.4444. Fortunately, in this case the confidence of the adversary is low with odds of a match at 3/4. In general, the strength of this approach is that the cases with the lowest fairness correspond with the lowest confidence values. This helps to impede any advantage for the adversary. In cases of early termination of the protocol with an odd number of bits released, the confidence and fairness index values increase monotonically with the number of bits as they approach the perfect confidence and fairness value of 1.0. Although the verification value V_{AB} may seem like a large number of bits to gradually release (e.g., 512 bits for SHA3-512), for most applications acceptable levels of confidence and fairness can be achieved with far fewer bits. For instance, greater than 99.99% confidence with a fairness index of 1.0 can be achieved by releasing only 28 total matching bits.

5   Performance Analysis

Due to multiple asymmetric encryptions in the protocol, assurance was desired regarding computational performance of the protocol. The number of rounds of communication required to achieve acceptable confidence and fairness via gradual release combined with the use of anonymous communication channels also motivated the need to evaluate feasibility before incurring the full costs of development. Consequently, testing consisting of phases evaluating computational and communication performance respectively was performed to answer the key feasibility questions for this study. In the complexity analysis presented in Table 2, c represents a small constant (e.g., 1 for communications based on push notifications or to 2–3 for polling) and λ

Table 2. Complexity analysis of the HN protocol

Type of operation	Alice	Bob	Matchmaker	Total
# of asymmetric encryptions	2	2	0	4
# of asymmetric decryptions	2	2	0	4
# of string concatenations	2	2	0	4
# of one-way hashes	3	3	0	6
# of messages	$c + \frac{\log(1-\lambda)}{\log 0.5}$	$c + \frac{\log(1-\lambda)}{\log 0.5}$	$2 \times \left(c + \frac{\log(1-\lambda)}{\log 0.5}\right)$	$4 \times \left(c + \frac{\log(1-\lambda)}{\log 0.5}\right)$

again represents the desired level of confidence in the result but disregarding the floor versus ceiling differences in the case of early termination attacks. We now discuss details of the experimental methodology and present results for each phase.

5.1 Computational Overhead

Methodology. Given that the matchmaker is just a database, and that a majority of the computationally intensive tasks occur on the client side, we concentrate on the runtime of computations performed by the client. We do not consider throughput given that the number of attempts by a client will likely be constrained to a small constant (e.g., via technical controls or associating a cost with each attempt) to mitigate potential brute force attacks. The most computationally intensive portions of the protocol are the challenge/counter-challenge steps and, to a lesser extent, the computation of the verifier V_{AB}. Our test program consisted of 100 iterations of the prom protocol selecting random users and random values for each execution. The implementation was instrumented with performance counters with <=1 μs resolution to measure execution time of the code segments implementing computation of the challenge, counter-challenge, and verification values. The test program was executed on a representative sampling of processors including legacy and recent architectures, budget to high-end processors, and desktop and mobile variants.

Results. The computational performance results are presented in Table 3. The average runtimes for the challenge and counter-challenge phases of the protocol ranged from just over 191 ms for the Intel® Atom™ Z3740D mobile processor running at 1.33 GHz to around 44 ms on the Intel® Core™ i7 CPU clocked at 3.4 GHz. Runtimes for computation of the joint verification value were considerably smaller and they are consequently insignificant when considering fitness for everyday usage. Thus, the most computationally intensive portions of the protocol have been demonstrated to be well-suited for usage on a variety of processors and the answer to the computational question is yes, the computational performance of the protocol is indeed practical.

Table 3. Computational performance results

CPU	Average runtime		
	Challenge (ms)	Counter-challenge (ms)	Compute verifier (ms)
Intel® Atom™ Z3740D, 1.13 GHz	188.123	191.255	0.0364
Intel® Pentium® N350, 2.16 GHz	114.779	109.071	0.0287
AMD Athlon™ 64 X2 4200+, 2.2 GHz	105.765	101.977	0.0215
AMD Athlon™ M320, 2.1 GHz	100.161	99.906	0.0145
Intel® Core™ i5 5200U, 2.2 GHz	57.591	54.978	0.0092
Intel® Core™ i7 4770, 3.4 GHz	44.158	43.963	0.0074

5.2 Communication Overhead

Methodology. The primary concern regarding communication performance is that of runtime rather than throughput. While database/server throughput challenges are significant, well-studied, and broadly applicable to many problem domains, common scalability solutions would be applicable such as employing clusters, geographic distribution, redundancy, and eventual consistency (e.g., see [18–20]). The key question pertaining to the HN protocol is whether the runtime performance of the gradual release process would be acceptable to users of the system. This concern is further amplified by the utilization of anonymous communication channels. The test program instrumented the gradual release with high resolution timers to measure runtime of the process ten times for each test case of releasing N bits where $N \in \{8, 10, 12 \ldots 58\}$ representing cases where confidence in the matching result ranges from 0.9375 to 0.999999998. In addition to testing a spectrum of the fairness index range, all tests were executed using multiple approaches to achieve varying degrees of anonymity including VPN services, onion routing, and combinations thereof. The test configuration used Tor onion routing and OpenVPN with 256 bit AES and SHA-256. The client portion ran from the Dallas, TX, USA area while the server portion ran on Amazon Web Services (AWS) at data centers in Portland and Boardman, OR, USA. The tests were first executed without extra layer(s) of anonymous communication channels for a baseline. The performance was then compared with use of Tor and VPN services with servers in Austin, TX, USA, Seattle, WA, USA, and Paris, France.

Results. The data of Fig. 1, sub-graph (a) represent the communication performance results for the gradual release of even numbers of bits from 8 to 58, corresponding with confidence values from 93.75% to 99.99998%. The mean runtimes are given in seconds. The communication costs per anonymity approach for each of the confidence values are depicted graphically as data points along with ellipsoid density which is composed of confidence curves and density contours derived from the bivariate normal

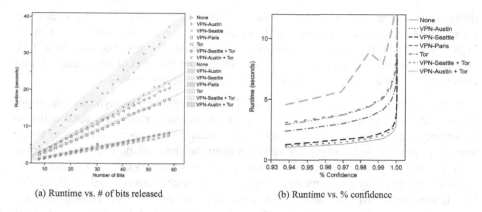

(a) Runtime vs. # of bits released   (b) Runtime vs. % confidence

Fig. 1. Communication performance results for the gradual release process

distribution. Sub-graph (b) of Fig. 1 depicts the runtimes corresponding with varying levels of confidence.

A High Degree of Confidence is Practical. The degree of confidence in the result is a function of the number of (correct) bits successfully released. Note also that the fairness index is closely related with a perfect value of 1.0 when even numbers of bits have been revealed and fairness index values that monotonically approach 1.0 for cases of early termination with an odd number of bits released. Extrapolating the average runtimes reflected in Fig. 1, maximizing confidence via gradual release of all bits of V_{AB}, where $|V_{AB}| = 512$ could take one minute or more depending on geographic distance, performance of the communication links, anonymity approach, and other factors. However, a high degree of confidence can be achieved with far fewer bits released and it is clear from the experimental data that a high degree of confidence is practical. For instance, 99.99998% can be achieved with 44 bits released and an average runtime t of $5 < t < 25$ s. Furthermore, this highlights one of the advantages of the approach. Parameters can be fine-tuned in a straightforward manner to achieve the appropriate tradeoff between runtime performance and the desired level of confidence in the matching result.

A High Degree of Fairness is Practical. The degree of fairness is also a function of the number of bits released. For even numbers, the fairness index is 1.0 reflecting that the parties have an identical level of confidence that they have computed the same matching result. Thus, a high degree of fairness can be achieved with even a small number of bits, but the confidence in that case might be low. The more important question is really the degree of unfairness that can be achieved by a misbehaving adversary. Recall that the lower bound on the fairness index is 0.4444 representing the worst case in which Alice's confidence is no better than randomly guessing while Trudy knows that there is a 3/4 chance of a matching result. The interpretation of unfairness at that point would require specific context but we believe that, in general, it would not be wise for anyone to act with no real proof or evidence and a 1/4 chance that their claims are false. As Trudy's confidence in the matching result increases, the difference between their confidence values becomes more negligible and f(x) approaches 1.0. Moreover, the experimental data under real-world conditions suggest that a high degree of both fairness and confidence is feasible. For instance, the 99.9939% confidence case with runtime $3 < t < 17$ s depending on the level of anonymity desired corresponds with a fairness index of $0.9998779 < f(x) < 0.9999389$.

A High Degree of Anonymity is Practical. The baseline of no anonymous communication was tested to quantify the relative costs of common, real-world approaches to anonymity. The results of Fig. 1 reflect mostly linear performance with respect to the number of bits released. But greater variation from the linear relationship was observed with Tor and especially with certain combinations of VPN service and Tor usage. To some extent, this may be exemplary of quality of service concerns such as those that [21] has expressed with the design and implementation of Tor. Considering now relative performance, the runtime with VPN service was roughly 1.1 to 2 times that of the baseline depending on server locations. Meanwhile, Tor required 2.5 to 3 times the runtime and combinations of Tor with VPN service cost between 4 and 6 times as much. Finally, when evaluating the communication costs of a relatively high degree of anonymity, even with high degrees of confidence and fairness, the runtimes were practical. Consider also that, rather than a user waiting in real-time, the matchmaking process will typically happen asynchronously over minutes, hours, or even days. That is, the gradual release would occur discretely in the background and be imperceptible to the user in most cases. From the users' perspectives, the next time they launch the app they would often have an answer.

6 Conclusion and Future Work

We have presented a feasibility analysis for an implementation of a previously proposed algorithm aimed at solving TPP. TPP represents a special class of matchmaking challenges requiring fair and privacy-enhanced matchmaking in addition to support for ILW. We have characterized fairness of the HN protocol, its relationship to confidence in the matching result, and proposed a fairness index to quantify the degree of fairness afforded by executions of the protocol. We summarized results from performance testing designed to answer key questions about the feasibility of the approach. Even the most computationally intensive portions of the algorithm were demonstrated to be practical across a wide range of processors with the worst-case protocol phase averaging less than 200 ms. The scrutiny on communication costs centered around the gradual release, particularly over anonymous communication channels given the increased overhead. The analysis evaluated runtimes for a broad range of confidence and fairness test cases with and without VPNs, Tor, and combinations thereof. The communication performance results showed that the protocol is practical even with high degrees of confidence, fairness, and anonymity. Furthermore, the relative impacts of varying each parameter are now well understood in the context of real-world networks and systems which will aid the application designers as the solution is applied to varying domains with different thresholds of acceptability for security and privacy.

Having quantified the fairness of the HN protocol and demonstrated its feasibility, we plan to incorporate the lessons learned into a full-featured implementation. While we believe that the Intel® Atom™ CPU was a reasonable proxy for other mobile processors, we will likely take advantage of opportunities to test on the ARM® architecture along the way. We are also evaluating the possibility of testing with I2P [22] for anonymity which could result in using I2P for the full-featured implementation and/or developing a separate I2P service for TPP. Another future consideration is the use of mix networks or an approach similar to Mix-In-Place Networks (MIPNets) [23]. Finally, we are planning for a number of enhancements to the basic protocol such as temporal constraints, geographic constraints, decoys, measures to detect and prevent certain brute force attacks, and an elegant mobile user interface to demonstrate the potential of this privacy-enhanced technology.

References

1. Baldwin, R., Gramlich, W.C.: Cryptographic protocol for trustable match making. In: 1985 IEEE Symposium on Security and Privacy, p. 92. IEEE (1985). doi:10.1109/SP.1985.10011
2. Meadows, C.: A more efficient cryptographic matchmaking protocol for use in the absence of a continuously available third party. In: 1986 IEEE Symposium on Security and Privacy, p. 134. IEEE (1986). doi:10.1109/SP.1986.10022
3. Lee, B., Kim, K.: Secure matchmaking protocol. In: Won, D. (ed.) ICISC 2000. LNCS, vol. 2015, pp. 123–134. Springer, Heidelberg (2001). doi:10.1007/3-540-45247-8_10
4. Zhang, K., Needham, R.: A private matchmaking protocol (2001). http://citeseerx.ist.psu.edu/viewdoc/summary?doi=10.1.1.54.835
5. Atallah, M.J., Cho, Y.: Private discovery of shared interests. In: Proceedings 9th International Conference on Information and Communications Security, ICICS 2007, Zhengzhou, China, December 2007
6. Patrick, K.N.: Comparison of documents possessed by two parties. U.S. Patent 8 032 747 (2011)
7. Veugen, P.J.M., Van Deventer, M.O., Klos, V.B.: Shared secret verification method and system. U.S. Patent 8 527 765 (2013)
8. Shin, J.S., Gligor, V.D.: A new privacy-enhanced matchmaking protocol. IEICE Trans. Commun. **96-B**(8), 2049–2059 (2013)
9. Horne, D., Nair, S.: The prom problem: fair and privacy-enhanced matchmaking with identity linked wishes. In: IEEE International Carnahan Conference on Security Technology (ICCST), pp. 115–122. IEEE (2016)
10. Bellare, M., Pointcheval, D., Rogaway, P.: Authenticated key exchange secure against dictionary attacks. In: Preneel, B. (ed.) EUROCRYPT 2000. LNCS, vol. 1807, pp. 139–155. Springer, Heidelberg (2000). doi:10.1007/3-540-45539-6_11
11. Canetti, R., Halevi, S., Katz, J., Lindell, Y., MacKenzie, P.: Universally composable password-based key exchange. In: Cramer, R. (ed.) EUROCRYPT 2005. LNCS, vol. 3494, pp. 404–421. Springer, Heidelberg (2005). doi:10.1007/11426639_24
12. Syverson, P.F., Goldschlag, D.M., Reed, M.G.: Anonymous connections and onion routing. In: 1997 IEEE Symposium on Security and Privacy, pp. 44–54. IEEE (1997)

13. Office of the Australian Information Commissioner and Office of the Privacy Commissioner of Canada: Joint investigation of Ashley Madison by the Privacy Commissioner and Acting Australian Information Commissioner (2016). https://www.oaic.gov.au/resources/privacy-law/commissioner-initiated-investigation-reports/ashley-madison.pdf

14. Bellare, M., Boldyreva, A., Desai, A., Pointcheval, D.: Key-privacy in public-key encryption. In: Boyd, C. (ed.) ASIACRYPT 2001. LNCS, vol. 2248, pp. 566–582. Springer, Heidelberg (2001). doi:10.1007/3-540-45682-1_33

15. Jain, R., Chiu, D.M., Hawe, W.R.: A quantitative measure of fairness and discrimination for resource allocation in shared computer system, vol. 38. Eastern Research Laboratory, Digital Equipment Corporation, Hudson (1984)

16. Joe-Wong, C., Sen, S., Lan, T., Chiang, M.: Multiresource allocation: fairness-efficiency tradeoffs in a unifying framework. IEEE/ACM Trans. Netw. **21**(6), 1785–1798 (2013). doi:10.1109/TNET.2012.2233213

17. Lan, T., Kao, D., Chiang, M., Sabharwal, A.: An axiomatic theory of fairness in network resource allocation. In: Proceedings of the 29th Conference on Information Communication, pp. 1–9. IEEE (2010). doi:10.1109/INFCOM.2010.5461911

18. Buyya, R., Ranjan, R., Calheiros, R.N.: Modeling and simulation of scalable cloud computing environments and the CloudSim toolkit: challenges and opportunities. In: International Conference on High Performance Computing & Simulation, pp. 1–11. IEEE (2009). doi:10.1109/HPCSIM.2009.5192685

19. Vogels, W.: Eventually consistent. Commun. ACM **52**(1), 40–44 (2009). doi:10.1145/1435417.1435432

20. Cardellini, V., Colajanni, M., Yu, P.S.: Geographic load balancing for scalable distributed web systems. In: Proceedings 8th International Symposium on Modeling, Analysis and Simulation of Computer and Telecommunication Systems, pp. 20–27. IEEE (2000). doi:10.1109/MASCOT.2000.876425

21. Pries, R., Yu, W., Graham, S., Fu, X.: On performance bottleneck of anonymous communication networks. In: 2008 International Symposium on Parallel and Distributed Processing, pp. 1–11. IEEE (2008). doi:10.1109/IPDPS.2008.4536239

22. Zantout, B., Haraty, R.: I2P data communication system. In: Proceedings of ICN, pp. 401–409 (2011)

23. Nipane, N., Dacosta, I., Traynor, P.: Mix-in-place anonymous networking using secure function evaluation. In: Proceedings of the 27th Annual Computer Security Applications Conference, pp. 63–72. ACM (2011). doi:10.1145/2076732.2076742

Fully Context-Sensitive CFI for COTS Binaries

Weizhong Qiang[1]($\boxtimes$), Yingda Huang[1], Deqing Zou[1], Hai Jin[1],
Shizhen Wang[1], and Guozhong Sun[2]

[1] Services Computing Technology and System Lab,
Cluster and Grid Computing Lab, Big Data Technology and System Lab,
School of Computer Science and Technology,
Huazhong University of Science and Technology, Wuhan 430074, China
wzqiang@hust.edu.cn
[2] Dawning Information Industry (Beijing) Co., Ltd., Beijing 100193, China

Abstract. *Control-Flow Integrity* (CFI) is a popular method against control-flow hijacking attacks. For *Commercial Off-the-Shelf* (COTS) binaries, in order to reduce the runtime overhead, traditional works provide coarse-grained CFI and thus are context-insensitive. Because of the inaccuracy of the *control-flow graphs* (CFGs), they can hardly defend against elaborately designed attacks. We present a fully context-sensitive CFI method (*FCCFI*), which determines the validity of the control flow of the current execution path through checking the whole execution path instead of the single edge or partial edges in the execution path. *FCCFI* gathers the control-flow information in the offline phase and tracks the execution paths to gather the process-tracking information during runtime. Then it compares the control-flow information with the process-tracking information to check the validity of the control flow. We implement the system and evaluate the security of the implementation. The evaluation results show that *FCCFI* can defend against most common control-flow hijacking attacks.

Keywords: Control-Flow Integrity · Context-sensitive CFI · Emulation execution

1 Introduction

Control-Flow Integrity (CFI) [1] is the most promising technique which prevents the code reuse attacks [4] by ensuring that the control flow of a program is consistent with its original *control-flow graph* (CFG). Several context-insensitive CFI solutions for *Commercial Off-the-Shelf* (COTS) binaries [7,8,10–12] check whether the control flow of the current execution path is valid by separately checking the validity of a single edge or partial edges of the path in the CFG. However, these context-insensitive CFI methods manually make some rules to generate CFGs which inevitably brings many invalid edges, which makes the CFGs inaccurate. Attackers can utilize these invalid edges to elaborately design some attacks to bypass this kind of CFI methods, which has been proven by many works [2–5].

© Springer International Publishing AG 2017
J. Pieprzyk and S. Suriadi (Eds.): ACISP 2017, Part II, LNCS 10343, pp. 435–442, 2017.
DOI: 10.1007/978-3-319-59870-3_28

In this paper, we present a novel method, shortly named *FCCFI*, which can achieve fully context-sensitive CFI. *FCCFI* is performed in the offline phase and the runtime phase. In the offline phase, the control-flow information is gathered through the emulation execution and the taint tracking. During runtime, it tracks the execution paths by using features of processors to gather the process-tracking information, which is then compared with the control-flow information to check the validity of the control flow. Especially, it can check the whole execution path instead of the single edge or partial edges in the execution path. In addition, the key properties and advantages are as below.

First, instead of injecting the checking code into the protected programs during runtime by using instrumentation, we separately place the checking code and the protected programs to ensure the transparency of the protection scheme. Because checking during runtime does not affect running of the protected programs, we can achieve the goal of transparency as well as the goal of low overhead. Second, because of the emulation execution, we do not need to make any rule to generate the CFGs. So it is compatible with sophisticated programs which are compiled from any compiled language. Third, we are able to support modularity since basic-block information for different executables and shared libraries is generated separately. When the different processes start with the same shared libraries, the basic-block information of these libraries can be reused. On the other hand, the control-flow information for the certain process can be used repeatedly when this process restarts.

In summary, the contribution is described as follows:

1. We present a fully context-sensitive CFI method for COTS binaries, *FCCFI*, which checks the validity of the control flow quickly by checking an execution path as a whole instead of checking each edge in this execution path one by one.
2. We present the architecture of *FCCFI* system, which gathers the control-flow information through the emulation execution and the taint tracking during the offline phase and uses features of processors to gather process-tracking information during runtime. It checks the validity of the control flow by comparing the control-flow information with the process-tracking information. If the invalid execution path is met, *FCCFI* will stop the execution of the protected program and gives the notification. *FCCFI* has many advantages, including compatibility, transparency, modularity support and so on.
3. We implement *FCCFI* on Ubuntu 14.04 32-bit and systematically evaluate the security of the implementation. The results show that *FCCFI* can defend against most common control-flow hijacking attacks.

2   Threat Model

The *trusted computing base* (TCB) contains the following components: operating system and its low-level environment including underlying software level, such as hypervisors if existing, and underlying hardware level like CPU as well as auxiliary computing units and I/O devices. Programs in the user-mode which are probably vulnerable are out of the TCB.

We assume that *Write XOR Execute* (W⊕X) and *Address Space Layout Randomization* (ASLR) are enforced, which can be satisfied easily on modern systems. Attackers can arbitrarily access and write data segments through exploiting vulnerabilities but cannot modify code segments and read-only data segments due to the enforcement of W⊕X.

There is no self-modified code or dynamically generated code in programs. Our method is not suitable for programs containing these codes because the control-flow information will not match the execution paths during runtime. Most programs generated by compiled languages meet this case.

3   CFI Policy

The traditional idea of CFI is to check the validity of partial edges of an execution path in the CFG which is constructed in the offline phase. However, in order to implement a fully context-sensitive CFI, a challenging task is to efficiently check all edges.

3.1   Control-Flow Checking for the Whole Execution Path

Since it costs too much time to check each edge of an execution path in proper order, we present a control-flow checking method which checks an execution path as a whole instead of checking each edge in this execution path one by one.

A code sample and its CFG are respectively illustrated in Fig. 1(a) and (b). The nodes in Fig. 1(b) are basic blocks which are numbered. The terminal instruction of basic block 9 is an indirect branch which targets the basic block 10 or the basic block 11. There are probably various valid execution paths. If the variable input is 3, the valid execution path (path A) is: $1 \rightarrow 2 \rightarrow 4 \rightarrow 6 \rightarrow 7 \rightarrow 1 \rightarrow 2 \rightarrow 4 \rightarrow 6 \rightarrow 8 \rightarrow 1 \rightarrow 2 \rightarrow 3 \rightarrow 9 \rightarrow 10$, which is supposed to be executed. The control-flow information of the execution path A can be gathered during the offline analysis. During runtime, our method checks the validity of the current execution path by using the information of the previous execution path. For example, if the execution path reaches basic block 9 by exactly conforming to the path A, the basic block 10 can be determined as the subsequent valid basic block. In other word, the basic block 11 will be determined as the invalid basic block. In this case, we check the validity of the control flow through checking the execution path A as a whole, which is reasonable because the value of each target-address variable can be uniquely determined for a certain execution path.

3.2   Control-Flow Checking with Hash

In order to check the whole execution path quickly, we compute the hash value for every execution path and check the execution path through matching the hash

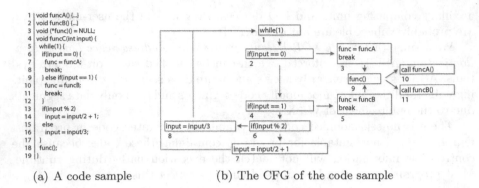

(a) A code sample   (b) The CFG of the code sample

Fig. 1. A code sample with the CFG for illustrating the idea of *FCCFI*

value. Whenever a branch is executed, the hash value of the current execution path is calculated. The format of a record for computing hash value is shown in Fig. 2, among which the previous hash value contains information of the previous execution path before the current branch is executed, and the pair of the file path and the offset in the file is taken as the address of the subsequent basic block. When the same executables or libraries are reloaded in different processes, the address of basic blocks can be calculated from the pair of the file path and its offset in the file, together with the load base address of these modules, thus we can achieve the support of modularity. Another advantage of using this format is that a hash value containing information of the whole execution path can be calculated quickly.

previous hash value	file path	offset
fixed-length related to the hash algorithms	variable-length and ending with ' \ 0'	4B or 8B

Fig. 2. The format of a record for computing hash value

3.3 Region-Based Tracking and Checking

There is a problem that the execution path may be pretty long and may even contain endless loops. Since all loops will be unrolled when tracking the execution path, the path information in a hash value could be too massive. Moreover, because the execution path is updated continually, new hash value will always be generated and stored, leading to the size of the storage consumed by hash value is very large, which brings in a path explosion problem.

In order to avoid the path explosion problem, we check execution paths in critical regions, rather than the execution path in the whole life cycle of the program. We specify critical regions by taking a suitable entry point as the start of tracking and setting up the upper limit for the number of basic blocks in a checked execution path. In general, an attack starts from a malicious input which will tamper with the value of a target-address variable used by a later indirect branch. As we know, the distance between the program point after the malicious input is taken and the program point before the affected indirect branch is executed is critical to attackers. The longer this distance is, the harder it is for the attackers to implement the exploits. Thus, we take some sensitive syscalls, which get inputs from users or external systems, as entry points, and set up a suitable upper limit for the number of basic blocks so that tracked execution paths can contain enough indirect branches that will most probably be manipulated by attackers. We only track and check the execution paths in the regions beginning with the entry points and ending with the end points which are determined according to the upper limit. In this way, the path explosion problem can be avoided and the hash value which has been calculated can be reused when the code in the same region is executed again, which results into higher efficiency.

4   System Design

We present the fully context-sensitive CFI (*FCCFI*) system, which consists of an emulation execution engine, a basic-block information generator, a process tracker, and a control-flow checker, as shown in Fig. 3.

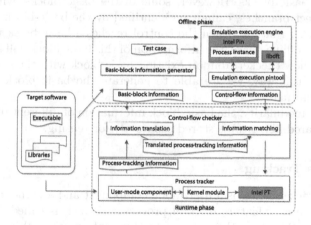

Fig. 3. *FCCFI* overview

4.1   Emulation Execution

The emulation execution engine is used to gather control flow information during the offline phase, which is implemented through instrumentation and standard I/O streams redirection. The standard input stream is redirected to a set of test cases which is configured by specifying predefined data and random data as seeds.

However, some of the input data could be invalid and might tamper with target-address variables. We introduce the taint tracking to solve this problem. We predefine some sensitive syscalls which take inputs from users or external systems, such as read and socket, and take the data returned from the sensitive syscalls or modified by these syscalls as taint data. If the taint data is propagated to target-address variables, the input data will be considered invalid and the control-flow information which is gathered this time will be discarded.

4.2   Basic-Block Information Generation

The basic-block information generator disassembles the binaries and identifies basic blocks to generate basic-block information used to translate the process-tracking information to be compared with the control-flow information gathered by the emulation execution engine.

Because the targets of unconditional direct branches are determinable, the basic-block information generator simplifies basic blocks into two kinds of basic blocks. One is a conditional basic block, the terminal instruction of which is a conditional branch. The other one is an indirect basic block, the terminal instruction of which is an indirect branch.

After disassembling the binaries, the basic-block information generator identifies basic blocks through identifying the entry instruction and the terminal instruction of basic blocks. However, some of the basic blocks, which are targeted by indirect branches, cannot be identified by the basic-block information generator. During runtime, when the control reaches a basic block which is not identified in the offline phase, the information of this basic block will be extracted by the control-flow checker from an existing basic block with the same terminal instruction. In this way, we are able to generate the basic block information lazily during runtime.

To support modularity, the basic-block information of different binaries (executables or shared libraries) is stored separately for reusing.

4.3   Process Tracking

The process tracker contains a user-mode component and a kernel module. The kernel module uses a feature of Intel processors, which is called *Intel Processor Trace* (Intel PT), to gather process-tracking information. When the control reaches the entry point, Intel PT will be enabled and the tracking will start. Intel PT is configured to store the process-tracking information in buffers which store redundant process-tracking information. When buffers are filled, the kernel module will disable Intel PT, trigger *Performance Monitoring Interrupt* (PMI) and notify the user-mode component to dump the process-tracking information into the storage.

4.4   Control-Flow Checking

The control-flow checker compares process-tracking information with control-flow information gathered by the emulation execution engine to check the validity of the control flow. When the control reaches an indirect branch, the hash value of the current execution path is compared with the hash value generated during the offline phase. If the control-flow checker detects the invalidity of the control flow, it will notify the process tracker to terminate the run of the program.

It is worth to mention that since the format of process-tracking information is different from the format of control-flow, the control-flow checker needs to translate the process-tracking information using the basic-block information before checking. During the information translation, the control-flow checker locates basic blocks from the basic-block information by going through each *data packet* of the process-tracking information. If a basic block is found, the hash value of the corresponding execution path is calculated. Otherwise, the control-flow checker generates a new basic block information and then calculates the hash value.

5   Implementation and Security

We implement the system and the emulation execution engine is on top of Intel Pin with libdft [6]. We run the experiments on Ubuntu 14.04 32-bit with Intel i5-5200U CPU 2.20 GHz and 4 GB RAM. We evaluate the security of *FCCFI* with RIPE [9], a security analysis benchmark, which provides many exploits to buffer overflow vulnerabilities. It attempts to perform control-flow hijacking attacks on the programs by using various dimensions. We modify the RIPE benchmark to make it take the inputs from a configuration file to trigger the vulnerabilities.

We test all of the 2770 exploits implemented by the current version of RIPE. On Ubuntu 14.04, with all protections (W⊕X, ASLR, stack cookies) disabled, 1582 exploits succeed, and 1138 exploits fail (because of the segmentation fault or the illegal instruction execution) but succeed to hijack the control flow. With all protections enabled, 67–69 succeed (due to the ASLR, some succeed probabilistically, hence the range), and 2011–2013 exploits fail but succeed to hijack the control flow. With *FCCFI* enabled only, all of the exploits that succeed to hijack the control flow are deterministically detected, and therefore none will do.

6   Conclusion

In this paper, we present a novel fully context-sensitive CFI method, *FCCFI*, which generates control-flow information by using the emulation execution and the taint tracking, as well as tracks execution paths by using features of processors. It separates the checking code from protected programs to offer the transparency and decrease the runtime overhead. Especially, it can check the validity of the control flow by checking an execution path as a whole instead of checking each edge in this execution path one by one. *FCCFI* has many advantages, including compatibility, transparency, modularity support, and so forth.

Acknowledgement. This work is supported by National Natural Science Foundation of China under grant No.61370106, and by National Key Research & Development (R&D) Plan of China under grant No. 2016YFB0200300.

References

1. Abadi, M., Budiu, M., Erlingsson, U., Ligatti, J.: Control-flow integrity. In: Proceedings of the 12th ACM Conference on Computer and Communications Security, pp. 340–353. ACM (2005)
2. Carlini, N., Wagner, D.: ROP is still dangerous: breaking modern defenses. In: Proceedings of the 23rd USENIX Security Symposium, pp. 385–399 (2014)
3. Davi, L., Sadeghi, A.R., Lehmann, D., Monrose, F.: Stitching the gadgets: on the ineffectiveness of coarse-grained control-flow integrity protection. In: Proceedings of the 23rd USENIX Security Symposium, pp. 401–416 (2014)
4. Göktaş, E., Athanasopoulos, E., Bos, H., Portokalidis, G.: Out of control: overcoming control-flow integrity. In: Proceedings of the 35th IEEE Symposium on Security and Privacy, pp. 575–589. IEEE (2014)
5. Göktaş, E., Athanasopoulos, E., Polychronakis, M., Bos, H., Portokalidis, G.: Size does matter: why using gadget-chain length to prevent code-reuse attacks is hard. In: Proceedings of the 23rd USENIX Security Symposium, pp. 417–432 (2014)
6. Kemerlis, V.P., Portokalidis, G., Jee, K., Keromytis, A.D.: Libdft: practical dynamic data flow tracking for commodity systems. In: Proceedings of the 8th International Conference on Virtual Execution Environments, pp. 121–132 (2012)
7. Pappas, V., Polychronakis, M., Keromytis, A.D.: Transparent ROP exploit mitigation using indirect branch tracing. In: Proceedings of the 22nd USENIX Security Symposium, pp. 447–462 (2013)
8. Wang, M., Yin, H., Bhaskar, A.V., Su, P., Feng, D.: Binary code continent: finer-grained control flow integrity for stripped binaries. In: Proceedings of the 31st Annual Computer Security Applications Conference, pp. 331–340. ACM (2015)
9. Wilander, J., Nikiforakis, N., Younan, Y., Kamkar, M., Joosen, W.: RIPE: runtime intrusion prevention evaluator. In: Proceedings of the 27th Annual Computer Security Applications Conference, pp. 41–50 (2011)
10. Xia, Y., Liu, Y., Chen, H., Zang, B.: CFIMon: detecting violation of control flow integrity using performance counters. In: Proceedings of the 42nd IEEE/IFIP International Conference on Dependable Systems and Networks, pp. 1–12. IEEE (2012)
11. Zhang, C., Wei, T., Chen, Z., Duan, L., Szekeres, L., McCamant, S., Song, D., Zou, W.: Practical control flow integrity and randomization for binary executables. In: Proceedings of the 34th IEEE Symposium on Security and Privacy, pp. 559–573. IEEE (2013)
12. Zhang, M., Sekar, R.: Control flow integrity for cots binaries. In: Proceedings of the 22nd USENIX Security Symposium, pp. 337–352 (2013)

Dual-Mode Cryptosystem Based on the Learning with Errors Problem

Jingnan He[1,2,3], Wenpan Jing[1,2(✉)], Bao Li[1,2,3], Xianhui Lu[1,2], and Dingding Jia[1,2]

[1] State Key Laboratory of Information Security,
Institute of Information Engineering
of Chinese Academy of Sciences, Beijing, China
{jnhe13,wpjing,lb,xhlu,ddjia}@is.ac.cn
[2] Data Assurance and Communication Security Research Center
of Chinese Academy of Sciences, Beijing, China
[3] School of Cyber Security,
University of Chinese Academy of Sciences, Beijing, China

Abstract. The existing LWE-based dual-mode scheme could not fit the framework of dual-mode cryptosystem very well. In this paper, we give two solutions of constructing "full-fledged" dual-mode cryptosystems based on LWE. In our first construction, we give a modified "dual version" of Peikert *et al.*'s (Crypto'08) construction, in which the simulated public keys can be uniformly and randomly chosen just like the real ones, thus it can fit the framework of dual-mode cryptosystem very well. Then, our second construction gets rid of the lattice trapdoor, which is known as lacking of efficiency and is used in our first construction as well as Peikert *et al.*'s construction.

Keywords: Dual-mode cryptosystem · Public key encryption · Learning with errors

1 Introduction

1.1 Background

Dual-mode cryptosystem is firstly proposed by Peikert *et al.* in [12], in order to construct oblivious transfer (OT) protocols that are efficient and universally composable (UC) in the common reference string (CRS) model. Oblivious transfer is a fundamental cryptographic primitive which is widely used in the secure multiparty computation.

A dual-mode cryptosystem has two modes: the messy mode and the decryption mode, depending on the CRS. The CRS for different modes are computationally indistinguishable. There always is a trapdoor generated along with

---

This research is supported by the National Nature Science Foundation of China (No. 61572495, No. 61379137 and No. 61502484), and the National Basic Research Program of China (973 project) (No. 2013CB338002).

J. Pieprzyk and S. Suriadi (Eds.): ACISP 2017, Part II, LNCS 10343, pp. 443–451, 2017.
DOI: 10.1007/978-3-319-59870-3_29

the CRS during the setup in both modes. In the messy mode, an algorithm FindMessy uses the trapdoor to identify the messy branch. In the decryption mode, an algorithm TrapKeyGen uses the trapdoor to generate a public key and two corresponding secret keys. And the simulated public keys generated by TrapKeyGen should be statistically indistinguishable with the real public keys generated by KeyGen. Wee [15] gives a framework of dual-mode cryptosystem based on smooth projective hash proof system.

Instances for the dual-mode cryptosystem based on DDH, QR, etc. assumptions that perfectly fit the framework is given by Peikert *et al.* in [12] and by Wee in [15]. However, the schemes they gave based on LWE can not suit the framework very well. It can only be performed by constant pairs of users, and the bound is predetermined while the CRS is set up. Therefore, the corresponding OT_2^1 can not be proved to be UC secure. Peikert *et al.* claimed that the reason is that the key generated by TrapKeyGen is only computationally indistinguishable with the real key for their construction. How to construct dual-mode cryptosystems based on LWE that the pairs of users are not bounded by the CRS is still an open problem [15].

1.2   Our Contributions

From our observation, the essential reason that the LWE-based dual-mode cryptosystem in [12] can not fit their framework well is that, the public key generating procedure of TrapKeyGen is deterministic while the real public keys are always generated randomly.

We give two new constructions of LWE based dual-mode cryptosystems that both solve the above problem. The first one can be viewed as a modified "dual version" of the LWE based construction of [12]. The second one further gets rid of the trapdoor of the lattice [1,4,7], which is used in the construction of [12] as well as our first construction.

The Design of Construction 1. To solve the problem, we try to make TrapKeyGen to choose the simulated public keys randomly and at the same time being able to generate corresponding secret keys to decrypt correctly. Based on the LWE problem, there are two types of encryption scheme in common, the Regev type [14] and the dual Regev type [7] encryption scheme. Instead of using the Regev type scheme in [12], we use the dual Regev type encryption scheme as the basic encryption system in our construction, so that we can uniformly and randomly generate a public key and then use the preimage sampling algorithm to extract secret keys with the help of a lattice trapdoor. Interestingly, the lattice trapdoor is used in FindMessy of [12] to find the messy branch of the CRS. Therefore, though the usage of the dual Regev type encryption scheme solves the problem in TrapKeyGen, it brings us new difficulties in finding a messy branch in FindMessy. We then briefly introduce our construction.

The CRS in our construction is in the form of $(\mathbf{B}, \mathbf{A}, \mathbf{U}_0, \mathbf{U}_1)$. In the messy mode, $(\mathbf{B}, \mathbf{A})$ are LWE instances $(\mathbf{B}, \mathbf{BC} + \mathbf{Z})$, and the trapdoor is $\mathbf{C}$. In the decryption mode, $(\mathbf{B}, \mathbf{A})$ are uniformly random matrices with a lattice trapdoor (using the trapdoor technique in [10]). Obviously, the messy mode is indistinguishable from the decryption mode based on the LWE assumption.

The design of TrapKeyGen in the decryption mode is natural. The public key generated by TrapKeyGen is $(\mathbf{U}'|\mathbf{U}'')$ where $\mathbf{U}'$ and $\mathbf{U}''$ are uniformly random matrices. With the help of trapdoors for lattices, TrapKeyGen can sample the secret key for these uniformly randomly chosen public key. Moreover, the public key generated by KeyGen is $(\mathbf{TB}|\mathbf{TA} + \mathbf{U}_\sigma)$, which is statistically indistinguishable from uniform distribution based on the leftover hash lemma [8]. Therefore, we have that the public keys generated by TrapKeyGen and KeyGen are statistically indistinguishable.

In FindMessy, to distinguish the messy branch, we basically view the CRS as the public key and the trapdoor as the secret key, then make KeyGen and FindMessy to be a pair of encryption and decryption algorithms in the Regev's LWE cryptosystem [14]. Then we let the public key for the dual-mode cryptosystem generated by KeyGen to be the "ciphertexts" of the message "0". When the branch is normal, FindMessy will decrypt the "ciphertexts" to "0" using the "secret key" (which is the trapdoor of CRS) in the Regev's LWE cryptosystem; and when the branch is messy, it will get a uniform matrix and by using error correcting code method, it will decrypt to "0" with negligible probability. And we use the lossy results [3,6] to achieve the messy encryption for the messy branch.

This scheme can be easily generalized to 1-out-of-k OT protocols by including the uniformly random matrix $\mathbf{U}_b$ for every $b \in \{0, 1, ..., k-1\}$ in the CRS.

The Design of Construction 2. The above construction we give and the construction in [12] all somehow rely on the lattice trapdoor, which is known as lacking of efficiency. We give our second construction that avoids using the lattice trapdoor. The basic encryption and decryption algorithms and FindMessy is similar with the first construction. The main difference is in the simulated key generation algorithm TrapKeyGen.

While the public key is uniformly and randomly chosen and the lattice trapdoor is used to extract secret keys in TrapKeyGen in our construction 1, in our second construction, we choose one of the secret keys first and generate the public key accordingly. Informally speaking, according to the leftover hash lemma, there is $(\mathbf{A}, \bar{\mathbf{R}}\mathbf{A}) \approx_s (\mathbf{A}, \mathbf{U}) \approx_s (\mathbf{A}, \mathbf{R}'\bar{\mathbf{R}}\mathbf{A})$, where $\mathbf{A}$ is a uniformly random matrix, $\mathbf{R}'$ and $\bar{\mathbf{R}}$ are matrices that each entry of $\mathbf{R}'$ and $\bar{\mathbf{R}}$ is randomly chosen from $\{0, 1\}$. So in our construction, we put $\bar{\mathbf{R}}\mathbf{A}$ in the CRS of decryption mode and use $\bar{\mathbf{R}}$ as the trapdoor. In the key simulation algorithm TrapKeyGen, we randomly choose a secret key $\mathbf{R}'$ to generate the public key $\mathbf{R}'\bar{\mathbf{R}}\mathbf{A}$ each time. We can obtain the other secret key $\mathbf{R}'\bar{\mathbf{R}}$ with the trapdoor $\bar{\mathbf{R}}$ directly.

In detail, in the decryption mode, the CRS consists of $(\bar{\mathbf{A}}_0, \bar{\mathbf{B}}_0, \bar{\mathbf{A}}_1 = \bar{\mathbf{R}}\bar{\mathbf{A}}_0, \bar{\mathbf{B}}_1 = \bar{\mathbf{R}}\bar{\mathbf{B}}_0)$ and the trapdoor is $\bar{\mathbf{R}}$. The real public key generated by KeyGen is $\mathbf{R}[\bar{\mathbf{A}}_\sigma|\bar{\mathbf{B}}_\sigma]$ where $\sigma \in \{0, 1\}$. The public key generated by TrapKeyGen is $\mathbf{R}'\bar{\mathbf{R}}[\bar{\mathbf{A}}_0|\bar{\mathbf{B}}_0]$, where each entry of $\mathbf{R}'$ is drawn from $\{0, 1\}$ randomly and freshly. The simulated secret keys are $\mathbf{R}'$ and $\mathbf{R}'\bar{\mathbf{R}}$ for branch 0 and branch 1 respectively.

By applying the fact that the distribution of $(\mathbf{U}, \mathbf{rU})$ is statistically indistinguishable from uniform distribution, where $\mathbf{U}$ is a uniformly random matrix in $\mathbb{Z}_q^{m \times n}$ and $\mathbf{r}$ is a uniformly random vector in $\mathbb{Z}_2^m$, the public keys generated by TrapKeyGen and KeyGen are statistically indistinguishable.

Our second construction gets rid of the lattice trapdoor and is more efficient than the prior construction. However, depending on the structure of the CRS, the first construction still has its advantage in extending to build OT_k^1.

2   Preliminaries

All operations are under the operation of modulo q. λ denotes the security parameter. Bold lower-case letters denotes vectors, and bold upper-case letters denotes matrices. $x \xleftarrow{\$} X$ denotes that x is drawn uniformly at random over a set X. $x \leftarrow \mathcal{X}$ denotes that x is drawn according to a distribution $\mathcal{X}$. For any $\mathbf{c} \in \mathbb{R}^n$, $s > 0$, and n-dimensional lattice Λ, the discrete Gaussian distribution over Λ is, $\forall \mathbf{x} \in \Lambda, \mathcal{D}_{\Lambda,s}(\mathbf{x}) = \frac{\rho_s(\mathbf{x})}{\rho_s(\Lambda)}$, where $\rho_s(\Lambda) = \sum_{\mathbf{y} \in \Lambda} \rho_s(\mathbf{y})$, $\rho_s(\mathbf{x}) = \exp(-\pi \|\mathbf{x}\|^2 / s^2)$ [2].

2.1   Dual-Mode Cryptosystem

As defined in [12], a dual-mode encryption system consists of seven algorithms:

- **SetupMessy**(1^λ): given security parameter λ, outputs (CRS,τ). The CRS is a common reference string for the remaining algorithms, and τ is a trapdoor value that enables the **FindMessy** algorithm. All the remaining algorithms take CRS as their first input, we omit it from the list of arguments.
- **SetupDec**(1^λ): the input and the output are same as **SetupMessy**. τ is a trapdoor value that enables the **TrapKeyGen**.
- **KeyGen**(σ): given a desired decryptable branch value $\sigma \in \{0, 1\}$, outputs (PK, SK) where PK is a public encryption key and SK is a corresponding secret key for the messages encrypted on branch σ.
- **Enc**(PK, b, μ): given PK, a branch value $b \in \{0, 1\}$, and a message $\mu \in \{0, 1\}^l$, outputs a ciphertext c encrypted on branch b.
- **Dec**(SK, c): given SK and a ciphertext c, outputs a message $\mu \in \{0, 1\}^l$.
- **FindMessy**(PK, τ): given a trapdoor τ for the CRS generated in messy mode and some (possibly malformed) public key PK, outputs a branch value $b \in \{0, 1\}$ corresponding to a messy branch of PK.
- **TrapKeyGen**(τ): given a trapdoor τ for the CRS generated in decryption mode, outputs (PK, SK_0, SK_1) where PK is a public encryption key and SK_0, SK_1 are the secret decryption keys corresponding to branches 0 and 1 respectively.

Definition 1 (Dual-Mode Encryption [12]). *A dual-mode cryptosystem is a tuple of algorithms described above that satisfy the following properties:*

1. **Completeness for decryptable branch:** *For every (CRS,τ)$\leftarrow$ SetupMessy(1^λ) or (CRS,τ)$\leftarrow$ SetupDec(1^λ), every $\sigma \in \{0,1\}$, every (PK, SK)$\leftarrow$ KeyGen(σ) and every $\mu \in \{0,1\}^l$, decryption is correct on branch σ.*

2. **Indistinguishability of modes:** *the first outputs of SetupMessy and SetupDec are computationally indistinguishable.*

3. **(Messy Mode) Trapdoor identification of messy branch:** *For every (CRS,τ)$\leftarrow$ SetupMessy(1^λ) and every (possibly malformed) PK, FindMessy(τ, PK) outputs a branch value $b \in \{0,1\}$ such that Enc(PK, b, $\cdot$) is messy. Namely, for every $\mu_0, \mu_1 \in \{0,1\}^l$, Enc(PK, b, μ_0) $\approx_s$ Enc(PK, b, μ_1).*

4. **(Decryption Mode) Trapdoor generation of keys decryptable on both branches[1]:** *For every (CRS,τ)$\leftarrow$ SetupDec(1^λ), (PK, SK$_0$, SK$_1$) $\leftarrow$ TrapKeyGen(τ), (PK$'$, SK$'$) $\leftarrow$ KeyGen(σ) and every $\sigma \in \{0,1\}$: PK $\approx_s$ PK$'$. SK$_0$ and SK$_1$ can decrypt properly for PK on both branches.*

2.2 (Decisional) Learning with Error (DLWE)

Let $m = m(n)$, $q = q(n)$ be integers, and χ be a distribution on $\mathbb{Z}_q$. Let $\mathbf{A} \xleftarrow{\$} \mathbb{Z}_q^{m \times n}, \mathbf{s} \xleftarrow{\$} \mathbb{Z}_q^n, \mathbf{e} \leftarrow \chi^m$, then the DLWE($m, n, q, \chi$) problem is that given $(\mathbf{A}, \mathbf{b})$, decide whether $\mathbf{b}$ is distributed by $\mathbf{As} + \mathbf{e}$ or chosen uniformly at random from $\mathbb{Z}_q^m$.

The hardness of DLWE is reduced to the hardness of the worst-case problems on lattices [5,9,11,13,14].

3 Construction

We just present our constructions in this section. In the full version, we show these two schemes both fulfill the properties of dual-mode cryptosystem based on the LWE assumption.

3.1 Our Construction 1

We use the lattice trapdoor in the algorithm TrapKeyGen, which helps us to extract corresponding secrets from the randomly generated simulated public key. The concrete construction is shown in Fig. 1. decode($\boldsymbol{\mu}'$) will decode each entry μ_i' of the vector $\boldsymbol{\mu}'$. For each bit, it outputs 0 if μ_i' is closer to 0 than to $\lfloor \frac{q}{2} \rfloor$ mod q; otherwise it outputs 1.

Parameters. $q > 4r_2 m\omega(\sqrt{\log n})$, $m > Cn\log q + w$, where $C > 1$ is some constant, $w = n\lceil \log q \rceil$, let $r_2 > \max\{r_1(n-l)m\omega(\sqrt{\log(n-l)}), \omega(\log n)$ $O(\sqrt{m-w} + \sqrt{w})\}$, $r_1 \geq 2\sqrt{n}$, and let $l \leq (n - 2\lambda + 2)/(\log q + 1)$, $k \leq (n - l - \lambda(\log m + \log q + 2) + 2)/\log q$.

---

[1] We do not require that SK$_\sigma \approx_s$ SK$'$, $\sigma \in \{0,1\}$ as in [12]. As Wee mentioned in [15] that the decryption mode is used in the case of a corrupted sender. And the corrupted sender sees only PK and not SK$_0$ or SK$_1$. As long as SK$_0$ and SK$_1$ can decrypt properly, we can extract both of its inputs. Therefore, this relaxed property is also sufficient for UC-secure OT.

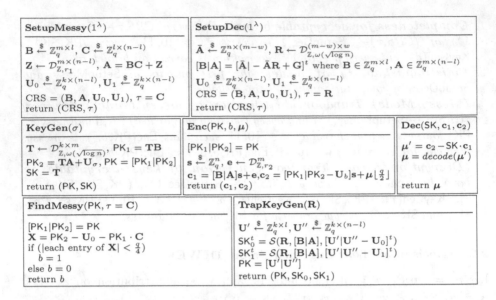

Fig. 1. Our construction 1 of dual-mode cryptosystem

The scheme in Fig. 1 is a dual-mode cryptosystem, assuming the DLWE(m, l, q, r_1) problem is hard. Just like [12], we can easily generalize this construction to a lager branch sets $\{0,1\}^k$ by including uniformly random matrices $\mathbf{U}_b$ for every $b \in \{0.1\}^k$ in the CRS.

3.2 Our Construction 2

In this construction, we do not use the lattice trapdoor which is used in the algorithm FindMessy of the construction in [12] and in the algorithm TrapKeyGen of our first construction. The concrete construction is shown in Fig. 2. This scheme is a dual-mode encryption, assuming the DLWE(m, l, q, r_1) problem is hard.

Parameters. Let $q > 4r_2 m$, $m > Cn \log q + n$ where C is a constant such that $C > 1$, let $r_2 \geq r_1 nm$, $r_1 \geq 2\sqrt{n}$, and let $l \leq (n - 2\lambda + 2)/\log q$, $k \leq (n - \lambda(\log m + \log q + 2) + 2)/\log q$.

3.3 Comparison

We give an efficiency comparison among Peikert *et al.*'s construction in [12] and both of our constructions as in Table 1 for an encryption of a k bits message.

Firstly, the size of the CRS of Peikert *et al.*'s construction and our first construction are related to k, but in our second construction, it is independent with the size of the secret message. However, when k is small, the size of the CRS in the second construction is bigger. Therefore, our second construction is more applicable to the case that each of the secret messages is big.

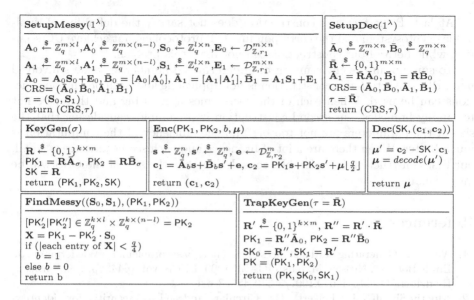

Fig. 2. Our construction 2 of dual-mode cryptosystem

Table 1. Comparisons among constructions of dual mode

	Peikert *et al.*'s construction [12]	Our construction 1	Our construction 2
CRS size	$m \times (n + 2k)$	$m \times n + 2k \times (n - l)$	$m \times 4n$
PK size	$m \times k$	$k \times n$	$k \times 2n$
SK size	$n \times k$	$k \times m$	$k \times m$
Ciphertext size	$n + k$	$m + k$	$m + k$
Parameters	$q = poly(n)$ $m = O(n \log q)$ $k = poly(n)$	$q = poly(n)$ $m = O(n \log q)$ $k = O(\frac{n}{\log q}), l = O(\frac{n}{\log q})$	$q = poly(n)$ $m = O(n \log q)$ $k = poly(n)$
Lattice trapdoor	Yes	Yes	No
Generalize to OT_d^1	Easy	Easy	Complex
Satisfy dual mode	✗	✓	✓

Secondly, our second construction is more efficient since it avoids using the lattice trapdoor and the preimage sample algorithm.

Thirdly, Peikert *et al.*'s construction and our first construction are easy to be generalized from two branches (OT_2^1) to d branches (OT_d^1), and the number of matrices in the CRS increases from three to $d+1$. But our second construction is inefficient to be generalized from two branches to d branches, since the number of matrices in the CRS will increase from four to d^2. Therefore, our second construction is not suitable for the case with too many branches.

At last, Peikert *et al.*'s construction does not satisfy the definition of dual-mode cryptosystem and the corresponding OT protocol cannot achieve UC security, while both of our constructions do not have this problem.

To sum up, in the environment of undetermined number of senders involved per CRS, Peikert *et al.*'s construction is not applicable and both of our constructions can be used. When each of the secret messages is big and there are not too many branches, our second construction is preferable, considering that the size of the parameters are not too big and the efficiency of the computation is much better. When there are a lot of branches and each secret message is small, our first construction is preferable, considering that the size of the CRS will be much smaller.

References

1. Ajtai, M.: Generating hard instances of the short basis problem. In: Wiedermann, J., Emde Boas, P., Nielsen, M. (eds.) ICALP 1999. LNCS, vol. 1644, pp. 1–9. Springer, Heidelberg (1999). doi:10.1007/3-540-48523-6_1
2. Alperin-Sheriff, J., Peikert, C.: Circular and KDM security for identity-based encryption. In: Fischlin, M., Buchmann, J., Manulis, M. (eds.) PKC 2012. LNCS, vol. 7293, pp. 334–352. Springer, Heidelberg (2012). doi:10.1007/978-3-642-30057-8_20
3. Alwen, J., Krenn, S., Pietrzak, K., Wichs, D.: Learning with rounding, revisited. In: Canetti, R., Garay, J.A. (eds.) CRYPTO 2013. LNCS, vol. 8042, pp. 57–74. Springer, Heidelberg (2013). doi:10.1007/978-3-642-40041-4_4
4. Alwen, J., Peikert, C.: Generating shorter bases for hard random lattices. Theory Comput. Syst. **48**(3), 535–553 (2011)
5. Applebaum, B., Cash, D., Peikert, C., Sahai, A.: Fast cryptographic primitives and circular-secure encryption based on hard learning problems. In: Halevi, S. (ed.) CRYPTO 2009. LNCS, vol. 5677, pp. 595–618. Springer, Heidelberg (2009). doi:10.1007/978-3-642-03356-8_35
6. Berkoff, A., Liu, F.-H.: Leakage resilient fully homomorphic encryption. In: Lindell, Y. (ed.) TCC 2014. LNCS, vol. 8349, pp. 515–539. Springer, Heidelberg (2014). doi:10.1007/978-3-642-54242-8_22
7. Gentry, C., Peikert, C., Vaikuntanathan, V.: Trapdoors for hard lattices and new cryptographic constructions. In: Proceedings of the Fortieth Annual ACM Symposium on Theory of Computing, pp. 197–206. ACM (2008)
8. Goldwasser, S., Kalai, Y.T., Peikert, C., Vaikuntanathan, V.: Robustness of the learning with errors assumption. In: Innovations in Computer Science (ICS 2010), Beijing, China, January 5–7, 2010, Proceedings, pp. 230–240. Tsinghua University (2010)
9. Micciancio, D., Mol, P.: Pseudorandom knapsacks and the sample complexity of LWE search-to-decision reductions. In: Rogaway, P. (ed.) CRYPTO 2011. LNCS, vol. 6841, pp. 465–484. Springer, Heidelberg (2011). doi:10.1007/978-3-642-22792-9_26
10. Micciancio, D., Peikert, C.: Trapdoors for lattices: simpler, tighter, faster, smaller. In: Pointcheval, D., Johansson, T. (eds.) EUROCRYPT 2012. LNCS, vol. 7237, pp. 700–718. Springer, Heidelberg (2012). doi:10.1007/978-3-642-29011-4_41

11. Peikert, C.: Public-key cryptosystems from the worst-case shortest vector problem. In: Proceedings of the Forty-First Annual ACM Symposium on Theory of Computing, pp. 333–342. ACM (2009)
12. Peikert, C., Vaikuntanathan, V., Waters, B.: A framework for efficient and composable oblivious transfer. In: Wagner, D. (ed.) CRYPTO 2008. LNCS, vol. 5157, pp. 554–571. Springer, Heidelberg (2008). doi:10.1007/978-3-540-85174-5_31
13. Regev, O.: On lattices, learning with errors, random linear codes, and cryptography. In: STOC, pp. 84–93 (2005)
14. Regev, O.: On lattices, learning with errors, random linear codes, and cryptography. J. ACM (JACM) **56**(6), 34 (2009)
15. Wee, H.: KDM-security via homomorphic smooth projective hashing. In: Cheng, C.-M., Chung, K.-M., Persiano, G., Yang, B.-Y. (eds.) PKC 2016. LNCS, vol. 9615, pp. 159–179. Springer, Heidelberg (2016). doi:10.1007/978-3-662-49387-8_7

Process Control Cyber-Attacks and Labelled Datasets on S7Comm Critical Infrastructure

Nicholas R. Rodofile[1(✉)], Thomas Schmidt[1,2], Sebastian T. Sherry[1], Christopher Djamaludin[1], Kenneth Radke[1], and Ernest Foo[1]

[1] Information Security Discipline, School of Electrical Engineering and Computer Science, Science and Engineering Faculty, Queensland University of Technology (QUT), Brisbane, Australia
{n.rodofile,christopher.djamaludin,k.radke,e.foo}@qut.edu.au,
sebastian.sherry@connect.qut.edu.au
[2] Fakultät für Elektrotechnik und Informationstechnik Ruhr-Universität Bochum, Bochum, Germany
thomas.schmidt-c2n@rub.de

Abstract. Cyber-security of their critical infrastructure is the current grand challenge facing nation-states. Development and research of cyber-security solutions for operational technology environments of critical infrastructure is being inhibited by the lack of publically available datasets. This paper provides a collection of labelled datasets containing attacks on the widely used STEP 7 (S7) protocol. To achieve this goal, we designed and executed a series of process-control attacks, using our physical critical infrastructure test-bed. The created labelled datasets, and the associated process logs, will directly aid in the development and assessment of intrusion detection systems (IDSs). We validate our dataset using Snort, configured with openly available S7 rule-sets.

Keywords: S7comm · STEP 7 · Cyber attacks · Datasets · Process control attacks

1 Introduction

Supervisory Control and Data Acquisition (SCADA) systems are significantly used around the world to provide automation to utilities such as water treatment, manufacturing, power transmission and transportation. As critical infrastructure and corporate networks interconnect using Internet technologies, critical infrastructure systems find themselves vulnerable to cyber-attacks that have the ability to impact SCADA [4]. In recent years, the world has been introduced to Stuxnet, Black Energy, Duqu, and Flame, which are some of the known cyber-weapons that have been used against SCADA [4]. Due to resource and process limitations in SCADA devices, researchers have identified intrusion detection systems (IDSs) and intrusion prevention systems (IPSs) to be an effective method for detecting and preventing cyber-attacks [6]. Attack datasets allow

© Springer International Publishing AG 2017
J. Pieprzyk and S. Suriadi (Eds.): ACISP 2017, Part II, LNCS 10343, pp. 452–459, 2017.
DOI: 10.1007/978-3-319-59870-3_30

IDS researchers to validate and evaluate the performance of their detection algorithms using techniques in machine learning, data or process mining [5]. However due to privacy issues, there is a lack of publicly available SCADA datasets for IDS verification, and validation [7].

In this paper, we provide a collection of unique process control attacks on a physical SCADA process control test-bed. Process control attacks focus on the disruption of physical processes that are required to complete a manufacturing or industrial process. Such attacks do not exploit vulnerabilities in SCADA protocols, but they make the use of textbook client-server attacks that target the procedures used to successfully complete an industrial process. From the process control attacks presented in this paper, we make available a labelled network traffic capture and a SCADA process log as datasets containing process control attacks against the widely used STEP 7 (S7) protocol.[1]

2   Background and Related Work

SCADA process control networks consists of various automation devices such as Programmable Logic Controllers (PLCs) or embedded, microprocessor-based devices that are networked via serial or Ethernet technologies. The majority of SCADA networks contains a hierarchy of master and slave devices, used to maintain an industrial automation process. The master device is often used to control, monitor and manage one or more slave devices. The communication adapts the client-server-model of traditional networking services: The master acts as a client and slaves provide services. The primary use of slave devices is to convert sensory signals into digital data [4].

The dataset contribution of this work could be used to test the proposed IDS, as the datasets contain extensive malicious activity on the S7 protocol. Recent works have used also datasets to investigate network traffic patterns of SCADA networks. Barbosa et al. [1] used multiple datasets to show that SCADA traffic has similarities to Simple Network Management Protocol (SNMP). In later work, Barbosa et al. [2] found that SCADA networks differ greatly from traditional IT traffic by "not presenting diurnal patters or self-similar correlations in the time series." Datasets have been created and used to train IDSs before. Gao et al. [3] created datasets of command injection, data injection, and Denial of Service (DoS) for Modbus, DNP3, and EtherNET/IP protocols. These datasets were used to help develop neural network based IDSs. This paper aims to contribute datasets for the S7 protocol to train IDSs against process control attacks.

3   Test-Bed and Control Processes

The test-bed simulates a mining refinery plant. The main process consists of three time-based sub-processes, which have to be executed in the order of *Conveyor*, *Wash Tank*, and finally the *Pipeline Reactor*. The Human Machine Interface (HMI) also provides historian logs which log the control processes during the experiment.

---

[1] Link: https://github.com/qut-infosec/2017QUT_S7comm.

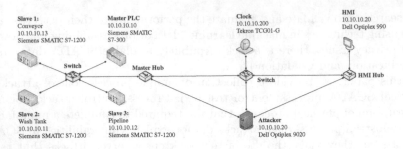

Fig. 1. Process control network test-bed structure.

An operator is to monitor the HMI, respond to unintended actions and only able to use functions available in the HMI, as each sub process can only be performed one-at-a-time via the HMI. A global reset button resets the process so that it has to be started from the beginning. Moreover, an emergency stop exists which pauses all processes for five minutes. Upon successful completion of the entire control process, the HMI will produce a log entry of "Master_Finish", in which the operator is to reset the equipment and start a new process, in which HMI will produce a log entry of "HMI_Master_Reset". The first process is to simulate splitting material with a conveyor system which simulates the separation of white impurities from raw black ore. This is done by detecting the colours with a sensor and sorting them with a solenoid driven arm. The sub-process is to run at least five minutes continuously. A successful separation is done, if all white impurities are on the left side whereas the raw black ore is on the right side. This will produce a log entry of "HMI_Conv_Finish" in the Master HMI log.

In the second step, a simulated chemical washing is demonstrated. The system consists of two tanks: In the first one the chemical wash is done; the second one is an underground reservoir tank which holds the chemical[2]. The sub-process can be run in Auto mode which controls a pump to ensure that the level in the Wash Tank is between 50% and 80%. In this interval the ore is completely covered and the tank can not overflow. This is done for eight minutes before the washed raw black ore is dumped into the Pipeline Reactor. In Manual mode the operator has to monitor the fill level – an overflow is not prevented by the control logic. Setting the switch from Auto to Manual also resets the timer for the sub-process. The successful completion of this process will produce a log entry of "HMI_Tank_Finish".

Finally, the end product is separated from the raw black ore with a catalytic reaction in the Pipeline Reactor. For that, the system is pressurised to 40 psi. Then, a solenoid valve opens and the pressure is dropped to 30 psi. This has to be repeated for at least two minutes. After that, the Pipeline Reactor vents and dumps the final product. The successful completion of this process will produce a log entry of "HMI_Pipeline_Finish".

---

[2] The Wash Tank runs with water. In a real world scenario, this could be any chemical.

Table 1. List of process attack.

Attack #	Description	Area	Address	Type	Log tag	Label
1.1	Turn Conveyor Belt off	0x83	0x0331	bit	HMI_Conv_Stop	ConveyorBeltOff
1.2	Turn Conveyor Belt on	0x83	0x0330	bit	HMI_Conv_Start	ConveyorBeltOn
1.3	Change direction of Conveyor Belt	0x83	0x0332	bit	HMI_Conv_Direction	ConveyorBeltGate ChangeDirection
1.4	Reset Conveyor Belt	0x83	0x0334	bit	HMI_Conv_Reset	ConveyorBeltReset
2.1	Turn Wash Tank off	0x83	0x0328	bit	HMI_Tank_Stop	WaterTankOff
2.2	Turn Wash Tank on (Auto)	0x83	0x0329	bit	HMI_Tank_In_Auto	WaterTankOnAuto
2.3	Turn Wash Tank on (Manual)	0x83	0x032a	bit	HMI_Tank_In_Manual	WaterTankOnManu
3.1	Turn Pipeline Reactor off	0x83	0x0320	bit	HMI_Pipe_Pump_On_SP	ReactorOff
3.2	Turn Pipeline Reactor on	0x83	0x0322	bit	HMI_Pipe_Pump_Off_SP	ReactorOn
3.3	Change upper threshold of Pipeline Reactor	0x83	0x0040	real	HMI_Pipe_Solenoid_On_SP	ChangeUpperThreshold
3.4	Change lower threshold of Pipeline Reactor	0x83	0x0060	real	HMI_Pipe_Solenoid_On	ChangeLowerThreshold
4.1	Reset complete systems	0x83	0x0339	bit	HMI_Master_Reset	GlobalReset
4.2	Emergency stop	0x83	0x033b	bit	Emergency_Stop	EmergencyStop

The network structure of our test-bed is given in Fig. 1. The simulated plant consists of three slave PLCs. Each of them is in charge of one of the sub-processes and is controlled by a master device. These components are connected via a managed switch. The operator monitors the process from the HMI. The Attacker and a Global Positioning System (GPS) clock are also connected to a network switch. For the dataset generation, we added two hubs to this network, which are captured by the Attacker to aid in the labelling process.

3.1 Process Attacks

The scope of the Attacker is to target the sub-processes via the Master PLC. Since this device stores important values for the sub-processes, it is possible to change the behaviour of sub-processes by manipulating registers on the Master PLC. The Attacker was modelled to only violate the control processes via TCP/IP connection. The process attacks are given in Table 1 outlining the attacks modelled in the Attacker. The attack script was implemented in Python using the Snap7 library to handle the communication.

The attacks which turn sub-processes off (1.1, 2.1, and 3.1) have a limited impact on the total process since the operator is able to start the process manually again. When such attacks were performed, the associated sub-process has to be started again. However, the Attacker is able to start sub-processes (1.2, 2.2, and 3.2) as well. Not only can already completed sub-processes be restarted by the Attacker, but also subsequent ones. This can cause serious damage in a real world scenario when the Pipeline Reactor is started while there is no washed material in it to be processed. In some circumstances, this will result in breaking the catalyser, which means that it has to be replaced. As consequences, there are long downtimes and therefore high costs.

The attack 1.3 changes the direction of the Conveyor Belt system so that the white impurities were sorted to the site where the raw black ore should be. As described above, the process can be completed even if the split process was unsuccessful. But this leads to a tainted end product, which is unusable. If it is detected in time the sub-process can be repeated which causes a loss of time. In addition, the Attacker is able to reset the sub-process (1.4) which causes an infinity loop since the sub-process timer is also reset but not restarted and the sub-process ends only when the timer has run down. The attack 2.3 turns the pump on and leaves it running until it is turned off. Therefore, the following situation is possible: An attacker turns the pump on but the operator is unable to stop it from the HMI even if he detects it. If the pump is not turned off the wash tank overflows which, in the real world, could cause an environmental catastrophe.

The Pipeline Reactor could be attacked by changing the pressure thresholds (3.3 and 3.4). Since the Attacker writes directly to the memory of the PLC the input validation of the HMI is bypassed. The damage can be caused by increasing the upper limit so that a pipe bursts or the compressor explodes. Moreover, it is also possible to set such a lower bound that this threshold is never reached and therefore the solenoid valve stays opened. Furthermore, the entire process can be disrupted by the Attacker by sending the command for the emergency stop (4.1) or global reset (4.2). In both cases in the simulation, the process has to be restarted and any previous progress in sub-processes is lost. Moreover, the system needs at least five minutes before it is operational after an emergency stop event.

Table 2. All process attacks from Table 1 and their time of occurrence in Fig. 2a and Fig. 2b. All attack numbers marked with "F" are flooding attacks.

Time	Attack	Time	Attack	Time	Attack	Time	Attack	Time	Attack	Time	Attack	Time	Attack	Time	Attack
2980	1.1	6198	2.1	8280	3.4	14517	2.1 F	17157	3.1	22971	1.2	25404	1.2	29968	4.2
3420	2.1	6237	2.2	8489	1.3 F	15457	3.1 F	17216	3.1	23367	1.4	25416	2.2	31326	1.1
3999	3.1	6796	3.1	8959	2.3 F	15861	2.2	20166	3.1	23369	1.2	26245	4.1	31332	1.2
4231	1.3	6826	3.1	9648	3.3 F	16575	3.1	21402	3.1	24098	1.2	27093	4.1	31340	1.3
4787	2.3	7057	1.3	9917	1.2 F	16605	3.1	21948	2.2	24107	1.4	27130	3.1	31359	2.3
5413	3.3	7146	1.3	10672	2.2 F	16655	3.1	21952	3.1	24109	1.2	27267	2.2	31377	3.1
5659	1.1	7460	2.3	12053	3.1 F	16753	3.1	22943	1.2	24113	3.1	27759	1.2	31388	3.3
5718	1.2	7648	2.3	12680	1.1 F	17087	3.1	22966	1.4	25401	1.4	28171	1.4	31396	3.4

4   Datasets and Results

As we have discussed the attacks that were implemented against the test-bed, in this section we present our attack datasets. The attack dataset, collected approximately over 9 h, consists of network traffic and process log data with 30 processes. The control dataset contains approximately 8.5 h of network traffic and process log data, with 32 processes. The datasets consists of network traffic from the perspective of the Master switch and the HMI. The control dataset contains an *Emergency stop* between the 22nd and 23rd process, and a *stop* of the process at process 28. Shown in Table 2 are the occurrences of the process control attacks on the test-bed. The table shows 64 attack instances over the data collection period. The attack datasets contain a network packet capture (pcap), and four process logs: *Master log*, *Conveyor log*, *Tank log*, and *Reactor log*. Each attack pcap and log is accompanied with a control pcap and log containing normal behaviour. The attack labels are correlated to the described attacks in Table 1 under labels. We have provided the raw network captures to allow IDSs developers to select their own features by preprocessing the pcaps with fields relevant to their detection methods. The labelling method was automated, in which packets that were produced by the Attacker was correlated against traffic collected by the Master and the HMI. We provide four logs, the *Master log*, *Conveyor log*, *Tank log*, and *Reactor log*. These logs were produced by the HMI by polling from the Master PLC in the test-bed. Each process log contains tag entries that identifies the state of the process during the time of polling.

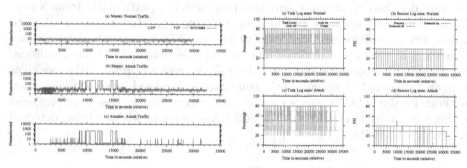

(a) Process Control Network traffic showing the differences between normal and attack traffic.

(b) Displaying reactor and wash tank statistics under normal and attack conditions.

Fig. 2. Results showing the impact of the attacks on the process control network.

The occurrence of each of the attacks during the data collection is outlined in Table 2. Each of the attacks is described in Table 1. Figure 2aa shows the test-bed network from the Master's interface under normal conditions. The flow of traffic seems consistent during the data collection period. Figure 2ab shows the test-bed network under attack conditions from the Master's interface.

Figure 2b consists of plots derived from logs collected from the test-bed. Figure 2ba shows normal conditions of the Wash Tank system, and Fig. 2bb shows normal conditions of the Pipeline Reactor. In both of the control plots, we can distinctly see 30 processes, however between the 21000 s and the 23000 s mark, we can see there is a distinct break between the 22nd and 23rd process, this break is to demonstrate an emergency stop process.

Figure 2bc shows the conditions of the Wash Tank under attack conditions. We can see, there is a significant impact to the Wash Tank during the data collection process. It also shows various inconsistencies with each Wash Tank process. We can see that the Wash Tank process continuously runs for approximately 1500 s instead of the 480 s (8 min) from the 10500 s mark. We can also see the Wash Tank process failing to run between the 12000 s and 14200 s mark. Around the 9000 s mark, we can see the Wash Tank level exceeding the 80% limit then reducing to below the 20% limit. These modifications were due to the Attacker setting the pump to manual, thus attempting to overflow, and under fill the wash tank. In Fig. 2bd, we can see various inconstancies in the pipeline reactor when comparing the processes to Fig. 2bb. During the 9700 s mark in in Fig. 2bd, we can see the alteration of the Solenoid on value, from 40 psi to 45 psi. Around the 31100 s mark, we can see the Solenoid off value, being altered from 30 psi to 20 psi.

To evaluate our attack dataset, we used the open source, signature-based IDS Snort. We configured Snort with S7 rules from the Digital Bond quick draw project[3]. We tested the rules with the provided pcap, by replaying the pcap to the IDS's interface. Snort failed to pick up the attacks as the rules are only designed to discover port scanning activity, particularly from Nmap. There were only two rules provided by the rule-set. They were described to detect any connection to port 102 (which is a S7comm port) with userdata requesting to read cpu functions. The second rule detects the same condition, but includes a specified master and slave IP address to prevent false positives from an authorized handshake. This demonstrates the need for smarter detection methods for the SCADA security community, as the attacks that were produced in this paper were able to impact the SCADA equipment without being detected by a widely used IDS.

5   Discussion and Future Work

Observations from our experiments show the attacker updating values via network. The captures show the Attacker connecting to the Master PLC, but does not interact with the process until the Attacker has updated a value in the PLC. So it might be difficult to correlate actions between the Attacker and the system logs, as the Attacker violates the system via the network.

The process logs produced in the presented work allows for the IDS development community to extend to process mining techniques in order to detect faults or attacks on process control systems. Finding the attacks in the logs requires

---

[3] http://www.digitalbond.com/tools/quickdraw/.

searching for process tag values and determining whether the process is violated based on the scenario described in Sect. 3.1.

One issue with using process logs to detect attacks, is the possibility of a Man-in-the-middle (MITM). Most process logs are extracted from the HMI via the communication protocol used in the network. During an attack with the ability to perform ARP poisoning and packet modification attacks, the process logs generated by HMI would be deceptive and unreliable for detecting attacks. MITM may have the ability to target feedback control messages, by sending false information back to the HMI or automated Master.

In our future work we will generate datasets containing a greater range of attacks, including attacks that target slave operations and the configurations of SCADA devices.

References

1. Barbosa, R.R.R., Sadre, R., Pras, A.: A first look into SCADA network traffic. In: 2012 IEEE Network Operations and Management Symposium, pp. 518–521. IEEE (2012a)
2. Barbosa, R.R.R., Sadre, R., Pras, A.: Difficulties in modeling SCADA traffic: a comparative analysis. In: Taft, N., Ricciato, F. (eds.) PAM 2012. LNCS, vol. 7192, pp. 126–135. Springer, Heidelberg (2012). doi:10.1007/978-3-642-28537-0_13
3. Gao, W., Morris, T., Reaves, B., Richey, D.: On SCADA control system command and response injection and intrusion detection. In: eCrime, pp. 1–9. IEEE (2010)
4. Knijff, R.V.D.: Control systems/SCADA forensics, what's the difference? Digital Investigation (2014)
5. Meshram, A., Haas, C.: Anomaly detection in industrial networks using machine learning: a roadmap. In: Machine Learning for Cyber Physical Systems, pp. 65–72. Springer (2017)
6. Morris, T., Gao, W.: Industrial control system traffic data sets for intrusion detection research. In: Critical Infrastructure Protection VIII, pp. 65–78. Springer (2014)
7. Rodofile, N.R., Radke, K., Foo, E.: Framework for SCADA cyber-attack dataset creation. In: Proceedings of the ACSW-AISC. ACM (2017)

Solving the DLP with Low Hamming Weight Product Exponents and Improved Attacks on the GPS Identification Scheme

Jason H.M. Ying[✉] and Noboru Kunihiro

The University of Tokyo, Tokyo, Japan
jason_ying@it.k.u-tokyo.ac.jp

Abstract. This paper describes methods of solving certain parameters of the discrete logarithm problem with low Hamming weight product exponents. Our approach is shown to be applicable for a concrete analysis of the GPS identification scheme. To achieve this, we introduce the notion of parameters dependent splitting system which served as tools to yield two improved results. The first attains a lower time complexity over the current state of the art without any compromise in memory. The second achieves the first known attack of the GPS scheme in a time complexity of under 2^{64} at the expense of some added memory requirements over the former.

Keywords: GPS scheme · Discrete logarithm problem with low hamming weight product exponents · Splitting system

1 Introduction

The GPS identification scheme is an interactive protocol between a prover and a verifier. It was introduced by Girault in [2] and later shown to be secure in [5]. This protocol is applicable for usage in low cost chips as the computational cost required by the prover is relatively low. Nevertheless, every operation incurred is still significant for low cost chips, like RFID tags. As such, Girault and Lefranc proposed in [7] for the private key exponent to be the product of two integers with low Hamming weight, thereby reducing the online computational cost. More specifically the private key was chosen such that the private key is a product of a 142-bit number with 16 random bits equal to 1 chosen among the 138 least significant ones and a 19-bit number with 5 random bits equal to 1 chosen among the 16 least significant ones (from which we henceforth refer to as GL parameters). In the same paper, it was computed that these parameters are not susceptible to a routine attack by exhaustive search. Subsequent work by Coron, Lefranc and Poupard [1] demonstrated a method of attack via Coppersmith's splitting system of the GL parameters with lower complexity than routine exhaustive search. As a result, they instead proposed a different set of parameters; namely that the private key be a product of a 30-bit number with 12 nonzero bits and

© Springer International Publishing AG 2017
J. Pieprzyk and S. Suriadi (Eds.): ACISP 2017, Part II, LNCS 10343, pp. 460–467, 2017.
DOI: 10.1007/978-3-319-59870-3_31

a 130-bit number with 26 nonzero bits (from which we henceforth refer to as CLP parameters). Moreover, they show that their line of attack is not effective against the CLP parameters.

Parameterized splitting system was first introduced by Kim and Cheon in [3]. Parameterized splitting system can be regarded as a generalization of Coppersmith's splitting system. Using this tool, they demonstrated an improved attack (with regards to speed) on the CLP parameters. They later further improve this attack over the previous work by applying a refinement [4]. Thus far, this is the current fastest known attack of the GPS identification scheme with CLP parameters.

Our Contributions. This work highlights general methods of solving various DLP with low Hamming weight product (LHWP) exponents by providing improved results for certain settings of the parameterized splitting system. We introduce the concept of parameters dependent splitting system which served as tools to solve such problems more efficiently. Moreover, we show that the GPS identification scheme utilizing CLP parameters satisfy such settings. There are two significant results that arise from this work. The first provides an improved attack on the GPS scheme with lower time over the most recent state of the art without any increment in memory. The second result shows for the first time that the GPS scheme can be attacked in time complexity of under 2^{64} with a slight increase in memory requirement over the former.

2   Preliminaries

Let G be a group, $g \in G$ be a generator of the group and z be an integer. Denote $\text{wt}(z)$ and $\text{ord}(g)$ to be the Hamming weight of z and the order of g respectively. The low Hamming weight DLP seeks solution z such that $g^z = h$ for given known G, g, $h \in G$, $\text{ord } g$ and $\text{wt}(z)$. The computational complexity of solving the low Hamming weight DLP has been well understood and a good exposition of known methods can be found in [6]. We denote CSS and PSS to mean Coppersmith's splitting system and parameterized splitting system respectively. In this work, we are interested to solve the DLP with LHWP exponents which has applications to the security of the GPS identification scheme. A definition of the DLP with LHWP exponents is given as follows.

Definition 1 (DLP with LHWP exponents). *Let* $z = xy$*, where* x*,* $y \in \mathbb{Z}^+$*. Given* G*,* g*,* $\text{ord } g$*,* $wt(x)$*,* $wt(y)$ *and* $h \in G$*, find* z *satisfying* $g^z = h$*.*

The Coppersmith's splitting system is described in [6] as follows.

Definition 2 (Coppersmith's splitting system (CSS)). *Let* n *and* t *be even integers such that* $0 < t < n$*. A* (N,n,t)*-splitting system is a pair of* $(X,\mathcal{B})$ *satisfying*

1. $|X| = n$.
2. $\mathcal{B}$ is a set of $\frac{n}{2}$-subsets of X called blocks and $|\mathcal{B}| = N$.
3. For every $Y \subseteq X$ such that $|Y| = t$, $\exists$ a block $B \in \mathcal{B}$ such that $|B \cap Y| = \frac{t}{2}$.

It was shown in [6] among others that N can be taken to be $\frac{n}{2}$. This result was applied in [1] to obtain improved attacks of the GPS scheme with GL parameters.

The parameterized splitting system was first introduced in [3]. It can be also be regarded as a generalized version of Coppersmith's splitting system and is given as follows.

Definition 3 (Parameterized splitting system (PSS)). *Let n and t be integers such that $0 < t < n$. For any t_s such that $1 \leq t_s \leq t$. A (N,n,t,t_s)-parameterized splitting system is a pair of $(X,\mathcal{B})$ satisfying*

1. $|X| = n$.
2. $\mathcal{B} = \{B \subset X : |B| = \lfloor \frac{t_s n}{t} \rfloor\}$ is a set of $\lfloor \frac{t_s n}{t} \rfloor$-subsets of X called blocks and $|\mathcal{B}| = N$.
3. For every $Y \subseteq X$ such that $|Y| = t$, $\exists$ a block $B \in \mathcal{B}$ such that $|B \cap Y| = t_s$.

In particular, when $t_s = \frac{t}{2}$, the parameterized splitting system corresponds to the Coppersmith's splitting system.

3 Improved Results on the Parameterized Splitting System

It was shown in [3,4] that the parameterized splitting system requires n blocks. We prove that for numerous classes of parameters, the number of blocks required in the parameterized splitting system is less than n. In particular, we show that the GPS scheme with CLP parameters is among those arising in such situations. As a result, we obtain a lower complexity attack on the GPS scheme.

We first provide a slight reformulation of the parameterized splitting system in order to distinguish and make a comparison of the number of blocks required of the splitting system. Let t_1, t_2, n_1, $n_2 \in \mathbb{Z}^+$ such that $t_1 \leq t_2$, $n_1 \leq n_2$, $t = t_1 + t_2$, $n = n_1 + n_2$ and $n_i = \frac{n t_i}{t}$ for $i = \{1,2\}$. With these added notations, we introduce the parameters dependent splitting system or PDSS as follows.

Definition 3* (Parameters dependent splitting system (PDSS)). *A (N, n_1, n_2, t_1, t_2)-parameterized splitting system is a pair of $(X,\mathcal{B})$ satisfying*
1. $|X| = n = n_1 + n_2$.
2. $\mathcal{B} = \{B \subset X : |B| = \frac{t_2 n}{t} = n_2\}$ is a set of n_2-subsets of X called blocks and $|\mathcal{B}| = N$.
3. For every $Y \subseteq X$ such that $|Y| = t$, $\exists$ a block $B \in \mathcal{B}$ such that $|B \cap Y| = t_2$.

Remark. t_2, n_2 can essentially be swapped with corresponding t_1, n_1 by considering the complement. For example, let $X \subseteq \mathbb{Z}_m$ so that $X = \{x = \sum_{i=0}^{n-1} x_j 2^j : x_j = 0 \text{ or } 1, \ \text{wt}(x) = t\}$. If $|B \cap Y| = t_2$ then $|(\mathbb{Z}_m \backslash B) \cap Y| = t_1$.

Theorem 1. *Let $n_1 > \frac{n_2}{2}$. For any n_1, n_2, let $k \in \mathbb{Z}^+\backslash\{1\}$ be the integer satisfying*

$$\frac{k+1}{2k+1}n_2 \le n_1 < \frac{k}{2k-1}n_2.$$

Suppose t_1 and t_2 satisfy the following:

$$\frac{2k+1}{k+1}t_1 - \frac{3k+1}{k+1} \le t_2 \le \frac{2k-1}{k}t_1 + \frac{3k-2}{k},$$

$$\frac{2k-1}{k}t_1 < t_2 \le \frac{2k+1}{k+1}t_1.$$

Then $N = 2n_2 - n_1 + 1$ suffices to generate a parameterized splitting system.

Recall that $N = n = n_1 + n_2$ was obtained in [3,4]. Since $n_1 > \frac{n_2}{2}$, $2n_2 - n_1 + 1 \le n = n_1 + n_2$, we derive a parameterized splitting system which requires a fewer number of blocks.

In situations where $t_2 \approx 2t_1$, we show that Theorem 1 can be further improved. In particular, we present the following result.

Theorem 2. *Let $\frac{1}{2}n_2 \le n_1 \le \frac{2}{3}n_2$. Suppose $t_2 = 2t_1, 2t_1 - 1$ or $2t_1 - 2$. Then*

$$N = \begin{cases} 2n_1\lceil\frac{1}{3}(t_1 - 1)\rceil - n_2(\lceil\frac{1}{3}(t_1 - 1)\rceil - 1) + 1, & \text{if } t_2 = 2t_1 \\ 2n_1\lceil\frac{1}{4}(t_1 - 2)\rceil - n_2(\lceil\frac{1}{4}(t_1 - 2)\rceil - 1) + 1, & \text{if } t_2 = 2t_1 - 1 \\ 2n_1\lceil\frac{1}{5}(t_1 - 3\rceil - n_2(\lceil\frac{1}{5}(t_1 - 3)\rceil - 1) + 1, & \text{if } t_2 = 2t_1 - 2 \end{cases}$$

suffices to generate a parameterized splitting system.

When $t_2 \approx 2t_1$, the results of Theorem 2 shows that fewer blocks than those obtained in Theorem 1 suffices.

4   Solving the DLP with LHWP Exponents and Applications

Upon obtaining improvements to the parameterized splitting system, the subsequent approach of solving the DLP with LHWP exponents is simply a meet-in the-middle technique. We provide an outline of it below.

The DLP with LHWP exponents seeks the solution z satisfying $h = g^z = g^{xy}$ given $\text{wt}(x)$ and $\text{wt}(y)$. Without loss of generality, suppose that $|X| > |Y|$. Then split $x = u + v$ for $u \in U, v \in V$ and where U and V are disjoint subsets of $\mathbb{Z}_m$ such that $X \subset U + V = \{u + v : u \in U, v \in V\}$. Denote n to be the maximum binary size of an element X. Hence $X = \{x = \sum_{j=0}^{n-1} x_j 2^{n-1-j} : x_j = 0 \text{ or } 1, \text{wt}(x) = t\}$. Now, by considering elements of X in their binary representations, say of the form $x_0 x_1 \ldots x_{n-1}$ where each $x_i = 0$ or 1, express them in a more concise form based off their indices via A_i and D_i where $A_i = \{i + j \bmod n : 0 \le j < n_1\}$ and $B_i = \{i + j \bmod n : 0 \le j < n_2\}$. For example $A_0 = \{0, 1, \ldots, n_1 - 1\}$ and this represents $x_0 x_1 \ldots x_{n_1-1}0 \ldots 0$.

Express $h = g^{xy}$ as

$$h^{y^{-1}} g^{-u} = g^v.$$

The method proceeds by computing and storing all the values of the left-hand side followed by computing each value of the right-hand side and check if it is in the list from the first part.

Let $t' \in \{1, 2, \ldots, \lceil \frac{t}{2} \rceil : \frac{nt'}{t} \in \mathbb{Z}\}$ be the value of t_1 that minimizes $|Y| \binom{n_1}{t_1} + \binom{n-n_1}{t-t_1}$. If t' and the corresponding $t-t'$ satisfy the conditions stated in Theorem 1 for the given k, then the computational complexity of solving the problem is given by

$$O\left((2n_2 - n_1 + 1) \left(|Y| \binom{n'}{t'} + \binom{n - n'}{t - t'} \right) \right)$$

where $n' = \frac{nt'}{t}$. The corresponding memory requirement is given by

$$O\left(\min \left\{ |Y| \binom{n'}{t'}, \binom{n - n'}{t - t'} \right\} \right).$$

This already provides a lower computational complexity over the results in [3] without any additional memory requirements via PDSS.

Improved results over [3] were subsequently obtained in [4]. Fix any subset $T \subseteq X$ such that $|T| = t$. The main improvement derives by noting that among all blocks B_i such that $|B_i \cap T| = t_2$, there exists block $B_{i'}$ such that $x_{i'} = 1$ and block $B_{i''}$ such that $x_{i''+n_2-1 \bmod n} = 1$. A similar property holds for A_i. However, this is not true in our PDSS. In the case of PDSS, there either exists block $B_{i'}$ such that $x_{i'} = 1$ and block $B_{i''}$ such that $x_{i''+n_2-1 \bmod n} = 1$. From the symmetry of t_1 and t_2 in PDSS, a similar property also holds for A_i. Crucially, there is no way to determine which of the two stated block properties will occur (or both). As such, a direct application of the PDSS as shown above while it yields improvements to [3], does not provide better results over [4]. Nevertheless, with some delicate refinements, we show how the results and properties of PDSS can be utilized to obtain two improved results over the existing state of the art. First, we present the following lemma.

Lemma 1. *Suppose for inputs t_i and n_i there exists some $s < n - 1$ such that for all $0 \leq i \leq s$ satisfying $|B_i \cap T| = t_2$, we have that $x_{i+n_2-1 \bmod n} = 0$. Then there exists some m satisfying $s < m \leq n - 1$ such that $x_m = 0$ and $x_{m+n_2-1 \bmod n} = 1$.*

With the results of Theorems 1, 2 and Lemma 1, we provide 2 possible ways via PDSS (dependent on parameters) to solve the DLP with low Hamming weight exponents more efficiently. We will also show in the subsequent section on how they can be applied to analyze or attack the GPS identification scheme utilizing CLP parameters.

From the result of Lemma 1, we can refine the earlier procedure of solving the DLP with LHWP exponent by computing g^v (or g^{-u}) where during the computation of all possible elements with hamming weight of t_2 in B_i, some bits are redundant and can be removed from the computations. More specifically for $i \leq s$, we first proceed with the assumption that one of the bits at the end edge of a block is 1. Hence, this requires a total of $(s + 1)\binom{n_2-1}{t_2-1}$ computations. If the above does not yield a valid solution, then for $i > s$, we can deduce from Lemma 1 that one of the bits at the initial edge of a block can be taken to be 0 and one bit at the end edge within this same block can be taken to be 1. This requires $(n - s)\binom{n_2-2}{t_2-1}$ computations. Lemma 1 ensures that ignoring these redundant computations will nevertheless still ensure the solution can be obtained. Without loss of generality, a similar result holds for A_i.

The roles of Theorems 1 and 2 arise in determining the values of s.

Our first improved result utilizing Theorem 1 and Lemma 1 is given as follows. Let $t' \in \{1, 2, \ldots, \lceil \frac{t}{2} \rceil : \frac{nt'}{t} \in \mathbb{Z}\}$ be the value of t_1 that minimizes $|Y|\binom{n_1-1}{t_1-1} + \binom{n-n_1}{t-t_1}$. If t' and the corresponding $t - t'$ satisfy the conditions stated in Theorem 1 then s can be taken to be $2n_2 - n_1$ and the computational complexity of solving the problem is given by

$$O\left((2n_2 - n_1 + 1)|Y|\binom{n' - 1}{t' - 1} + n\binom{n - n'}{t - t'} + (2n_1 - n_2 - 1)|Y|\binom{n' - 2}{t' - 1} \right)$$

where $n' = \frac{nt'}{t}$. The corresponding memory requirement is given by

$$O\left(\min\left\{ |Y|\binom{n' - 1}{t' - 1}, \binom{n - n'}{t - t'} \right\} \right).$$

This provides a strict improvement over the current best known result of [4] with regards to time complexity while maintaining an equal amount of storage required.

We can further improve on this result if $t_2 \approx 2t_1$ using Theorem 2. Let $t' \in \{1, 2, \ldots, \lceil \frac{t}{2} \rceil : \frac{nt'}{t} \in \mathbb{Z}\}$ be the value of t_1 that minimizes $|Y|\binom{n_1}{t_1} + \binom{n-n_1-1}{t-t_1-1}$. If t' and the corresponding $t - t'$ satisfy the conditions stated in Theorem 2 then s can be taken to be $2kn_1 - (k - 1)n_2$, where the value of k depends on the relation between t_1 and t_2 as highlighted in Theorem 2. For brevity, let $k' = 2kn_1 - (k - 1)n_2$. The computational complexity of solving the problem is then given by

$$O\left((k' + 1)\binom{n - n' - 1}{t - t' - 1} + n|Y|\binom{n'}{t'} + (n - k' - 1)\binom{n - n' - 2}{t - t' - 1} \right)$$

where $n' = \frac{nt'}{t}$. The corresponding memory requirement is given by

$$O\left(\min\left\{ |Y|\binom{n'}{t'}, \binom{n - n' - 1}{t - t' - 1} \right\} \right).$$

5   Application to the GPS Scheme

In this section, we provide 2 improved approaches of attacking the GPS identification scheme utilizing CLP parameters. The CLP parameters for the GPS scheme based on the DLP with LHWP exponents were proposed in [1]. We show that these parameters satisfy the conditions to utilize the PDSS and provide concrete security evaluations. Furthermore, we demonstrate additional enhancements which can be applied to provide further improvements for these specific parameters. One caveat is that the ord(g) is kept secret in the GPS. However, it is already known (for instance in [1]) that this can be circumvented without any significant increase in computational resources.

The CLP parameters are that the private key be a product of a 30-bit number with 12 nonzero bits and a 130-bit number with 26 nonzero bits. As such, $|Y| = \binom{30}{12}$, $n = 130$ and $t = 26$. Moreover, some simple computational checking reveals that $t' = 10$ is the value of t_1 which minimizes $|Y|\binom{n_1-1}{t_1-1} + \binom{n-n_1}{t-t_1}$. Hence $t_1 = 10$, $t_2 = 16$, $n_1 = 50$ and $n_2 = 80$. It is easily verified that $k = 2$ in Theorem 1 and the conditions for t_i are also satisfied. As a result, $2n_2 - n_1 + 1 = 111$ and so only 111 blocks are required as opposed to 130 required in [3,4]. In fact, by applying a more deliberate argument for this particular set of parameters, it can be further show that only 106 blocks are required. The computational complexity of this attack can now easily be computed to be $2^{64.49}$ exponentiations with memory requirement of $2^{54.58}$ which is an improvement in time complexity over the results of [4] without any added storage requirements.

Our second improvement is achieved by minimizing $|Y|\binom{n_1}{t_1} + \binom{n-n_1-1}{t-t_1-1}$. The minimum is attained when $t_1 = 9$, $t_2 = 17$, $n_1 = 45$ and $n_2 = 85$. In this case, we have that $t_2 = 2t_1 - 1$ and thus Theorem 2 can be applied. From the result of Theorem 2, we obtain $N = 96$. By applying a more deliberate argument for this particular set of parameters, it can be shown that only 95 blocks are required. The computational complexity of this attack can now easily be computed to be $2^{63.95}$ exponentiations with memory requirement of $2^{55.83}$. It is of note that this second approach yields the first known result that achieves a time complexity of under 2^{64} at a slight additional expense of memory space.

6   Results

Table 1 presented on the next page highlights this results of this work when compared with other existing state of the art.

Table 1. Results

Attacks	Method	Exponentiations	Storage
[1]	CSS	$2^{77.3}$	$2^{43.9}$
[3]	PSS	$2^{65.48}$	$2^{56.09}$
[4]	PSS	$2^{64.53}$	$2^{54.58}$
[This work]	PDSS	$2^{64.49}$	$2^{54.58}$
[This work]	PDSS	$2^{63.95}$	$2^{55.83}$

As evident from the results of Table 1, the method of PDSS introduced in this work provides improvements to current known attacks and analysis of the GPS identification scheme. They are two ways of approach to apply the PDSS method. The former provides a reduced complexity of the best current known GPS scheme without additional increment in storage requirement. The latter provides an even lower time complexity that falls under 2^{64} for the first time at the expense of some storage increment.

7 Conclusion

In this work, we introduce a method of parameters dependent splitting system (PDSS) which can be applied to analyze the security of the GPS scheme which invokes the DLP with low hamming weight exponents as its security basis. The method is shown to provide better results over existing state of the art. In particular, we show for the first time that the security barrier for the GPS scheme is under 2^{64}. The analysis of the minimum number of blocks required in the parameterized splitting of given inputs might also be of independent interest in the field of Combinatorics.

Acknowledgement. This research was partially supported by JST CREST Grant Number JPMJCR14D6, Japan and JSPS KAKENHI Grant Number 16H02780.

References

1. Coron, J., Lefranc, D., Poupard, G.: A new baby-step giant-step algorithm and some application to cryptanalysis. In: Rao, J.R., Sunar, B. (eds.) CHES 2005. LNCS, vol. 3659, pp. 47–60. Springer, Heidelberg (2005)
2. Girault, M.: Self-certified public keys. In: Davies, D.W. (ed.) EUROCRYPT 1991. LNCS, vol. 547, pp. 490–497. Springer, Heidelberg (1991). doi:10.1007/3-540-46416-6_42
3. Kim, S., Cheon, J.H.: A parameterized splitting system and its application to the discrete logarithm problem with low hamming weight product exponents. In: Cramer, R. (ed.) PKC 2008. LNCS, vol. 4939, pp. 328–343. Springer, Heidelberg (2008). doi:10.1007/978-3-540-78440-1_19
4. Kim, S., Cheon, J.H.: Parameterized splitting systems for the discrete logarithm. IEEE Trans. Inf. Theory **56**(5), 2528–2535 (2010)
5. Poupard, G., Stern, J.: Security analysis of a practical "on the fly" authentication and signature generation. In: Nyberg, K. (ed.) EUROCRYPT 1998. LNCS, vol. 1403, pp. 422–436. Springer, Heidelberg (1998). doi:10.1007/BFb0054143
6. Stinson, D.: Some baby-step giant-step algorithms for the low hamming weight discrete logarithm problem. Math. Comput. **71**(237), 379–391 (2002)
7. Girault, M., Lefranc, D.: Public key authentication with one (online) single addition. In: Joye, M., Quisquater, J.-J. (eds.) CHES 2004. LNCS, vol. 3156, pp. 413–427. Springer, Heidelberg (2004). doi:10.1007/978-3-540-28632-5_30

Author Index

Printed in the United States
By Bookmasters